Faith
and
Fraternalism

Faith and Fraternalism

The History of the

KNIGHTS OF COLUMBUS
1882–1982

Christopher J. Kauffman

1817

HARPER & ROW, PUBLISHERS, New York

Cambridge, Philadelphia, San Francisco, London, Mexico City, São Paulo, Sydney

71496

FAITH AND FRATERNALISM: THE HISTORY OF THE KNIGHTS OF COLUMBUS. Copyright © 1982 by Christopher J. Kauffman. All rights reserved. Printed in the United States of America. No part of this book may be used or reproduced in any manner whatsoever without written permission except in the case of brief quotations embodied in critical articles and reviews. For information address Harper & Row, Publishers, Inc., 10 East 53rd Street, New York, N.Y. 10022. Published simultaneously in Canada by Fitzhenry & Whiteside Limited, Toronto.

FIRST EDITION

Designed by Ruth Bornschlegel

Library of Congress Cataloging in Publication Data

Kauffman, Christopher J., 1936–
   Faith and fraternalism.

   Includes index.
   1. Knights of Columbus—History 2. Catholics—
United States. I. Title.
HS1529.K583K38 1982   267′.24273   81–47660
ISBN 0–06–014940–X   AACR2

82 83 84 85 86 10 9 8 7 6 5 4 3 2 1

TO
The Most Reverend Charles Pascal Greco, D.D.
SUPREME CHAPLAIN

A Knight who has lived the Order's history for more than six decades;

·

A State Chaplain of Louisiana for three decades;

·

Supreme Chaplain for more than two decades;

·

A man of learning, of personal charm, of love for the unfortunate
flowing from his great love for Our Lord and His Blessed Mother;

·

A man who proclaims that, next to his faith and priesthood, his
membership in the Knights of Columbus has been the greatest blessing in
his life;

·

One who has been acquainted personally with seven Supreme Pontiffs
from Benedict XV to John Paul II;

·

One who, as a priest, has spread the love and spirit of Christ as reflected
in his episcopal motto, *"Vivat Jesus"*;

·

A successor of the apostles whose guidance, inspiration and friendship
have always been available to every Brother Knight;

AND IN HIS PERSON TO ALL CHAPLAINS
WHO SO SELFLESSLY SERVE THE ORDER,
THIS VOLUME IS RESPECTFULLY DEDICATED.

Founders' Day — March 29, 1982

This dedication of the History of the Order was adopted unanimously by formal
resolution of the Board of Directors on the feast of Corpus Christi, June 21, 1981.

Virgil C. Dechant Supreme Knight

ATTEST:

Howard E. Murphy Supreme Secretary

FREDERICK H. PELLETIER	JOSE LUIS GONZALEZ, M.D.	ROBERT J. HISEL	ALFRED N. NICOLAS
DANIEL L. McCORMICK	LESLIE D. LEMIEUX	WILLIAM J. VAN TASSELL	CHARLES P. RIESBECK, JR.
JOHN M. MURPHY	JOHN F. BARRETT	JULIAN F. JOSEPH	GERMAIN A. FORTIER
JOHN H. GRIFFIN, M.D.	MEDARD R. YUTRZENKA	W. PATRICK DONLIN	JOHN R. PLUNKETT
MAURICE PERRON	HILARY F. SCHMITTZEHE	THOMAS J. KEATING	

Contents

Photographs follow pages 208, 336, and 400.
A section of color plates follows page 432.

Preface

WHEN I WAS COMMISSIONED to write this history I was delighted to discover that I would be exploring such fascinating topics as nativism, anti-Catholicism, the revolution in Mexico, McCarthyism and the preservation of fraternalism in contemporary society. Because the project has been such a stimulating experience, I am deeply indebted to Father Colman Barry, O.S.B., who introduced me to the Knights and who has provided much encouragement over the years ever since I was a student of his at St. John's University. He also introduced me to Father Robert Trisco, who has taken a keen interest in this work. No student of American church history can approach any aspect of this field without explicitly acknowledging his indebtedness to the dean of Catholic Church historians, Monsignor John Tracy Ellis. I am also grateful to Justus George Lawler for sharing with me his broad vision of religious and cultural history.

From our first meeting to the present, Supreme Knight Virgil C. Dechant has always been extremely supportive of every aspect of the history project. His primary concern has been that the Order's past be accurately recorded so that the members will have a strong sense of their roots and so that they and the general public will appreciate the significant roles the Order has played in American church and social history. For the opportunity to pursue these ends in an atmosphere of integrity and freedom I am very grateful. Through his history committee, composed of Supreme Advocate John M. Murphy, Supreme Physician John H. Griffin, M.D., and former Supreme Secretary Richard B. Scheiber, I received many helpful suggestions and strong encouragement. Paul M. McGlinchey and Elmer Von Feldt assisted the committee in the tedious task of proofreading. From Supreme Treasurer Daniel L. McCormick, Supreme Secretary Howard E. Murphy, Deputy Supreme Knight Frederick H. Pelletier, former Deputy Supreme Knight Charles J. Ducey, former Supreme Advocate Harold J. Lamboley, former Assistant Supreme Secretary William L. Piedmont, and several Supreme Directors I have received many insights. I am especially grateful to Past Supreme Knight John W. McDevitt for sharing with me the wealth of his knowledge of the Order's history.

I am indebted to Professors Jay P. Dolan and Dolores Ann Liptak, R.S.M., for reading portions of the manuscript and offering valuable suggestions. I am deeply grateful to Professor Joseph Chinnici, O.F.M., for his critique of the entire manuscript. His advice on the crucial issues of analysis and of interpretation was extremely helpful. Of course I am entirely responsible for whatever inaccuracies may have crept into the text.

It has been my good fortune to have two excellent research assistants gifted with keen intelligence, sharp wit, and an easy tolerance for my moodiness. Carmen Garcia organized nearly twenty-five file drawers of the Luke E. Hart Papers and arranged the primary and secondary material according to topics. Hugh MacDonald arrived just in time to become the major proofreader for the content of the text. Because he is the son of the first Assistant Supreme Secretary and because he has been employed by the Knights for more than fifty years, he was able to combine historical criticism with his proofreading.

I am grateful to Kim Perry, a history student at Albertus Magnus College, who worked with me as an intern at the Order's archives. I am thankful to Mary Lou Cummings, the archivist-curator for the Knights of Columbus, for her valuable assistance with many problems and particularly for her work on the illustrations for this book.

My family's spirited interest has been a constant source of joyful amazement. Because of the warm wisdom and understanding of my wife, Helen, and because of the gentle goodness of our children, Jane, Christopher, and Kathryn Ann, this book was written by a happy person.

Introduction

ONE OF THE PASSWORDS by which a late-nineteenth-century Knight identified himself as a member in good standing was "diligence, devotion, and defense." This piece of alliterative fraternal coinage, minted in 1895, reveals several marks of the Order's historical character. "Diligence" was a Knightly virtue in the sense that a hard-working, persevering, serious man was one who could be relied upon to care for his family through the Order's insurance program. The diligent member was counseled to aid his brother Knights in distress, to attend meetings of his council, and to project a respectable image before those Protestant guardians of the host culture ever suspicious of the immigrant Catholic. Indeed, diligence had been enshrined as one of the cardinal virtues of the Protestant work ethic.

"Devotion" symbolized the primary qualification for Knighthood. Every Knight pledged that he was a "practical Catholic." He was not a theoretician of Catholicism, but rather a layman who was actively engaged in the liturgical and spiritual life of the Church. Devotion also evoked a sense of piety and religious commitment well beyond the bonds of Sunday obligation. The Knight was also expected to be devoted to his Order and to demonstrate his devotion to the Knights' principles: Charity, Unity, Fraternity, and Patriotism.

"Defense" conveyed a sense of alarm, as if the ideal Knight were always to be on guard against attacks from those ubiquitous enemies of nativism and anti-Catholicism. This organization of laymen, which subsequently evolved into an unofficial Catholic anti-defamation society, defended the faith not with the weapons of vindictiveness but rather with those of open encounter, respect, and civil discourse. Indeed, the ceremonials or rituals of the Order formally instructed the candidates to behave as Catholic gentlemen.

The secret character inherent in the use of the password implied the belief that the enemies of Catholicism were ceaselessly attempting to infiltrate the Order; however, such passwords were also intended to remind the members of their duties as Knights. Other passwords, such

xi

as "Christopher Columbus" or "Commodore Barry," were symbolic of the Order's celebration of the American-Catholic heritage. Columbus and Barry were viewed as heroes not because of their Italian or Irish nationality but because they represented the enormous Catholic contribution to the life of the nation. By placing the Catholic component of American culture before the public, the Knights asserted the legitimacy of Catholic citizenship in pluralist, democratic American society.

Though the first-generation Knights were predominantly Irish Americans, the organizing impulse of their sense of peoplehood was Catholicism. Fraternalism was the chosen medium for fashioning a unique expression of Catholic Americanness, one which appealed to Catholic men of all nationalities. The ceremonials of the Order instructed the initiates in these lessons and satisfied their need for forging strong fraternal ties in an otherwise antagonistic social and cultural climate.

During their first hundred years, the Knights' strong sense of Catholic identity allowed them to respond to the needs of Church and society in remarkable ways. If social history is defined as the story of ordinary people, then this institutional history of the Knights of Columbus is the history of an organization of ordinary people united in a variety of rather extraordinary causes. Whether they were raising money for the Catholic University of America, manning social and recreational centers for servicemen in World War I, or struggling against the Ku Klux Klan or against religious persecution in Mexico, their fraternal sense of Catholic peoplehood was strongly manifested in their drive to personify "diligence, devotion, and defense."

Public expressions of the themes of these passwords were balanced by many more privately oriented social events such as parties, clambakes, parades, and pilgrimages. There were, of course, also those men who joined the Order primarily for economic and political reasons. However, because these reasons are common motives for membership in any fraternal organization, they are not unique traits of the Knights of Columbus.

The preceding character sketch of the Order may be said to illustrate the predominant methodology adopted for this history of the Knights. The life of an institution is best understood by allowing its most articulate spokesmen to express its personality, its self-image, its role within the various social contexts of the times, its idealism, and the general means by which it attempts to achieve its goals. The purpose of institutional historiography is to chart the evolution of a given institution's consciousness, a task which presupposes the historian's empathetic immersion in the documentary fragments of the past with a view to discerning those key components of its inner life and spirit. Passwords, symbols, and metaphors embedded in the Order's ceremonial character convey a portion of this spirit. Moreover, the institutional historian must attempt to reconstruct the historical events by examining the internal motives of the participants in these events and the ways in which the institution was influenced by or reflected the dominant forces of a particular period. As the narrative moves closer to the present, the perspective narrows and the methodology becomes less historical and more journalistic. The reporter's questions on current events dominate the final chapter until the conclusion, where the historian's questions lead to the discernment of the significance of the present in the light of the Order's past.

Because there is little extant correspondence of the Knights of Columbus leaders prior to World War I, it has been necessary to rely upon official minutes of meetings and upon public statements to discern the Order's early character. Though there is always a gap between public expressions and private motivations, such public rhetoric does nevertheless reveal much of the Order's ideals of contemporary and Catholic Knighthood. For the post-World War I periods, this history is largely dependent upon the Luke E. Hart Papers (1918–64). Hart was Supreme Director 1918–64, Supreme Advocate 1922–53, and Supreme Knight 1953–64. His papers not only provide a participant's perspective on the formation of policies and the subsequent development of strategies but—because Hart and several leaders with whom he corresponded reflected the evolution of the Order's own self-understanding—form the core of the historical narrative from the Church of Cardinal Gibbons to the Church of the Second Vatican Council.

From its origins to World War I, the Order's goals were most visibly expressed in its assertion of the social legitimacy and patriotic loyalty of Catholic immigrants. By accepting—indeed, extolling—the religious and ethnic pluralism of American society, by portraying Catholic citizenship as the highest form of American citizenship, by promoting American-Catholic culture (symbolized by their strong support of the Catholic University of America), and by expressing a firm belief that the American Catholic experience has had a transforming effect upon Catholicism and upon American society, the Knights generally reflected the optimism characteristic of several ecclesiastical leaders associated with the "Americanist" posture in American Catholicism.

Though there were divergences within "Americanist" and "anti-Americanist" groups of bishops, the Knights seem to have been unaware of such distinctions as they absorbed the general ethos of a natively structured religious vision.

With American Catholicism as the organizing principle of their sense of mission the Knights embraced the Church's ethnic pluralism and promoted the American way of life as a means of dissolving some of the more divisive customs of the Old World. Indeed, one of the most articulate spokesmen of the spirit of the Order, Thomas H. Cummings, reflected what sociologists have subsequently labeled the "triple melting-pot" view of American society. He foresaw the contours of American society as being formed on Jewish, Protestant, and Catholic lines, with these groups living together in a spirit of respect and cooperation. This strand of what the Knights called "Columbianism," in its extolling of religious civility, closely resembled what has recently been known as "civil religion." However, the Order's interpretation of the American-Catholic heritage prevented it from an uncritical endorsement of the implicit creed of American "civil religion."

The Order reached a new phase in its evolution when, in 1917, it was recognized as the official Catholic service agency for the armed forces in World War I. In the immediate post–World War I period, the Order experienced a vast increase in membership and reflected the general trend toward centralization as the larger society also became preoccupied with institutionalization and corporate order. Centralization and corporate growth generated certain stresses among the membership and led to a dissident movement, which exploited the emerging strain between leadership and rank and file.

The centralization of the Church, symbolized in many ways by the evolution of the National Catholic Welfare Conference (N.C.W.C.), also had a strong impact upon the Order's development. In the struggle against anti-Catholicism in Oregon (the Oregon School case) and in Mexico, the Order and the N.C.W.C. clashed on goals and strategy. When the N.C.W.C. was recognized as the official Catholic community-service organization immediately prior to World War II, it was evident that the Order could no longer assume that it was the only effectively organized arm of the Catholic laity. Though there was a time when it could have been absorbed by the N.C.W.C., the Order maintained its autonomy while also maintaining its deference toward the hierarchy.

Traditionally, the Order reflected the social mentality associated with what was called "ghetto Catholicism." However, its fraternal sense of Catholic peoplehood was not expressed in diffident tones of defensiveness but in tones of confidence in the essential legitimacy of American Catholicism, symbolized by Columbus's act of consecrating the New World. The Knights did not view the "ghetto" as a refuge from the mainstream of American life, but rather as a healthy preserve of Catholic culture.

In the post–Vatican II períod, the ghetto walls have crumbled and overt anti-Catholicism and nativism have been relegated to the extreme fringes of American society. Though the Order's self-understanding was deeply affected by the political and religious trends in the aftermath of the election of John F. Kennedy and the Second Vatican Council, its fundamental spirit has persisted to the present. Supreme Knights John W. McDevitt and Virgil C. Dechant committed the Order to the promotion of *diligent* Knights, loyal to their families through insurance, to a membership *devoted* to the traditions and practices of its faith, and to the *defense* of Church against those forces of secularism which are offensive to Catholic social morality. Though fraternalism in general has experienced a severe decline, the Order of the Knights of Columbus today is composed of 1.3 million Catholic Knights located in nearly 7,000 councils—and is continuing to flourish.

I

Origins in New Haven

THE ORIGINS OF THE KNIGHTS OF COLUMBUS follow a pattern deeply etched in the history of most institutions and large social movements. A small group of men gathers together in an obscure, seemingly insignificant meeting to discuss ways in which they can forge an organization to respond to deeply felt social and religious needs.

On October 2, 1881, such a group met in the basement of St. Mary's Church on Hillhouse Avenue, New Haven, Connecticut, to discuss the formation of a fraternal benefit society. Convened at the request of Father Michael J. McGivney, a twenty-nine-year-old curate well known "among the young go-ahead men of the city,"[1] this obscure meeting marked the foundation of what became the largest body of Catholic laymen in the world. Four months after this first meeting, the group adopted the name "Knights of Columbus"; twenty-five years later, Knights were located in every state, in most of the provinces of Canada, in Mexico, and in the Philippines and were prepared to enter Puerto Rico and Cuba.

Although leaders of the first-generation Knights, particularly Father McGivney, established a strong base for the Order's growth and expansion, they had no idea that the unique blend of Catholic, fraternal, and insurance features which they were designing would have such widespread international appeal. Because these features were planned by and appealed to Catholics of Irish descent (with potential appeal to second-generation immigrants of various nationalities), one must attempt to discern the specific social, economic, and religious needs of the Catholic minority in America—particularly of those Irish-American New Englanders—in the last quarter of the nineteenth century. To examine the historical context which gave rise to this singular expression of American-Catholic fraternalism also raises questions related to fraternalism in general as well as to the secular, religious, and ethnic antecedents of the Knights of Columbus in particular.

II

When John Carroll was consecrated bishop in 1790, his Baltimore diocese encompassed the entire nation, with thirty priests ministering to nearly 25,000 Catholics, the vast majority of whom lived in Maryland and Pennsylvania. Although about four hundred French Catholics had been forcibly settled in Connecticut in the early eighteenth century and although there was a smattering of Irish Catholics in this state (fifty-six Irishmen from Connecticut fought the British during the American War for Independence), Catholic communities were priestless enclaves in a militantly Protestant society. Church and state were so intimately linked in Connecticut that it was not until the passage of a new State Constitution in 1818 that the Congregational Church was formally disestablished and religious liberty guaranteed by law. In 1810, Connecticut Catholics were incorporated into the Diocese of New England under Boston's first bishop, Jean Louis Lefebvre de Cheverus (1768–1836).[2] In 1828 his successor, Bishop Benedict Joseph Fenwick, S.J. (1782–1846), appointed the Reverend Robert D. Woodley pastor of all Catholics in Connecticut and Rhode Island. A year later Bishop Fenwick purchased a church from the Episcopal Bishop of Hartford, Bishop Thomas C. Brownell, and appointed the state's first resident pastor. In his history of the Catholic Church in Connecticut, Thomas S. Duggan wrote of the first meeting of the two bishops. " 'Well, Bishop Fenwick,' said Bishop Brownell, 'as we have a fine new Church building we will let you have the old one.' 'Yes,' Bishop Fenwick rejoined, 'and you have a fine new religion and we will keep the old one.' " One New Havener recalled the historic event of Connecticut's first Catholic church: "When we heard that a church had been purchased at Hartford, and was about to have a priest, we were delighted."[3]

In 1834 a New Haven congregation numbering some two hundred became the second official parish, when on May 8 of that year their new church, Christ Church, was consecrated by Bishop Fenwick with Father James McDermott the first pastor. The next year Father William Wiley became pastor of Christ Church. Nine years later, Father William Tyler became the first bishop of the Hartford diocese, which embraced all of Connecticut and Rhode Island. A convert related to a famous family of converts, Bishop Tyler was consecrated on St. Patrick's Day 1844 at the age of thirty-seven.

With 4,817 Catholics in Connecticut and 5,180 in Rhode Island,

Bishop Tyler chose Providence, with a Catholic population of 2,000, rather than Hartford, with only 600, as his episcopal seat. Bishop Tyler's Providence home, described as "a mere shanty," was symbolic of the poverty of the diocese. His successor, Bernard O'Reilly (1803–56), presided over the diocese for six years and as the first bishop of Irish extraction he symbolized the growing ascendancy of the Irish within the nineteenth-century Catholic Church, including the budding diocese of Hartford-Providence.[4]

In 1850 (two years before the birth of Michael J. McGivney), the United States had an Irish population of 961,700. The Great Famine in Ireland of the mid-1840s resulted in the emigration of hundreds of thousands to the United States. The flood of Irish immigrants continued to inundate America's shores after the famine of 1846–49; 900,000 entered the United States between 1850 and 1860, and New York became the "largest Irish city in the world." By 1850 Hartford had 2,300 Irish-born citizens, while New Haven had about 3,400. Besides a goodly number of second- and third-generation Irish-American residents, the total of first-generation Irish in Connecticut in 1860 was 26,689.[5]

Just as construction on the Enfield Canal during the 1820s had attracted many Irish workers to Connecticut, so the famine exiles were drawn to that state by the jobs available on the railroads and in the factories. In 1850 Connecticut was the third largest state in manufacturing; New Haven, the state's largest manufacturing center, attracted the greatest supply of alien laborers, particularly the Irish.[6]

Among those historians who have described the life of Irish immigrants, Thomas N. Brown has succinctly captured its full dimension. He portrayed the Irish as

"like tired migratory birds. Prisoners of their own poverty, they were confined to the cities in which they landed or those of the interior, on rivers and railways where work was available. The potato culture of Ireland had not prepared them for the hard ways of the frontier farm, nor given them the skills to work the land the Yankees left behind. Everywhere the Irish performed the crude labor of the factory, construction gang, and mine; the women, when fortunate, worked as servants in homes of the wealthy. The Irish were the 'hewers of the wood and the drawers of water,' as they had been at home."[7]

Though the transplanting process was economically and socially painful, the Irish brought to America much of what was even then being called the spirit of the old sod to nourish them in their adjustments to the new soil. In 1850 that included the nutrients of a strong sense of nationality and a deep identity with Catholicism. In Ireland the great "Irish Liberator," Daniel O'Connell, had forged a Catholic nationalist alliance in his battle for political liberty. In the 1820s O'Connell's struggle for Catholic emancipation—that is, full civil liberties and the franchise—appealed enough to the priests that they urged the laity to join his Catholic Association. In their Sunday sermons, Irish-Catholic clergymen described emancipation as both a holy and a patriotic cause, and Catholic peasant and urban working-class people flocked to enroll. The Catholic Relief Bill of 1829 was not a total victory, but it did enfranchise many upper- and middle-class Catholics. More importantly, the reform movement provided the Irish masses with the rudimentary political skills necessary for success in a modern democratic system and also symbolized the historic identity between Irishness and Catholicism.[8]

The lines of warfare between Ireland and England had long been drawn on religious as well as on political grounds. Though English incursions into Ireland began in the late twelfth century, it was Protestant Britain which succeeded in the long subjugation process during the sixteenth and seventeenth centuries. The fusion of nationality and religion in Ireland resulted in a unique form of cultural Catholicism. Without native Catholic political leaders, Irish loyalty to Rome was strengthened. Without a class of clerics allied with the social and political elites, loyalty to the native clergy was far greater than on the continent. Hence Daniel O'Connell's Catholic Association was founded upon what Alexis de Tocqueville—probably looking back to the disastrous example in his own country of Félicité de Lamennais—referred to as "an unbelievable unity between the Irish clergy and the Irish population."[9] In a traditional society, priests had been called upon to assume the roles of doctor, lawyer, teacher, and economist, as well as serving as spiritual and liturgical functionaries. In Ireland this was grounded in popular affection as well as in sheer practical necessity. So deep was this affection that "the people referred to their clerics by the Gaelic phrase *soggarth aroon,* or 'priest dear.' "[10] The Irish immigrant to the United States was more likely to be better schooled in politics than were most other immigrants and more accustomed to struggling with a militant Anglo-Saxon Protestantism. And nowhere was Anglo-Saxon Protestantism more entrenched than in the stratified society of New England. Though the acculturation process of the Irish Americans was fraught with the problems of ghetto life—poverty, illiteracy, gang violence, and alcoholism—these transplanted Irish Americans were prepared to stand firm against the anti-Catholicism endemic among the "native" New Englanders.[11]

The large influx of immigrants into America created a severe backlash of that intense anti-foreigner complex which has spasmodically surfaced in American society whenever a seemingly alien minority appears to be threatening the majority's notion of "the American way." Though nativism and anti-Catholicism were not quite synonymous, the strong anti-Catholic residue of the Protestant Reformation frequently manifested itself in nativist attacks. Since the foundation of the Knights of Columbus represents, in part, an Irish-American response to the anti-Catholic hostility which still lingered after the flood tide of nativism before the Civil War, it is necessary to examine more fully this anti-immigrant movement.[12]

American Protestants, infused with traditional antipathy to the Church of Rome, viewed Catholic Europe as antidemocratic and the Pope as a tyrannical despot ever conniving to extend his empire. The nativist, motivated by obvious economic interests, magnified this view and found it strategically effective to vilify the immigrants as pawns in a papal conspiracy to win America over to the old superstitions of Romanism; they then developed political strategies aimed at stiffening the naturalization laws and excluding Catholics and foreigners from public office. Anglo-Saxon racism also expressed itself against the allegedly shiftless, irresponsible Celts. Paradoxically, while many Protestants viewed the immigrant Catholics as antidemocratic conspirators in a papist plot, others feared the immigrants as the fomenters of revolution.[13]

Nativism expressed itself in a plethora of pamphlets, books, and soapbox and pulpit oratory lashing out at the "Catholic menace" to American institutions. Bizarre tales, frequently pornographic in tone or content, circulated in which Catholic priests and nuns were portrayed as at least sexually frustrated, at most, sexually fiendish. The most infamous was the bogus autobiographical exposé *Awful Disclosures of the Hotel Dieu in Montreal* (1836), by "Maria Monk," in which a known "mentally retarded and deranged Protestant girl" described the sexual lives of priests and nuns in lurid detail.[14] Anti-Catholic sentiment reached violent proportions in the early 1830s. An Ursuline convent was burned in Charlestown, Massachusetts, in 1834; in 1844 a nativist mob attacked an Irish neighborhood in Philadelphia, setting fire to homes and bombing churches; anti-Catholic violence also occurred in Boston, New York, Louisville, New Orleans, and other Irish settlements in urban America. In the wake of the Philadelphia incident, Bishop John J. Hughes of New York posted Irishmen as guards to protect the churches of the diocese, which proved to be a successful deterrent to nativist invasion. Some of these incidents were triggered by anti-Catholic extremists overreacting to the Catholic appeal for state aid for parochial schools, while others were either spontaneous or well-planned violent incursions by anti-Catholic hoodlums.[15]

Many Protestant clergymen deplored the violence. However, for a short period the anti-Catholic "neurosis"[16] (Laurence McCaffrey's term for the nativist xenophobia) gained political respectability when, in 1854, the anti-Catholic American Party (an offshoot of the secret society, the Order of the Star-Spangled Banner) was founded. Because its members refused to reveal their aims and objectives, it was called the Know-Nothing Party. With sectionalism and the slavery issue inflaming the body politic, the Know-Nothing Party (its goals were immigration restriction, revision of the naturalization laws, and exclusion of immigrants from the opportunity of holding office) had broad appeal not only to the anti-Catholic element but also to respectable citizens alienated by the urban decay symbolized by the rise of the immigrant ghettos. By avoiding the slavery issue, which had split both the Democrats and the Whigs, the Know-Nothing Party soon became a refuge for disaffected members of both major parties until the Republicans evolved into a national organization. In 1854 and 1855 the Know-Nothings gained local, state, and national election victories in eleven states. They controlled both houses of the legislature and the governor's office in Massachusetts and had surfaced in Connecticut as early as July 1853, where their constitution revealed their true character: "Its object shall be to resist the insidious policy of the Church of Rome and all other foreign influences against the institutions of our country, by placing people, whether by election or appointment, none but native-born Protestant citizens [sic]."[17]

In the 1854 mayoral election in New Haven, a majority of the citizens voted for the Know-Nothing candidate. Though the New Haven Times attempted to expose the anti-immigrant bias of the nativist party, Know-Nothings were victorious in many towns in Connecticut. One reporter stated that there were 169 Know-Nothing lodges and 22,000 members in Connecticut in November .1854. The Hartford Courant supported the Know-Nothing Party, noting, in an editorial, "The individual Catholic votes as the priest dictates; the priest follows the dictates of the prelate, and he so controls the elections as shall best serve the interests of the Pope, the establishment of the Church, and its subsequent complete rule over the country."[18]

From 1855 to 1858, Know-Nothing leader, William T. Minor, was governor of Connecticut. Under his leadership, naturalization laws became more stringent, all militia organizations composed of foreign-born were proscribed, and a law was passed which forbade the registration of Catholic property in the bishop's name.[19] By 1860 the sectional conflict had become the central issue, and the Republican Party was clearly heir to the Whigs as the Democrats' major opponent. The Democrats had been the party of the immigrant before the rise of nativism pinned upon it (in the election of 1884) the label of "Rum, Romanism, and Rebellion," the three Rs of the anti-Catholic animus. But the anti-Catholic nativists' attacks upon the Irish only served to strengthen the latter's unified loyalty to Church and country.

The American Catholic Church of the mid-nineteenth century, in which Irish-American bishops were in the ascendancy, reflected the Catholic revival occurring in Ireland. Recently entitled the "devotional revolution," this revival was characterized by an intensive building program, an enriched pastoral commitment by the clergy, a highly popular devotionalism among the laity and a considerable increase in vocations to the priesthood and religious life.[20] The revival of parish life in Ireland was reflected in the parishes of "little Irelands" in America.[21] At the First Plenary Council of Baltimore (1852), the bishops were vitally concerned with forging a strong parish life. The fiber of this life, strengthened by the mid-century revival, continued to expand and develop in the post–Civil War period. Economic and social improvement among many of the Irish immigrants contributed to the institutional growth of the Church.[22] Dwelling within a hostile environment, the American Catholic Church established its own separate educational and charitable institutions. The immigrant groups also established their own separate benevolent societies, the first of which for the Irish was the Ancient Order of Hibernians (A.O.H.).

Established in the United States in 1836, the Hibernians trace their putative origins as far back as 1565, when Irish Catholics were struggling against Elizabethan imperialism and Catholic persecution. The American A.O.H. became a Catholic defense organization during the nativist period; Bishop Hughes called upon it to provide guards for the churches of New York when they were threatened with anti-Catholic violence.[23] From 1862 to 1876, A.O.H. lodges in the coalfields of Pennsylvania were meeting halls for the Molly Maguires, militant Irish miners organized for industrial conflict with their employers. Because the conflict frequently became violent (eleven Molly Maguires were hanged for murder in 1877), the A.O.H. subsequently disassociated itself from the miners' movement. However, the local Hibernian lodges represented the Irish layman's loyalties to church and country, and it was the A.O.H. which was almost solely responsible for the institutionalization of the St. Patrick's Day parade.[24]

German Catholics also formed their own societies, of which the most prominent was the Catholic Central Verein of America, established in Baltimore in 1855. The Central Verein was concerned with preserving the faith of German Catholics in a society charged with Know-Nothingism, with unifying all benevolent societies, and with sponsoring spiritual, social, and educational programs for the edification of its members and the general improvement of society.[25] It evolved along the lines of the German-Catholic community, with its emphasis upon preserving the German culture and language. Later in the century, conflicts between German and many of the leading English-speaking Irish bishops became intense over the questions of Catholic accommodation to the New World. These conflicts, which included the propriety of Catholic membership in secret fraternal societies, reached crisis proportions in the 1890s in the Americanist controversy.

The proliferation of fraternal societies in America during the latter half of the nineteenth century is a relatively unexplored chapter of American history. Though secret societies also flourished in England and Ireland and on the Continent, no other nation exceeded the United States in sheer variety; during the nineteenth century around six hundred such societies were established in America.

Of course, one may trace the origin of such organizations throughout history, but the economic and social matrix of the nineteenth century shaped a specific type of fraternal society. As industrial capitalism and urbanization advanced, communal life and communities diminished. Though modern Freemasonry, which has middle-class origins, was established in London in 1717 prior to widespread industrialization, its evolution represented a response to men's social need to organize themselves into some kind of brotherhood during a period when the dominant social ethic was becoming individualism. Individualistic, theistic, and anti-Catholic, the Masons organized a collective force infused with brotherly humanism and based on elaborate ritual. The Odd Fellows, the Woodmen, and scores of other societies adopted many of the Masonic principles, such as their three-degree initiation rite, secret passwords, special handshakes, and promises to aid one another in distress and sickness. Subsequently many of these brotherhoods monitored sick benefits and some form of life insurance. These elements were solidified over the decades, so that during the depression of the 1870s, when many commercial insurance companies collapsed, fraternal insurance societies, which were managed by un-salaried or low-salaried confreres, had great appeal to members of all classes seeking communal or economic security. In America, where there was an even stronger individualistic ethic than in Europe, mid-dle- and lower-class Anglo-Saxons, as well as various immigrant groups, organized themselves into hundreds of fraternal organizations ranging from ritualistic Masonic-like societies to temperance and liter-ary groups.[26]

Among Catholics, the Irish Catholic Benevolent Union (I.C.B.U.) was an early attempt to organize all Catholic benefit societies on a national scale. In 1877 a group of Irish Americans in Nashville, Tennessee, founded a fraternal life insurance society, the Catholic Knights of America; a similar insurance society, the Western Catholic Union, was founded in Quincy, Illinois, the same year. The Massachu-setts Catholic Order of Foresters (M.C.O.F.) and the Catholic Benevo-lent Legion (C.B.L.) of Brooklyn, also fraternal insurance societies, were founded in 1879 and 1881 respectively.

Besides the Catholic fraternal insurance societies there were hundreds of smaller death-benefit and burial societies among Catho-lic immigrant groups in the United States. Considering the economic precariousness and absence of social security, these organizations, particularly among immigrant groups, were designed not only for the cultural edification of their members but for the economic necessity of providing financial aid to families in times of sickness and death, and frequently for the preservation of the language of their home-land. The Knights of Columbus originated as one such society, but in a unique way, emphasizing not so much Old World ties as loyalty to the new republic. Unlike most immigrant organizations, it looked more to the potential of the United States than to the traditions of Europe. As will be fully explored in later Chapters, it is this ardent assimilationism, this devoted Americanism—in an era when "Ameri-canism" was to become in many Catholic circles a code word for heresy—that accounts for the continuous expansion of the Knights of Columbus even into the present, while scores of other nineteenth-century movements have in the twentieth century either atrophied or disappeared.

III

Although a lodge of the Ancient Order of Hibernians was located in New Haven, it was a local Irish-American fraternal society named the Red Knights which had a direct influence upon the formation of the Knights of Columbus. Indeed, all the original incorporators of the Knights of Columbus (those men whom the State of Connecticut recognized as the charter members of the Order when it affixed its seal to the articles of incorporation), except Fathers Michael McGivney and Patrick Lawlor, pastor of St. Mary's Church, belonged to the Red Knights. Daniel Colwell, a Grand Knight of the Red Knights (and Supreme Secretary of the Knights of Columbus for twenty-five years), traced the origins of this fraternal society to that period of nativism when William T. Minor, governor of Connecticut, proscribed all Irish-Catholic militia organizations.[27] At the end of the Civil War, in which many Connecticut Catholics served with distinction, Catholics were formally invited to reestablish militia units which were to be incorporated into the National Guard of Connecticut. Indeed, James T. Mullen, who was to become the first Supreme Knight of the Knights of Columbus, was a leader of one of these militia units, the Sarsfield Guards.[28]

The Red Knights (so-called because at their first spontaneous initiation the members covered themselves with red blankets from their Sarsfield knapsacks) was a social organization founded in 1874 at the suggestion of James Mullen. A three-degree initiation was developed, and the Red Knights soon became, in the words of Daniel Colwell, "the most popular social organization of our people in the state."[29] As William Geary, a Red Knight and an incorporator of the Knights of Columbus, noted, speaking for Irish Catholics in general, "Membership in the Red Knights was considered a necessary qualification for young men looking for political, business, and social advancement."[30]

The desire for self-improvement, the drive for respectability, and the recognition of the need for Irish Catholics in New Haven to sustain each other in times of crisis permeated the constitution of the "Sarsfield Council No. 1, Order of Red Knights." The preamble states the order's general goal as "the advancement and mutual improvement of the young men of our race . . . [and] to bring about an acquaintance and maintain a feeling of friendship and brotherly love between young men of our race." The specific objectives were:

1. Mutual improvement in literature.
2. To promote harmony, concord, and good fellowship among all men, and particularly among ourselves.
3. To extend a helping hand to needy Brothers, and to assist them in the time of sickness and death.

To implement the third objective, the Red Knights established a benefit fund out of which was paid $5.00 a week during a member's illness and funeral expenses upon a member's death. Membership was open to men "between the ages of twenty-one and thirty-five years and in good health and possessing good moral character."[31] With "Semper Fidelis" imprinted on their emblem, the Red Knights were dedicated to their motto: Charity, Friendship, and Unity. The order's literary character took the forms of Irish, Catholic, and American cultures and of the staging of dramatic productions for the general public. But according to William Geary, it was none of these that was primarily responsible for attracting members; it was the ceremonial character of its degree work that was the cause of the order's appeal.[32] The March 18, 1875, edition of the *New Haven Morning Journal and Courier* reported that the Red Knights Club was "a new and flourishing secret society of young men, originating among members of Sarsfield Guards."[33]

Catholic parishes in the diocese also sponsored literary societies, but the Red Knights was the first New Haven Irish society to blend literary, sick-and-death-benefit, and ritualistic features into an original fraternal order. However, in 1880 the Red Knights disbanded. William Geary claimed the cause was simply that the leading members had become married.[34] It is more likely that the real reason was that there was no strong economic tie within the membership because the order had a relatively weak death-benefit feature.

In 1878, New Haven Catholics, representing the city's six parishes, formed a strictly death-benefit organization, the St. Vincent's Mutual Burial Association. Like the Red Knights, this burial society included several future incorporators of the Knights of Columbus, among them Cornelius T. Driscoll, the first legal officer (Supreme Advocate), and Matthew C. O'Connor, M.D., the first Supreme Physician. By May of 1881 the association numbered 382, and it nearly doubled in membership the following year.[35] It was an assessment death-benefit society without any of the social and literary characteristics of the Red Knights.

In 1881, twenty-nine-year-old Father Michael J. McGivney, the curate at St. Mary's Church, was chaplain of the "St. Joseph's Young

Men of New Haven,"[36] a total abstinence society attached to St. Mary's parish. (The temperance movement had gained strong momentum within Irish-Catholic communities in the United States, and nearly every Irish-American parish in Connecticut formed what was colloquially called a TAB society—for "total abstinence.")[37] Though there is no strong relationship between the foundation of the Knights of Columbus and the temperance group, Father McGivney was active in both societies, as was Cornelius T. Driscoll, who served as president of the Connecticut Catholic Temperance Society in the mid-1870s. Also, it was not unusual for a TAB society to form a council of the Knights of Columbus, such as the foundation of Russell Council in New Haven in the nineties.

Father McGivney's leadership of the St. Joseph's TAB was of great historical significance, because he soon attempted to incorporate the group into the Ancient Order of Foresters (A.O.F.), a fraternal insurance society. According to Daniel Colwell's recollections, "The reverend gentleman volunteered to lay the matter before his lordship, Bishop [Lawrence S.] McMahon. This was done but the proposition did not meet with the bishop's approval and the matter was quietly and finally abandoned."[38] We have no evidence of Father McGivney's views of the Red Knights or of the St. Vincent's Mutual Burial Association, but Colwell's remarks indicate that the young priest was seriously concerned with the need for a fraternal benefit society. Indeed, Colwell's recollections are substantiated by William H. Sellwood, one of the incorporators of the Knights of Columbus. "I always think of the Knights in connection with a temperance society to which I belonged a good many years ago."[39]

The Ancient Order of Foresters, one of three Forester fraternal societies, formed its ceremonial character upon the legends of "Robin Hood and his merrie men." Though we have no evidence of Bishop McMahon's reasons for disapproving Father McGivney's proposal to incorporate the TAB society into the A.O.F., he probably considered that secular fraternal society within the general context of secret societies condemned by the Church. Since the proposal to join the A.O.F. occurred in the fall of 1881 (Colwell's recollection of the date), and since the first meeting of what was later the Knights of Columbus occurred in October 1881, there is probably a strong causal relationship between the two. Daniel Colwell, perhaps influenced by hindsight, recalled that Bishop McMahon and Father McGivney "freely discussed the topic of a National Fraternal Association for Catholics."[40] At this juncture Father McGivney appears to have been driven, and perhaps encouraged by Bishop McMahon, to explore various alternative paths rather than to establish a particular society. Though there is no evidence revealing Father McGivney's views during this crucial period, there is no doubt that he was deeply interested in pursuing the topic of a Catholic fraternal insurance society among groups of Catholic laymen of New Haven.

Thus the Knights of Columbus did not originate out of some plan for a national organization but developed from the simpler notion that some sort of local fraternal insurance society was needed. This notion was discussed at gatherings of two groups of laymen, one in the basement of St. Mary's Church on October 2, 1881, the other at 157 Church Street (the offices of Daniel Colwell and Cornelius T. Driscoll) on January 9 or 15, 1882. As several incorporators recalled:

The project of an association of some form for the material and social advantage was met by him [Father McGivney] with enthusiasm. He increasingly urged activity in advancing the desire for the establishment of some kind of an association. It was always in a vein of seriousness and optimism of the success of the project that he counselled with his associates, and he would not be put off with promises they would look into the matter. It was this earnest, persistent attitude of his that finally resulted in a call for a meeting, which was held in the basement of St. Mary's Church and attended by about eighty men.[41]

The minutes of that first meeting in the basement of St. Mary's Church further illustrate the significance of the young curate, but they are frustratingly general:

The meeting was called to order by the Reverend M. J. McGiveny [sic], who explained the object of the meeting. Michael E. Tracy was elected chairman and John F. O'Brien was elected secretary. There were 80 present at the meeting from the different parishes. After some discussion a motion was made that the chair appoint a committee of 10 on Constitution and By-laws. The chairman appointed the following to that committee: Reverend M. J. McGiveny [sic], C. T. Driscoll, John Tracy, John F. O'Brien, Bart Healy, Thomas McCurry, Michael Curran, Thomas Leddy, John T. Cerrigan [sic], Patrick Madden. Then a motion was made and carried that the chairman be added to the committee to be its chairman. The meeting adjourned to meet the third Sunday at the same time and place."[42]

These minutes reveal not the birth of a dream but the businesslike pursuit of practical needs. One should note that though Father McGivney called the meeting, he deferred to lay leadership from the very beginning. His role as the organizer and catalyst, however, continued to develop. At the third meeting, on November 6, 1881, he "reported that he wrote to some of the clergy in this diocese and had received some encouragement from them."[43] At the next meeting, two weeks later, a motion was passed that "Rev. M. J. McGiveny [sic] go to Boston and get what information he could from the Catholic Societies of Boston."[44] At the fifth meeting on December 4, the election of officers for a six-month term resulted in Father McGivney's election as Financial Secretary.[45] It seems that the laymen considered their priest the officer responsible for handling the day-to-day business of the society; the remaining offices, except for medical examiner, appear to have been limited to a general executive character. C. T. Driscoll was elected President; M. E. Tracy, First Vice-President; John T. Kerrigan, Second Vice-President; Michael Curran, Treasurer; John F. O'Brien, Recording Secretary; Dr. M. C. O'Connor, Medical Examiner. These titles show that at this juncture the group was certain of its insurance character, but the lack of any fraternal titles such as Supreme or Grand Knight indicates that its future as a fraternal society was indefinite.

According to the minutes of December 18, Father McGivney reported "that he went to Boston and was treated very nicely but they [the Massachusetts Catholic Order of Foresters] did not want anything to do with us." After delivering his report he was "instructed . . . to go to Brooklyn and find out what he could about Catholic Societies there."[46] At this point the minutes of the St. Mary's group run contrary to the minutes of the 157 Church Street group, which had its first meeting on either January 9 or 15. Since the extant minutes of both groups are not original transcriptions, it is possible that chronological and other inaccuracies could have crept in during the copying process. Daniel Colwell wrote that Father McGivney had experienced "indifferent success" with the men of St. Mary's, and that it was only after he had met with a representative of the defunct Red Knights, who was interested in reviving the association, that the Church Street group was called together for its first meeting.[47] William Geary and others view the St. Mary's group as a continuous body out of which developed the Church Street group,[48] while Colwell points to the Church Street group as a separate organization which Father McGivney welded to a dormant St. Mary's group.[49]

According to the minutes of January 9, 1882, the Church Street group discussion centered on Father McGivney's proposed visits to Boston and Brooklyn, where he would explore the possibility of associating his New Haven organization with the Massachusetts Catholic Order of Foresters and the Catholic Benevolent Legion respectively.[50] The meeting adjourned with the understanding that it would reconvene upon Father McGivney's return from his journey to Boston and Brooklyn.

Regardless of the exact dates of his visits with representatives of these two societies, the results were that the C.B.L. (for reasons unknown) had no appeal, while the M.C.O.F. rejected the proposal to expand into Connecticut because it considered "it could not accept us [i.e., the Church Street group] as insurance risks."[51] Because the professional character of the M.C.O.F. impressed the group, it was decided to form a similar organization which they called the Connecticut Catholic Order of Foresters (C.C.O.F.). Patrick H. Carrigan's original application for membership into the C.C.O.F. was dated January 15, 1882. On the "Report of the Investigation Committee" located on the reverse side of this application appears the following: "To the Officers of St. Mary's Court No. 1, C.C.O. of Foresters." Above the words *St. Mary's* is written *K.C.* and stamped above the words *C.C.O. of Foresters* is *Knights of Columbus*. M. J. McGivney's signature appears at the top of the list of committee signatures. The date of March 12, 1882, is scratched out; below it is written April 8, 1882. On the application for medical examination, attached to the application for membership, *St. Mary's* was not deleted, but *Knights of Columbus* was stamped above the title *Connecticut Catholic Order of Foresters.* It also provides us with Carrigan's initiation date as February 2, 1882.[52] The information on this document is in agreement with the recollections of Geary, Driscoll, and others: "The decision then was to organize a similar society to be known as the Connecticut Catholic Order of Foresters. Application blanks were printed with the applicant's declaration on one side and the medical examination on the reverse. . . . The organization was perfected February 2, 1882. On that date eleven men were examined for insurance in the St. Mary's Court No. 1 Catholic Order of Foresters."[53]

However, as the minutes of the Church Street group for February 2, 1882, report, "a motion was made and unanimously carried that 'we organize a purely original organization.' It was moved and seconded and carried that the society be known as the 'Connecticut Knights of Columbus.' "[54] The Geary-Driscoll history states that sometime between February 2 and February 6 the name K. of C. was adopted. We do know that by February 7 the organization had adopted Knights of Columbus, for the *New Haven Morning Journal and Courier* of Wednesday, February 8, reported, "The first meeting of those interested in the Catholic organization known as the Knights of Columbus was held in St. Mary's Church, Monday [Feb. 6] evening, and was presided over by James T. Mullen . . . about sixty were present."[55]

In the February 11 *Connecticut Catholic* (an Irish-American newspaper owned and edited by a layman but "in the service to Catholics of the Diocese of Hartford"), the reporter from New Haven stated that the meeting was held on Tuesday rather than Monday: "Pursuant to a call issued by Reverend Fr. McGivney over sixty young men assembled in the basement of St. Mary's Church last Tuesday evening [February 7, 1882] and formed a cooperative benefit order to be known as the Knights of Columbus."[56]

Daniel Colwell wrote that Father McGivney first thought of Columbus as the patron, with "Sons of Columbus" as the name of the society; whereupon James T. Mullen, the former Supreme Knight of the Red Knights and the first Supreme Knight of the Knights of Columbus, successfully urged the adoption of the name "Knights of Columbus" to better symbolize the ritualistic character of the Order.[57] Others attributed the origin of the name to Dr. O'Connor and C. T. Driscoll.[58] Dr. O'Connor recalled the discussion of the name during which he suggested "The Columbian Order." He invoked the cause of Catholic civil liberty as he asserted that the Order's patron signified that, as Catholic descendants of Columbus, "[We] were entitled to all rights and privileges due to such a discovery by one of our faith."[59] William Geary substantiated O'Connor's recollection when he stated that the name clearly signified that Catholics "were not aliens" in America but rather participated in the foundation of the country. Geary also envisioned a Columbian movement—perhaps anticipating the quadricentennial of the discovery of America in 1892—and said that "the name Columbus would be a tower of strength" for expansion as well as abundant with themes "upon which a ritual could be written."[60]

The adoption of the name Knights of Columbus represented a profoundly significant phase in the origins of the Order. Father McGivney's first attempt to establish a fraternal benefit society failed when Bishop McMahon rejected his proposal to incorporate the St. Joseph's TAB society into the Ancient Order of Foresters; his persistence led his followers to consider a Catholic Foresters motif. Yet it soon became obvious to both the founder and his associates that the Robin Hood legend was not in accord with their need to portray their ideals ritualistically. By adopting Columbus as their patron, this small group of New Haven Irish-American Catholics displayed their pride in America's Catholic heritage. The name Columbus evoked the aura of Catholicity and affirmed the discovery of America as a Catholic event.

An 1878 editorial in the *Connecticut Catholic* illustrated the devotion to Columbus among a portion of the American-Catholic community: "As American Catholics we do not know of anyone who more deserves our grateful remembrance than the great and noble man—the pious, zealous, faithful Catholic, the enterprising navigator, and the large-hearted and generous sailor: Christopher Columbus."[61]

Though the notion of knighthood had been popularized by the New Haven Red Knights, the term "Knights" symbolizes the deep conviction that to pledge one's fealty to the Catholic ideals of Columbus involved one in a militant struggle against the strong anti-Catholic and, therefore, anti-Irish sentiment so prevalent in traditional New England society. Had these men developed their ceremonial character under the patronage of St. Patrick or upon the Robin Hood Forester model, Father McGivney's society would never have achieved international stature; but all North American, Caribbean-, and Pacific-Island Catholics could identify with Columbus as a Catholic hero. Other Catholic fraternal insurance societies, such as the Catholic Knights of America and the Catholic Foresters, became large organizations, but eventually the Knights of Columbus exceeded them in membership, influence and range of activities. Though the Columbian themes were barely discernible in the American-Catholic landscape, Catholic journalists and scholars, as well as such leading members of the hierarchy as James Gibbons of Baltimore, John Ireland of St. Paul, and John Lancaster Spalding of Peoria, were strongly urging their immigrant flocks to accommodate themselves to an American way of life.

As founder of the Knights of Columbus, Father McGivney deeply believed in the compatibility of Catholicism and American fraternalism. No doubt Father McGivney was motivated by the wish to keep young Catholics from entering the ranks of condemned secret societies and by the need to protect families during sickness and death, yet he was equally persistent in his aim to establish a Catholic fraternal society imbued with a zealous pride in one's American-Catholic heritage. In early February 1882, when only a handful of Catholic men had adopted the idealism of the discovery event, no one could have predicted the remarkable expansion of the Order. On the contrary, as we will see in the next chapter, the men of '82 confronted severe criticism, experienced deep disillusionment, and seriously doubted the value of their efforts. It was Father McGivney's persistence and optimism that carried the Order through its infancy. As he later wrote of those days in January and early February, "the Order I was endeavoring to establish fell back almost lifeless, but not dead."[62]

Though it had not developed its by-laws, ritual, and organizational structure, the Church Street group established a Supreme Council and incorporated itself under the laws of Connecticut. The Supreme Council minute book reports that election of officers occurred on February 2, 1882. Since documents do not reveal the formation of the Supreme Council before May, it is likely that the February elections were temporary and that the election of permanent officers occurred when the by-laws and constitution of the Order, which granted the authority to the Supreme Council, were completed in mid-June. The Church Street group elected the following by unanimous vote: James T. Mullen, Supreme Knight; John T. Kerrigan, Deputy Supreme Knight; Reverend Michael J. McGivney, Corresponding Secretary; Michael Curran, Treasurer; James T. McMahon, Financial Secretary; Cornelius T. Driscoll, Advocate; Reverend Patrick Lawlor (pastor of St. Mary's Church), Chaplain; Dr. Matthew C. O'Connor, Physician; Daniel Colwell, Lecturer. The minutes of this February 2 meeting also report that Colwell was appointed a committee of one to draft articles of incorporation to be presented to the state legislature.[63] Colwell recalled that he drew up articles of incorporation based upon those "of a well known fraternal organization and approved by the Legislature of Massachusetts." He submitted his draft to Father McGivney, who filed it with the Connecticut legislature. Because Colwell's draft did not include a section on the property rights of the Order, it was not in accord with Connecticut's laws on incorporation. C. T. Driscoll, an incorporator and a member of the lower house of the legislature, assisted by A. Heaton Robertson, a state senator from New Haven, guided the amended articles through the legislature and on March 29, 1882, the Knights of Columbus assumed the legal status of a corporation.[64]

Resolved by this Assembly:

SECTION 1.

That Michael J. McGivney, Patrick Lawlor, Matthew C. O'Connor, Cornelius T. Driscoll, James T. Mullen, John T. Kerrigan, Daniel Colwell, William M. Geary, Thomas M. Carroll, Bartholomew Healy, Michael Curran, and all such persons as may from time to time be associated with them, with their successors be, and they are hereby, constituted a body corporate and politic by the name of the Knights of Columbus of New Haven, for the purpose of rendering mutual aid and assistance to the members of said society and their families; and by that name shall have perpetual succession, and be capable in law to purchase, receive, hold, and convey all kinds of property, real and personal, requisite or convenient for the purposes of said society; may have a common seal, which they may change and renew at pleasure; may sue and be sued, defend and be defended, plead and be impleaded, answer and be answered unto, by their corporate name, in all courts and places whatsoever; may elect such officers and agents as they shall deem necessary, and may make and execute necessary by-laws, rules, and regulations for the proper management of said society and its property; "provided," such by-laws, rules and regulations shall not be inconsistent with the general laws of this state.

SECTION 2.

This resolution may be amended or repealed at the pleasure of the general assembly.[65]

During the spring of 1882, Father McGivney was immersed in committee work on the by-laws and permanent organization of the Order. Almost immediately after the incorporation of the Knights of Columbus, he wrote a letter (dated April 1882) to all pastors of the Diocese of Hartford. Clearly the first diocesan-wide promotional endeavor by the founder of the Order, this is the earliest document which details Father McGivney's pastoral concerns. He prefaced his introduction to the aims and objectives of the Order by stating its religious and civil credentials. "By permission of our Rt. Rev. Bishop, and in accordance with an Act of the Legislature of the State of Connecticut, we have formed an organization under the name of the Knights of Columbus." Father McGivney was deeply concerned about the numbers of young Catholic men who were attracted to secret fraternal societies. "Our primary object is to prevent our people from entering *Secret Societies* by offering the same if not better advantages to our members."[66]

Though a Catholic fraternal order struck him as a pastoral necessity in protecting the faith, "Unity and Charity"—the Order's motto until 1885, when "Fraternity" was added—were expressed through its sick-benefit and life-insurance feature. "Secondly, our object is to unite the men of our faith throughout the Diocese of Hartford, that we may thereby gain strength *to aid* each other in time of sickness; *to provide* for decent burial, and *to render* pecuniary assistance to the families of deceased members." The founder's letter concluded with his hope that the Knights of Columbus would be represented in every parish throughout Connecticut. He urged each of the pastors to "exert your influence in the formation of a council in your parish."[67]

Knowledge of Bishop Lawrence S. McMahon's role in the foundation of the Knights of Columbus is limited to Father McGivney's remark, "By permission of our Rt. Rev. Bishop." Though a strand of oral tradition virtually places Bishop McMahon as the founder of the Order, there is no documentary evidence revealing his views on any of its aspects other than Father McGivney's statement that the group received the Bishop's consent to embark on this venture. Historians agree that Bishop McMahon was a practical man of few words. An astute administrator who viewed his role as shepherd along the simple theoretical lines that he was the implicit spiritual director of all organizations of Catholics, Bishop McMahon would not have given his consent without serious consideration. Though we have no documentation evidencing Bishop McMahon's views on the Knights of Columbus foundation, there is one document which reveals his strong views on the principles for ecclesiastical recognition of a lay society of Catholic men. Writing to the president of the Connecticut Total Abstinence Union in 1885, the Ordinary of the Hartford diocese stated that recognition of lay organizations "is not given indiscriminately even though the organization be comprised of Catholics. She [the Church] has a right to expect that the members of these societies shall show themselves conspicuous by their loyalty toward her principles, their respect and obedience to her clergy, and their fidelity to Catholic methods in the advancement of their ends."[68]

During a period when the Catholic Church viewed secret societies as suspect, at best, Bishop McMahon's approval of this experiment in Catholic fraternalism represented a bold move. It is uncertain whether it was upon the insistence of the Bishop or the advice of Father McGivney that the office of Supreme Chaplain was established, but according to Bishop McMahon, a chaplain within a lay society should never be "simply a figurehead." However, the Knights of Columbus has never been considered a canonical lay society legally attached to the authority structure of the Church, even though the presence of a chaplain symbolized to Bishop McMahon the Church's implicit authority. "It is a fundamental principle that no association of men, even though comprised of Catholics alone, can attain a position of a Catholic organization unless they have to direct them a Chaplain . . . who represents to them the Church, and speaks with her authority. It is essential also that the official [Chaplain] should be canonically appointed."[69]

With a Supreme Chaplain elected rather than "canonically appointed," the Knights of Columbus did not qualify for recognition as a canonical organization. Nevertheless, from the fact that it has always been spiritually directed by a priest who could not have held that office unless he had the bishop's implicit endorsement, the Knights of Columbus may be considered from its foundation a society which Catholics are permitted to join in good faith.

Bishop McMahon's approval of the young curate's venture into Catholic fraternalism did not have an immediate effect upon the expansion of the Knights of Columbus, and Father McGivney's letter to the pastors did not elicit one positive response in the formation of a parish council. Though there was discouragingly little interest in the new fraternal order, Father McGivney was confident of its success. On June 7, 1882, he wrote to the High Court Secretary of the Massachusetts Catholic Order of Foresters that "our beginning is extremely slow but I think that when our by-laws are distributed we will advance more rapidly."[70] On June 15 Father McGivney placed before the Supreme Council the Constitution and By-laws of the Order.

Although this constitution was frequently amended during its first fifteen years, much of the general authority structure of the Order has been preserved to the present. The Supreme Council, composed of Supreme Officers, Grand Knights, and Past Grand Knights, was the highest tribunal and legislative body, meeting annually to make laws, "receive appeals, and redress grievances." The Supreme Committee, composed of the Supreme Officers and elected by the Supreme Council, was vested with "all executive authority." Instructed to meet at least once a month, the Supreme Committee was granted responsibility for all the processes involved in new-council development, for the property held in the name of the Supreme Council, for investigating and adjudicating charges against subordinate council officers and members, and for suspending councils in violation of their charter. It was accountable to the Supreme Council in the form of an Annual Report on the general condition of the Order.[71]

The major duties of the Supreme Knight were set by his responsibility as the presiding officer of the Supreme Council and Supreme Committee. In addition, he was charged with deciding "all questions of order and usage, and all constitutional questions subject to an appeal." Anticipating that period when a large number of councils would preclude his personal visitation, he was granted the authority, with "the advice and consent of the Supreme Committee," to appoint a Deputy Supreme Knight "who would act on his behalf in the installation of officers of the subordinate councils in his district." The District Deputy Supreme Knight was envisioned as the equivalent to today's State and District Deputies, the representative of the Supreme Knight in the formation of new councils and in the ceremonial work of the Order.

The Supreme Secretary was the most responsible administrative officer, particularly as the central coordinating figure in the insurance aspect of the Order and as the general correspondent in all matters between the Supreme Committee and the subordinate councils. Because his position was considered a full-time occupation, he was one of two salaried officers. The Supreme Council was empowered to fix his salary at its annual convention. The Supreme Treasurer was in charge of all moneys of the Supreme Council and, with the approval of the Supreme Knight and attested by the Supreme Secretary, was to pay all bills regularly. The Supreme Financial Secretary would collect all moneys to be turned over to the Supreme Treasurer. The Supreme Physician was to confirm or veto all subordinate council appointments of examining physicians as well as decide on all appeals from applicants refused admission by subordinate council physicians.

The Supreme Chaplain "shall conduct all religious exercises of the Supreme Council" and shall open and close meetings with prayers. The Supreme Advocate was the chief legal officer, responsible for advising the Supreme Committee on constitutional issues and, more importantly, representing the Order in all legal matters. The Supreme Lecturer acted as the guardian of the fraternal ideals of the Order. At the direction of the Supreme Knight, he was to instruct the various councils of the Order. He was also a salaried officer, which salary was to be fixed by the Supreme Council, and could receive honorariums from the local councils. The duties of the Supreme Chancellor, Warden, and Guard were not specified.

The subordinate councils' officers were modeled on the Supreme Committee: Grand Knight, Deputy Grand Knight, Recording Secretary, Financial Secretary, Treasurer, Lecturer, Advocate, Physician, Chaplain, Warden, and Guard. The constitution stipulated that each council should form an investigating committee, to pass on the physical and personal qualities of candidates for membership, and on a board of trustees which was empowered to supervise and approve all financial dealings of the council. The insurance program entailed a $1.00 per-capita assessment upon the death of a member, with the hope that the Order would soon reach one thousand members, thereby providing a $1,000 death benefit. Initiation into the Order was restricted to men between the ages of eighteen and fifty, with a graduated initiation fee: $3.25 at age eighteen plus 25 cents for each additional year, with a fifty-year-old paying $11.25. Officers were elected by a simple majority, but two thirds of the council's membership had to be present and voting as a condition for a constitutional election.

The duties assigned to these offices were theoretically identical to those of the Supreme Committee; the Grand Knight, Financial Secretary, and Physician were the key offices in the supervision and promotion of the fraternal and insurance character of the Order on the local level.

The organizational structure of the Knights of Columbus reflected the democratic features of the American system of government. Subordinate councils elected their own leaders as well as representatives who, with Grand Knights and Past Grand Knights, composed the Supreme Council, which elected the Supreme Committee officers. The Supreme Council was the legislative branch; the Supreme Committee was the executive branch. However, because the Supreme Committee was responsible to the Supreme Council, it was analogous to a parliamentary-cabinet system of government rather than to the American constitutional separation of powers. The Supreme Knight was the chief executive officer in that he was charged with executing the law, but he was subject to the advice and consent of the Supreme Committee. However, because the Supreme Knight embodied the fraternal ideals of the Order, he possessed moral authority far beyond the letter of his mandate. The Supreme Secretary was implicitly the chief administrative officer, symbolized by his responsibility for the Seal of the Order. Since the management of the insurance and sick-benefit business was lodged in the Supreme Committee, the duties of the officers reflect the corporate structures which were evolving during the period of the rapid expansion of American industry and commerce. This elaborate system of government clearly indicates the long-range intentions of Father McGivney and his founding Knights. They envisioned the Order as a statewide organization, the Connecticut Knights of Columbus. Though based upon sound business practices, the Knights were unlike commercial insurance companies, as they were motivated by charity rather than profit: "The object of this association is to promote the principles of unity and charity . . . so that in our unity we may gain strength to bestow charity on each other."

In an undated circular, *Connecticut Knights of Columbus . . . Objects, Benefits, and Instructions for Forming New Councils,* signed by "M. J. McGivney, Supreme Council Secretary," the practical character of the Order was clearly projected. After noting the advantages of belonging to an Order founded on unity and charity, one which would pay $5.00 per week during sickness and $1,000 upon the death of a member (once there were 1,000 members), Father McGivney provided detailed instructions on the process of forming new councils. The minimum membership for a new council was twelve gentlemen who had passed the physical examination. After a council was formed, new councils were instructed to adhere to the following directives:

1st.   Have the Treasurer and Financial Secretary furnish the required bonds.

2nd.   Have stringent medical examination of all new members.

3rd.   Appoint thoroughly efficient officers and committees.

4th.   Invest all surplus funds profitably, safely, and legally in the name of the council.

5th.   Keep the management expenses low.

6th.   Have thorough and regular audits of all accounts.

7th.   File all documents, communications, bills, vouchers, receipts, memorandums, etc., etc., and destroy none.

8th.   Pay direct rents for the council room, and have written agreements therefor.

9th.   Make all returns regularly, promptly, and correctly.

10th.   Read the reports and other documents issued by the Supreme Council as soon as received.

11th.   Impress upon members the importance of being present at all meetings to guard the interests of the Council, and zealously assist in its advancement.

12th.   Adhere strictly to the Laws and Rules of the Order, and avoid strife, discord, and personality.

13th.   Keep the cash in the Treasurer's hands as low as possible, and within the amount of his bond.

14th.   Transact the business of the Council promptly, and in a businesslike manner; also, discourage carelessness, frivolity, and levity during the session of the Council.

15th.   Do not put off until tomorrow that which can be accomplished today.

16th.   Do not accept an office if you cannot attend to the duties; nor retain an office if you cannot attend to the same.[72]

Father McGivney's principles for sound management appear very extensive. Obviously he was quite concerned that the council leaders realize their responsibilities as "field agents" in an insurance business, as respectable representatives of the Order's motto, "Unity and Charity," and as symbols of its reliability as a repository for the savings of their members. Since there was a strong likelihood of uneducated and inexperienced men rising to positions of leadership, it was particularly necessary to instruct them in the principles of effective business practices.

Charity and Catholic brotherhood within the Order were the twin virtues; it was not until the Knights of Columbus became a strong national organization that it broadened the notion of charity to include the general needs of church and society. In 1882 the Order faced the enormous task of convincing first- and second-generation immigrants to assume financial responsibility for their families. Within the extended family structure of Irish village society, kinship ties provided for social security and insurance was unthinkable, but within the Little Irelands in urban industrial America it was rapidly becoming a necessity. However, breaking down the attitudes of the Irish village was an extremely slow process.

The first council, instituted on May 15 (though initiation was held on June 15), chose to name itself San Salvador in commemoration of that island upon which Columbus first set foot in the New World.[73] It is significant that two of the men listed as incorporators, Thomas M. Carroll and Bartholomew Healy, were not initiated into the Order's first council. According to one source, Bartholomew Healy quarreled with other incorporators over Father McGivney's leadership. Healy allegedly stated that he never knew a society to prosper which had a priest at its head, and Carroll seems to have sided with Healy in this dispute.[74]

William Geary recalled that on May 15, 1882, James Mullen stated that if the Order succeeds it will be because of Father McGivney's "indomitable will" to succeed and his "faith" in the ultimate success of the Order. Geary paraphrased Mullen's remarks: "Fr. McGivney is too modest to assume to himself any honor. But Brothers, if this Order succeeds . . . as we fervently hope, in uniting the Catholic men of the state, the honor as its founder will be his." Then Geary added his own comment: "No commission from Church or State gave to him [Father McGivney] the honor, it was given to him on that 15th day of May by twenty-four men with hearts full of joy and thanksgiving recognizing that without his optimism, his will to succeed, his counsel and advise [sic] they would have failed, they gave to him the honor which attached to his name as founder of the Knights of Columbus, and which no power on earth can disassociate from his name."[75]

With an average age of thirty-four and with a majority being native-born Americans, the charter members of the Knights of Columbus belonged to that generation whose childhood experienced the most intense period of anti-Catholic nativism, whose teenage years witnessed the Civil War and reconstruction, whose early manhood encountered the severe depression of the mid-'70s. Reaching their thirties by 1880, these charter members also represent that post-famine generation of Irish Americans characterized by a strong loyalty to their parish and its clergy, an increasingly improved economic condition, a growing sense of confidence in America, and an emotional attachment to the cause of Irish nationalism.[76]

As Supreme Secretary, Father Michael J. McGivney was entrusted with the daily management of the infant Order, a position in accord with his role as founder, organizer, and ambassador of the Knights of Columbus. Born in Waterbury on August 12, 1852, the eldest child of thirteen children, Michael was baptized by Father Michael O'Neale, the first pastor of Waterbury's only Catholic church, St. Peter's, later named Immaculate Conception. He must have been a rather precocious youngster, for at the age of seven he was admitted to what would be considered today as the third grade. "The principal, Thomas Meagher, was charmed with the boy's manner and from the date of his entrance into the classroom . . . he was noted for excellent deportment and proficiency in his studies."[77] After completing his grade-school education, he worked in the spoon department of Holmes, Booth and Haydens. The registrar at St. Mary's Seminary, Baltimore, recorded, after his name, "was in spoon factory from 13teen to 16teen [sic]."[78]

Father Thomas F. Hendricken (1827–86), pastor of Immaculate Conception and later bishop of the Providence diocese, took a strong interest in the boy and, in 1868, personally accompanied him to the College of St. Hyacinth in Quebec, Canada, where McGivney spent two years in preparation for entering the seminary. In 1869 he was awarded the prize for excellence in English, as well as an honorable mention in Latin translation and grammar. There is no extant record of his studies in 1870.

In 1871–72 McGivney studied philosophy at Our Lady of the Angels Seminary, attached to Niagara University in New York.[79] Though there is no written record of his seminary training in 1872–73, oral tradition locates him at St. Mary's Seminary in Montreal. Since he lacked funds for tuition, Bishop Francis P. MacFarland of Hartford paid his seminary expenses, and at the Bishop's request he entered St. Mary's Seminary in Baltimore in the fall of 1873. Prior to McGivney's ordination, Father Joseph P. Dubruel, S.S., the rector of St. Mary's Seminary, Baltimore, wrote Bishop Thomas Galberry, "Mr. McGivney is a very good and pious young man, with good and attractive manners, and much address and industry, exceedingly sensitive *usque ad lacrymas* [even unto tears]." History clearly contradicts Father Dubruel's concluding remarks: "[He is] rather weak-headed both mentally and morally, not able to control great difficulties, he will please and succeed in an ordinary situation."[80] On December 22, 1877, Archbishop Gibbons ordained him.

After celebrating his first Mass at Immaculate Conception in Waterbury, Father McGivney moved to New Haven, where he began his life as a curate at St. Mary's Church. William Geary recalled the personality of the young priest: "Father McGivney was a man of simple character, pleasant, light-hearted, and delighted [sic] in the companionship of children; although rather retiring in his disposition, he possessed an indomitable will and never was discouraged no matter what obstacles might come his way."[81]

Father William Slocum, pastor at Immaculate Conception, Waterbury, in an address on June 10, 1900, told a story which reveals Father McGivney's keen sensitivity. A young man under the influence of liquor shot and killed a policeman who had been his close friend. Tried and convicted for first-degree murder, the young man was sentenced to death by hanging. Father Slocum recalled that Father McGivney became the convict's spiritual director during the period prior to his execution.[82] The young man was the convicted murderer James (Chip) Smith, who, according to the *Connecticut Catholic* of July 29, 1882, was "visited every day by Father McGivney."[83] Father McGivney celebrated a High Mass for Smith; "many tears were shed when the Reverend Father spoke of the unfortunate fate of the young man." As Father Slocum concluded the story, "In the death cell, preparatory to the march to the scaffold, Father McGivney was deeply affected and extremely nervous, so much so that the condemned man begged him not to break down. 'Father,' he said, 'your saintly administration has enabled me to meet death without a tremor. Do not fear for me, I must not break down now.' Father McGivney did not recover for some time."[84] The New Haven reporter for the *Connecticut Catholic* wrote that Chip Smith "went bravely to his death, and let it be said to the honor and credit of his spiritual adviser, Rev. Father McGivney, that he so braced him with the comforts of his religion that Smith could not help but die as he did."[85]

Father Gordian Daley recalled his only meeting with Father McGivney: "I saw him but once and yet I remember his pale, beautiful face . . . it was a face of wonderful repose, there was nothing harsh in that countenance although there was everything that was strong . . . guile and ambition were as far from him as from heaven." Daley noted of his prison ministry that "at the city jail the wardens still hand down anecdotes of what Father McGivney said and did during visits which he paid the prisoners."[86]

Father McGivney's influence among young people was particularly well known. He was gifted with an endearing personality and an easy temperament, infused with a strong sense of charity, "never known to cherish the slightest feeling of resentment towards those who differed with him; his great charity in this respect being one of the marked features of his whole life."[87] Because he elicited great trust and possessed that "indomitable will," Father McGivney persevered against great odds. Father Slocum recalled the many priests and laymen who bitterly criticized his work on behalf of the Knights of Columbus and how he "was made the laughing stock of those who thought themselves more wise and far seeing than he."[88] William Geary also remembered how Father McGivney suffered abuse for establishing what his critics referred to as the Catholic Masons. The young priest persevered because he was convinced of the necessity of establishing an order which would respond to the need for financial protection during illness and at the time of death and the need to bind Catholic men's loyalties to one another in a deeply Catholic-oriented ritualistic Brotherhood.

Though the ritual was not completed until the following year, the Columbian theme was eagerly promoted. As Father McGivney installed the officers of San Salvador in the late spring of 1882, he had no idea of the Order's bright future. Yet when he presided over the opening of this "Holy Redeemer" Council, he may have sensed in the spirit of the gathering that unique blend of loyalties so implicit in the foundation of the Knights of Columbus: loyalty to their Church, to each other, and to America, mediated by the Columbian theme, pride in the Catholic heritage of America. Indeed, this first generation of the Order viewed the discovery of America as a Catholic event, just as Anglo-Saxon Protestants viewed the landing at Plymouth Rock as a Puritan event. With the establishment of San Salvador Council No. 1, the Knights of Columbus were implicitly celebrating the landing of the *Santa Maria,* the Catholic counterpart to the Protestants' *Mayflower* and a ship which had arrived 128 years earlier. As a member of the Massachusetts Catholic Order of the Foresters was to write in early 1883:

One is particularly struck with the appropriateness of the official seal of the Supreme Council. This is a very fine cut, representing the landing of Columbus. The grouping of the figures and the entire surroundings portray a truly Catholic scene. In these days of political subserviency, when it is sometimes thought a crime to assert [Catholic] rights, it is truly consoling to find a sister Order come out with a design that would seem to insist that somebody landed in America before the saintly pilgrims.[89]

2

Conflict and Expansion in Connecticut

By the summer of 1882 the Knights of Columbus had developed a well-defined organizational scheme for a diocesan-wide order. From the outset it was apparent to Father McGivney and the charter members that if they were to develop a popular society they needed to devise strict procedures to assure that the Order's professional business was seen to be of the highest stature. The Columbian themes were not to be viewed as a commercial trademark but rather as ideals of "Catholic manhood" permeating the Unity and Charity motifs. These ideals were not grounded in rituals or ceremonials (nor were they consciously perceived in refined terms) until the spring of 1883. In the summer of 1882 the men of San Salvador were expressing the felt need to display their pride as Catholic Americans. Though they had a diocesan-wide structure, a clear idea of their good works in times of sickness and death, and a notion of lay-Catholic Columbian spirituality, the Order was limited to a small group of men who continued to meet in the basement of St. Mary's Church.

During the summer of 1882, many of the young Knights began to experience deep disillusionment and discord. Father McGivney's letter to the pastors of the diocese and his printed brochure on new-council development did not elicit one positive response, not one application for a new council. On the contrary, the infant Order was subjected to criticism from layman and cleric alike. As was noted earlier, many considered the Knights of Columbus a mock form of Catholic Masonry, and Father McGivney was derided by critics who distrusted his motives. Though the Supreme Officers were prominent men among the Irish Catholics of New Haven, they were immersed in other positions of responsibility and had only a limited amount of time for the task of promoting a volunteer society, and Father McGivney's parish work was extremely demanding.

The minutes of San Salvador Council from July through November reveal various tensions among the members. On July 2 Michael Tracy, who had faithfully attended every meeting of the St. Mary's group since October 2, 1881, proposed "that should any officer be absent three successive times without a reasonable excuse that office be declared vacant."[1] Since Grand Knight James Mullen (also Supreme Knight) was absent for the July 2 meeting, Tracy was obviously challenging the Grand Knight to assume his responsibilities. At the July 16 meeting, with Mullen in the chair, the council incorporated Tracy's amendment into the by-laws. Tracy's proposals continued to dominate the meetings through November. On August 6 he urged all the members to "send circulars to our friends in various towns and try to induce them to start new councils."[2] On August 20, Tracy indicated his disillusionment with the lack of clerical support for the Order: "If we cannot get a notice of a meeting announced in the churches or any encouragement from the clergy, I think it is time we found some other quarters and I move we appoint a committee of three to procure other quarters and that the next meeting be subject to their call."[3] Since San Salvador was meeting in the basement of St. Mary's Church, Tracy's motion, which was carried, may have been prompted by the members' desire to project accurately their diocesan-wide aspirations and not to be viewed as a parish organization.

At the first meeting at Tyler's Hall on September 21, only seventeen members were present. Since James Mullen had not attended a meeting since July 16, the office of Grand Knight was declared vacant.[4] Disillusionment was evident during the next three meetings. On October 5 Peter Clancy moved that the council either consider becoming a "court of the Foresters" or disband.[5] On October 19, by a vote of thirteen to five, the council decided to appoint a committee to confer with the District Chief Ranger of the Foresters on the feasibility of transforming San Salvador into a court of that order.[6]

On November 2, the Feast of All Souls, San Salvador grappled with the issue of simple survival. It was reported that the Foresters would not accept them as a separate court, but they were invited to join "Court Sarsfield or Court of the Guiding Star." With thoughts of disbanding circulating throughout the council chamber, "Brother Tracy appealed to the members to stick and not give up. Dr. O'Connor also appealed to the member [sic] and said that [their] work would be rewarded in the future."[7] O'Connor later recalled that eventful meeting.

At this proposed action [disbanding and joining the Foresters] I strongly protested and declared that we had started out with our drums beating and our flags flying; not to antagonize but to provide a more suitable organization. . . . I said if we were going down, let it be with honor . . . and I said, there was no necessity for any such action, but if we kept up our courage, worked shoulder to shoulder, success would crown our efforts.[8]

The Supreme Physician's impassioned address proved effective, for "a unanimous vote was taken to stick together."[9] The leadership issue remained volatile. On November 16 it was resolved: John T. Kerrigan was unanimously elected Grand Knight; Patrick Kearny, Deputy Grand Knight; James T. McMahon, Financial Secretary; Michael Curran, Treasurer; Dr. O'Connor, Medical Examiner; and William Sellwood, Recording Secretary. Michael Tracy, John F. Moore, and Father McGivney were elected Trustees. The pastor of St. Mary's Church remained as Chaplain. James T. Mullen, a chronic absentee Grand Knight during this critical period, still presided as Supreme Knight, but as long as there was only one council that office was insignificant.[10]

Though San Salvador had revived in November 1882, it was not until the following March that the Columbian spirit caught hold outside Council No. 1. In a March 9, 1883, response to a letter of inquiry (which is not extant), Father McGivney wrote to P. J. Ford of Meriden, who, according to Father McGivney's remarks, had discovered the existence of the young Order via the *Pilot,* which was the Catholic newspaper for Boston. Under the letterhead "Supreme Council, Connecticut Knights of Columbus, Rev. M. J. McGivney, Financial Secretary," he enthusiastically stated, "I am glad to hear that the Meriden Catholic young men are not behind their age in looking for their own benefit. I send you copies of our by-laws, etc. After perusing them I hope you will come to the conclusion of forming a council in Meriden." With characteristic optimism, Father McGivney went on to assure Ford "that when we are well established in the diocese we can bid defiance to the secret societies and bring our fellow Catholics to enjoy, without any danger to their faith, all the benefits which those societies offer as inducements to enter them."[11]

Though Ford garnered interest in forming a council in Meriden, Father Thomas Walsh, pastor of St. Rose of Lima Church in Meriden and vicar general of the diocese, seems to have been reluctant to approve the Order's extension into his parish. Without such approval, Father McGivney delayed his visit to Meriden, with the result that Ford's group considered joining the Foresters. On April 17, Father McGivney explained his position to Ford.

Your dispatch this morning occasioned both joy and sorrow. Joy at the thoughts of your being so anxious to form a council and sorrow to hear that you had it in mind to join the Foresters which I hope you will never do. I sent a dispatch this morning and one tonight. I hope you have not acted one way or the other yet. You know that one cause of delay, and I may say the principal one, was my waiting a letter from Fr. Walsh. Not receiving it I had to prepare one of the other members of the Supreme Council to go to Meriden and I was about to telegraph tonight to say a delegation of two would go up Friday to organize, but unfortunately I am held in suspense by the sickness of one of the delegates' wives.[12]

Father McGivney would have made the trip himself but, as he wrote to Ford, "if I did Father Walsh would come out against the Order and destroy all our hopes." With only this cryptic remark, it is impossible to detect whether Father Walsh was opposed on principle to the Knights or merely resentful of any outside clergymen organizing the men of his parish. Father McGivney assured Ford that a delegation of the Order, which "is purely civil and businesslike in all its transactions," would be sent to Meriden, and that "if the young men in Meriden intending to join our band will be a little patient I promise you everything will come out satisfactory."[sic][13] Since this delegation successfully negotiated the formation of a council in Meriden, Father Walsh's reluctance seems to have stemmed from his opposition to the New Haven priest rather than the Order itself. The Meriden reporter for the *Connecticut Catholic* wrote, "A new Catholic benevolent Order has been founded in this State to be known as the Connecticut Knights of Columbus. Delegates Kerrigan, McMahon and Sellwood of New Haven, members of the Supreme Council, were in town Monday night [April 23, 1883] and instituted a new council here."[14]

However, the council was not formally instituted until May 16, 1883, when Mullen, Kerrigan, Sellwood, McMahon, and Colwell installed the officers of Council No. 2, which adopted the name Silver City, representing the members' pride in Meriden's reputation as a center for the manufacture of quality tableware. On one level the name may be viewed as local chauvinism, but one may also see the charter members of Council No. 2 to have been stating implicitly that as first- and second-generation Catholic immigrants they were as loyal to the traditions of Meriden as were the descendants of the Puritans.

Though the vast majority of the officers of Silver City were Irish Americans (John Dowling, Joseph Curran, John B. Glynn, P. J. Ford, John Scully, and Dominic Brennan), P. T. Marchand was of French extraction, and the chaplain, Father A. Van Oppen, was Flemish.[15] Hence, the Knights of Columbus showed themselves as not exclusively Irish Americans; indeed, it was the only American fraternal society which did not, by its constitution, prohibit Negro membership. Because the Columbian themes were thoroughly American Catholic, the Order gradually appealed to a variety of ethnic groups, particularly those of the second generation who were groping for a fraternal medium through which they could express their pride in Catholicism and their loyalty to America. However, since the Order was promoted by the Irish Americans and since other ethnic groups founded their own benefit societies, the Order's membership reflected the predominance of Irish Americans in the Northeast until it spread into the towns of the middle Atlantic and midwestern states, where there were increasing numbers of non-Irish ethnic groups.

The *Connecticut Catholic* did not refer to an initiation rite in its article on the installation of the officers for the Silver City Council. According to a strand of oral tradition still circulating in 1981, Daniel Colwell wrote the initiation ceremonial during the train ride from New Haven to Meriden. Colwell recalled that James Mullen assigned him the task of developing ceremonials in the spring of 1882. They agreed that there should be three sections in accord with the "Trinity of Virtues, Charity, Unity, and Brotherly Love."[16] Though the first section of the initiation rite had been prepared in time for the opening of San Salvador Council, the entire ceremonial was not ready for Bishop McMahon's approval until the spring of 1883. After frequent consultation with Mullen, Colwell devised the rituals. As Geary and Driscoll recalled, "Father McGivney advised that all the ritual and secret work be laid before the bishop of the diocese. . . . A few members of the committee [probably Colwell and Mullen], with Father McGivney, met with the bishop at the rectory of St. Mary's Church and he heartily approved of the work and bade the committee and the new Order God speed."[17]

When the ceremonials were first printed in 1885, the Seal of the Order revealed only two virtues, "Unity and Charity," and the handbook contained only two sections, as if there were a two-degree initiation. However, articles in the *Connecticut Catholic,* which reported on various initiations in 1885, referred to a three-stage initiation. One infers that the third degree was in an experimental phase during these early years until the Order officially adopted a specific ceremony for "Fraternity" in 1891.[18]

Since the ceremonials were intended as a "rite of passage" into "Catholic Columbian manhood" they allowed a broad margin of innovation and experimentation within the specified formulae. Those presiding could ask the candidates to elaborate on the articles of Catholic belief and on their application in the Order and in society in general, and there might also have been some sort of theatrical performance of one or more of the cardinal principles of Knighthood. Certainly, defense of the faith and pride in the Catholic foundation of America were two of the most impressive lessons of the ceremonials. One newspaper account in the *Connecticut Catholic* praised the way in which Supreme Knight Mullen presided at an initiation rite. "Mullen . . . conducted the ceremonies through the Three Sections of the Order. To say that he did his work well, and himself justice, is but faint praise. The exercises were very instructive and gratifying to the . . . brethren, who were very loud in their praise of its many excellencies."[19]

With Silver City established and San Salvador flourishing, the June 15, 1883, convention took place in an atmosphere of confidence and hope. In attendance were nine Supreme Officers (Father Lawlor, Supreme Chaplain, was absent); two representatives from San Salvador, Thomas Leddy and Henry P. Kenny; and the delegate from Silver City, P. J. Ford. William Geary was also a delegate, according to his status as one of the incorporators.

Supreme Knight Mullen opened the convention. After noting that there had been no lapses (nor had there been a death in the Order), Mullen congratulated the delegates for "having passed the dangerous days of infancy" and for displaying "the splendid manhood on which our Order is made." As if he were participating in a ceremonial instructing his brothers in a valuable lesson on fraternal charity, Mullen said, "I am not a prophet nor yet the son of a prophet. There is a voice low and soft that tells me that many homes and many families in the future will bless your unselfish efforts—and that in years to come your names and deeds will be inscribed upon the rolls of modest honor."[20]

With two councils securely founded, with the preliminary work completed for the formation of two additional councils in Middletown and Wallingford, and with "our ritual completed," Mullen was confident that "the way is paved for a grand advance." Then he concluded, "Let us gird our loins, each one resolved to do the best in the interest of a United Catholic Fraternity, bearing malice for none and with a charity broad enough to embrace all worthy men, we will do our duty to our God and our fellow man."[21]

Besides unanimously reelecting each of the Supreme Officers for another one-year term, the most significant item of business concerned the symbols of the Order. The Supreme Knight's design, with the symbols of the anchor, the compass, and the sextant for the three degrees, was approved. The delegates also voted that Mullen be a committee of one "to design a suitable emblem to be identified with the Order."[22] According to William Geary, James Mullen developed the K. of C. emblem from his prior design for the Red Knights. The latter was a shield with the letters R.K. (Red Knights) interwoven in the center, a Maltese-like cross at each of its three corners, "Semper Fidelis" along its base, and the letters C, F, and U (Charity, Friendship, and Unity) embossed upon a crown at the top. The outline for the Knights of Columbus emblem was a shield imposed upon a Maltese-like cross as the general symbol for Catholic Knighthood. Within the shield Mullen placed the specific symbols: a vertical mace representing the ideals of unity and authority, with an anchor and a sword crossed behind it, emblematic of the Order's patron, Columbus, and the knightly virtues of honor and mercy. "K. of C." was placed on the bar at the top of the shield. Geary recalled that Mullen had proposed maintaining "Semper Fidelis" along the bottom of the shield to indicate the continuity from the Red Knights to the Knights of Columbus, but that proposal was rejected.[23] Except for later innovations in colors and shading, Mullen's design is still the official emblem of the Knights.

Supreme Knight Mullen, the leading fraternalist of the Order, presided at the installation of council officers and at the three sections of the initiation rites, a role which was in accord with his experience as a Red Knight and, one might add, as an amateur actor in local theatrical productions. On the other hand, Father McGivney kept aloof from the social dimension of the Order. Though he seems to have been well aware of the value of ceremonials as the binding force for fraternal unity, he spent his energy in promoting the insurance feature. Underlying his emphasis on business was his pastoral concern for the social and financial security of the family. Traditional Irish folk wisdom viewed any attempt at advance preparation as a fool's ploy to outwit "Mr. Death"; such folly would only provoke from Death an early invitation. Not only did Father McGivney battle this residue of Irish folk culture, he also was determined to instill a sense of moral responsibility among the Catholic wage earners in Connecticut. For this, he could draw on his own experience as he recalled his widowed mother raising a large family. In his capacity as Corresponding Secretary (he was also referred to as Supreme Secretary and wrote under the letterhead of Financial Secretary), Father McGivney wrote a long letter to the editor of the *Connecticut Catholic* (August 25, 1883), in which he informed "the public of the good the Order of the K. of C. is destined to bring about in the future." He clearly revealed his intention to limit the Order to the State of Connecticut and explained the reasons why the K. of C. should not become a national organization.

First, we can always more readily command a knowledge of the financial condition of the Order and thereby prevent fraud—a most important item in the maintenance of unity and charity, peace and order in an endowment and benevolent corporation such as ours. Secondly, because much labor and unnecessary expenses are avoided in the case of delegates traveling to conventions, in collecting assessments, etc., etc., etc.

He then elaborated on the Order's motto, "Unity and Charity."

Unity in order to gain strength to be charitable to each other in benevolence whilst we live and in bestowing financial aid to those whom we leave to mourn our loss. The manner in which we effect this is by monthly payments for the "benevolent fund," from which members when sick receive five dollars a week . . . , and for the "endowment fund" by a per capita tax of one dollar at the death of a member in good standing.

He explained the $1,000 limit of the endowment: that after the Order exceeded one thousand members the assessment would decrease according to the rate of the increase in membership, that each officer was obliged to be bonded for twice the amount of the moneys entrusted to him, and lastly that "the strictest vigilance" would be maintained over the financial affairs of the local councils, which were required to operate according to stringent procedures of responsibility and accountability. "Everything is worked on strictly business principles, as we are solely a business corporation." With only two councils in existence at the time, Father McGivney strongly stressed the professionalism of the Order's benevolent character in order to reassure potential candidates of its financial reliability.[24]

Hopeful that "before long" councils would be formed "in many of the parishes throughout the diocese," the founder of the Order noted that "similar organizations are promoted by Catholics in nearly every state in the union. We have it is true begun at a rather late hour to do what should now be well on the road to completion. However we have set the wheel in motion, and with willing cooperation in a work that lends so much to our own welfare, we venture to say that soon, very soon, the Order of the Knights of Columbus will hold a prominent place among the best Catholic cooperative corporations in the union."[25]

Father McGivney mentioned that the K. of C. developed along the lines of its sister society, the Massachusetts Catholic Order of Foresters

(M.C.O.F.). However, a member of the M.C.O.F. in a letter to the editor of that Order's publication, the *Catholic Forester,* which was reprinted in the *Connecticut Catholic,* pointed out the distinctions between the two Catholic cooperative insurance societies. Upon the death of a member, the M.C.O.F. assessed the local court while the K. of C. assessed the individual. "Here is an improvement of no small effect, for it does away with a cumbersome system of collection which is in vogue with us." The correspondent indicated that both societies assessed individuals equally regardless of age. "This plan of equalized assessment is not strictly an equitable one, for the longer the member continues in the Order, the more he pays, while an older person, who enters the Order later on, brings with an older age the increased risk without a corresponding increase in his assessment." However, the Forester pointed out that "if the fraternal spirit be such that young and old are to be treated alike then the Knights of Columbus was destined to be for the Catholic of Connecticut what the M.C.O.F. is for us today." He also noted the appropriateness of the Columbian themes, concluding with "one more word; the Financial Secretary of the Supreme Council is the Rev. M. J. McGivney of New Haven. Let this fact speak."[26]

Father McGivney's letter to the editor so impressed the latter that he urged his "male readers" to consider the benefits "to be derived from this great organization." He also pointed out that Father McGivney was "laboring hard to call the attention of the Catholics throughout the state to the Knights." The editor proudly concluded that "Rt. Rev. Bishop McMahon most heartily approved of the organization, and it is to be hoped that very soon branches will be established in every parish in the Hartford diocese."[27]

The Meriden Knights of Silver City Council promoted the Order so vigorously that by the end of October they had recruited eighty-four members, over twice the number then enrolled in San Salvador, New Haven. On October 19, delegations from New Haven and Meriden participated in the opening of a new council in Middletown. Named Forest City Council No. 3, it began with a membership of fifty men. Apparently there was no clerical reluctance at Middletown such as had delayed instituting a council in Meriden, since Father McGivney was present at the ceremonials for the initiation and installation of officers.[28]

Because Silver City was growing so rapidly—125 members by mid-November—the need for establishing another council in Meriden surfaced in December 1883.[29] In order to entice men to join the proposed new council, the organizers were allowed to offer a reduced initiation fee. Whoever joined during the first six months would be required to pay only $3.00. After that the fee would be charged according to the age of the applicant.[30]

Wallingford, adjacent to Meriden, was also actively pursuing a new council. The *Connecticut Catholic* reported that at "the first organizational meeting at Wallingford a number of prominent Catholic gentlemen had gathered at National Hall to consider forming a council. There will, no doubt, be a good council established here, as some of our best men have taken hold of the matter."[31] Dr. Andrew W. Tracy of Meriden's Silver City Council was actively promoting new-council development in Wallingford as well as in his hometown. Though the Wallingford council was instituted before Meriden's second council, the latter's application was accepted by the Supreme Committee first. Hence Meriden's Washington Council received the number four and Wallingford's Pinta (one of the three ships in Columbus's first voyage) the number five. The names of councils Nos. 4 and 5 clearly represent the character of the Order's pride in the Catholic contribution to America and its loyalty to the founding fathers of the nation.

The institution of Washington Council (February 28, 1884) was a gala event with twenty-five members from San Salvador, twenty-five from Pinta, and one hundred from Silver City present for the occasion. Representing the Supreme Committee were Kerrigan, Colwell, James T. McMahon, and Sellwood; the "Rev. M. J. McGivney, founder of the Order and present Supreme Secretary" was also in attendance.[32] For the Meriden reporter of the *Connecticut Catholic* to designate Father McGivney as founder of the Knights of Columbus as early as 1884 reflects the general recognition bestowed upon him early in the Order's history. His attendance at the opening of councils in Middletown and Meriden (Father Walsh had died the previous summer) no doubt symbolized to the new members the integrity of an Order with a priest as founder and chief administrative officer.

II

In April 1884 Pope Leo XIII published an encyclical letter, *Humanum Genus,* denouncing Freemasonry as an abominable form of naturalistic religion.[33] The letter reflected the definition found in the then current edition of the *Catholic Dictionary* as "essentially opposed to the idle belief in the personality of God whose name in the Masonic rituals veils the doctrine of blind force only guiding the universe. It is essentially subversion of legitimate authority."[34] Though the latter statement was not entirely applicable to American Masons, the European lodges were frequently centers of political dissent and anti-Catholicism, which, though more impassioned in Europe, were characteristics of all Masonic lodges in the nineteenth century. In the fall of 1883, American archbishops and their representatives met in Rome to discuss problems of the American Catholic Church preparatory to convening a Plenary Council the following year. One of the major topics discussed was the issue of secret societies. Since seventy-eight such societies had been formed prior to 1880, and 124 new ones originated during the 1880s, the American hierarchy found it extremely difficult to forge a consensus position on all secret societies. Should the Odd Fellows, Knights of Pythias, Ancient Order of United Workmen, and the Ancient Order of Foresters all be proscribed along the lines of the Church's proscription of Masonry?[35]

John Gilmary Shea, the leading Catholic historian of the day, wrote an article for the April 1884 issue of the *American Catholic Quarterly Review* in which he discussed the vast popularity of secret societies. Though he cited their ceremonials as sources of great appeal, he viewed their life-insurance feature as the major attraction:

But a still more powerful attraction was the establishment in the lodges of a system of cooperative life insurance, by which in case of death assessments were made on all who joined the project, to pay the amount insured. As the payment thus required was far less than the premiums demanded by ordinary life insurance companies, many became Freemasons in order to be able to insure with them. Other secret associations adopted the same system, and out of this grew mutual cooperative insurance associations which took the form of secret societies, but which, from the low rate at which insurance was given, became very popular.[36]

D. J. Donohue of Forest City Council, Middletown, was impressed with the relationship between the encyclical of Leo XIII and the burgeoning Order of the Knights of Columbus. His letter to the editor of the *Connecticut Catholic* appeared in the May 10, 1884, issue.

Two events have recently occurred which cannot fail to set our Catholic people thinking; namely, the Holy Father's indictment against Freemasons, at Rome, some days ago, and the First [actually the second] Annual Convention of the Connecticut Knights of Columbus at New Haven Tuesday last. The serious danger to which young Catholics are exposed by the workings of the first society, and the need of the second for their protection and to supply the social and beneficial assistance, which men in a community like ours find most imperative, could not better be set forth than by these two important events. Indeed, the Holy Father has recommended the formation and fostering of societies which will counteract the effect and ward off the dangers of those secret societies which are [proscribed] by the Church. For these great purposes the Knights of Columbus, as an organization, is eminently fitted. It has among its members several priests and carries with it the God speed of the bishop.[37]

After introducing his readers to the features of the K. of C. insurance program, Donohue stressed the privilege associated with membership in the K. of C., which was, he concluded, "one of the highest distinctions a man can enjoy."[38]

III

The second annual meeting of the Supreme Council was held at the San Salvador Hall in the Hoadley Building, New Haven, on April 29, 1884. The delegates met between sessions again on June 15 to consider a new constitution which had been prepared for the Supreme Council. The constitution, which was ultimately approved and printed in 1884, was not a drastic departure from the 1882 constitution; its major innovation was to refine the duties of Supreme Council officers as well as the procedures for accountability.[39]

One such refinement in the 1884 constitution was an increase in the authority of Deputy Supreme Knights. Because the Supreme Knight could not attend every initiation ceremony and supervise every council, District Deputy Supreme Knights were appointed to act on behalf of the Supreme Knight in their districts. The proliferation of councils required this constitutional change. The District Deputy Supreme Knight, empowered to organize and institute councils within his district, was the precursor of the present state and district deputies. He was the liaison officer between the Supreme Council and specific subordinate councils as well as the representative of the Supreme Knight in supervising the insurance and fraternal aspects of each of the councils in his district.[40]

Supreme Knight Mullen opened his address to the June 15 convention by discussing the origins of the Order and its rather late appearance on the fraternal scene:

It will be admitted that up to this time we, as a distinct people [i.e., Irish Catholics] had been sadly behind the times. . . . The practical example set us by our non-Catholic and German-American friends and neighbors was so manifest as to make our position almost intolerable to the thoughtful and patriotic Catholics. To know that we were the only element, in this community at least, that did not properly provide a reasonable protection for our kind, at the most critical and distressing situations [sickness and death] likely to visit our hearths at any time, and often without warning, was not flattering to our self-interest, and the dictates of charity and brotherly love. This then to a people who in all other respects were freely abreast of the times was indeed humiliating.[41]

After this rather dramatic introduction to the historic conditions which engendered the origin of an Irish-American Catholic fraternal society, Mullen expressed his gratitude for the expansion of the Order and his confidence in its future.

Though there probably was some campaigning before the meeting, the minutes reveal that the election of officers proceeded without contest. However, after James Mullen was unanimously elected Supreme Knight and John Dowling of Silver City Council unanimously elected Deputy Supreme Knight, Mullen "announced that he had been instructed by Father McGivney to inform the council that under no consideration could he [McGivney] serve as Supreme Secretary and that he desired, through the Supreme Knight, to express his warmest thanks to the brethren for their great kindness to him during his service as secretary and that he would ever aid in the work of advancing the prestige of the Order when his sacred duties would permit." Mullen informed the convention of his efforts to persuade Father McGivney to continue as Supreme Secretary, but "he was reluctantly obliged to yield to the arguments of the worthy priest."[42] The conflict between his parish duties and those incumbent on his office in the Knights of Columbus must have become rather intense as the Order expanded. With five councils and the promise of many more in the near future, Father McGivney removed himself from the demanding office of Supreme Secretary and accepted the office of Supreme Chaplain, an office which removed him from daily business concerns and was more compatible with his other priestly duties.

After Mullen announced Father McGivney's wishes, he took himself out of the chair in order to nominate Daniel Colwell, "a brother . . . who had been of great service to the Order . . . at many critical times, to succeed Father McGivney as Supreme Secretary."[43] Colwell was unanimously elected and continued to serve as chief administrator of the Order until 1909. The remaining offices were filled by leaders of the various subordinate councils: Supreme Treasurer, John F. Butler, Washington Council; Financial Secretary, William Hassett of Pinta

Council; Supreme Lecturer, D. J. Donohue of Forest City Council; Supreme Warden, James McCarthy of Forest City Council. New Haven members filled the remaining offices; Supreme Advocate, C. T. Driscoll, and Supreme Physician, Dr. M. C. O'Connor. The total membership of the Order came to 429: San Salvador, New Haven, 98; Silver City, Meriden, 159; Forest City, Middletown, 80; Pinta, Wallingford, 32; Washington, Meriden, 60. The Order had collected $100 during what was called "the fraternal year" (time between conventions) and had expended $168.60, $135.65 of which was spent on printing.[44] San Salvador advanced the money necessary to cover the deficit. There is no extant record of the councils' sick benefits, but there had been no need for death assessments, as not one member had died since the Order's foundation.

At the first session of the Second Annual Convention, the committee on the constitution voted unanimously "to request the *Connecticut Catholic* to lend its assistance to the Order, and to support it in such matters as it may deem fit; and as may be compatible with the aims of that journal." The committee instructed Chairman D. J. Donohue and Secretary William Geary to write a letter to the *Connecticut Catholic* explaining why the newspaper should support the Order. Their letter appeared in the June 7 edition of the weekly newspaper and noted that because the *Connecticut Catholic* was a recognized organ of the Roman Catholic Faith it should encourage "all societies whose objects tend to bring a better condition of things, both morally and socially,"[45] among the people of the Hartford diocese.

Donohue and Geary listed seven ways in which the Knights of Columbus qualified as a society worthy of the journal's encouragement:

a. It receives within its body only recognized Catholics.
b. It requires them to be men of good moral character.
c. It has, as the basis of its entire structure . . . unity and brotherly love.
d. Its charity consists in furnishing both moral and material assistance to members in need. . . .
e. It also requires members to render all the aid to worthy brothers in distress which can be rendered without great injury to the relieving member or those dependent upon him.
f. It guards against the vices of poverty, want, and lack of friends, by providing necessary and reasonable means in case of death or sickness, and supplying in strange places friends [easily] recognizable to any true brothers, and all the kindness which the word friend implies.
g. It fosters a unity among its members which can only be found in

associations bound together by the strongest human ties. By means of this unity the Order possesses strength and standing sufficient to make its charitable objects perfectly feasible.

Geary and Donohue also stressed the role of the Order as a respectable alternative to those secret societies proscribed by the Church. "How many young [Catholic] men, tempted and seduced by the false glare of virtue, charity, and fraternity issuing from the lodges and council chambers of the Free Masons and other dangerous organizations, have been drawn away from the Church, can never be known; but it is safe to say that there is not a single parish in the diocese that has not by this means suffered more or less." The Knights of Columbus, "within the limits of the Church," promoted virtues "in as full a perfect manner, in fact, as any of these dangerous organizations pretend to do."[46]

Though the *Connecticut Catholic* had previously endorsed the Order, Geary and Donohue continued their promotional efforts through published correspondence to the editor. On June 14, 1884, a letter from Geary appeared. Once again he urged Catholic men to enjoy the benefits of a fraternal society "and at the same time not violate their consciences or antagonize their Church." Though he referred to "exemplification of the life and work of our patron," Geary stressed the insurance benefits of the Order. He wrote of the poor unfortunate man who failed to consider insurance "until surrounded by sorrowing wife and little ones." Geary concluded his letter in an equally emotional tone. "Let us live, not as bubbles upon the waves, which when bursted, vanish and leave no trace of their existence, but rather in the language of our ritual: Let us live for those who love us, for those we know are true; for the heavens that smile above us, and the good that we can do."[47] Two weeks later, D. J. Donohue's letter appeared in the newspaper. Though it reads as a pamphlet on the organizational structure and insurance benefits of the Order, Donohue noted, introducing his readers to the ceremonials of the Order, that "the social side of the Order is perhaps the most beautiful, impressive, and magnificent ceremony . . . and is one of the vital parts."[48]

May and June were prosperous months for the Order: On May 30, DeSoto Council No. 6 and Freestone Council No. 7 were instituted in Cromwell and Portland respectively. On June 21 the second council in New Haven was instituted, Santa Maria No. 8. Meriden maintained its leadership in both councils and members; on June 23, Genoa No. 9 was instituted in the Silver City. Branford, just ten miles east of New Haven, opened its first council, El Dorado No. 10, on August 10. The

Connecticut Catholic had been instrumental in spreading the news of the Order, and in September 1884 its editor hosted an organizational meeting for a council in Hartford. With thirty men present, the group unanimously adopted the name Green Cross Council. "The appropriate and historic name was chosen as it was the name of the banner or device that Christopher Columbus selected when he first started to discover America. This was the same banner that fluttered in the breezes when he and his followers first landed and knelt in fervent thanksgiving to God for bringing them safely to the New World."[49]

On October 9, Green Cross Council No. 11 received its charter and the officers were installed. Bishop McMahon, who had returned from Rome on September 19, just six days before the election of officers, was the first chaplain of the Hartford council. The *Connecticut Catholic*'s coverage of the ceremonials did not include references to either Bishop McMahon or Father McGivney. However, the founder of the Order was in Hartford that day, as he was listed as one of the priests in attendance at an anniversary memorial Mass for former Bishop Galberry, celebrated by Bishop McMahon.[50]

The Hartford reporter for the *Connecticut Catholic* provided his readers with an eyewitness account of the initiation ceremonies for Green Cross Council. The two-and-a-half-hour ritual climaxed with Supreme Knight Mullen conferring "the Third and most important Degree." The curious and even outlandish element in this affair is brought out by the newspaper report.

On all sides and by each one about to be let into the mysteries of the Knights much speculation and interest were manifest. Finally when the large trunk of the Supreme Council was deposited in the ante-room, the anxiety of all was raised to the greatest tension. It was supposed to be where the sturdy goat, that each one was to ride about the hall, bareback, three times, was therein confined. Some even alleged they heard him kick the sides of the iron bound and spacious trunk. No one fainted, however, and each one said he was willing to ride a goat in order to become a member of the Knights of Columbus.

After the ceremonies, over 125 Knights met at St. Patrick's Hall for refreshments, dinner, and entertainment. "Thursday evening, the 9th of October, will long be remembered by the Knights of Columbus. Friendships were made on that evening that can only be broken by death."[51]

Though the formulae for the Third Degree had not been formally adopted by the Order, the theme of Catholic fraternalism with its emphasis upon friendship seems to have made a lasting impression upon the men who passed through the ceremonials. It was not simply "friendship," in the general sense of the term, but Catholic Columbian friendship. The Order cultivated Catholic friendship in its councils because the ceremonials were designed to foster mutual loyalties among brother Catholics in a social atmosphere charged with intense animosity toward Irish and Catholics.

A month after Bishop McMahon and Father McGivney shared in the memorial Mass for Bishop Galberry, Father McGivney was appointed pastor of St. Thomas' Church, Thomaston, Connecticut. On Sunday, November 9, he preached his farewell sermon to the parishioners of St. Mary's. After seven years of service in New Haven, "his words of parting brought tears to the eyes of many."[52] The *Connecticut Catholic* continued its commentary on Father McGivney's farewell sermon.

He said that, like St. Paul, he has been called upon to depart. He was before them today to say those sad words "good-bye." . . . He had prepared the little ones for their First Communion, and had late and early visited the sick as well as attending to the other duties of a priest. If he had ever been seemingly severe or austere he asked forgiveness. Whatever he had done had been in the interests of morality, in justice to religion, and for the people's spiritual welfare. He prayed that they would finally meet in Heaven, where there are no partings, and where no one is called upon to say "good-bye."[53]

That Sunday evening a meeting was held in St. Mary's hall during which the pastor, Father Lawlor, and others spoke of the general sadness created by Father McGivney's departure. (William Geary was appointed chairman of a committee to draft resolutions honoring the priest.) Father McGivney left for Thomaston on November 13 but returned to St. Mary's on November 30 for a reception in his honor, when testimonial resolutions of deep fondness and a gift of $400 were presented to him.[54] Three of his fellow incorporating officers of the Knights were members of the resolution committee: C. T. Driscoll, William Geary, and James Mullen. Though such testimonial resolutions were not uncommon, the committee seems to have designed this resolution with deep fondness for those qualities of compassion and selfless service which were so characteristic of Father McGivney's general ministry to both his parish and his Order.

The parishioners of St. Mary's clearly demonstrated their devotion to their departed curate when they commissioned F. A. Cargill to print the testimonial resolutions in an elaborate and ornate script. The following text was superimposed upon a drawing of a large chalice and host:

Whereas our Right Reverend Bishop has in his wisdom seen fit to call the Rev. M. J. McGivney from St. Mary's Parish to labor in another part of Christ's vineyard, therefore be it resolved, that the Rev. M. J. McGivney has, by his courtesy and kindness, by the purity of his life, and by the faithful discharge of the duties pertaining to his HOLY OFFICE, secured the love and confidence of the people of St. Mary's, which will follow him in every future field of labor. Resolved, that it is to be especially remembered of him that while yet young in the service of his Master, and his ministrations to us, he devotedly and nobly bore burdens and afflictions with us while acting as pastor [sic] of this Church.[55]

Since Father McGivney had reduced his service to the Knights of Columbus from Supreme Secretary to Supreme Chaplain the previous June, the move to Thomaston did not greatly affect his association with the Order. Thomaston, the home of the Seth Thomas Clock Company, was just ten miles north of his hometown, Waterbury.

By the end of 1884 the Order had expanded to twelve councils, when Ferdinand Council No. 12 in New Britain was instituted on December 29. With the *Connecticut Catholic* energetically advertising the benefits of the Knights of Columbus, the first five months of 1885 witnessed more growth of the Order, as the following twelve councils were instituted between February 17 and May 3: White Cross in Norwich; San José in Willimantic; Isabella in Southington; Park City in Bridgeport; Seaside in New London; Atlantic in Thomaston; Charter Oak in Hartford; Columbia in New Haven; Narragansett in Westerly, Rhode Island (a council for Stonington, Connecticut, it was instituted across the river in Westerly because of a fire in its originally selected hall); Winsted in Winchester; Valley in Ansonia; and Sheridan in Waterbury.

Though Father McGivney played a role in the institution of Atlantic Council in Thomaston, the appearance of a new council in his hometown of Waterbury must have given him singular satisfaction. The formation of Sheridan Council No. 24 at Waterbury was well recorded in its minutes, which are still preserved today, and are representative of the early stages of the council during the Order's infancy. Parliamentary procedure, an efficiently organized order of business, and the delegation of specific matters to committees characterized these minutes. On April 27, 1885, nine Irish-Americans met "for the purpose of organizing a council of the Knights of Columbus."[56] Cornelius Maloney, publisher and editor of the *Waterbury Democrat*, was elected chairman. After the secretary read the constitution and by-laws of the Order, the members voted to call their council Sheridan in honor of General Philip Sheridan, an Irish-American Catholic Civil War hero and in 1885 the commanding general of the U.S. Army. In accord with the Columbian theme, the name commemorated the Catholic contribution to American society.

At the second organizational meeting, on May 1, 1885, the committee to select a physician reported "having secured Dr. Neville." Committees were then formed to "secure a suitable room for the installation of the council" and to be a reception committee "to receive the officers of the Supreme Council."[57] Five additional applicants were approved on May 1 and six more on May 3, the date on which officers were elected and installed by Supreme Knight Mullen, "the ceremonies being performed in a satisfactory manner to all concerned."[58] Cornelius Maloney, who was elected Grand Knight, recorded that the members of the Supreme Council led "the new members into the mysteries of the [Order]. A great deal had been said with reference to the severity of the test for Knighthood and while nobody evinced signs of fear at the coming ordeal, still there was great pause when the officer announced that the Third Degree would be exemplified."[59]

Characteristic of the first-generation Knights, all charter members of Sheridan Council were of Irish descent. However, the Order was no longer exclusively Irish. Among the first 1105 members, 450 were born in Ireland, 548 were American-born of Irish descent, 67 were also of Irish descent though born in England, Scotland, and Canada; but there were 11 German-born and 1 from each of the following nations: Belgium, France, Denmark, Italy, and Switzerland. (In 24 cases there was insufficient information.) The statistical breakdown according to age indicates that the Order appealed to younger Catholic men of Connecticut: Of those 1105 who entered the Order before May 1, 1885, 465 were under thirty and 413 were in their thirties. The occupations of the first eleven hundred Knights were typical of the general trend in ethnic history during the 1880s. The Irish Americans were primarily members of the working classes but were already evidencing significant upward economic mobility: 754 were laborers and craftsmen, while 351 were engaged in business and the professions. Most of the council officers were drawn from the professional and business groups.[60]

Sheridan Council was instituted just two days before the third annual convention of the Supreme Council, held in Meriden on May 5, 1885. Supreme Secretary Colwell presented the statistical evidence of the Order's growth: May 1884, five councils, 380 members; May 1885, twenty-four councils, nearly 1,500 members. Councils had been established in nineteen towns; Meriden and New Haven each had three councils while Hartford had two. Between March 1 and April 6, 1885, the first four deaths occurred among the membership. The family of Dennis J. O'Brien of Hartford received $970; the families of James Creed, Dennis Devine, and Jeremiah Mulcahy, all of Meriden, received $1,000. Since the Order had been in existence for nearly three years before a death occurred and since its membership had reached well over a thousand by the time of the first death, Father McGivney's promise of a society characterized by financial integrity and moral responsibility had clearly been fulfilled. Except for Philip J. Markley, who was elected the Supreme Lecturer, all the officers were reelected for a one-year term.[61]

The three Meriden councils entertained the delegates "in handsome style." Because of the rapid growth of the Order, two special meetings were held in conjunction with the convention. Grand Knights met to discuss, among other topics, "the secret workings of the Order." Thirteen council physicians discussed common features of their vital work of examining candidates for the Order. The *Connecticut Catholic* went on to comment proudly that since the paper "began to take a lively interest in the Order, the Knights of Columbus had achieved gratifying success."[62]

A correspondent, under the pseudonym "Clericus," challenged the editor of the *Connecticut Catholic* to explain what he meant when he reported that at the third annual convention the Grand Knights discussed "the secret workings of the Order." "Clericus" wrote that "your assertion . . . that the Knights of Columbus is to be classed among secret societies has caused no little surprise among your readers" since "no secret society," properly so called, "can exist in the Church." "Clericus" requested the editor to explain "in what this secrecy consists" and if indeed the Order was secret, was it "not going beyond the intention of its founder."[63]

The editor of the *Connecticut Catholic* replied that though he was a Knight he was not authorized to speak as a representative of the Order, only as the editor of a journal which aims "to always give the truth." Such a line of reasoning in which he separated his Knighthood from his editorship protected him from violating his promise not to reveal the ceremonials of the Order. Instead he stressed good business reasons as the rationale for secrecy. "Insurance companies and banking institutions do not tell every Tom, Dick, and Harry about their financial ventures"; so, as a mutual assistance society, the Knights of Columbus conduct their meetings "with closed doors and with only members present." Since the Order had been approved by Bishop McMahon, the editor stated that "it is not necessary for us to be an apologist for the Knights of Columbus." After citing the pastoral letter issued by the Thrid Plenary Council of Baltimore of the previous November, the editor concluded, "Any organization, as we understand, gotten up for a good purpose, and proposing to attain the end in view by legitimate moral and legal means, will meet with the approval of the Church. The mere fact of secrecy does not bring condemnation to any society."[64]

Father McGivney also responded to "Clericus," with some remarks on the editor's comments as well. Appearing in the May 30 issue of the *Connecticut Catholic,* Father McGivney's letter to the editor reveals a side of his personality seldom expressed. "Since the article in question seems to reflect upon the 'founder' as belonging to a secret society and since he (the founder) is supposed to have known what he intended when he organized the Knights of Columbus, I deem it but justice to the young men of the diocese to permit 'the founder' to make known his intentions." Father McGivney went on to explain that the Order was not a Church society: "It is composed of Catholics and instituted for the welfare of Catholic families in the State of Connecticut. It has no connection whatever with the Church, except that Catholic priests are among its members and Catholic priests, whether members or not, can attend any of the meetings. From the fact that the Order had been formed upon purely business principles, it has not asked for, nor did it need, the approbation of the authorities of the diocese any more than an insurance company composed of Catholics would ask the Rt. Rev. Bishop to approve its by-laws and constitution." Later in the letter, Father McGivney once again emphasized that the Order "has not been approved" by the Bishop.[65]

In light of the many documents which explicitly refer to Bishop McMahon's approval of the Order, and indeed of Father McGivney's role in seeking this approval, the founder appears to have been somewhat disingenuous. However, in light of ecclesiastical laws governing lay societies, his comments were accurate. One may recall his April 1882 letter to the pastors of the diocese: "By *permission* of our Rt. Rev. Bishop . . . we have formed an organization under the name of the Knights of Columbus." There is a thin line separating "by permission" and "with the approval," but the distinctions are profound. Father McGivney seems to have implied that Bishop McMahon permitted Catholics to establish the Order, thereby allowing the laity of his diocese to pursue the aims and objectives of the fraternal benefit society.

He may have even enthusiastically *permitted* the Order to be established. When the rituals were submitted to him he obviously saw no conflict between their contents and the Catholic faith and morals, thereby *permitting* their use by the Catholic laity. If he were to *approve* the Order and its ceremonials, he would have crossed that legal line between freedom and authority. In that event the Knights of Columbus would have become a Church society under the direct authority of the ordinary of the diocese, with all the limitations upon freedom of action entailed in that status. Instead, the Order was permitted as a society which Catholics could join in good faith. As Catholics they were under the authority of their bishop; as Knights of Columbus they were autonomous. A permitted society may be fostered by the Church without being regulated according to ecclesiastical law. As Father McGivney stated, "The authorities of the Church are only too anxious to foster any society which will better the conditions of her children provided that the by-laws and constitution do not conflict with the rules and regulations of the Church. . . . Had there been anything objectionable in the business of the different councils, I would be most likely to have seen it in my connection with the Order since its foundation."[66]

Though the founder of the Order did not elaborate on the topic of secrecy, he did emphatically state that "the Knights of Columbus is not a secret society."[67] To resolve the conflict between the secret ceremonials of the Order and Father McGivney's denial that it was a secret society, we must attempt to disentangle the issue from its semantic web. Father McGivney's notion of a secret society seems to have been derived from the traditional position of the Church on Masonry, which viewed the Mason's oath of secrecy as a naturalistic religious rite, and the general character of Masonic ritual as grounded in occult superstition bordering on blasphemy. The earliest extant document on the ceremonials of the Order does not include an oath but a promise, and the K. of C. ceremonials have never smacked of religious ritual. The opening prayer by the Chaplain was an orthodox Catholic invocation, and embedded in the Order's ceremonials were lessons in the Knights' moral, religious, and civic duties. Hence, in Father McGivney's sense of the term, the Order was not a secret society.

Though the founder of the Order had intended his letter to be a way of "enlightening" "Clericus," the latter opened his response by stating, "That the founder of the Knights of Columbus totally misapprehended the purpose of my queries . . . goes without saying. By some perverse and inexplicable mode of reasoning he tortured my note into a declaration of war against himself and his organization and thereupon he launches against me a number of alleged sarcasms." After explaining how his sense of priestly duty compelled him to question the propriety of the organization in order to "lead souls into the right path," "Clericus" reminded "the founder of the Knights of Columbus [of] the sad fact that secret societies have time and again corrupted the pure stream of faith." Though at the conclusion of his note he once again said that he was "assaulted without reason," his final remark was conciliatory: "That, in the spirit of utmost charity, I say to the founder of the Knights of Columbus: Let peace reign between me and thee."[68]

This rather impassioned exchange of views between the priest founder and his clerical opponent illustrates the doubts and misunderstandings which haunted the Order in its early days. Since there seem to have been pockets of clerical opposition from the time when the founder first introduced the K. of C. to the pastors of the diocese (April 1882), the exasperated tone of Father McGivney's letter may have stemmed from the fact that even with almost 1,500 members located in nineteen towns in Connecticut, all of whom were committed to fraternal charity in distress, sickness, and death, he was still being called upon to defend its orthodoxy. He must have thought that the battle for the Order's legitimacy and respectability had already been won. And indeed it had. "Clericus" represented a position which was rapidly dissolving. Bishop McMahon and eighteen other priests had accepted the position of council chaplain. All the local reporters for the *Connecticut Catholic* wrote of the Order as attracting the "cream of Catholic manhood," as performing the crucial task of protection in illness and death, as a refuge for deep friendships in a hostile society, as inculcating pride in Catholic Columbian themes, and as possessing a beautiful and effective ceremonial character. Hence by 1885 the Order had reached the first stage of maturity as a unique Catholic fraternal benefit society.

3

The Vitality of the Order and the Death of the Founder

FROM 1886 TO 1892 THE KNIGHTS continued to expand throughout Connecticut. In his first letter to the editor of the *Connecticut Catholic* (August 25, 1883), Father McGivney had clearly stated his intention to limit the Order to that State. However, the *New Haven Union* reported that in the fall of 1884 Supreme Knight Mullen had received a letter of application from Lawrence, Massachusetts. According to the *Union,* the delegates to the Supreme Council meeting of the previous June discussed the issue "whether the organization should branch out into other states or confine its labor to Connecticut"; the delegates then deferred to the wisdom of the Supreme Knight, "and if he deems it advisable he can order an extension of the organization to other states." The article concluded with a remark of Supreme Knight Mullen indicating that he himself was an "expansionist"; he said "that its benefits should not be confined to one state."[1]

There is no evidence to indicate a McGivney-Mullen conflict on interstate expansion during the 1884–86 period. Since fourteen Connecticut councils were formed during the year between the 1884 and 1885 Supreme Council meetings, the development of a strong base in the home state took precedence over interstate expansion. Because, as previously noted, the institution of Narragansett Council No. 21 in Westerly, Rhode Island (May 1885), was accidental, necessitated by a fire in the meeting hall in Stonington, Connecticut, the Order's presence in that state was unrelated to the expansionist issue.

In early April 1885 the Supreme Committee wrote a letter to each of the Grand Knights in which the problems of assessment collections were clearly stated. The first death occurred on March 1, 1885, when there were 1,047 members; however, only $970 was collected in assessments. Therefore, councils were not reporting suspensions and lapsed members to the Supreme Secretary. In March 1885 the latter requested an updated list of members from each council. When three more deaths occurred within five weeks, the Supreme Secretary once again requested lists. To remedy the problems of council responsibility and accountability, the Supreme Council of 1885 amended that article of the constitution for the subordinate councils which specified the duties of the Financial Secretary. The responsibilities for the endowment fund entailed very precise procedures for collection and distribution which, when combined with the broad duties of the office, placed a heavy burden upon the Financial Secretary. Hence the amended constitution made the Financial Secretary a salaried officer, the amount of which was to be specified by the local council.[2]

The delegates to the Supreme Council meeting of 1885 struggled with many constitutional issues related to the rapid growth of the Order. In Chapter Two it was noted that the Supreme Council held its May 1885 meeting at Meriden. The *Connecticut Catholic*'s article on that meeting stressed the festive atmosphere in which the delegates discussed the accomplishments of the Order.[3] However, when the convention reassembled in New Haven on May 12 (at the Hoadley Building on Church Street), the issues related to the sudden expansion of the Order were discussed. A resolution was passed stating the need for constitutional revisions and requesting each council to authorize the delegates to the 1885 convention to reconvene for the purpose of revising the constitution.[4] At a June 9 meeting, Supreme Knight Mullen appointed a constitution revision committee of seven in accordance with the resolution.

There seems to have been some tension within this June 9 meeting. John F. Butler, the Supreme Treasurer from Washington Council No. 4, refused an appointment to the committee and later in the meeting announced his resignation as Supreme Treasurer because he was withdrawing from the Order. Upon a motion by Andrew Smith of Hartford, Butler's resignation as Supreme Treasurer was rejected. Since we may infer that Supreme Knight Mullen appointed him in good faith, Butler's announcement must have shocked the convention. Between Butler's refusal to serve on the committee and his stunning revelation, Father McGivney "made some remarks for the good of the Order, which were heartily applauded."[5] Though his words were not recorded, it appears that the founder assumed the role of a peacemaker. Since Butler's resignation from the constitution revision committee occurred immediately after James Mullen and C. T. Driscoll were voted to it, his resignation may have symbolized a Meriden–New Haven conflict. Because the New Haven delegates included Grand Knights and Past Grand Knights from three councils as well as incorporators, who by the constitution were granted voice and vote at conventions, Butler's resignation may have reflected a swelling anti–New Haven sentiment which became evident in later meetings of the convention. Butler may not have been immediately appeased, but eventually he decided not to withdraw from the Order.

One constitutional change occurred at the June 9 meeting when it was decided to change the age limit of new members from fifty to forty-five years old. Obviously the four deaths that year had created a sentiment against elderly members—a sentiment not grounded in fact, however, as each of the deceased was under forty.

On October 29 the committee presented its draft of a new constitution for the subordinate councils. Before discussing the revisions, a debate ensued on the forty-five age limit passed at the previous meeting. After this was resolved in the affirmative, the delegates debated the legal basis for constitutional revision. The question which arose was central to the authority of the Supreme Council, viz., whether the Supreme Council had the final word on constitutional issues or whether its decisions had to be submitted to the subordinate councils for their ratification. With only twenty-one out of sixty-seven eligible delegates present, it seems the New Haven contingency was conspicuous by its absence. Was this challenge of the Supreme Council's authority another expression of the provinces' disenchantment with the leadership of the central government in New Haven? Since this and another challenge (demanding that the Supreme Secretary issue regular reports on the financial status of the Order) were defeated, the apparent anti–New Haven sentiment was unable to gain the ascendancy.

Supreme Knight Mullen did not chair the meeting but rather, as a member of the constitution revision committee, was a strong advocate of the proposed changes in the laws governing subordinate councils which were drafted by William Geary, the untiring incorporator. John J. Phelan of Bridgeport's Park City Council No. 16 strongly supported tightening those laws which governed the accountability of council officers. He was particularly forceful in his remarks on the need to provide greater flexibility in the rules related to suspension of members who were in arrears. The original law on suspensions stipulated a one-month grace period for late payment, which Phelan considered so stringent that council officers refused to enforce it. Upon Phelan's motion the law was changed to a two-month grace period.

Besides lowering the maximum age at initiation to forty-five, the convention raised the initiation dues by a considerable amount. While the original schedule began at $3.25 for eighteen-year-olds and rose by 25 cents a year from nineteen through fifty, the new schedule levied a $5.25 fee for eighteen-year-olds and graduated at a 25-cents-a-year rate only to age twenty-five. Twenty-six-year-olds were levied $7.25, and the fees then rose $1.00 per year, with forty-five-year-old members paying an initiation fee of $26.75 in contrast to $10 under the old schedule.[6] The costs of administering a rapidly growing society had obviously risen since the time of the 1882 constitution, when there was only one subordinate council.

Though one should be reluctant to accept ethnic generalizations, the Irish themselves admitted a penchant for political animosities. For example, the *Connecticut Catholic* published a long editorial on the K. of C. as an Irish Order.

For if we [Knights] prove in our actions and deliberations by the three great principles upon which our organization is established, unity, charity, and brotherly love, then the Order will have made great strides beyond the limitations of Irish Americans. Lack of unity, want of charity, and personal antagonism in place of brotherly love have characterized Irishmen's relations with one another in this country. They can never appreciate the fact that a member of their own nationality can be just as intelligent either in business pursuits or professional callings, for example, as a German or English.

The editor viewed "lack of educational facilities" as a "principal drawback" for Irish-American harmony.

But apart from all of this, there seems to be some innate perversity in the Irish character, which does not permit the Irishman to see the same intellectual qualities in a fellow Irishman as are witnessed in others. It is mainly owing to this perversity, this particular jealousy, that the Irish Americans have not made the advances in this country that they should have.

In a sense the editor was preaching the nineteenth-century equivalent of consciousness-raising: that members of any persecuted minority need only develop self-confidence and mutual respect for one another and they will enjoy success and affluence. Change a few words here and there, and the following exhortation could apply to the role of the B'nai B'rith among the Jews, the N.A.A.C.P. among the blacks, or any organization representing the aspirations of a suppressed minority group.

The future of the Irish race in the state, to a great degree, lies within the province of the [K. of C.] Order. Teach Irishmen to rely on one another, to have trust and confidence in each other, and not to display their petty jealousies and clannish feelings upon every occasion, and the work performed will reflect unbounded credit on the organization.[7]

The editor did acknowledge the unique character of the Order. As a cooperative insurance society it fostered interdependence and mutual loyalty among its members. It also engendered a sense of religious and national pride within the Irish-American minority. Members passed through ceremonials which ritualized the Catholic contribution to America, the harmony between Catholic faith and American freedom, and the need to display loyalty to country and to be ever ready to defend the faith against anti-Catholic enemies with a distorted view of the Church and American religious liberty. But he also scored the Irish penchant for "petty jealousies and clannish feelings." He warned his brothers:

Let not any man strive to make political capital out of the Knights. Let politics and political discussion be entirely eschewed, and with its extensive membership, with its representation in every trade and profession, in a word by its exercise of judicious influences over its members, the future of the Knights will not only be brilliant but lasting.[8]

Though the Order had experienced a period of political discord associated with its growth in 1885, it clearly displayed its unity at its first annual state parade and clambake held on August 12, 1885. In early July each council was invited to participate in the festivities. The occasion provided the opportunity to celebrate the extraordinary growth of the Order during the previous year; the invitation stated that the parade was "for the purpose of bringing together our forces, that those who are not of us, but who are eligible to participate in the benefits of our organization, may see for themselves the class of men who are enrolled beneath our banners." In gilded prose the invitation stressed the membership-development theme of the parade. "Flourishing as has been the past of the organization, there is yet a brighter future before it, if our hearts and hands go together in sowing the seeds that will ripen into a large membership. The enthusiasm that has cradled the young organization must not slumber till the prophesy of its founders has been fulfilled, and the glorious pennant of Columbus waves over all who are worthy to have its beneficial fruits."[9]

The parade and clambake were a historic success. All but three of the twenty-four councils were represented. The *New Haven Register* reported that "fully 12,000 men were in line," while the *Hartford Telegram* noted that "well over 1,000 men were in line."[10] Father Michael J. McGivney was in a carriage leading the parade as it wended its way through New Haven to Branford Point. Some well-intentioned doggerel, "To the Knights of Columbus" by J.T.M. (presumably James T. Mullen), was composed in honor of the occasion.

> We meet today with those we love most dear—
> Our sweethearts; wives and little ones, and brothers far and near—
> And at the altar of our love, will keep the flame alive—
> And cherish in our hearts this day in '85—
> With nature fair and salt sea air, our hearts with love inspired—
> And let the God of mirth and song add fuel to the fire—
> May God bestow his love on all assembled here today—
> And every blessing grant to them, for this Lord we pray.[11]

The editor of the *Connecticut Catholic* wrote a long editorial on the parade, in which he extolled the virtues of the Knights.

We never witnessed a more creditable display by any organization in Connecticut, or elsewhere. All the members were well-dressed and in the parade, as well as in the streets, presented an excellent appearance. . . . The meeting will be beneficial to the Order. It has proven that most of our prominent and representative men in the state are enrolled as true Knights under the banner of Columbus. It has also proven to the inhabitants of the state . . . that our people are an exceedingly well behaved and orderly class of men.[12]

By "our people" the editor meant not Catholics but Irish-American Catholics. He proudly quoted from the *Hartford Telegram:* "We overheard an ex-governor of the state remark as the procession passed by, 'That parade is an honor to the Irish race,' and it was." The *Hartford Telegram* editorial quoted by the *Connecticut Catholic* included an insightful commentary of the strong American patriotism displayed by second-generation Irish Americans in the K. of C. parade.

There are some narrow minded people living in New England yet who imagine that the Irish race are idle, slovenly, and often vicious. They judge the whole stock by the few unfortunates they meet. It is a fact, however, that the Irish will compare favorably with every other nationality in all that goes to make up good citizenship. The second generation in this country are intensely American in their instincts, and they are forging ahead to prominent positions in commerce, trade, and in the professions.[13]

Since one of the fundamental motivations in the formation of the K. of C. was to prove to the "narrow minded people living in New England" that Irish-American Catholics were just as patriotic as the descendants of the Pilgrims, the *Hartford Telegram* editorial indicates that by 1885 the Order had successfully made its point.

The publicity resulting from the parade must have had some impact upon new-council development; thirteen councils were instituted between August 12, 1885, and May 17, 1886, the date of the annual convention. However, when the delegates met in Hartford on that day, the name of the meeting had been changed from Supreme Council to Board of Government.[14] The events leading up to the altered form of governance were related to the rapid growth of the Order.

As previously noted, the constitutional revision in the autumn of 1885 had focused upon the laws governing the subordinate councils, such as the expanded duties of the Financial Secretary, the lowering of the age limit for members from fifty to forty-five years old, and the substantial increase in initiation fees. The tensions between the subordinate councils and the Supreme Council officers, as well as those between the "provinces" and the New Haven "capital," seem to have emanated from many sources: the rapid proliferation of councils without adequate introduction to business and governance principles and procedures; the heavy demands placed upon volunteer officers to issue quarterly reports for accurate death-benefit assessments; the young members' resentment against equal assessment without consideration of age; the preponderance of New Haveners at the Supreme Council meetings; and perhaps a normal amount of that Irish jealousy and distrust of those in authority already discussed.

In the autumn of 1885 the Supreme Council, acting as a "constitutional convention," grappled with the issues related to the subordinate councils. Rather than adjourning and deferring the crucial constitutional problems to the next annual convention, the 1885 "constitutional convention" authorized a committee of eleven to submit proposals for reforms prior to the annual convention of 1886. Since this committee, chaired by John J. Phelan of Bridgeport, met as late as April 1886, the Supreme Council of 1885 had several sessions over a span of nearly a year.

William Geary and William Sellwood, as incorporators and thereby delegates to the convention, wrote a letter to the *Connecticut Catholic* in which they elaborated on the political climate surrounding the events leading to the convention of 1886. They considered the conflict between the subordinate council and the Supreme committee as the manifestation of petty complaints. According to Geary and Sellwood, the tensions created in the minds "of the most intelligent and best informed men [the opinion] that a crisis was at hand, that not only was the . . . Supreme Council to be assailed [at the 1886 convention] and perhaps its existence annihilated, but that the very life of the

Order itself was threatened."[15] The committee of eleven was, there-fore, charged with drafting new laws governing the central legislative and executive authority of the society in order to avert this putative crisis and to assure confidence from below (subordinate councils) and administrative efficiency from above (Supreme Council and its offic-ers).

When the committee reported to the convention, the delegates were stunned with its report, which included proposals to dissolve the Supreme Council and the Supreme Council Committee and to estab-lish in their place a Board of Government composed of Grand Knights and immediate Past Grand Knights of each council, and a Board of Directors composed of the Supreme officers and one representative from each of the nine districts. It was proposed that the Board of Government would meet annually to elect officers and would be the highest lawmaking body. The Board of Directors would meet quarterly and would be the highest executive authority. Geary and Sellwood described the scene:

The convention was as silent as the house of death. . . . The crisis had arrived. What would be the reception of this radical change? Would a motion be made which would be its death blow? The silence was broken with a motion that the new constitution be accepted and that it be adopted section by section. The crisis was passed; the champions of the document would forcibly advocate and explain its provisions and if defeated it could be only after every feature had [been] lucidly explained.[16]

The May 3 session of the constitutional convention fully debated each section, but ultimately the entire constitution was given unani-mous approval. The new authority structure was in a sense less demo-cratic than its predecessor. A Supreme Council convention was com-posed of Grand Knights and all Past Grand Knights as well as elected representatives of each council. The Board of Government was limited to Grand Knights and immediate Past Grand Knights of each council. But the representative character of the executive authority was en-larged by the new constitution. The Supreme Council officers had composed the Supreme Committee; the 1886 constitution replaced it with the Board of Directors, which included, besides the officers, nine additional directors representing the districts.

The titles of Supreme and Deputy Supreme Knight were con-tinued, but the other officers—Chaplain, Secretary, Treasurer, etc.,—were changed from Supreme to General. Without any documentary evidence as to why these titles were changed, one presumes that "Gen-

eral" was considered more in accord with the business side of the
Order than "Supreme." The Supreme Knight was ex-officio president
of the Board of Government and Board of Directors, while the General
Secretary, Treasurer, Advocate, and Physician were ex-officio members of the Board of Directors. We may infer that it was understood
that Father McGivney would be General Chaplain for as long as he
wished and that he accepted the completely lay character of the Board
of Directors which, by the constitution, removed the priest founder
from the business concerns of the Order.

The new constitution did contain an important provision to ensure the membership's right of redress: A majority of councils could
mandate a convention of the subordinate councils composed of one
elected representative for every fifty members enrolled. For the first
time, the qualifications for membership included the stipulation that
one must be a "Practical Roman Catholic."[17] To accommodate the
younger members who resented equal assessments, a new law was
adopted providing for rates based on age. For every year younger or
older than the average age in the Order, members were assessed 3
percent less or more than average-age members. For example, if the
whole membership of a council was one hundred, if the endowment
assessment was $50, and if the average age of the Order was thirty-five
years old, the thirty-five-year-old would pay 50 cents, the thirty-four-
year-old 48 cents, and the thirty-six-year-old 52 cents, etc. On this
scale the twenty-year-old would pay 10 cents and the fifty-five-year-old
80 cents.

The assessment collection process was improved at the 1886 convention. Previously the Financial Secretary of the council which had
experienced a death would notify the Supreme Secretary, who would
assess each council according to its membersip, with each council
sending its assessment to the originating Financial Secretary. According to the 1886 law, each council would send its assessment to the
General Treasurer, who would send the entire assessment to the Financial Secretary for paying the death-benefit claim. Another section
of the 1886 Constitution stipulated that sick benefits were optional
according to the by-laws of each council.

The change from Supreme Council and Supreme Council Committee to Board of Government and Board of Directors symbolized a
shift in emphasis from fraternal to business concerns. Between May 30,
1884, and May 6, 1886, the Order had grown from five to thirty-eight
councils. The leaders of the 1886 convention must have felt that if this
volunteer society were to function efficiently and equitably, proce-

dures for accountability at all levels had to be refined and the governance system had to be enlarged at the executive level and reduced at
the legislative level.

On May 17, two weeks after the constitution had been adopted,
the first meeting of the Board of Government was held. Composed
only of Grand Knights and immediate Past Grand Knights, the new
legislative body, by unanimous vote, invited James Mullen and Daniel
Colwell to participate in this meeting. Chaired by John J. Phelan, one
of the chief advocates of the new form of government, the meeting
proceeded to elect a Supreme Knight. Of the thirty-seven votes cast,
Mullen received twenty-three, Phelan thirteen, and James Hurley of
Bridgeport, one. When Mullen's election was made unanimous by an
informal ballot, "he declined the honor . . . in a very feeling speech."
The Board of Government then elected Phelan Supreme Knight. At
this juncture the minutes record that "Rev. M. J. McGivney be invited
to a seat in the body."[18] There may be some irony in the fact that the
founder was not a delegate to the meeting, but since the Supreme
Council had been dissolved, each officer of that defunct body had to
be invited unless he were a Grand Knight or immediate Past Grand
Knight. The following list of officers elected in 1886 illustrates the shift
from New Haven to the "provinces":

> Deputy Supreme Knight, William Hassett, Pinta Council No. 5, Walling-
> ford
> General Treasurer, Henry T. Downs, formerly of Silver City Council
> No. 2, Meriden, then a member of Genoa Council No. 9, also of Me-
> riden
> General Secretary, Daniel Colwell, San Salvador Council No. 1, New
> Haven
> General Advocate, Philip J. Markley, Ferdinand (now Daly) Council
> No. 12, New Britain
> General Chaplain, Rev. M. J. McGivney, also chaplain at Atlantic Council
> No. 18, Thomaston
> General Physician, Andrew W. Tracy, M.D., Silver City Council No. 2,
> Meriden
> National Warden, Matthew McNamara, Seaside Council No. 17, New
> London[19]

The offices of Supreme Lecturer and Supreme Guard were discontinued, but a new office, Director General of Ceremonies, was
created at the May 17 meeting. It was designed particularly for James
Mullen, who held the position until his death in 1891. According to the
Connecticut Catholic, Mullen's business considerations prevented him

from accepting the office of Supreme Knight in 1886.[20] In his new position Mullen could continue to serve as master of ceremonies for the Order.

William Geary reported an incident which reveals the integrity of Mullen as the first Supreme Knight as well as the rising stature of the Order among the business community of New Haven. In February of 1886 Mullen was notified that the Order faced a legal suit if it did not pay a $900 debt. Though Geary did not disclose the source of the debt, it seems to have been related to expenses for the parade and clambake. Since the Order's treasury was empty and since a public display of indebtedness would jeopardize confidence in the Order, both agreed to seek a solution privately and quietly. Without collateral or an endorsement by a person of means, Mullen and his fellow incorporator sought a loan of $1,000 from the First National Bank of New Haven, "whose president [Harman W. Welch] they both knew personally." Mr. Welch, who, as Geary stated, "was not what his name may indicate, an Irishman . . . [but] an American and a Protestant," responded to their request. "You gentlemen are known to me and the community as possessing qualities that make for honor and high character and integrity and I am pleased to loan you the money without any security but your note." Geary reported that the loan was eventually paid in full from the per-capita taxes on the members and related this incident to illustrate how the Order "came close to disaster."[21]

II

The election of John J. Phelan as the second Supreme Knight marks a significant phase in the Order's history. Since he did not join the Knights until Park City Council No. 16 was instituted on March 22, 1885, he did not help found the Order, but as the first Grand Knight of his council he was a delegate to the long-drawn-out constitutional convention of that year. Because he was a skilled lawyer, a successful politician—in 1885 he was elected to the Connecticut General Assembly—and a captivating orator, he displayed strong leadership qualities in the debate on constitutional reform. Indeed, he was credited with writing the constitution for the Board of Government.

Born in Wexford, Ireland, on June 24, 1851, John Phelan entered the stonecutting business with his father after he completed his studies under the Irish Christian Brothers. In 1870, after the death of his parents, he emigrated to Bridgeport, Connecticut, where he continued to pursue his stonecutting trade. His ambition to be a lawyer was so strong that he commuted daily to attend classes (on a part-time basis) at the University of the City of New York. In 1878 he received his law degree, was admitted to the bar in Connecticut, and established his practice in Bridgeport.

Though he was not involved in the formation of the Order, his attitude toward the role of Irish-American Catholics in the struggle against prejudice and discrimination shows him to have been in close accord with the spirit of the Knights. One biographer remarked, "His great ambition on becoming a lawyer was not only to win approval in his profession, but to win such worthy prominence in social and political life as would by example allay race and religious prejudice and tend to prove the loyalty and integrity of Roman Catholics as American citizens."[22] John Phelan was ably qualified not only as an administrative and political leader but also as a strong fraternalist within a society dedicated to the Columbian ideals of publicizing the Catholic contribution to America and the compatibility between Catholicism and patriotism.

During the first year of Phelan's leadership, the Order grew by four councils, with the addition of Cecil Calvert No. 38 in Bridgeport, Orinoco No. 39 in Greenwich, Housatonic No. 40 in New Milford, and St. Augustine No. 41 in Stamford. Though the preceding two years had witnessed considerably more growth in the number of councils, membership in the Order advanced in 1886–87 by seven hundred members, which represented a growth of over 20 percent. In his opening remarks to the 1887 meeting of the Board of Government, Phelan congratulated the subordinate councils for their adaptability to the new form of government. He gave particular praise for their "allegiance" to the graded system of assessments "despite the prejudices and sophistries fostered by the inequitable and old fashioned precedent [equal assessments without consideration for age] established in primitive organizations." He advocated advancing beyond "the progressive thought" of the 1886 convention by recommending the establishment of a commission "to carefully investigate the different plans of life insurance reserve funds." Without adopting a reserve fund, the Order's "permanence must of necessity be seriously jeopardized." It was Phelan's intention to place before the 1888 meeting of the Board of Government a proposal for a sustaining fund suitable to the needs of the Order. The Supreme Knight also strongly recommended an alteration of the laws governing the council physicians' examinations. Because there was a reluctance among physicians to reject an applicant, all examination reports should be sent to the General Physician for approval. The Board favorably passed on this recommendation, which significantly strengthened his authority and which to this day is still in effect.

Expanding upon the Order's motto, "Unity, Charity, and Fraternity," Phelan proposed the creation of a special fund, developed by a 50-cent per-capita tax, "for the assistance of needy orphans of deceased members, a project appealing for consummation to the finest sentiment of humanity."[23] Though Phelan frequently urged the Order to establish such a fund, it never received the majority support of the Board of Government.

Since the Supreme Knight devoted more than a quarter of his address to the topic "Practical Roman Catholic" as a qualification for membership, this must have reflected a serious problem. He defended it as nothing more than "declaring of the then implied law, that the Order as such, in membership and practice, should be, and continue to be, Roman Catholic absolutely." He noted that the Order was founded "as a refuge for Catholics only," who by becoming Knights implicitly rejected membership in those "societies condemned by the Church." No Knight who held allegiance to a condemned society "can be tolerated within our ranks. The Order cannot stultify itself or allow itself to masquerade in the garb of a sanctity it willingly desecrates." Phelan was aware that false accusations of violating this law could be made in witch-hunting or vindictive ways. To remove authority for expulsion of non-practicing Catholics from the council chambers, Phelan successfully urged the delegates to "invest the Supreme Knight with full powers to suspend or expel" such violators.[24]

By 1887 the Order had reached that stage in its maturity at which John Phelan could accurately remark, "The Order is destined to become in the near future the ideal of its founders, as well as a powerful factor in the elevation of the social and moral status of the Catholic people in this and neighboring states."[25] Though the Order had become a moral force in the diocese of Hartford (the lone council in Rhode Island was under the ordinary in Hartford), it relied upon its strong insurance base for its sustenance. Indeed, the moral responsibility engendered by the cooperative insurance program whereby the "brother's keeper" message was expressed in terms of hard-earned dollars was fundamental to its fraternal life. Serving over three thousand members in 1887 entailed complex business and accounting procedures which, in a voluntary society, required a deep sense of dedication and a broad political consensus. John Phelan led the Order to accept the 1886 constitution with its rationalized governance system and insurance program, even though these changes provoked strong political dissent.

The three issues fueling the fire of disagreement were the power of the Board of Directors, the undemocratic features of the Board of Government, and the rise of administrative costs. The Board of Directors, composed of the Supreme Knight, the General Secretary, Treasurer, and Advocate, and representatives of the nine districts, was granted broad authority by the constitution. Because the Order's business concerns had expanded, it was necessary to hold several special meetings. As compensation for their time and travel expenses, the Board of Directors voted a $5.00 per diem payment and travel allotment for each of its members. Though the exact salary is difficult to determine from the reports, it appears that they each received $30 per month plus expenses. The Board of Government authorized a $90 monthly salary for the General Secretary, the only full-time salaried officer.

Upon reading the printed treasurer's report for the fraternal year (between meetings, 1886–87), some members noted with anger that administrative costs, the bulk of which was in the form of salaries and expenses for directors, amounted to $4,171.17. Though this figure represented only a little over $1.00 per member for increasingly heavy administrative responsibilities, dissident members, who for political reasons or distress at the rapid pace of change were eager to return to the regulations of the past, focused on the salary issue as a rallying point. Above the signature T.F.C., a Knight from Meriden wrote a lengthy letter to the editor of the *Connecticut Catholic* in which he strongly asserted that the Order was "run on too expensive a scale for the class of men that make up the society. I believe in less officers and less salary. . . . In the first place, the Supreme Knight should not have any salary attached to his office, but allow him his expenses. Second, do away with the office of Supreme [General] Treasurer, as we have no need for one at all." After referring to other insurance companies which did not have treasurers but relied instead on their secretary for both administrative and financial tasks, he lashed out at the Board of Directors as not only "a very expensive body" but one which had far too much power, particularly the authority to virtually veto actions by the Board of Government. He would reduce its number to five and place all executive power in the Board of Government. He also advocated abolishing all district deputies and investing their duties in immediate Past Grand Knights. Writing his letter just a week before the 1888 meeting of the Board of Government, he made an impassioned plea for the delegates not to just "sit there and allow the same old clique to run the convention as usual."[26]

Though the minutes for the 1888 Board of Government do not include roll-call votes, the action of the Board was in accord with the ideas of T.F.C. of Meriden:

1. The number of districts was reduced from eleven to seven.
2. The authority to fix salaries and expenses shifted from the Board of Directors to the Board of Government.
3. Salaries were reduced by $500.
4. The salary of the General Treasurer was reduced to $150 and the per diem for Directors reduced to $3.00.
5. The Supreme Knight's salary was set at $250.
6. The veto power of the Board of Directors over the action of the Board of Government was abolished.
7. The per-capita tax was also abolished.
8. The meeting of the 1889 Board of Government was to be extended, allowing time for constitutional reform with the implication that democratic (i.e., provisions for elected delegates) reforms would be introduced.[27]

Since John Phelan was re-elected Supreme Knight by one formal ballot, it appears that he had sensed the political climate and made the necessary adjustments, accommodations, and compromises without undermining the new constitutional foundation of the Order. However, Phelan was unable to garner majority support for his two major proposals, the orphans' home and the reserve fund, probably because of the membership's sentiments against rising administrative costs.

Although the Board of Government passed resolutions reflecting the thoughts of T.F.C., one resolution was passed which condemned members who abused the spirit of fraternity by venting their criticisms in the press: "Resolved that any member of the Knights of Columbus who shall publish or cause to be published in the public press or in any circulating newspaper . . . any document . . . tending to create disorder or dissension among the members thereof, be expelled, suspended, or punished in such other manner as the Board of Directors may determine."[28]

By 1888, the K. of C., like any institution based upon elections and open discussion of issues, was a highly politicized organization. The above resolution adopted in 1888 was not intended to suppress political interchange but rather to restrict disagreements to the council chambers and other internal platforms. Implicit in the resolution was the notion that as an Order of Catholic gentlemen the Knights must keep their conflicts within the confines of the fraternity and project a united front against those detractors who would unjustly criticize "the ignorant bungling Irish."

On June 9, a week prior to the meeting of the Board of Government, the Board of Directors voted to establish a new council in Providence, Rhode Island. Subsequently the Board of Government passed a resolution to authorize the General Advocate, Philip J. Markley, to revise the Order's articles of incorporation in order to protect the legal status of the Order as it expanded into other states as well to guarantee the jurisdictional authority of the parent organization within Connecticut.[29]

Daniel E. Sullivan, Dennis F. McCarthy, and a Dr. McNally, members of San Jose Council in Willimantic, had moved to Providence and "after working hard for two months . . . succeeded in getting twenty signatures for the granting of a charter." The pioneer Knights in Providence chose the name Tyler Council in honor of Bishop William Tyler, the first bishop of the Hartford-Providence diocese. One of the charter members proudly remarked that "we would now have a name distinctly Catholic and also American, Tyler being one of our Presidents."[30] Since Bishop Tyler was a member of an old New England family and a convert to Catholicism, the council was implicitly honoring the advance of Catholicism into a Protestant stronghold as well as illustrating its loyalty to American tradition.

On July 8, 1888, Phelan and Colwell, along with Knights from New Haven, Norwich, New London, Stonington, and Westerly, traveled to Providence for the institution of Tyler Council, the installation of officers, and the initiation rites of the charter members. When Bishop Tyler died in June 1849, there were only six small parishes in Providence. By the time Bishop Matthew Harkins was consecrated bishop of Providence on April 14, 1887, the diocese was flourishing with a population of predominantly Irish-American and French-Canadian Catholics. But apparently this Boston-born bishop was reluctant to support Tyler Council, and without episcopal and clerical endorsement the infant council floundered with low membership and poor morale. On the recommendation of Supreme Knight Phelan, Father McGivney traveled to Providence in January 1889 and "layed the object of the Order and the good work it is accomplishing before Right Reverend Bishop Harkins." One Providence Knight wrote that Father McGivney's visit resulted in Bishop Harkins's "approbation" of the Order and "naturally that of his priests."[31]

With only one letter to the editor of the *Connecticut Catholic* written by "Tempus" of Providence as evidence of the McGivney-Harkins meeting, it is not clear what was the basis for the Bishop's apparent indifference to the fate of Tyler Council. Harkins was, however, a stringent conservative on the issue of secret societies, by contrast with Gibbons and Ireland's more accommodationist position. Also, since the Catholic Knights of America, a fraternal insurance society, had been very successful in recruiting members in Providence, Harkins may have concluded that there was no need for the K. of C. there. Known for the strict way in which he controlled every facet of Church life in his diocese, the introduction of an autonomous order with headquarters outside Providence may have appeared to him as a threat to his administrative authority.

In any case, Father McGivney must have succeeded in convincing Harkins that the Order would be a valuable asset to him, for on January 22, 1889, after McGivney's visit, Tyler Council held a "public" meeting (an open house) which "was full to overflowing with interested friends waiting . . . enlightenment." Grand Knight Sullivan "introduced the first speaker of the evening in the person of the Reverend founder of the Order, whose remarks were listened to with close attention." The *Providence Visitor,* Rhode Island's counterpart to the *Connecticut Catholic,* did not cover the meeting between Father McGivney and Bishop Harkins, but it did report on the "first public meeting" of Tyler Council. The *Visitor* stated that "the founder of the Order . . . gave an interesting history of the organization, its struggle for existence during the first two years, and finally its wondrous growth."[32] "Tempus" noted that Phelan and Colwell also gave "stirring speeches."[33] After this auspicious public meeting, Tyler Council prospered in membership and influence. One lesson was clearly illustrated by this experience: Without the support of the local ordinary and his clergy, no council could hope to flourish.

III

Father McGivney's views on the interstate extension of the Order had changed considerably since his 1883 statement in which he limited the Order's growth to the towns of Connecticut. As a very active pastor in Thomaston concerned with the heavy indebtedness of St. Thomas' Church, he deferred to the lay leaders of the Order. Though he must have been intimately concerned with its development and personally gratified by its "wondrous growth" (over five thousand members and fifty-one councils in June 1889), there are no extant documents revealing his role in the business of the Order. However, he resumed an active role in this critical situation which indicated his consistent concern for the welfare of his Order.

At the Board of Government meeting on June 27, 1889, Supreme Knight Phelan made an impassioned plea that the Order express its gratitude to its founder:

I am reminded that in this era of prosperity we should be loath to deny to any amongst us that proper need of appreciative loyalty that to them justly belongs, to them that so deserve it should be our pleasurable duty to do honors, then permit us not to overlook in the march of time, the sturdy pioneers . . . , let us be mindful of their labors, those devoted few whose increasing interest in the Order made our triumphs possible, those who launched the ship "Columbus" and through whom, as her trusty mariners, seas unknown and unexplored were traversed, to these and to him who was her architect and master, we owe a lasting gratitude. It is the Rev. Chaplain of the Order in particular of whom I speak. . . . I commend this convention that it take such proper steps through the usual channels in presenting an appropriate testimonial to the Rev. M. J. McGivney, our worthy Chaplain, as will attest the esteem in which he is held by our organization.[34]

The committee on the Good of the Order proposed a resolution authorizing the Order to pay $1,000 to Father McGivney "as a testimony of the gratitude of the Order for his past services on its behalf." The resolution was "adopted by a rising unanimous vote."[35]

The priest founder, re-elected General Chaplain, returned to Thomaston, where he resumed his ministry. Never a man of robust health, Father McGivney had sensed at a young age the precariousness of existence. The early death of his father must have had a strong effect upon him during his seminary days. To have been a priest witness at bedside and graveside, and to have been involved in the foundation of a sick-and-death benefit society, meant that he and death were more than mere acquaintances. Pneumonia struck him in January 1890. After traveling south on two occasions and after treatment by an "eminent medical staff in New York," the thirty-eight-year-old priest died on August 14.[36]

On the Feast of the Assumption, the day after he died, the *Waterbury Republican* simply stated, "Father McGivney was well-known throughout Connecticut. His conception and successful execution of the idea of organizing the Order of the Knights of Columbus brought him great prominence. Unassuming in manners, he was full of vitality and energy. His efforts were uniformly successful."[37] His unassuming manner was symbolized at his funeral: "as it has been requested by the deceased . . . there should be no flowers."[38] Father T. M. Crowley, curate at St. Thomas', arranged the funeral. "All business was suspended in Thomaston" on the morning of August 18 as a solemn requiem Mass was celebrated with Father Charles Foley of Southold, Long Island, as celebrant, Father James J. Walsh of Waterbury, deacon, and Father J. F. Crowley of Cromwell, subdeacon.[39] With Bishop McMahon "on the episcopal throne" and many priests in attendance, the church was overflowing with mourners.[40]

Four extra cars were added to the train to accommodate the Waterbury friends of Father McGivney. When the funeral cortege reached Waterbury by train, Knights from three Waterbury councils, Sheridan, Carrollton, and Barcelona, "were drawn up in a line wearing mourning badges and white gloves."[41] With more than 250 Knights in attendance, including Supreme officers and delegates from almost all the fifty-six councils in the state, "the funeral procession was the largest ever seen in Waterbury, nearly every hack [horse-drawn taxi] in this and nearby towns [was] pressed into service."[42] The cortege terminated at St. Joseph's Cemetery, where Father McGivney's remains were buried in the family plot.

Though the various funeral eulogies went unrecorded, less than a year later Edward Downes, who was master of ceremonies at a gathering honoring the deceased members of the Order, eulogized the founder.

He was a man of the people. He was ever zealous for the people's welfare and all the kindliness of his priestly soul asserted itself most strongly in his unceasing efforts for the betterment of their condition. . . . Oh Reverend Founder, if [naught] else in all thy holy priestly career merited for thy heavenly rest, that act alone of thine, which gave life to the Knights of Columbus, has surely secured for thee everlasting joy and eternal peace. Comfort and help are not the only fruits of our organization, its province is more far reaching. . . . The very name of our Order, bespeaking the wisdom of our founder, necessarily inspires our members with renewed patriotism and makes us better citizens. The name stands as a beacon light reminding us of the duties we owe our country, and reminding us that unrivaled civil liberty on the one side and unrivaled religious liberty on the other demand of us cultivation and exercise of the most ardent patriotism.[43]

Father McGivney was indeed a "man of the people." He seems to have easily bridged the then abysmal gap between priest and laity. He inspired his brother Knights not by rhetoric but by practical work as organizer and ambassador. The Order he founded inspired thousands to view the ideals of Columbianism in terms of fraternal charity, mediated by sick- and death-benefit assessments on the practical plane. The ceremonial character of Father McGivney's society led the initiates on a journey into the council chambers, where, with symbol, metaphor, and an occasional dash of tomfoolery, they were taught the lessons of Columbianism: pride in America's Catholic heritage, its religious and civil liberty; the duty to defend the faith against its enemies and display loyalty to the cross and flag.

Other Catholic fraternal societies such as the Catholic Knights of America also aimed at providing Catholics with an alternative to the Masons and other proscribed societies; they too demanded that their members be practicing Catholics and even required proof that each member made his Easter duty. But the Knights of Columbus was more than a society of Catholics, it was a uniquely American cultural phenomenon. Built upon a strong foundation of mutual need and fraternal charity, Father McGivney's Order provided first- and second-generation immigrants a "rite of passage" into American society. The enthusiasm engendered by the ceremonials was not merely the ritualized mumbo-jumbo of continental secret societies but, rather, symbolized the heightened consciousness among Knights that as Catholics they could be religiously proud and as immigrants they could be patriotically loyal. By proclaiming the nobility of the American-Catholic experience and by conspicuously avoiding any association with the Old World, the Knights of Columbus are a classic instance of a minority's drive to assimilate into the larger society.

Unlike, say, the Ancient Order of Hibernians, which mediated the struggle in American society by parading their Irish heroes before the Protestant public, frequently reaching a higher pitch of nationalism than that which had existed in Ireland, the K. of C. was an ethnic association in which the struggle for Catholic legitimacy was fought by the rules of the American battlefield. For this reason the Knights paraded American-Catholic heroes, descendants of Columbus, and through their ceremonials they instilled within the Order the confidence to defeat Anglo-Saxon prejudice on its own terms and on its own grounds of respectability and civility. The Order never exhibited European-Catholic triumphalism, nor did it limit membership to those of Irish descent. Indeed, its blend of Catholic-American and assimilationist attitudes indicates that it had a heavy investment in American religious pluralism.

The K. of C. displayed a robust Catholicism which reflected the strong institutional fabric of the American Church, with its schools, orphanages, hospitals, and historical and literary societies, and variety of Catholic newspapers serving the ever-increasing number of immigrants faithful to their Church. Though there were dozens of death-benefit societies developed by ethnic groups, only the Knights of Columbus evolved as a broad movement grounded in a burgeoning American-Catholic culture. Two years after Father McGivney died, the Order expanded into New York and Massachusetts, and twelve years later there were councils in nearly every major American city from Portland, Maine, to Los Angeles, California. Such rapid growth marked not only the westward expansion of Catholic society but also the advance of a strong fraternal movement, with Catholicism as its organizing impulse and with a cooperative insurance program to fulfill its economic needs.

4

Columbianism, Anti-Catholicism, and Americanism

As THE KNIGHTS OF COLUMBUS EVOLVED into a nationwide organization, its structure, spirit, and mission underwent a profound transformation. Supreme Knight John J. Phelan, who presided from 1886 to 1897, nurtured a national vision without relinquishing his loyalty to the Order's roots in Connecticut. A successful lawyer in Bridgeport who was twice elected Secretary of the State of Connecticut, Phelan had the legal and political skills so necessary during the transitional phase from local to national organization. Philip J. Markley, General Advocate 1886–99, was also an eminent lawyer and a successful Democratic politician. Born in New Britain, Connecticut, in 1855, Markley represented the economic ascendancy of a growing proportion of second-generation Irish Americans. After receiving his B.A. and M.A. degrees from Holy Cross College, he studied law at Columbia University. Elected to the state legislature in 1890, Markley was a valuable asset to the Order during its period of expansion.[1]

The new 1889 charter included four sections, each with an elaborate statement of purpose, of which one was "to promote such social and intellectual intercourse among its members as shall be desirable and proper, and by such lawful means as to them shall seem best."[2] By explicitly dedicating themselves to very broad social and cultural goals, the Knights were revealing a self-image far beyond the scope of merely a cooperative insurance society. In his annual address to the 1890 Board of Government, Supreme Knight Phelan blended the economic and social advantages in extending "the hand of fellowship to the Catholics of other jurisdictions."[3] Phelan's expansionist policy did not receive unanimous support. M. F. Sullivan, a New Haven Knight recalled "an undertone of protest in New Haven" against the extension of the Order throughout New England. He explained the anti-expansionist rationale: "They feared that a large influx of new members would in some way increase the insurance rates."[4]

These fears seem to have been based on the assumption that expansion would result in an ever-increasing number of high insurance risks entering the Order, and so result in a proportionate increase in the death rate. Because Phelan's expansionist policy included the Order's traditional requirement that all prospective insurance members take a stringent physical examination, and because eventually the Order welcomed those who failed the exam as noninsurance members, per-capita death assessments actually declined during the expansion period. However, as we shall see in Chapter 6, the assessment basis of the insurance program could not withstand the weight of national expansion.

Phelan was so confident of the Order's broad appeal that he sensed its destiny as a national society. "It has yielded to no other in its allegiance to Church and State and stands with any as an example of charity and integrity. It has with solicitous patience guided the future of the widow and orphan and directed their footsteps along life's tangled pathway. Its influence has dignified the deathbed of poverty and made happy and consoled him whose fast-ebbing breath gave it praise and whose offspring live to bless, nay pray for, its continued prosperity."[5] Phelan's rhetoric may strike a discordant note today, but it was characteristic of the idealistic language common among stump orators of the era. No doubt Phelan was deeply touched by his experiences in guiding the Order from a path of relative obscurity to the threshold of national prominence. At that 1890 convention the delegates (all Grand Knights and immediate Past Grand Knights of each of the fifty-six councils) approved a new constitution which provided for the governance of a national organization.[6] Lawyers Phelan and Markley were foresighted in establishing the legal ground for the future, when several state jurisdictions would be absorbed into the authority structure of the Order.

The new constitution provided for a National Council to replace the Board of Government as the "supreme governing body" of the Order. The State Councils, counterparts of the National Council, were composed of representatives of the subordinate councils, Grand Knights and immediate Past Grand Knights, while the National Council was composed of representatives from each State Council, State Deputies, and immediate Past State Deputies. Both State and National Councils also included delegates elected on a proportional basis. The

Supreme officers remained as before, but only the Supreme Knight kept the traditional title; the remaining officers' titles were changed from General to National. The State Deputy was the Supreme Knight's counterpart for each state jurisdiction; other state officers included State Treasurer, Secretary, Warden, Chaplain, and Advocate. The National Council was to meet biennially and the national officers served two-year terms, but the State Councils met annually and state officers were elected for a one-year term. Though the executive authority still resided in the Board of Directors, its composition was changed from representatives of districts to members of the National Council, who were chosen annually. Only the Supreme Knight, National Secretary, and National Advocate were ex-officio members, and the total number of districts was never to be less than five nor more than twelve.

The new constitution, which was to go into effect when four (later changed to three) state jurisdictions had been formed, added a new state tier to the governance structure. However, federalism remained the basic principle. State and subordinate councils possessed a high degree of autonomy, as exemplified by election of officers, authorship of their own constitution and by-laws, and the control of funds unrelated to moneys collected for insurance and the national administration of the Order. There was one exception to the federal system. The Supreme Knight, with the approval of the Board of Directors, appointed one local officer, the District Deputy Supreme Knight. Since this office was the extension of the Supreme Knight's supervisory and ceremonial authority, its appointive character may be viewed as illustrative of the principle of checks and balances incorporated into the federal system. Biennial meetings of the National Council and two-year terms for national officers were departures from tradition, but Phelan and Markley, the major authors of the 1891 constitution, were obviously concerned with the expense involved in annual meetings of delegates from several states. Though the constitution would be amended during the next period, the basic structure has remained intact to the present.

At the 1891 convention, Supreme Knight Phelan reported that the Order's expansion was obstructed by three factors: the need to perfect its rituals, the need to enact laws suitable to the insurance regulations of the various states, and the need to commission an organizer empowered with responsibility for new-council development.[7] Though Phelan hinged the success of expansion to his annual plea for a monetary reserve fund to guarantee financial solvency during epidemics (*la grippe* had been responsible for several deaths in 1890 and 1891), the delegates rejected the reserve-fund proposal but did approve the hiring of an organizer.[8]

Ironically, the first council beyond the Connecticut–Rhode Island limits was founded not by the organizer but rather by Knights who had moved from Connecticut to New York. Samuel D. Cronin and John Clark, members of Silver City Council No. 2, Meriden, and employees of Ansonia Clock Company, were transferred to Brooklyn, where the clock company was establishing a factory. Cronin and Clark were such enthusiastic missionaries that within a short time they had gathered together the nucleus of a new council. In late June of 1891, Supreme Knight Phelan and National Secretary Colwell traveled to Brooklyn for a meeting in the basement of St. John the Evangelist Church where twenty-nine men "signified their willingness to become Knights." The *Connecticut Catholic* went on to report that the local pastor was supportive of their efforts and that "nearly all of the [Brooklyn] members are total abstainers."[9]

When Brooklyn Council No. 60 was instituted on September 16, 1891, forty members, "representing several of the leading families of Brooklyn," were initiated into the Order. Philip Markley, John Phelan, and Daniel Colwell participated in the ceremonies with "a large delegation of Connecticut Knights in attendance." The reporter for the *Connecticut Catholic* was very optimistic about the Order's future in the Brooklyn–New York area.[10]

To encourage new-council development in the area, Brooklyn Council hosted a "grand entertainment in a full dress reception," the main attraction being a three-act drama entitled "Tom Cobb." S. D. Cronin, one of the Knights transplanted from Meriden, extended an invitation to all the Connecticut Knights through the *Connecticut Catholic.* Though Cronin was confident of success, he ended his letter on an ambivalent note: "Our council has not been long in existence and in a large city like our own, a handful of men cannot be readily noticed. Indeed our council will meet with many opponents, and whatever you can do, brothers, will be for the betterment of all."[11] Though there is no evidence of attendance figures for the reception, the hope of engendering new councils in the area was frustrated.

When Cronin referred to opponents of the K. of C. he was probably alluding to members of the Catholic Benevolent Legion (C.B.L.), which had originated in Brooklyn in 1881 with the enthusiastic support of Bishop John Loughlin, ordinary from 1853 to 1891. In April 1892, Bishop Charles E. McDonnell was consecrated the second ordinary of this fast-growing diocese. According to the Constitution of the Catholic Benevolent Legion, the bishop of Brooklyn was ex officio its Supreme Spiritual Advisor. With over 28,000 members located in several states in 1892, the C.B.L. was a far more powerful society than the K. of C.[12] And so without the support and endorsement of the bishop and clergy, the Order had only one council in the area for the next few years.

The expansion into Boston also occurred more by accident than design. In late 1891, Phelan and Colwell journeyed to Providence to attend a ball hosted by Tyler Council. Three Bostonians were also present: James H. Conley, Edward W. Dunn, and Thomas Dunlon. Impressed with the Tyler Knights and the national officers, the Bostonians became strong advocates of the Order's extension into Massachusetts.[13] In March 1892, Phelan and Colwell were invited to Boston by forty-two interested candidates to whom the organization and character of the Order were explained. The pioneer council in the Old Bay State was instituted on April 10, 1892.[14] M. F. Sullivan of Rodrigo Council No. 44, New Haven, who was a member of the degree team for the institution of the first Boston council, recalled the social composition of its charter members as "high class men, merchants, doctors, lawyers, State and City officials." Sullivan's role was to present "the panoramic lecture of the then second degree . . . with the lecture requiring fifty minutes to deliver."[15] James H. Conley, one of the three Bostonians introduced to the Order in Providence, was elected first Grand Knight, and James E. Hayes, later to be elected first State Deputy of Massachusetts and Supreme Knight (1897–98), was chosen Deputy Grand Knight. Located in the Charlestown section of Boston, the Irish-American charter members illustrated their American patriotism by naming their council Bunker Hill.[16]

Conley and Hayes were second-generation Irish Americans who clearly represented that group's economic ascendancy. Conley was born in Deer Isle, Maine, on January 12, 1857. Upon moving to Boston in 1873, he entered the machinist trade while he pursued secondary education in night school. After thirteen years as a machinist, he established his own laundry business, which provided him with increased status and wealth. Conley was also a very active member of the Catholic Total Abstinence Society and a popular lecturer on the temperance circuit. Hayes, also active in the temperance movement, was a native of Charlestown. Born in 1865, he attended Prescott Grammar School and in 1885 received his Bachelor's Degree, with highest honors, from Boston College. While teaching six years at the Frothingham Grammar

School, he pursued training in law under a private tutor and was admitted to the Suffolk County Bar in 1891. From the fall of 1892 until his death in 1898 he was the Democratic choice for state representative (1892–96) and state senator (1896–97).[17]

The large number of socially and economically ascendant Irish-American Catholics in Boston, symbolized by the election of a mayor from their ranks in 1884, provided a fertile field for the growth of the Order, even though the Catholic Knights of America, the Massachusetts Catholic Order of Foresters, and the Catholic Benevolent Legion were already providing fraternal insurance. Though the K. of C. offered a rich ceremonial in which its ideals were firmly embedded as unique marks distinguishing it from other Catholic fraternal societies, its appeal was further enhanced in 1892 when the Board of Government allowed noninsurance, or associate, members to join its ranks, expanded its insurance plan to include three alternative policies, $1,000, $2,000 and $3,000; it also established a reserve fund to protect the membership during epidemics.[18] Reforms in the insurance program were explicitly intended to enhance the Order's competitiveness in the fraternal field, but it was the creation of associate membership which had the greatest impact upon the character and appeal of the K. of C.

The earliest evidence of support for noninsurance membership appeared in the *Connecticut Catholic* for March 28, 1885; a New London Knight wrote a letter to the editor in which he advocated making the insurance plan optional in order to attract "the vast number who would be drawn to the Order for the sake of sociality, good fellowship, and brotherly instincts, which are the natural outcome of organizations of this nature." Signed "Semper Idem," the letter concluded that if the plan were optional, "young men would, in time, be educated to the benefits of the insurance plan and would be gradually absorbed in that scheme of the organization."[19]

When John Phelan introduced the notion of associate members, he included in that category only those "of our faith, whose age, health, or calling debars them from an active participation in the benefits of the Society as ordinary members." Referring to the new category as "honorary or associate members," Phelan did not agree with Semper Idem's optional plan but rather opened the door to those unqualified for full membership. However, by advocating the new policy he emphasized the moral purposes of the Order: "This suggestion is born of the thought that our usefulness and prestige might, from social, intellectual, or other points, be materially improved by [their] advice, example, and companionship."[20] Phelan's basis for the qualification for associate membership was drastically redesigned during the subsequent year. Apparently there was strong sentiment favoring a totally nonrestrictive policy because of the strong social appeal of the Knights. "Thoroughly imbued as I am in the conviction that the growth and anticipated greatness of this society lies in and through the development, for Catholics, of the great moral and social forces, with the insurance or other pecuniary features as a vital appendage, I cherish the hope that through an extension of our scheme of associate membership, a mighty stride will have been taken in the coveted direction." The Supreme Knight not only advocated amending the laws "to permit all Catholics, whether eligible for insurance or not, to join and swell our Brotherhood,"[21] but also instituting Associate Councils. Though the laws regulating the status of associate members were frequently modified, practical Catholicity was the only consistent qualification from its inception to the present day. Also, the noninsurance members passed through the same three-degree ritual as insurance members, and this forged strong bonds between both groups.

II

The tenth anniversary of the Order called for a celebration in 1892; the expansion into Boston, the adoption of a reserve fund and alternative insurance policies, and the establishment of the associate membership were marks of progress far beyond the vision of the Knights of a decade earlier. However, the quadricentennial of the discovery of America by the Order's patron preempted their own anniversary and became a national celebration in which the Knights could more freely display their own participation in the spirit of Columbianism.

At the 1891 meeting of the Board of Government, John Phelan received a strong vote of confidence to proceed, through a committee, in planning for an appropriate celebration of the quadricentennial.[22] By the summer of 1892, extensive plans for a large parade were well under way, and Phelan enthusiastically urged the membership to support this demonstration which promised "to rank with the foremost civic events of the period." He also referred to the insurance and sick benefits as "incidental to, and not the final purpose of the Order." The moral, social, and intellectual "acquirements," which he considered as advancing the "magnificent possibilities for citizen culture," formed the spiritual nature of the Order.[23]

The *Connecticut Catholic*'s endorsement of the Catholic Columbian celebration was based on the fact that "the discovery of America [was] within itself a Catholic event . . . and the first act of Catholic worship."[24] Hence when nearly 6,000 Knights paraded through the streets of New Haven on October 11, 1892, it was not merely a commemoration of one of the many historical events in the life of the nation but rather, in the minds and hearts of the Knights — descendants of Columbus—it was a commemoration of a sacred event, the Catholic baptism of the country. When Phelan referred to the Order's purpose as the promotion of "citizen culture," he implied that those who formed their lives according to the principles of Columbian Knighthood derived their civic virtues from their patron's heroic deed.

Because Catholic immigrant families were viewed by many as suspect, loyal only to one master, the Pope, the promotion of "citizen culture" was also expressed in explicit displays of loyalty to purely civic events; thus within the Order, San Salvador and Green Cross Councils shared a fraternal spirit with Washington and Bunker Hill Councils. With the fear of anti-Catholic prejudice and discrimination ever circulating through the Catholic community, a vigorous adversary position was implicit in the Order's promotion of "citizen culture."

The 1892 Columbus Day Parade was expressive of the Order's spirit: six thousand Knights, thirty-six bands, eleven drum corps, "pretty little girls in white, who carried shields with the names of the states and territories,"[25] floats depicting the Catholic King and Queen, Ferdinand and Isabella, a Bishop blessing the sailors in preparation for embarking on the perilous journey and the landing of Columbus. After parading down Church Street—it took forty-five minutes for the marchers to pass by the reviewing stand—the celebrants reassembled for an afternoon program. Nearly 40,000 people gathered on the New Haven green, where three churches stand as sentinels of the Protestant heritage of America. Among those on the speaker's stand were Bishop Lawrence S. McMahon, Father W. J. Maher, Chancellor of the Diocese of Hartford, and Supreme Knight Phelan. A thousand-piece band, under the baton of the musical director of the U.S. Military Academy at West Point, and a six-hundred-voice choir, directed by the choir leader of St. Mary's Church, joined in a concert which included "Hail Columbia, Ode to Columbus," an original anthem written by Judge D. J. Donohue of Forest City Council No. 3, Middletown, the national anthems of Spain, Italy, France, Germany, and Ireland, and culminating in "America." Between the singing of the "Ode to Columbus" and the national anthems, Father Maher delivered an oration on Columbian themes. In his introductory remarks he reminded the Knights of their debt of gratitude to Bishop McMahon, "who has been an active and earnest factor in the establishment of your organization . . . one whose name, with that of the lovingly lamented Father Michael J. McGivney, should be listed in your annals as best deserving your gratitude and esteem." Then followed a collage of Columbian themes:

"Columbia—Columbia—what a name and what a nation. The one an emblem of truest Christianity: The other, a pledge of highest civilization . . . his flagship was named after the Virgin Mother of the Savior of mankind, Santa Maria . . . the first act of the glorious admiral . . . was to plant the Cross of Christ on the shore, a symbol of his sacred commission to take possession of Columbia . . . as the viceroy of a Christian kingdom and representative of the faith of the Catholic Church. . . . We enter the wake of the modern march of American progress . . . there is no land, however far, fertile, or fortunate, like our beloved 'Columbia.' "[26]

III

Thomas Harrison Cummings, charter member of Bunker Hill Council No. 62, became the most articulate spokesman of these Columbian themes. A Boston native, born in 1856, Cummings was educated in the classics both at American and European universities. A curator at the Boston Public Library, business manager of the *Boston Pilot* (a Catholic newspaper with a circulation of over 100,000), lecturer and photographer, Cummings enthusiastically immersed himself in a number of intellectual and artistic pursuits.[27] Even before he entered the Order he was lecturing on the saga of Christopher Columbus.

Cummings succeeded to the office of Master of Ceremonies, vacant since the death in 1891 of James T. Mullen, first Supreme Knight. Elected to that office at the October 24, 1893, meeting of the National Council (when three state councils had been instituted, the Board of Government, a purely Connecticut authority, was dissolved), Cummings's position was that of both Master of Ceremonies and National Organizer.[28] The new ceremonials, which were approved by the Board of Directors in March 1891, bore the mark of Mullen's theatrical flare and of Cummings' literary aspirations.

The Second Section of the three-degree ritual was in the form of a melodrama. The degree team could choose one of three scripts, each of which was a depiction of Columbus's voyage woven together around the principle of Unity. And the whole fulfilled the criteria for successful melodrama as defined by George Bernard Shaw, who noted that it "should be simple and sincere drama of action and feeling, kept well within the vast tract of passion and motive which is common to the philosopher and the laborer. . . . The whole character of the piece must be allegorical, idealistic, full of generalization and moral lessons."[29] Before the "Unity" melodrama began, the candidates for the Second Degree renewed their promise to live according to the principle of the First Degree, Charity. The Deputy Grand Knight then addressed them on the meaning of unity.

Unity is the all powerful ally of that God-given attribute implanted in the human heart, charity. Unity is the force and power that makes the march of armies enlisted in sweet charity's name, as restless as the ocean's sweep, that causes charity as a sentiment to attain the magnitude of a passion, and becomes the expounder of its divinity. Unity in our Order comprehends a mighty host of Christian men welded together for their social and moral welfare, unswerving in their loyalty to the country's flag, to the principles of our Order, the Catholic Church, and God, our Father.

The Chancellor then addressed the candidates in the form of a prologue to the Columbus melodrama:

I beg to remind you that there is no more truthful and beautiful lesson and example of the limitless, boundless consequence of Unity afforded in the world's history than that of the great exemplar of our Order himself, in his mighty achievement of the discovery of America, and from none other lips than his can we more aptly find prophetic vision and hopeful anticipation so brilliantly realized.

The melodrama's rising action proceeds through scenes of mutinous protest against Columbus which cause the admiral to address his sailors on the need for faith and unity. Then, as he is prayerfully reflecting on God's will, land is sighted. The mutinous sailors kneel before their admiral beseeching forgiveness. He responds:

Now rise, my friends; no sincere christian soul could bar forgiveness for errors past, nor shall the shadow cast o'er future joy. Then up, my friends; unbolt the gates of love, all, all is past, forgiven.

It is suggested that they name the land Columbia in honor of the discoverer, but Columbus responds that, though his "heart is touched at your kind words," a name nobler than his deserves the honor. After one sailor suggests the Spanish King or Queen, Columbus delivers an impassioned peroration on the sacred nature of the discovery event:

Great, honored names indeed are those, good friends,
And yet, withal, a nobler still remains.
'Tis Friday morn; upon this fateful day
A sacred life was given for fallen man,
And Calvary's mount, with cruel thirst deep, drank
Of blood divine, the price of man's redemption.
Then shall this new found land be named for him,
And in the soft, sweet language of Castile
Let it be called San Salvador.
And, in the years to come when we're but dust,
And but faint memory of our deeds remain;
When millions yet unborn shall seek this shore,
And make their homes upon its fruitful breast,
Sweet reverence shall they pay when grateful
Souls breathe forth the Saviour's name, San Salvador.[30]

IV

When Thomas Harrison Cummings spread the Columbian message throughout Boston (1892–93), where Irish-American Catholicism was militantly assertive on the one hand and institutionally well grounded on the other, his success had an extraordinary impact upon the Order. According to statistics published in May 1893, the Archdiocese of Boston numbered 550,000 Catholics, served by 380 priests, and 170 churches, with a total parochial-school population of nearly 30,000 children.[31] For more than five years Boston Catholics had been engaged in a struggle with a variety of anti-Catholic groups.

The Columbian themes were developed in Connecticut during the eighties but Columbianism was greatly influenced by the expansion into Boston, where the Knights militantly defended the Catholic presence in America. Because the Knights' battle was repeated in Chicago, St. Louis, Memphis, Louisville, Los Angeles, and other urban centers in the United States and Canada during the subsequent ten years, and because the Order emerged from these battles as a kind of Catholic anti-defamation league, a brief summary of later-nineteenth-century nativism and anti-Catholicism is crucial to understanding the character of the Knights of Columbus.

During the first decade of the Order's history, the leadership expressed a buoyant confidence in America's capacity to assimilate Catholic immigrants peacefully. The social atmosphere contained strong anti-Irish and anti-Catholic biases, but overt anti-Catholicism within Connecticut was limited to peripheral expressions of traditional distrust of "Romanists," particularly of the combative Irish.

The situation in Massachusetts was not so calm. With Irish-Catholic mayors elected in Lawrence (1881), Lowell (1882), and Boston (1884), the Catholic issue was injected into politics. Anti-Catholicism vigorously asserted itself in Boston in 1887; anti-Catholic organizations, lecturers, and demonstrations revived the crusading of the Know-Nothing movement with the distinction that nativism played a secondary role to the primary drive, anti-Catholicism. Nativism was fed by the competition for jobs between the "natives and the swelling ranks of Irish Catholics." The political ascendancy of Catholics was viewed in terms of papal imperialism, while the Catholic parochial-school movement "was distorted into a 'papal aggression against American institutions,' an attempt to wreck the public school system by withdrawing from it a great part of the nation's school children and building up a rival system of 'priest controlled schools,' which would then demand a major part of the public school funds."[32]

The religious tensions in Boston were parallel to the conflicts in Ireland. Though there was a large Catholic population, nearly 40,000 Protestants—the vast majority of whom were of Scotch-Irish descent —had immigrated to the area since the Civil War. Just as the Irish Catholics established the Ancient Order of Hibernians in America, so many of these Scotch Irish brought with them the Loyal Orange Institutions, a fraternal society grounded in anti-Catholicism. The religious warfare between the various anti-Catholic groups and the Irish Catholics occurred on three fronts. Books such as *Why Priests Should Wed* (1887) and *My Life in a Convent* (1892) were bizarre pornographic barbs hurled at traditional theological and devotional practices; *Washington in the Lap of Rome* (1885) caricatured the Democratic President, Grover Cleveland, as a victim of the papacy, which was aiming "to awe the state, control the people, and banish liberty."[33] The publication *Women's Voice and Public School Champion* also attacked Catholics' allegiance to Rome as contrary to their American citizenship, and focused on the public school as the fortress of democracy vis-à-vis the parochial school as a training ground for papal imperialism.[34]

By 1893 a national movement which attempted to define political loyalties on religious grounds was under way. Many anti-Catholic organizations such as the Junior Order of the United American Mechanics achieved a strong national following (160,000 members in 1890), but none rivaled the American Protective Association (A.P.A.) in membership and influence. Founded in Clinton, Iowa, on March 13, 1887, the A.P.A. was in the vanguard of a national Protestant crusade to make democracy safe from papal imperialism. Though the A.P.A. exploited nativist xenophobia, it admitted foreign-born into its ranks. Henry Francis Bowers, its founder, gathered together a militant group of followers who were frightened at the increasing political power of the Catholics attracted to Clinton's lumber mills and factories. In the 1887 mayoralty contest, the Catholic vote organized by the Knights of Labor was a strong factor. Bowers, who had achieved notoriety as a lecturer on the Masonic circuit in Iowa and who had attained the level of the thirty-second degree in Scottish Rite Masonry, organized his followers into a ritualistic secret society aimed at protecting American republican institutions from the Romanist enemy. Besides taking oaths to struggle against Romanism in all its manifestations, every member swore not to hire or do business with Catholics. Unlike the Know-Nothings, the A.P.A. did not attempt to form an independent political party but rather aimed at influencing existing parties, particularly the Republican Party. The A.P.A. exploited nativist fears that Catholic immigrants were radical unionists of the Haymarket riot stripe.[35]

The Catholic presence had certainly become more evident by the late 1880s and early 1890s. At the Third Plenary Council of Baltimore in 1884, the Catholic hierarchy energetically called for the establishment of parochial schools. The Knights of Labor included many Irish Catholics and was supported by the American-Irish press such as the *Connecticut Catholic.* By arguing against the papacy's near condemnation of the Knights of Labor, Cardinal Gibbons was viewed by many as the friend of foreign radical groups. Displays of institutional strength such as the foundation of Catholic University in Washington, D.C. (1888), the presence of Pope Leo XIII's emissary, Archbishop Francesco Satolli, at the Columbian Exposition in 1892, and the establishment of Satolli's residence in Washington, D.C., struck anti-Catholic groups as institutional counterparts to the ascendancy of Catholic politicians in many of the urban areas throughout the nation.

Until 1890 the A.P.A. was only one of many nativist anti-Catholic organizations; it was limited to Iowa, Illinois, and Nebraska but it had one council in Jonesville, Wisconsin, and one in Detroit, Michigan. During the next three years, when the Catholic issue was inserted into the Congressional election of 1890 and the Presidential election of 1892, it gained in strength as local councils became political clearinghouses for other patriotic societies concerned with the Romanist menace. Through affiliation with other nativist, anti-Catholic societies, it exercised a national influence.

In 1893, a year characterized by economic collapse, which engendered a four-year depression, the A.P.A. had supporters in twenty-two states and Canada. During these depression years a confused and discontented public was highly vulnerable to the simplistic solutions of nativist anti-Catholic rhetoric.[36] Though there were Catholic extremists who exacerbated these tensions, many Catholic leaders were confident that the American spirit of liberty and fair play would prevail. In response to news of the growth of the A.P.A., the editors of the *Connecticut Catholic* stated, "There's no danger; America owes much of its present strength and influence in advancement to its Catholic element."[37]

Thomas Cummings's first published piece on the K. of C. Order reflected the way in which the Knights incorporated their battle against anti-Catholicism into Columbian themes. Appearing in the May 1893 edition of *Donahoe's Magazine,* a Catholic monthly in Boston, Cummings's article included a concise statement of Columbianism within the context of anti-Catholicism:

With true American patriotism they [the K. of C.] demand from their members respect for manhood and liberty for the individual, particularly that liberty which is the essence of all liberty and which was first planted on this continent by Roman Catholics, viz: Freedom to worship God according to one's conscience. They ask that no man's social and civil rights be affected by his religious beliefs. Accordingly, the unjust and un-American attempt on the part of a certain coterie of bigoted writers to belittle the character of Columbus simply because he was a Roman Catholic, naturally meets with their dissent and disapproval.[38]

His reference to anti-Catholic bigotry as un-American was not, in itself, distinctively Columbian. Many leading Protestant ministers had articulated the same general principle. However, when patriotism was linked with the Catholic heritage of America, including Catholic respect for freedom of worship as in the colony of Maryland, the notion that anti-Catholicism was un-American meant that the former was viewed as a distortion of the historical events in which Catholics and Catholicism had played such significant roles.

Cummings published and edited a monthly, *Columbiad,* "a paper devoted to interests of the Knights of Columbus."[39] In defense of the Church against attack by the A.P.A. and other "patriotic societies," *Columbiad* frequently included articles and addresses extolling the Catholic contribution to American progress. Cummings incorporated a speech by William J. Coughlin in the January 1894 edition of *Colum-*

biad, one which clearly illustrated the principle and symbols of Columbianism. In his address to a gathering in the new home of Lowell Council No. 72, Lowell, Massachusetts, Coughlin stated that

we are privileged to enjoy the rich heritage bequeathed by noble ancestors. The humblest Roman proudly boasted of his citizenship apostrophizing liberty, whilst yet a thrall to the "blood-red spirit of Brutus." How infinitely more proudly should we boast of our political, social, and religious enfranchisement, sanctified as it is by the "snow-white spirit of Christ." [The root of "Columbus" is dove and, by extension, Holy Spirit.] Yet we, the Americans . . . should in our self-congratulation hold in sweet remembrance, the honest hearts, the brawny hands, the independent, liberal minds of those patriot pathfinders, who blazed a thoroughfare . . . through the everglades and morasses of the fierce wilds of fanaticism and intolerance—those evangelists who bore aloft . . . the sterling principles of the Declaration of Independence.[40]

After establishing that fanaticism and intolerance are contrary to the American spirit, Coughlin lashed out at the "ignorant, malevolent clique" who parade their Americanism as they intolerantly trample upon the rights of immigrant Catholics.

Intelligent and cultural persons, mostly of Anglo-Saxon lineage—forgetting that the cradle of their immediate ancestors was rocked on the banks of the Severn or the Thames—demand recognition of their Americanism, yet deny the same title to those whose ancestoral homes lay in the Valleys of the Rhine, the Tiber, the Seine, the Shannon, or the St. Lawrence. Coupled with such antecedents, if these latter profess the Catholic religion, the distinction is more clearly defined, and patriotism is usurped by a prejudice which of all national ills is the most mischievous, as it is the one most difficult to eradicate and cure.[41]

Coughlin proceeded to attack those who call Catholic priests "masters of machiavellian intrigue," and the Catholic laity disloyal "knaves or imbeciles" who are unable "to distinguish between the debt due to Caesar and the tribute due to God." He concluded on a note struck by earlier Knights:

As if it were not history that long before that solitary adventurous vessel, the *Mayflower,* of forlorn hope, debarked her sturdy pilgrim passengers by the rock of Plymouth, the towns of St. Augustine in Florida and Sante Fe in New Mexico had been founded and the discoveries of Cortez, Denys, Ponce de Leon . . . and Cartier, supplementing those of the good Columbus, were surely no less important than the distinguished performances of Drake, Raleigh, and the adventurous Cabot, in whose glory we all aspire to participate.[42]

Coughlin linked Columbus's discovery to the evolution of liberty and the progress of American civilization. He implicitly referred to the melting-pot theory of immigrant assimilation into American life: "Such has been our progress under free institutions that the crude material of the old world is received and converted, as if by magic, into the finished product of modern civilization." Though militant in defense of the faith and the American loyalty of Catholics, Coughlin's view of the "mission of the Knights of Columbus" was "not to disrupt or disunite, but to unify and to heal—not to bear down, but to build up . . . the precepts of fraternity, unity, and charity which we teach are as Catholic as Christianity, and as universal as humanity itself."[43]

Thomas Cummings believed that Columbianism not only legitimized the Catholic presence in America but actually implanted within each Knight "the best type of American citizenship." Though the Order was predominantly Irish-American it had always viewed itself as cosmopolitan. Cummings boasted that

like the crew who sailed with Columbus on the first voyage to America, we have men of various races and languages. But by drawing close the bonds of brotherhood, we make for the best type of American citizenship. For the best American is he who best exemplifies in his own life, that this is not a Protestant country, nor a Catholic country, nor a Hebrew country, any more than it is an Anglo-Saxon or a Latin country, but a country of all races and all creeds, with one great, broad, unmolturable [sic] creed of fair play and equal rights for all.[44]

The ideal Columbian citizen was not to be arrogantly Catholic but rather, with the cosmopolitan Protestant and Jew, was to exemplify the utmost of civility within his pluralistic society, i.e., the "unmolturable [sic] creed of fair play and equal rights for all." As he passed through the ceremonials, the Columbian citizen was to be so immersed in the Catholic heritage in America that he could feel confidently secure and proud of his American character.

Cummings's notion of Columbian citizenship as the major force in struggling against anti-Catholicism was clearly expressed in an article he wrote for *Donahoe's Magazine* entitled "Catholic Gentlemen in Fraternity." After introducing his readers to the cooperative insurance program, Cummings elaborated on the "Fraternity side, perhaps the most beautiful and useful feature of the Order."[45] By joining the Knights, Catholics could develop "social and fraternal instincts by which men grow in civilized feeling and in the kindlier emotions of the heart." However, Columbian fraternalism was more than a civilizing or taming process; it was a unifying spirit motivating Catholic men to forge a common defense of the faith. Though the Catholic population was "numerically large, professing one Lord, one Faith, one Baptism," each parish was "in a sense an isolated community and each individual parishioner stands by himself." Besides the social isolation of the parishioner, political, economic and social differences "tend to break up the unity and harmony of Catholic society."[46] The major role of the Knights of Columbus was to provide an organization which transcended parish lines, which healed divisions within Catholic society, which promoted Catholic cultural interests, and which proudly and civilly defended the faith.

Much as their adversaries may storm and rave about the Catholic vote, and the political power of Rome in America, Catholics know that in political, material, and social affairs they are really more divided than their Protestant neighbors. . . . It can safely be asserted that not until Catholic men have learned the lessons of fraternity and mutual sympathy, will die away the misrepresentations, abuse, contempt, and caricature to which all Catholics are now subject. There is full need and place for an intelligent organism such as the Knights of Columbus to step to the front, to work for the advancement of Catholic social and material interests, and in its own name and in that of justice, reason, and humanity, to cry out to the opposing forces—Halt![47]

Other Catholic societies were dedicated to pursuing "the relief of suffering," but they were concerned "chiefly [with] one of the many wants of humanity." Because the Knights of Columbus possessed "a wider scope, influence, and power and greater facilities for the accomplishment of their benevolent purposes," they alone could pursue a dignified crusade in the promotion and defense of Catholic society. Cummings compared the ideal Columbian fraternalism to the "kinship of spirit and brotherly love"[48] of the early Christians. These were ideals which were imbedded in the "beautiful ritual" aimed to unite secular society "by the mystic tie of charity and the golden chain of brotherly love." Inspired by Columbus, who was "a prophet and a seer, an instrument of Divine Providence [and] a mystic of the very highest order," each true Knight "becomes a better Catholic and a better citizen."[49]

In response to those who considered the Order just another secular fraternal society with Catholic trappings, Cummings stated:

Catholicity is the essence and central idea of the institution. The sentiment of religion pervades all its ceremonies. The great mysteries of life and death, accountability to God, a future life—all these facts are kept constantly before the minds of the brothers. In this respect it stands prominent over all existing Catholic societies . . . one thing above all else the Order lays claim to, and that is the evolution of Catholic Gentlemen in Fraternity. The principles of the Order, if rightly applied and honorably practiced, mean the creation of a new type of Catholic manhood. They mean that the young men who are in touch with the world and its affairs are creating a new spirit in the Church by illustrating what a layman can and ought to do, in the active work of life. They stand for what is clean, moral, wholesome, and effective in American manhood when that is crowned by the teachings of Mother Church, and as a grand result, they must achieve in time the social uplift of the entire Catholic people.[50]

Cummings's effusive flow of idealism marks him as the most impassioned exponent of Columbianism during the nineties.

Columbianism illustrates Timothy Smith's notions of the relationship between faith and ethnicity among immigrant groups within pluralistic, industrial, urban America. According to Smith, "As a consequence of uprooting and repeated resettlement," American ethnic groups experienced "an intensification of the psychic basis of theological reflection and ethno-religious commitment." Cummings's imagery of the Order as bound "by the mystic tie of charity and the golden chain of brotherly love" and as promoting "fraternal instincts by which men grow in civilized feelings and in the kindlier emotions of the heart" certainly represents such "theological reflection and ethno-religious commitment." Though most students of ethnicity focus on ethnic associations as essentially nostalgic in the cultivation of Old World customs, Smith views their experiences in American society as engendering a "sense of peoplehood" which was "more future oriented than backward looking."[51] The K. of C. looked back to the discovery event but primarily to its sense of peoplehood, i.e., Columbianism, with the promise of a new age, a new Catholic manhood, characterized by an end of Protestant hegemony, and full civil and social rights for persons of all religions.

Thomas Cummings's views are reminiscent of those of Isaac T. Hecker, the founder of the Paulists, a society of priests dedicated to the evangelization of American society. Hecker's vision of the Church in America, though developed on more deeply spiritual and intellectual levels, was thoroughly Columbian. He stated that

so far as it is compatible with faith and piety I am for accepting the American civilization with its usages and customs . . . it is the only way by which Catholicity can become the religion of our people. The character and spirit of our people, and their institutions, must find themselves at home in our Church . . . and it is on this basis alone that the Catholic religion can make progress in this country.[52]

Hecker saw Catholicity and American democracy as not merely compatible but rather complementary. "The form of government of the United States is preferable to Catholics above other forms. . . . This government leaves man a larger margin for liberty of action, and hence for cooperation with the guidance of the Holy Spirit, than any other government under the sun."[53]

Add to Hecker's ideas those of Archbishop John Ireland, who was a great admirer of Hecker, and one receives a stronger sense of the spiritual roots of Columbianism. In an introduction to an 1894 biography of Hecker, Ireland wrote:

The Republic, he [Hecker] taught, presupposes the Church's doctrine, and the Church ought to love a policy which is the offspring of its own spirit. . . . Not minimizing in the least the dreadful evil of the absence of the supernatural, I am not afraid to give as my belief that there is among Americans as high an appreciation and as lively a realization of natural truth and goodness as has been seen in any people, and it seems as if Almighty God, intending a great age and a great people, has put here in America a singular development of nature's power and gifts.[54]

Hecker and Ireland have been portrayed as liberals, but perhaps a more accurate descriptive label for their spiritual perspective on America is *transformationist,* since they believed that as a result of the encounter between Catholicism and American culture both experienced a positive change, as if Catholicism would be renewed within the freedom of the New World republic and American culture would be refined by its contact with the ancient faith of Western civilization.

Archbishop Ireland's faith in America as the promised land where natural and supernatural virtues would be blended by the Catholic spirit to form a new man glorifying God is analogous to Cummings's faith in Catholic America's heralding a new age. Just as Cummings wrote on Catholic gentlemen in fraternity, and on the need for Catholics to dispose themselves with civility at all times, Ireland wrote, "Today we need the Christian gentleman and the Christian citizen. An honest ballot and social decorum, [and] civility will do more for God's glory and the salvation of souls than midnight flagellations or Compostelan pilgrimages."[55] Ireland also spoke of how the American Catholic Church embraced many immigrant groups, a condition acting as a mirror to the "growth of the country into a new and vigorous spiritual commonwealth." Just as Cummings projected the appearance of a new type of humanity, so Ireland projected "a new people in a new age."[56]

There is, of course, no direct causal relationship between the spiritual ideals of Hecker and Ireland and the principles and symbols of Columbianism. However, as the spirit of the Knights evolved, it absorbed from the Hecker-Ireland climate many of its American-Catholic ideals of transformationist spirituality, as both the spiritual leaders and the fraternalists were reconciling religious loyalties and patriotic affections. This effort at reconciliation was shared by several leading members of the Catholic hierarchy, including James Cardinal Gibbons of Baltimore and bishops John Lancaster Spalding of Peoria and John J. Keane, rector of Catholic University. But they were opposed by a group of conservative bishops, such as Archbishop Michael A. Corrigan of New York and Bishop Bernard J. McQuaid of Rochester, along with most German-speaking bishops, who were fearful that Catholics would lose their faith if they accommodated themselves to the prevalent forces in American society. The Germans regarded their language and customs as necessary safeguards of their Catholicism, and they eagerly supported national parishes and organizations and a German-language press. The conservatives also criticized the establishment of Catholic University of America, the Knights of Labor, and the school plan of Archbishop John Ireland (a parochial system established by Catholics but supported by public funds and subject to local school boards) and were strongly opposed to all secret societies.[57] Hence, in opposition to the transformationists, these were *preservationists,* reluctant to risk the integrity of the faith in a democratic, pluralist society. To illustrate how the conflict infiltrated relatively minor issues: When Cardinal Gibbons responded to President Cleveland's 1888 proclamation making Thanksgiving a national holiday by publicly encouraging prayers for civil authorities on that day, Father Benjamin Keiley, later Bishop of Savannah, remarked that Gibbons had "out heroded Herod" by recognizing "the damnable puritanical substitute for Christmas."[58]

Though realignments occurred on specific issues, the conflict over the proper strategy for relating to the social forces in America continued throughout the 1890s and reached grotesque proportions in France where, upon the 1898 French publication of the life of Father Hecker, liberal Catholics popularized the progressive spirit of the American Church as the harbinger of a new age for the universal Church. The liberal-conservative (or transformationist-preservationist) tensions were muffled when Leo XIII condemned "Americanism" in an encyclical letter addressed to Cardinal Gibbons.

Under this heading the Pope listed such principles as that the Church should adjust her structure and dogma to fit the demands of modern civilization, that the individual should form his conscience according to the prompting of the Holy Spirit and to natural truth and virtue, and that the active religious life is preferable to the spirituality of the cloister. Pope Leo considered Americanism a tendency rather than an established movement based upon heretical theses. Cardinal Gibbons, Archbishop Ireland, and other progressives considered these tendencies to have been extremely remote from the life of the Church in America, while their conservative opponents congratulated the Pope for his strong stand against a clear and present danger.[59] Archbishop Ireland, the most vociferous liberal, immediately responded to the encyclical with a letter to the Pope in which he stated, "I repudiate and condemn these opinions without exception as literally as your holiness repudiates and condemns them." Ireland told the Pope that the entire American Church felt "indignant" at being wronged by "enemies of the Church of America . . . false interpreters of the faith, who 'imagine' that there is, or who wish to establish in the United States a Church which differs one iota from the Universal Church . . . which Rome herself recognizes, and cannot but recognize as the infallible guardian of the revelation of Jesus Christ."[60]

Though the liberal prelates continued to express their confidence in the harmony between Catholicism and the American way of life, there is no doubt that Ireland and Gibbon's vision of an American Catholic Church loyal to Rome but possessing a distinctive character in accord with a progressive democratic spirit was gradually replaced by a more conservative vision which emphasized the Romanness of the Church, its separation from modern culture, and its hierarchical structure. However, the American Church had absorbed so much of the American ethos that, in fact, it did evolve its own distinctively American identity, characterized by social activity and the development of strong economic bases for its myriad organizations.

Columbianism was in a sense a fraternal expression of these prevalent "Americanist" trends in the Church. Though the Knights shared many principles with the liberals, the Order seemed to have been more apprehensive of anti-Catholicism than were some of the liberal bishops. On the other hand, the most vigorous lay spokesman for German-American conservatism, Arthur Preuss, lashed out at the K. of C. as a "pernicious" secret society, a Catholic capitulation to American secularism and materialism. Preuss's *Review* became a forum for a barrage of anti–K. of C. criticism. The ceremonial character of the Order was particularly offensive to conservative Catholics in general, striking them as pseudo-Masonry in Catholic garb.[61]

And Conservative Irish prelates such as Corrigan and McQuaid were also extremely reluctant to endorse the Order. However, on July 24, 1895, Archbishop Satolli, who was deeply involved in attempting to settle the conflict between liberal and conservative bishops, granted the Order his "warm approbation and apostolic blessing."[62] Though Satolli had leaned toward Archbishop Ireland in the 1892–94 period, by the time he gave his apostolic blessing to the Knights he had shifted to the conservative camp. Ironically, he illustrated his conservative views by disagreeing with Ireland and Gibbons precisely on the issue of secular secret societies. The liberals were not proponents of such societies as the Odd Fellows and the Knights of Pythias, but when the Vatican condemned them, the liberal bishops were less than diligent in enforcing the condemnation, fearing to alienate many who were otherwise amenable to the Church. Hence, Satolli's endorsement of the Knights of Columbus during this conflict over secret societies set him apart from his conservative allies and his approbation was accepted more readily than it would have been while he was in the liberal camp.

The American hierarchy, however, did not immediately follow Satolli's lead in embracing the Knights. As late as 1902 the archbishops, at their annual meeting, refused to make a public endorsement of the Knights of Columbus, the Catholic Order of Foresters, and other Catholic societies. Though one Church historian concluded that "it is not possible to say" just what "lay behind this reluctance of the archbishops to give their formal blessing to these Catholic societies,"[63] one may infer that in this period the archbishops decided to table the proposal for endorsement rather than revive an issue embedded in the Americanist controversy.

5

International Expansion

AFTER COUNCILS HAD BEEN ESTABLISHED in Rhode Island (1885), New York (1891), and Massachusetts (1892), the Order spread at such a rapid pace that by 1905 it was in every state in the union, in Mexico, the Philippines, Newfoundland, and in five of the nine Canadian provinces. Though regional variations gradually developed in accord with the variety of cultures within the Order, the unifying force throughout was Columbian fraternalism, with which Catholics of all regions could identify.

There were, as we have seen, many causes for this rapid growth of the Order. Its ceremonial character instilled a sense of pride in the Catholic roots of New World civilization, satisfying a strong need among second-generation immigrants to harmonize Catholicism with loyalty to country. The insurance feature, a strong component of the Order's generally attractive fraternal character, provided it with the financial solvency to undertake a strong expansionist policy. Its social-club dimension appealed to those men who sought a Catholic milieu for their leisure, recreation, and intellectual stimulation, while expressions of anti-Catholicism led many to join an organization dedicated to defending the faith. The farsighted vision and strong leadership of Supreme Knights Phelan, Hayes, John J. Cone, and Edward Hearn (1886–1909), manifested in national organizers delegated to spread Columbianism, were crucial to the success of expansion. The Order's friends among the hierarchy of the Church provided prestige and dispelled suspicions that the K. of C. was a Masonic-like secret society. Catholic journalists, like many other professional men, were attracted to the Order and liberally spread the Columbian message across the continent. Members who had business contacts in distant areas of the country or who had been transferred to these areas were also energetic missionaries of Columbianism.

Because by the mid-1890s the majority of second-generation Catholic immigrants were of either Irish or German descent, and because the Germans were drawn to national benefit societies, Irish-

Americans continued to dominate the Knights. However, there were several German-American councils within the Order. Just as parishes tended to be divided along national lines, so there was a growing number of K. of C. councils formed according to nationalities. For example, in Boston the Germans formed Teutonia Council No. 225, instituted in May 1897, and the Italians later founded Ausonia Council No. 1513. As the Order spread into smaller midwestern towns in Indiana, Illinois, and Kansas, the K. of C. councils reflected the large proportion of German-American Catholics within these communities, and occasionally non-Irishmen such as Warren Mosher of Youngstown, Ohio, and Ferdinand Kuhn of Nashville, Tennessee, achieved leadership roles as State Deputies. Before 1900 the Catholic Benevolent Legion and the Catholic Knights of America absorbed many more German-Americans than the K. of C.; indeed, the C.B.L. had so many German-speaking members that a section of its magazine was published in that language.

Rather than detailing the society's growth, this chapter on international expansion will limit its focus to the Order's entrance into the various regions of the United States and into Canada, Mexico, and the Philippines. Though the Supreme Office embarked on a policy of expansion, it appears that the leadership was unprepared for the breadth of the Order's appeal. No sooner had the Order expanded into a given state than local leaders would begin new-council development in adjacent towns and states. Hence, this chapter on expansion is, in a sense, the success story of Columbian fraternalists, those national, regional, and local organizers who so vigorously promoted the Order. Their achievements were particularly impressive because the vast majority were volunteers, and many confronted opposition from bishops, priests, and laymen who were suspicious of the Order's ceremonial character and its noncanonical, autonomous basis.

II

As the ambassador of Columbianism and as National Organizer from 1893 to 1899, Thomas H. Cummings was directly involved in new-council development throughout New England and the mid-Atlantic states and into such distant midwestern areas as Detroit and Chicago. According to Charles S. O'Neill, who wrote a series of articles on "The Story of Columbian Knighthood," Cummings's efforts were decisive. "A dry rot had set in in the Order and during the years 1892 and 1893 the losses exceeded the gains by several hundred. . . . The sudden and almost continuous growth of the Order outside the state of Connecticut helped to save it unquestionably from the ruin that was inevitable. . . . It was by preaching this doctrine of Columbianism and by emphasizing the fraternal side of the Order that National Organizer Cummings was able to meet the crisis in its affairs."[1]

Cummings's strategy for expansion appears to have been composed of three basic moves: to introduce Columbianism and its insurance benefits informally to prominent laymen of the community, to garner support from their bishop and priests, and to host a public meeting of interested laymen and priests in preparation for instituting a new council. Though the first component varied—several new councils were pioneered in grass-roots fashion by members who were relocated (viz., Brooklyn Council)—the support of prominent men, the hierarchy, and the clergy was crucial to the proliferation of new councils.

During 1893, Cummings limited his organizational efforts to Massachusetts. Archbishop John J. Williams, whom scholars have placed alternately in both liberal and conservative camps, was certainly not conservative in his views on the natural harmony between Catholicism and the American way of life. Ordained in 1845 and consecrated bishop in 1866, Williams was a strong proponent of Catholic assimilation. He represented Yankee Catholicism (vis-à-vis immigrant Catholicism) and, even in the midst of the American Protective Association attack on the Church described in Chapter Four, he lauded Massachusetts' "strong liking for fair play."[2] There is no extant documentation of his views of the Order, but we may infer that he was sympathetic to Columbianism and in no way interfered with those priests who became enthusiastic Knights. Between January 8 and December 13, 1893, Cummings organized thirteen councils throughout the Bay State, which rapidly became the predominant jurisdiction, with over one hundred councils by the end of 1897.

The Order entered New Hampshire in 1893 through the efforts of Cummings in the episcopal city of Manchester. Bishop Denis M. Bradley, an ardent admirer of Cardinal Gibbons during the liberal-conservative conflict,[3] was very supportive of Columbianism. On April 22, 1893, Massachusetts State Deputy James E. Hayes, accompanied by seventy-five visiting Knights, presided over the initiation ceremonies for thirty-four candidates. The list of charter members shows that the entire group was composed of Irish Americans. Though there were various other Catholic ethnic groups living in Manchester, particularly

French Canadians attracted by the mills, they appear to have been reluctant to shed their ethnic loyalties in favor of Columbian patriotism. However, when Concord Council was instituted in 1895, there was a smattering of French names on the charter, indicating the Order's gradual appeal to non-Irish Americans: E. St. Hillair, H. Pelletier, P. A. Benoit, W. Depont.[4]

Unlike its entrance into the diocese of Manchester, the Order's expansion into Portland, Maine, was not with the enthusiastic support of Bishop James Augustine Healy. Consecrated in 1875, Bishop Healy was the first black prelate of the American Church. He was aligned with the conservative bishops on several issues, particularly on the evils of secret fraternal societies. When Portland Council was instituted on August 12, 1894, more than five hundred Knights, representing councils in Massachusetts, Connecticut, Rhode Island, and New Hampshire, chartered the ship *City of Portland* to transport them to the site of the initiation ceremonies.[5] Without adequate documentation it is difficult to discern Bishop Healy's attitude. One infers that since no chaplain appears on lists of council officers until 1896, Healy only gradually and perhaps reluctantly recognized the benefits of the Knights of Columbus.

In September of 1894, Cummings extended his missionary efforts into New York City, bearing with him letters of introduction from Boston Knights to two prominent Catholics, Dr. James K. Lee of Manhattan and William Harper Bennett of Brooklyn. A delay of nine months preceded the institution of councils in these two large dioceses.[6] Archbishop Corrigan, a vigorous conservative, was not sympathetic to Columbianism. However, because the Order attracted many of New York's most active Catholic laymen, he seems to have reluctantly tolerated its expansion into his archdiocese. Though Brooklyn Council was instituted as early as 1891, it was more by accident than design. Bishop McDonnell's views were in accord with those of Corrigan and, as the Supreme Spiritual Director of the Catholic Benevolent Legion, he was naturally protective of its interests in the face of competition from the Knights.[7] William Harper Bennett, who became the first Grand Knight of the second council in Brooklyn, Columbus Council No. 126, and who was a journalist on the staff of the *New York Herald,* wrote of the difficult challenges confronting Cummings in Brooklyn:

The outlook for a numerous establishment in the Knights of Columbus was not promising. For Brooklyn, New York, is the birthplace of one of the strongest Catholic insurance bodies in the country, viz., The Catholic Benevolent Legion, numbering 1,400 members in that city alone. Furthermore, within its borders 13,000 members of Royal Arcanum, 1,300 Foresters, 8,000 Legion of Honor, and more than 1,000 Catholic Knights will be found. The ablest organizers in the country have gone over every section of this city thoroughly. . . . As a matter of fact the executive body of one organization pays a bonus of twenty-five dollars for every council of eight members instituted. . . . The apostle of the new K. of C. was regarded with suspicion naturally, and soon found himself among the breakers. The mission of the Order, its financial standing, its ritual, its standing with the ecclesiastical authorities, and every possible weapon was employed in the attack and each assault was ably met and repulsed by him; and the good work of spreading the Order went on quietly but effectively. As the result of his [Cummings's] wise policy the foundations of the Order were laid deep and strong, its upbuilding was phenomenal.[8]

The institution of New York Council No. 124 and Columbus Council No. 126 (Brooklyn) occurred on May 12 and May 26, 1895, respectively. On June 5, John J. Derry, one of the men initiated into New York Council, wrote to Archbishop Corrigan that he considered the initiation ceremonies to be so "outrageous" that he decided to withdraw.[9] In a June 15 letter, Richard L. Walsh, a friend of Derry's, informed Corrigan that Derry had accurately reported on "the outrageous indignities inflicted on the Catholic men who had assembled in good faith . . . a few Sundays ago to join an Order which they believed would forward Catholic interests." Walsh, who had previously been initiated, recalled "the brutal treatment . . . which I with others had to endure." Though he did not mention the name of the council in which he was initiated, he did state that he was subjected to "a howling, brutal mob of two hundred [Knights] from Boston and New England." Despite his distressing experience, Walsh told Corrigan that he would remain a member and join the new council in Brooklyn, "for the good that I might do." However, because he feared scandal resulting from this "vile conduct" at initiations, he urged Corrigan to "take action" against the ceremonials.[10] Since all the Supreme Officers were present at the initiation of New York Council, references to the outrages which occurred at that initiation must have been particularly damaging to the Order's image in the eyes of Corrigan. Though there is no documentation evidencing the archbishop's explicit response to these letters, he did investigate the initiation procedures.

Apparently, Supreme Knight Phelan submitted to Corrigan a copy of the ceremonials, but unless it was accompanied by a handbook on the "unwritten work" during the Third Degree, he would not have understood the experiences of Derry and Walsh. Their outrage at the staged behavior during the ceremonials was actually the intentional object lodged in the shock value of the Third Degree. One still hears of some degree teams which engaged in harassments, but for every Derry-Walsh report there were hundreds of reports on the beautiful lessons of the ceremonials in general and the profound impact of the Third Degree in particular. The typical college fraternity's initiation was grounded on individual harassment, ideally intended to test the mettle of those aspiring to bind their loyalty to an elite group. Portions of the K. of C. initiation were general group deceptions rather than individual harassment, and each of these deceptions included in the Order's Third Degree were later unraveled as a test of the candidates' moral and religious ideals. Degree teams were instructed never to harass an individual. Indeed, the ideal K. of C. candidate was one who stood up and challenged deceptions, while if a candidate for a college fraternity challenged the individual harassment, such behavior would tend to lead to his immediate expulsion from the initiation class.

Most importantly, the initiation ceremonies of the Order were intended to dramatize the moral and religious duties of all practical Catholics and to instill the social responsibilities of all Knights to promote Catholic interests within a society given to spurts of anti-Catholic behavior. Some degree teams and individual councils violated this general code and alienated men from the K. of C., but the successful expansion of the Order illustrates that such abuses were quite uncommon.

It is very doubtful that the principles underlying the Order's ceremonial structure were explained to Corrigan, as the Order's status in the archdiocese remained an issue after the Derry-Walsh correspondence. As late as the October 15, 1895, meeting of the National Council, Supreme Knight Phelan reported that "it is regrettable that our work [in New York State] has been and now is seriously embarrassed through the delay occasioned by ecclesiastical inquiries relative to our ritualistic forms." However, he indicated that he was "hopeful that pending negotiations for the elimination of objection, actual or possible, in the eye of the Church, may be accomplished for all time to the entire satisfaction of the most exacting Churchman." He specifically referred to his hope for a speedy resolution to "the points in issue in the Brooklyn Diocese."[11]

Phelan explained how the difficulties in New York and Brooklyn led him to seek Archbishop Satolli's approbation. Stressing the disadvantages of a noncanonical society in receiving public endorsement from bishops, he said, "In view of the desire to spread the Order outside of New England, it early became important to us as a secular [noncanonical] society, not having the prestige of public, as distinguished from private endorsement, of eminent churchmen, to dissipate the apprehensions of clergy and laity in various localities as to our moral standing." He told the delegates that he had petitioned the Apostolic Delegate, Archbishop Satolli, for his blessings upon the work of the Order. Though the Supreme Knight did not quote from Satolli's "complimentary and vigorous testimonial,"[12] it was published in full in the August 21, 1896, edition of the *Connecticut Catholic.* After extending his and Pope Leo XIII's apostolic blessing, Satolli stated that "we also wish to express our great pleasure, after learning of the merits of this splendid Catholic organization, that in the present active period of social and fraternal alliances in America, there exists a society for practical advancement of insurance, benevolence, and fraternity, proffered by the most popular secular societies without any of the disadvantages of prohibited companionship."[13] This letter must have been influential in Phelan's negotiations with McDonnell and Corrigan, for within six months after Phelan's address new councils were formed in Brooklyn and New York. Hence it appears as if both prelates were not actively obstructive.

The 1894 papal condemnation of the Knights of Pythias, the Odd Fellows, and the Sons of Temperance was still an issue in 1895. No doubt Satolli's emphasis upon the Order within "the social and fraternal alliance in America" reflected his concern that Catholics provide an orthodox alternative to the condemned organizations.

Of all the bishops in the American Church, none was more adamant in his condemnation of secret societies than Bishop McQuaid of Rochester. Though Rochester Council No. 178 was instituted on June 24, 1896 (the first council in western New York), it did not receive any encouragement from McQuaid.[14] According to his biographer, McQuaid had "never entered into cordial relations with them [the Knights of Columbus]." As late as September 20, 1897, he wrote to Archbishop Corrigan, "In a word, all the forms and tomfoolery of the Masons and Odd Fellows are imitated by the Catholic Knights of Columbus, thus familiarizing the rising generation with their dangerous customs and ways." He told Corrigan that in deference to his priests who were members of the Order he would "withhold all public action" against the Knights until the priest members met with the leaders to effect a change quietly. New York's first State Deputy, John J. Delaney, had a meeting with McQuaid, at which time "he promised to lay all their [the Knights'] methods" before Archbishops Corrigan and Williams and Auxiliary Bishop John Farley of New York. McQuaid advised Corrigan to include Bishop McDonnell of Brooklyn and Archbishop Patrick John Ryan of Philadelphia in the meeting with Delaney. Though McQuaid said that "the present gentlemen [in the K. of C.] mean well," he doubted that the "next generation would be equal to them in their Catholicity." He ended his letter to Corrigan on an ominous note. "Should the change not take place within a reasonable time, I will request all my priests to withdraw and bring all my influence to bear against the organization, for I foresee great danger in the future." McQuaid appears to have been unimpressed by Satolli's public endorsement. He also viewed the ritualistic work of the Order "as objectionable features [which] ought to be removed without delay."[15]

There is no extant documentation of Delaney's meeting with Corrigan and other members of the hierarchy, but since Rochester Council continued to thrive and since fifty-four councils were instituted in New York between the time of the 1897 McQuaid letter to Corrigan and 1900, McQuaid's attitude did not seriously impede the growth of the Order in the Empire State. However, in 1898 the Board of Directors "for prudential reasons" did decide to have the Third Degree entirely revised.[16] By 1898 the Order had spread through New Jersey, Delaware, Pennsylvania, and Maryland and had even leaped into Illinois.

During this expansionary period, few bishops were willing to endorse the Order publicly. McQuaid, Corrigan, and McDonnell were extremely suspicious. Archbishop Satolli's favorable testimonial letter seems to have had little effect in dispelling rumors of the mischievous character of the Knights' rituals or ceremonials. As Supreme Knight Phelan intimated, the secular or noncanonical basis of the Order precluded a public endorsement simply because many bishops seem to have considered such a statement as applicable only to those organizations such as the Holy Name Society, which were officially instituted within the diocesan structure. Theoretically, the Knights did not require the approval of an ordinary, but on the practical plane they would never have succeeded without his permission to recruit chaplains for new council development within a given diocese. Columbianism's stress upon practical Catholicity and its accent upon deep loyalty to the Church must have constituted a counterweight to those bishops who were fearful of its ritualistic character. The negativism of Bishop McQuaid was the exception. Thomas Cummings and the Supreme Officers were very deferential to episcopal authority, as exemplified by two notations in the diary of Matthew Harkins, bishop of the Providence diocese:

May 7, 1896. T. H. Cummings about Knights of Columbus—said it was reported that I am opposed to them—told them I am aloof from them.

May 27, 1896. Fr. Treanor Supreme Chaplain of Waterbury—who came about Knights of Columbus. He wishes me to examine & advise about new councils and induction thereinto.[17]

Bishop Harkins's attitude was not atypical. He neither strongly encouraged nor discouraged the Order's growth in his diocese. Though its expansion throughout the nation stirred controversies in a few chancery offices, by and large most bishops were either very supportive, like Cardinal Gibbons, or were aloof, like Bishop Harkins. With fourteen councils and 1,248 members in Harkins's diocese by the fall of 1897, his reserved attitude seems to have had little or no effect upon the growth of the Order in Rhode Island.

Cummings's strategy was to focus on large metropolitan areas for the institution of the first council in a jurisdiction, and to encourage that council to form a degree team for new council development within the state. Shortly after the institution of new councils in New York and Brooklyn, he traveled across the Hudson to Jersey City, where, on November 3, 1895, with a degree team from New York Council, he initiated thirty-two charter members of Jersey City Council No. 137. One hundred and fifty Knights from the New York area witnessed the ceremonies in which John J. Cone, a businessman active in the local Democratic Party, became New Jersey's first State Deputy.[18] Cone was also the state's first member of the Board of Directors, and while serving in both capacities he was elected Deputy Supreme Knight in 1897. Upon the death of Supreme Knight Hayes, Cone became Supreme Knight on February 8, 1898. Like his predecessors, Mullen, Phelan, and Hayes, Cone was an enthusiastic fraternalist, a characteristic best expressed by his membership on a degree team. For example, he directed the ceremonials for the institution of Hoboken Council No. 159 (April 12, 1896); Santa Maria Council No. 195, Wilmington, Delaware (December 13, 1896); and Baltimore Council No. 205 (February 21, 1897).[19]

After Cummings had organized a group of candidates in Philadelphia he called upon Delaney, first State Deputy of New York, to direct the initiation ceremonies for Philadelphia Council No. 196 (November 26, 1896). Forty-two men, headed by Grand Knight James A. Flaherty, passed through the three degrees with nearly six hundred visiting Knights in attendance (Flaherty later became Supreme Knight). Like Boston and New York, Philadelphia possessed a large Catholic population predominantly of Irish extraction, with a sizable upper middle class. "Thousands of Irish Catholics who became middle class in the 1880's moved to ornate Victorian houses in West Philadelphia, Oak Lane, and Germantown. . . . They had their own coteries and literary salons in which Maurice Francis Egan, Eleanor Donnelly, and Martin I. J. Griffin held forth."[20]

Though not all the Philadelphia Knights were recruited from the middle class, both Griffin and Egan ultimately joined the Order. Indeed, Egan, with John B. Kennedy, wrote a history of the Knights of Columbus.[21] While Philadelphia Council was in the organizational process, Cummings traveled to Baltimore, where he easily found ready recruits. Winand Michael Wigger, Bishop of Newark, New Jersey, and Archbishop Patrick John Ryan of Philadelphia had been moderately supportive of the Order's expansion into their dioceses, but James Cardinal Gibbons enthusiastically welcomed the Knights into Baltimore. John Cone and James Flaherty participated in the rituals instituting Baltimore Council No. 205 early in 1897. Within a few months a new council was formed in the District of Columbia.[22]

Cummings and Delaney also worked in tandem in Chicago. Catholics in this city were introduced to the Order in 1893, when many Knights from the East visited the Columbia Exposition. Thomas S. Kiernan, a former New Yorker who traveled extensively in the East on business, was attracted to the Order in Boston and passed through the degree ceremonies at a combined initiation of two local councils in 1894. Determined to import Columbianism to his new midwestern home, Kiernan was unable to muster enough interest to establish a council in Chicago.[23] It was reported that Kiernan remarked, "Indeed, the Chicago men in general seemed to adopt the attitude that we were overrun with societies, and were skeptical of the success of a new one."[24] For that reason Thomas Cummings was sent to assist Kiernan. After twenty-three candidates had been recruited, Delaney was chosen to direct the ceremonies instituting Chicago Council No. 182. Joseph J. Thompson, a Past State Deputy who wrote a thorough history of the Illinois jurisdiction, reported that since the nearest council was several hundred miles from Chicago, the vast majority of those Knights who witnessed the ceremonies were delegates and visitors to the National Democratic Convention then in progress.

Before appearing at this initiation they had come under the spell of the rising young orator William Jennings Bryan and his renowned "Cross of Gold" speech. No doubt many of the applicants also had been thrilled by that epoch making utterance but all survivors assure us that the degree was a thriller; and as most members maintain with reference to the occasion when they received their degrees, that the performance of July 7, 1896, was the "greatest in the history of the Order."[25]

As first Grand Knight, Thomas S. Kiernan was a very successful missionary; by the end of 1896, membership in the Chicago Council had reached nearly five hundred. Chicago's Archbishop Patrick Augustine Feehan was one of the founders of the Catholic Knights of America, but he "permitted the establishment of the Order, and through his representatives sent the necessary support and encouragement."[26] Perhaps because he was generally an ally of Archbishop Ireland, he looked favorably upon Columbianism.

The void between Chicago and Philadelphia was filled by Philadelphia Council's degree team, led by James Flaherty, which instituted councils throughout the state. Warren E. Mosher, the founder of the Catholic Summer School, introduced the Order into Ohio with the institution of Youngstown Council No. 274 on October 24, 1897. Mosher, who, like Kiernan, had been initiated into a council in the East, was a member of the Youngstown's Young Men's Catholic Institute. Through his influence the Institute, which had been foundering because of its lack of insurance- and sick-benefit programs, evolved into Youngstown Council of the K. of C. The institution of Ohio's first council was an extremely festive occasion; Knights from New York, Boston, Philadelphia, Buffalo, Chicago, Pittsburgh, and other cities traveled to Youngstown for the ceremonies. Delaney and Flaherty also made the journey; it was Delaney who conducted the Third Degree ritual. W. A. Maline, former president of the Young Men's Catholic Institute, was elected first Grand Knight, while Warren E. Mosher was appointed Territorial Deputy of Ohio by the Supreme Knight. Within a year Mosher had formed councils in Cleveland, Canton, Ashtabula, and Cincinnati.[27]

John J. Delaney was also instrumental in the institution of a Detroit Council. Edward H. Doyle, industrialist, financier, and part owner of the Detroit Base Ball Club, was a frequent visitor to New York, where he met Delaney and other prominent Knights. Ultimately initiated into New York Council No. 124, Doyle was determined to spread the Columbianism message throughout Wayne County, which included well over 100,000 Catholics. By February 13, 1898, Doyle and Jeremiah Buckley (initiated into Southington, Connecticut, Council No. 15) had gathered more than one hundred candidates for Knighthood. A large contingency from Buffalo Council No. 184 was on hand for the occasion, with its degree team working the first and second parts. The Third Degree was worked by Delaney, who by this time had achieved national stature as a master of ceremonials. Immediately after the initiation a young Detroit attorney, George F. Monaghan, became Michigan's leading ceremonialist, which led to his election as first State Deputy (1901–02) and as Supreme Director (1902–20). By 1905 Michigan had twenty-six councils. In 1898, the Order also spread southward into Virginia and Kentucky. Among those initiated into Norfolk Council No. 367 was Daniel J. Callahan, first Grand Knight, Territorial and State Deputy, and Supreme Treasurer from 1909 to his death in 1942. Callahan was the South's leading fraternalist, who participated in the institution of many councils below the Mason-Dixon line.[28]

However, expansion in the South was obstructed by the fear that the region was generally a high-risk area for insurance. "The climatic conditions, danger of epidemics, etc., affecting our insurance system, stand in the way."[29] The high incidence of yellow fever and other epidemics in portions of the South, particularly New Orleans, prompted many insurance societies and companies to shun the region. Yet as soon as councils were instituted in Louisville, Norfolk, and Richmond, the southward momentum had been established and it was merely a matter of time before Catholics throughout the South would be requesting councils. After receiving news of the formation of a council in Louisville, a delegation from Nashville approached the Supreme Office for permission to gather candidates for the first council in Tennessee.[30] Though the National Physician was reluctant to endorse southward expansion, a compromise was devised by which councils in specific areas of the South were to be composed entirely of associate members. All of Louisiana, Mississippi, and Florida and portions of Tennessee, Alabama, Texas, Georgia, and South Carolina were designated as noninsurance areas of the South.

Ferdinand Kuhn was one of the Nashville Catholics who had advocated expansion into Tennessee. The 1900 compromise allowed for the formation of Nashville Council No. 544.[31] Kuhn, who became Tennessee's first State Deputy, succeeded Daniel J. Callahan as the master ceremonialist, presiding at the institution ceremonies of councils in Florida (1900), Alabama (1902), Louisiana (1902), and Georgia (1902). His degree work at the opening of New Orleans Council No.

714 in November 1902 was long remembered as "something out of this world."[32]

Columbianism was particularly appealing to southern Catholics. Though several areas possessed a rich Catholic heritage, many portions of the South were mission territories with tiny Catholic enclaves. Conscious of their minority status and frequently victims of prejudice and discrimination, Catholics were strongly attracted to an Order which ritualized the Catholic contribution to American culture and extolled the virtues of religious liberty, patriotism, and defense of the faith. Catholic fraternalism provided the organizational unity so necessary to the survival and growth of the Church in the South. Priests and bishops were generally very grateful that the Order was organizing Catholic laymen in their parishes and dioceses. For example, before Ferdinand Kuhn exemplified the degrees to the candidates of Alabama's first council, Birmingham No. 635 (January 12, 1902), the eighty-seven charter members and visiting Knights gathered in St. Paul's Church for a Solemn High Mass and for welcoming remarks from the Bishop of Mobile, Edward P. Allen.[33] The vast majority of bishops welcomed the Order, but it was rare for a bishop to participate in the ceremonies instituting a council in his diocese.

To illustrate the society's deep attachment to the South, the National Convention of 1909 was held in Mobile, Alabama. Since yellow fever had been largely eliminated by Walter Reed's research, the Supreme Board of Directors in 1909 lifted the insurance ban in Louisiana and other areas of the South. By the time all the southern states were represented in the Order (1902), the first councils were being established on the West Coast.

The story of the westward expansion begins in St. Paul, Minnesota, and St. Louis, Missouri. With Columbianism so closely related to the vision of Archbishop John Ireland of St. Paul, Minnesota possessed an ideal ecclesiastical climate for the growth of the Order. As in Chicago and Detroit, the first council in Minnesota was pioneered by local men who had been previously initiated into the Order. Father Richard Cotter of the St. Paul Seminary faculty and a colleague from St. Thomas College began recruiting candidates in late 1898.[34] Their labors were rewarded on February 22 when a degree team from Chicago, led by District Deputy L. E. Sauter, exemplified the degrees at the institution of St. Paul Council No. 397.[35] One of the charter members recalled the initiation experience with such verve that there is no doubt of the crucial role of the ceremonials in the appeal of Columbian fraternalism.

The event is one that will ever remain memorable in the estimation of all the participants. The ceremonies were impressive, interesting, and replete with historical, scholarly, and religious significance. . . . Seldom has a task of this kind ever been attempted by a coterie of men so gifted with varied talent as were the gentlemen from Chicago who conducted this initiation and installation. The Deputy Grand Knight [sic], Sauter, is a man of fine presence, brilliant oratorical talent, and creates about him wherever he goes an atmosphere of wholesome thought, religious zeal, and knightly courtesy. The spectacular and symbolic features of the ritual were so well managed as to create a profound impression, and the whole was beautiful with excellent music.[36]

St. Paul's twin city, Minneapolis, housed Minnesota's second council, Hennepin Council No. 435, on June 26, 1899. From the twin cities the Order spread north and east to Duluth and into Superior, Wisconsin. Ten charter members of Duluth Council No. 447 (instituted September 4, 1899) were residents of Superior. Because the Order was not licensed to sell insurance in Wisconsin, the council was not established until June 17, 1900, when Superior Council No. 499 was instituted.[37]

A week later Milwaukee Council No. 524 was begun, and within five years there were councils throughout the state. Illinois State Deputy Patrick T. McArdle, responsible for organizing the first council in Wisconsin, led the exemplification of the three degrees in both Superior and Milwaukee and, along with his fellow Chicagoan, L. E. Sauter, was active in degree work in Indiana. After John W. Ward, a temporary national organizer, had pursued new-council development in Indiana, Sauter exemplified the degrees at the institution of Indianapolis Council No. 437 on June 25, 1899.[38] The following October 15, Patrick McArdle presided at the institution of Fort Wayne Council No. 451.[39] In 1902, John G. Ewing, Grand Knight of South Bend Council, was elected State Deputy. A professor of history and law at the University of Notre Dame, Ewing rapidly gained national stature as a Catholic intellectual and an expert ceremonialist. Another national organizer, M. W. Gleason of Chicago, teamed up with McArdle to establish the Order in Iowa. On April 29, 1899, McArdle, assisted by members from St. Paul and several Illinois councils, led fifty-three candidates of Dubuque Council No. 510 into Knighthood. By this time McArdle had already organized a council downriver from Dubuque.

When he arrived in St. Louis, McArdle found "great eagerness" among "many prominent residents who were interested in the movement from the start."[40] On October 8, 1899, fifty-six men passed through the three degrees and St. Louis Council No. 453 was instituted. It was a festive occasion; the degree team from Mt. Pleasant Council No. 98 had traveled all the way from Boston to initiate the first class in the "gateway to the West." The minutes of a special meeting of Mt. Pleasant Council held in St. Louis on the day of the initiation marked the occasion:

The First and Second Degree was confered [sic] on 56 candidates composed of some of the prominent clergy and laity of the city of St. Louis. . . . After a collation the Third Degree was conferred by Bro. McArdle, District Deputy of Chicago, Illinois. Large delegations were present from different parts of adjoining states. Some of the delegations . . . came in special trains for 500 miles and more, remaining until the close of the degree and requiring of them a loss of 3 days in coming and going therefrom.[41]

The twenty-seven members of Mt. Pleasant and other Boston councils, led by Grand Knight T. E. Masterson, left Boston on October 6 in a "special pullman car."[42] To participate in the institution of the first council within a state was a thrilling adventure for these fraternalists eager to see their society move westward. One St. Louis Catholic weekly, *Church Progress,* projected a bleak future for the K. of C. in St. Louis. According to an editorial in the *Columbiad, Church Progress* considered that "Catholicity . . . is almost dead in St. Louis."[43] *Columbiad's* editor responded by stating that the Catholics of St. Louis were

not dead, but sleeping; they just want a little rousing up. It will not be the first time that the Knights of Columbus have encountered similar conditions, have met the lukewarm and indifferent and, by appealing to their intelligence, by arousing them to the sentiment of their better selves, have created a marvelous change. . . . We have not the slightest doubt that the zeal and devotion of the gentlemen who founded the Knights of Columbus in St. Louis will stimulate the flagging energies and invigorate the spirit of Catholic enthusiasm and Catholic loyalty.[44]

Another St. Louis Catholic weekly, the *Sunday Watchman,* projected a more promising future than *Church Progress.* In an article probably written by its editor, Father John Phelan, the *Watchman* endorsed the Order as "the flower of the Catholic population." This article, which introduced the K. of C. to its readers, captured an aspect of the Columbian spirit. "With true American patriotism they demand of their members respect for true manhood and liberty for the individual, particularly that liberty which is the essence of all liberties and which was first planted on this continent by Roman Catholics; freedom to worship God according to one's conscience. They ask that no man's social and civil rights be affected by his religious beliefs."[45]

Led by Grand Knight Condé B. Pallen, who had achieved national fame as a Catholic intellectual, the St. Louis Council progressed rapidly; within a few months after its institution it had doubled its membership. An old friend of Supreme Knight Hearn, Valle Reyburn, was appointed Territorial Deputy of Missouri. Dr. H. B. Zwart, who had been initiated into an Illinois council, "was one of the most active promoters" in Kansas City. After several informal meetings an organizational meeting was held in Kansas City at the Baltimore Hotel on May 27, 1900. Reyburn spoke on the "purposes and benefits of the Order. He told what results, from a social and commercial standpoint, would accrue to membership."[46] He encouraged them to plan for the institution of the new council either on or before July 4, the date when the National Democratic Convention would convene in Kansas City. According to the minutes of subsequent organizational meetings, "enthusiasm was rampant" throughout the group and several visiting Knights attended, "each of whom spoke on the greatness of the Order." On July 1, "with the thermometer playing about the 100° mark," forty-nine members were initiated into Kansas City's first council. More than two hundred visiting Knights, representing councils in St. Louis, Chicago, New York, Boston, St. Paul, Youngstown, and other cities, witnessed the event. A degree team from St. Louis Council led the ceremonies, with J. J. Kelly of Chicago conferring the Third Degree. The day opened with a High Mass at the cathedral ("permission from Bishop [John] Glennon was secured for reserved seats") and closed with a gala banquet. "The event was carried out very successfully. Wine was not served," recorded the secretary in the minute book.[47]

On July 14, Judge William B. Teasdale was elected Grand Knight and within two weeks he was contacted by National Organizer James J. Gorman of Fall River, Massachusetts, to assist him in establishing a council in Topeka, Kansas. Thomas McAloon, a Knight from Washington, D.C., had been recuperating from an illness at his brother's home in Topeka during 1900. "He it was who prevailed upon J. J. Gorman to come to Topeka and organize the Knights of Columbus in Kansas."[48] At an August 29, 1900, meeting of Kansas City Council, "Bro. Gorman was loud in praise of the 32 applicants for membership at Topeka. He stated that they were representative of the 6,400 Catholic population of that city."[49] Gorman turned to the Kansas City Council to conduct the initiation ceremonies for the new council. Though it "lacked sufficient confidence to undertake the conferring of the Three Degrees . . . Kansas City [Council was] determined to take charge of the work."[50] After two rehearsals, the degree team boarded the train for the institution of Topeka Council No. 534 on September 9, 1900. Though a jubilant spirit surrounded expansion west of the Missouri River, it was not until over a year later that the second council was established in Kansas. One Knight explained that the slow growth was "due to the difficulty of providing degree teams."[51] However, once the K. of C. achieved momentum in Kansas in 1901–2, they experienced steady growth. By 1907 there were thirty-nine councils with 3,300 members.[52]

National Organizer Gorman must have been very pleased with the Kansas City degree team, for in early October of 1900 he requested it to "assist in the institution of a Council in Denver."[53] The national leadership of the Order placed such a high priority on westward expansion that the Supreme Office offered $150 to the Kansas City Council "toward defraying expenses of Brothers who would accompany the . . . council officers, provided that amount would prove an incentive."[54] Though we have no record of the response, the degree team of Kansas City Council did preside at the November 17, 1900, institution of Denver Council No. 539.[55] John H. Reddin, a young lawyer, and Father William O'Ryan were Gorman's chief lieutenants in organizing the new council with its fifty-one charter members. Knights from Fall River, Massachusetts; Chicago, Joliet, and Peoria, Illinois; Dubuque, Iowa; and Topeka joined those from Kansas City in witnessing the historic occasion.

Reddin was elected first Grand Knight and appointed Territorial Deputy. Later he became Colorado's first State Deputy and first Supreme Director. His artistry as a ceremonialist and his strong fraternalist zeal soon won him national recognition. Reddin's Denver Council degree team made its first of many trips outside Colorado in September 1901. James Gorman's "indefatigable labor" resulted in the institution of Salt Lake Council No. 602 on September 8, 1901. One charter member praised the degree work of Denver Council in general but was particularly struck with John Reddin's skill: "His work was of surpassing excellence. Men who have witnessed many institutions of councils declared that it surpassed in beauty and effectiveness anything they have ever witnessed."[56]

According to the *Columbiad,* the bishop of Salt Lake City was very supportive of the Order's entrance into his diocese.

One of the pleasantest features of the exemplification of the first and second degrees was the presence of the Right Rev. Bishop Scannel, bishop of Salt

Lake City. It was a promising sign when a society and a bishop extend such mutual courtesies to each other. . . . It shows in a marked degree that the members of the new council know what is due their leader and their love and trust in him. On the other hand, it is also indicative of the loyal faith that the reverend bishop reposes on the professions of his children.[57]

The anonymous author of this statement misled his readers. The bishop's name was not Scannel but Lawrence Scanlan, and though he may have been present during the degree program his presence was not a sign of support. Bishop Duane G. Hunt, who was State Lecturer in Utah 1915–16, wrote in 1950, "It was generally understood . . . that Bishop Scanlan had forbidden his priests to be members of the Order or to be Chaplains."[58]

As early as November 1899 the editor of the *Columbiad* had marked the institution of St. Louis Council as the beginning of an "onward march to the Rockies—with the sturdy Missourians as a vanguard. Few months need elapse before we may glory in a council on the Pacific Coast." He quoted a letter from a Knight who had moved to San Francisco: "So far, I have excited a local enthusiasm among my friends here, and I am glad to say that my efforts have borne fruit and with very little additional work, I shall be able to secure men in numbers large enough to form a council."[59]

Though the railroad provided rapid communication from St. Louis to San Francisco, National Organizer Gorman's trek to the Pacific entailed the hard work of organizing councils and degree teams in states along the route. According to the recollections of California's first State Deputy, Joseph Scott, Gorman "worked indefatigably through the Spring and Summer of 1901 in San Francisco and Los Angeles." Advance work in the bay city by Neal Power, a member of the Order and probably the San Francisco author of the letter quoted by the editor of the *Columbiad,* had paved the way for Gorman's efforts. Scott also recalled, "In Los Angeles great credit should be given to Bishop George Montgomery, who gave unstinted support to the efforts of Mr. Gorman."[60]

Gorman and his assistant organizers decided to form councils in each of the two principal cities from which other councils in the state would originate. On January 19, 1902, John Reddin led the Denver team in instituting San Francisco Council No. 615, and on January 26, Richard Hayden of Topeka exemplified the Third Degree assisted by the Denver team.[61] Scott's zeal for spreading Columbianism placed him on a level with John Reddin, Patrick McArdle, John Delaney, James Flaherty, and Supreme Knight Hearn.

Two years after the first councils were instituted in California, Scott wrote a piece for the *Columbiad* entitled "The Mission of the Order in the Land of the Missions." As had earlier Knights, Scott countered the Puritan–Plymouth Rock story of the origins of American civilization by focusing on the civilizing forces of the Catholic missionary schools in Mexico and the American Southwest. Though the thesis of his article was based upon historical interpretation, its thrust was to place the role of the Order in the West within the then current religious and social trends. According to Scott, Catholic immigrants had so frightened the descendants of the Pilgrims that there was a Puritan invasion of the Catholic West. "To my mind it seems a bounden duty on the part of the men responsible for expelling the Puritans from their native hearth into this land of the mission Fathers to give the faith in this southwest country an antidote against the poison of Puritan doctrine." Implicit in Scott's reasoning was his identification of Puritanism with anti-Catholicism, which he had personally witnessed in the rise of the A.P.A. in California: "the Knights of Columbus did well to send in after the retiring Puritans the degree teams of our noble Order to cheer their brethren in the task they must meet, and to prepare them for this fight in the southwest, which is one of no small dimension." Scott distinguished between his native Los Angeles, which had been inundated by a large influx "of Puritan stock from the East [and] a second crop of Yankees via Kansas and the Middle West," and San Francisco, where "conditions are very different [with its] enormous Catholic population [which] is enough to scare away any hard headed [i.e. anti-Catholic] New Englander." He envisioned the day when eastern and western Knights will "converge their lives until their hands meet in a clasp that will signalize the control of this country for the faith of Columbus and for the faith of the Mission Fathers."[62] Anti-Catholics may have scoffed at Scott's hope that Catholics aimed to "control" the Southwest, but the impassioned young lawyer seems to have believed that Los Angeles was already under the control of the enemies of the Church.

While Scott was establishing new councils in California, James J. Gorman was organizing the Northwest. Though he had hoped to return to his hometown of Fall River, Massachusetts, after the institution of San Francisco and Los Angeles councils, Supreme Knight Hearn wired him instructions to continue his new council development in Washington, Oregon, and Montana. In August of 1900 the *Columbiad* had reported that "Brother James P. Lavin of New York Council . . . has found a number of Knights in [Seattle] . . . who were anxious for the establishment of the Order" in the western seaport.[63] Hence, when Gorman arrived in Seattle in late February 1902, he had a core of Knights ready to support his organizational efforts. Before making final arrangements for the institution of a new council in Seattle, Gorman traveled to Portland, Oregon, to meet with Archbishop Alexander Christie, who was very supportive of the Order's entrance into his archdiocese. During early June, Gorman successfully laid the groundwork for a council in Portland. On June 15, Portland Council No. 678 was instituted, with Deputy Supreme Knight Patrick McArdle of Chicago, assisted by John Reddin and the Denver Council degree team, exemplifying the Third Degree. The San Francisco degree team was on hand for the exemplification of the first two degrees. The following Sunday, June 22, Seattle Council No. 676 was instituted by the same degree teams. John Reddin's team also led the ceremonials instituting Spokane Council No. 683 on July 6 and the first council in Montana, Butte Council No. 668, on July 9, 1902.[64]

The remaining northwestern states of Wyoming and Idaho were absorbed into the Order with the institution of Council No. 801 in Cheyenne on July 12, 1903, and Council No. 892 in Pocatello on May 15, 1904. Three upper midwestern states, Nebraska and South and North Dakota, were brought into the Order in 1902–3; Council No. 652 in Omaha on March 16, 1902; No. 782 in Fargo on May 30, 1903; No. 815 in Sioux Falls on October 22, 1903.[65]

James J. Gorman was so impressed with the Pacific Northwest that he settled in Seattle, where he became first State Deputy of Washington, 1904–5. Like portions of the Deep South, the Northwest was mission country desperate for priests. In 1904 there was only one priest (seventy years of age) in Seattle, with a population of 20,000. Gorman reported that the role of the Order in this frontier situation was to work with unchurched Catholic men. He noted that he had organized a new council with thirty-five charter members, twenty-five of whom were not known as Catholics, either by the local priest or by active Catholics in the parish. Thus in many instances Gorman's recruits reentered the Church as a step toward entering the Order.[66]

While Gorman was pioneering the Northwest, John Reddin's ceremonial talents were being sought for the institution of the first council in New Mexico: Albuquerque No. 641 on February 2, 1902. The story of the Order's origin in New Mexico begins in Port Henry, New York, where Owen N. Marron was actively promoting the Democratic standard-bearer, Grover Cleveland, in the election of 1888. Cleveland lost to William Harrison, and Marron was financially stranded. Subsequently, he appealed to the state chairman of the Democratic Party, who found him a position in the Albuquerque Indian School. Marron, together with Father Alphonse Mandari, S.J., pastor of Immaculate Conception parish, energetically pushed for a council in their hometown. By the time the Supreme Council issued a charter for Albuquerque, Marron had been elected Mayor. At a February 1 meeting in his office, he was elected first Grand Knight and later held the office of Territorial and State Deputy. Though there were a few other charter members of Irish descent, Spanish Americans formed the majority. It was not until 1913 that the Order entered Santa Fe, the principal Catholic city in the state. José D. Seña recalled that it took twelve years to persuade diocesan authorities to look favorably upon the Order.[67]

The first Texans to enter the Order were Father James M. Hayes, rector of the cathedral in Dallas, and two prominent businessmen, Michael J. Carver and W. G. Crush, also of Dallas, who "in their impatience to become members of the Knights of Columbus, had been initiated in the Order at Parsons, Kansas . . . on April 20, 1901."[68] However, El Paso had the first council. Michael F. Burke, a member of Terre Haute (Indiana) Council No. 541, had engendered interest in the Order while on business there. James Clifford, E. V. Berrien, and Father Francis Roy, S.J., encouraged by Burke and William S. McNary, a new council organizer in the South and Southwest, were determined to achieve the honor of forming Texas' first council. After garnering forty candidates, the Supreme Office authorized the council and delegated John Reddin to exemplify the Third Degree on April 13, 1902.[69] (Owen N. Marron led a team for the exemplification of the first two degrees.) E. V. Berrien was elected first Grand Knight of El Paso Council No. 638 and later was appointed Territorial Deputy. After organizing councils in Dallas, Fort Worth, Galveston, and San Antonio, Berrien chartered a Pullman car for twenty-four members of his council, and between May 8 and 17, 1903, these four councils were instituted.[70]

The Indian Territory (Oklahoma) received its first council on November 22, 1903. Teams composed of Knights from Topeka and Wichita exemplified the degrees for fifty "energetic and enthusiastic" candidates for Council No. 767 in El Reno. The following day another council was instituted in the south Indian Territory. Council No. 775 in McAlester was honored with the initiation of Bishop Theophile Meerschaert as a charter member.[71]

The El Paso degree team was assigned to the institution of the first council in Arizona, Bisbee Council No. 863, on March 27, 1904.

Bishop Henry Granjon of the Tucson diocese had been an opponent of the Order, but when he was "permitted to witness the proceedings of a council [he became] an enthusiastic admirer."[72] After the banquet honoring the new council, "Bishop Granjou [sic] spoke eloquently on behalf of the Order."[73]

The last state to be organized was Nevada. Territorial Deputy George J. Gibson conducted the ceremonials for the institution of Reno Council No. 978 on April 9, 1905. Knights from Salt Lake City, San Francisco, Sacramento, and several eastern councils were on hand. "Some of the most prominent men in Nevada joined the Order. . . . The people of Reno gave the visiting Knights a royal welcome. . . . Many of the stores were decorated with American flags, purple and white bunting."[74] By the time Nevada was absorbed into the Order, the Canadian Knights were preparing to celebrate their eighth anniversary and councils were about to be introduced into the Philippines and Mexico.

III

Before Catholics of the northwestern United States had heard of the Knights of Columbus, Quebec Catholics had established a council. The story begins in Cliff Haven, New York, where the Catholic Summer School was in session. Primarily concerned with religious education, the Summer School represented the increasing maturity of the Church in America. On August 8, 1897, the school was the setting for the institution of Plattsburg Council No. 255. Of the sixty-six members initiated on that day, two were former residents of Plattsburg who had moved to Montreal but were attending the Summer School. These Montrealers, J. P. Kavanaugh and Charles F. Smith, returned home with the determination to pioneer a new council. Among their interested friends, Dr. J. J. Guerin, a former mayor of Montreal and then a minister in the Quebec government, became the most enthusiastic advocate for a K. of C. council in the city. After Kavanaugh and Guerin had successfully gathered together enough men they met with Archbishop Paul Bruchési. Though he stated that there was no need for another society within the archdiocese, through the intervention of Father John Quenlenon, pastor of St. Patrick's Church, he reluctantly gave his permission. On November 22, 1897, the Plattsburg degree team, accompanied by more than one hundred Knights from its council, exemplified the three degrees for the sixty-eight charter members of Montreal Council No. 284. Dr. Guerin was elected first Grand Knight. However, the council was composed almost entirely of men of Irish descent, with only six French Canadians on the charter list.[75]

British Canadians dominated the political and economic life of the nation. Though the Catholic Church was allowed to develop its own social and educational institutions, Catholic laymen, predominantly of French and Irish descent, were victims of prejudice and discrimination. Because American and Canadian Catholics shared common needs, Columbianism was easily transplanted beyond U.S. soil. On November 25, 1897, J. P. Kavanaugh was appointed District Deputy for all of Canada, with the authority to organize new councils. In 1899 his efforts led to the institution of Quebec Council No. 446 in Quebec City and the second Montreal Council, Dominion No. 465.[76] As late as February 1899, Archbishop Bruchési was considering public condemnation of the K. of C.; like Bishop McQuaid of Rochester, he seems to have identified the Order with secret societies proscribed by the Church. Bruchesi sought Cardinal Gibbons's opinion. The vice-rector of Catholic University, Reverend Philip J. Garrigan, related the story to the delegates at the 1899 convention and concluded with the remark, "It is needless to say that the Cardinal wrote a very strong letter of recommendation and thereby saved the Knights of Columbus in Canada, at least from a fatal blow, which would give us all a black eye, even in America."[77]

The first Canadian council outside of Quebec, Ottawa No. 485, was instituted on January 28, 1900. J. P. Kavanaugh conducted the ceremonies; visiting Knights from Montreal, Quebec City, northern New York, and Vermont "applauded his work heartily and complimented him for his skill and proficiency."[78] By the end of 1903, Ontario councils included Ottawa, Kingston, Cornwall, and Peterborough.

Prince Edward Island was the next Canadian area to be settled. An organizer, G. H. Kelley of Massachusetts, had succeeded in gathering eighty-four men to form Charlottetown Council No. 824. Instituted on December 13, 1903, by a team from North Easton, Massachusetts, the council included eighteen priests, eleven of whom held Doctor of Divinity degrees. A charter member reported, "The degree work was most impressive; and after the rites a banquet was served at which appropriate brilliant speeches were made. This is the first council in the district, and the enthusiasm of the members shows the broad humanity of the Order."[79] With the institution of St. John (New Brunswick) Council No. 937 on November 14, 1904, and Sydney (Nova

Scotia) Council No. 1060 on November 12, 1905, Eastern Canada (with the exception of Newfoundland and Labrador, which formed a British Crown colony) was firmly anchored in the Order. Like the United States, Canada possessed an enormous amount of diversity. Just as the Mobile Knights drastically differed from their brothers in Boston, Baltimore, and Boise, so the Sydney Knights were very different from their brothers in Quebec City, Montreal, and Ottawa. Columbianism engendered a loyalty throughout the diverse fraternal society, even to the remote port city of Manila.

The Spanish-American War resulted in U.S. annexation of the Philippine Islands. President McKinley had stated his rationale for this adventure in empire building as primarily religious, viz., that it was America's responsibility to "Christianize" the Filipinos. After a Filipino insurrection (1898–99) had been suppressed and an American civilian government had been established (1902), many volunteers in the U.S. armed forces chose to remain in the Philippines, where they worked in the civil administration.[80] Archbishop Jeremiah J. Harty, the first American ordinary of the Manila archdiocese, drew a large American following to Cathedral Parish, several of whom had been initiated into the K. of C. back in the States. By 1905 these men had formed a close association and had successfully appealed to the Supreme Board of Directors for a council charter. On April 23, 1905, Manila Council No. 1000 was instituted. Because the Order would not extend insurance coverage to what it considered such a high-risk area, Manila Council was granted associate status.[81] Though the charter members were all Americans, Filipinos joined the council as early as 1907. After 1916, when the civil administration passed out of American hands, Manila Council was composed almost entirely of Filipinos. Since the Board did not envision more than one council in the Islands, it placed Manila within the California jurisdiction.

The editor of the *Columbiad* doubted the American government's ability to deal justly with Filipinos, since its record of dealing with American blacks and Catholics was characterized by injustice.[82] Hence, the presence of the K. of C. in Manila symbolized the defense of the faith in a situation in which the Catholics were struggling against "delegitimacy," as opposed to the American and Canadian situation where Catholics were struggling for legitimacy.

The Order's entrance into Mexico entails a story replete with coincidence. John B. Frisbie, Jr., son of an American general who had fought in the Mexican War and later married the daughter of the Mexican general he had defeated, was an owner of a large plantation in Guerro, Mexico. According to an article in the *Columbiad,* Frisbie "had begun a study of American-Catholic organizations with the idea of introducing one of them into that country to work in English among the English-speaking Catholics and in Spanish among the Mexicans." In January 1905, while he was still deliberating the matter, Frisbie met Father William McMahon, editor of the Cleveland *Catholic Universe,* and another Cleveland priest, Father Francis McMahon. The result of this encounter was that these two priests "convinced him, [i.e., Frisbie] that the Knights of Columbus would be the best society to introduce, not only for the beneficence of its works, but also for the charm of its name, and its international character."[83] Frisbie was so impressed that he journeyed to Los Angeles the following June, where, while the National Convention was in session, he joined the Order and was immediately appointed Territorial Deputy for Mexico.[84]

In September 1905, Supreme Knight Hearn visited Mexico City to install the officers of Guadalupe Council No. 1050. "He was given a most cordial welcome by the leading Catholics in the city of Mexico and was received in audience by President [Porfirio] Díaz, who manifested great interest in the work of the Order."[85] On September 18, Hearn exemplified the first two degrees at the institution of the first council south of the Rio Grande. This historic event occurred at the home of General John B. Frisbie, who was granted the honorary title of "Past Grand Knight." Judge Ignacio Sepulveda, a retired California jurist then serving in the American embassy in Mexico City, was elected first Grand Knight. The ten other original members of the council were prominent American bankers and businessmen.[86] Since these men did not receive the Third Degree until Hearn's second visit the following February, the official charter-member class of Guadalupe Council actually numbered fifty men, including a large representation of Mexicans.[87]

A strong contingency of American Knights, led by Supreme Knight Hearn and National Chaplain Father Patrick J. McGivney (the founder's brother), journeyed to Mexico for the festive degree work in February 1906. After John Reddin, the master ceremonialist in the West, conferred the Third Degree, the council hosted a "grand banquet" in honor of Supreme Knight Hearn. The week-long visit was also highlighted by a meeting with Archbishop Próspero Alarcón.[88] During this period, the Mexican Church, inspired by Pope Leo XIII's 1891 encyclical *Rerum Novarum,* had organized a series of Catholic Social Congresses, 1903–9. As the ordinary of the capital city, Archbishop Alarcón played a significant role in these congresses and viewed the entrance of the Order in his archdiocese as another sign of the revival of lay Catholicism.[89]

Though the Mexican Knights were of necessity associate members, they persisted in their strong attachment to the Order. By 1911 they had their own Spanish ritual and had successfully incorporated the principles of the Order into Mexican culture. Like the French-speaking councils in Quebec and like the Filipino councils, the Mexican councils reflected the growing international character of the Knights of Columbus. By the turn of the century, the Church in Mexico had experienced several decades of anticlerical conflict. During the twenty years prior to the dictatorship of Porfirio Díaz (1877–1911), the state had confiscated most ecclesiastical property, and reform statutes had stripped the Church of its privileged status. Díaz pursued a conciliatory policy, but Church property and privileges were never fully restored. Hence, when the early leaders of the Order in Mexico pledged their loyalty to Díaz, they viewed him, as did most middle-class Mexicans, as the guardian of social order. In such a precarious ecclesiastical situation, Mexican Columbianism sought to defend the Church against further encroachments at the hands of the state. Though they developed along their own cultural lines, all Knights were united in Columbianism, a spirit which manifested itself in pride in one's Catholic heritage whether American, Canadian, Filipino, or Mexican.

IV

Of all the reasons why Columbianism expanded so rapidly throughout the United States, Canada, the Philippines, and Mexico, the popularity of the ceremonials and the enthusiasm and expertise of the degree teams were most significant. Columbianism may mean social and/or economic advancement, but almost all Knights placed primary importance on the lessons embodied in the rituals. This historian interviewed Eugene Donahoe, a past State Deputy of Michigan, who was initiated in 1906 in O'Neill, Nebraska. When asked what the ceremonials meant to him, he responded that they embodied the "great lessons of Catholicism."[90] By this he did not mean explicit catechetical training; rather, he said that as a result of experiencing the dramatic rituals on immortality, the cardinal virtues, and the traditions of the Church, he became a more serious practical Catholic. Passage through the ceremonials engendered an enthusiasm in new members to encourage

their friends to join the Order. Donahoe was so inspired that he became a member of a degree team and took great pride in his ability to
convey the Columbian themes to the initiates.

Though Columbianism was primarily a religious spirit, it assumed
specific social and cultural forms according to the historical context in
which it took root. Loyalty to the Church was expressed in a variety of
ways, reflecting the diverse needs of the Church in North America and
the Philippines. In rural Oregon or along the coast of Newfoundland
it was expressed in the actual building of a church; in Boston, Montreal, or Philadelphia it was expressed in supporting the ordinary's
parochial-school development or seminary drive. However, that cultural strand which was basic to Columbian Knighthood in all regions
was the drive to assert what sociologists term social legitimacy, i.e.,
Catholic legitimacy. Derived from its minority consciousness, the
Order's pursuit of Catholic legitimacy was first manifested in the adoption of Columbus as its patron. Just as Columbus was an Italian in the
service of the Catholic King and Queen of Spain, so the Irish-American
founding Knights were not honoring their national origins but rather
their Catholic heritage in the New World. Hence the Order was cosmopolitan in the sense that it embraced Catholics of all nationalities, best
symbolized by its expansion throughout Canada and into Mexico,
Puerto Rico, Cuba, and the Philippines. Even in traditionally Catholic
Mexico the drive for legitimacy was basic, because anticlericalism and
anti-Catholicism were so strongly infused into that nation's revolutionary ethos.

In 1907 the Order's ceremonials were changed as a tribute to its
multinational character. From this time on the initiates were introduced to heroic laymen of many nationalities: Ludwig Windthorst, one
of the founders of the Catholic Center Party in Germany; Antoine
Frédéric Ozanam, the French founder of the St. Vincent de Paul Society; and Daniel O'Connell, the Irish patriot who founded the Catholic
Association.[91] As will be noted in the next chapter, the Fourth Degree
ceremonial, which was thematically based upon patriotism, stressed
the multi-ethnic character of the Catholic contribution to the New
World, a ceremonial which was easily incorporated into the world
views of Canadians, Mexicans, and Filipinos, as well as of Americans
of all regions, as symbolic of their Catholic legitimacy.

6

Insurance Reforms, Patriotism, and Catholic Culture

THE ORGANIZATION OF THE KNIGHTS OF COLUMBUS became increasingly complex as the Order expanded. The present chapter will explore the ways in which quantitative growth effected qualitative changes in its structure and character. The best way to perceive these changes is to focus on the national leaders, particularly the Supreme Knights, who were responsible for guiding the Order through this transition from a regional to an international society. Since Supreme Knight James Hayes died shortly after his election to office and his successor, John Cone, served only the remaining thirteen months of Hayes's term of office, the leadership of John Phelan (1886–97) and Edward Hearn (1899–1909) dominated the period. To place national governance within its proper context, one should recall that the national officers did not live in New Haven. The only exception was the National Secretary, who was the chief administrative officer responsible for the everyday business of the Order. From 1884 to 1909 Daniel Colwell served as the National Secretary. However, because his position did not involve the formation of policy, Colwell's contribution, though significant, will not be examined in this chapter.

Though each of the officers shared executive authority as members of the National Board of Directors, the Supreme Knight was the chief architect of national policy as well as the moral leader of the group. Only Supreme Knight Hearn's fragmentary memoir of his decade in office provides us with an eyewitness account of events which occurred behind the public scene. Since all the national officers were elected (with the exception of the national chaplaincy, which became appointive in 1902), National Council meetings were highly charged political affairs. Phelan, Hayes, and Cone had all been successful politicians outside the Order and therefore were skilled leaders experienced in the art of consensus and compromise.

John Phelan, of Bridgeport, Connecticut, was the first Supreme Knight to articulate explicitly the ideals of the Order in terms of moral, intellectual, and cultural roles within the Catholic laity. His strong promotion of the associate (noninsurance) membership; his insurance reforms, i.e., the reserve fund and the three grades of insurance (later reduced to two grades, $1,000 and $2,000); his alteration of the constitution to provide for national expansion with corporate headquarters in New Haven; his reforms in the ceremonials and his strenuous efforts to satisfy members of the hierarchy (particularly Archbishop Corrigan and Bishop McDonnell)—all these were clear marks of Phelan's national leadership.

Confident of Columbianism's general appeal, Phelan referred to the "mystic, moral, and material fascination of the Organization."[1] During the first decade, Supreme Knights stressed the insurance program, but as the Order expanded, Phelan and others began explicitly to underline its social and moral goals. At the first meeting of the National Council in October 1893, Phelan spoke of the "higher social development of Catholics . . . yearning for the day when Catholics for whom . . . we labored finally emerged from contracted environments will displace prejudice and distrust with love and confidence of their fellows, and honorably occupy their proper sphere as citizens in the march of their own and their country's welfare."[2]

To allay distrust and prejudice and to project an honorable image in opposition to those who caricaturized Irish Catholics as alcoholics, the Order placed in a special category any applicant for membership who was connected with the manufacture or sale of intoxicating liquor. For several years the Order's National Physician had listed the number of deaths in the Order due to alcoholism. In 1895 liquor manufacturers, dealers, and bartenders were prohibited from insurance membership and had to be approved by a special examining board to qualify for associate membership.[3] Seven years later the blanket prohibition was extended to associate members as well.[4] During the late 1890s, other temperance laws were passed, prohibiting liquor at degree work and at banquets held under the auspices of the K. of C. Just as Archbishop Ireland had identified good Catholic citizenship with civility and temperance, so the Order went on record as identifying Columbian citizenship with sobriety.

John Phelan's most innovative proposal, one which had the unanimous endorsement of the Board of Directors, was his 1895 recommendation to the National Council that the rules be amended to allow women into the society.[5] Perhaps he and other directors were influenced by the Massachusetts Catholic Order of Foresters, which had passed such a law the previous year.[6] Regardless of its origin, Phelan was committed to the reform.

Personally, I am convinced of the usefulness of women's cooperation in enlarging and developing our social area, and am imbued with the advantages that would accrue as a result of the joining of forces, not the least of which would be felt in the family circle, and in many places, wherever in fact the influence of women ardently identified with our purposes in the development of the best in the Catholic people could be appropriately exercised, and further, in this regard, it is not untruthful to assert that no sufficient reason exists why women equally eligible as insurance risks with men should not be insured in the same manner as their more highly favored brothers.[7]

The resolution limited women to membership in women's councils, to a maximum of $1,000 insurance, and to associate status in legal and political rights—which meant that they would be subject to the Board of Directors and the National Council without direct representation in either body.[8]

The Massachusetts Catholic Order of Foresters admitted women on an equal footing with men.[9] Had the Knights of Columbus followed suit, it would have entailed a drastic alteration of its character. Traditional notions of the male role permeated every aspect of Columbian fraternalism. The ceremonial "rite of passage" was intended to imbue the member with a "manly" sense of pride in his Catholicism and a strong dedication to defend the faith. The insurance program was a medium for expressing the breadwinner's economic responsibility for his family. The K. of C. council was a place where Catholic men could find social sustenance for their struggle as a minority group within a hostile society and where they could unite in the militant promotion of Catholic interests. Had its fraternalism been merely peripheral to the insurance program, the Order would probably have easily accommodated itself to feminine membership. However, as we have noted in previous chapters, Columbian fraternalism, which extolled the "manly" virtues of modern Knighthood, formed the core, while the insurance program was viewed as a "vital appendage." This identification with masculinity was so strong that the resolution admitting women into the Order never reached the floor of the National Council, either in 1895 or at any subsequent meeting. Since it had the unanimous support of the Board of Directors, the majority of whom were from Connecticut, one concludes that on this issue the Board was ignorant of the membership's opinion.

Ladies' auxiliaries to various councils did emerge in the late 1890s. Though they were never absorbed as members of the K. of C., some of these auxiliaries were active in the social life of the local councils. The first such organization was the ladies' auxiliary to Russell Council No. 65 of New Haven, which evolved into a national organization.[10] Daniel Colwell, an incorporator of the K. of C. and then National Secretary, played a supervisory role in its foundation and was the major author of its ceremonials. Columbian themes were incorporated into the women's organization, as illustrated by the ceremony dramatizing Queen Isabella's pledging her jewels to support Columbus's voyage. After a new member passed through the ritual, the "crown of Isabella" was placed upon her head. Rituals, songs, pins, and insignia were the general symbols of the women's organization. On March 7, 1904, the society was incorporated in Connecticut as "Daughters of Isabella, Circle No. 1, Auxiliary to Russell Council No. 65, Knights of Columbus." Its charter was similar to that of the K. of C.: "The objects and purposes of the said corporation shall be to render pecuniary aid and assistance to sick and distressed members and to beneficiaries of members whether such sickness be temporary or incurable and to render pecuniary aid toward defraying the funeral expenses of members; and to promote social and intellectual intercourse among its members."[11]

The Russell Circle Daughters of Isabella received a charter from the State of Connecticut in 1904. Circle No. 1 had its title changed by the Connecticut General Assembly (July 1907) to "National Circle, Daughters of Isabella."[12] Gradually the Order expanded throughout the United States. It entered Canada in 1925 and later established circles in the Philippines and Mexico. Though it never achieved the size of the K. of C. in membership or in its insurance program, the Daughters of Isabella paralleled the K. of C. in its promotion of Catholic culture. Other Knights of Columbus councils formed ladies' auxiliaries, such as the Columbiettes in New York, New Jersey, and Connecticut, but only one other group, the Catholic Daughters of America (C.D.A.), managed to achieve national status.

The C.D.A. originated in Utica, New York, in 1899 as the Daughters of Isabella, which was incorporated in New York State in 1903 and in 1905 received a national charter as the National Order of the Daughters of Isabella.[13] Imported into Utica by Michael F. Kelley, without prior authorization from the New Haven society, the two Daughters societies collided in their national recruitment efforts. After several court struggles, the New Haven group won, and in 1921 the Utica society became the Catholic Daughters of America.[14] In their successful drive to unify Catholic women for sick and death benefits and for the pursuit of Catholic charity, these two national women's societies, and other ladies' auxiliaries movements within the K. of C., illustrate that the authors of the proposed 1895 resolution to establish women's councils were correct about the need but incorrect about the strategy to satisfy it. Phelan referred to the resolution in his 1896 address, but once again it never reached the floor.

From 1895 to 1897 the major concerns of the national leadership were related to the expansion of the Order. The National Advocate, Philip Markley of New Britain, Connecticut, had to file more and more applications with various state insurance departments. A steady increase in membership enlarged the duties of the National Treasurer, P. D. Ryan of Hartford, Connecticut, and the National Physician, Andrew W. Tracy of Meriden, Connecticut. The former was responsible for investing a portion of the money from the Reserve Fund (over $12,000 in December 1896),[15] while the latter had to approve an ever-increasing number of insurance applications. Since the National Chaplain was not a member of the Board of Directors, Father Hugh Treanor of Waterbury, Connecticut, was relatively free to pursue his pastoral duties. However, whenever there was an inquiry from a bishop or priest regarding the nature of the Order, Father Treanor was called upon to reply. (It was he who appealed to Archbishop Satolli for his approval of the Order.) Of all the officers, the National Secretary, Daniel Colwell, was most affected by expansion. As the only full-time officer, Colwell assumed an ever-increasing load of daily administrative affairs. He was the chief correspondent in all official fraternal and insurance matters and was responsible for keeping the officers informed on important matters, as well as for recording the proceedings at Board and National Council meetings. His office was in the Hoadley Building on Church Street until 1906, when the Order had its own building constructed on Chapel Street. The National Secretary and the Supreme Knight were the only salaried officers during the 1890s. Salaries were set by the Board, with the approval of the National Convention, and were raised in 1897. The Supreme Knight received $1,500 and expenses, while the National Secretary received $2,000.[16]

The business of the Order expanded at such a rate that by 1897 the finance committee of the Board of Directors reported to the National Council that "the volume of rapidly increasing business calls for increasing vigilance and labor in the national office and foreshadows the necessity, in the near future, of requiring the whole time of the chief officer of the Order to the care and direction of its affairs."[17] Hence, it recommended enlarging the staff and creating a chief business officer to work under the General Secretary.[18] When John Phelan became Supreme Knight in 1886, there were twenty-seven councils, with 2,700 members, located in Connecticut and Rhode Island. By 1897, the figures had risen to 195 councils, with 16,651 members located in eight states.

The Order thrived during the mid-nineties, even though this was a period of severe depression. Supreme Knight Phelan described the economic and social climate of the day when he addressed the 1897 convention: "The year of 1896 [was] fraught with adversity to commercial and industrial life. . . . To many persons and to many vocations it was a year of gloom, during which the sun of material prosperity was veiled by clouds of evil aspect."[19] The delegates confronted the conditions of economic and social distress when they voted to pass a resolution establishing charity funds within the local councils "for the purpose of retaining their worthy members in good standing who are in need and in distress [and] who are absent from home."[20] Fraternal charity was strongly accented in Phelan's 1897 address. Harking back to the distrust and discord that had characterized the Catholic laity in America, he said, "Solicitude to participate in developing dormant sympathy of love of Catholics for each other's sake and welfare, seems to have supplanted the indifference, jealousy, and distrust of the past. It seems destined in the providence of God that through the medium of this society will the kindliness of the Catholic heart find consolation to the fullness of content in loving his neighbor as himself and in divinely sharing his joys and sorrows."[21]

Upon the completion of his address, the delegates voted in a new Supreme Knight, James E. Hayes, immediate Past State Deputy of Massachusetts. Though there was no roll-call vote, the strength of the non-Connecticut vote was enough to defeat Phelan by a vote of 17 to 13 and one abstention. The Hayes forces joined with New York and New Jersey, for John J. Cone of New Jersey was elected Deputy Supreme Knight by seven votes over Eugene J. McCarthy of Rhode Island, and William T. McManus of New York defeated Andrew W. Tracy of Connecticut by five votes. However, Connecticut retained the office of National Treasurer with the reelection of P. D. Ryan, while Colwell and Father Treanor's elections were uncontested. Hayes nominated John Ward of New York for the office of National Organizer and Director of Ceremonies in opposition to his fellow Bostonian, Thomas H. Cummings. After debate, Ward withdrew his name and Cummings was unanimously elected.[22] Without documents revealing the behind-the-scene politics, one can only infer that the majority of the delegates considered it was time for a change. Since Massachusetts had seventy-six councils in 1897 and Connecticut had fifty-eight, Hayes's victory may be viewed as the political reward for the Order's phenomenal success in the Bay State.

The careers of Phelan and Hayes evolved along parallel lines. Both were university graduates, attorneys, successful Democratic politicians, and highly skilled orators. However, Phelan was born in Ireland and worked his way through college, while Hayes was a native Bostonian and attended Prescott School, a prestigious private preparatory school. Hayes was only thirty-two years old when he was elected Supreme Knight, the youngest occupant of the office in the history of the Order. Apparently destined to achieve great prominence in the Order as well as in politics, Hayes's career was tragically terminated when he succumbed to peritonitis and died on February 8, 1898. The *Columbiad* reported the Order's expression of grief:

The Knights of Columbus mourned the loss of their Supreme Knight and more than one thousand members of the organization, not only representing the councils in Boston and vicinity, but from the other New England states, who acted as escort and bodyguard to the remains of their associate, paid him all the honor and respect due to one who had risen to the highest position in the gift of the fraternity. . . . Members of Beacon Council, of which the late Senator Hayes was the first Grand Knight, headed the procession, and were followed by the Bunker Hill, Mt. Pleasant, Redberry, and other Councils, all of which turned out in a body. The State Council of the Knights of Columbus, made up of Grand Knights and Deputy Grand Knights, to the number of more than one hundred, and delegations from several of the Councils in and about Boston, swelling the number to more than 1,000, all of whom wore crepe rosettes on their left arm, comprised the Knights of Columbus representation."[23]

James E. Hayes had presided at only three meetings of the Board of Directors and had never chaired a meeting of the National Council. Hence, there is no evidence of his specific goals and priorities for the future of the Order.

On March 5, 1898, less than a month following the death of Hayes, the National Council met with John J. Cone, Deputy Supreme Knight and acting Supreme Knight, presiding. Cone did not present a formal address. After the regular business reports were presented, the delegates confronted the unprecedented situation, the death of an incumbent Supreme Knight. Cone requested a vote for a successor to Hayes, but Phelan countered with the personal opinion that Cone should fill the unexpired term and discharge the duties of Supreme Knight. John Delaney of New York presented "contrary views," but Phelan's opinion carried: "RESOLVED, that the death of our late lamented Supreme Knight, James E. Hayes, created a vacancy which cannot be filled until the next succeeding regular biennial election, and that the Deputy Supreme Knight in the discharge of the duties of Supreme Knight receives the salary attached to said office." The delegates also passed a resolution lamenting the death of Hayes. It extolled his "boundless zeal, matchless mind, and devoted heart," and by way of extending the Order's sympathy to his family, the delegates agreed to send to his mother (Hayes was a bachelor) money equivalent to the salary of his unexpired term.[24]

John Cone had been a Knight only two and a half years when he ascended to the position of Supreme Knight. Indeed, he had been elected first State Deputy of New Jersey and a member of the Board of Directors only in the previous year.[25] Though he was an enthusiastic fraternalist, he was not familiar with the complex cooperative insurance program. He was a successful businessman and politician who served as fire commissioner of Jersey City, but, unlike Phelan and Hayes, he did not bring a lawyer's background to the position. Nevertheless, Cone was not a caretaker Supreme Knight. Under his leadership the Board of Directors responded patriotically to the Spanish-American War by subscribing to war bonds and by removing the disqualification for insuring members who were soldiers and sailors.[26]

When the National Council convened on March 7, 1899, Supreme Knight Cone reported on the most significant trend of the preceding year, the vigorous expansion of the Order. Cone's speech was a summary of the "history of Columbianism for 1898" and of the society's financial condition.[27] In contrast to previous and later Supreme Knights' reports, Cone's was an exercise in brevity. However, the reports of the National Treasurer, Secretary, and Physician were extremely detailed. Contrary to tradition, the election of officers did not occur at the end of the Supreme Knight's address but rather at the second session, on the following day, March 8. According to Edward Hearn's recollections, the election was preceded by a long night of caucusing. Hearn's account of the events leading to his own election as Supreme Knight reveals a crisis of leadership which, because it was recorded forty years later, may be exaggerated. Nevertheless, it is the only document of its kind and is worthy of consideration.

When the Convention adjourned on the first day, I went to my hotel (The Old Tontine). After dinner I went to my room and then after reading the papers I retired. About two o'clock in the morning I was awakened by pounding on my door. Surprised, I asked, "Who is there?" Congressman William S. McNary of Boston answered and said, "It is me, Ed, let me in; I want to talk to you." I hesitated to let him in, fearing some mischief, but he seemed excited and when I opened the door, he and others walked in. They were all excited. McNary spoke up and said, "Ed, we are going to elect you Supreme Knight." I said, "You are not going to give me any office." But they insisted that I dress and go with them to the New Haven house, where seventeen delegates were in session and going over the situation of the Order in deadly earnest. When I entered the room and was seated, John J. Delaney, Corporation Counsel of New York City, arose and said, "No use wasting time going over the condition of the Order, you know it. Something has to be done to save the Order and we have decided on you for Supreme Knight." Pulling myself together I said that I had had all the office experience I wanted and that I would not take any office. A long talk followed and Delaney finally said, "You are a loyal member of the Order and you should do your part in trying to work matters out." I responded by saying that the Order was financially broke and they knew it. "It has $93,000 in death claims over ninety days old and not a cent with which to pay them. To save the Order you should be making plans to meet and pay off these claims right now instead of talking about office." Mr. T. D. O'Brien of St. Paul, Insurance Commissioner of Minnesota and Territorial Deputy from that state, arose and asked me to repeat what I had said. This was his first convention and I had not met him nor did I know who he was. Therefore, I rather hesitated in replying and he again asked me to please repeat what I had just said. Carefully I repeated my statement. Mr. O'Brien then said, "You don't know it, but you are going to be Supreme Knight." I said, "It is impossible for me to take any office. My time is not my own. I am a traveling salesman and my time belongs to the concern I represent." It was finally agreed that I would call my office at nine o'clock that morning and ascertain what the firm would say about arranging things so that I could give some time to the Knights of Columbus. I left the meeting around three or four o'clock A.M. and went to the Yale Turkish Bath for the rest of the night.

As agreed, I called my office in Boston the next morning and talked with Mr. J. R. Entwistle, a member of the firm and the business manager. I explained the situation to him and he was just splendid. He said, "You take the office and I will arrange matters for you. But I want you to promise that if you are elected you will come and see me the minute you return to Boston." Several of the delegates were waiting for my answer and when I told them I would accept the office, we went at once to the Poli Building, where the convention went into session at ten o'clock. The first order of business was the election of officers and I was elected Supreme Knight over John J. Cone by a vote of 30 to 26 [sic].[28]

Hearn's recollection of the Order's indebtedness does not square with the 1899 reports of the various officers. For example, the National Treasurer reported that "cash on hand" amounted to $93,933.80, with only $40,133.65 in unpaid death claims and other liabilities. Neither the financial statement of 1899 nor that of 1900, after Hearn had presided for a year, substantiates Hearn's contention that the Order was close to bankruptcy. But his account of the political events is more credible. Of the four delegates who nominated Hearn, two were from Massachusetts, one from Rhode Island, and Delaney was from New York. Delegates from New Jersey, Pennsylvania, Maine, and New York, along with John Phelan of Connecticut, supported Cone's nomination.[29] Since it was not a roll-call vote there is no evidence of how the votes were patterned, but Hearn won 33 to 26. Phelan's endorsement of Cone, along with that of the delegates from most of the smaller jurisdictions, appears to indicate that there was concern over a Massachusetts–New York domination. The election results of the remaining offices substantiated such concern: Deputy Supreme Knight, John W. Hogan of New York; National Physician, Dr. William T. McManus of New York; National Advocate, James E. McConnell of Massachusetts. John H. Drury of Rhode Island, who supported Hearn, was elected National Treasurer over P. D. Ryan of Connecticut. National Secretary Colwell and National Warden McNamara, both of Connecticut, were the only survivors among the incumbent officers.[30] However, a spirit of loyal opposition prevailed; each vote was followed by a motion to make the election unanimous. Unity was maintained, illustrated by Hearn's appointment of Phelan and other supporters of Cone to positions on various committees.

The National Council of 1899 marked a new era in the history of the Order, not only because Edward Hearn was destined for ten years of leadership but also because it was during these years that the society experienced its greatest growth and became the foremost representative of organized Catholic laity. At this 1899 meeting, three issues surfaced which indicated the impact of expansion: the need to reform the insurance program drastically to suit the needs of a burgeoning national society, the need to provide the membership with an additional ceremonial degree representing national patriotism, and a plea from the Catholic University of America for the endowment of a chair in secular history.[31] Had the Order remained a regional society, these developments would never have occurred.

II

Edward Hearn was only thirty-four years old when he became Supreme Knight in 1899. Unlike his predecessors, Hearn was not involved in politics. After attending public schools in Boston, he became a journeyman in the shoe trade; four years later he was employed as a salesman for a large wholesale shoe company. William O'Neill, the first historian of the Knights of Columbus and a friend of Hearn, wrote, "He has been more than ordinarily successful in a business way, and holds a high place in the confidence of the firm by which he is employed."[32] A charter member and first Grand Knight of Coeur de Leon Council No. 87, which was instituted in South Framingham, Massachusetts, in early 1894, his rise to prominence in the Order was extremely rapid: 1894–96, Grand Knight; 1895–99, Member of National Board of Directors; 1897–99, State Deputy; 1899, Supreme Knight. A year before Hearn ascended to the highest position of the Order, the *Columbiad* published his ideas on "True Knighthood." After quoting Edmund Burke on the demise of chivalry, Hearn said, "The Knights of Columbus are doing a noble and a beautiful work in seeking to re-establish those old ideals. The finer graces and charms of manner which are the fruits of a high social development blossom to the fullest extent in the social life of the K. of C." He viewed the K. of C. council as a school for the restoration of chivalric ideals within a society replete with materialism. In contrast to "the feverish desire for material success which characterizes American life, with all its hurry and unrest," the desire of the ideal Knight is to live according to the virtues of loyalty, charity, courtesy, and modesty, "self-denial and a careful respect for the feelings of others . . . a readiness to relieve want, and a liberality in all things." Just as the medieval Knight represented the ideal Christian layman, so the modern Knight of Columbus should represent the ideal American Catholic layman. "To make the type of Catholic gentleman the highest of American types is the ideal of the Knights of Columbus."[33] But Hearn's idealism was tempered by his pragmatic businessman's perspective. Hence, he stressed the practical advantages of belonging to the Order.

The question is often asked, of what advantage to a business man is membership in the Knights of Columbus? The answer is, that it gives him an opportunity to attract the favorable attention of his "brothers" by conscientious work among them, endeavoring at all times to advance the objects of the society, to make himself strong in the confidence and respect of his fellow-members.

... The idea that a businessman would deliberately join the Knights of Columbus to advance his business interests is not to be entertained, but that our Order has for its object the advancement of the social and business interests of its members is true, for we are a body of Catholic men associated for our common good.[34]

Hearn was only sixteen years old when Father McGivney chaired the first meeting in the basement of St. Mary's Church. He never experienced the early days of struggle in Connecticut but rather was initiated into the Order during the period of its triumphal expansion through New England. When he became a Knight, Columbianism, that set of symbols, beliefs, and principles to guide Catholic men in their struggle for legitimacy, had evolved into an explicit ideology. Hearn was a product of the robust Catholicism of Boston, which in the mid-nineties was vigorously struggling against the American Protective Association; he was a second-generation leader who inherited a sound governing structure infused with a militant spirit dedicated to its well-defined economic, social, and religious mission. Under his leadership (1899–1909), membership climbed from 40,000 to nearly 230,000, councils from 300 to over 1,300. In terms of territorial expansion, councils were instituted in thirty-one states in the United States, in the nine provinces in Canada, in Newfoundland, in Mexico, in the Philippines, in Cuba, and in the Panama Canal Zone.

It has already been noted that delegates to the 1899 convention which elected Hearn Supreme Knight confronted three major issues: the need to reform the insurance program; the need for an additional degree, the Fourth Degree, explicitly to express patriotism; and Catholic University's appeal for financial support to endow a chair of American history. Upon his election, Hearn's political leadership was severely put to the test. National expansion was occurring simultaneously with the development of state regulations of commercial and fraternal insurance programs. A report presented by an ad hoc committee on insurance to the 1899 convention included a lengthy analysis of the unstable and inequitable nature of the assessments for the insurance program.[35] The instability derived from the fact that only a small reserve fund, incapable of meeting a significant rise in death claims, was available. The inequitability stemmed from the fact that members were assessed according to the relationship between their age and the average age of the Order. The National Secretary computed the average age and the individual member's age according to the age listed on the member's application. Members were assessed

3 percent more or less for every year their age was above or below the average figure. The entrance application age never changed, and once a member's rate was determined it remained such for life. Since this rate was not calculated on actuarial tables of mortality, there was no relationship between the premiums paid by a member and the cost of providing his insurance. Also there was not being set aside, out of premiums collected each year, an adequate reserve for payment of future claims. Hence, the Order's solvency was based entirely upon a strong continuous flow of new members entering the Order. To illustrate this, the committee pointed out that death claims in 1898 came to $144,000 while the total amount these 144 members paid into the Order was slightly over $9,000.[36] The committee on revision of the insurance rates was established in 1898, but it was not until 1901 that it submitted its program for reform. More importantly, because the committee's task necessarily entailed raising the insurance rates, it had time to wage an extensive campaign of education during which it sent to every member a circular outlining its proposals and soliciting responses.[37] Nevertheless, the attempt to change the old permanent assessment structures created a heated controversy.

Supreme Knight Hearn was not a member of the insurance committee, but he did authorize it to employ a nationally recognized actuary, David Parks Fackler.[38] Though the committee submitted three alternative programs to the delegates at the March 1901 Convention, and though Hearn had urged them to resolve the issue which had been pending for three years, it became obvious that, amid all the other business on the agenda, the delegates would be unable to grapple with such a complex issue. Hence, a special session of the 1901 National Council was held the following August at the Catholic Summer School in Cliff Haven, New York. By this time, the committee had unanimously endorsed one proposal which, after considerable confusion and much debate, the convention passed: a step-rate plan (to be implemented on January 1, 1902) which Fackler had designed using the Fraternal American Table of Mortality.[39] The step-rate plan was designed along the lines of a renewable-term policy issued by commercial companies. Whereas the latter policy called for an annual increase of the premium as the policy was renewed, the step-rate plan devised by Fackler called for an increase in premiums in five-year periods. For example, if a member entered the Order at age twenty-one, he paid a monthly premium of 76 cents for a $1,000 policy. From age twenty-six through thirty his premium was 81 cents. A member entering at age thirty paid 85 cents a month, and at age thirty-five his premium rose to 90 cents. Hence, each class of members paid for the cost of its own protection as calculated by the actuary. In addition, in the premium, each member was assessed an additional 30 cents per month in order to build up a reserve so that his payments after he reached sixty (later set at age fifty-five) would not continue to increase at a high rate; optional plans were available for members when they reached fifty-five.[40]

The younger members were relieved of the burden of compensating for the low assessment rates for the older members, but the latter were confronted with a considerable increase in their monthly assessments. The Connecticut members, many of whom had been paying assessments for over ten years, felt that the reform placed an unjust hardship upon them, because their monthly rate tripled or quadrupled. Though these older members never gained enough political power to restore the level-rate plan, the Connecticut State Convention consistently sought some compensation for its older members. As the insurance funds of the Order grew, many members concluded that part of the surplus should be distributed to compensate the older members. Rather than considering the long-range liabilities built into such insurance revenues, those seeking compensation were considering only the immediate circulation of surplus. As late as 1907 the Connecticut group was advocating compensation.[41] They gained strong moral support from Father Timothy Crowley, who had been Father McGivney's curate when he was pastor of St. Thomas' Church, Thomaston, Connecticut. In a letter published in the May 23, 1907, edition of the *Catholic Transcript,* Father Crowley urged the Order to set aside "a portion of the surplus . . . to relieve the condition of the older members upon whose shoulders the step-rate falls as a heavy burden." Crowley invoked the memory of the Order's founder to substantiate his position:

Perhaps few were closer to the Reverend founder of the K. of C. than I was in the days when he labored in season and out to build up an organization that has been such a boon to Catholics. In the declining years I was still closer to him, as I was then his assistant, and I feel sure nothing could be further from his mind than that the "Old Guard" should at the end of their days be practically forced out of membership. . . . A quarter of a century has passed away since the K. of C. was organized and the younger generation should remember that when it was a struggling infant, when it had to face almost insurmountable obstacles, when for a time the clouds of uncertainty hung dark and lowering over it, when the Reverend founder was making herculean efforts to place it on a sound foundation, it was the "Old Guard" that ably and generously seconded his efforts and not only paid their ordinary dues and assessments but went down into their own pockets to meet expenses.[42]

Father Crowley's letter may have created a stir among the officers and directors, but older members remained uncompensated for their increased premiums. However, the Connecticut movement continued to gain momentum, culminating in a 1909 suit in which Patrick Kane, a member since 1885, contended that the Mortuary Reserve Fund of 1892 and the Surplus Death Benefit Fund of 1897 should be allocated to all members who had paid five dollars into the funds between 1892 and 1897. These funds had been combined into the one Death Benefit Fund in 1902. Among those representing the plaintiffs was John J. Phelan, Past Supreme Knight, who ironically had been one of the members of the committee which had revised the insurance rates. Joseph C. Pelletier, Supreme Advocate, was the major defendant representing the Order. Mr. Justice Wheeler of the Supreme Court of Errors of Connecticut decided against the Order in its transference of the Mortuary Death Fund to the Death Benefit Fund, because the former fund was established solely for use during epidemics and its transfer was a violation of a trust. However, because the Order held the fund in trust for all its members, Wheeler concluded, "It does not follow that its contributors are entitled to its distribution, or to have it set apart for their ultimate benefit."[43] The separate fund for epidemics was therefore reconstituted and, during the influenza epidemic of 1918–19, was very useful in paying the increased death claims.

Starting in 1910, the Order offered an Economic Plan beginning at age sixty (later fifty-five). For a reduced premium a member could maintain a $1,000 policy until age sixty-one. Annual $50 reductions would then reduce the insurance to $250 at age seventy-five. Because of the Order's growth and its sound actuarial basis, several dividends were issued in the form of waivers of monthly premiums. Though the older members were enrolled in an extremely secure program, the Connecticut faction remained alienated from the leadership for many years. Terence O'Donnell, who wrote a comprehensive history of insurance, cited the Knights of Columbus as one of the earliest fraternal assessment societies to adopt a program grounded in the new actuarial science.[44] He also praised the Order's stability and concluded with the remark, "Few Third Degree exemplifications in any fraternity equal the psychological dynamite let loose upon the candidates at that phase of passage into the Knights of Columbus."[45]

To maintain that delicate balance between a vibrant fraternalism and a strong insurance program was the top priority of all administrations. Without a rich social, intellectual, and religious fraternal life to draw new members, the insurance program would suffer; without the economic strength derived from the insurance program, the fraternal expressions of charity and the society's promotion of Catholic culture and Catholic interests would suffer. The Hearn administration was the first to experience the need to maintain this delicate balance. As it was responding to the challenge to restructure the insurance program, Hearn's administration also established a new fraternal degree, the Fourth Degree, Patriotism.

III

The Fourth Degree was first considered in 1886 when the Order was in its infancy. Enthusiasm over the degree work led various councils to seek an additional one. Supreme Knight Mullen had even recommended that the Supreme Council consider establishing two degrees, which he referred to as commandery degrees. Because the Supreme Council of 1886 was immersed in establishing a new governance structure and insurance reforms, as well as electing a new Supreme Knight, the degree proposals were set aside for future action. However, a *Connecticut Catholic* editorial entitled "Knights of Columbus in Uniforms" indicated that at least one council had established a new degree program in 1886 without prior approval. "Our New Haven correspondent says 'the first regular meeting of the proposed uniformed legion will be held Monday evening, July 12.'" The editorial also quoted from an untitled New Haven newspaper which reported on the new uniformed degree:

The uniform of the Knights of Columbus [will consist] of a black Prince Albert coat, black trousers, black soft felt hat, with an ostrich feather encircling the crown, similar to that worn by Columbus as represented in his pictures, a reversible cape, black on one side and scarlet on the other, white cross and waist belt, sword and gauntlet. The officers of each commandery will consist of a commander, vice-commander, sub-commander, ensign, and first, second, third, fourth, and fifth orderlies. When five commanderies are established, a battalion will be formed.[46]

The editor of the *Connecticut Catholic,* who was a Knight in Hartford's Green Cross Council, was considerably disturbed by this report on the unconstitutional behavior of his New Haven confreres. After scolding the latter for presuming "to speak for others in the state not represented" in the decision to embark on a new degree, the editor indicated that he was opposed to a uniformed degree on democratic grounds. "A complete uniform, as proposed, could not be purchased for much less than $100. We hardly think that many would care to go to this extraordinary expense. . . . It is hardly the proper thing to set up *class distinction* in a benevolent association where charity and unity should dwell."[47]

The reluctance to pursue seriously additional ceremonials may be explained by the fact, as we have seen, that the Order had been criticized for its Masonic-like character by such members of the hierarchy as Bishop McQuaid of Rochester and had had to defend its ritualistic structure to Archbishop Corrigan of New York and Bishop McDonnell of Brooklyn. Though, as an organization, it was free from the direct authority of the Church, the Knights were very sensitive to the need for the general approval from members of the hierarchy.

Whatever apprehension over additional degrees might have existed prior to 1899, it does not appear to have had any impact upon Supreme Knight Edward Hearn. With the Order expanding westward across the Mississippi, Hearn, shortly after his election, urged a special committee to design a new degree immediately. Serving on the committee with Hearn was Daniel Colwell, National Secretary and one of the authors of the first three degrees; Charles A. Webber of Brooklyn, a National Director; John J. Delaney, first State Deputy of New York and a nationally recognized master of ceremonials; Right Reverend Joseph H. Conroy, Vicar-General and later appointed Bishop of the Diocese of Ogdensburg; Patrick T. McArdle, a National Director and one of the oustanding fraternalists of the Midwest. New York was also represented by John Hogan of Syracuse and William H. Bennett of Brooklyn. William S. McNary and William T. Cashman were the Boston members of the committee.[48] A subcommittee composed of Webber, Conroy, and Delaney was authorized actually to prepare the ceremonials while the full committee considered qualifications and organizational matters.[49] Since New York was the center of interest for a new degree, there was a strong preponderance of New Yorkers on the committee.[50]

The ceremonial for the new degree was approved in August of 1899. To qualify for the Fourth Degree one had to have been a member for three years and to have served the Order, the Church, and the community with distinction. The first exemplification of the new degree was on February 22, 1900. The Order had intended to use the Astor Hotel in New York, but with 1,100 Knights qualified to receive the degree, the Lenox Lyceum, "a large frame building erected to display a mammoth painting of the Civil War," was chosen for the gala occasion.[51] The following May 8, another 750 Knights received the Fourth Degree in Boston.

Fourth Degree districts were formed representing the distribution of membership: For example, seven districts were established in New York, five in Massachusetts, two in Connecticut, eight for the remaining states, and two for "the rest of the West." Each district was headed by a master who was appointed by the National Board of Directors. Until 1910, when there was a major restructuring of the organization, there were no Fourth Degree assemblies, nor was there a Supreme Master. Instead, Fourth Degree members, called Sir Knights, were lodged within local councils, and all district masters reported to the National Board. However, between 1900 and 1910, Sir Knights in various cities gradually adopted the custom of meeting separately to discuss ways in which they could pursue their own specialized activities.

The ceremonial for the Fourth Degree was orchestrated on the theme of Catholic citizenship. "Proud in the olden days was the boast; 'I am a Roman Catholic'; prouder yet today is the boast, 'I am an American citizen'; but the proudest boast of all times is ours to make, 'I am an American Catholic citizen.' " The lessons of Catholic citizenship entailed a lengthy litany of the Catholic contribution to America. "To Catholics, America can give thanks for her discovery, her exploration, her very name. They baptized this continent, our rivers, our lakes, our mountains, our valleys, and our hearthstones." After a long discourse on Christopher Columbus, whose "prophetic name," translated to "Christ-bearer Dove," symbolized the Catholic baptism of the New World, the candidates were introduced to other Catholic explorers: Amerigo Vespucci, Cabot, Verrazano, Cartier, LaSalle, DeSoto, Cadillac, Father Marquette, Balboa, and the missionaries who brought Christianity to the New World. The Catholic contribution also included the principle of religious toleration in Lord Baltimore's colony. "What he did in Maryland, the 'land of sanctuary,' Dongan, a Catholic governor, did in New York. The two oldest and grandest movements of religious toleration in the world are, therefore, to be credited to the sons of the Catholic Church." The Catholics of the revolutionary periods, such as John Carroll and John Barry, were also extolled as noble predecessors of the Sir Knights. The degree ceremonial also praised the "grand, staunch, fearless, patriotic prelates—Carroll, Hughes, Ireland, and Gibbons"—as illustrations of the

Church's "weighty influence in the crises of the nation."[52]

After listening to the lessons on the Catholic discovery, exploration, settlement, and evangelization of the nation, the candidates were reminded of "what our republic has done for the Church." In accord with Columbianism's strong affinity to the "Americanist" ideals of Archbishop Ireland, the ritual read: "Under laws of toleration and freedom she [the Catholic Church] has enjoyed a peace and progress, a prosperity and growth unequalled and beyond all expectation." Just as Catholics nobly shaped the past, so must they be aware of their duty to preserve "the virtue and permanence of our republic. If it is to endure in the future as in the past, the Catholic Church must be a potent and indispensable agent. Her sons, by the morality of their lives, their loyalty to the constitution and their conscientious performance of the duties of citizenship and, above all, by their steadfast adherence to Catholic principles, must strengthen the Church, stem the tide of irreligion, preserve the reign of God in the land, or see the republic perish." Because the Sir Knights "ought to be, must be, nay will be . . . the flower of Catholicity" they must be in the vanguard of Catholic-American citizenship.[53]

To place the spirit of the Fourth Degree within its proper perspective, one should recall specific trends within the Order, the Church, and American society at the turn of the century. We have noted that Columbianism, so impassionedly expressed by Thomas H. Cummings in the mid-nineties, was a Catholic fraternal spirit analogous to the Americanist ideals of Archbishop John Ireland. Both Cummings and Ireland identified America as a land where Catholicism and democratic freedom existed in a symbiotic way. In the relationship, Catholicism brought out the best in American freedom, and within American freedom Catholicism progressed to a higher stage in its development. Columbianism and Ireland's "Americanism" extolled the Catholic ideals infused into American culture as well as the American ideals infused into Catholicism. "The great theologians of the Church lay the foundation of political democracy which today attains its perfect form. They [the Knights of Columbus] stand for what is clean, moral, wholesome, and effective in American manhood when that is crowned with the teachings of Holy Mother Church, and as a result, they must achieve in time the social uplift of the entire American people."[54]

In early 1898, when the United States and Spain were on the brink of war, the major spokesmen for the Church, including Archbishop Ireland and Cardinal Gibbons, expressed "a very restrained and peaceful attitude."[55] However, once this easily avoidable (and clearly unjust) war began, Cardinal Gibbons stated the Church's position as in accord with the government's call to arms. The Order reflected the position of Cardinal Gibbons. State Deputy John F. Crowley of Maine reported to the 1899 State Convention that "while our people, as did the people of other faiths, differed as to the means of bringing about a satisfactory settlement of the trouble, still at the declaration of war all personal opinions as to the wisdom of such a course were forgotten, and the Catholic people, imbued with the teachings of our Holy Church, to be always ready to sacrifice everything for our Faith and Country, offered themselves by the hundreds to fight and, if need be, to die in defense of our Country's cause." Crowley implied that the K. of C. response to the war should be viewed as a strenuous "reply to the cheap agitators whose only principle is hatred to Catholics and who, although professing ardent love for America and American institutions, fly to the woods whenever danger threatens the flag they profess to love so much."[56] The Board of Directors approved the purchase of $100,000 in War Bonds, in the event that such bonds were issued. It also waived the armed forces disqualification for its insurance members who joined the armed services. Crowley proudly commented that "this . . . is the Order who a few months ago . . . [was] denounced by Catholic haters as non-American simply because it was Catholic."[57]

Dorothy Dohen, a sociologist, regards the spirit of anti-Catholicism as a factor within the atmosphere of the late 1890s, but she does not consider it to have been a mitigating factor in what she views as Gibbons's failure to lead the American Catholic Church in its prophetic mission to oppose an unjust war.[58] Unfortunately, her judgment is anachronistic. The model of the Church as prophet was almost entirely dormant in Europe during the nineteenth century. Ireland, Gibbons, and others broke from the European tradition by extolling the modern spirit of American liberty and thereby expressing a prophetic hope in American culture. Because they were misunderstood by American and European conservatives within the Church, who caricatured them as deviants from orthodoxy, Rome responded with a condemnation of Americanism. Though confident of the Church's future in America, Gibbons was particularly aware of both the anti-American attitude of many conservative Catholics and the widespread anti-Catholicism endemic to nineteenth-century America. Hence, one can admire his prudence in not opposing the war on the grounds that the Church was adjusting to American pluralism and was still a suspect minority institution. To accuse Gibbons of capitulating to the forces of nationalism is to judge him by standards other than his.

Catholic patriotism during the Spanish-American War derived from complex motivations, including the immigrant's drive to certify loyalty to one's adopted country and express gratitude for the enormous growth of Catholic culture in America. Hence, it was not excessive nationalism but rather a tempered patriotism. If it were an unreflective nationalism which motivated the Knights of Columbus to establish a Fourth Degree based upon patriotism, then in the postwar period one would expect the Knights to be uncritical of the nation's imperialistic ventures resulting from its victory in the Spanish-American War. In fact, the monthly magazine devoted to K. of C. interests severely criticized the U.S. government for failing to behave according to the "essentially Catholic concept respecting the natural right of all men [sic]."[59] The editor of *Columbiad,* D. P. Toomey, stated that because the United States "was imposing our civilization on Filipinos and Porto [sic] Ricans . . . it looks as if all the old national ideals have been discarded by our government, and that bloody conquest and greed of gain have taken their place in the national mind."[60] Though the *Columbiad* had maintained a strongly patriotic line over the years, this editorial clearly reveals that Catholic patriotism was not overcome by excessive nationalism. Toomey was so deeply opposed to imperialism (which may have derived from his antipathy to British imperialism in Ireland) that he saw American domination of Puerto Rico and the Philippines as "a curse to them if not to ourselves."[61]

According to Toomey, "Protestant nations who have acquired dominion over weaker races have exterminated the latter, or . . . the so called inferior race has been held in a state of vassalage and exploited in the commercial interests of the conqueror. . . . To all practical intents and purposes our republic is a Protestant nation, that is to say the dominant thought of its people, even of some who call themselves Catholics, is Protestant or Pagan, respecting so called inferior races. This has been exemplified by our treatment of Indians and Negroes."[62] Toomey linked the problems of imperialism abroad to industrial conflict and attacks upon the liberty of the Church at home. Though his immediate frame of reference may have been Protestant domination of Catholic Ireland, he contended that the "Church militant has always been and will always be engaged in a bitter contest with the powers of darkness."[63] Toomey's magazine was not the official organ of the Order, but it did become so several years later with Toomey as its editor. It is impossible to discern the extent to which his thought was representative of the Order. Yet he was and remained a leading spokesman for the Knights of Columbus, one who was patriotic, but who did not view American Catholicism as swept up in a frenzy of unreflective nationalism.

The emblem of the Fourth Degree symbolized the primary significance of Catholicism in Catholic-American citizenship. The uniform of the Fourth Degree was originally styled according to the formal wear of the day: top hat, Prince Albert coat, etc., with a red, white, and blue baldric upon which was pinned an emblem depicting the U.S. Constitution. Sir Knights wore a sword with a cross-handle grip signifying Christian Knighthood. From its foundation, the Fourth Degree provided honor guards for religious and civic ceremonies. To appreciate this uniformed degree fully, one must recall that before the age of radio and television, civic parades and religious processions played a much more important role in America's public life than they do today. For Catholics to wear their Catholicism literally on their sleeves evoked an experience analogous to that of the patriot witnessing the national flag ascending against a clear blue sky as a band played the national anthem. A later Supreme Knight, John McDevitt (1964–77), proudly recalled his father commenting that he experienced "goose bumps" when he marched in a Holy Name Society parade.[64]

IV

At the 1899 Supreme Council Convention, the Reverend Dr. Philip Garrigan, vice-rector of the Catholic University of America, addressed the delegates on a proposed K. of C. chair of American History at the university. Speaking on the day before Edward Hearn was elected Supreme Knight, Father Garrigan prefaced his remarks on the chair by noting the strong ties between the university and the Order. "The Keane Council, organized in honor of our late rector, formed its nucleus in the Catholic Univeristy."[65] Because he himself was a leader of the movement to establish Keane Council, he addressed the delegates as his Brother Knights.

Garrigan's plea for the K. of C. chair echoed the basic themes of Columbianism: that "we are attacked by anti-Catholic spokesmen on every side, partly because we have no historian among us." He noted the valuable contribution of John Gilmary Shea to the field of American Catholic Church history but lamented the fact that "he died a poor man with his work unfinished." Though he said that Protestant historians "do not mean to be unfair . . . they cannot take Catholic facts and analyze them and give the mainspring of the action and estimate fairly the character of the men. . . . We have to take, after all, Protestant history and call it Catholic history. We have become accustomed to it. It is the old story of England's lying about Ireland. She did it so systematically and persistently that we have come to accept it as truth and to repeat it, to our shame."[66]

Garrigan envisioned the occupant of the chair to be of such high stature that "the defamer of Catholic truth will be silenced" in his presence. He injected a note of competition into his appeal when he informed the delegates that the Ancient Order of Hibernians had presented the university with a check for $50,000 for a chair in Celtic Literature and Language.[67] With the vast majority of the K. of C. delegates of Irish descent but committed to the promotion of American-Catholic culture, Garrigan's comment on the A.O.H. chair must have had an impact.

At the 1894 A.O.H. convention, Father Thomas J. Shahan, former vicar general of the Hartford diocese and then professor at Catholic University, had successfully garnered support for the chair in Celtic studies.[68] Perhaps Garrigan was chosen as ambassador to the K. of C. not only because he was a Brother Knight but also because he was from the diocese of Springfield, Massachusetts, as was the rector, Monsignor Thomas J. Conaty. With four of the twenty-four professors from the archdiocese of Boston (and with three Massachusetts Knights elected to national office at the 1899 convention), Massachusetts had almost a vested interest in Catholic University. The leader of the New York delegation, National Director John Delaney, had proposed a chair in K. of C. American history for the Catholic Summer School at Cliff Haven in 1897 when Monsignor Conaty was its president.[69] With such strong religious, political, and personal ties of loyalty between the leaders of the largest delegations and the univeristy, it comes as no surprise that when John Delaney proposed a motion, which was followed by "spirited remarks" by twenty-two delegates, to establish a K. of C. chair of American History at the university, the convention enthusiastically responded to the appeal.[70]

The K. of C. commitment to Catholic University, with Cardinal Gibbons as its chancellor and prominent members of the hierarchy as its directors, signaled the realization of Phelan's dream. At the same time the Order was crossing the Mississippi River on its way to the West Coast, as it was grappling with the problems entailed in establishing a sound actuarial system for its insurance program, and as it was developing a ritual and organizational structure for the Fourth Degree, it assumed a task beyond that of serving its members. Supreme Knight

Hearn and the other national officers who so enthusiastically attached the Order to the cause of Catholic University manifested their implicit confidence that the membership would immediately contribute to the $50,000 fund drive. Perhaps the K. of C. leadership was unaware of the fact that it took over seven years for the A.O.H. to achieve the goal, or that the Catholic Total Abstinence Union never exceeded half its goal in funding a chair in honor of the Irish temperance leader, Father Theobald Mathew, O.F.M. Cap. (1790–1856).[71] Had Hearn known of these other societies' difficulties in funding a chair, he might not have been so sanguine that by 1901 the fund would reach its goal. Indeed, the indifferent response of the subordinate councils appears to illustrate the wide gap between the broad cultural vision of the national leaders and the relatively narrow perspective of the Knights of the local councils.

In his address to the National Council on March 5, 1901, Hearn lamented that only $10,000 had been contributed. "If we do not discharge this obligation in the very near future, the Order will not receive the praise it should merit from the accomplishment of so glorious a work."[72] One may recall that on January 1, 1902, the insurance rates rose considerably, which placed a heavy financial burden upon the older members. Finally, after five years and several pleas from Supreme Knight Hearn, the $50,000 goal was achieved, and at the presentation ceremonies on April 13, 1904, over ten thousand Knights and their families were in attendance, indicating a widespread pride in the Order's first response to a call from the American Church. Indeed, never before had the K. of C. been so honored by the American hierarchy. Present for the ceremonies were Cardinal Gibbons, Archbishops Ireland, Ryan, Keane, Glennon, Chapelle, Riordan, and Elder, and Bishops Spalding, Garrigan (the former vice-rector of C.U. who had first proposed the chair at the 1899 convention and subsequently became bishop of Sioux City), Horstmann, John S. Foley, Harkins, and Maes.[73] The Order's pride in establishing the chair was symbolized by the proportion of the check for $55,633.79, which measured ten feet in length and four feet in width. Monsignor Denis J. O'Connell, rector of Catholic University, opened the proceedings:

The University receives this endowment with gratitude, and pledges itself to administer with fidelity your sacred trust, remembering always to teach, in this capital of the nation, the history of that land which was discovered by Columbus, and which ever since has been so dearly loved and bravely defended by all those who, following in his wake, have come to these shores, bringing in their hearts the faith that animated the heart of Columbus.[74]

Supreme Knight Hearn viewed the K. of C. chair of American History in terms of the Order's role as a kind of Catholic anti-defamation league, noting that

the spirit of intolerance fostered by our New England Puritans is still rampant, and seems to seize particularly upon non-Catholic historians who find no room in their histories to laud the magnificent work done in the early days of the nation by the Catholic missionaries and the Catholic pioneers. Converging lines of evidence from many sides tend to prove that our histories are discriminating, and go far to justify our rejection of present histories, because of discrimination and incompleteness. These are the evils we seek to remedy by founding this Chair of American History. We have been apathetic too long, and our apathy long indulged has led almost to inertia.[75]

Cardinal Gibbons saw the K. of C. chair as a symbol of a united effort of the entire American Church which should dispel any suspicions that the Order was merely a social organization with no strong Catholic core.

Gentlemen of the Knights of Columbus, you do not possess royal titles, nor regal purses, but you have proved today that you possess royal hearts, and deserve the noble title which you bear. May you increase in numbers and in usefulness, and may you continue to merit in the future, as you have deserved in the past, the confidence and support of the prelates and clergy of the United States.[76]

John J. Delaney, the celebrated fraternalist from New York and a former National Director, evaluated the K. of C. chair as a sign of the Order's strong loyalty and devotion to the American Catholic Church. He responded to a noted scholar of the day, Goldwin Smith, who had concluded that the proliferation of fraternal societies symbolized the deterioration of religious faith and the growth of secular humanism, by saying that

whether it be in the work of reforming delinquents, or whether it be in the work of alleviating pain or remedying diseases, if that be the manifestation of benevolence, it is the manifestation of the spirit of Christ in modern society, and the greatest possible assurance that religion is increasing rather than decaying. Yet this man is one of the philosophers of history, and I have no doubt you dip into his books and permit your children to dip into his books, although Mr. Goldwin Smith turns and twists every fact against your religion.[77]

The first occupant of the chair was Dr. Charles H. McCarthy, who had received his training at the University of Pennsylvania and had been teaching American political and constitutional history at the

Catholic High School in Philadelphia. His candidacy for the appointment had been promoted by Thomas B. Lawler of Ginn & Company.[78] Since McCarthy had not published in the field of American Catholic history and since he was not a member of the Order, his appointment engendered a heated controversy. John G. Ewing, a history professor at the University of Notre Dame and the first State Deputy of Indiana, was considered by some the logical choice.[79] Martin I. J. Griffin, editor and publisher of the *American Catholic Historical Researches,* was particularly bitter at the appointment of McCarthy, saying that "the Catholic aspect of his mind has not been manifested"; Arthur Preuss, the conservative Catholic who was ever anxious to popularize criticism of the K. of C., quoted Griffin's remarks in his periodical, the *Review.*[80] Despite such attacks, McCarthy proved to be a worthy occupant of the chair. He frequently and vigorously challenged other scholars whose errors seemed to him to be derived from anti-Catholic prejudices. He also directed graduate students in researching Catholic topics; among his students was Matthew J. Walsh, C.S.C.,who later became professor of history at the University of Notre Dame and author of *The Political Status of Catholics in Colonial America.*[81]

Less than a year after the Knights had established their chair, Catholic University once again turned to the Order for help. Because of a severe financial situation caused by the failure of speculative investments made by the university's treasurer since 1885, Thomas E. Waggaman, prospects for meeting operating costs were dismal. Cardinal Gibbons, chancellor of the university, deeply distraught at the critical situation, appealed to friends among the hierarchy and laity.[82] On December 12, 1904, Cardinal Gibbons wrote a letter addressed to "Dear Sir Knights," in which he sought contributions from the Knights to "guarantee funds to help meet the deficit resulting from the Waggaman failure."[83] Referring to the Knights' "princely munificence" for endowing the chair which "signaled their devotion to Catholic University," the Cardinal was "emboldened to make a special appeal." He did not propose a specific goal; "any amount will be gratefully accepted, for I know that your bounty is limited only by your means."[84] State Deputy Thompson of Illinois devised a fund-raising effort which called for a series of lectures by prominent bishops, priests, and laymen, but Archbishop James E. Quigley of Chicago "advised against the prosecution of the plan, and the lecture feature was omitted."[85] However, Illinois Knights did collect $300 for the guarantee fund, while the entire Order contributed nearly $25,000.[86]

By 1907, the university had recovered almost 45 percent of the

Waggaman indebtedness, but the financial situation was still very grave. At a meeting of the trustees of the university, April 10, 1907, a committee was formed, chaired by Archbishop Glennon of St. Louis and charged with the responsibility of formulating procedures for collecting funds for a $500,000 endowment fund which, together with the recovered funds from the Waggaman indebtedness and the annual collection from the dioceses, would accrue enough interest to maintain solvency. The committee decided that the Knights of Columbus was the only organization which could manage the collection of so great a sum. On July 18, 1907, Archbishop Glennon directly appealed to the Order to establish a K. of C. $500,000 endowment fund. He prefaced his appeal by summarizing the financial condition of the university and concluded by noting that "it is known to the archbishops and has been frequently urged by representatives of your society that you always stand ready to work for the Church, and to do so intelligently and efficiently." However, he reminded them that "no object worthy enough, definite enough, and Catholic enough, has been laid before you." Glennon acknowledged the many local appeals placed before the Knights, but he urged them to "centralize your Catholic activities . . . and fuse the activities of your Society into one grand movement that would stand out at the head of all Catholic National and Charitable movements in the United States." He pointed out two further factors which would enhance the Order's prestige. This project would "give you the position your friends believe you are entitled to, namely the leading Catholic Society of the leading Catholic people of the United States." It would also provide the Order with "the strategic value [of] silencing criticism that appears here in America as unjust, and upbuilding your good name forever."[87]

Hearn expressed his gratitude for the honor bestowed upon the Order by this appeal from the "united hierarchy of America." However, he did not enthusiastically endorse the cause but rather left the matter to the "serious and careful thought of the delegates" and, if they felt "equal to the task," then "I am confident you will respond in the affirmative to this position."[88]

According to the Missouri State Deputy and National Director, John S. Leahy of St. Louis, Hearn's response to Archbishop Glennon's appeal was, at best, cool. Leahy recalled in a 1924 letter to another Past State Deputy of Missouri that while he was driving to the depot where he was to board a train for the 1907 convention in Norfolk, Virginia, he "noticed Archbishop Glennon sitting on his lawn at 3810 Lindell Boulevard, whereupon [he and his fellow delegates] stopped for a chat

with the archbishop." Glennon "stated that if he were invited to attend
the convention he would accept and present a . . . plan for the purpose
of paying off the deficit of the Catholic University." Leahy stated that
upon arrival at Norfolk he "presented this matter to the Board of
Directors and by a very close vote the motion to extend the invitation
to Archbishop Glennon carried."[89] The minutes of the Board of Directors meeting of August 5, 1907, verify Leahy's recollection, but since
there was no roll-call vote it is impossible to verify his further contention that Hearn voted against the motion.[90] Leahy was so suspicious
that Hearn would not send a telegram to the archbishop, as another
motion had mandated him to do, that Leahy decided to wire the archbishop himself. "Afterwards he [Glennon] stated that it was the only
telegram he received."[91]

On August 8, three days after Leahy had wired the St. Louis
prelate, "Brother Leahy of Missouri asked the privilege of the floor"[92]
to allow Archbishop Glennon to address the convention on the
$500,000 endowment fund for Catholic University. The text of his
speech was not reprinted; Hearn could have influenced the editor of
Columbiad not to print the address. Since Leahy was supporting the
election of John G. Ewing, State Deputy of Indiana, for Supreme Knight
in 1907, the matter may also have been entangled in a political conflict.

Upon the completion of Glennon's address, a resolution was submitted which called for the appropriation of $500,000 to be collected
by an increase of 35 cents over the usual January and July per-capita
dues for a five-year period. This resolution was immediately tabled.
The following day another resolution was defeated which would have
appropriated funds only if four fifths of the local councils voted in
favor of the proposal. Though charter restrictions precluded the
Order from any such levy, the National Council did accept, in principle, Catholic University's proposal, and Hearn was directed to appoint
a committee to establish ways of raising the necessary funds.[93]

Hearn appears to have been ambivalent toward the project. On
December 7, 1907, he wrote to the chancellor of the University, "Now,
my dear Cardinal Gibbons, let me say that there really is not the
enthusiasm for this work that perhaps one would expect." He then
protested—perhaps to excess—his own devotion to the cause: "My
energy, my enthusiasm is given to this project because of my affection
for yourself" and "every ounce of energy and power I have got" will
be directed to the success of a K. of C. endowment fund for Catholic
University. He explained the delay in appointing an endowment committee by the need to find qualified leaders to engender a strong

national movement on behalf of Catholic University. He mentioned three candidates: Festus J. Wade, St. Louis, Missouri; Thomas P. Fay, Long Branch, New Jersey; and Louis E. Sauter, Chicago, Illinois. However, because of New York's prominent place and large membership in the Order he hoped to find a New York Knight "who would arouse the enthusiasm of the membership." To emphasize that his commitment to the prelate was far greater than that to Catholic University, Hearn closed with the remark, "I want you to know that the source of all my courage and strength in this great task is born of the affection I entertain for you, and the desire I have to see this enterprise a monument to your labors in the Catholic Church."[94]

Cardinal Gibbons sent Hearn's letter to Archbishop Glennon, who was disappointed with Hearn's delay in appointing a committee. Though Glennon noted Hearn's "strong personal interest . . . his delay now makes it impossible to take advantage of the enthusiasm" generated at the National Convention. He related to Gibbons reports from "gossips . . . who state that Mr. H's delay . . . is due to advice received from the Archbishop of Boston and the Jesuit Fathers and that his great friendship for the measure in the beginning was based on the belief that it would never carry." Glennon advised Gibbons not to attach too much importance to the gossip, which originated from "sources in the Order hostile to Mr. H. (It appears as if many in the Order are opposed to him.)"[95]

In early January 1908, Hearn appointed the committee: Thomas P. Fay, chairman; Festus J. Wade; and Maurice Breen of Brooklyn, New York. Fay was in favor of a tax levy rather than further delay the project by polling individual councils, a strategy which ran counter to the consensus of the National Convention of 1907 as well as that of 1908. Hearn resolved the conflict in late 1908 by removing Fay and Breen from the committee and appointing Edward H. Doyle of Detroit and Philip A. Hart of Philadelphia. Later Wade resigned because of other commitments and was replaced by Joseph M. Byrne of Newark, New Jersey.[96]

In a November 1908 letter to Cardinal Gibbons, Hearn reported on the formation of the new committee and expressed his confidence in the "energy, intelligence, ability, and financial standing" of the new members and in the success of the entire project. He suggested that the next meeting of the committee be at the Cardinal's residence in Baltimore.[97] On December 5 and 6, 1908, the committee together with Cardinal Gibbons devised a plan for voluntary contributions to the endowment fund. The committee's actions were confirmed by the

Board of Directors in April 1909, and a letter was mailed to every Knight outlining the details of the plan. Each Knight was *voluntarily* assessed $1.00 per year for a five-year period, to be collected by the financial secretary of his council and transferred to the National Secretary to be deposited in a separate fund, "Knights of Columbus Catholic University Endowment Fund." For each $10,000 contributed, the Order was to receive a free perpetual scholarship for a full course of studies in pursuance of an M.A. or Ph.D., for which Knights and their families were granted a preference. In accord with the principles embedded in the K. of C. chair of American History, each graduate student was required to take a course in American history, and it was the hope that the Fellows would excel as teachers in Catholic and secular institutions of higher education. The Board of Directors indicated its enthusiasm for the project by a $25,000 subsidy to the committee for expenses in promoting the fund. At the 1909 National Council meeting, 830 councils with a total membership of 137,654 were committed to the fund, representing a pledge of $344,135.[98] By February 1910, the fund was enriched by an average of $17,000 per month, and on December 6, 1913, exactly five years from the day of the first meeting in Baltimore when Cardinal Gibbons, Hearn, and the committee had designed the fund-raising plan, the goal was reached.

The presentation ceremonies of the K. of C. endowment were hosted by Cardinal Gibbons at his residence in Baltimore on January 6, 1914.[99] James A. Flaherty, Supreme Knight since 1909, paid tribute to his predecessor, Edward Hearn—"that great leader of men"—and to the committee for their successful fund-raising efforts.[100] After the committee chairman, Edward H. Doyle, presented the securities, valued at $500,000, he stated that he hoped the Order would raise another $100,000 within the year to cover the cost of a dormitory to house the fifty K. of C. Fellows. Cardinal Gibbons compared the Knights' work on behalf of Catholic University to the "building of a great medieval Cathedral by the loyal and devoted merchant guilds of those faraway Catholic days."[101] Monsignor Thomas J. Shahan, rector of the University, congratulated the Order for having "founded a Knights of Columbus College" in the tradition of Robert Sorbonne, the thirteenth-century patron of the University of Paris.[102] Supreme Advocate Joseph Pelletier responded by congratulating Cardinal Gibbons, "the friend and protector of the Knights of Columbus."[103] The original intention of the endowment fund was to provide for the University's general operating cost. By the 1908 agreement between Cardinal Gibbons and the committee, later ratified by the boards of both institutions, interest from the fund was to be used for the fellowships. If the revenues of the fund exceeded the amount necessary for the K. of C. Fellowship program, C.U.A. could use the surplus for general expenses. According to the plan, when the securities representing the endowment were turned over to the university, a joint board representing both the K. of C. and C.U.A. administered the fund. By 1922, 146 K. of C. Fellowships had been awarded.[104]

The Order's drive to promote Catholic interests had achieved national momentum in its relationship with Catholic University. The American hierarchy had recognized its strength in numbers, organization, and commitment. When Father Garrigan approached the Knights in 1899 for a chair of American History, there were 40,267 members. By the time Cardinal Gibbons received the $500,000 Endowment Fund, the membership exceeded 300,000.

7

The Catholic
Anti-Defamation Projects

WHEN FATHER MICHAEL McGIVNEY and the founding Knights chose Christopher Columbus as the patron for their infant Order, they were, as noted earlier, tacitly asserting the legitimacy of the Catholic minority in American society. However, the spirit of Columbianism was not fully articulated until the Order spread into Boston, New York, and Philadelphia in the 1890s, where it encountered virulent anti-Catholicism ignited by militant organizations such as the American Protective Association. Previous chapters have quoted from the writings of Thomas H. Cummings, from the speeches of Supreme Knights Phelan and Hearn, and from the ceremonials of the four degrees in order to describe the essential features of the Order's unique spirit. Such phrases as "Catholic Gentlemen in Fraternity," "Catholic Citizenship," "The pursuit of Catholic interests," and "Catholic anti-defamation society" have been incorporated as thematic strands woven into the narrative to illustrate this Columbian consciousness.

This chapter is primarily concerned with internal and external events related to the evolution of the Order's character, and culminates in a discussion of its work as a "Catholic anti-defamation society." The foremost Jewish fraternal society, the B'nai B'rith, established its Anti-Defamation League (A.D.L.) in 1913,[1] even though the preamble to the constitution of the B'nai B'rith (1843) included as one of its objectives "alleviating the wants of the victims of persecution."[2] The Knights of Columbus established its Commission on Religious Prejudices in 1914, but, as with the B'nai B'rith, the struggle for religious freedom goes back to the society's origin. Unlike the founders of the Jewish fraternal society, Father McGivney's followers did not include this struggle as a specific objective. However, the B'nai B'rith and the K. of C. shared many characteristics. Each society offered an insurance feature to protect the widow and orphan; each was based on the principles of unity, charity, and patriotism; each developed a fraternal goal of absorbing immigrants of all nationalities who shared a common religious tradition; each society sought social legitimacy for all members of its faith.

The K. of C. Commission on Religious Prejudices was conceived in 1914, constituted in 1915, and terminated with the U.S. entrance into World War I. This commission represents a historic response to anti-Catholicism, a response which expressed itself in a variety of ways. For example, the establishment of the K. of C. chair of American History was motivated by a drive to combat the anti-Catholic prejudices and biases in school history books. The B'nai B'rith's A.D.L. had for its "original tentative name" the "National Caricature Committee."[3] The development of the K. of C. as a Catholic anti-defamation society entails its struggle against not only the anti-Catholic caricature but also the anti–K. of C. caricature which was promoted by Catholic as well as by anti-Catholic spokesmen.

As mentioned in Chapter 4, the most ardent Catholic anti–K. of C. exponent was Arthur Preuss, editor and publisher of the *Review,* later called the *Fortnightly Review.* His father, Arthur Preuss, Sr., was a well-known convert from Lutheranism and was editor of the German-American newspaper *Amerika.* A journalist and polemicist, the younger Preuss was allied with the conservatives in the "Americanist" controversy.[4] His anti–K. of C. animus derived in part from his antipathy to ritualistic fraternalism, which he saw as the symbol of materialistic and Masonic decadence. In 1901 he published a portion of the script for the Knights' First Degree entitled "An Extract from the Ritual of the Catholic Elks" in which the candidate was instructed on the importance of secrecy. His primary reason for publishing the ritual was to illustrate that it was "little more than a hodge-podge of Masonic apery diluted with religion."[5]

Preuss's first conflict with the Order occurred during the period when the conservative bishop of Belleville, Illinois, John Janssen, had refused to allow the formation of a K. of C. council within his diocese.[6] In a December 1900 letter to his clergy, Bishop Janssen explained that he was opposed to the "Catholic Knights of Columbus" solely because a new organization in his diocese "would be a detriment to the Catholic cause [and would tend] to split the Catholic forces still more."[7] However, the letter did not successfully obstruct the effort to form a new council in East St. Louis, Illinois. The Bishop responded with a letter, dated June 29, 1901, to all pastors in that city in which he reviewed his reason for opposing the K. of C., noted that a council was to be instituted on the following day (June 30, 1901) without episcopal sanction, and urged the pastors "to persuade their people not to join said organization."[8] On the day the contents of this letter were to be communicated at Sunday Mass, thirty-four candidates became members of East St. Louis Council No. 592.

The Belleville situation achieved notoriety as the first public episcopal ban of the K. of C. within the American Church, and both the bishop's action and the open violation of his ban stirred considerable controversy and misunderstanding. D. P. Toomey, editor of the *Columbiad*, reported that Bishop Janssen's ban allegedly stemmed from his view that the Order "came within the category of secret societies condemned by the Church." Toomey acknowledged the bishop's right to issue such a ban but was confident that when he became fully informed of the nature of the Order "he may see fit to revise his judgement."[9] Toomey juxtaposed the Janssen censure with the public approval of Archbishop Corrigan of New York. Corrigan admitted that at one time the Order was suspect, "that it was tending toward a forbidden society . . . that, however, is being gradually dispelled . . . you have the good will of the bishops and clergy throughout the country. . . . I trust you will continue to be of great service to the Catholic cause by being what you are, practical Catholic Knights of Columbus."[10] One may recall that Archbishop Corrigan's reservations about the orthodoxy of the Order prompted Supreme Knight Phelan to seek the Apostolic Delegate's approbation in 1895. Corrigan was a strong critic of Archbishop Ireland's "Americanist" tendencies, and this too endeared Corrigan to Arthur Preuss. Hence, when he heard of Corrigan's public endorsement of the K. of C. during the period of the Janssen controversy, he expressed great disappointment.[11]

Father John Walsh, chaplain of Troy, New York, Council No. 176, wrote a lengthy letter to the *Troy Press* which was later reprinted as a pamphlet entitled *Some Words Explanatory and Defensive of the Knights of Columbus Against a Recent Episcopal Censure.*[12] Father Walsh also viewed Janssen's action as based upon the general condemnation of secret societies by the Council of Baltimore (1884). Walsh concluded that "the Fathers of Baltimore would never dream of branding such a society with the papal ban. There is no oath of secrecy. . . . There is no offer of blind servitude to other cliques high or low. There is only devotion for and submission to papal authority."[13] Toomey was forced to retract the *Columbiad*'s suspicion of Janssen's opposition to the Order as a secret society when he received word of the bishop's expressed rationale, viz., Belleville already had too many Catholic organizations. He reprinted the bishop's June 29, 1901, letter and regretted that his Brother Knights in the Archdiocese of St. Louis, contiguous to the diocese of Belleville, did not "get at the facts . . . and report the same to the Supreme Council." Had the truth been known, "considerable anxiety would have been avoided and the daily press would have little to say on the matter."[14]

Though no new councils were formed in the Belleville diocese after East St. Louis Council had violated the bishop's ban, many Catholic men joined existing councils in East St. Louis and Alton, Illinois, and St. Louis, Missouri. By 1905 thirty-three men from the bishop's city of Belleville had become members of the Order. One such Belleville Knight wrote that these thirty-three Belleville Knights formed an organization known as the Pius Guards "who, by reason of a lack of friendship on the part of the Reverend Bishop, sailed under an assumed name so as not to give scandal by permitting people to believe that they were in existence contrary to the wishes of the Reverend Bishop, and in open hostility to him."[15] Ultimately the Pius Guards, i.e., Belleville Knights attached to councils outside the diocese, organized a committee which sought Bishop Janssen's approval to establish a K. of C. council in Belleville and other towns in the diocese. Though the bishop received the committee in a "most cordial, courteous, and respectful manner," he rejected its petition. The committee, "feeling that his Lordship was ill-advised concerning the Knights of Columbus," appealed to the Apostolic Delegate, Archbishop Diomede Falconio, who responded "that the establishment of councils of the Knights of Columbus in a diocese is left to the prudence and discretion of the Right Reverend Bishop." Since Falconio was in no way critical of the Order, the committee renewed its efforts to seek the bishop's approbation. On March 7, Bishop Janssen wrote the following letter of approval:

To whom it may concern:
In his letter of February 25th of this year, His Excellency, the Most Rev. Apostolic Delegate Archbishop Falconio, writes to us that the Knights of Columbus certainly made a mistake in not giving us their regulations and rituals in order to be sent to Rome for examination. He then continues: "I have seen them and have a copy of them in this Delegation. I told the Grand Knight that in the regulations, the law of the secret should be modified, etc., and they agreed to it." We have now concluded to tolerate the organization of councils of the Knights of Columbus in Belleville, East St. Louis, Cairo, and Murphysboro. It is understood that the rules of the Diocese applying to Catholic societies must be observed.
(*Signed*) John Janssen, Bishop of Belleville[16]

From this letter it is obvious that the real reason for the bishop's ban was in fact his suspicion of the secret character of the Order. On July 1, 1905, thirty-one members of the Pius Guards formed Belleville Council No. 1028. The vast majority of the charter members were of German descent. August Barthel, who was elected Grand Knight, wrote a brief historical sketch of the council, from which was derived the story of the evolution of the Pius Guards. In gratitude to Bishop Janssen, Belleville Council immediately initiated a fund-raising effort which netted $1,000 for St. John's Diocesan Orphanage.[17]

The charge of Masonry also haunted the Knights of Columbus. As early as 1899 the *New York Herald* noted the growth of the Knights of Columbus as a sign that "the future of Catholicism in America is Free Masonry." Because of the initiations, grip, password, and titled officers, the *Herald* was convinced of the K. of C.'s Masonic core.[18] The Order had confronted such slurs, based upon the bias of guilt by association, but this was the first such attack by a prominent newspaper of wide circulation. The *Catholic Transcript,* descendant of the *Connecticut Catholic* and the official newspaper of the Diocese of Hartford, referred to the charges of the *Herald* as "ridiculously spurious and utterly unworthy of a moment's serious attention."[19] However, because it was taken seriously in the West, where the Knights of Columbus were not well known, the *Transcript* did seriously attend to the charges by vigorously defending the Connecticut-based Order:

We, here in Connecticut, must deplore the spread of this senseless but damaging rumor. We are proud of the Knights of Columbus. They sprang from our soil. . . . They are true to their Mother Church and to their country, and being such their organization has appealed to the fraternal and religious instincts of the Catholic young men of the nation. We glory in the gigantic growth of the society whose humble beginnings were with us. We delight in honoring the memory of the zealous and far-seeing founder, and we are justly indignant of any attempt to cast suspicion upon a fraternity whose high aims and beneficent deeds entitle it to the approval of all serious Christian men. The Knights of Columbus enjoy ecclesiastical sanction. The clergy are with them. They are Catholic to the core. Herein is to be found the secret of their wondrous growth.[20]

The Order seems to have considered the charges of Masonry as unworthy of a serious consideration until the spring of 1904, when a Mason was actually discovered among the members. When Patrick Coughlin, Past Grand Knight of Rodrigo Council (1893–94) and a former mayor of Bridgeport, died in late March 1904, much to the shock of his brother Knights he received a Masonic funeral.[21] Father Thomas S. Duggan, editor of the *Catholic Transcript,* severely criticized the Order for harboring a Mason within its ranks. "But what is to be said of a Catholic organization which takes to its bosom and places in its seat of honor those who defy bishop and pontiff, laugh at the penalty of mere excommunication, and make friends with those whose ultimate aim is to overthrow and annihilate the religion of Christ? Does it require a prophet to foresee the final outcome of such a course?"[22] Since Duggan had defended the Order against those who criticized it for its Masonic-like character, his remarks constituted a serious warning that the K. of C. should remedy this situation or suffer the official censure of the hierarchy.

Arthur Preuss quoted portions of Duggan's editorial, and another Masonry–K. of C. editorial from the *Providence Visitor,* to substantiate further his contention that the Order should be listed as a forbidden secret society.

The Knights of Columbus is indeed a dangerous organization, and the sooner our Catholic editors see this and warn their readers against it, the better will it be for the cause of religion—the number of bishops who look with disfavor and alarm upon the spread of this society is continually increasing, and the time cannot be far off when the "Knights" will either be condemned by the Church or compelled to abolish the objectionable features and will collapse when forced to do away with them.[23]

At its April meeting, the Board of Directors voted to censure those officers and members of the council who were "responsible for permitting Patrick Coughlin to exercise the privileges of a member after knowledge of his affiliation with Masonry." The Board also voted to establish a committee to ascertain who was responsible for allowing Coughlin to remain a member and to investigate the entire matter of dual membership in the K. of C. and a prohibited fraternal society.[24] According to its board minutes, the committee never reported to the Directors, but there is evidence that when Coughlin's beneficiary was unable to collect on his insurance because Coughlin was in arrears on monthly payments, the beneficiary sued the K. of C. on the grounds that failure to pay monthly insurance premiums did not constitute the loss of membership, as it was a uniform practice among financial secretaries to pay the monthly premiums for those in arrears until they could afford to pay. On February 26, 1906, Judge Curtiss of the Connecticut Court of Common Pleas decided in favor of the Order. The common practice among financial secretaries does not "effect a waiver of compliance with its laws"; hence, Coughlin was disqualified as an insurance member. The *Columbiad* reported that Coughlin's Masonic affiliation had caused "quite a stir . . . in Knights of Columbus circles,"[25] but Preuss's prediction that the Coughlin scandal would lead to the bishops' proscription of the Order proved false. Instead, in April of 1904, just a few weeks after the scandal was disclosed, fourteen members of the hierarchy paid tribute to the Order's promotion of Catholic interests at the presentation of the chair of American History for Catholic University. In July of 1904, Cardinal Satolli, the former Apostolic Delegate, enthusiastically endorsed the Order: "I declare that henceforth I shall cherish a special regard for the Knights of Columbus, and I trust it may have a field growing wider with years and a future blessed with prosperity."[26] Even Archbishop Bruchési of Montreal, who had seriously doubted the orthodox character of the Order, lauded the Knights for their Catholic idealism at a 1906 banquet.[27]

By 1906 the Knights of Columbus were so deeply rooted in American Catholic culture that Preuss's barrage of criticism may have struck the leadership of the Order as harmless rhetoric. But while the strong institutional evolution of the Order tended to diminish the significance of the anti–K. of C. caricature among Catholic spokesmen, anti-Catholic groups viewed this same institutional strength as evidence of the increasingly dangerous power of the Roman Catholic Church in America. However, before tracing the story of this anti-Catholic animus, it is necessary first to chart the extent to which the Order had grown in stature and influence within the American Church itself.

II

The National Convention of June 1906, which convened in New Haven for the dedication of the Order's new national headquarters, was an extremely festive expression of the Knights' growing prominence. Downtown New Haven was extravagantly decorated for the occasion. The city's principal buildings were adorned with colorful displays, while the New Haven Green featured "a tri-colored canopy of seven thousand incandescent lights." Cardinal Gibbons was greeted by thousands, who lined the streets as a carriage carried the prelate to Yale's Woolsey Hall for an organ recital. Arthur T. Hadley, president of Yale, welcomed the Knights and their guest, noting that both Yale and the K. of C. were educational institutions. "You, in your turn . . . represent an educational institution, for does not such an organization as yours instill a regard for the rights of others, a regard for the law and for morality? I believe it is this responsibility of citizenship which gives us the pleasure tonight of the presence of His Eminence Cardinal Gibbons."[28] The Baltimore archbishop echoed the remarks of the president of Yale when he commended the Order as a combination of education, morality, and religion. And he added that its success was dependent upon a union of bishops, clergy, and Knights. Bishop Michael Tierney of the Hartford diocese lamented the absence of the founder, Father Michael McGivney, who "did not live to see the great results of his work in founding this Order."[29]

The new K. of C. national headquarters, located on Chapel Street at the southern edge of Yale's campus, was an impressive four-story building symbolic of the Order's maturity. Lyman Faxon, its architect, wrote that "the style of the building is modern French Renaissance, a form of treatment selected because it combines grace and dignity, is free of excessive . . . ornamentation, and meets the requirements as to future enlargement."[30] The cost of the new headquarters was $113,275, but the figure represented less than 10 percent of the Order's total assets. The financial growth of the Order between 1899 and 1906, nearly 700 percent, provided it with the treasury to lend money to dioceses and to wage such drives as the endowment fund for Catholic University.

The subordinate councils were also developing strong institutional roots. Florentine Council No. 304 of Poughkeepsie, New York, initiated in 1902 what became known as the "permanent-home" movement.[31] Florentine's home, called the Columbian Institute, was a large four-story building which housed the council chambers, auditorium, store, and office space for rental income. One floor was designated the club floor, with library, reading, and recreation rooms. The lodge floor, where the council chambers were located, was reserved for members and candidates.

The *Columbiad* enthusiastically endorsed the permanent-home movement. It viewed the K. of C. home as a Catholic alternative to the social clubs of non- and anti-Catholic organizations which were attracting Catholic youth. Because the appeal of these latter groups may result in "hundreds of cases of defection from the Church," the *Columbiad* urged the local councils to take the leadership in making a "determined effort to stop the leakage." It also urged the local Knights to view the home as a way of letting "down the barriers which so unfortunately prevent us from gathering together for our social and business benefit."[32] The *Columbiad* was confident that the K. of C. home would be a self-supporting social and intellectual center of Catholic culture, a "Catholic Y.M.C.A." The movement caught on and, by World War I, council homes were established in New Haven, Pittsburgh, St. Louis, St. Paul, San Francisco, Seattle, Toronto, Detroit, Memphis, Louisville, Galveston, Fort Wayne, and many other cities and towns in the United States and Canada. The K. of C. homes in Buffalo, New York, and St. Paul, Minnesota, were also hotels, which became models upon which other councils developed residential quarters attached to their homes.

In the late 1890s the chapter movement was initiated among subordinate councils in Long Island. On January 19, 1897, seven Brooklyn councils formed the Long Island Chapter. William Harper Bennett, then District Deputy in Brooklyn, conceived the idea of councils joining together to pursue projects which were too large for individual councils to undertake.[33] One such project was the establishment of a central K. of C. building for the use of many councils. When the Spanish-American War broke out, the Long Island Chapter also established social clubs for soldiers in three camps. It also founded a chapter Hospital-Bed Fund and sponsored retreats, lectures, and various other social and intellectual gatherings which were beyond the means of the subordinate councils.[34]

The K. of C. permanent-home and chapter movements, which had gained strong momentum by 1910, were very visible expressions of Columbianism's vitality. Knights throughout the United States, Canada, and Mexico were uniting in common social, intellectual, and charitable endeavors not solely for their own membership but for the entire Catholic community. In 1903 the Order raised nearly $5,000 for a Kansas Flood-Relief Fund from which grants and loans were disbursed to Catholic churches and K. of C. councils.[35] In response to the Catholic victims of the San Francisco earthquake of 1906, the Order collected over $100,000. By 1908 over half the funds allocated for the San Francisco victims had been paid back by the local K. of C. councils.[36] Building permanent homes, engaging in locally sponsored charities, and raising funds for Catholic University and for the victims of disasters illustrate the Order's strong financial base. Because the assets of the Order were almost entirely invested to protect the insurance program, the membership was the primary financial source of all these endeavors. Had the Order not contained many middle-class business and professional men, Columbianism would never have achieved such a strong institutional and charitable expression.

The *Columbiad* had long advocated the Order's affiliation with the American Federation of Catholic Societies, which was formed in 1901 to cement "the bonds of fraternal union among the Catholic laity and Catholic societies of the U.S. in order to promote Catholic intellectual, charitable, pious, educational, and social interests."[37] Like the K. of C., the Federation struggled against anti-Catholic discrimination and publicized Catholic contributions to American society. Established right after the Spanish-American War, when the religious problems of the Philippines clearly illustrated the need for a strong Catholic voice at the national level, the Federation attempted to foster Catholic lay leadership in social affairs.[38] The impact of the "Americanist" crisis precluded widespread support among the hierarchy, while the Federation's exclusion of the clergy was an obvious weakness. Hence, the Federation became, in fact, an organization with a weak central authority and strong local autonomy.[39] Many leading Knights urged their National Council to join with other societies in this common Catholic endeavor. After several resolutions to that effect had been introduced at annual meetings, the National Council finally established a commission to consider the merits of affiliation based upon a national poll of the subordinate councils. At the 1908 convention, the commission reported that the overwhelming sentiment was in opposition to affiliation, on the grounds that the K. of C. could best fulfill its goals by following a totally independent course. Though the commission had favored permitting local councils to affiliate, the delegates rejected the proposal.[40] The anti-Federation consensus within the Order seems to have derived from its fear that its unique spirit as a ritualistic fraternal society might be diminished, and from its realization that it had in fact little to gain by affiliating.

The institutional influence of the K. of C. was evidenced not only within the Catholic community but also American society in general. Largely through the lobbying efforts of the Order, the U.S. Congress passed a law which mandated the establishment of a Columbus Memorial in the nation's capital and appropriated $100,000 to cover construction costs. A commission was established composed of the secretaries of State and War, the chairmen of the House and Senate Committees on the Library of Congress, and the Supreme Knight of the Knights of Columbus. On June 8, 1912, the memorial, dominated by a large statue of Columbus, was unveiled. Though Edward Hearn had decided not to stand for reelection as Supreme Knight in 1909, he continued to serve on the commission and was in charge of the unveiling ceremonies. President William Howard Taft, accompanied by most of his cabinet, several Supreme Court justices, and many congressmen, was on hand for the occasion.[41] After Monsignor Thomas J. Shahan, rector of Catholic University, led the invocation, Victor J. Dowling, a former National Director of the K. of C. and a Justice of the New York Supreme Court, gave a brief address on the historical significance of the discoverer. Dowling's speech, like the Fourth Degree ritual through which he passed as a charter member, was another tribute to the Catholic contribution to the American heritage. "Here was no Alexander, sighing for new worlds to conquer, but here was the apostolic spirit for one who sighed for quicker ways to make known to distant lands the sweetness of Faith and the light of Hope. Here was one who, like Napoleon, believed in his star; but the star of Columbus was the star of Bethlehem."[42]

President Taft followed Dowling to the podium to laud the discoverer's courage and daring, noting how appropriate it was that the Columbus Memorial was situated across from Union Station, where visitors could view the symbol of the nation's origin in its capital city.[43] Shortly after the President's speech there was a parade. After 2,500 soldiers and sailors passed the reviewing stand "came the Knights of Columbus—the men who made possible this great demonstration. There were surely nineteen or twenty thousand of them in line— perhaps more—and from first to last they made a showing of which not only they themselves may be proud, but which must have been a source of pride and pleasure as well to every Catholic who viewed them."[44] That evening the K. of C. banquet marked the culmination of an important occasion for the Order. With twelve hundred in attendance, including Cardinal Gibbons, Champ Clark, Speaker of the House of Representatives, and several other prominent politicians, ambassadors, and clergymen, the banquet symbolized the Order's growing stature. A reporter of the *Washington Star* remarked that, "like the ceremonies of the unveiling itself [the banquet] marked anew the important position of the Knights of Columbus as an Order in the social fabric of the United States."[45] Past Supreme Knight Hearn declared, "Never in the history of the Nation's Capital, a city rich in memories of pomp and pagentry, has any civic demonstration equalled, in point of numbers, genteel appearance and orderly demeanor, the patriotic display made by the Knights of Columbus. The spectacle of over 20,000 men representing the flower and chivalry of Catholic manhood, marching in well ordered ranks through the streets of Washington, would thrill and gladden the heart of any Christian man."[46]

The K. of C. promotion of a national celebration of Columbus Day on October 12, which began in Colorado with the governor's proclamation of Columbus Day, had reached national proportions by 1912, with thirty states following Colorado's lead. Hearn's stress upon "genteel appearance and orderly demeanor" and patriotism illustrates the K. of C. drive to rescue the image of immigrant Catholics from the regnant caricature, which depicted them as unruly and even bestial. A national K. of C. lecture movement was also launched to dispel ignorance of the Catholic faith. Cedar Rapids (Iowa) Council No. 909 was one of the first to sponsor a series of lectures to inform non-Catholics of the beliefs of the Church. James J. Keane, bishop of Cheyenne, Wyoming, lectured to overflowing audiences in October 1908. Because Keane was a Minnesota priest consecrated bishop by Archbishop John Ireland, and was "Americanist" in spirit, he was an appropriate choice as a Catholic spokesman to a broadly ecumenical audience. The *Cedar Rapids Republican* complimented the Knights for their "lofty idea of brotherly love . . . Christian charity [and] for their gentlemanly way in which they undertook and carried out this work." The *Republican* also noted that Bishop Keane warmly appreciated the entire experience and "gratefully acknowledged the attention shown to him by the city and visiting clergy."[47] With over 85 percent non-Catholics in attendance for the lectures, Bishop Keane and the Cedar Rapids Knights were confident that the series had achieved its goal.

In February 1909, Bishop Keane presented a week-long series of lectures sponsored by Denver Council No. 539. The invitation to the lecture series clearly stated the council's intentions. "This is not intended as a controversial movement but is offered by the Knights of Columbus, a lay fraternal organization, as an intellectual and educational gift to the people of Denver, and with the spirit of fostering an era of good feelings among all religious bodies in the city." Bishop Keane expressed his "Americanist" nonpolemic spirit when he stated that "I have not come prepared to show any man that he is wrong, but to bring us all closer to God Almighty." The lecture topics substantiated this irenic intent: "The Reasonableness of the Belief in God," "What Manner of Creed Can Satisfy Man's Religious Wants?" "Jesus Christ, His Origin and Mission," "Christianity and the Pope," "Christianity and the Bible," "Why I Am a Catholic."[48] Bishop Keane's lectures were so popular that councils in Milwaukee, Buffalo, Houston, Los Angeles, and several other cities sponsored them. In his last speech as Supreme Knight, Edward Hearn enthusiastically praised Bishop Keane and the councils which had sponsored his lectures. "For this kind of work I believe our Order is especially equipped. The work of Catholic truth and Catholic education appeals particularly to the class of men that form the membership of the Knights of Columbus. To utilize the great resources of this Order in the cause of Catholic education, and to raise its mighty voice in the cause of Catholic truth, is especially its mission."[49]

In response to these sentiments of the retiring Supreme Knight, the National Council established a committee on Catholic Truth and commissioned James C. Monaghan, a professor of economics at the University of Wisconsin, to give lectures throughout the Order, open to members and friends and free of charge. "The subjects of his lectures include Catholic Truth, Educational, and Historical Matters."[50] Monaghan had joined the Order in Providence, Rhode Island, while he was a graduate student at Brown University. He had studied extensively in Germany, served in the diplomatic corps, and was a nationally recognized author. At the National Council meeting in August 1910, the Committee on the Good of the Order noted the "invaluable" lectures of Monaghan and urged the delegates to pursue strongly this and other Catholic efforts, such as distributing council subscriptions to the K. of C. edition of the *Catholic Encyclopedia* and cataloguing Catholic literature in public libraries.[51] Hearn later wrote of these educational undertakings. "Splendid results have attended the lectures so far delivered. They have led to a better understanding of the Catholic faith on the part of non-Catholics, and a more friendly attitude towards it; they have shown that bigotry is on the wane, and that the non-Catholic mind is open to conviction."[52] Hearn said this in the article on the Knights of Columbus in the *Catholic Encyclopedia*. The latter was incorporated into the Order's Catholic Truth program when in 1913 it subsidized a special K. of C. edition of the encyclopedia.

Hearn's confidence in the expansion of religious liberty and in the constriction of anti-Catholic prejudice was in accord with the generally optimistic mood of the nation during the first decade of the twentieth century. The American Protective Association, which had successfully promoted vicious anti-Catholicism in the early nineties, had gradually declined to political impotency by 1900. Internal conflicts, disillusionment with its simplistic identification of Catholicism as the source of all the nation's social and economic problems, and the abundance of Catholics in positions of prominence and respectability contributed to its demise. However, nativist groups continued as a social and political force but shifted their strategies from anti-Catholic nationalism to anti-immigrant restrictionism.

The most salient political force in the first decade of the century was Progressivism, a reform movement which attempted to broaden democracy and to rid the nation of political bosses, corporate trusts, and the dominance of privileged interests. Since the Order did not officially involve itself in political or social issues unless they touched upon Catholicism or fraternal insurance, it did not officially promote the specific reform agenda of the Progressives, such as the initiative, the referendum, and the recall, nor did the Order champion trust-busting or attacks upon privilege. However, the Knights did sponsor several lecturers who were sympathetic to the reform spirit. For example, on Columbus Day in 1906, fifty-two councils from the boroughs of Manhattan, the Bronx, and Richmond joined for a "grand patriotic demonstration" at Carnegie Hall.[53] The featured speaker was Senator Albert J. Beveridge, a prominent Progressive, who lectured the Knights on the patriotic roots of such reform principles as the government regulation of business and corporate accountability to the public.[54] Similarly, the official K. of C. lecturer, James C. Monaghan, frequently endorsed Progressive causes. In an article written for the *Columbiad* (December 1911), Monaghan lashed out at sweatshops: "If we are not only wise, but Knights, loyal to Cross and Flag, to Christ and Country, we will stand up in every big city of this country and call for active, energetic, earnest, honest men to enter the [anti-sweat-shops] cause. . . . Is life no more than the massed up money of Wall Street and the money centers of the large cities of our land?" His notion of social causation, though rhetorically overblown, was lodged in a view of the rise of Protestantism and capitalism later identified with Max Weber. "A time came when the greed for gold spread with the dangerous doctrines of Luther and the Protestant Reformation. This greed grew so strong that it crushed like an Indian Juggernaut all over the Protestant world. Relief is coming at last. The whole world is realizing that not by faith alone, but by good works, mankind shall, as it should, be saved." Though he severely criticized the ways in which the poor were exploited "as cheap labor furnished to Mammon worshippers," Monaghan was also critical of those who viewed American society as a "huge sink of falsehood and corruption. This is not true. Wonderful women and wonderful men are working and working hard to save society from itself."[55]

As an institution responsive to the social currents of the day, the K. of C. reflected the dominant trends of the early twentieth century. K. of C. councils had been traditionally social-welfare agencies for those in need. Councils, chapters, and institutes established unemployment bureaus for Catholic men and women, nonmembers as well as members. They were also dedicated to education, to relief for the poor and sick, and to a variety of charitable causes. Such a strong social emphasis predates the Progressive reform movement, but when the latter did gain momentum the Order's general character was in accord with much of its agenda. But it was definitely not in sympathy with those Progressives who advocated immigrant restriction or claimed the superiority of the Anglo-Saxon race. John Higham has remarked that "if some progressives were nativist, Progressivism was not."[56]

Many immigrant leaders struggled against the immigrant restrictionist movement. Indeed, it was during this period (1908) when Israel Zangwill wrote his play *The Melting Pot,* which "permanently attached a vivid symbol to the old assimilationist ideal of American society." The moral of Zangwill's melodrama was that "America . . . was God's fiery crucible, consuming the dross of Europe and fusing all of its warring peoples into 'the coming superman.' "[57] Another immigrant writer, Mary Antin, wrote in her autobiography, *The Promised Land,* of her total transformation from a Czarist Russian to an American.[58] The spirit of Columbianism, which was in general accord with the optimistic mood of the Progressive era, also extolled the melting-pot ideal of American nationality. One may recall the ideals expressed by Thomas H. Cummings, when he noted that "like the crew who sailed with Columbus on the first voyage, we [the K. of C.] have men of various races and languages. But by drawing close the bonds of brotherhood, we make for the best type of American citizenship."[59] However, because Cummings stressed the continuity of religious distinctions, he anticipated the sociologist's model of the triple melting pot. "For the best type of American is he who best exemplifies in his own life, that this is not a Protestant country, nor a Catholic country, nor a Hebrew country, any more than it is an Anglo-Saxon or a Latin country, but a country of all races and all creeds, with one great, broad unmolterable [sic] creed of fair play and equal rights for all."[60]

Columbianism also stressed the complementary relationship between the idea of natural law embedded in the American Constitution, which transcends ethnicity, and the universality of Catholicism, with its multinational diversity. I have already noted the transformationist theological tendency of both Americanist and K. of C. spokesmen, who viewed Catholicism and American democracy as dwelling in a complementary, almost symbiotic, relationship. Cummings referred to the Knights as representative of a "new type of Catholic manhood," as if the blend of Catholicism and American society made for a totally transformed believer. Columbianism was expressed in persistently optimistic and idealistic terms but, given the K. of C. consciousness of the ever-present threat from the forces of anti-Catholicism, Columbianism was also, of necessity, a rallying ground for the defense of the faith. The optimism of the Progressive era was countered by those groups which feared that the increased immigration from southern and eastern Europe (which totaled nearly seven million between 1897 and 1914) would ultimately result in the breakdown of "American" folkways. Anglo-Saxon nativism included anti-Semitism, widespread antagonism to Italian and Slavic peoples, a resurgence of racism in the South and North, and the growth of anti-Oriental sentiment in the West and Northwest, symbolized by the canard of the "Yellow Peril." This type of nativism was in the ascendant by 1907, when the new immigration reached its peak, and was expressed in secular, even scientific, terms. Primarily aimed at immigrant restriction, it was popular among urban middle and upper classes. It did not spill out as overt anti-Catholicism, because by this time these classes had developed a secular perspective through which to filter their anti-foreigner animus.[61]

The anti-Catholicism which emerged around 1910 was centered in small rural towns where traditional Protestant prejudices lingered. While the A.P.A. feared Catholicism as a menace to both liberty and capitalism (Catholic immigrants were equated with anarchists), the new religious xenophobia was popularized by those who felt that Progressive reforms had failed because of a grand papal conspiracy. John Higham suspected that the new anti-Catholic sentiment "came from a displacement or distortion of antimonopolistic sentiment. . . . It is hard to explain the rebirth of anti-Catholic ferment except as an outlet for expectations which Progressivism raised and then failed to fulfill."[62]

One such frustrated progressive, Wilbur Franklin Phelps, became one of the most impassioned spokesmen of the new anti-Catholicism, which he vented in his weekly newspaper, *The Menace.* Founded in the Ozark town of Aurora, Missouri, in 1911, *The Menace* waged incessant war on Catholicism. Because the Knights of Columbus had become such a strongly visible Catholic institution, the Order became a symbol of Rome's alleged menace to American political liberty and social reform. Thomas Watson, also a frustrated reformer, became, by 1910, a major figure in the new anti-Catholic campaign through the medium of *Watson's Magazine.* He too viewed the Knights of Columbus as a sort of a fifth column in the papal conspiracy to persecute heretics—i.e., all Protestants—and to abolish American liberty.[63] Another anti-Catholic force, the Guardians of Liberty, was garbed in respectability, founded as it was in 1911 by retired army and navy officers in northern New York. General Nelson A. Miles, who had been U.S. Chief of Staff, was the head Guardian. The Guardians' political strategy was to struggle against any political appointee or candidate "who owes superior temporal allegiance to any power above his obligation to . . . the United States."[64]

Though *The Menace* and *Watson's Magazine* were far more actively anti–K. of C. than the Guardians, it was this last group which first came to the notice of the Order. In an April 1912 editorial in the *Columbiad*, D. P. Toomey responded to news of the formation of the Guardians by referring to the group as composed of the "discarded rags of the foul A.P.A." Toomey reported that the Guardians considered the K. of C. as a "secret military Order," but he considered the group as "of little or no concern" and expressed his "sincere regret . . . that a brave and distinguished soldier should prominently appear as one of the sponsors of the new movement."[65]

III

The new wave of anti-Catholicism became a factor in the election campaign of 1912. Because the K. of C. had become such a strong force, symbolized by the Columbus statue-unveiling ceremonies in June of that year, the Order was portrayed as the advance guard of papal aggression. To certify the Order's role in this Roman conspiracy, a spurious Fourth Degree oath was circulated during the campaign by several anti-Catholic groups. The oath appears to have been invented by William C. Black, a lecturer for the Guardians of Liberty, who altered the three-centuries-old "Jesuit Oath of Secrecy" and the more recent "Priest's Oath" (both fabrications) to conform to the Knights' fraternal character.[66] Though it has often appeared in abbreviated form, the entire creation is cited here—grammatical errors and all—to illustrate the extent to which the K. of C. was vilified by its enemies:

I, ———— ————, now in the presence of Almighty God, the blessed Virgin Mary, the Blessed St. John the Baptist, the Holy Apostles, St. Peter and St. Paul, and all the saints, sacred host of Heaven, and to you, my Ghostly Father, the superior general of the Society of Jesus, founded by St. Ignatius Loyola, in the pontification of Paul the III, and continued to the present, do by the womb of the Virgin, the matrix of God, and the rod of Jesus Christ, declare and swear that His Holiness, the Pope, is Christ's vice-regent and is the true and only head of the Catholic or Universal Church throughout the earth, and that by virtue of the keys of binding and loosing given his Holiness by my Savior, Jesus Christ, he hath power to depose heretical kings, princes, States, Commonwealths, and Governments, and they may be safely destroyed. Therefore, to the utmost of my power I will defend this doctrine and His Holiness' right and custom against all usurpers of the heretical or Protestant authority whatever, especially the Lutheran Church of Germany, Holland, Denmark, Sweden, and Norway, and the now pretended authority and Churches of England and Scotland, and the branches of same now established in Ireland and on the Continent of America and elsewhere, and all adherents in regard that they may be usurped and heretical opposing the sacred Mother Church of Rome.

I do now denounce and disown any allegiance as due to any heretical king, prince, or State, named Protestant or Liberals, or obedience to any of their laws, magistrates, or officers.

I do further declare that the doctrine of the Churches of England and Scotland, of the Calvinists, Huguenots, and others of the name of Protestants or Masons, to be damnable, and they themselves to be damned who will not forsake the same.

I do further declare that I will help, assist, and advise all or any of His Holiness' agents, in any place where I should be, Switzerland, Germany, Holland, Ireland, or America, or in any other kingdom or territory I shall come to, and do my utmost to extirpate the heretical Protestant or Masonic doctrines and to destroy all their pretended powers, legal or otherwise.

I do further promise and declare that, notwithstanding that I am dispensed with to assume any religion, heretical for the propagation of the Mother Church's interest to keep secret and private all her agents' counsels from time to time, as they instruct me, and not divulge, directly or indirectly, by word, writing, or circumstances whatever, but to execute all that should be proposed, given in charge, or discovered unto me by you, my Ghostly Father, or any of this sacred order.

I do further promise and declare that I will have no opinion or will of my own or any mental reservation whatsoever, even as a corpse or cadaver (perinde ac cadaver), but will unhesitatingly obey each and every command that I may receive from my superiors in the militia of the Pope and of Jesus Christ.

That I will go to any part of the world whithersoever I may be sent, to the frozen regions of the North, to the jungles of India, to the centers of civilization of Europe, or to the wild haunts of the barbarous savages of America without murmuring or repining, and will be submissive in all things whatsoever is communicated to me.

I do further promise and declare that I will, when opportunity presents, make and wage relentless war, secretly and openly, against all heretics, Protestants, and Masons, as I am directed to do, to extirpate them from the face of the whole earth; and that I will spare neither age nor sex, or condition, and that I will hang, burn, waste, boil, flay, strangle, and bury alive these infamous heretics, rip up the stomachs and wombs of their women, and crush their infants' heads against the walls in order to annihilate their execrable race. That when the same cannot be done openly, I will secretly use the poisonous cup, the strangulation cord, the steel of the poniard, or the leaden bullet, regardless of the honor, rank, dignity, or authority of the persons, whatever may be their condition in life, either public or private, as I at any time may be directed to do so by any agents of the Pope or superior of the Brotherhood of the Holy Father of the Society of Jesus.

In confirmation of which I hereby dedicate my life, soul, and all corporal powers, and with the dagger which I now receive, I will subscribe my name written in my blood in testimony thereof; and should I prove false or weaken in my determination, may my brethren and fellow soldiers of the militia of the Pope cut off my hands and feet and my throat from ear to ear, my belly opened and sulphur burned therein with all the punishment that can be inflicted upon me on earth and my soul shall be tortured by demons in eternal hell forever.

That I will in voting always vote for a K. of C. in preference to a Protestant, especially a Mason, and that I will leave my party so to do; that if two Catholics are on the ticket I will satisfy myself which is the better supporter of Mother Church and vote accordingly.

That I will not deal with or employ a Protestant if in my power to deal with or employ a Catholic. That I will place Catholic girls in Protestant families that a weekly report may be made of the inner movements of the heretics.

That I will provide myself with arms and ammunition that I may be in readiness when the word is passed, or I am commanded to defend the Church either as an individual or with the militia of the Pope.

All of which, I, ———— ————, do swear by the blessed Trinity and blessed sacrament which I am now to receive to perform and on part [sic] to keep this, my oath.

In testimony hereof, take this most holy and blessed Sacrament of the Eucharist and witness the same further with my name written with the point of this dagger dipped in my own blood and seal in the face of this holy sacrament.[67]

The "bogus oath," as it became known, first surfaced on September 1, 1912, in Seattle, Washington, when a preacher at the First Methodist Church included it in his sermon.[68] The Seattle Knights responded by voluntarily submitting the actual Fourth Degree pledge to three prominent Protestants. In contrast to the bogus oath, the pledge is characterized by its patriotism and its deep but unostentatious loyalty to the Church:

"I swear to support the Constitution of the United States. I pledge myself, as a Catholic citizen and Knight of Columbus, to enlighten myself fully upon my duties as a citizen and to conscientiously perform such duties entirely in the interest of my country and regardless of all personal consequences. I pledge myself to do all in my power to preserve the integrity and purity of the ballot, and to promote reverence and respect for law and order. I promise to practice my religion openly and consistently, but without ostentation, and to so conduct myself in public affairs, and in the exercise of public virtue, as to reflect nothing but credit upon our Holy Church, to the end that she may flourish and our country prosper to the greater honor and glory of God.[69]

Seattle Protestant groups issued a public statement on October 12, 1912 (Columbus Day), in which they criticized the bogus oath as a "blasphemous and horrible travesty upon the real oath" and praised the actual pledge as indication of the "highest type of American citizenship."[70]

The bogus oath was the focal point for a contested congressional election in Philadelphia in which Eugene C. Bonniwell, the defeated Democratic candidate and a Fourth Degree Knight, accused Thomas C. Butler, his victorious opponent, of libel by circulating the bogus oath during the campaign. Though a congressional committee investigating the election concluded (on February 15, 1913) that Butler was not directly responsible for circulating the oath, it also reported, "This Committee cannot condemn too strongly the false and libelous article . . . the spurious Knights of Columbus oath."[71] Since the bogus oath was submitted as evidence, it was included in the *Congressional Record.* Subsequently, when anti-Catholic newspapers and pamphlets printed it, they quoted it from the *Congressional Record,* which ironically lent the oath an aura of authenticity.

The first criminal libel suit for the circulation of the bogus oath was initiated by Charles B. Dowds, a member of Brownson Council No. 993 of Philadelphia. Charles Megonegal, a printer, and Clarence H. Stage, a barber, were charged with "willfully and maliciously exposing the Knights of Columbus as a body and Charles B. Dowds; . . . James Flaherty, Supreme Knight; and Philip A. Hart, Master of the Fourth Degree to public hatred, contempt, and ridicule, to their great damage, disgrace, scandal, and infamy."[72] Megonegal stated that he had purchased a large number of copies of the oath from *The Menace* before he printed his copies.[73] *The Menace* responded to the Philadelphia case by defending Megonegal's right of free press, asserted its readiness to defend itself on "every utterance we have made about the Knights," including the oath, and threatened the Order with full publication of the K. of C. "complete ritual and secret work"[74] if it attempted to embroil *The Menace* in the Megonegal controversy. During the trial

(January 1914), Supreme Knight Flaherty explained the Order's reason in seeking a legal remedy for the circulation of the injurious oath:

This alleged oath is a tissue of falsehoods from the first word to the last— absolutely false. This prosecution was brought simply to vindicate the Knights of Columbus on account of wide circulation given to this vile and scurrilous circular, the purpose of which was to breed strife and to arouse religious bigotry. The alleged oath is absolutely baseless, and of such a flagrant character that it is indeed surprising that any one would give it the slightest credence. It was so persistently circulated that the Knights of Columbus were compelled to take some steps to refute it, and we thought criminal prosecution would be the best way.[75]

Megonegal pleaded guilty and Stage pleaded *nolo contendere* to the charges of criminal libel. The prosecution, apparently with the consent of Flaherty, Hart, and Dowds, agreed to a suspended sentence. The presiding judge, "a prominent Presbyterian layman in Philadelphia," stated that "my personal acquaintance with Mr. Flaherty . . . leads me to accept his statement without hesitation."[76] In a letter to Megonegal and Stage's attorney, the editor of *The Menace* advised him that "it would be folly for you to undertake to base your defense on the authenticity of this document [i.e., the bogus oath]." He admitted that "the alleged oath . . . was circulated in practically every state during the late campaign [1912] and the demand upon us for this document was something great . . . and while we have no apologies to make for doing so, we do not have any evidence that the oath is the one which is taken by the members of the Knights of Columbus."[77]

To illustrate the extent to which the oath was circulated, it reached St. John's, Newfoundland, where, in February 1913, another distributor of the oath was charged with criminal libel.[78] Charles O'Neill Conroy of St. John's Council was the complainant, Charles A. Swift the defendant. After listening to testimony by members of the K. of C., Swift admitted his guilt and made a lengthy apology for his "false representation."[79] Since Newfoundland Knights, Catholics of Irish extraction, were accustomed to strong expressions of anti-Catholicism from the dominant Anglo-Saxon Protestant class, this was a particularly rewarding case.

In the late summer of 1914, H. S. Turner, the editor of the *World Issue,* a socialist newspaper in Santa Cruz, California, was charged with criminal libel for publishing the bogus oath.[80] Knights from Santa Cruz Council No. 971, from Oakland and San Francisco, testified to its libelous character. After a preliminary hearing, the case went to the

Superior Court, where a jury found Turner guilty. The case was appealed to the District Court of Appeals, which upheld the lower court's verdict.[81] The significance of this particular case was that it demonstrated the prejudice of some socialists toward Catholicism. Because of deep misunderstanding of the bogus oath in California, particularly among the Masons, who felt that it was an anti-Masonic vow, the California State Deputy, Judge Paul J. McCormick of Los Angeles, submitted the ceremonials for the four K. of C. degrees to a committee of prominent Masons.[82] On October 9, 1914, the committee reported that the "alleged oath is scurrilous, wicked, and libelous and must be the invention of an impious and venomous mind."[83] It completely cleared the K. of C. of the charges that its ritual contained negative references to Masonry and Protestantism. "The ceremonial of the Order teaches a high and noble patriotism, instills a love of country, inculcates a reverence for law and order, . . . and holds up the Constitution of our country as the richest and most precious possession of a Knight of the Order."[84] On January 29, 1915, a California member of the U.S. House of Representatives and a thirty-third-degree Mason filed the Masonic report in the *Congressional Record* with the remark, "I esteem it a privilege to present this report . . . on a subject [the bogus oath] which has been grossly misrepresented and has caused religious bitterness and strife."[85]

On July 25, 1914, two Supreme Officers were witnesses for the prosecution in a Waterville, Minnesota, case. A. M. and G. E. Morrison were charged with criminal libel for having printed in their newspaper, the *Mankato Morning Journal,* the charge that E. M. Lawless,[86] editor of the *Waterville Sentinel,* had taken the bogus oath. Supreme Physician Edward Buckley of St. Paul, Minnesota, testified to the patriotic character of the Fourth Degree; Supreme Secretary William J. McGinley testified to the fact that there were no references to Protestants within any of the rituals of the Order and submitted the actual Fourth Degree pledge as evidence of the oath's fraudulent nature. The Morrisons were found guilty and sentenced to thirty days in jail, which, upon appeal, was changed to a $25 fine. According to Reverend Thomas Billing, pastor of the Methodist Episcopal Church of Waterville, Minnesota, and a member of the jury in the Morrison's case, the sensationalism surrounding the Waterville trial was "the result of an anti-Catholic spirit . . . stirred up by the advent of Annie Lowry, the pseudo nun, whose trail across the state is quite visible, and certainly not enviable. Such things exhibit the strange anomaly of a religion of love producing the keenest of haters."[87]

The Menace responded to the Order's public exposure of its Fourth Degree pledge with repeated sarcastic expressions of doubt as to the authenticity of the real pledge. As a way of expressing its hostility to the Order, it referred to the Knights as the "Nits," a slang word for lice. "The Nits and their patron saint are great discoverers and if the original Columbus discovered the new world it would be easy for his numerous Nits to discover a new oath when so badly needed." *The Menace* insisted that the anti-constitutional behavior of the Knights revealed their true papal colors. "We know that they are a secret military body; that their membership is restricted to subjects of the pope; that they are armed, drilled, uniformed, and commanded by good Catholics; and that as such they are licensed, and are to be rewarded, for the extirpation of heresies and heretics."[88] Hence, *The Menace,* with a 1914 circulation of nearly 1.5 million, continued to refer to the bogus oath as a verification of the papal conspiracy against American liberty and Protestantism.

The Order's response to the new wave of anti-Catholicism was influenced by European political and social movements which were infused with anti-Catholic hostility. In 1907 the National Council established a committee to investigate "the cause of the oppression of Catholic interests and confiscation of Church property in France and the anti-Catholic troubles in Italy." The committee, composed of Father Thomas P. Phelan, State Chaplain of New York, John M. Cleary of Kansas City Council, and James E. Reilly, a Past State Deputy of Rhode Island, reported its findings to the National Council meeting of 1908 in St. Louis, in which it concluded that "Free Masonry and Socialism were responsible for the state's seizure of Catholic institutions and property in France." The report warned American Catholics not to be duped by the French government's suppression of religious liberty on the grounds of furthering the separation of church and state. The committee distinguished between French and American Masonry by pointing out that, in France, Masonry was "anti-Christian and anti-religious," while in America "the Masonic Lodges are regarded as fraternal and social organizations." The report condemned "the devotees of socialism [who] have denounced the Church as 'the enemy of civil society' and 'the upholder of tyrannical government.' "[89] The delegates passed a resolution approving the committee's report, which mandated the *Columbiad* to wage a campaign to enlighten the membership to the dangers of such European movements and requested the committee to report to the 1909 convention in Mobile, Alabama, on ways in which the Order could most effectively respond to anti-Catholicism in Europe.[90] When the committee submitted its 1909 report, it appealed to the Order "to unite in supporting our Catholic schools, academies, and colleges." The Order was also advised to scrutinize legislative and philanthropic proposals to discern their impact upon Catholic education. Because education was the focal point for anti-Catholicism in Europe and for the attack by the A.P.A. in America, "the Knights of Columbus, as the flower of Catholic manhood, should be the leaders" of the American laity in safeguarding Catholic education.[91]

IV

Edward Hearn had decided to retire as Supreme Knight after presiding over the Order for ten years, during which time forty new jurisdictions were established, while membership increased from 42,267 to 226,289 and assets from $253,774 to $2,763,243. Still vigorous at age forty-five, Hearn turned his full attention to his business efforts as vice-president of a commercial insurance company. However, as the immediate Past Supreme Knight, he continued as a moral leader of the Order, symbolized by his work on behalf of the Columbus Memorial and the endowment fund for Catholic University.

While Hearn had met the challenges of expansion, the establishment of the Fourth Degree, the insurance reforms, and the appeals from Cardinal Gibbons and Catholic University, his successor, James A. Flaherty, was almost immediately confronted with a new wave of anti-Catholicism. As a former Deputy Supreme Knight, Flaherty was well aware of the problems which confronted the Church in Europe, and as a lawyer he was sensitive to the periodic outbursts of anti-Catholic hostility which had surfaced in his own city, Philadelphia. Indeed, Henry D. Warren, a Protestant bishop there, was listed as one of the honorary vice-presidents of the A.P.A. in 1896.[92]

James Flaherty was fifty-six years old when he was elected by unanimous vote at the 1909 National Convention in Mobile. Upon his arrival in Philadelphia after the convention, five thousand Knights jubilantly met his train. Such a show of loyalty by his Brother Knights illustrated the popularity of Flaherty's leadership. He had been elected first Grand Knight of Philadelphia Council No. 196 in 1896 and first State Deputy of Pennsylvania in 1897. The following year he had been elected to the National Board of Directors and in 1905 was elected Deputy Supreme Knight. He was extremely fond of Shakespeare and had been drawn to amateur acting in his youth, characteristics which were expressed in his skills as a K. of C. ceremonialist and as a powerful and eloquent speaker. Admitted to the Pennsylvania Bar in 1874, he was a well-established lawyer by the time he joined the Order in 1896, a year which also marked the last major election-campaign effort by the anti-Catholic A.P.A.[93] Though Catholics had achieved political prominence and social stature in Philadelphia by the turn of the century, even as late as 1908, during the dormant period of anti-Catholicism, resolutions of the Philadelphia conference of Baptist ministers included the statement that Catholics accept the separation of church and state and religious liberty "as a matter of necessity or expediency."[94]

I have already noted Flaherty's testimony in the Philadelphia criminal-libel case against Megonegal and Stage in February of 1913. In his 1913 New Year's greeting to his Brother Knights, Flaherty did not refer specifically to the bogus oath. However, he did note the rise of anti-Catholicism. "Only a few years ago we had reason to resent the unkindness, in some cases cowardly conduct, shown to our Church and its children. In the future we will have to fight the enemies of our Church in connection with great questions touching taxation, education, divorce, and socialism. We will be fair, always fair, and our enemies will find us in the open. . . . The future is to be ours but, as counsellor, I can give no better advice, to every council in our Order, than is conveyed by the word 'Prepare.' "[95] Though Flaherty did not elaborate on the anti-Catholic aspect of socialism, the editor of the *Columbiad,* D. P. Toomey, lashed out at that "foul socialist publication, *The Menace,* " in the same issue in which Flaherty's article appeared.[96] The *Catholic Columbian,* a K. of C. publication of Columbus, Ohio, also linked *The Menace* to socialism: "Seeing that the Catholic Church is the greatest obstacle to the success of materialistic and anti-Christian Socialism, socialists have started *The Menace* to destroy the Catholic Church. *The Menace* is simply the tool of socialism."[97]

American socialism, stimulated by the reform consciousness of the Progressive movement, had gained national momentum by 1912, when Eugene V. Debs stood as the Socialist Party candidate for the presidency. Since *Watson's Magazine* and *The Menace*'s anti-Catholicism appear to have represented expressions of the excessive frustration of the left-wing element of the Progressive reformers, since many varieties of socialist ideology contained strong antireligious, particularly anti-Catholic sentiment, and since the K. of C. had vigorously opposed the socialist attacks upon the Church in France and Italy, the Order viewed the bogus oath and other manifestations of anti-Catholicism, including the socialist brand, as requiring a vigorous response. Thus articles on the evils of socialism, as a manifestation of anti-Catholicism, appeared frequently in the pages of the *Columbiad*. One such article, "How to Successfully Combat Socialism," pointed out that the founder of *The Menace* was the former editor of the Socialist journal *The Appeal to Reason*. The author, Edwin A. Daly, elaborated on the nationwide Socialist propaganda network and urged the Order to consider sponsoring an anti-Socialist lecture movement to accord with the strong anti-socialism resolutions passed by the 1913 Supreme Convention. (The title "Supreme" was revived in 1912.) Daly praised the lecture efforts of David Goldstein, a member of Mt. Pleasant Council in Boston and Secretary of the Boston School of Political Economy: "Mr. Goldstein is the first layman to give his whole time to the public work of defending Christianity versus Socialism. . . . Mr. Goldstein's success has been phenomenal."[98]

Born of a Jewish working-class family, Goldstein became a prominent member of the Socialist Labor Party in the late 1890s. However, he was soon disillusioned with socialism and took up the cause of trade unionism and became a leader in Samuel Gompers's American Federation of Labor. First influenced by Pope Leo XIII's encyclical *Rerum Novarum*, which denounced both atheistic socialism and laissez-faire capitalism, and later by experiences with Catholic friends, Goldstein began to study the teachings of the Church and was baptized on May 21, 1905.[99] In 1911–12, Goldstein was commissioned by the German-American Catholic organization, the Central Verein, to lecture on the evils of socialism and the Christian virtues embodied in *Rerum Novarum*.[100]

In January 1914, the Supreme Board of Directors commissioned Goldstein and Peter W. Collins, a member of Newton Council No. 167 and general secretary of the Brotherhood of Electrical Workers, as K. of C. lecturers to present the Catholic views on social issues in general and socialism in particular.[101] With the Order paying the lecturers' salaries, subordinate councils were instructed to open the lectures to the public free of charge. Goldstein's and Collins's itineraries were soon completed. Collins limited himself almost entirely to the South and Southeast, while Goldstein's travels included the major cities and towns of the Midwest and Northwest and northwestern Canada. John Reddin, who had successfully garnered support for this campaign at the 1913 Supreme Convention, viewed the lecture series within the spirit of Columbianism. Reddin prefaced his remarks on the series with an elaborate commentary on the character of the Order in light of the attacks by its enemies.

Some good people, honest people—but dupes, nevertheless of designing, wicked, and bigoted men—believe that the Knights of Columbus have grown up in a night to tear down the great structure of American liberty which we and our forebears helped to erect. They are builders, these Knights of Columbus—not wreckers—builders of education—builders of those things that make for honesty and morality in public and private places.[102]

After introducing his readers to the cosmopolitan character of the Order, characterized by its multi-ethnic composition, Reddin wrote:

This free lecture movement is a gift of the Knights of Columbus to the American people. It is to be a nationwide education campaign. No other social body —no organization, no government, no church even—ever attempted a work of such magnitude. . . . Socialism is the present day peril of America. It must be met with the weapons of Catholic truth in the one hand and education in the other.[103]

David Goldstein visited Denver, John Reddin's home city, in the spring of 1914. He later recalled that "the anti-Catholic spirit was intense." Immediately prior to his arrival, Otis L. Spurgeon, "an anti-Romanist agitator connected with *The Menace,*" had been kidnapped, miserably beaten, and abandoned in a desolate place outside Denver. "This incident added considerable interest to my coming," wrote Goldstein. After he had addressed a large gathering of about three thousand, "one third socialist," Goldstein opened himself to questions from the audience.

The Socialists could not wait for the Query Period; they shot out the query, "Who mobbed Spurgeon last Saturday night?" Knowing the question would arise, I was prepared to shoot back at once, "Some lawless citizens of Denver!" Yet, let me say to you that very little sympathy is due a man who deliberately assaults the integrity and morality of God's holiest men and women, the priests and sisters. I believe such a man deserves a thrashing. Still no private citizens have any right to kidnap and mob a man, no matter what his opinions or expressions of opinion may be. . . . I believe Rev. Spurgeon ought to have been arrested and put in jail. But remember this—the Order of the Knights of Columbus is a law abiding and liberty loving body of American citizens, and it, therefore, repudiates the action of the men who assaulted Spurgeon.[104]

Since both the K. of C. and the Socialists gave advance notices of Goldstein's tour, large audiences attended his lectures throughout the United States and Canada. Anti-Catholic agitators, Socialist and non-

Socialist, heckled him ceaselessly. On one occasion the anti-Catholic abuse was so venomous that a Socialist came to Goldstein's defense.[105]

Collins does not appear to have been as flamboyant as his colleague on the lecture circuit. However, as a well-known figure in the trade-union movement, his talks were well received. Goldstein tended to be theoretical and drew upon his experience as a Socialist while Collins stressed his practical experience. Both were advocates of social reform and sought to dispel ignorance and to enlighten non-Catholics on the Church's teachings, particularly her social doctrine and its compatibility with American ideals. Columbianism was never more forcefully represented than in this lecture tour. The *Columbiad* proudly reported on the large enthusiastic audiences, the tour's progress in spreading Catholic truth, and the lecturers' many victories over Socialist and anti-Catholic opponents. Thus, it noted after Collins's lecture in Fort Worth, Texas, that "a Methodist gentleman . . . said, 'We have been holding missionary meetings in this very auditorium, yet I have never heard a stronger plea in the cause of God and country than the lecturer made this evening.' " Collins achieved such fame that Eugene V. Debs, the Socialist Party candidate for president in 1912 who polled over one million votes, accused Collins of "following him throughout the country."[106]

Supreme Knight Flaherty reported to the delegates to the 1914 Supreme Council in St. Paul, Minnesota, that the Goldstein-Collins lecture series, "our latest effort for God and Country . . . has been a most unprecedented success, and must certainly bring its full share of glory to the Order as it will bring its benefit to the country."[107] By this time Collins and Goldstein had delivered 148 lectures, traveled 27,000 miles, and addressed 200,000 people, "perhaps a majority of whom were non-Catholic." As chairman of the Committee on the Good of the Order, William Mulligan of Connecticut strongly endorsed the lecture series and called for its continuation as a fine illustration of the Order's constructive, rather than defensively negative, program of "enlightenment." "The law of Christian charity contains no behest which commands us to sit supinely still while unfriendly men attempt to despoil us of our cherished treasures." As in his 1913 report, Mulligan warned the delegates to be cautious as to the choice of means employed in defending the faith. He reminded them that the lay status of the Order prevented it from organizing an independent K. of C. "evangelizing body, as do laymen in other communions." Instead, the Knights "must wait upon the invitation of competent ecclesiastical authorities before we launch forth on any spiritual conquest." The committee also warned that unreflective protest against anti-Catholic journalists and spokesmen might prove damaging. "Constant complaint may cause irritation, whereas the evidence of our sincere desire to be known as we are must inevitably, though perhaps slowly, win over fairminded people. . . . In other words, true to the spirit of our Order we must be less censorious than optimistic; less bent on cultivating a belligerent manner than peacefully aggressive in spreading the truth; less prone to answer every unspeakable taunt that vile creatures hurl against our name than anxious to show forth to the really honorable men of the world what we actually stand for."[108] Hence, the committee advocated the Order's support for relatively moderate means of constructive enlightenment, such as the lecture series, educational initiatives, and the Catholic press.

Patrick Henry Callahan, State Deputy of Kentucky, submitted a resolution on the Good of the Order which was in the spirit of the committee's report but one which called for an innovative measure in the K. of C. war against anti-Catholic hostility:

RESOLVED, That the Board of Directors be authorized to expend a sum not exceeding Fifty Thousand Dollars to study the causes, investigate conditions, and suggest remedies for the religious prejudice that has been manifest through press and rostrum in a malicious and scurrilous campaign that is hostile to the spirit of American freedom and liberty and contrary to God's law of "Love Thy Neighbor as Thyself," and that the Supreme Knight shall be authorized to appoint a Commission to be known as the Commission on Religious Prejudices, consisting of five members of the Order to conduct such investigation under the direction of the Board of Directors.[109]

Callahan had submitted a resolution following Mulligan's committee report, but it was tabled. The above resolution, submitted on the following day, seems to have been discussed outside the convention, because it specified a $50,000 limit and was almost immediately passed with the approval of Mulligan's committee and without opposition from the Supreme Officers. Callahan later recalled how a Congregational minister, Dr. Washington Gladden, had inspired him to develop the Commission idea: "It was the thought contained in the 'Anti-Papal Panic,' that all classes do their utmost for peace and harmony, and the example of Dr. Gladden that gave me the inspiration to suggest to the St. Paul Convention, August 1914, the idea that developed into our Commission on Religious Prejudices."[110]

Dr. Gladden's article, "Anti-Papal Panic," had appeared in *Harper's* and was reprinted in *Columbiad.* Gladden, who had severely criticized the A.P.A., lashed out at the revival of anti-Catholicism and urged Protestants and Catholics to seek mutual understanding.[111] Later referred to as the "Father of the American Social Gospel," he was in the forefront of the Protestant movement aimed at achieving social reforms according to scriptural directives and in tandem with secular progressive movements.[112] P. H. Callahan's social thought was also infused with a reform spirit. Influenced by *Rerum Novarum*'s insistence on the workingman's right to a living wage and by Father John A. Ryan's vigorous pursuit of that ideal, Callahan, president of the Louisville Varnish Company, initiated in 1912 a profit-sharing scheme for his workers which he called the "Ryan-Callahan Plan." According to this plan, profits and losses were divided equally between employees and stockholders.[113]

Callahan was State Deputy of Kentucky when Flaherty appointed him chairman of the Commission on Religious Prejudices in the fall of 1914. The other appointments were determined by the criteria of regional representation, prominence in the Order, and stature in the community: Joseph Scott, Past State Deputy and president of the Los Angeles Board of Education; Albert G. Bagley, State Deputy of British Columbia and president of the Vancouver Board of Trade; Thomas Lawler, State Deputy of Michigan and former state assistant attorney general; Joseph C. Pelletier, Supreme Advocate 1907–1922 and district attorney of Suffolk County (i.e., Boston). Benedict Elder, lawyer, journalist and a close friend of Callahan, was the chairman's administrative assistant.[114] Callahan's commitment to labor-capital reconciliation was in accord with the spirit of the resolution establishing the commission: "American Freedom and Liberty . . . [and] God's Law of 'Love Thy Neighbor as Thyself.' "[115] Later it affirmed, "The fundamental governing our Commission is that tolerance begets tolerance, whereas 'intolerance begets intolerance.' " It also noted that some of the members of the K. of C. were prejudiced against Protestants. "We have members who think there is no prejudice on our part, but this is not so. We must cultivate the gift, as the Scot [Robert Burns] put it, 'to see ourselves as others see us.' "[116]

Though the members were appointed in October, the Commission on Religious Prejudices did not formally meet until January 1915. At this New York meeting, it decided: (1) to investigate the sources of religious prejudice by researching newspapers, periodicals, and lectures, and by polling the membership for information on anti-Catholic manifestations; (2) to conduct an education campaign by informing and correcting editors and journalists who allowed religious prejudice to surface in their newspapers and by seeking the "cooperation of all fair-minded citizens showing that the Catholic, as a citizen, is the equal of any other"; (3) to support the Department of Justice in its criminal libel prosecution against "bigoted publications" and to urge the Postmaster General to ban such publications.[117] Though the Canadian government had banned *The Menace* from its mail service in April 1914, the U.S. Postmaster, rather than proscribing it, deferred to the Justice Department to prosecute *The Menace*.[118] After its March 1915 meeting, the commission published the results of its investigation on the causes of religious prejudice, locating it within three groups:

> First—Those who fail to appreciate the constitutional provision regarding freedom of religious worship or to understand the belief of those professing a religion other than their own.
> Second—Those whose purpose is to destroy not only the Catholic religion but all religion and all duly constituted government.
> Third—Perhaps the worst class comprises those who, despite their expressed motives of high purpose, are actuated solely by sordid mercenary considerations.[119]

At this March meeting the commission met with a representative of the Associated Press. Callahan and Melville E. Stone, general manager of the Associated Press, had been corresponding with one another over the Order's strong feeling that the A.P. was anti-Catholic because it had failed to report the successful criminal-libel suits related to the bogus oath. Stone sent Edgar E. Cutter to the commission meeting in Chicago, which "was very satisfactory," as the commissioners were convinced of the "good intention of the Associated Press."[120] Cutter assured the commission that a K. of C. or other Catholic news release would be considered solely on news value "without reference to its religious bearing."[121] By the summer of 1915, the commissioners were convinced that the "press had been generally fair. From editorial expressions and news items coming from every part of the country, it seems that the object of the Commission, its policy and its work, are endorsed by practically every newspaper of note." However, they noted that "only a few" of the periodicals were concerned with the K. of C. "movement to eliminate religious prejudice." Among those listed as sympathetic to the movement were *The Century, North American Review, Literary Digest,* and *Harper's*.[122] By the end of its first year, the commission had successfully recruited several Protestant clergymen: Washington Gladden (Congregational), J. Faville (Congregational), W. M. Walker (Baptist), Eugene Rodman (Unitarian), D. M. Milner

(Presbyterian), and George A. Cartenson (Episcopalian).[123] Besides listing its friends among the press and among the Protestant clergy, the commission published a list of all anti-Catholic newspapers and societies.

During Callahan's first year as chairman he wrote hundreds of letters on Catholic support of public education, on Catholic independence of the pope in civil matters, and on religious prejudice and discrimination as violations of constitutional freedom and of the Protestant heritage. Together with his assistant, Benedict Elder, he wrote to editors of all anti-Catholic newspapers and leaders of anti-Catholic societies, answering their attacks with clarity and dignity. Civility, candor, and toleration thus became the commission's major weapons against anti-Catholicism. "If a kindly personal letter to thousands, bespeaking justice and fair play and informing them in Catholic teaching on matters that excite prejudice, can be counted on as something done, if fair and honest answers make this a worthy accomplishment in the breaking down of prejudice—then has this much been effected."[124]

The commission submitted seven recommendations to the Supreme Council of 1915. The first two were aimed at errors about Catholic loyalty and about the Church's attitude toward public schools; it urged the Order to strive to enlighten public opinion on the civil allegiance of Catholics and on the fact that the Church had no design to hinder or control public education.[125] Noting how social problems engender the growth of prejudice, the commission urged the Knights to become aware of social issues and to join forces with those of "all other creeds and stand as a body for the betterment of public morals, the furtherance of social justice, and the very best in citizenship."[126] It also strongly endorsed the Catholic press, especially *Our Sunday Visitor,* as an educational medium not only for Catholics but for non-Catholics as well.[127] In regard to the general press, it recommended that at least one member of every council be responsible for submitting articles "setting forth the position of Catholics on matters of interest to the public." The commission also endorsed lectures "calculated to neutralize the activity of the bigots who stir up enmity and hate among men of different faiths."[128] Lastly, it recommended that the commission be continued under its 1914 mandate but with its budget reduced from $50,000 to $20,000.[129]

In his report to the 1915 Supreme Convention, Supreme Knight Flaherty congratulated the commission for its successful efforts in countering prejudice with Catholic truth. He was particularly proud of its spirit of civility and fair play. "The day of polemics and controversy is, generally speaking, over and gone, and the old methods of encounter and attack have given way to what might be called a meeting under truce for the simple exposition of Catholic doctrine."[130] With the Supreme Council's confirmation of its 1915 report, the commission entered its second year. To further incorporate local councils in its efforts, it undertook a survey of the 1,800 subordinate councils to ascertain the ways in which local councils were attempting to improve their members and the general welfare of their communities, "both of which will go far in the way of producing more friendly relations between Catholics and non-Catholics."[131] The lecture series was strengthened by the addition of Joseph Scott of Los Angeles, who toured sections of the country twice during 1916. In his speeches Scott emphasized Catholic loyalty and love of America, and the hope and trust that all Americans would respect religious liberty. At the conclusion of one tour he stated, "I think we cannot be too emphatic in applauding the cooperation of our non-Catholic citizens in the cordiality of their response to the invitation of the local committees to attend these lectures."[132]

Among the pamphlets distributed by the commission, the most popular was *A Message to All Patriotic Citizens,* a compilation of "eloquent tributes to the Catholic Church, spoken by members of the great body of non-Catholic ministers and public men who are fair minded toward her and her teachings and her people." During the first seven months of 1916, over 500,000 copies of *A Message* were distributed. Besides quotes from the sermons and writings of over twenty Protestant clergymen, the pamphlet included an explanation of the Fourth Degree pledge and the testimony submitted by California Masons on the slanderous character of the bogus oath.[133]

Callahan met daily with his commission staff. His major correspondence during 1916 was to poll each council for a list of the twenty-five most prominent persons within the council's community, whereupon he sent to each of them the 1915 Commission Report, accompanied by a letter in which he sought their support in breaking down religious prejudices. In his letter Callahan stated, "We are opposed to all manner of discord. We frown on religious prejudices and stand for religious liberty; we plead for that sympathy and unity among neighbors which the common history, the common interest, the common destiny of the whole American people make imperative in the fulfillment of their hopes and aims."[134] Callahan was so confident that his candid broad-minded style would disarm the most bitter bigots that he personally met with General Nelson Miles, the most notable leader of the Guardians of Liberty. Callahan later described the incident in a letter to H. L. Mencken:

We had a very lengthy and satisfactory discussion—largely due to my approach —which was a reference to my father's having served in the Army of the Potomac, of which General Miles led a division. . . . The General, until the days of his death at least a dozen years afterwards, never allowed his name to appear in any anti-Catholic program or anti-Catholic movement of any kind and ceased issuing those statements and interviews attacking our Church, which was his custom from time to time and for years before.[135]

In a letter to members, Callahan also described his meeting with Jacob I. Sheppard of *The Menace:*

I succeeded in selling Sheppard, the publisher, as I did Miles, that Catholics were good and worthy citizens. . . . It resulted in his issuing orders to his editors . . . to the effect that . . . there should be nothing appearing on any of its pages or in the contributions that would be featuring the alleged immoralities of the clergy and of the sisters. Furthermore, that all criticism of the Catholic Church must be confined to its interfering in strictly political questions, which policy was maintained as long as the paper was published.[136]

The Menace's response to Callahan under the title "Callahan the Varnisher, Varnishing Romanism," indicated that it would now distinguish between the innocence of the Catholic people and the corruption of the "Roman Hierarchy."[137] It even praised Callahan for formulating, albeit in an incomplete manner, his ideas of the causes disturbing the peace and serenity, "which we hope to secure some day for the benefit of all, without distinction to race, creed, sex, caste, or color."[138] This spirit of détente between Callahan and *The Menace,* however, was quite short-lived, as the latter soon resumed its anti– K. of C. forays in its general assault on the "papal conspiracy." Nevertheless, the temporary relaxation of tensions between the K. of C. and *The Menace* illustrate the remarkably persuasive powers of Patrick H. Callahan.

The commission's investigation of the causes of religious prejudices was further refined during its second year. "Religious prejudices have come down to us through many generations, from centuries of enmity and strife when Catholics and Protestants took turns persecuting one another and together persecuted the Jew."[139] The commission distinguished between individual bias, which was considered endemic to human nature, and social prejudice, the product of "conditions and circumstances in our country, whose democratic form of government has given rise to any number of popular movements."[140] It discerned five waves of anti-Catholic prejudice, with the last developing in reaction to Pope Pius X's elevation of the Church in the United States from its status as a mission country. The first overt manifestation of the new wave occurred after a November 1908 meeting of the First American Catholic Missionary Society. The commission observed that "before this meeting had adjourned, the New York Synod of a Protestant denomination addressed an open and labored letter to the President of the United States, which in brief asserted that the Catholic Church was a menace to American institutions."[141]

As other symbols of the growth of Catholic prominence surfaced, noted the commission, "more resolutions were passed by apprehensive Protestants." This increase of anti-Catholic sentiment engendered the rise of the "shrewd professional agitator" who founded secret societies, established newspapers, and sponsored professional propagandists "of the ex-priest and ex-nun type." The commission viewed the culmination of this fifth wave of anti-Catholicism in terms of a well-organized national movement by the election of 1912. It was in response to "these professional hate breeders [who] take advantage of the predilections of Protestants" that the K. of C. Commission on Religious Prejudices was founded in order to restore peace by appealing to the constitution and the basic goodness and spirit of fair play of the American people.[142]

The 1916 report included detailed suggestions on ways in which the Order could better implement the commission's 1915 recommendations. For example, to improve the Order's work in alleviating social problems, the commission urged the Knights to study Pope Leo XIII's encyclical *Rerum Novarum*. Callahan's personal involvement in a profit-sharing plan was evident in the report's choice of quotes from the encyclical, particularly that portion which asserted, "The first concern of all is to save the workers from the cruelty of grasping men who use them as instruments to make money."[143] The 1916 report concluded with a lengthy peroration on the education of both Protestants and Catholics as the only means of breaking down the walls of prejudice. It called upon the Knights to wage a "courteous" campaign against anti-Catholic prejudices and sentiments which had crept into many textbooks used in the public schools. Members of the Order were also urged to examine textbooks in Catholic schools "to see that they are not only fair, but sympathetic, in regard to those matters which usually excite ill-feeling between class and class."[144] The eight recommendations submitted to the Supreme Council meeting of 1916 in Davenport, Iowa, were related to ways in which the local and Supreme Councils might be fully incorporated into the commission's task of public enlightenment. In his 1916 report to the Supreme Council, Supreme Knight Flaherty once again congratulated the commission for effecting "a marked falling off in the attacks of professional anti-Catholics" and for the "remarkable tact" with which it had expressed the Catholic positions on civic, educational, and social aspects of American society.[145] The commission's recommendations, which included that it be continued for another year with a $30,000 budget, were approved by delegates to the 1916 convention.

Callahan broadened the scope of the commission during its third year by establishing a clearinghouse for "the exchange and dissemination" of projects, programs, and publications related to either the promotion of or opposition to religious prejudice. However, when the United States entered World War I in April 1917, the commission decided to terminate its work at the close of the fraternal year on June 30. In his introduction to the commission's final report, Callahan summarized its purpose, its strategies, and the character and tone of its operations. After noting again the distinction between individual and social prejudice, he confidently stated that the commission had contributed to the demise of the anti-Catholic movement. "For the first time in the history of anti-Catholic campaigns one of them has been peacefully broken at high tide."[146]

The commission had persistently viewed the "professional propagandists" as the central force of the campaign. To show how this force had lost its momentum, Callahan pointed out that between August 1914, when the Commission on Religious Prejudices was established, and January 1917, the number of anti-Catholic publications dropped from sixty to two or three. He pointed to the absence of bigotry in the national elections of 1916 and to the few anti-Catholic bills introduced in state legislatures in 1916 as further illustrations of the weakness of the movement.[147] He credited the commission's success to the dignified way in which it had comported itself, elevating the discussion of religious prejudices from the heated arena of passion and bitter invective to the dignified realm of "sane, calm, composed discussion,"[148] and recommended that "the Commission ought to be discontinued because its work is done, and, we venture to think, not altogether badly done. Not that bigotry is dead, not by any means, that will never be. But the wave of bigotry that a little while ago was spreading over the country has subsided and its bitter waters lie stagnant."[149] In its final report, the commission stated:

The war will kill bigotry. Not the individual sentiment, but the movement. That personal dislike or disbelief which one may have for this or that religion, that spirit of adverse though sincere criticism which is the salt of intellectual life, will abide as long as personal preferences and individual initiative remain characteristics of free men. But the jealousies, enmities, bitterness and hate, wholesale inventions of scandal, studied falsehoods, agitated feelings of anxiety, fear and suspicion born of dark thoughts and evil rumors, all played against each other with diabolical cunning, these the war will quiet and the social ferment arising from their systematic exploitation will stagnate and die.[150]

For three years the Commission on Religious Prejudices had waged a national campaign against anti-Catholicism with studied respectability and candor. It rationalized its efforts not along the lines of a defense of the Church, which it explicitly stated needed no *apologia*, but rather on the basis of the constitutional guarantees of freedom of religion. Callahan's wealth allowed him the time to respond vigorously to every manifestation of religious prejudice. He possessed boundless energy, which was expressed in a variety of causes, but none took precedence over his commitment to enlighten those who were subjected to the cant of the professional anti-Catholic propagandists. As a Catholic social reformer who implemented his own profit-sharing scheme, Callahan seems to have been very confident of the role of personal initiative in the solution of social problems. His confidence in the American spirit of fair play and in the Church's progress in a democratic society was in close accord with Archbishop Ireland's views, as well as with those other strands of Columbianism which extolled the harmony of Catholicism and American freedom.

The Commission on Religious Prejudices was the Order's first institutional manifestation of its traditional characteristic as a Catholic anti-defamation society. Though both the B'nai B'rith Anti-Defamation League and the Knights of Columbus Commission on Religious Prejudices aimed to enlighten the public on the un-American character of religious discrimination, the Commission dissolved because it had concluded that the anti-Catholic movement had reached its nadir as a force in society, while the Anti-Defamation League has continued to struggle against anti-Semitism, which has been firmly embedded in American social attitudes. However, in the 1920s the Knights once again found themselves confronting a revival of anti-Catholicism, and though the Order did not reestablish the commission, its anti-defamation character was strongly expressed in a massive struggle against the most virulent anti-Catholic organization, the Ku Klux Klan.

8

Serving the Servicemen in World War I

DURING WORLD WAR I the Knights of Columbus was recognized as the preeminent Catholic lay organization. On April 2, 1917, President Woodrow Wilson appeared before a joint session of Congress seeking a declaration of war against Germany. Fifteen days later, Supreme Knight James Flaherty informed President Wilson of the "devotion of 400,000 members of this Order in this country to our Republic and the Congress of this nation in their determination to protect its honor and its ideals of humanity and right."[1] The following May 23, Flaherty wrote to Wilson a brief letter in which he reported that the Order proposed "to establish centers for the large body of men who will be concentrated in training and mobilization camps. These will be for the recreation and spiritual comfort not only of members of the Order and Catholics, but for all others, regardless of creed."[2]

The story of the Order's social service to soldiers begins not with World War I but rather with the U.S. Army's incursion into Mexico in retaliation for General Francisco ("Pancho") Villa's March 9, 1916, attack upon Columbus, New Mexico.[3] Nearly 250,000 National Guardsmen were encamped along the Mexican border during the year preceding the U.S. entrance to World War I. Several K. of C. councils in New Mexico, Arizona, and Texas spontaneously responded to the religious and social needs of the thousands of Catholic troops. For example, Knights of El Paso Council No. 638, led by Joseph I. Driscoll, Daniel Long, and Joseph M. Nealon, laid the foundation for a K. of C. recreation center which was to be open to everyone, "regardless of creed or color," and which was also to serve as a chapel for Catholic services.[4] Until such a center materialized, the council entertained the soldiers in its large three-story home. After they completed a local fund drive for the center, the need for further funds compelled them to appeal to the Supreme Council for financial aid. The national leadership responded with $1,000, followed by subsidies to other councils that had also established such centers. In July, the Board of Directors committed the K. of C. to the establishment of recreation centers and dispatched Special Agent W. J. Moriarty of St. Louis to the border states to supervise this new aspect of the Order's work.[5]

The Y.M.C.A. had been involved in such social work for decades and had forty-two recreation facilities and 376 secretaries in border camps.[6] From its origin, the permanent-home movement within the K. of C. had emulated the Y.M.C.A., with the implication that Catholics should develop their own social centers. Though the K. of C. centers welcomed all soldiers, the Order's primary purpose was to provide religious and social support for Catholics. The need for such service was desperate. Shortly after General John J. Pershing had been ordered to the border, he "asked for association [i.e., Y.M.C.A.] facilities to follow the punitive expedition to Mexico." C. Howard Hopkins, the historian of the Y.M.C.A., referred to the association's work on the border as a "mission" and quoted Pershing's attitude toward its wartime service as "as much a part of army equipment as the army mule or commissary cook."[7] The general disregarded the religious character of the Y's mission as secondary to its social dimension and appears to have been unaware that the thousands of Catholic soldiers under him would generally view the association as an agency of Protestant proselytization. W. J. Moriarty, the Supreme Council's representative to the border camps, reported that the "Knights of Columbus buildings were not as commodious or so [sic] expensively equipped as those of the Y.M.C.A. and the voluntary labors of brother Knights attending the hall will cut down the costs of salaried secretaries in many instances."[8] Within two months the Order established nine centers, ranging from makeshift frame buildings to tents and located in nearby towns, on the edges of and within the camps.

Moriarty's reports included many references to the paucity of chaplains. "Yesterday afternoon we made a visit to all the camps in the [Brownsville, Texas] area and here we find there are no Catholic chaplains. They had a field Mass last Sunday at the Illinois camp, and they asked us for one at the Iowa camp for tomorrow, but I am afraid we cannot supply their wants just at this time. We are badly handicapped for priests here, and at many of the small towns along the border."[9] With the Y.M.C.A. providing religious services for Protestant soldiers, Knights were hard pressed to coordinate Mass schedules for the Catholic troops. Several priests responded to the call for volunteer chaplains, such as Father O. G. Magnell of Hartford, who joined the Connecticut Guardsmen as an auxiliary chaplain. General C. T. O'Neill, commander of a Pennsylvania brigade, was an "enthusiastic Knight, and had the warmest commendation for the Supreme Council for its care in providing for 5,000 Catholic lads" at Camp Stewart.[10]

To illustrate the nondiscriminatory character of the K. of C. effort, several centers displayed signs which read KNIGHTS OF COLUMBUS FIELD HEADQUARTERS—ALL WELCOME. Because many centers were equipped with baths, library, billiard tables, and parlors, soldiers of all faiths could find social refuge with the K. of C. After the centers had been established and thousands of non-Catholics entertained, it became apparent that they could serve the Order's mission to break down anti-Catholic prejudice. As one observer wrote, Protestants "have come to the halls for amusement, and have learned something more than how to pass the time of leisure—they have come to learn something of the Catholic religion; they have come, in some cases, to let toleration take the place of ignorance or intolerance; they have come to see that a man can be both a devout Catholic and a loyal patriot."[11] Special agent Moriarty viewed the border work as an adjunct to the K. of C. Commission on Religious Prejudices: "as a destroyer of religious prejudice this movement will be a most valuable aid to the Order's zealous and efficient Commission."[12] The centers included an abundance of Catholic literature, but there appears to have been no direct attempt to convert Protestant visitors. "And although . . . the Knights of Columbus never at any time went down to the border to proselytize, if through the needs of the natural man some message of truth can be brought home to the spiritual man, then the work of the recreation centers will be doubly justified."[13]

II

With Collins and Goldstein lecturing throughout the nation on the evils of socialism and the need for constructive reform, with Callahan's commission communicating with tens of thousands on the need for religious understanding and peace, and with fifteen recreational centers along the Mexican border, the Knights of Columbus was engaging in a wide variety of works, each of which was an ad hoc response to clearly perceived needs of society and the Church. Though the cost of the Mexican border work was less than $20,000, it entailed coordinating hundreds of volunteer Knights in a new project, one which provided the Order with the experience to realistically seek the Wilson Administration's recognition of the Knights of Columbus as the official

Catholic service agency in World War I. On May 23, 1917, Flaherty wrote to Wilson:

As you know we conducted fifteen such centers at the Mexican front, with the permission of the military officers in charge of the various camps, but as this undertaking will involve a much greater expenditure, we have felt that we ought to secure your approval and helpfulness. . . . May we, in modesty, add that we expect to furnish more men for service than any other organization, and while this work may be largely impelled by the thought of helping them, it will, as with the case at the Mexican front, be open to all men in the service.[14]

Nearly a month earlier President Wilson had issued Executive Order No. 57, in which he directed the officers of the armed services "to render the fullest practicable assistance and cooperation in the maintenance and extension of the association [i.e., the Y.M.C.A.], both at permanent posts and stations and in camps and field."[15] During the seven-week interval between the declaration of war and Flaherty's May 23 appeal to Wilson, events were occurring on all levels of the Order which impelled it to assume the leadership role as the only organized group of Catholic laymen with the resources to become the Church's counterpart to the Y.M.C.A.

As early as April 14, A. G. Bagley, a special agent living in Berkeley, California, and a former member of the Commission on Religious Prejudices, wired Supreme Secretary William McGinley recommending that the Board of Directors (then meeting in Washington, D.C.) consider establishing recreation centers "similar to those on the border"[16] and offering to take charge of such work on the West Coast. In another letter on the same day, Bagley elaborated on the motivation behind his proposal. He described his visit with two officers at the Presidio (in San Francisco) who "were fervent in their hopes" that the Order would once again provide recreation centers. "The Y.M.C.A. took over the gymnasium and recreation equipment of the soldiers some time ago and the men now have to pay for the use of it. Therefore, their admiration of the K. of C.'s [charitable] method of conducting their recreation quarters is very high."[17]

Bagley appears to have been deeply concerned with the antiwar attitudes of American "German Catholics and Sinn Feiners [Irish nationalists who led the Easter Rebellion of 1916 against Great Britain] . . . which will bring the patriotism of Catholics into question." He told McGinley that a group of Germans had protested against Archbishop Edward J. Hanna's statement of Catholic loyalty to the President, and that Father Peter Yorke's Irish nationalist newspaper, the *Leader,* had referred to Wilson as a "Judas Iscariot" for allying with England. "If we establish Knights of Columbus quarters in the training camps, our activities and the publicity which we could get for our people would counteract"[18] accusations of Catholic disloyalty. McGinley responded to Bagley's proposal by informing him that the Board considered the project so far beyond the scope of the border work that it "deemed it inadvisable to take any action at this time."[19]

According to P. H. Callahan's recollection, Supreme Advocate Joseph Pelletier said that "it was out of the question, with our meager resources, to consider the idea of erecting a K. of C. house in every camp."[20] However, two weeks after Bagley's letter, Supreme Physician Buckley of St. Paul, Minnesota, circulated a letter among several Board members in which he urged passage of the recreation-center proposal (including the lecture series): "I feel that we should abandon all work along the lines of religious prejudice and blazon to the country the fact that we have given up this work and directed our energies to aiding the government along other lines, leaving to the 'Menace' and the so-called 'patriotic societies' the duty of guarding the Palladium of liberty which they claim to fear we may steal if they relax their vigilance." Buckley's enthusiasm for the project derived from his many encounters with strong local sentiment evidenced in the upper Midwest. He was convinced that the membership in general would favorably respond to an appeal for a contribution of $1.00 per member.[21]

Buckley's letter elicited positive response from most of the directors. As chairman of the Commission on Religious Prejudices, P. H. Callahan wrote that he was "heartily in accord" with Buckley's suggestion "to cease all of our extraordinary expenses, such as the Commission," but he too doubted the Order's capability to extend the border work into every army and navy training center throughout the country.[22] William P. Larkin, Supreme Director from New York, was in full agreement with the proposal and submitted to McGinley a letter from Father John J. Wynne, S.J., of Fordham University, who added a note of urgency to implementing the proposal: "I think Mr. Buckley's letter contains a solution of the religious prejudice problem now and for fifty years."[23] Wynne expressed his distress that Secretary of War Newton Baker had appointed a committee dominated by "Rockefeller and Y.M.C.A. managers to look after the recreation centers but did not appoint a Catholic or Jew." He was convinced that if the Order worked closely with Father Lewis J. O'Hern, C.S.P., head of the Catholic chaplains, that the recreation centers "would not be exclusively in the hands of the money foundations and the Y.M.C.A."[24] The only known

Board member who was thoroughly opposed to the Buckley proposal was William J. Mulligan of Connecticut. Though he favored allowing state councils to fund and maintain social service centers within their jurisdictions, he believed that "no action should be taken by the Supreme Officers or Directors in establishing recreation halls." Because Mulligan anticipated a need for severe wartime austerity, he advocated conserving the Order's resources "so that we may be able, in the first place, to look after the dependents of our own." In response to Buckley's views on the need for the Order to silence the anti-Catholic forces by displaying Catholic loyalty, Mulligan stated that "we neither have to talk, write nor build recreation halls to show our patriotism. Men of our class have demonstrated where they stood by carrying the musket in all of this country's difficulties and there will be no attempting to hide nor shirk their real duty at this time."[25]

The movement to immerse the Order in war work, initiated by Buckley's letter, gained momentum during May, when the states were holding their annual conventions, and when the Supreme Officers were preparing for a June Board meeting and an August Supreme Council meeting. At their May 8–9 convention, the Missouri Knights contributed $3,000 "to provide for the wants of the Catholic service men at Jefferson Barracks."[26] Under the direction of State Deputy Joseph Kane, the Missouri K. of C. recreation center was formally dedicated on June 17, followed by a Mass celebrated by one Father McFadden, a Fourth Degree Knight stationed at the barracks.[27] On May 8, at the Vermont state convention, $500 was donated "to furnish literature, religious articles, and other comforts for the soldiers of the state." Later the Vermont State Council erected a K. of C. building at Fort Ethan Allen, near Burlington.[28] During their May convention the Ontario Knights contributed $7,000, and the Manitoba and Saskatchewan state conventions accepted a $1.00 per-capita tax to provide chapels and other services for Canadian troops in Europe.[29]

Board members and Supreme Officers were in constant communication during late May and early June. As noted, P. H. Callahan was moderately supportive of Dr. Buckley's proposal, but he was more concerned with strategically countering the Y.M.C.A. "Realizing the great necessity of looking after the spiritual requirements of Catholic young men and how much it meant to the morale of the Army, and knowing the attitude of most of these young men toward the Y.M.C.A. on account of its organization and personnel being confined to members of the Evangelical religion in all its activities, it occurred to me that something must be done quickly." On May 21, Callahan wired the members of the Commission on Religious Prejudices, proposing the possibility of working out "arrangements with our own clergy and Dr. John R. Mott, general secretary of the Y.M.C.A., so that we could bring about a full cooperation without a compromise of our principles, for it is impossible to think of the Knights of Columbus duplicating this work and the Catholics will be neglected if the Knights don't get busy."[30] The following day he wrote to the Supreme Officers, informing them of his views and seeking advice. Since Flaherty's letter to Wilson, appealing for official recognition of the K. of C. as the Catholic service organization, was dated May 23, 1917, two days after Callahan's letter proposing negotiations with the Y.M.C.A., it is evident that the consensus policy of the officers was to establish independent war work. Callahan's communications with the Y.M.C.A. failed to convince them to drop their commitment to religious proselytization or admit Catholics to their staff and grant them a voice in designing the daily programs in the centers. Callahan contended that had John Mott not been visiting Russia during that period, negotiations would have been successful.[31]

President Wilson did not directly reply to Flaherty's May 23 letter but rather submitted it to Raymond B. Fosdick, chairman of the War Department's Commission on Training Camp Activities. In a June 1 letter, Fosdick informed Flaherty that Wilson "was impressed with the opportunity for service contained in your suggestion," and Fosdick himself said that he "was confident that the Order can play a very useful part in stimulating the tone of camp life." Fosdick also reported that Supreme Treasurer D. J. Callahan had been in touch with Charles P. Neill of New York, a member of the commission and a Knight of Columbus, and proposed further consultation between the Order and Neill "to discuss specific plans which you have in mind." He also proposed meeting with Neill and a representative of the Order at his office after the specific plans had been formulated.[32]

The result of these meetings was a June 12 letter from Flaherty to Fosdick in which the Supreme Knight proposed that the commission arrange for central locations at designated camps upon which the Order would erect buildings to accommodate five hundred to one thousand soldiers. Flaherty told Fosdick that these K. of C. centers would be used for "recreation purposes, reading and writing, a place for men to assemble, get up their own entertainments if they wish, and beyond this, in order to avoid duplication, the buildings will be open for such use as your commission may desire. We will not undertake athletics or gymnasium work."[33]

On the day Flaherty wrote this letter, he also wrote to the Grand Knights of all the U.S. councils, urgently appealing for a $2.00 contribution from each member to go into a $1-million War Camp Fund. He informed them that the Board of Directors had decided to expand and enlarge the border work to provide Catholic soldiers "with every spiritual comfort and the service of priests." K. of C. recreation centers were to be located at sixteen training camps, with probable future expansion into regular army camps. Though it was clearly stipulated that the centers were open to soldiers of all faiths, Flaherty's appeal was to the members' Catholic patriotism. "Is our Order of nearly four hundred thousand men prepared and willing to take up this service for God and country, this duty to fellow-man, to fellow Catholics, and to Brother Knights of Columbus?"[34] The Board action on the centers project and Flaherty's subsequent letter to the Grand Knights preceded the Order's proposal to Fosdick, but, as William McGinley explained to Director Thomas A. Lawler of Lansing, Michigan, after consultation with Fosdick and Neill, "we feel warranted in going ahead with the appeal pending official approval of the commission." McGinley also confided to Lawler the general Catholic attitude toward the Y.M.C.A.: "For more reasons than one . . . we cannot become the tail of the Y.M.C.A., and this institution has not [been,] and never will be, of any real service to our fellows."[35]

A variety of motivations stirred the Order to adopt the center project speedily: a genuine concern for the spiritual and social welfare of Catholic soldiers who otherwise would have been subjected to the Y.M.C.A. mission social work, a deeply felt need to demonstrate Catholic loyalty and patriotism, the self-confidence to assume the task derived from experience on the Mexican border, widespread interest on the local level and from strong leadership on the Supreme level, the realization of the vast amount of publicity entailed in a work of such scope, and the general mood. Infused in this attitude was the Order's traditional Catholic anti-defamation purpose; one of the most active Knights promoting the K. of C. war work was the Chairman of the Commission on Religious Prejudices, P. H. Callahan. Because he was also active in the Democratic Party, he had several valuable contacts in Washington, through whom he promoted the Order's initial phase of wartime activities. A longtime friend of Secretary of War Newton D. Baker, Callahan was confident that when Baker "learned exactly what our object was, and that there would not be any propaganda or the remotest sort of [Catholic] proselytiing [sic], but only an opportunity given soldiers of our faith to worship God in camps in the same manner as they did at home, he would not permit anything to stand in our way." After visiting with Baker in mid-June, he was assured, as were the Supreme Officers who visited with Chairman Fosdick, that the K. of C. would have the same privileges as the Y.M.C.A.[36] On June 21, Fosdick officially approved the Order's proposal, but he stressed the social-service side of its work, with no reference to the religious dimension. However, Fosdick did note the Order's "strong position [on] the moral hazards surrounding a young man's life" and stated his confidence that the K. of C. "influence in the camps will add much to their general tone."[37]

The American hierarchy's official representative to Fosdick's commission on training camp activities was Father Lewis J. O'Hern, C.S.P., of the College of St. Paul the Apostle, attached to Catholic University. Cardinal Gibbons specified one of O'Hern's duties as the "spiritual care of Catholic soldiers in . . . the provision of halls for services."[38] After he had become aware of the K. of C. proposal and had been notified that P. H. Callahan was "an old friend" of Secretary Baker, O'Hern contacted Callahan for assistance at the War Department in negotiating an equitable figure for the percentage of Catholic chaplains permitted to serve in the armed forces.[39] Callahan and O'Hern, supported by statistics abstracted from a religious census conducted by the Federal Council of the Churches of Christ which showed Catholics constituting one third of the churchgoing population, convinced Baker that Catholics were entitled to nearly 35 percent of all chaplains.[40] Because the K. of C. war project entailed volunteer chaplains, O'Hern worked closely with the Order and was later provided office space in its Washington headquarters.

At its Detroit meeting on June 24, the Board of Directors heard reports from Callahan and others who had initiated work in Washington which resulted in Fosdick's June 21 approval. Callahan emerged from the meeting as chairman of the Supreme Board of Directors' Committee on War Activities. Flaherty, Supreme Treasurer Daniel J. Callahan, McGinley, and Supreme Director J. J. McGraw of Ponca City, Oklahoma, were also appointed to the committee.[41] As has been noted, P. H. Callahan was president of the Louisville Varnish Company, a position he easily vacated to devote his entire efforts to the Order's war work. The other commissioners were also in positions which allowed them freely to assist the chairman on a part-time basis. Supreme Treasurer Daniel Callahan, formerly of Norfolk, Virginia, was the manager of the N & W Steamboat Company and president of the Washington, D.C., Chamber of Commerce; McGraw was president of the Ponca National Bank. However, from his Washington headquarters P. H. Callahan dominated the committee, whose staff included a permanent secretary (A. G. Bagley, a former member of the Commission on Religious Prejudices) and the four regional "managers" of the centers' project.[42]

The committee was charged with formulating policy as well as administering every aspect of the wartime programs. At its first meeting (July 9, 1917), it was decided that each center (or "hut," as it was called) would be administered by a volunteer K. of C. "secretary" (the Y.M.C.A. title for such an office) and that the Order would seek volunteer K. of C. chaplains to live within the center but independent of the chaplain corps of the Army. P. H. Callahan recalled the evolution of the K. of C. chaplain. "We all saw the great need of our religion to preserve the morals, build up the morale, and intensify the patriotism of the soldier, which made it necessary for us to utilize more and more K-C chaplains."[43]

By the time of the Supreme Council meeting in Chicago on August 7–8, plans for the centers had undergone considerable expansion. The original project envisioned sixteen centers, but Fosdick's committee urged the Order to construct, furnish, and maintain forty-eight buildings at National Guard, regular army, and auxiliary camps. Some camps were to have one large, easily accessible center and two small ones in remote areas. Each was designed like a church building to distinguish it from the standard barracks structure. The large buildings were to be 60 by 100 feet, with a gallery and a stage at opposite ends. The latter was symbolic of the dual character of the center: the altar, sacristy, and confessional were located on the stage, while the gallery was a recreation hall suitable for motion pictures and general entertainment. The stage was draped with a curtain to assure "ample room for private meditation." Though the committee held tight controls over the management of the buildings, the secretaries were instructed to encourage the soldiers to initiate their own forms of entertainment, such as choirs, debates, reading groups, and chess and checkers tournaments. Sensitive to the need "to minimize the dangers and evils which, at best, are all too numerous in connection with the soldier's life," the Order was dedicated to maintaining a high moral tone in the camps. "Literature of an interesting, clean, and instructive character . . . should be plentiful, as this is one of the very best ways for bringing our Catholic boys in touch with their separated brethren whom they can edify, both by word and example." Callahan concluded his report by emphasizing that this war work was not only "a Knights of Columbus movement."[44] The Order held the administrative authority over the work, but it was intended for the common good of all.

Callahan's plea for Catholic cooperation was evidenced by the fact that the Order's $1-million fund drive was enthusiastically endorsed by the vast majority of the hierarchy. Less than a week after Flaherty had announced it, Cardinal Gibbons "congratulated the Order for planning to cooperate so extensively with our Government in caring for the temporal and spiritual wants of the soldiers, regardless of their creed or membership in your Order." In this July 4 letter, Gibbons stressed the practical organizational skills of the Order represented by the drive. "The Knights of Columbus *do* things. . . . Your noble gift of a million dollars to furnish decent places for these splendid young American Catholic soldiers to hear Mass and receive the sacraments and other consolations of our holy faith, should forever stamp the Knights of Columbus as men of practical forethought, timely patriotism, and true Christian charity."[45]

The fund drive attracted contributions from a variety of non-Catholic sources as well. William Jennings Bryan, an old friend of Callahan, sent him $10, John D. Rockefeller sent $1,000, and Fosdick also contributed an undisclosed amount, which Callahan said was "not large."[46] Several local and state councils exceeded their goals. Bay City (Michigan) Council, with five hundred members, successfully raised $1,000 in a one-day drive which they delivered to Callahan at the June 24 Board meeting in Detroit. By the August convention, Indiana had raised $90,000. After Callahan's report to the convention, the delegates unanimously voted to expand the drive from $1 to $3 million.[47] Though the fund drive elicited a united Catholic endorsement of the Order's war work, Callahan feared that fragmentation would jeopardize the efficiency of the Knights' center project.

As early as July 9, Father John J. Burke, C.S.P., editor of the *Catholic World,* told Callahan of the formation of the Catholic Interests Committee of New York, "which included about a hundred members of wealth and influence, and to whom we [i.e., Callahan and other Knights] humorously used to refer as 'Wall Street Catholics.' "[48] Burke reported that the New York Committee had initiated a general meeting of what was later entitled the National Catholic War Council, composed of two delegates from every diocese in the United States and representatives from all national Catholic societies and the Catholic Press Association, in order to plan and coordinate Catholic war activities and formulate policy on the Y.M.C.A. and the Red Cross (rumored to be anti-Catholic), on anti-war Catholic newspapers, and on the

Order's war project.[49] As one of the organizers of this meeting, which was scheduled to convene at Catholic University on August 12, Burke invited Callahan and his committee to present the K. of C. war plans to the delegates. Callahan recalled that at the August meeting of the Supreme Council, the Board of Directors decided not to affiliate with the new organization, "owing to the scant courtesy extended to us, and especially because of their having conferences and making all their plans with the Knights not represented, although we were the only agency working for the Church, had taken the initiative, raised the money, and were doing the work."[50] Though Callahan viewed the lay leaders of this organization as unsympathetic to the Order, he attended its August 12 meeting as a delegate of the diocese of Louisville.

According to his 1919 recollections of this organizational meeting of the National Catholic War Council (N.C.W.C.), Callahan was confronted with an enormous amount of anti-K. of C. sentiment. As a member of the Resolutions Committee, he found it impossible to dissociate himself from the chairmanship of the War Activities Committee. The overwhelming consensus of the Resolutions Committee was that the Knights had no right "to do this work in the name of the Church [and] . . . should not be allowed to pursue a policy where other Catholic societies would not have the same privileges." Callahan did not agree "that the Knights should be a subsidiary agency" of this new organization, and "lacking the usual tact and diplomacy the situation demanded," he informed both the committee and the convention of the full scope of the K. of C. program.[51] Monsignor Michael J. Lavelle, rector of St. Patrick's Cathedral of New York, responded favorably to Callahan's speech and called upon the delegates dutifully to support the Order's fund campaign. After the convention passed resolutions organizing the National Catholic War Council from the parish level to a national executive committee, it unanimously resolved that "the convention most heartily commends the excellent work . . . [of] the Knights of Columbus . . . and that [they] should be recognized as the representative Catholic body for the special work they have undertaken."[52] However, the Executive Committee of the N.C.W.C., dominated by the committee of Catholic laymen of New York, pursued a strategy contrary to the spirit of the resolution. In general, the Executive Committee was critical of the Order's center project, was distrustful of its autonomy, and was determined to assert some form of control.[53]

The conflict between the Order and the N.C.W.C. Executive Committee occurred at a crucial stage in the development of the K. of

C. effort. During the six weeks following the August meeting of the N.C.W.C., Callahan's committee was administering the construction of nearly forty buildings, placing secretaries and chaplains, and planning its overseas work. Because the directives from the N.C.W.C. implied that it would be the sole agency for Catholic war work, many members were confused as to the Order's role and status, a situation which threatened to have an adverse effect upon the fund drive. Since the vast number of wealthy Catholics in New York was tied to the N.C.W.C.'s Executive Committee, the Order's hopes for large donations were dimmed by the K. of C.–N.C.W.C. conflict.

John G. Agar and J. C. Walsh, who were leaders of the committee of Catholic laymen of New York and were on the Executive Committee of the N.C.W.C., led the anti–K. of C. forces. In late August, Callahan suspected that the Executive Committee was "going to interfere materially" with the Order's program. To remedy the problem, Callahan proposed the establishment of an advisory committee of the N.C.W.C. "that would be a fair representation of all the interests involved."[54] Though it appears that Father Burke and others were supportive of closer ties between the K. of C. and the N.C.W.C. Executive Committee, Agar and Walsh were adamant in their opposition.

After a conference between the K. of C. and the so-called "Wall Street Catholics," Callahan was of the opinion that Agar "desires to supervise the entire work, namely, that we are to submit our ideas and plans for their approval, and then they will raise the money in a campaign of their own."[55] Hence, he was ready "to nicely break away from these people."[56] Callahan seems to have been convinced, since Agar and others had raised only $20,000 for the K. of C. in six weeks to supplement the K. of C. membership drive, that the New York leadership was hopelessly alienated. Urged by Flaherty and McGinley, he continued to seek support from Agar and was willing to compromise on the issue of sponsorship of the fund drive. He wrote to Agar, "Have you any plan whereby a million dollars can be raised in New York for Catholic war work; no matter under whose auspices it is conducted?"[57]

Agar's reply illustrated his total lack of confidence in the Knights' war program. "You have so long stated that you are going to put up recreation halls and supply secretaries and provide chaplains that the public have begun to realize that you have not only not begun this work, but are unable to do it." Though Agar stated that he did "not share in this mistrust," he told Callahan that "the time has come when the promise should be made performance. You need assistance and should not hesitate to receive it." He said that because of widespread criticism of the Order it could not presume to be representative of the whole Church, nor could it raise an additional $1 million "until you have accomplished some definite results." Agar closed with the remark that the Y.M.C.A. progress in the field "should at least be a spur to you."[58]

Agar's opinions did not square with the facts. In September the Order was in the process of erecting forty-eight buildings in twenty-four camps. There is no evidence of widespread opposition but rather of general endorsement by the hierarchy and laity of the Church. In three months the Order had raised $85,000. Since the Red Cross and the Y.M.C.A. had successfully raised one third of their funds in New York, the Knights were disappointed with the situation there, particularly since Agar's group was, for a time, unwilling to transfer even the $20,000 that it had collected. William P. Larkin, Supreme Director from New York, reflected the general sentiment of the Board when he stated that "we will have to cut adrift from the Wall Street Committee as it seems impossible to get anything from them except efforts at domination."[59] At its October meeting the Board gratefully acknowledged receipt of nearly $20,000 from the Committee of Catholic Laymen of New York.[60] Relations between the Order and the Wall Street group and the N.C.W.C. remained cool until early January, when the latter was reorganized and a new Administrative Committee composed of four archbishops was established. However, the Knights' old opponent, John Agar, remained influential in both Church and War Department circles.

Ever concerned with projecting the image of a unified Catholic laity, the Order's problems with the "Wall Street Catholics" were viewed as family squabbles not to be vented publicly. However, as the K. of C. war work gained broader coverage by the press, several groups challenged the propriety of the War Department's approval of the Order's official status as a social service agency. Since the Y.M.C.A. had received widespread publicity for its war work, news of the K. of C.'s entrance into the field elicited charges of wasteful duplication. Throughout the autumn of 1917, members from all parts of the nation sent Callahan newspaper articles and editorials which reflected this charge. Public opinion tended to view the Y.M.C.A. as a nonsectarian organization. Hence, Callahan wrote letters to "scores of newspapers" and to periodicals such as *Collier's* and *Life,* informing their readers of the Evangelical Protestant character of the Y.M.C.A.'s mission. In several letters, he elaborated on the *raison d'être* of the Order's war work, stating in one such letter that "it may be news to you to learn that the

Y.M.C.A. does not allow Catholics any representation, voice, or control, and especially are they not to hold any office, and as we form about 35 per cent of the Army, the government requested us to look after Catholic necessities in the Army and Navy, although our advantages are open to everyone, regardless of creed."[61]

In a September 15 editorial, the *Columbia* (South Carolina) *Record* sympathized with the Masons' charge that the War Department was discriminating against all other fraternal societies by granting the Knights privileges to establish centers in the camps.[62] Callahan replied to the charge by making the distinction between the Knights as a Catholic society and as a fraternal Order. He stated that the Order had no official status; "we [were] selected as an agency to supply the spiritual necessities of Catholic soldiers, and incidentally furnish recreation under the auspices of the War Department." He further explained that each K. of C. center was open to all, regardless of creed, and was not in any way used as a K. of C. lodge for fraternal business. Callahan sent this letter to Fosdick with a note encouraging "either the Secretary, or even the President, [to respond] to this matter along the lines of what was in my mind."[63]

Secretary Baker issued a public statement on September 22, 1917, in which he said that he had received numerous communications from societies and fraternal organizations "protesting alleged discrimination by the War Department in allowing the Young Men's Christian Association and the Knights of Columbus to erect recreation buildings while forbidding other societies the same privilege." Baker explained that both organizations "had already been identified with recreation work" prior to the war and that each represented two of the three major denominations. He assured his critics that, though the K. of C. was a fraternal society, its relations to the soldiers would be the same as those of the Y.M.C.A. In the same vein, he announced that the Young Men's Hebrew Association (Y.M.H.A.) had been approved and was also successfully "ministering to the social needs of the soldiers." To satisfy the many organizations excluded from official recognition, he encouraged them to establish in-town social activities for the armed forces.[64]

Baker's statement did not satisfy the fraternal orders. Indeed, Callahan later remarked that "it seemed that we were jumping out of the frying pan into the fire,"[65] for after Secretary Baker's statement further protests were made. The news media circulated reports that a bitter religious struggle had developed between Catholics and Protestants.[66] The situation became politically charged when it was discov-

ered that over 70 percent of the U.S. Congress belonged to the protesting societies. To settle the issue peacefully, Baker held a meeting
at the War Department for representatives of twenty-six fraternal societies. Callahan recalled that, after he had attempted to explain the K.
of C. nonfraternal, religious role in the camps, "there was some con-
sternation," anger, and general suspicion regarding the motives of the
Knights. Baker's explanation of the Knights as a kind of Catholic
Y.M.C.A. had a positive impact upon the fraternalists; Callahan remarked that "the air immediately cleared and with a much better
feeling all around [I] explained our plans and programs and how
members of any fraternal society were just as welcome to our buildings, and included in our entertainment and recreation programs, as
our own members."[67]

As a result of this meeting, Baker issued another statement inviting all fraternal societies to work with the official organizations and to
erect their camp buildings or tents either singly or in common for their
fraternal work with the stipulation that they could not recruit new
members. "After all this fuss and feathers," wrote Callahan, "not a
society attempted to avail itself of the privilege."[68]

Though the Order experienced further conflict with ecclesiastical
and civil authorities during the war, it no longer had to defend itself
as the Catholic counterpart to the Y.M.C.A. It appears to have been
almost inevitable that its role would be challenged by those who misunderstood the Catholic attitude toward the religious character of the
Y.M.C.A. as well as by Catholics who for various reasons doubted its
motivation and its abilities. The Order had successfully grappled with
these challenges and had asserted itself as the only viable social organization capable of attending to the social and religious needs of Catholic servicemen. In the process, P. H. Callahan's leadership was crucial.
He was a well-known figure in political and ecclesiastical circles, was
a thorough and forceful administrator, and possessed an independent,
critical mind. He prided himself on his diplomacy and tact, particularly
within an interfaith situation, but he was also quite candid in expressing his opinions and seems to have relished controversy. His voluminous correspondence with Grand Knights, Supreme Officers, archbishops, cabinet members, and prominent politicians reveal his
seasoned poise in dealing with a wide variety of people on a limitless
variety of issues. For example, amid the conflicts with the "Wall Street
Catholics," with the Masons, and with those who criticized the Order
for duplicating the work of the Y.M.C.A., he wrote to William Jennings
Bryan—a fellow prohibitionist Democrat—"You could have been of

immense help to me in my work had you had an opportunity while in Washington, for things are not running so smoothly . . . so much so that your influence with the War Department and Y.M.C.A. would help matters materially; but you will perhaps be up this way again, in which event be sure and let me know as far in advance as possible."[69]

In August and September, Callahan's staff had been enlarged to include an architect and directors of construction, operations, and publicity. Regarding salaries, Callahan stated that "our work here is of such a patriotic character that we expect a lot of volunteer service, and have made it a rule that we will not pay over $125.00 a month."[70] Francis W. Durbin, director of operations, was responsible for selecting and training the camp secretaries. Clarence E. Manion, who later became Dean of the Law School at the University of Notre Dame, was the first secretary appointed by the Committee (ca. September 1, 1917). A K. of C. scholar at Catholic University and a Knight from Henderson, Kentucky, Manion was assigned to a camp at Gettysburg, Pennsylvania; because "he made such a record at the camp," he was selected to open and administer the main K. of C. center at Camp Jackson, Jacksonville, Florida. He later joined the Army and became a commissioned officer.[71] The Order was commended by the provost marshal general's office, which administered the draft, for not seeking immunity from conscription for its secretaries.[72]

During this period the Knights were frequently criticized for usurping ecclesiastical authority by hiring and directing Catholic chaplains. In October 1917, the *Catholic Transcript* of the diocese of Hartford challenged the Order's right to supply, select, and instruct chaplains. Callahan replied that the Knights were not engaged directly in such activity; rather, it "was in its entirety" directed by Father Lewis J. O'Hern, the official representative of the hierarchy. He further stated that he was "at a loss to understand the criticism aimed at our work. . . . We merely supply the 'sinews of war.' "[73]

Father A. J. Ohlingschlagger was the first K. of C. chaplain and was assigned to Camp Taylor, Louisville, Kentucky. Both secretaries and chaplains received a salary of $125 per month, but the chaplain's salary was paid through his ordinary. The Y.M.C.A. depended upon volunteer secretaries, for whom they paid living expenses. However, their salaried secretaries received $200 to $300 a month.[74] By December 1, 1917, the Knights had erected seventy-three buildings at various military and naval camps (they were prohibited from establishing centers at regular army camps), and had appointed 165 secretaries, but only

45 chaplains, because many were then regular-army chaplains assigned to training camps.[75]

Local councils throughout the nation were also initiating war work of a social and religious nature. The Chicago chapter established its own K. of C. recreational chapter on 26th Street and Karlov Avenue, which was designed particularly for "the comfort of the Motor Transport Corps, the members of which were obliged to stop for a short period en route across the country."[76] Since Chicago was the largest railroad center in the nation, local Knights were assigned to the various stations, where they distributed free candy, cigarettes, and postcards to departing soldiers and sailors.[77] Many State Councils established their own War Activities Committees, the most significant task of these committees was the $3-million fund drive which involved thousands of Knights on the local and state levels. Since the Order's work was continuously expanding, and since it had always intended to establish operations in Europe, its budget, as well as its entire operations, was heavily dependent upon grass-roots support.

III

Callahan's committee considered work abroad as its most important task. Shortly before the August convention in 1917, Father Joseph Pontur of Norwood, New York, and Felix Limongi, resident secretary of the K. of C. home in New Orleans, both French-speaking Americans, independently volunteered to work for the Order overseas. After Callahan and Father O'Hern interviewed them, they were sent to France in late August as scouts for other K. of C. forces that would be following. They were directed to inform Callahan of the regulations relating to official recognition of the Knights' work, which he projected as being "highly technical."[78] Since the War Department would not interfere with General Pershing's policies regarding the establishment of social and religious centers in Europe, the War Activities Committee had to proceed along independent lines. Before it could devise the proper strategies for seeking Pershing's approval, for receiving the French hierarchy's permission, and for accommodating its work to the needs of the soldiers overseas, it was necessary to send such "scouts" to Europe and to proceed very cautiously.

The need for overseas work was quite evident among Catholic soldiers. Three Knights, who were serving "somewhere in France,"

wrote to Supreme Secretary McGinley (September 17, 1917) informing him that their regiment was 40 percent Catholic, with a large
representation from the Order. Though they appreciated the "noble
work" of the Y.M.C.A., they noted that it had "a religious atmosphere
that is not wholly our own, one somewhat foreign to us, which sometimes leaves the impression that the Catholic boys have been forgotten." Unaware of the Order's intention to establish centers in Europe,
they encouraged such a move with confidence "that it would [be] a
greater work than the Y.M.C.A. can accomplish, for with the cooperation of Catholic France and her wonderful soldier priests, we will be
enabled to put things over with a punch and leave a favorable impression for the introduction of Columbianism in more favorable times."[79]

During early September, while Pontur and Limongi were scouting
in Paris, Walter N. Kernan was appointed "Commissioner in Charge
of War Activities with the Overseas Armies," with authority to seek
General Pershing's permission to establish K. of C. centers and to
administer the entire overseas project. A native of Utica, New York,
Kernan was a wealthy railroad executive, then residing in New York
City, who had donated his services to the Order. On October 9, after
visiting with the Secretary of War and Cardinal Gibbons, and after
several consultations with Callahan, Kernan sailed to Europe with
instructions to investigate the situation in London before establishing
headquarters in Paris.[80] Shortly before he left, Pontur cabled Father
O'Hern: AMERICAN FORCES IN PARIS REFUSE TO RECOGNIZE KNIGHTS OF
COLUMBUS UNTIL THEY RECEIVE INSTRUCTIONS.[81] Callahan and O'Hern
presented the cable to the Secretary of War, who immediately informed General Pershing of the Order's work in the United States and
its intention to send chaplains overseas to erect recreation centers or
huts.[82] Callahan had informed Pontur of Kernan's appointment as the
Order's commissioner and was extremely disturbed that Pontur had
exceeded his authority by unilaterally seeking permission to establish
huts in France. On October 1, he cabled Pontur to that effect and
concluded with the following order: YOU HAVE NOT COMPLIED WITH OUR
INSTRUCTIONS AND ANY AUTHORITY TO REPRESENT US IN ANY WAY IS
HEREBY REVOKED. RETURN TO AMERICA AT ONCE.[83] When Kernan arrived
in Paris on November 1, he reported that Pontur was preparing to sail
for home in a day or so. He was grateful that the priest scout was
relieved of duty, as he had heard that "Pontur had made an unfavora-
ble impression."[84]

By the time Kernan had established his Paris headquarters, there
were about 150,000 soldiers in the American Expeditionary Forces in

Origins in New Haven

Father Michael J. McGivney

St. Mary's Church

Incorporators

John T. Kerrigan

James T. Mullen

Cornelius T. Driscoll

Daniel Colwell

William M. Geary

Matthew C. O'Connor, M.D.

A Century of Supreme Knights

James T. Mullen, 1882–1886

John J. Phelan, 1886–1897

James E. Hayes, 1897–1898

John J. Cone, 1898–1899

Edward L. Hearn, 1899–1909

James A. Flaherty, 1909–1927

Martin H. Carmody, 1927–1939

Francis P. Matthews, 1939–1945

John E. Swift, 1945–1953

Luke E. Hart, 1953–1964

John W. McDevitt, 1964–1977

Virgil C. Dechant, 1977–

The McGivney Legacy:
Reverend Michael J. McGivney's two brothers and nephew

Monsignor Patrick J. McGivney,
Supreme Chaplain, 1901–1928

Monsignor John J. McGivney,
Supreme Chaplain, 1928–1939

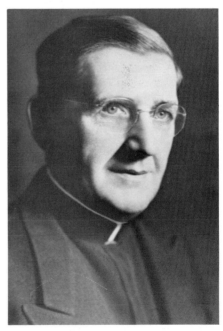

Monsignor Leo M. Finn,
Supreme Chaplain, 1939–1960

Columbian Patriotism

Charter members of the Fourth Degree, which is founded upon patriotism

Over five thousand Knights paraded at the unveiling on June 8, 1912, of this Columbus Memorial in front of Union Station, Washington, D.C.

Knights of Columbus center in the Argonne region of France

Longacre Hut recreation center at Broadway and 46th Street, New York City

A secretary of the Knights of Columbus gives sustenance to a young refugee.

The 3rd Division outside the Knights of Columbus clubhouse in Andernach, Germany

France.[85] When Kernan approached Pershing for permission to erect K. of C. huts (the American units did not actively participate in battle until March 1918), Pershing responded favorably but asked that Kernan consult with the Y.M.C.A. and the Red Cross to avoid duplication.[86] Kernan reported that E. C. Carter of the Y.M.C.A. and J. H. Perkins of the Red Cross agreed that the Knights should "have the same rights as the Y.M.C.A."[87] Callahan had urged Kernan to cooperate with the Y but stated that "our work wants to be directed . . . so that it will have the Catholic personal aspect, and in making all arrangements [with the Y] be careful that the Catholic identity and activity is not submerged."[88]

Satisfied that there would be no duplication among the three organizations, Pershing issued, on November 20, General Order No. 63 by which he recognized the Knights on an equal footing with the Y.M.C.A. and the Red Cross. He was favorably disposed to Kernan and remarked that he was the first American civilian he had met in France who did not request a visit to the front. Pershing arranged for Kernan to tour the various camps, determine the needs of the soldiers, and return to the States in order to recruit a staff and develop an organization necessary for the large task.[89] By this time the Y.M.C.A. had about 115 huts while the Order had only seven K. of C. chaplains. Before Kernan left for the States, he provided his staff with enough money to lease suitable buildings or erect temporary huts, two of which were eventually located in towns where American troops disembarked, a move which was in accord with a suggestion by Callahan.[90] The latter had intended to direct the overseas operation from Washington, D.C., but Kernan reported that the Paris office must have that responsibility and that he planned to return to France "as soon as possible."[91] During his absence, Mrs. Kernan was in charge of the office and authorized to "keep in touch" with the chaplains and to provide them with stationery and other supplies.[92]

Kernan's proposals for the overseas program, which he presented to the Board of Directors, involved erecting large centers at the three major disembarkation ports and smaller huts in each regimental headquarters near the front (which could be easily transported as the army advanced), purchasing automobiles and trucks to resolve the transportation problems resulting from nearly three years of war in Europe, and recruiting secretaries of advanced age, i.e., forty or over, who would be able to meet the practical and social demands of huts which might be located in isolated, remote areas. Kernan reported that the organizational problems would be resolved if the Order could attract the volunteer services of six or eight "of our best known, biggest business Catholic laymen," who would provide "the benefit of their extended business experience" and whose names would be helpful in fund-raising campaigns.[93]

Kernan also submitted reports to the restructured and reconstituted National Catholic War Council, met individually with Cardinal Gibbons and William Cardinal O'Connell of Boston, and finally in early February met with Callahan, who concluded that Kernan was "a chinese puzzle to me; and that it is going to require the most delicate handling to make the headway we anticipated."[94] He was particularly disturbed at Kernan's deference to the National Catholic War Council, which, though reconstituted, included the leader of the "Wall Street Catholics," John Agar. Since Kernan was hoping to attract wealthy Catholics to volunteer for overseas administration work, Callahan no doubt feared another round of conflicts with the "Wall Street Catholics," who he thought were determined to dominate the K. of C. war work. Indeed, he felt that the overseas commissioner "had broken away" from him "and seems to feel that his work should be apart from our Committee, which will not do at all."[95] With little or no confidence in Kernan's practical ability and alienated by his independent attitude, Callahan, without the approval of the Board of Directors, sent Dillon E. Mapother, a staff member of his committee, and Christopher Connolly, a Catholic journalist, to Paris in mid-February, two weeks before Kernan was scheduled to return to Europe. Mapother, who had been secretary of overseas operations, was instructed to select appropriate sites for huts, while Connolly was appointed secretary to Callahan, with the explicit charge to investigate the overseas situation and report directly to him.

Within the next several weeks, others were assigned to the Paris staff to supervise construction, supplies, transportation, and the general office affairs of the Paris bureau. When Supreme Advocate Joseph Pelletier learned of the appointments of Mapother and Connolly, he was incensed. He told Callahan that the Board would never have confirmed these appointments. "It looks to me from this distance as if you are trying to beat out Kernan in sending these men over at this time, and personally I think you have sent over two misfits." Pelletier considered Connolly to have been a "misanthrope" who had been consistently critical of Catholic affairs. "They are always doing things in the wrong way; they are always making mistakes." He concluded by urging Callahan to be more accountable to the Board in order to engender unity in the Order's war work.[96] Callahan responded with a warning that since he would be held responsible for the results of the work, "there should not be any interference" with his administration of the War Activities Committee.[97]

During the weeks immediately prior to Kernan's March 15 departure for Paris, Callahan strongly asserted his authority over the overseas commissioner. He instructed Kernan to seek his permission for any expense of $10,000 or over.[98] He was extremely critical of Kernan's plan to include the services of some of his Protestant friends in the K. of C. Paris headquarters. Callahan told his committee that he intended "to put our foot down on this proposition for if the Y.M.C.A. is conducting an Evangelical institute, it is very essential that we conduct a Catholic program."[99] Callahan was so apprehensive of Kernan's ability that he made overtures to Past Supreme Knight Edward Hearn as to his willingness to "head an expedition to Great Britain or Ireland. . . . Then, if the Kernan project does not work out satisfactorily, we will have a man on the other side big enough for the job, and one of our own crowd."[100] Thus, by the time Kernan departed for Paris, a triangle of conflict had developed among the three centers of authority: Washington, Paris, and New Haven. Kernan alienated Callahan, who retaliated with appointments of men loyal to him; this in turn alienated Supreme officers and Board members. Since Kernan was outside the Order's political structure, he approached his responsibilities with the utmost caution and diffidence. As Callahan later remarked, Kernan expressed "a most exaggerated formality as well as other mannerisms which . . . did not go with a 'regular' fellow."[101] Both men appear to have been genuinely motivated to establish first-rate centers and to develop a strong Catholic presence overseas, but Callahan distrusted Kernan's ability to design effective practical strategies to achieve these goals while Kernan seems to have, at least unintentionally, ignored Callahan's directives.

Kernan, accompanied by three K. of C. chaplains, eight field secretaries, and four staff members, arrived in Paris on March 25. According to Pelletier, Mapother, representing Callahan, caused a "tremendous row. . . . All through a mistake of yours [Callahan's] in instructing Maypother [sic]." Pelletier went on to tell Callahan that the Board had agreed on Kernan's authority, and "yet the very first thing that happens upon his arrival is to find a denial from the mouth of Maypother under your instructions."[102] Five days after Pelletier had excoriated Callahan, the latter submitted his resignation as chairman of the War Activities Committee. The resignation occurred at the April 15 meeting of the Board of Directors. According to the minutes of this meeting, Callahan did not specify the reasons for his resignation, though it must have been apparent to all present that the conflict between the Board and Callahan over Kernan had reached a breaking point.[103]

In a letter to Supreme Knight Flaherty (April 20, 1918), Callahan stated that "the immediate cause of my resignation" was the Order's forwarding to Kernan $250,000. He asked Flaherty to explain the authorization of such a large amount because Kernan was bonded for only $50,000 and because "it was directly contrary to my own orders in the series of letters written him surrounding our funds with every possible precaution, as we all were aware of his great personal indebtedness, as well as agreed on his lack of capacity as an executive."[104] Flaherty explained that the $250,000 advanced to Kernan was in response to a request from Monsignor James N. Connolly, who was in Paris to determine the need of both army and K. of C. chaplains. Flaherty further told Callahan that he had consulted with McGinley and Pelletier and reminded Callahan that the action had been ratified by unanimous vote of the Board meeting on May 14. Flaherty also expressed his implicit trust in Kernan's integrity and executive ability.[105] It is likely that Callahan first heard of Flaherty's action at that May meeting and, given the intense conflict between himself and Kernan, viewed the bank draft as a strong repudiation of his chairmanship.

William J. Mulligan replaced Callahan as chairman of the War Activities Committee, and Pelletier was appointed as a member. In reaction to Callahan's excessive independence in his Washington-based office, the Board reasserted its authority over the committee. At the request of the Board, Callahan remained on the job in Washington until mid-June, during which time he worked "ten or twelve hours a day carrying out our plan of getting twenty-five [secretaries] across each week."[106] Upon Callahan's termination, William Larkin, Supreme Director from New York, opened an office in Manhattan to administer overseas work and to supervise the training of secretaries.

By mid-June, however, the overseas operation had become a source of embarrassment for the Order. Early that month, Father Thomas F. Oakley, an army chaplain serving in France, wrote a letter intended for publication in several Catholic newspapers, in which he lamented the fact that Kernan had

unlimited funds at his disposal [but] there are no salaried Knights of Columbus secretaries serving in France . . . unless the Catholic American people, and the Knights of Columbus . . . wake up and wake up promptly to the crisis which now confronts them . . . the Catholic Church will receive a serious blow . . . practically every soldier the American chaplains meet in France is loud in his complaint against the K. of C. . . . what the soldiers want is secretaries, not excuses. . . . Too long have they been fed on promises, and we are tired of such unsubstantial pablum.[107]

In a private letter to Oakley, Callahan stated that such criticism was justified, but he blamed the failure of the overseas program on "interference by officials of the Order with my plan of action, being my reason for resigning the chairmanship." He urged Oakley to consider "the facts" before he rushed "to the defense of Mr. Kernan. . . . Mr. Kernan at first only wanted to take back with him bankers, capitalists, railroad men, and executives as commissioners, and, if it was not for myself, 'taking the bull by the horns,' there would perhaps be no secretaries over there now. . . . Mr. Kernan never fell in with the idea of sending secretaries across until the 10th of February."[108]

The Board of Directors was supportive of Kernan throughout April and May, but by June the Supreme Officers became disillusioned with his lack of communication on specific needs of the overseas program, with the particulars of his budget, and with his apparent lack of progress in establishing huts. Mulligan and the Supreme Chaplain, Father Patrick McGivney, returned from a two-month visit to France in mid-June with news that they had successfully initiated the construction of many huts, but they did not diminish the disenchantment with Kernan's leadership. Ironically, it was Pelletier, Kernan's most vigorous proponent on the Board, who took the lead in seeking his resignation. In a June 21 letter to Walter Kernan's brother, John, he stated, "My own notion . . . as one who has been Walter's friend, having written him several leading letters to Paris asking for a report, is that he ought to resign at once. He has proven himself absolutely helpless and hopeless, in my opinion." Pelletier listed ways in which Kernan had "failed us most miserably," most of which pertained to his lack of communication and accountability, and the glacial pace at which he moved in establishing huts. "Here we are, some of us officers of the Order, collecting millions of dollars, people clamoring to know what is done, boys writing back letters, and fathers and mothers asking questions."[109]

Six days after Pelletier had written this letter, Kernan cabled his resignation to Flaherty, prefacing it with the remark ADVICE RECEIVED FROM HOME RENDERS ABSOLUTELY NECESSARY MY RETURN SHORTLY AMERICA.[110] Hence, Pelletier's letter to his brother allowed Kernan to resign graciously with the minimum of embarrassment. Mapother and Connolly resigned on the same day. Flaherty accepted the resignations and appointed Kernan's deputy commissioner, Lawrence O. Murray, acting commissioner. In accord with the ironic character of these events, in which both Callahan and Kernan fell from grace, the Order ultimately appointed Past Supreme Knight Edward Hearn, once Callahan's strongest supporter, to replace Kernan as permanent overseas commissioner.

As Kernan later reported, when he returned to Paris in late March, he had faced a situation which explains his lack of communication and progress.[111] The German offensive (i.e., Somme offensive) which began on March 1 included periodic shelling of Paris and required a continuous flow of soldiers and supplies to the front. Because the Y.M.C.A. had established many huts by this time, they could advance as the front advanced. However, since the supply lines and roads received top military priority, and since throughout March and April the Paris business community was preparing to evacuate the city, it had been impossible to initiate the Order's work until late May, when the Allies began to control the situation on the western front. Kernan later explained, "Nothing more of importance than contained in my cables would pass the censor . . . any letter I wrote, if containing more than I cabled about conditions, would have caused friction with him and constant waste of time in getting his consent."[112] However, by the time he left for home, the overseas operations included twenty-four secretaries, eight of whom were stationed at the front, nineteen K. of C. chaplains, and eleven staff members in the Paris office. Besides the huts at the front, the Order had established twelve K. of C. clubs in ten French towns.[113]

In hindsight, Kernan regretted that he did not remain in France and develop a strong base before the March offensive rather than return to America. General Pershing, who was well known for his stress upon planning and training before entering battle, urged Kernan to return and develop a stronger organizational structure. Since he, as well as Callahan and the entire leadership of the Order, was utterly inexperienced in administering such work, it appears extraordinary that within a year after the project had been approved by Pershing, there were over three hundred secretaries and dozens of huts overseas.

One of these secretaries who was appointed to serve in France in the summer of 1918 was Frank A. Larkin of the Washington Heights section of upper Manhattan. Larkin was just over the conscription age when he resigned as Grand Knight of Mystic Rose Council No. 268 to become a K. of C. secretary.[114] His diary, covering the first several months of service in France, provides us with a personal glimpse of the

Order's overseas work "from below"[115] in contrast to the administrative point of view already set forth. Shortly after his July 5 arrival in Paris, Larkin was assigned by Acting Commissioner Murray to work in the Red Cross Hospital No. 1, located in Neuilly. His secretarial duties were frequently interrupted by emergency situations which required volunteers to help with the scores of injured soldiers transported from the front. "Commissioners Murray and Scott [the Board of Directors had sent Joseph Scott of California to investigate the overseas program and gather material for a lecture series in the United States] joined our workers and aided in carrying stretchers and undressing the wounded. They left instructions with our force to spare no expense in order to alleviate the sufferings of the soldier boys. The sight of our superiors working along side of us gave us new life and every member of the party pledged to work until they dropped, if necessary."[116]

Larkin recorded one of his most poignant experiences as a secretary. After he had returned from work in the operating room, "a young voice called out to him weakly, 'Have you a minute to spare, Casey [a name for a K. of C. secretary coined by the American soldiers]? . . . Can you write a little letter for me?' Larkin replied, 'Now what do you want me to say to her, buddy?' He said, 'Casey, I'm one of your kind [i.e., a Catholic] and I'm going to get a little confidential with you. I ran away from home and I faked my papers. I'm not quite 18 yet and this girl I want you to write to is my sweetheart and the only living person who knows where I am. . . . Casey, I am badly wounded. Fritz got me in both arms and just below the left lung and I'm worse. But don't tell her, just say I'm only slightly wounded and that I'll be all right in a few days.' The boy's last words were, 'Casey, get a priest!' And as the good chaplain bent over the cot and gave the last rites of Holy Mother Church, the soldier hero, with a smile on his lips, closed his eyes in death and another gold star was added to the firmament."[117]

On July 25, Larkin was transferred to Dijon, where the Order had one "of the finest" clubrooms in France.[118] He and Secretary Mark Shriver of Maryland managed the recreation center, where each evening over 150 soldiers gathered for relaxation. Once a month the secretaries arranged "a large program of entertainment embracing boxing, wrestling, moving pictures, and vaudeville numbers. The hall would be packed to overflowing; as many as 500 soldiers being jammed in every available space. . . . We always ran a show that would not in any way offend anyone."[119] Because the Dijon Club was so popular, the secretaries frequently sought additional staff from the

Paris headquarters. By October, when there were over 500 secretaries in France, the Paris office assigned five to Dijon. Hence, a few months after Kernan resigned, the overseas operation was thriving. Larkin was later assigned to the front, where he was seriously injured by mustard gas.[120]

When Larkin left France, the overseas operation had reached its peak with over 1,000 secretaries and nearly 150 clubs and huts located throughout the western and eastern war zones. The enormous cost of such an extensive program ultimately entailed the Order's cooperation with the reconstituted National Catholic War Council and other service organizations. However, during the first year of the war work, the Knights raised funds independent of any other organization. The hierarchy had enthusiastically supported the Knights' $1-million fund drive initiated in June 1917, but the Order had never received a public endorsement from President Wilson. Flaherty had attempted to arrange an interview with Wilson in September, but he was advised by the President's secretary, Joseph Tumulty, a member of the Order, that because of Wilson's "overcrowded calendar . . . I suggest that you write the President. . . . I shall be glad to bring to his attention any communication you may care to send."[121]

Flaherty's subsequent letter to Wilson was a forceful expression of the Supreme Knight's disappointment with the President's silence regarding the Order's war efforts. He reported to Wilson that word had reached him via Tumulty that the President "would not agree to give us a written endorsement for fear that many other organizations would be asking for a like favor." Flaherty said that "we were surprised at this statement," since Wilson had publicly endorsed the Y.M.C.A., the Playgrounds Association, and the American Bible Society. He reminded him that the Order was not seeking a presidential endorsement as a fraternal society but rather "as the agents of the Catholic people, and with the endorsement of the three American Cardinals, the entire Catholic Hierarchy, the National Catholic War Council, and the Catholic Federation of the United States." He informed Wilson that the Order had successfully raised $1 million but that it needed three times that amount. In consideration of this need and of the several endorsements granted to other organizations, Flaherty asked the President, "will you therefore pardon me if I seem to be overzealous in asking for the Knights of Columbus a few words of encouragement for its work in the War Camps?"[122] The Order published Wilson's October 23 reply in the *Columbiad* within the context of its $3-million fund drive, but it was far from an enthusiastic endorsement.

My dear Mr. Flaherty:

Pray pardon my delay in replying to your letter of October tenth.

Inasmuch as the campaign for funds for the Knights of Columbus has been brought to a successful conclusion and the work of the organization is now actively in progress in the camps (very much to my satisfaction), it only remains for me to speak of the sincere gratification with which I have learned of the cooperation of the Young Men's Christian Association and the Knights of Columbus and their harmonious and successful work in the training camps.

Cordially and sincerely yours,
Woodrow Wilson[123]

By noting the termination of the Order's drive for funds rather than encouraging the public to support the ongoing fund drive, Wilson refused to lend his explicit support for the Knights' appeal for money. Though he parenthetically remarked that he was pleased with the Order's war work, he seems to have been more pleased with the Order's cooperation with the Y.M.C.A. In his characteristically patrician style, Wilson's minimalistic endorsement of the Knights' work was, at best, a patronizing gesture of good will.

But the President's guarded endorsement did not appear to hurt the Order's appeal for funds. Councils throughout the nation, working in tandem with diocesan and parochial leaders, were continuously campaigning for contributions from both Catholics and non-Catholics. By the end of 1917, more than $2 million had been collected and, with plans to develop an overseas operation, the Order initiated a $10-million effort. The drive to display Catholic patriotism and to dispel anti-Catholic prejudice, which motivated the leaders of the Order to engage in war work, was evident in the grass-roots enthusiasm in the war fund campaign. Thus, the New Jersey State Council, under the direction of State Deputy John F. O'Neill, raised $600,000 between January 19 and 29, while in Detroit the Knights' campaign totaled $325,000.[124] Such drives engendered a spirit of ecumenism, as prominent Protestant and Jewish leaders actively participated in the cause. John Agar, the leader of the "Wall Street Catholics" and, as we have noted, a bitter critic of the Order, was Cardinal Farley's lay leader of the New York Catholic War Drive which netted $5 million, two thirds of which was donated to the K. of C. Committee on War Activities. The Knights organized parish teams which collected more than $3 million, but there were many large donors; the Carnegie and Rockefeller Foundations donated $250,000 and $100,000 respectively, while wealthy Catholic families such as the Bradys, Ryans, and Dohertys each contributed $50,000.[125] While this campaign was in progress, Agar and

Pelletier were negotiating over the role of the Order in the reconstituted N.C.W.C.

Originally, Father Burke's executive committee was accountable to the fourteen American archbishops but, because the latter only met once a year, there was no way in which the hierarchy could provide support and direction to the committee. In early December, Cardinal Gibbons appointed bishops Peter J. Muldoon (Rockford, Illinois), Joseph Schrembs (Toledo, Ohio), Patrick J. Hayes (auxiliary bishop of New York), and William T. Russell (Charleston, South Carolina) as members of the administrative committee of the N.C.W.C., with Muldoon as chairman. To promote harmony between the Order and the N.C.W.C., the latter formed an executive committee composed of six Supreme Officers of the Order and six representatives of the old N.C.W.C. executive committee. The N.C.W.C.'s immediate work was assigned to two subcommittees, one of which, the committee of the Knights of Columbus, was chaired by Supreme Secretary McGinley, who was authorized to oversee the work of the Order, particularly on budgetary matters. John Agar and Father Burke, who had appeared unsympathetic to the Knights' independent role, served on the other subcommittee, charged with directing the council's non–K. of C. war work.

Unlike the original N.C.W.C. Executive Committee, which threatened to absorb the Order's work into a national Catholic organization, Bishop Muldoon's Administrative Committee assured the Supreme Board that it did not want to reduce the independent identity of the Knights' war activities but merely to place it within the authority structure of the Church's united war effort. Muldoon attended Board meetings in the spring and summer of 1918, pledging the N.C.W.C.'s enthusiastic support for the Knights' war work. During a May 26 meeting of the Board of Directors, when there was deep concern over the lack of progress overseas, Muldoon told the Directors that he was "glad to hear you criticize yourselves. It is safe . . . so long as you do not criticize yourselves outside the fold of your organization. All the difficulties you are having, the Y.M.C.A. are having them, everyone. . . . Let our criticism be with the idea of betterment." He assured them that he was "sure the Bishops of the country are . . . highly pleased" with the Knights' work. "Do not become downhearted or discouraged. . . . War Council or no War Council, we stand behind the Knights of Columbus everywhere." Muldoon promised that the N.C.W.C. had no intention of interfering with the Order's work. "Whatever may come in the future we cannot interfere with the government's statement that you are standing for the Catholics of the country. We do not want to interfere. Consequently, see that you stand true." The bishop concluded his remarks with an impassioned pastoral message:

[You] are the most important body of Catholic laymen that has ever existed in this country. . . . The Catholic Church is looking to you to make a record, you Grand Knights of the Gospel of Jesus. . . . The Knights of Columbus are doing a sacred work, a truly priestly work . . . you are one in Christ and in His Prayer. You have behind you a united Catholic people. Therefore, go forth for Jesus Christ and for the Glory of the Church.[126]

The only major conflict between Muldoon and the Order centered on budgetary authority and methods of fund-raising. Since, in the summer of 1918, the War Department recognized the N.C.W.C. as the official Catholic organization for war work, with the Knights of Columbus as its agent for recreational work, the Order had to submit its budget to the N.C.W.C. However, because the Order had raised funds independently for over a year, it considered that it held these moneys as a public trust, which precluded merging them with those of the N.C.W.C. Indeed, the Knights financed their fund drives from their general fund rather than from contributions, and had widely publicized the fact that their financial statements were open to inspection. After some confusion, a formula for a united fund-raising method was achieved whereby the campaign would be under the auspices of the N.C.W.C., but "the symbol of the Knights of Columbus should be given every possible prominence and their achievements and their needs in this war brought strikingly before the public."[127]

At the 1918 "Victory Convention" of the Supreme Council in New York, several distinguished speakers congratulated the Order for its war work. Raymond Fosdick reported that the K. of C. efforts in Europe "will receive lasting commendation." French High Commissioner Marcel Knecht stated that "the devoted secretaries in khaki, wearing on their arms the well known K.C., have been always ready to give their complete services not only to the Catholics, but to all the soldiers of Democracy." John Agar, Father Burke, and bishops Hayes, Russell, and Muldoon were also guests of the convention. Muldoon explained the role of the Order within the N.C.W.C. and its proposed campaign for funds.[128] While the Order and the N.C.W.C. were planning their fund drive, the White House announced a plan for a combined drive for all the service organizations. The Knights had long advocated a united campaign but vigorously protested against the War Department's decision to split the drive in two. According to the

August 14 directive, the Y.M.C.A. and Y.W.C.A., the War Camp Community Service, and the American Library Association would conduct a combined drive in November, while the K. of C., the Jewish Welfare Board, and the Salvation Army would wait until January for their drive.[129]

A few days later, Flaherty issued a press release in which he explained the Order's opposition to the fragmented campaign. In response to the War Department's statement that the different fiscal years among the organizations precluded a united drive, Flaherty noted that this issue had never surfaced during discussions on the combined drive. He said that the Knights were "honored with the association with the Jewish Welfare Board, to whom we have extended the use of our buildings for their religious services, and with the Salvation Army, whose wonderful work at the front has won the heart of every boy and every Mother and Father." But he considered it a "pity" so to divide the agencies during "this time of stress and universal desire to help the government win the war." Flaherty criticized "the unfairness" of the directive which placed the Catholics, Jews, and Salvation Army drive in January "when they are left to get what is left" after the Y.M.C.A. and others collect their funds. Flaherty reported that the Order had been cooperating with over four hundred local groups throughout the country and that there was "an almost unanimous opinion in favor of one joint war chest for all the activities, except for the Red Cross which . . . stands by itself."[130]

The *Columbiad* reported that Dr. John R. Mott, general secretary of the Y.M.C.A., had been the major spokesman against a combined drive, but ultimately his opinion did not prevail as the War Department announced in September that the seven agencies would conduct a united campaign scheduled to commence on November 11. By this time the N.C.W.C. had been approved as the official Catholic organization, but with the qualification that funds would be solicited "for the Knights of Columbus."[131] Indeed, of the $30-million-budget that the N.C.W.C. submitted for the $170-million combined drive, $25 million was earmarked for the Order, which had raised more than $14 million on its own during the previous year. A committee of eleven, representative of the seven agencies, was formed within Fosdick's office to administer the fund. John Agar and James Phelan, a Knight from Boston, represented the N.C.W.C. Ironically, the combined drive commenced the very day on which the Armistice was signed. Peace prevented the early success of the drive, but the goal was ultimately achieved the following spring. The Knights and the bishops' committee of the N.C.W.C. continued to cooperate, but there were many conflicts between the Order and Father Burke and John Agar, particularly over the latter's attempt to interfere with the N.C.W.C.'s subcommittee on K. of C. war activities.

IV

With the signing of the Armistice, the Allied armies moved across the borders into Germany and Belgium and, since the K. of C. huts followed the troops, the Order established numerous recreation centers to serve the occupation forces. Within the next ten months, thirty-two K. of C. clubs were opened in Germany. Many of these clubs included makeshift hotels for soldiers on leave, nearly all provided baths and showers, and some had gymnasiums and theaters for entertainment.[132] Though all the organizations engaged in a variety of services, the Y.M.C.A. gained fame through its canteen service, the Salvation Army through its coffee and doughnuts, and the Knights of Columbus through its athletic contests. Frequently two or more organizations cooperated in special entertainment programs. One such cooperative endeavor occurred in Antwerp, where, on July 3, 4, and 5, 1919, a series of musical shows was presented. The theater was provided by the Knights, the entertainment by the Y.M.C.A., and the orchestra by the Jewish Welfare Board.[133]

The Order responded to the large number of American soldiers and sailors passing through Great Britain by enlarging its operation, which by August 1919 included nine clubs under the direction of Edgar A. Sharpe, assistant commissioner for Great Britain and Ireland. From his London headquarters on the Haymarket, Sharpe administered four clubs in London and those in Southampton, Winchester, and Knotty Ash, near Liverpool; two in Scotland; and a large club and hotel in Dublin. The Canadian Knights, who had initiated their war work shortly after their American brothers, also had an extensive network of clubs in the British Isles. Though there were only 19,000 Canadian Knights in 1917, they managed to collect over $1 million for their program, which, unlike the Americans, was limited to clubs outside camps.

Under the direction of Secretary Jere J. Ormand, the Order opened a club in Rome in November 1918. He secured seven rooms in the Hotel Minerva, where, on Thanksgiving night, the Order hosted a dinner for over two hundred guests, including Vatican and civil dignitaries.[134] The club could sleep twenty and was a center of tourist activity in arranging for sightseeing trips and audiences with the Holy Father. When William P. Larkin, the New York–based director of overseas work, visited Rome he was privileged to receive an audience with Pope Benedict XV, who "was enthusiastic concerning what the Knights had accomplished in Rome for the American soldiers. He expressed the hope that the Order would maintain a permanent club building in that city."[135] The Rome club was closed in late 1919, but at the request of Admiral Harry R. Knapp the Order opened clubs with hotel facilities in Venice, Spoleto, and Constantinople.[136]

K. of C. work in France remained the major zone of operations after the Armistice. By August 1919 nearly one hundred clubs had been established and over four hundred secretaries and thirty-six chaplains were stationed there. Le Mans and Bordeaux were two of the major K. of C. recreation centers. Immediately after the Armistice, the secretaries devised special postcards known as "Safe and Sound" cards by which soldiers notified their families that they had survived the war. Upon boarding ship for home, each soldier was provided with a free K. of C. gift pack with cigarettes, sweets, handkerchiefs, and shaving material in accord with the motto, "Everybody Welcome, Everything Free."[137] The free-gift policy became controversial during late February 1919, when General Pershing sent a directive to the War Department requesting that a limit be placed on free distribution because it was an unnecessarily patronizing policy, because it placed an undue burden on transportation facilities in Europe, and because it was injurious to the health of the soldiers. After the War Department passed a resolution which limited free distribution to 10 percent of an agency's budget (the Order and the Salvation Army's free distribution allotments were 20 to 30 percent), the Supreme Board of Directors responded with a vigorous protest. The Board's position was that since the Order solicited public funds on the "Everybody Welcome, Everything Free" policy, it could not alter the policy without violating a public trust.[138] Ultimately a compromise was reached whereby the 10 percent principle did not apply to stationery and periodicals. However, an Army directive overseas limited free distribution to locales where supplies were low. This, however, proved to be unenforceable, and the K. of C. secretaries continued to distribute everything free according to their traditional practice. In an article in *America*, D. J. McCarthy viewed the entire controversy as emanating from other organizations which, out of jealousy, aimed "to curtail their [the Knights'] popularity." To those who condemned the free distribution of candy and gum as detrimental to the health of the soldiers, McCarthy sarcastically retorted, *"O Tempora! O Mores! O Spearmint!"*[139]

William Alan Wolff, in an article in *Collier's,* testified to the soldiers' view of the Order's free distribution policy. "For one thing, Casey managed to eliminate red tape entirely. Since nothing was sold, there was never a chance for a timid secretary to make the mistake of refusing supplies to a hungry outfit that had missed connections with its payroll. Man after man would go to a K-C hut, get cigarettes, or whatever, and then ask: 'How much?' 'Son—this stuff doesn't belong to Casey!' the secretary would answer. 'It was just handed to us by your folks back home to pass on to you. Your money's no good with Casey —get that.'"[140]

However, as late as mid-April, the Order's free policy was still controversial. Raymond Fosdick wrote to John Agar from Paris informing him of the K. of C.'s "open defiance to General Pershing and the whole administrative staff" and asking him to notify Bishop Muldoon.[141] It appears that Fosdick's efforts to have Muldoon order the Knights to conform to army regulations were ineffective. On several other minor issues, Fosdick voiced complaints to Mulligan and Edward Hearn. Generally, the War Department was very grateful for the Order's war work, as symbolized by Secretary of War Baker's awarding Supreme Knight Flaherty the Distinguished Service Medal.[142]

In early December 1919, just as the Order was terminating its operations in Europe, William Fox, Supreme Director from Indiana and former assistant overseas director, sailed for Siberia, where several K. of C. secretaries had established huts to serve the American soldiers and sailors stationed there. Fox arrived in Vladivostok on New Year's Day, 1920. He reported that the Order's work "was done under the most trying circumstances, three revolutions having taken place during our stay there." To serve American soldiers stationed along the Trans-Siberian Railroad, one of the secretaries had converted a boxcar into a K. of C. hut on wheels, equipped with writing desks and a record player and stocked with foodstuffs. Occasionally the hut was transformed into a theater whenever talent was available. The K. of C. terminated this operation in January 1920 when the American troops were ordered out of Siberia.[143]

Fox also visited Japan and China, where he arranged for entertainment for American sailors and for permission to erect portable altars for Mass and other conditions to facilitate their spiritual welfare. He met many civilian members of the Order in Yokohama and Shanghai who were eager to establish councils. He was encouraged by the well-managed huts in the Philippine Islands, where the Order had established a council (Manila Council 1000) in 1905. In his diary, he recorded that the Catholic hierarchy urged the extension of the Order in the Philippines noting "that membership in the Knights of Columbus would be the salvation of Catholicity among the [Filipino] men who were being pressured to join the Masons."[144]

V

While the Order's hut program was expanding to meet the demands of the Army and Navy's postwar condition, it was also expanding its own reconstruction program to facilitate the veterans' adjustment to civilian life. On November 22, 1918, just eleven days after the armistice was signed, the Supreme Board of Directors voted "that the Knights of Columbus as part of their community and welfare work adopt an educational, vocational, occupational, and employment program at once."[145] In cooperation with the U.S. Employment Service of the Department of Labor, the Order initiated a national employment campaign which incorporated the local councils as employment bureaus. In the larger cities, councils cooperated with central committees on the chapter level. On January 8, 1919, Supreme Secretary McGinley wrote to over seventeen hundred Grand Knghts of the local councils, urging them to coordinate their employment efforts and to seek out the best men to serve on employment committees, even nonmembers and non-Catholics.[146] A few weeks later, McGinley sent a memo to all K. of C. secretaries scheduled to return aboard transport ships, directing them to distribute and collect employment application forms and to return them to the Supreme Office, which in turn was distributing them to local council representatives. "[It] is expected that former employers will, even at some financial risk or loss, if necessary, make immediate provisions for the reabsorption of the returning men into industrial life."[147] This hope never materialized; unemployment reached three million in February 1919.

In April, Peter W. Collins, the former head of the Electrical Workers and a leader in the A.F. of L., left his position with the League to Enforce Peace to assume the administration of the Order's employment service. As noted in Chapter 7, Collins was a lecturer in the Order's anti-Socialist campaign and in that capacity had visited every state in the union and every province in Canada. He devised an extensive and detailed plan which called for the establishment of five committees within each local council under the headings agricultural, business, industrial, professional, and vocational. Each committee was to seek its members from appropriate occupation groups, keep accurate statistics, and coordinate its efforts with district and state deputies, with the Supreme Office, and with private and public employment bureaus.[148]

From the turn of the century, local councils had served as employment agencies. The War Activities Committee had organized the councils into a national network for fund-raising, so that when Collins introduced this plan there was the tradition and the organization ready to implement the employment scheme. The N.C.W.C. had also established employment bureaus, many of which were administered by Knights. Under the direction of Father John J. Burke's Committee on Special War Activities, Father John O'Grady had developed a national employment program. Though Burke and O'Grady attempted to curtail the Knights' program, the Order resisted the pressure, knowing full well that the N.C.W.C. could not compete with the more than seventeen hundred K. of C. councils.[149]

Less than a year after he had been appointed director general of the Order's reconstruction and employment work, Collins reported that "the story of what had been done by the K. of C. to open the door of opportunity to overseas men reads like a romance of the modern business world."[150] Indeed, the statistics for the first ten months were impressive. The Knights sponsored a canvassing drive in which almost 450,000 employers were contacted in the New England and mid-Atlantic states and nearly 150,000 veterans were placed in jobs. A *Saturday Evening Post* article illustrated the nondenominational character of the employment work. "'The K. of C. gets jobs for only Catholics,' said the employer. 'That's funny,' said the canvasser. 'I'm a Presbyterian and they pay me $4.00 a day to find jobs for other Presbyterians and any other kind of creed-holder.' "[151] Collins viewed the reconstruction work within the context of the Order's traditional struggle against socialism, and he applauded the trade-union movement's commitment to economic progress and social reform.[152]

By 1921 the postwar recession had ended and unemployment had dropped substantially. The Order discontinued its employment service, after having found jobs for over 300,000 veterans. To those veterans who could not seek work because of injuries, the Order responded by assigning over two hundred secretaries in nearly five hundred hospitals throughout the country.[153]

Another dimension of the Order's postwar general reconstruction work was its broad education program. The first K. of C. venture into education occurred at Camp Devens, Massachusetts, in June of 1919, where camp secretaries sponsored vocational courses for soldiers entering the civilian job market. By November 1919, the date upon which the War Department assumed the work performed by voluntary organizations, there were K. of C. schools in twenty-five camps with a total enrollment of nearly seven thousand students. The core of the curriculum was vocational, but courses were also offered in English, government, history, and religion. Many nonveterans and some women became students for a slight fee.

Encouraged by such a widespread response, the Board of Directors established an Education Committee composed of Flaherty, Pelletier, and McGinley in June 1919. After the committee had consulted with prominent educators during a week-long conference, it embarked on the establishment of a national evening-school program which would be tuition-free for veterans. The evening-school program was organized along professional lines with highly trained national and regional directors, administrators, and faculty. The program reached its peak in the spring of 1920 when over a hundred schools had a combined enrollment of over fifty thousand students. Simultaneous with the establishment of the evening schools, the Order developed a correspondence school, administered by the Supreme Office, with an enrollment of almost 25,000 students, and awarded over four hundred college scholarships to veterans. The entire educational program may be viewed as a precursor to the G.I. Bill of Rights and was a unique development, as no other wartime social-service agency entered into these fields.[154]

The Order financed its entire reconstruction work from its own war fund and the balance of the united war fund. The education programs, all of which were terminated by 1926, except for the correspondence courses, cost nearly $10 million. Though it depended on outside funds, reconstruction entailed tens of thousands of volunteers throughout the nation. Supreme Knight Flaherty reflected on such a blend of practical services with the idealism of Columbianism when he remarked, "We have served men and women of all colors and creeds in these schools; we have been enabled to better the lives of white and colored, Protestant, Jew, and Catholic alike—and it is my hope . . . that we may always provide these opportunities for our fellow citizens, for in providing them we are adding immeasurably to the quality of citizenship."[155]

Never before or since has an organization of Catholic laity had such an impact upon American society as did the Knights of Columbus in their war and reconstruction work. Though there were several periods of tension and conflict, they never impeded the work, which literally stretched around the globe. The Knights succeeded in demonstrating Catholic loyalty, and, as Callahan had predicted, anti-Catholicism subsided during the war. Other than *The Menace*'s weekly attacks upon the Order, there were few incidents of anti–K. of C. activity.

The Knights achieved great popularity among the soldiers. "Casey" became a well-known nickname among the armed forces, symbolized by a U.S. ship christened *Casey*. To the non-Catholic soldier, the K. of C. secretary was "a regular guy who never pushed his religion," but to the Catholic he was one of his own who provided a Catholic chapel, confession, and Mass. The American hierarchy, President Wilson, General Pershing, Marshal Ferdinand Foch, Desiré Cardinal Mercier, and others paid tribute to the Knights' war and reconstruction work. However, the greatest tribute to the Knights was the admiration demonstrated by the nearly 400,000 men who joined the Order between 1917 and 1923.

9

The Mission Abroad and Divisions at Home

THE KNIGHTS OF COLUMBUS WAR AND RECONSTRUCTION WORK constituted the opening of a new era in the history of the Order. During the twenties, the leadership became conscious of the Knights' prestigious social and religious stature. Because it had successfully mobilized thousands of men in support of the war effort, the Order was infused with the self-confidence that it could respond with organizational skill and with social and political power to any need of Church and society. In this sense, the K. of C. reflected the passage of American Catholicism from an immigrant Church to a well established and respected religious denomination which had proven its patriotic loyalty in the acid test of the Great War. By 1920 both the Church and the Knights had achieved a sense of maturity within the fabric of American culture. Nevertheless, the religious perspective precluded a comfortable conformity to many trends within this society. Indeed, the story of the Knights of Columbus is best understood as a series of conflicts with some of the major forces in this period of rapid social change.

In general, the Order assumed a conservative position on divorce, abortion, and the role of women, but on other issues of social justice it advocated liberal reform in opposition both to unrestricted capitalism and to doctrinaire socialism. Editorials and articles in *Columbiad* (renamed *Columbia* in August 1921) clearly illustrate these positions, as well as the Order's general perspective on what was being widely discussed as the "crisis of civilization." Thus, *Columbia* published several articles by Hilaire Belloc, G. K. Chesterton, E. I. Watkin, and Theodore Maynard, authors who lashed out at the relativism of contemporary philosophy, the breakdown of the family, and the inhumane components of industrial capitalism. These writers tended to view the origin of the "crisis" in the Reformation's successful attack upon a unified Christendom and to view the remedy as a revival of an integrated society animated by Catholic principles of culture and social justice. Postwar disillusionment, derived from industrial conflicts, from severe economic and social dislocation, and from the realization that great technological progress is no preventive for the conflagration of war, appeared to justify such deep questioning of the very foundations of modern life. Though the leaders of the Knights of Columbus did not explicitly concur in the views expressed in *Columbia,* they did deplore many of the symptoms of the crisis and established programs and sponsored projects which were intended to remedy many of the ills of society. For example, Peter W. Collins and David Goldstein continued their K. of C. lectures on the evils of socialism and the virtues of the principles of social reform embedded in *Rerum Novarum.* Condé B. Pallen (an editor of the *Catholic Encyclopedia*) and James J. Walsh (author of many historical books, including *The Thirteenth, the Greatest of Centuries*) lectured on the irreligious tendencies in contemporary culture.

Supreme Knight Flaherty's report to the 1919 Supreme Council included several references to the Order's prestige and self-confidence as well as to its determination to struggle against the forces putatively eroding Western civilization. He explicitly identified the prestige of the Order with that of American Catholicism:

Brothers, our record is part of the national record, our name is written large in the glorious history of the greatest war the world has ever seen. God has so guided us that today we stand more powerful than ever and with ever increasing power, acknowledged throughout the world as a force for good. It is, indeed, a time in which he who wears the badge of knighthood may raise his head among his fellowmen; it is, indeed, a time when the word Catholic signifies more than it ever did in the history of the Church.[1]

After reviewing the Order's reconstruction program, aimed at alleviating unemployment and providing education as the Order's means of combating "the fermenting forces of socialism and anarchy," Flaherty elaborated on the need for a revival of faith as the integral principle of a civilized society.

We know there is a danger ahead. . . . short-sighted men on both sides of the dispute between extreme radicalism and oppressive plutocracy are blindly driving the established order of society towards catastrophe. It is the majority of sane, industrious citizens—of men and women who hold their faith and live up to it, who scorn the cynical iconoclasm which describes religion as a panacea for the weaker in the struggle for wealth—who scorn it through the unfailing conviction that God is greater than his world, and who know that human evils can be remedied by Faith, more effectively than by reason—for Faith is the divine inspiration and guide of reason, and reason, when an instrument of Faith, works at its best; when the enemy of Faith, it is merely destructive —it is the vast majority of industrious, God-fearing Americans who will save our country from ruin when reckless anarchy and grasping plutocracy have wreaked their utmost evil, when fallible statecraft has miserably failed.[2]

Flaherty's criticism of "oppressive plutocracy" was in accord with the Catholic bishops' program of "Social Reconstruction" of 1919, which called for a series of liberal reforms to control the self-serving biases of American capitalism. Written by P. H. Callahan's friend, Father John A. Ryan (Callahan-Ryan profit-sharing scheme) the program advocated many state measures later incorporated into the New Deal.[3] At the 1919 Supreme Council Convention, the delegates concurred with the Committee on the Good of the Order's "endorsement of the sentiments expressed in the bishops' manifesto . . . that employees should receive a living wage, and be surrounded by proper working conditions and proper home environment."[4]

Like the Church in general, the Knights did not vigorously pursue the implementation of the specific goals of the bishops' manifesto, but its employment bureaus and educational projects were strong expressions of their own reconstruction program. Except for the promotion of Columbus Day, the Knights had never been active lobbyists for specific legislative measures on either state or federal levels. Though the Order assumed strong positions and articulated the enlightened Catholic layman's moral concern over issues ranging from censorship of motion pictures to capital-labor relations, the means for implementing these positions were generally moral persuasion and education.[5] In some instances, the Order engaged in direct-action measures by establishing its own programs.

In response to a plea from the Vatican, the Knights established playgrounds in Rome, a project which enhanced the Order's prestige and manifested its enormous international strength. This chapter opens with an exploration of developments related to the K. of C. presence in the Eternal City and closes with the story of other youth programs. The central focus of this phase of the narrative is an examination of a major dissident movement, a reaction against growing power of the national officers, which severely challenged the administration of the Order, The increased concentration of power and *Columbia*'s projection of the Order's cosmopolitanism were viewed by the dissenters as symbols of the growing gap between the Supreme Office and the membership, and the Order's Roman project seemed indicative of this trend. Instead of a direct-action effort, the dissidents advocated financing the playgrounds but leaving their administration to Rome; they thus intimated that the Supreme Office was more concerned about the prestige of the K. of C. and its leaders than it was about the common good of the rank and file.

II

The Knights' path to Rome led through France. The "Peace Convention" of 1919, held in Buffalo, New York, celebrated the strong ties between France and the Order; Marcel Knecht of the French High Commission bestowed the cross of the Legion of Honor upon James Flaherty; the delegates assembled at the Lafayette memorial to pay tribute to the French defender of American liberty; and the convention unanimously voted to offer an equestrian statue of Lafayette to the city of Metz, where, as a young army officer, he had decided to take part in the American war of independence. The statue was intended to commemorate the "glorious dead of the American and French armies" who struggled to capture Metz, which had been seized by Germany in the Franco-Prussian War of 1870. Marshal Ferdinand Foch, "soldier of civilization and of Christ," was educated at the Jesuit College in Metz, Marcel Knecht's grandfather was from the city, and General Pershing was partially of Alsatian heritage.[6] Within a month, Knecht informed Flaherty that the French government and the city of Metz enthusiastically accepted the Order's offer. Though the Supreme Council of 1919 had unanimously endorsed the statue proposal, there was considerable controversy among the councils within the German-American community. Several German-language newspapers severely criticized the Order for honoring Lafayette, who was a nominal Catholic and a Freemason. For example, in May 1920, the *Familien Blatt* of Techny, Illinois, published a caustic article, "A Freemason Saint of the K.C.," which condemned Lafayette as a supporter of anticlerical and anti-papal laws. Following the lead of Arthur Preuss, the *Familien Blatt* attacked the Knights for posturing as "Catholic *par excellence*" when actually their forthcoming Metz pilgrimage "was a disgrace to true Catholic feelings."[7]

One German-American Knight, J. M. Weinzapfel of Scotland, Texas, wrote to Supreme Secretary McGinley, "Practically all the German newspapers are taking this matter in the same light [as the *Familien Blatt*]. . . . The councils in the German communities are having very serious discussions over this and for defense of the Order it is quite difficult." Though he then stated that such anti–K.C. criticism was derived from "bigotry, malice, and contempt," he asked McGinley to advise him how the national leadership "has handled this matter."[8] McGinley responded by explaining that the gift of the statue was not intended "to glorify Lafayette as a Catholic" but rather "to express appreciation of the aid and assistance given by France to the struggling colonies, in which Lafayette was a leader, standing beside Washington almost from the beginning." McGinley reminded Weinzapfel that though the American Catholic hierarchy had not endorsed the gift of the statue, "all the bishops and archbishops of France are expected to attend the ceremony at Metz."[9] McGinley also could have pointed out that there was strong precedent for the Order honoring Freemasons, as most of the heroes of the American Revolution were enrolled in Masonic lodges. In his report to the 1920 Supreme Council, Flaherty briefly referred to "the objections . . . whispered against the gift" and, in defense, repeated these comments by McGinley.[10]

On August 5, 1920, at the close of the New York meeting of the Supreme Council, called the "Lafayette Convention," 235 Knights sailed for France. John Reddin, Supreme Master of the Fourth Degree, recorded in his diary that the New York police band and more than one hundred taxis carrying friends and relatives "gave a fitting send off to the Pilgrims going to Metz."[11] On August 15, Marshal Foch met the Knights' ship at Le Havre and accompanied them for several days. In Paris, they were greeted by Leon Cardinal Amette and had luncheon at Versailles. After visiting several battlefields, the Knights journeyed to Rheims, where they met various ecclesiastical and civic dignitaries, including Premier Alexandre Millerand. On August 20, thousands of people welcomed the Knights to Metz. "The city was profusely decorated with French and American flags. The streets were lined with many thousands of people, waving flags and shouting 'Vive l'Amérique, vive les Chevaliers de Colomb.' Everybody agreed that royalty never received a greater welcome than did the Knights of Columbus."[12]

On the next day, proclaimed a regional holiday for Alsace-Lorraine, a Solemn High Mass was offered at the Metz Cathedral, followed by the unveiling of the Knights' memorial. The bronze equestrian statue, nearly eighteen feet in length and height, was a reproduction from the cast of a Lafayette statue which Paul Bartlett had sculptured and which is located in the court of the Louvre. Reddin described the statue, saying that "the whole image appears to the observer a life-like, living, breathing object. Lafayette's face sharp featured, intelligent, aristocratic."[13] He also provided an impression of the pedestal, designed by the New York architect Thomas Hastings: "The bas-reliefs are finished in Tennessee marble and the front of the pedestal pictures General Pershing at the tomb of Lafayette, on the arrival of the American army in France, uttering the famous words 'Lafayette, we are here.' The back depicts Columbus discovering America. One side shows President Wilson delivering his great war speech to Congress, the other Marshal Foch, whose genius . . . made possible the victory over Prussianism."[14]

After Hugh Wallace, the American ambassador to France, spoke, Flaherty presented Foch with a marshal's baton designed by Tiffany and costing $15,000. Marshal Foch embraced the Supreme Knight and rendered his gratitude: "I welcome you, Knights of Columbus, as the representatives of America. I know your merits because of what you have done in the war. The sentiments that led Lafayette to go to America to fight have prompted you to come to Metz to reassure France that America is ever ready to do her part."[15] These events culminated in a banquet, hosted by the Order, for over four hundred guests, when once again several speeches on Franco-American unity were delivered.

The following day the Knights visited Verdun, escorted by Marshal Henri Philippe Pétain, whose fame was associated with the war-torn battlefield. After tours of Nancy and Strasbourg, where thirty thousand people and five thousand French soldiers hailed their arrival, the Knights set off for Rome on a train provided by the French government.

Just before noon on Saturday, August 28, carriages carrying nearly 235 Knights arrived in St. Peter's Square. Dressed in silk-hat white-tie evening dress, they filed into the Consistorial Hall to be received in private audience by Benedict XV. After the Pope ascended the throne, Supreme Knight Flaherty, on behalf of the entire Order, extended gratitude for the "privilege of an audience with your august person." He identified the ideals of the Order as "wrapped up in the well-being of the Church." Echoing Belloc and Chesterton's "crisis of civilization" theme, Flaherty stated that "all the blessings of modern civilization we owe to the Church, which has the secret of peace for the turmoil and unrest with which the world is now seething." Flaherty proudly referred to the Knights' war work as proof that "Catholic ideals are not incompatible with the most complete devotion to country." After noting that Benedict XV, like Christopher Columbus, was born and raised in Genoa, he remarked to the Pope that "the Knights of Columbus claim kindred with you." Pledging the Order's "love and support [and] all the energy of our Catholic manhood," he petitioned the Pope for his blessing. "With that blessing we will go back to America strengthened in our resolve to work for God and country. In that giant land where the genuine notion of freedom is a glorious heritage, your blessing will help us to give our fellow citizens an example of Catholic Knighthood and be an incentive to labor for the common good and the glory of God."[16]

Benedict XV welcomed the Knights with sentiments of "sweet comfort and good hope." He praised them for their deep loyalty to the faith, exemplified by their strong support for the Catholic University of America and by the "unfailing help that [they] give both to bishops and parish priests for the carrying out of their pastoral ministry." He lauded the K. of C. war work, which had "gained the praise and admiration not only of Catholics, but of all of good heart." He urged the Knights to maintain their reverence to the episcopate and their determination never to involve the Order's program with that of a political party.[17]

Prior to concluding with his blessing, the Pope urged the Knights to expand their work to Rome in such a way as to combat Protestant proselytization, which was

trying to rob our children nearest to us of the most precious heritage left them by their forefathers, the Catholic faith. . . . They are trying to attract our young men who are so inclined to the pleasures of sport into associations which, while they give facilities for satisfying that inclination, tend to make insidious attacks in the hearts of the young men on the sacred treasure of Catholic principles. . . . You, noble Knights of Columbus, are not ignorant of the work of propaganda of which all speak, and all glory in the hope that, in conformity with the aims of your association, you will set your good propaganda here in Rome, too, against the wicked propaganda, which to our sorrow we see so widely spread in this dear city. There is another field of competition before you. May this struggle bring you as much merit as it brings us hope.[18]

After Flaherty had knelt to kiss his ring, the Pope "with democratic simplicity announced that he would go among the assemblage, instead of requiring them to kneel before him singly."[19]

The next day, Sunday, the pilgrims gathered in the Vatican gardens, where Benedict XV celebrated Mass and distributed Communion to each of the Knights. The morning culminated with movie cameramen photographing the event. Hearn reported that it was the first time a pope had permitted himself to be filmed for motion pictures.[20] The following evening the Order hosted a banquet at the Grand Hotel in honor of Monsignor Bonaventura Cerretti, Papal Undersecretary of State and former representative of the Vatican in Washington. Cerretti expressed the Pope's delight "on the piety and devotion shown by the Knights." He also reiterated Benedict's "invitation to the Knights to establish themselves in Rome, and assist in combatting the religious propaganda against the Church." Cerretti also noted that "this invitation coming from the Pope is the equivalent of a demand. The Pope gave his unqualified approval to the Knights of Columbus."[21] These latter comments, and others recorded by John Reddin, convey the deep impression the Pope had made upon the Knights. Never before had a body of American Catholic laymen been so honored by the Papacy. Another precedent was broken when the Pope personally announced from the papal throne that Flaherty was to be named a Knight Commander of the Order of St. Gregory. As a further tribute to the Order, the American flag flew over the Vatican throughout the Knights' visit. On October 2, less than two weeks after the Knights had landed in New York, Flaherty reported at a meeting of the Board of Directors that the Pope was "very anxious" that the Knights "counteract American anti-Catholic propaganda" in Rome.[22]

Rome had been absorbed into the Italian state in 1870, and the constitutional guarantees for religious toleration followed the Italian flag into this last center of papal temporal sovereignty. Various Protestant denominations established churches in Rome, most of which ministered to the Anglo-American community. The American Methodist Episcopal Church had initiated a program of evangelization when its first missionary, Leroy McVernon, established residence in Rome in 1874 and on Christmas day 1875 "dedicated . . . the first Protestant Italian Church within the city walls." In 1895 a new church, located on the Via Firenze, was dedicated; the memorial tablet was inscribed as "solemnly dedicated on the 20th of September 1895, the Twenty-Fifth Anniversary of the Downfall of Papal Power."[23]

To loyal Catholics, particularly to the Knights, the Methodist evangelization program was intrinsically pernicious. In August 1921, Edward Hearn reported to the Supreme Office his own impressions of this Methodist program as well as the views of European Catholic journalists and added that "the American Methodists are the most belligerent and hostile to the Catholic church, of all the Protestants. They have a vast program which is covered by other objects [i.e., sports programs for youth], is fiercely anti-Catholic, anti-Latin, and has for its end American imperialism, which is contrary to the sentiments of the national organizations of other peoples."[24]

Arthur Benington, in a November 1921 article in *Columbia,* substantiated Hearn's impressions. He criticized the Methodists for "working openly with the anti-clerical element" and accused the Methodist pastors of being "as savage in their attacks upon the Pope and the Church as ever was Tom Watson." Benington, who was president of the Catholic Writers' Guild of New York, informed his readers that copies of an anticlerical weekly, *"L-Asino* [sic], which regularly publishes vile and filthy cartoons and jokes directed against the Church and its clergy," were on sale at a Roman bookstore "managed by the American Methodist Church."[25] When this church announced that it had purchased nearly forty-five acres on the Monte Mario for a large complex of religious and educational structures,[26] Supreme Knight Flaherty remarked, "They [the Methodists] have in their brazen egotism, which they mistake for audacity, dared to insult the Head of the Church, the Vicar of Christ on earth—for only recently have we heard of their attempt to build on Monte Mario, one of the seven hills of Rome opposite the Vatican itself, a Methodist Seminary. Think of it, in Rome!"[27]

An American spokesman for the Methodist Church denied any attempt "to fight . . . the Roman Catholic Church" and invoked the principle of "fair play." In a caustic response, John B. Kennedy, editor of *Columbia,* wrote that the Methodists certainly had a right to build their seminary but that actually to implement that right in Rome would be a violation of Christian ethics. Kennedy placed the Methodists within the anti-Catholic camp which disseminated lurid tales of "ex-priests and ex-nuns and . . . other like propaganda which portrayed the authority of the Vatican as a superstitious despotism of the dark ages."[28] And in an article in *L'Osservatore Romano,* the official newspaper of the Vatican, a writer explained that "the Society of the Knights of Columbus was founded about thirty years ago in order to force public opinion to recognize the rights of Catholic citizens. Instead of Methodist strongholds they hope that parks of remembrance may be planted on Monte Mario in memory of Roman soldiers who fell in the Great War, and a monument erected to Christopher Columbus 'to remind the forgetful that he brought the light of the faith and civilization to a land which is now responsible for an un-called-for outrage.' "[29]

Edward Hearn had made preliminary reports on the Roman situation throughout 1921 as he was preparing to close the war activities office of the K. of C. in Paris. However, he presented a personal report to the Board of Directors on January 15, 1922. He said that Benedict XV's invitation "came as much as a surprise to him as it did to any other person present, that this request was born in the mind of the Holy Father, and as far as he knew it was his individual suggestion."[30] Upon the request of Pietro Cardinal Gasparri, the Vatican Secretary of State, Hearn prepared an outline of the Order's projected work in Rome. He proposed that the first phase of the operation should be the establishment of a K. of C. headquarters, "with reception facilities where English-speaking visitors to the Eternal City may find a welcome with arrangements made for the furnishing of guides to English-speaking tourists. These guides are to be of a type entirely different from the common type who for years have found it profitable to speak with revilement of the Father of All Christendom."[31] The second phase should include the construction of at least two athletic fields equipped with locker and shower facilities and supervised by Italian instructors. Hearn offered his services as director of the program but stipulated that he must have the Board's "absolute confidence."[32] The Board approved Hearn's proposals and appointed him director at an annual salary of $6,000, which was later increased to $10,000, and requested that Hearn submit monthly reports to the Supreme Office.

In late April, after an intensive search and extensive legal difficulties, Hearn found a suitable location for the Order's headquarters in Rome at 25 Via della Muratte. He wrote to Flaherty that "the people in the Vatican are simply delighted that the Order has started work here and they expect of course great comfort and consolation will come to them as the result of [our] work and presence." He referred to the methods and tactics of the American Protestant proselytizers: "Business cards peddled through the streets announcing St. Paul's Methodist Episcopal Church as the 'American Church,' pamphlets distributed entitled 'The Pretensions of the Papacy.' "[33] On February 6, 1922, while Hearn was seeking a suitable site for his office, Benedict XV, who had died on January 22, was succeeded by Pius XI. After a May 14 audience with the Pope, Hearn cabled to Supreme Secretary McGinley, AT GREAT AUDIENCE TODAY, HOLY FATHER EXPRESSED ENTHUSIASTIC APPROVAL OF PROPOSED WORK, ENDORSING IT COMPLETELY, DONATING ONE PARTICULAR SITE WHERE HE SAID I CAN SEE THE DEVELOPMENT FROM MY WINDOWS.[34] Hearn's detailed account of this twenty-five-minute private audience was published in *Columbia*. He wrote that he explained to the Pope that the Order did not intend to extend its fraternal organization to Rome but rather that the Roman project was undertaken "as a tribute to the memory of Columbus . . . and to the memory of the late Pope Benedict XV." Upon hearing of Pius XI's donation of property within the shadows of the Vatican, he said that he was "amazed, and so, too, I think was the Papal attendant present in the room." Hearn quoted Pius as saying that the K. of C. presence in Rome was "very fitting . . . for it is no less important than any other kind of relief work. You will bring closer the relations between your country and Italy. I have a profound admiration for the idealism of America which is none the less practical and can see the advantage to domestic morale of the extension to other countries of advantages which America enjoys." Pius also said that the Knights' "achievements for America [have] aroused my admiration." Hearn said that Pope Pius "shares the opinion of Pope Benedict regarding foreign missionary intervention in Rome as every cultured Italian does." Pius indicated that non-Catholics should be allowed to enjoy the Knights' athletic facilities—which pleased Hearn, as he had hoped to extend the motto of the World War I huts, "Everybody Welcome, Everything Free," to the K. of C. playgrounds in Rome.[35]

Postwar Italy had suffered severe economic decline, unemployment, social dislocation, and political polarization ranging from Anarchists and Communists on the left to Mussolini's black-shirt Fascists on the right. Within this context, Pope Pius XI's reference to the morale of the youth gains added significance. Since the Italian government assumed control of Rome in 1870, each Pope had protested the loss of papal sovereignty by proclaiming himself a prisoner in the Vatican. Given these economic, political, and diplomatic conditions, the Pope realistically referred to the Order's Roman project as relief work. When the 1921 Supreme Council unanimously approved the establishment of a million-dollar fund to implement the wishes of Benedict XV, it was entitled the Italian Welfare Fund. Though the Board of Directors approved a semiannual per-capita tax of 50 cents, it was decided not to levy the January 1922 assessment because "economic and industrial affairs of the country [i.e., the U.S.A.] were in such [bad] shape."[36] Since the Italian Welfare Fund became the locus of contention within the Order, the Supreme Officers were compelled to dispel anti-administration as well as anti-Catholic rumors that the cost of the Roman project was to be illegally financed from the War Fund. After the January 1922 Board meeting, Flaherty issued a press statement in which he clarified the issue. "It is our desire . . . to make clear from the outset that none but private funds will be used for this work. The impression is held in certain parts of the country that the

K. of C. War Fund might be applied to this work. That is tantamount to saying that the Knights of Columbus will steal from disabled veterans. The K. of C. record is clean: not one penny entrusted to us for the servicemen will go to any other purpose."[37]

Throughout the next two years Hearn expressed increasing frustration over financial matters both in Rome and in the Supreme Office. Costs of playground construction and building renovation far exceeded his budget projections. Relations with the various bureaus of the Italian government entailed complex legal negotiations to settle the issue of the incorporation of an American philanthropic organization. Hearn considered himself fortunate that he had contracted the services of Giulio Galeazzi, a lawyer, whose brother Enrico spoke excellent English and was in charge of all construction aspects of the playgrounds, from their design phase to their actual use by the youth of Rome.

Between 1924 and 1927 the Order opened five recreation centers. St. Peter's Oratory, located on the site donated by Pius XI, was dedicated April 9, 1924. In the process of demolishing the old structures which had housed a foundry, the fifteenth-century coat of arms of Pope Innocent VIII was found.[38] Since he had reigned during the time of Columbus, it was salvaged and placed on one of the new buildings as an appropriate symbol of the Columbian heritage.[39] Once the site of the Circus of Nero, where Christians had been martyred, the land was regarded by the Knights as sacred soil. St. Peter's Oratory included two modern buildings, a large two-story school, and a modern gymnasium. The school, which housed a thousand-seat theater, was so designed that boys and girls could have their own separate wings, each of which included a chapel and access to its own athletic field. The school concentrated on technical training and the fine arts as a supplement to the students' regular curriculum. The boys were under the direction of secular priests appointed by the Pope, while the girls were supervised by the Daughters of Charity.

The boys' chapel was the former Church of St. Salvatore in Ossibus. Constructed in the mid-tenth century, this ancient church was renovated according to the designs of Enrico Galeazzi, who had the emblem of the Order prominently placed in two of the lovely stained-glass windows. Though St. Peter's Oratory was moved outside the Vatican in the early 1960s to make way for the present Paul VI Audience Hall, the chapel was preserved and the Order's emblem still occupies a commanding position in the church windows, the only nonecclesiastical coat of arms displayed in Vatican City.

Prior to the dedication, the Knights had presented the center to Pius XI. In a *motu proprio* dated March 25, 1924, Pius XI accepted the gift and recalled the Oratory tradition dating back to St. Philip Neri of Rome and St. Charles Borromeo of Milan.[40] The Pope had intended to be present at the dedication but, after discovering that a portion of the center extended into what was then considered territory of the Italian state, he preferred to remain in the confines of the Vatican. Instead, he sent his Secretary of State, Cardinal Gasparri, as his representative. Among the ten cardinals present for the April 9 dedication of the Oratory were George Cardinal Mundelein of Chicago and Patrick Cardinal Hayes of New York. After the ceremonies, the cardinals and Edward Hearn returned to the Vatican apartments, where Pius XI received them. In his address commemorating the occasion, which contained several references to the unsolved "Roman question," the Pope commented on the appropriateness of the presence of American cardinals, "for it must be said that we owe it not only to American munificence, but better still to the intelligence, generosity, and charity of the American heart and soul, and especially of that real honor of the United States of America, which the Knights of Columbus are, Knights of honor and love for the Holy See." Pius XI congratulated Enrico Galeazzi when he applauded the center as a splendid work "as much from the artistic as the construction point of view."[41] He then noted that St. Peter's Oratory was a work of "redemption and mission. Redemption of so many youth; mission in an area of Rome that needs, so greatly, care for its spiritual interests." The Pope then expressed his gratitude to Edward Hearn as the representative of the Order and asked him to convey to the Knights his "expression of true paternal recognition." He noted the Order's many "crusading and missionary" works, placing the Order's presence in Rome within the context of an American Catholic response to the "propaganda of error." As an expression of his gratitude, Pope Pius XI elevated Hearn and Flaherty to the ranks of the Grand Cross of St. Gregory, McGinley to the Commandership of St. Gregory, Supreme Chaplain Patrick McGivney to Domestic Prelate, and Enrico Galeazzi to Commandership of St. Gregory. As a final tribute, Pius XI ordered a special medal to be designed and coined to commemorate the establishment of the Oratory.[42]

Four more recreation centers were established during Flaherty's term of office: Benedict XV Playground (January 1926), located in the San Lorenzo quarter, one of Rome's most densely populated areas; Pius XI Playground (May 1926), on the Gelsomino; the Valle Giulia Playground; and the Tiber River Playground (May 1927). Each was designed by Enrico Galeazzi in accord with the natural and architectural features of the environs, and each possessed a unique character.

The development of the Order's strong presence in Rome was recognized by both the Pope and the officers as a crusade against the Protestant invasion of the Holy City. However, during 1922–23, several prominent U.S. local and state leaders formed a strong anti-administration movement within the Order, and among their long list of grievances was a criticism of the Order's Italian welfare program. This dissent movement, which adopted the title "Reconstruction Program," gained momentum as a result of a scandal surrounding the political activities of a prominent Knight, Joseph Pelletier, district attorney of Suffolk County (Boston). Thus, at a time when the Order was gaining great prestige through its Roman projects and was on the brink of a major battle with the gathering forces of anti-Catholicism in America, it was also to confront public scandal and internal divisiveness.

III

Joseph Pelletier, of French-Canadian and Irish parentage, experienced a rapid rise to leadership both within the Order and within Boston politics. Joining Franklin Council No. 168 in 1896, by 1901 he was elected State Deputy and chosen to fill an unexpired term on the National Board of Directors. His close friendship with then Supreme Knight Edward Hearn (also of the Boston area), led to his election as National Advocate in 1907. Two years later the Democrats of Boston elected him district attorney of Suffolk County. Unlike New York's Democratic Party, which was tightly controlled by the Tammany Hall leadership, Boston political leaders such as Martin Lomasney, John F. ("Honey Fitz") Fitzgerald, and James Michael Curley developed a personal ward-based following and competed with one another for major political offices.[43] Because the Boston Irish dominated the Democratic Party, they formed a united religious and ethnic opposition to the largely Protestant Yankee-dominated Republican Party. Indeed, in no other American city was there so intense a political struggle between Catholic Irish and Protestant Yankees. Though Pelletier continued to be reelected until his 1922 downfall, he was the persistent target of the Yankee Watch and Ward Society, with Godfrey L. Cabot, one of the most prominent of the Boston Cabots, as its treasurer and driving force. The Watch and Ward Society originated in 1878 and was a citizens' organization ostensibly dedicated to detecting crime overlooked by the police. Pelletier and Cabot clashed on several issues relating to the methods by which the society gathered evidence for the cases it brought to the district attorney's office. Angered by Pelletier's refusal to prosecute such cases, Cabot unsuccessfully attempted to have Pelletier removed from office through legislative investigation and a State Supreme Court trial. In November 1919, Pelletier discovered that a recording device had been concealed in his office and that the wires had been traced to the office of Godfrey Cabot.[44] In a headline article in the *Boston Evening Record* it was reported that Cabot justified the installation of the "detective machine" in 1917 on the grounds that he needed incriminating evidence to support another suit in the State Supreme Court to remove Pelletier from office. It was also reported that the Watch and Ward Society had hired a detective who kept Pelletier under surveillance for over two years. The society's motives derived from Pelletier's failure "to take steps to close Rovere House and other Boston hostelries against which the Watch and Ward Society had evidence on the grounds that they were houses of assignation."[45] According to a friend of Pelletier, the reason why he refused to prosecute these cases was that the evidence was "gathered immorally by hiring college boys as decoy clients in these houses."[46] When the suit to remove Pelletier from office was accepted by the Supreme Court, the case did not include the latter incident; rather, Pelletier was charged with several counts of extortion and blackmail, as well as failure to prosecute known criminals. Since this was a civil suit, Pelletier did not face the possibility of imprisonment, but by the time the court heard the case in January 1922, he and the Knights of Columbus had received a vast amount of adverse publicity.[47]

Declaring that he did not have enough time during an election year to prepare adequately, Pelletier did not take the stand as a witness in his own defense. Instead, U.S. Senator James A. Reed (Democrat, Missouri) and Louis C. Boyle (former attorney general of Kansas) pleaded his case. In his closing argument, which amounted to over fifty pages of detailed scrutiny of the state's case against his client, Senator Reed asked, "Does this diabolical prosecution spring from religious prejudice? Is that the thing that inspires Cabot and his crew, that makes them gather witnesses from the four corners of the earth, that gives protection to the criminal and near criminal? [Many of the state's witnesses were convicted felons] Is that [i.e., religious prejudice] the sinister shadow which rises back of the scene?"[48] On February 21, 1922, the court unanimously decided that several of the allegations against Pelletier were true, and he was removed from office.

The following day, Pelletier issued a press release in which he contended that he had been tried "without the presumption of innocence" and that the court considered the testimony of "crooks, libertines, and their kind" as credible.[49] Pelletier traced the case back to his attack upon the Watch and Ward Society.

So the expected has happened. Planned long before but started in the winter of 1917, the scheme of Godfrey Cabot and his minions stung by my rebuke for the immoral methods of the Watch and Ward Society has been completed. Applications to the legislature for my investigation met with unanimous refusal; applications to the Supreme Court for my removal twice refused; engagement finally of the assistance of a high brow group of the bar association [who paid] $5,000 to manage the campaign against me; use of the peeping-tom method of dictograph in my office; stealing papers; . . . use of crook and criminal detective and sleuth without numbers—all have now culminated in securing my removal from office."[50]

In conclusion Pelletier elaborated on his notion of justice.

"My picture of justice has not been that of a blind pagan goddess with sword in one hand and scales in the other; but rather a wide-eyed, far-seeing, Christ-like figure with outstretched hands offering succor, hope, and consolation to all who have transgressed the law and are truly repentant."[51]

There is little doubt that Pelletier was juxtaposing the image of justice allegedly held by descendants of the Puritans to that of the working-class Irish Catholics who were, presumably, victimized by self-righteous, unmerciful Anglo-Saxons. He closed his statement with the announcement that he intended to run for reelection the following November.

The Pelletier case was so controversial that few seemed free of bias; his enemies within both the Democratic and Republican parties were convinced of his guilt while his friends viewed the court's decisions as a clear illustration of religious prejudice.[52] Supreme Knight Flaherty issued a press release on February 21, the day on which the court handed down its decision, in which he implied that despite the fact that two of its justices were Fourth Degree Knights, the Court had been swayed by anti-Catholic propaganda. "The fact that the plea of a priest to Pelletier for an erring member of his flock is characterized inferentially as a 'sinister influence' is, to my mind, sufficient indication of the philosophy against Pelletier." Flaherty expressed the "unwavering faith of his colleagues [i.e., Supreme Officers] in his integrity" and announced that "his position of great trust" as Supreme Advocate "is in no way affected by his removal from political office." *Columbia* compared Pelletier to Alfred Dreyfus, the nineteenth-century Jewish-French army officer convicted of treason on forged evidence. "That is the only reasonable epithet to apply to the case manufactured against Joseph C. Pelletier by his enemies in Boston. The smoke screen of privileged lying and near-lying cannot obscure the fact that religious prejudice is at the bottom of the case."[53]

Flaherty's support for Pelletier, published in the *New York Times,* and *Columbia*'s "American Dreyfus case" piece became more controversial than the case itself. *The Nation* stated that "militant championship of Pelletier" was tantamount to making his defenders "moral accessories after the fact to his crimes."[54] According to William J. Mulligan, a Supreme Director during this period, all the members of the Board except himself decided to "stand by Joe."[55] At their April 1922 meeting, Mulligan criticized Flaherty for "bringing the Order into the Pelletier case" and told the Board that as a result of his defense of Pelletier there was a groundswell of anti-Flaherty sentiment in the Order.[56] Mulligan's contention was substantiated by the fact that, at the state conventions in May, eight states passed resolutions condemning Flaherty's defense of Pelletier and his implicit attack upon the integrity of the Massachusetts Supreme Court; there were also several resolutions aimed at limiting terms of Supreme Officers to six years.[57] An anti-Flaherty pamphlet entitled *Authority or Anarchy,* anonymous but distributed by a Bernard Rothwell of Boston, was mailed to Grand Knights and ecclesiastical authorities throughout the country.[58] Rothwell was a member of the Catholic Laymen's Committee of Boston, which, in a letter to all the delegates to the 1922 Supreme Council Convention at Atlantic City, severely lashed out at Flaherty for his attack upon the Massachusetts Supreme Court, an act which "deliberately aligned the great organization of which he is the head . . . with those destructive forces—avowedly anarchistic—whose persistent aim is to tear down and to destroy the very foundations of constitutional liberty, law, order, and legitimate authority." Signed by 101 members of the Laymen's Committee, some of whom were Knights and all of whom were members of the business and professional classes, the letter also attacked Flaherty for "his baseless, indefensible, [and] vicious attempt to rekindle the consuming flames of religious and racial intolerance, which, happily, here, had been dying out, and for whose lingering embers those outside the Faith are not solely responsible." These Boston Catholics were lobbying the Supreme Council Convention for the passage of a strong anti-Pelletier resolution. Since Flaherty was not up for reelection until 1923, such a resolution was the only tactical maneuver available to them. The letter concluded with a plea that the delegates "feel a personal responsibility to weigh in conscience the [results] of your action in this vital crisis [and] act solely with a view to promote the glory of God, the welfare of his Church, and the safety of the Nation."[59]

On June 29, 1922, exactly one month before the foregoing letter was posted, Pelletier submitted his resignation as Supreme Advocate. He explained that he had "contemplated resigning some time ago, but when my enemies outside the Order commenced a propaganda within it to force trouble upon me, I decided to wait and watch developments." Since he viewed the anti-Pelletier resolutions emanating from the state conventions as representing "a mere handful [who] have succumbed to this hostile propaganda,"[60] he considered himself vindicated by the vast majority of the Order and therefore tendered his resignation free from the onus of having been pressured to resign. In response to the passionately anti-Flaherty letter from the Catholic Laymen's Committee, Pelletier stated that "it was a piece of impertinence." He said that Flaherty had never criticized the Supreme Court of Massachusetts; "I challenge proof of any assertion to the contrary." He labeled the signers of the protest "Goos Goos [sic], reformers, and largely what we call 'Castle Irish.' " He expressed his confidence that the Supreme Council will not "yield to the false accusation of 100 picked would-be reformers, whose signatures were obtained only after a thorough canvass of the city extending over several weeks."[61]

At the July 1, 1922, meeting of the Supreme Board of Directors, Pelletier's resignation was accepted. Flaherty appointed Luke E. Hart, a member of the Board, Supreme Advocate. Hart could never have publicly opposed Flaherty in the Pelletier matter and have maintained his trust, but as early as March 20, Hart wrote to the State Deputy of Missouri stating his confidence in the administration's ability to overcome an anti-Pelletier, anti-Flaherty movement. However, he was uncertain "whether or not it is good policy to do so."[62] As a member of the Board, Hart was the target of anti-administration protests in Missouri. In late March he wrote that reprints of Rothwell's letters and other anti-Flaherty protests were freely distributed at the churches on Sunday. Though Hart rightly stated that such open display of fraternal dissension was a violation of the Order's rules, he did not advocate charges against the protesters. Yet he was deeply concerned with the adverse publicity, noting that "something must be done to stop this or the Order will become a laughing stock."[63] Hart seems to have sympathized with Pelletier, but concern for the good name of the Order appears to have been his overriding consideration.

Luke Hart, later to become Supreme Knight, was born in Clinton, Iowa, in 1880. After studying law at the University of Missouri, he moved to St. Louis, where he took up legal practice and entered local politics. Because the founding families of St. Louis were French Catholics, its political life was not affected by the Yankee–Irish-Catholic conflicts which dominated Boston politics. Anti-Catholicism was frequently injected into St. Louis politics, but it never became a persistent feature of its political climate. Hart was a successful Republican alderman (1915–23) who had been urged to run for mayor. He joined Kenrick Council No. 686 in 1908, served as Grand Knight 1913–15, as District Deputy 1916–18, as State Deputy 1918–20, and as Supreme Director 1918–22, when he became Supreme Advocate (an ex-officio member of the Board). During his tenure as State Deputy he founded the Catholic Home for students at the University of Missouri and successfully led a K. of C. fund drive for the Jesuits of St. Louis University.[64]

Dr. John H. Coyle, the State Deputy of New York, led the insurgent faction at the Supreme Convention of 1922. At the New York State Convention, he had successfully run for election on a platform which called for Pelletier's removal, for a vote of censure against him, and for the dismissal of John B. Kennedy, the editor of *Columbia* and the Order's chief publicist. The resignation of Pelletier did not deter the insurgents; Coyle still demanded "a thorough housecleaning" and anticipated much strife at the Atlantic City Convention.[65] The battle centered on the anti-Flaherty and anti-Pelletier resolutions and the election of a Supreme Advocate. Though Hart had been appointed in July, he still had to face a contest at the convention. In opposition to the administration's candidate, the insurgents supported William J. Mulligan, former chairman of the War Activities Committee and a Supreme Director. A Hartford lawyer and the most powerful Knight in Connecticut, Mulligan had been a dissenter on the Board even before the Pelletier case. In a letter to Archbishop Edward J. Hanna of San Francisco, he explained his opposition to Pelletier and Flaherty and objected to Flaherty's appointment of Hart just three weeks before the convention. He told Hanna he had opposed the administration on several issues. "I have my own ideas as to the present national publication [*Columbia*] and have expressed myself as being opposed to the make-up of the paper." Mulligan advocated widespread coverage of Knights' news and full disclosure of Board meetings rather than the popular magazine format which Kennedy had developed. He also explained his opposition to the Order's work in Rome, saying that "our membership should not [have been] taxed for the maintaining of a central place in Rome where American visitors could locate and that it was impossible to feel that we could keep the Italian people in the Church by teaching them base ball [sic]." Instead he proposed giving "a lump sum of money and let Rome use it as it desired." He concluded by informing Hanna that friends had urged him to become a candidate for Advocate and that "while I have no desire to inject myself into a fight, I feel a little contest in the Convention ought not to result in any harm."[66]

When the Supreme Council convened on August 1, Archbishop John J. Glennon of St. Louis made a visit to the convention, a visit arranged through Luke Hart, his close friend. According to Hart, Glennon was "not in sympathy with the tactics of our friends on the other side."[67] In his address to the delegates, Glennon referred to the current "crisis" within the Order and told them that "you must put aside personalities for the sake of the cause you serve, at least you should not ventilate your personal grievances on the public highways."[68] Implying that Glennon's address had a positive pro-administration effect, the Boston *Globe* said his speech "was a master stroke of policy . . . [which] must have sent a chill through the veins of the reforming group."[69] But the *Catholic Transcript* referred to his "unexpected" appearance as a "coup d'état," or a "desperate stroke," and as "unwise from many points of view." The *Transcript* intimated that the archbishop was being used by Hart to bolster his support in the election for Supreme Advocate, and the paper expressed the fear that this would establish a dangerous precedent.[70]

Despite Glennon's admonitions, the three-day convention was the stormiest in the Order's forty-year history. Flaherty's report reflected Glennon's sentiments on the impropriety of ventilating "personal grievances on the public highways," but he was considerably more impassioned in his attack upon the insurgents: "I, for one, openly condemn that man who openly calumniates his brother of the Faith, for he is wantonly injuring his brother, traitorously denying the justice and fairness which even those opposed to us religiously would give if they had but the knowledge of this insult. I say to such a man who by pen or tongue knowingly injures his brother of the Faith, that he merits the most unendurable epithet ever applied to a human being—the epithet of 'traitor!' "[71] Led by Coyle of New York, the insurgents submitted resolutions ranging from a demand that Flaherty resign to limiting the term of the Supreme Knight to three years. Each of the eleven "reform" resolutions failed to achieve a majority vote. Mulligan's challenge to Luke Hart also ended in failure. However, because he lost by the narrow margin of eleven votes, the convention closed with the Order still polarized. Indeed, within six weeks, J. G. Hargrove of Milwaukee was circulating a petition to call a special session of the Supreme Council which he assumed would culminate in a majority anti-administration vote.[72] Though the petition failed to muster the necessary support, the insurgents met again in Detroit on February 11, 1923.

Dr. Coyle had been in touch with P. H. Callahan, who had been publicly critical of the Order's leadership since 1919, with the result that Callahan became a driving force among the dissidents.[73] The selection of Detroit for the location of the meeting was made, according to Callahan, because "we think the psychology of Michigan logically makes it the place."[74] The "psychology" related to the fact that Judge Joseph A. Moynihan, State Deputy, was a vigorous insurgent. Also, Bishop Michael J. Gallagher of Detroit was supportive of Moynihan's anti-administration position. With twenty-three Knights in attendance, the group divided into three committees: platform, organization, and finance, with P. H. Callahan chairman of the first and William Mulligan and Martin E. Galvin (Detroit) chairmen of the others. In mid-April, Callahan, assisted by Benedict Elder (see Chapter 7) and Dr. Coyle, submitted the Reconstruction Program to the chairman of the entire organization, Joseph Moynihan, who distributed it to Supreme Officers, Directors, present and past State Deputies, Grand Knights, Financial Secretaries, Delegates to the Supreme Council, and the members of the Catholic hierarchy.[75] Callahan explained the group's strategy: "it is our aim to have interested in the cause some State Deputy or Past State Deputy in every jurisdiction, who, having the privilege of the floor [at the State Convention], can introduce and speak for the "Reconstruction of our Order."[76] Mulligan was responsible for organizing the movement at the state level, while the headquarters for the national movement was in Detroit.[77]

The Reconstruction Program was actually a thirty-five-point platform which included several reforms to reduce salaries of Supreme Officers and expenses of the Supreme Office, to decentralize the Order's authority structure, to alter the format of *Columbia,* to compel Supreme Officers to be more accountable, and to revise the Order's rules. It attempted to appeal to the Canadian and Latin-American members by calling for an additional Deputy Supreme Knight for

Canada and a Latin-American representative on the Supreme Board. There were several points aimed at limiting the authority of the Board, such as calling meetings of District Deputies within a state jurisdiction so that the Directors would be able to influence the election of State Deputies and delegates to the convention. That section of the platform entitled "Conservation" urged the Order to work for the reclaiming of fallen-away Catholics and to establish a Catholic Interest Committee aimed at "elevating Catholic status, dissipating religious prejudices," and fostering a "cordial relationship among all citizens regardless of creed." The group opposed the Order's administration of the Roman playgrounds by advocating financial help to the Church overseas "without undertaking supervision of the work."[78]

In two memoranda, the administration responded to the Reconstruction Program point by point. In general, the Supreme Officers considered the insurgents "self-seeking and inordinately ambitious men who crave the honors and embodiments of office and who do not hesitate to use any means to attain their ends."[79] On the financial issue, the administration pointed out that Flaherty's $12,500 salary was exactly one half that of the president of the Woodmen of the World, a comparable fraternal benefit society, and that the entire administrative expenses of the Order amounted to 87 cents per member. Similar statistics on the K. of C. per-capita tax, the cost of *Columbia,* and quotations from Church and civil dignitaries were published by the Supreme Office in response to the insurgents' program.[80]

Bishop Gallagher of Detroit, State Chaplain of the Michigan Knights, became so infuriated with the Flaherty administration that he publicly referred to the Supreme Officers as "ambitious office seekers [who] are intoxicated with the glory that is theirs."[81] The immediate cause of this attack upon the Supreme Officers was a movement by pro-administration Knights in Detroit to form a new council. Had there been no national dissent movement in the Order, the institution of a new council would not have become a major issue, particularly since Detroit Council had over 8,000 members and was the only council in the city. However, the polarization within the Detroit Council was extremely severe. Michigan's State Deputy, Joseph Moynihan, chairman of the Reconstruction Group, was bitterly opposed by pro-administration Knights there, who attempted to form a new council in order to send delegates to the State Convention, where they could promote the administration's anti-Reconstruction Program and challenge Moynihan's election as State Deputy.

The issue came before the Supreme Board in January 1923 with

Father John F. Doyle, Chancellor of the Diocese, representing the bishop, who was opposed to the new council, and four members of the Gabriel Richard Club composed of pro-administration Detroit Knights seeking new council status. Board action was postponed until April pending a meeting between the petitioners and Bishop Gallagher. On April 8, in Washington, D.C., the Board convened a hearing which was charged with emotion because the petitioners had decided to pursue their aims in direct opposition to the wishes of the bishop.[82] Frederick McGraw, one of the petitioners, presented a lengthy argument for instituting a second council in Detroit based upon statistical evidence indicating widespread support among Catholic men. He reported on the February 24 meeting with the bishop, at which Gallagher had informed them of his desire that "not from fraternal, social, or religious standpoints [but for a] personal, private reason" he was opposed to a new council. The bishop had stated that he hoped to support the new council in six to eight months depending "upon developments of a certain undisclosed reason or circumstance."[83]

Deputy Supreme Knight Carmody expressed his respect for his former pastor and former bishop of Grand Rapids and testified that he was completely aloof from the group forming the new council. However, he stated that he would still consider the case on its merits.[84] John Babcock, another representative of the Gabriel Richard Club who had met with the bishop, summarized the controversy and expressed his strong loyalty to Bishop Gallagher. However, he stated that the bishop should not have the final word on the case.

It seems to me, gentlemen, that, unless some fraternal, some social, or some religious reason affecting Columbianism or Catholics, locally or nationally, is given in this matter, that his Lordship put aside his mitre, take from his shoulders his cloak, and stand before us as a Knight of Columbus. And for that reason, and having that in mind, and appreciating the fact that we are all apt to make a mistake—except possibly, on a question of faith or morals when his Lordship is not—we feel that he is mistaken in this case; consequently our membership has asked your body for a charter.[85]

That evening the Supreme Board hosted a dinner in honor of the Apostolic Delegate, Archbishop Pietro Fumasoni-Biondi. Though there is no evidence revealing discussion between the Supreme Officers and the Apostolic Delegate on the Detroit situation, it may be that such a discussion occurred, for immediately after the dinner the Board met and voted to grant the charter. William Mulligan and Patrick H. Rice voted in opposition, while Father Patrick McGivney, Supreme

Chaplain, abstained. Mulligan, who was campaigning as the Reconstruction candidate for Supreme Knight, had had two visits with Gallagher prior to the April hearing. He strongly urged the Board to support Gallagher, quoting the bishop's request to "ask for no reasons but do as we say."[86]

Shortly after the Board had granted the charter for the new Gabriel Richard Council, Bishop Gallagher delivered his impassioned attack against the Supreme Officers in a sermon at the Detroit Assembly's (Fourth Degree) Communion Mass. He rejected the principle upon which the Board decided to institute the new council in Detroit against the wishes of the ordinary, viz., that the Order is not a Catholic organization but an organization of Catholics. He contended that the assertion of such a principle was analogous to stating that one could establish an organization of Americans, not an American organization, which would be free from the authority of the government. Gallagher criticized the apathy of the majority of the Knights for not challenging the leaders, who "have set themselves up from selfish motives for the emoluments of office, for the advertising of their business or profession." He went on to say that he had information from priests and bishops that "a spirit of anticlericalism" was growing "within the ranks of many Councils" throughout the country. "There is a persistent tendency to criticize their pastors, to find fault with their conduct of parish affairs. . . . Many of the archbishops and bishops in the United States have expressed the fear that unless the Knights of Columbus are officered by thorough Catholics, they would in time become a menace to the Church and to America." To illustrate his case, he cited the Pelletier scandal and the Supreme Knight's "attack upon the Supreme Court of Massachusetts. . . . In trying to hide behind the skirts of Mother Church, they got all Catholics into trouble. In the arrogance of power, they are intoxicated with the glory that is theirs."[87]

Gallagher explicitly denied that he had some "undisclosed private reason" for opposing the new council. "I asked the men who interviewed me on the matter to delay for six months. I hoped that the coming elections, within that period, would result in placing thoroughly Catholic men at the head of the organization." He accused the Supreme Officers of abusing their powers "in behalf of a couple of only half-Catholics, to split Detroit Council and get the votes to keep themselves in office." He responded to Babcock's assertion that the bishop should take off his mitre, etc., by exclaiming that "any such utterance is anti-Catholic. Any such utterance is heresy." He severely criticized the Supreme Officers for not having "rebuked this outburst of anticlerical spirit." He reminded those who would follow such "false leaders" that a canon of the Church grants the ordinary the authority to approve Catholic organizations. Gallagher then set himself squarely behind the insurgents: "In the life of every organization it is necessary to have a revival of the ideals and principles that prompted its founding. Such a revival, in the form of a reconstruction program, is under way in the Knights of Columbus." He closed by asking the Detroit Knights "to cling to that spirit of loyalty and cooperation—of instant cooperation—that is required by a Catholic organization."[88] Arthur Preuss, ever ready to grasp at any Catholic anti–K. of C. expression, published extracts from Gallagher's sermon in his *Fortnightly Review* and circulated reprints throughout the country.

It is possible that some bishops may have held views similar to Gallagher's but, unlike him, they were guided by the principle enunciated by Archbishop Glennon at the 1922 Supreme Council meeting: not to "ventilate [our] personal grievances on the public highways." But it is probable that most bishops considered the reconstruction movement as a matter for the Order to resolve by itself. Thus, in May 1923, representatives of the reconstruction forces from Steubenville, Ohio, appealed to Bishop Joseph Schrembs of Cleveland to attend the Supreme Council Convention in August 1923 "and clean up with the politicians by a strong and straight forward talk." Schrembs wrote to Bishop Peter J. Muldoon of Rockford, Illinois, about the Steubenville delegation. "I told them that this was quite out of the question—that the present trouble of the Knights of Columbus was a purely internal affair and they would have to do their own housekeeping."[89]

Supreme Treasurer Daniel Callahan, with characteristic understatement, described Bishop Gallagher's address as "some warm baby" and said that "his Lordship must have been a little displeased with something that has recently happened." However, he knew that the Detroit matter would be an explosive issue at the state conventions in May, and he was in full accord with the other Supreme Officers that the situation required a great deal of political planning to ensure that a sizable majority of pro-administration delegates would be elected to the Supreme Council Convention.[90] Their strategy included publicizing the administration's response to the Reconstruction Program and dividing the country into districts where local caucuses would be held, sponsored by Supreme Agents, Directors, and Officers.[91] Such strategies proved effective. For example, the Wisconsin State Convention, which was anti-administration in 1922, elected pro-administration delegates by a nine-to-one ratio. Though the Wisconsin insurgents "fortified their position by reading Bishop Gallagher's tirade," they experienced a resounding defeat.[92] After receiving reports of the state conventions, Luke Hart wrote to Edward Hearn in Rome "that we will be much stronger than we were last year."[93]

But William Mulligan, a leader of the insurgent forces, was also optimistic. He told Bishop Muldoon in mid-July that "at present time the vote I figure is mighty close."[94] He was particularly hopeful that the convention would decide to limit the terms of the officers, except for the Supreme Secretary, an office which requires continuity. On August 6, the eve of the meeting, the Supreme Board adopted a resolution in response to Bishop Gallagher's sermon. After quoting Babcock's full statement from the April hearing, which included the remark "that his Lordship put aside his mitre," the resolution stated:

The Board of Directors hearing the speaker, and having before them the full context of his remarks, did not then have conveyed to them, nor do they now feel that there was any lack of respect or loyalty to His Lordship. If any such had been evidenced either by word or conduct, it would not have been permitted by the Board to go unchallenged. There was nothing either in the language used or in the manner of statement that the Board believed to be anti-Catholic or heresy as stated by His Lordship. If, however, in the language as actually used, His Lordship still feels that proper respect was not being given to Episcopal authority, the Board of Directors deeply regrets the use of the same, and most respectfully assures His Lordship that no offence, no matter how slight, if so understood, would have been permitted before it.[95]

Later Flaherty sent an explanatory letter and copies of this resolution and of the entire hearing to leading members of the American hierarchy. He referred to Gallagher's statement as the result of a misunderstanding and reaffirmed the Order's obedience "to the Hierarchy in all matters of Faith, Morals, and Discipline"[96] as well as its loyalty and devotion to the clergy.

Entitled "Progress and Prosperity," Flaherty's report to the Supreme Council meeting was framed as a response to the insurgents.[97] He pointed to the growth of the Order's assets to over $17 million and to the fact that the actuary had twice waived insurance assessments during the past year. He then outlined the Order's many programs, ranging from the Roman playgrounds to its educational and hospital work with the veterans of the World War. He energetically defended *Columbia,* a prime target of the insurgents, on the grounds that "the names of eminent men of the Church and of the State appear frequently in its pages, and it is generally conceded to be among the most quoted publications in the English speaking world." After noting the rise of anti-Catholicism, Flaherty closed his address with a plea for internal unity. "There may be contests among us; but there must not be conflict. The man who, through purpose of ambition, would drag this Order's repute and the repute of its Officers through the mire . . . is rendering service to the enemy."[98]

The election of Supreme Officers and five of the ten Directors revealed a two-to-one pro-administration majority. William Mulligan's challenge to Flaherty resulted in Flaherty's reelection, 210 to 117.[99] The twelve states which submitted anti-administration amendments based on the Reconstruction Program also failed to muster the necessary majority vote. However, after each vote the results were made unanimous.[100] The printed proceedings do not include the long caucuses which lasted into the early morning hours. Luke Hart recalled the exacting pace of this strife-ridden convention. "I never went through a Convention which was so wearing on the officers as this one was. Six thirty in the morning was our usual time for going to bed, and as I was there a week and got up at eight each morning . . . I was pretty well fagged out before [we] adjourned." According to Hart, the "great battle" occurred on the night before elections of Supreme Officers and Directors. "The antis selected the Detroit Council matter and Bishop Gallagher's speech as the issue to be fought out before the delegates [in caucus]. It required nearly five hours to dispose of it and the result was a complete vindication of the Supreme Board." Hart quoted the views of one of the delegates who shifted from a neutral to a pro-administration position. "After that memorable session which lasted until 2 A.M., I cannot understand how any delegate could fail to realize that the organization is in the hands of men who are competent and who have the interests of the Order at heart."[101]

Though the reconstruction movement failed to achieve its major goals, it did illustrate a need for the Supreme Officers and Directors to be more accountable to the membership. Indeed, the entire movement may be viewed as a reaction to the rapid rise of the Order's growth and prestige. Though the Pelletier case and Flaherty's defense of his Supreme Advocate set the movement in motion, it gained its strength from those members who felt that the Supreme Officers had become so immersed in international matters that they had lost sight of the needs of the membership. *Columbia,* which aimed to influence the general public, was viewed by the insurgents as symptomatic of the myopia of the leadership. Just as the officers dined with premiers and cardinals in Paris and Rome, so *Columbia* projected a cosmopolitan image as it published articles by representatives of the Catholic intellectual elite, the American hierarchy, and the political and academic establishments.

Circulating throughout the leaders of the insurgents were motives of various shades of ambition and idealism, but they seem to have gained a strong following from those who viewed the rise of the Order to the pinnacle of prestige in terms of "bigness is badness," as if the leaders had become too big to recognize the needs of the ordinary member. From the Supreme Officers' points of view, the marked rise in membership and in insurance business of the Order, and its vast amount of postwar social programs, compelled them to centralize authority and to view the Supreme Council not as a policy-making body but a convention of representatives to whom measures were presented for their advice and consent. As early as 1918, P. H. Callahan noted the need for changes in the nature of the Supreme Council, changes later symbolized by its being renamed a Supreme Convention. There is no evidence of a drive for self-aggrandizement by the Supreme Officers. It was rather that the business and fraternal programs of the Order had so expanded that the Board and the Officers were confronted with a plethora of situations demanding speedy decisions.

IV

At the two Supreme Council meetings (1922 and 1923) in which the insurgents challenged the administration, both sides were in agreement that the Knights should establish a junior Order that "will serve to unite, entertain, and safeguard the Catholic boys in America."[102] At the Atlantic City meeting (1922), the delegates listened to the remarks of Bishop Thomas J. Walsh of Trenton, New Jersey, who urged the Order to emulate the Trenton Knights and other organizations which contributed to the development of Catholic recreation centers in his diocese. "If the Knights of Columbus will take care of the growing boy . . . then the boy grown into manhood will take care not only of the Knights of Columbus, but of the Church and the nation as well."[103] There had been strong grass-roots support for the idea prior to Walsh's address, and six State Councils had submitted resolutions calling for a junior branch of the K. of C. This culminated in a Supreme Council resolution endorsing the proposal, and the Supreme Board established a Committee on Boy Movement, chaired by Deputy Supreme Knight Carmody.

The Order's interest in youth reflected a national trend manifested by development of the Boy Scouts of America and the Big Brother movement. Local councils and chapters had established youth programs, and Knights were actively involved in Catholic Big Brother and Boy Scout organizations. The Roman playgrounds appear to have strengthened the Order's interest in youth, while the Order's "Catholic Y.M.C.A." work in World War I stimulated the Knights to expand such social-service efforts. Besides competing with Protestant youth organizations, the Order was emulating the Scottish Rite Masons, whose junior order, the DeMolay organization, had been established recently and had experienced rapid growth.

After receiving responses to its questionnaire from Grand Knights thorughout the country, the Committee on Boy Movement met with several Knights involved in boys' work, as well as Brother Barnabas McDonald, F.S.C., a Christian Brother who had gained a national reputation for his pioneering efforts with delinquents and orphans. The result of this June 11 meeting in Chicago was the recommendation that the Order establish within its structure a junior organization of boys between the ages of fourteen and eighteen, that each council decide on the sponsorship of this youth organization, and that the approval of the ordinary be secured before introducing it into any diocese.[104] The Supreme Council meeting at Montreal approved the establishment of the junior Order, entitled the Columbian Squires, as well as three other youth programs originally drafted by Brother Barnabas.

Upon the request of members of the Canadian and American hierarchy, Brother Barnabas had prepared a leadership training program. He had been involved in all phases of social service for delinquent and orphan boys since 1894 and was deeply concerned about the dearth of professionally trained leaders in his field. As a consultant to the Committee on Boy Movement, he submitted his training plan as a necessary corollary to the development of the Squires program. It included the Order's awarding graduate scholarships for the pursuit of M.A. degrees in child guidance, offering intensive ten-day practical training courses in what was called "boyology" on the local level, and encouraging local councils to sponsor Boy Scout troops. In the fall of 1923, Brother Barnabas was appointed Executive Secretary of the Committee on the Boy Movement (later named Boy Life Committee) at an annual honorarium of $1,000 and expenses.[105]

His top priority was to develop a two-year graduate program in Boy Guidance in cooperation with Father Matthew Walsh, C.S.C., an educationist at the University of Notre Dame, and Father William Cunningham, C.S.C., president of the university. Brother Barnabas had selected Notre Dame because its "Catholic spirit and atmosphere is the strongest in America."[106] In February 1924, the university incorporated the Boy Guidance program as a separate department within its school of education. Raymond A. Hoyr, who had been involved in boys' club work and was a friend of Brother Barnabas, was appointed director of the program. The curriculum was interdisciplinary and included such courses as Introduction to Boys' Work, Principles and Theory of Boys' Work, Administration, Physical Education, Psychology of Adolescence, Religion for Adolescence, and practical field work. Theologians, philosophers, and athletic coaches, including Knute Rockne, were instructors in the Boy Guidance program.[107]

The K. of C. Boy-Guidance Scholarship program guaranteed a large entrance class each year as it awarded a $1,000 scholarship for each of the archdioceses in the United States, Canada, Mexico, Newfoundland, Cuba, and the Philippines. Eventually State Councils also awarded full scholarships: New York, six; Wisconsin, two; Pennsylvania, Illinois, Texas, and New Jersey, one each. The ordinary of each of the archdioceses was authorized to select the K. of C. Boy-Guidance Fellow. In a letter to Cardinal O'Connell, Supreme Knight Flaherty explained the criteria for selecting the candidate: "First, that the candidate shall be a practical Roman Catholic and a member of the Knights of Columbus; second that he shall be a layman—not a member of any religious body; and third, that he must be a graduate of a university or college having a course equivalent to the four-year undergraduate university course."[108] By the time of the program's termination in 1940, 187 K. of C. Fellows had graduated from the University of Notre Dame with an M.A. in Boy Guidance.

In order for the Knights to train local leaders to supervise their own junior orders, as well as provide volunteers for other youth organizations, Brother Barnabas designed a thirty-hour course in boyology.[109] While Notre Dame was assembling a faculty for its academic program, Brother Barnabas was recruiting a volunteer faculty to offer boyology courses sponsored by a local K. of C. council but open to anyone interested in volunteer work with boys. Besides Brother Barnabas and Deputy Supreme Knight Martin Carmody, the volunteer faculty included local and national executives of the Boy Scouts and the International Boys' Club Federation, a judge of probate court, and a supervisor of a boys' vocational school. The course occupied an entire weekend and seven weekday evenings and featured lectures on principles and methods of boys' work, adolescent psychology, and classes in camping, athletics, etc.[110] Class enrollments frequently exceeded two hundred men, many of whom were non-Catholics. The pastor of the First Christian Church of South Bend, Indiana, praised the Knights for sponsoring the course, which illustrated to him that "the Roman Catholic Church has gained a point in introducing a movement that is to touch all religious bodies."[111] Over a ten-year period (1925–35), 75,000 men attended Boyology Institutes in 187 cities in the United States and Canada.

Less than a year after he had assumed the position of executive secretary of the Boy Life Committee, Brother Barnabas was also developing the organizational structure, character, and ritual for the Columbian Squires. He was very insistent that two years of study and consultation on "this very delicate and very vital subject" were required before the Squires program could be properly established.[112]

To assist him in developing a suitable constitution and an initiation ceremony for the Squires, Brother Barnabas turned to his confrere, Brother Herman, principal of St. Patrick's School, Montreal. In late December 1924, a conference "of representative boy experts, religious and lay," convened in Chicago to draw up the final draft for the Squires program. After initiation ceremonies had been rehearsed in South Bend and Montreal, Brother Barnabas prepared for the institution of the first Columbian Squires circle in Duluth, Minnesota, where the delegates assembled for the Supreme Convention of 1925 could witness the historic event.[113] He stated that the major objective of the Squires "is character building . . . a program of activities, fivefold in nature [spiritual, intellectual, cultural, social, and civic] pursued throughout an extended period to prepare the young Squire for Knighthood in our glorious order."[114] The emblem, an S and a C interwoven into a Maltese-like cross with S.I.P. and C on each of the branches of the cross and with a K at its center, represents Columbian Squires (CS) dedicated to Christ (C), and to the improvement of the spiritual (S), intellectual (I), and physical (P) condition of the members under the guidance of the Knights of Columbus (K). The five major committees, and the themes upon which Squires' programs were designed, reflected the fivefold object of the Order.[115] At the time of organization, each circle was to include not less than twenty or more than forty members and was to be supervised by members of its sponsoring council, two of whom must have attended a boyology institute.

The officers of the circle consisted of Chief Squire, Chaplain, Chancellor Squire, Notary Squire, Bursar Squire, and Guard. A

Spiritual Director, a priest, was selected according to the regulations of the diocese. Membership was limited to practical Roman-Catholic boys between the ages of fourteen and eighteen. During the initiation ceremonies the candidates were instructed, primarily through symbols, on the Squires' motto, "Know Thyself," on their model, the youth Christ, on their dedication to sound mind and healthy body, and on the Columbian loyalties to God, Church, and Country.[116]

After the institution of the first Columbian Squires circle in Duluth, August 1925, circles were instituted in South Bend, Quebec, Montreal, Portsmouth, New Hampshire, and El Paso during the next fourteen months.[117] By September 1, 1940, there were only about 250 circles within the Order. The stipulation that two members of the sponsoring council must have been trained in a boyology institute hampered their growth. Though boyology institutes had been held in many cities and summer courses had been established at the University of Notre Dame, at the Catholic Summer School in Cliff Haven, New York, and at St. Edward's University in Austin, Texas, K. of C. attendance was far below expectations. The depression caused a decline in K. of C. membership and also obstructed the progress of the Squires, because money for initiation fees and membership dues was considered by many members to be an extravagance. Only after the Supreme Office established its Service Department in the late thirties, and hired Charles Ducey and later William Piedmont, graduates of the Boy Guidance program at Notre Dame, to administer it, did the Columbian Squires experience a revival.

To coordinate all the youth activities of the Order, Brother Barnabas established the Boy Life Bureau. Upon assuming his position with the Order, he had envisioned such an office to "serve as a clearing house for all the activities of the Knights of Columbus in this Boy Work Program."[118] When it was established in 1925, its role had expanded to include an employment bureau for boys interested in working in youth programs sponsored by local councils and a resource center for members of the hierarchy concerned with establishing or improving diocesan youth programs. It was also cooperating with other youth organizations, such as the Boy Scouts of America, the Federation of Boys' Clubs, and the National Big Brothers Association.[119] Brother Barnabas pursued his work with the Order with vigor and enthusiasm. Nearly sixty years old when he began it, he realized that "this is to be the last effort of my life. . . . I have passed over the age when men may look for continued years."[120] With nearly forty years' experience in boys' work, he had developed a broad historical perspective on the

problems of modern youth. He frequently spoke on how industrialization and urbanization had contributed to an expanded leisure time for
young people, to the breakdown of the family, and to the development
of the gang, conditions which could only be remedied by professionally trained men working within highly organized structures and dedicating themselves to the spiritual, moral, and physical improvement of
youth as a supplement to church, school, and family. His own dedication was an inspiration to the Order." I pray almighty God to give our
men [in the K. of C.] the wisdom and guidance that will make them
appreciate fully the sacredness of the lives of our boys."

Brother Barnabas's health declined in 1925, but he continued
working until his death on April 22, 1929. He had a profound impact
upon the Order which is still manifested today in the Columbian
Squires. An editorial in the *New York Times* clearly conveys the deep
impressions he made upon youth, upon the profession of boys' work,
and upon the general public.

Brother Barnabas was a saint walking amid the crowded, busy modern ways
of men, in active ministry to boyhood—or, rather, for many years to individual
boys wherever he could lend a brother's hand, and then, when infirmities came
upon him, to boyhood in general through his preparation of others to carry
on in a more widely helpful way. . . . His voice was raised against making
factories out of institutions for children and always in behalf of finding suitable
homes for boys where they might make their own way. To how many thousands of individuals he has given a helping hand no one can estimate. He has
helped indirectly many years. He found that, while frequently communities
wished to do something for their youth outside of school, there was no one
to be found able to do it. So he began to teach "boyology" to others out of
his own experience and wisdom, wishing to make boy leadership a profession.
He was never able to take the longed-for pilgrimage to the Holy Land, but he
has helped to invest with a certain holiness the places in which he himself
labored for boys and for boyhood.[121]

IO

Historical Revisionism
and the Ku Klux Klan

THE ORDER'S ASSERTION OF CATHOLIC PATRIOTISM, so strongly manifested during the war and so dramatically symbolized by the pilgrimage to Metz, derived from its view of the American Catholic past and from its effort to demonstrate the compatibility of Roman Catholicism and American democracy. To the Knight, particularly the Fourth Degree member who had participated in the ceremonial thematization of patriotism, Columbianism represented a deep respect for the Catholic baptism of America and for the ideals enshrined in the Declaration of Independence and the Constitution. The Irish-American influence upon the Order's historical consciousness was expressed in pride at America's successful struggle against the colonialism of Protestant England. The Knights cherished the ideals of religious liberty and the heroic deeds of the many Catholics who contributed to the cultural, religious, and political development of the nation.

Historical scholarship of the early twentieth century tended to deemphasize the libertarian ideals of the revolutionary period and to stress instead the economic and social aspirations of the founding fathers. There was also a tendency among historians, particularly those who wrote textbooks, to demythologize the heroes of the American Revolution and to portray the Revolution itself as the result of a mercantile quarrel among Anglo-Saxons rather than as a new experiment in democratic self-government. The typical nineteenth-century textbook was anti-Catholic, but it was exceedingly patriotic.[1] Catholic historians responded to this anti-Catholic bias by rejecting much of the new economic interpretations (which debunked heroism and patriotism) on the grounds that such historiography denigrated the nobility of the Catholic experience within the idealistic streams of the American past.

Catholic historians were also offended by those history textbooks which assumed that "Americanizing" the millions of new immigrants from southern and eastern Europe meant stressing almost exclusively the Anglo-Saxon roots of the American heritage. Though some of these textbooks extolled patriotism, they emphasized the English origins of the American concept of liberty and viewed the Revolution primarily in practical economic and political forms.[2] As the foremost Catholic fraternal society dedicated to the preservation of the American-Catholic heritage (which was in fact almost entirely non–Anglo-Saxon), the Knights of Columbus decided to establish a historical commission to combat the revisionism which they felt was gradually subverting the nation's youth.

Edward F. McSweeney of Boston first suggested the need for the commission. Born in Marlboro, Massachusetts, in 1864, McSweeney was a self-educated trade unionist who edited the newspaper of the Lasters' Union. A founder and later president of the union, he was also active in the Democratic Party and was the publicity organizer in Massachusetts for Grover Cleveland's successful campaign in 1892. Later he managed the political campaigns of Colonel William A. Gaston, who ran unsuccessfully for governor and senator in Massachusetts. However, it was his experience as assistant U.S. Commissioner of Immigration at Ellis Island from 1893 to 1902 which seems to have had a significant influence upon his suggestion for a K. of C. historical commission.[3] In 1920, when he was actively opposing restrictive immigrant legislation (particularly aimed at southern and eastern Europeans), he published a pamphlet entitled *De-Americanizing Young America* in which he criticized those American history textbooks whose Anglo-Saxon emphases implicitly supported restricting immigration.[4] McSweeney referred to "sinister influences" behind a campaign to "de-Americanize America," and he noted the strong relationship between American and British spokesmen for Anglo-American superiority and the publishers of American history texts.[5] He quoted George Haven Putnam, executive secretary of the Society to Promote American-British Union and also president of the American Book Sellers of North America: "The influence of the British elements in our population has proved sufficiently strong to enable the English Americans to bring under control and weld into a nation . . . the great medley of [British] racial factors that make up the population of the continent. . . . Text books are now being prepared which will present a juster historical account of the events of 1775–1783, 1812–1815, and 1861–1865."[6] McSweeney also quoted a 1919 article by John Wister, known to be a vehement de-Americanizer: "A movement to correct the school books of the United States has been started. It will go on . . . if ever we (the United States) cease to be like you (England); if ever the streams of foreign blood (Jews, Italians, Slavs, Scandinavians, Irish, etc.) that have poured into us, pollute the race current that flows through our veins from yours, we (the United States) shall perish from the list of free nations."[7] The historians most commonly cited as pro-British revisionists were George Louis Beer, Charles McLean Andrews, Herbert L. Osgood, Sydney George Fisher, Claude H. Van Tyne, and Albert Bushnell Hart.[8]

McSweeney's struggle against such authors was brought to the attention of the Knights of Columbus in 1921 by his friend Joseph Pelletier. Pelletier introduced McSweeney to Supreme Master John Reddin, who successfully sponsored a resolution passed by the Supreme Assembly of the Fourth Degree (Chicago, May 28, 1921) that the Fourth Degree establish the K. of C. Historical Commission. The purpose of the commission was to combat "propaganda . . . inundating our country" aimed at undermining "the spirit of American nationalism and solidarity" by obscuring and falsifying the "story of the events in our early national history" and by erasing "from the minds of the pupils the significance of the Declaration of Independence and the struggle of 1776." The commission was charged with the responsibility "to investigate the facts of history, to correct historical errors and omissions, to amplify and preserve our national history, to exalt and perpetuate American ideals, and to combat anti-American propaganda by means of pamphlets, each to be complete and authoritative in itself . . . and by other proper means and methods as shall be approved by the Supreme Assembly."[9]

In his address to the Supreme Council meeting held in San Francisco, August 1921, Supreme Knight Flaherty enthusiastically endorsed the idea.[10] John Reddin introduced the commission, which included the following: Edward McSweeney, chairman; Admiral William S. Benson, former Chief of Naval Operations and a convert to Catholicism; Charles H. McCarthy, Ph.D., occupant of the K. of C. chair of American History at the Catholic University of America; George Hermann Derry, Ph.D., professor of political economy at Union College, Schenectady, New York, and a prominent Catholic lecturer; and Maurice Francis Egan, former U.S. ambassador to Denmark and co-author of *The History of the Knights of Columbus in Peace and War,* an authorized two-volume history of the Order published in 1920. Additional appointments were made later that year: Henry Jones Ford, Ph.D., a convert to Catholicism and a professor of political science at Princeton; Harris Taylor, Ph.D., an authority on American and English constitutional law and former ambassador to Spain; and Joseph Dunn, Ph.D., occupant of the chair in Celtic languages and literature at Catholic University, who was to replace Maurice Francis Egan.

Reddin announced the commission's $7,500 history awards, which included prizes in six categories for "the best studies, based as far as practicable on original research in the field of American History."[11] The categories were divided according to the backgrounds of the contestants: Class A, a $2,500 prize, which was later raised to $3,000, for the best scholarly monograph submitted by professors of history; Class B, $1,000 prizes for best studies submitted by school superintendents and schoolteachers in the United States who specialized in history curricula and teaching methods; Class C, members of the general public who were interested in social sciences and biography; Class D, students of American foreign relations who had access to documents in countries in the western hemisphere; Class E, students of American history who had access to documents overseas; Class F, students in colleges in the United States. To assure that a special board of judges would evaluate the studies with maximum objectivity, each manuscript was to be signed with an assumed name, while the author's real name was to be mailed to a bank in Boston, to be divulged only after the judges had selected the prize manuscript.

The delegates to the 1921 convention were extremely supportive of the commission, but there was some misunderstanding of its role within the academic community. In late September 1921, a press release clarified the commission's purpose: "The Knights of Columbus do not intend to rewrite American history. What the organization has in mind is to produce authoritative chapters on phases and personalities in American history that have been insufficiently treated and even obscured and totally neglected in certain text books." In the release, John Reddin stated that the commission's purpose was not to "promulgate controversy" but to encourage "scholarly research" which will be published in pamphlets "containing complete bibliography and references to documentary evidence."[12] *The Pilot* (Boston) reported that millions of the pamphlets were to be distributed throughout the country by the local councils and that the entire cost of the commission's publishing efforts would reach nearly $1 million in time and material.[13]

McSweeney, who had left school at the age of eleven, was a self-educated specialist in American history. Though he lashed out at the revisionists in a polemical rather than scholarly fashion, he articulated his ideas with finesse.

In our democratic government there is unhappily little symbolism—the flag, a regiment of militia passing by, the stately progress of a naval squadron, or the imposing majesty of the entrance of the judges of the Supreme Court into their great tribunal, are but occasional and transitory manifestations of the dignity and majesty of our government soon forgotten. It is in the lives of the patriots who worked and suffered to establish our great country that we must hope to find our abiding inspirations.

McSweeney discussed the ideals of liberty cherished by these patriots by noting the penny and half-penny coins issued around 1795, upon which were inscribed the words "Liberty and Security" and "an asylum for the oppressed of all nations." He implicitly blamed revisionist propaganda for debunking these ideals and encouraging immigrant restrictionism. He condemned the Anglo-Saxon historiography emanating from the eastern seaboard and wanted the commission's publications to be "Free from sectionalism, bigotry, and from race prejudices which weaken and divide."[14]

McSweeney's reference to bigotry and race prejudice was understandable. The commission was established during that period which witnessed the rise of the modern Ku Klux Klan; indeed, there were 100,000 Klansmen in the summer of 1921 when the commission was founded.[15] Though the Klan extolled Americanism, its impassioned nativism and racism and virulent anti-Semitism and anti-Catholicism were predicated upon white Anglo-Saxon racial myths. McSweeney later recalled that one of the motives for establishing the Historical Commission was to offset "the discordant . . . appeals to hatred, racial and religious prejudice [which] were manifested everywhere."[16] Because the Klan had widely disseminated the bogus Fourth Degree oath, the Supreme Board of Directors authorized the publication of a new edition of the pamphlet *Knights of Columbus vs. Criminal Libel and Malicious Bigotry.*[17]

McSweeney traced the origins of Anglo-Saxonist revisionism to the mid-1890s and cited the Rhodes Scholarship fund and the Carnegie Foundation as major supporters of the propaganda effort. He stated that the "Anglo-Saxon tradition is pure myth. To verify it is like looking at midnight for a black cat that isn't there." According to McSweeney, the putative "Anglo-Saxon impulse [was not] in the least responsible for the progress of the United States. It had nothing to do with the Spanish in Florida; the Huguenots in Virginia; the Swedes in

Delaware." He quoted an article in the *London Times* that exemplified the Anglo-Saxon point of view. "Nothing in American life, however, has been more remarkable in the past than the completeness with which the Anglo-Saxon core of the nation has succeeded in imposing its character and dominating the whole people." He accused the "promoters of the Anglo-Saxon cult" of engendering racial "caste dominance" which must be checked by "ardent American patriotism" enabling Americans to be "virile and strong enough to assimilate the many races to find a home within our borders."[18]

In his address to the Supreme Convention in August 1922, McSweeney placed the economic historians, who viewed the idealistic patriotism of the founding fathers as a mask for greed and cupidity, in the same camp with the Anglo-Saxonists. Because they stressed a kind of "economic determinism," many of these historians focused primarily upon the post–Civil War period of American history when the nation was rapidly industrializing. McSweeney noted that the era of industrialism was marked by the advancement of technology and the accumulation of wealth, but, he added, with such progress came "greed, sloth, intellectual pride, and social arrogance." The revisionists, he declared, ignore the fact that during the period after the Civil War the "Spiritual impulse and moral urge [had] been supplied by the Catholic Church and the despised aliens who have been the custodians of the spiritual forces without which the nation could not long endure." He believed that "deep in the heart of the American people lingered a strong patriotic sentiment . . . only waiting the call to respond."[19]

The commission's drive to reassess history text books was shared by many other organizations and societies: the American Legion, the Descendants of the Signers of the Declaration of Independence, the Grand Army of the Republic, the Sons of the American Revolution, the Daughters of the American Revolution, the United Spanish War Veterans, and the Patriotic League. In 1922, these groups officially condemned ten school histories written in "the spirit of Benedict Arnold."[20] Such popular historians as David Saville Muzzey, Willis Mason West, Albert Bushnell Hart, William B. Gutteau, and Claude H. Van Tyne were among those proscribed by these organizations.[21] The Hearst newspaper chain also took up the cause and campaigned editorially among parents, politicians, and educators for an investigation of school textbooks. Most state legislatures had passed laws requiring all students to study American history and government. During World War I, several states required teachers to take loyalty oaths.

McSweeney testified before a committee in New York City's school system on the need for patriotic history textbooks, and the commission published a strongly anti-revisionist pamphlet (reprinted in *Columbia*) by Charles Edward Russell, editor of the *New York Herald* and a leading publicist of the Patriotic League for the Preservation of American History.[22]

One of the history textbooks frequently cited as riddled with Anglo-Saxon myth was David Saville Muzzey's *American History,* published in 1911. As Frances FitzGerald has pointed out, it is still in print and relatively popular. FitzGerald notes Muzzey's Anglo-Saxon biases, his anti-immigrant attacks, and his flaws in social and economic analysis. She also records the decline in popularity of Muzzey's text during the 1960s when blacks, white ethnics, native Americans, and women protested against its obvious biases. Curiously, she is unaware of the fact that the Knights of Columbus Historical Commission was the first national group to challenge that textbook and many others on the same basis—in the case of Muzzey, nearly six decades before FitzGerald's exposé.[23] The following partial list of suggested topics for graduate students interested in entering the commission's American history contest is remarkable as an agenda for dissent in the 1960s: "The American Indians, Past and Present," "Contributions of the Negro to American History," "Contributions of Alien Races to American Nationality," "Democracy vs. 'Caste' in the United States."[24] It is notable that, in reaction to the Anglo-Saxon revisionists, the K. of C. Historical Commission encouraged research on topics which became associated with a totally different school of revisionist American history in the 1960s.

Though the commission's statements were popular and polemical, its publications were academic and scholarly. In 1922 it awarded its first prize of $3,000 in Class A, limited to professors of history, to Samuel Flagg Bemis for his manuscript *Jay's Treaty: A Study in Commerce and Diplomacy.* The committee of judges was chaired by Dr. Gaillard Hunt, chief archivist of the State Department, and consisted of Frederick A. Cleveland, Ph.D., of Boston University; David A. McCabe, Ph.D., of Princeton University (the only Catholic on the committee); Frank I. Cobb, editor of the *New York World;* and John H. Edmonds, archivist of the Commonwealth of Massachusetts. At the 1922 Supreme Convention, Gaillard Hunt reported that all the monographs submitted in Class A achieved a "high degree of excellence," and he announced the winning manuscript and its author's pseudonym—fittingly "Christopher Columbus."[25]

In his preface to *Jay's Treaty,* which Macmillan published as the first in the Knights of Columbus Historical Series, Bemis acknowledged his gratitude to the Knights for their generosity and their Americanism and his indebtedness to several Harvard historians under whom he had studied.[26] Frederick Jackson Turner, whom McSweeney had mistakenly placed among the Anglo-Saxonists, was at the top of Bemis's list. Prior to Bemis's study, Jay's treaty had been considered symbolic of America's capitulation to British interests. Though Bemis admitted that Jay was "somewhat outplayed" by England's Foreign Secretary, Lord Grenville, he concluded that, because the treaty removed the threat of war, the United States was granted the "opportunity to develop in population and resources, and above all *in consciousness of nationality* [italics added] to a large degree which made possible in the War of 1812 a far more effective resistance than could have been afforded in 1794."[27] The book launched Bemis's career; he became Sterling Professor of Diplomatic History and Inter-American Relations at Yale University and twice won the Pulitzer Prize. It also brought prestige to the commission and illustrated its deep commitment to encouraging serious historical scholarship.

Bemis's work was the only prizewinner in 1922; the judges decided that the manuscripts submitted in the other categories were not of sufficiently high quality. Concurrent with the encouragement of research through the contest, the commission established a noncompetitive history series which ultimately overshadowed the contest itself. Publications in 1922 included *The Monroe Doctrine* by Thomas A. Mahony, and *The Origins of the Propaganda Movement* by Charles Edward Russell. The latter was an exposé of the various agencies, publishing houses, and historians who popularized the Anglo-Saxon myth aimed to promote British-American solidarity.[28] Mahony, McSweeney's son-in-law and Pelletier's assistant district attorney, published his pamphlet *The Monroe Doctrine* on the centennial of its promulgation. His thesis was that the doctrine emerged from the ideals of the American Revolution and the diplomatic needs of the young republic rather than from a maneuver to further British commercial interest. Mahony strongly advocated maintenance of the doctrine and supported a neutralist foreign policy.[29] Though historians today might debate with such a thesis, it was a thoroughly documented albeit polemical work.

Admiral William S. Benson, a member of the commission, was the author of *The Merchant Marine,* published in the K. of C. series by Macmillan in 1923. Since Benson's book was a comprehensive treatment of the entire history of the Merchant Marine and set forth its past contribution to American commerce, as well as its then present need for progress and development, it aptly fulfilled the purpose of the series "to encourage investigations into the origins, achievements, and problems of the U.S."[30] In accord with the commission's goal to foster scholarship in those areas where American principles have had great impact, it sponsored the publication of *The Open Door Doctrine in Relation to China* by Mengchien Joseph Bau, Ph.D.[31] McSweeney praised this analysis of American policy in the Orient and concluded that "it becomes evident that this doctrine is applicable not only to China but to the entire range of our commercial and political relations with foreign nations." He explained that the commercial aspects of Benson's and Bau's work served a practical purpose by suggesting ways in which America's growing economic wealth might be employed in world markets.[32]

Cables and Wireless, by George Abel Schreiner, was published by the commission to illustrate the ways in which international communications had been subjected to nationalistic propaganda purposes in the past and to advocate the need for international regulation on an equitable basis.[33] McSweeney was particularly proud of the pamphlet, *Charters of Liberty* by Frederick J. Kinsman, who sought to demonstrate that "progress in human freedom is a heritage of the Christian era" and should not be credited to the Anglo-Saxons.[34] McSweeney referred to Kinsman as "our American Newman" as he had been the Episcopal Bishop of Delaware before he converted to Catholicism.[35] The most prominent author whose work was sponsored by the commission was Allan Nevins. His book, *The American States During and After the Revolution, 1775–1789,* is an extremely detailed history of the transition from colonial status to self-government.[36] Nevins was associate editor of the *New York Evening Post* when he wrote this book, and though he had written several books prior to this one *The American States* was his first major scholarly effort. A few years later he entered academic life and eventually became one of the most distinguished historians of the century.

In the autumn of 1922, McSweeney designed a unique set of historical studies entitled "The Knights of Columbus Racial Contribution Series." He explained its rationale:

Immediately after the war, an army of propagandists proceeded to expound the theory that the bulk of the nation are "hyphenates" who are not, and never can be, true to the United States. This was accompanied by special drives on the Negroes and Jews, but particularly on Catholics of all racial derivation.

More than a score of organizations with a wide diversity of methods but identity of aim, in which the false history textbooks were common to all, have been at work on this program steadily for five years. To assert that . . . a citizen of the United States is unworthy of the right of citizenship because of color, racial descent, or religious belief is abhorrent to the spirit of the Declaration of Independence and the Constitution of the United States, but this attempt is being made nevertheless, and openly supported by agencies and organizations that pretend to work under the cloak of "Americanization."

This series is unlike any heretofore published, since it gives the actual history of racial contributions to the making of the United States, not from the isolated viewpoint of a single race, concerning other races, but *from the viewpoint of each race concerning itself.* [37]

Three monographs were published in this ambitious series: *The Gift of Black Folk* by W.E.B. DuBois, *The Jews in the Making of America* by George Cohen, and *The Germans in the Making of America* by Frederick Franklin Schrader. In his introduction to each of these books, McSweeney summarized the history of immigration to America, the waves of nativism, anti-Catholicism, and anti-Semitism, and the persistence of racial prejudice in the life of the nation. He concluded with a commentary on the immigrant-restriction movement which culminated in legislation in 1921 limiting the number of aliens from any one nation to 3 percent of the total foreign-born of that nationality living in the United States in 1890. Particularly the "new immigrants" from Southern and Eastern Europe, who settled in America from 1890 onward, were the butt of this discriminatory law. McSweeney referred to the law as the result of a movement aimed at classifying them as "hyphenates" and "mongrels." "These laws are haphazard, unscientific, based on unworthy prejudice, and likely, ultimately, to be disastrous in their economic consequences. . . . Such laws, worked out under the hysteria of 'after war psychology,' seem to be one of the instances so frequent in history, where Democracy must take time to work out its own mistakes. Under these circumstances, there is all the more reason that the priceless heritage of racial achievement by the descendants of various racial groups in the United States be told."[38]

W.E.B. DuBois was the most prominent black historian of the early twentieth century. Editor of *The Crisis,* DuBois was the first black man to attempt to write scholarly black history. In the foreword to his book in the K. of C. series, he noted that it was "not uncommon to view America as a continuation of English nationality."[39] In accord with McSweeney's ideas on the nature of America, DuBois stated, "America is a conglomerate. This is at once her problem and her glory—perhaps indeed her sole and greatest reason for being. . . . American history has no prototype and has been developed from the various racial elements. . . . And finally the American spirit is a new and interesting result of diverse threads of thought and feeling coming not only from America but Europe and Asia and indeed from Africa." He presented the thesis of his book as "that despite starving, war, and caste, and despite our Negro problem, the American Negro is and has been a distinct asset to this country and has brought a contribution without which America could not have been."[40]

In response to a letter from a Catholic priest who informed him of the Catholic Church's educational efforts for blacks, DuBois criticized the American Catholic Church for its "color separation and discrimination," which, he said, was unequaled by any church in America, "and that is saying a great deal." He pointed to the Church's Jim Crow system, illustrated by the ways in which its private schools, universities, and seminaries excluded blacks. He pointed to the anti-black admissions policy at Catholic University of America as an example of racial discrimination. However, DuBois praised the "great tradition of Catholicism throughout the ages." He concluded that the appearance of his book in the K. of C. series was an exception to the rule. "I have just written, for the Knights of Columbus, a volume in their admirably conceived series of monographs for inter-racial understanding of the making of America. But because Catholicism has so much that is splendid in the past and fine in its present, it is the greater shame that 'nigger' haters clothed in its episcopal robes should do to black Americans . . . all that the KKK ever asked."[41] DuBois played a leading role in the N.A.A.C.P. for years, was on the faculty at Atlanta University, and became the leading black exponent of a Marxist interpretation of American history.

George Cohen, the author of *The Jews in the Making of America,* wrote his book under the direction of a group of Jewish editors. Cohen discussed every aspect of Jewish life in America, including a chapter on "the psychology of the Jew" in which he traced the evolution of the Jewish stereotype from the figure of "the wandering Jew" to the then current popular conception of "the mysterious Jew."[42]

While anti-Semitism was on the rise in the 1920s, Germanophobia was still alive in the aftermath of the war. Frederick Franklin Schrader, writer, editor, playwright, and publicist, was American-born but of German ancestry. His book, *The Germans in the Making of America,* was a popular history, a synthesis of secondary works in the field; like DuBois and Cohen, Schrader focused on ethnic character.[43] Monographs on the contributions of various other groups were planned but never published, because the Historical Commission was soon subjected to severe criticism from several sources within the Order.

In the winter of 1923 a special financial committee of the Supreme Board of Directors was established to investigate the commission's program. To save it, McSweeney volunteered to give up his salary, but the committee still decided to limit publications to those for which contracts had been made.[44] During this period, a group of insurgents, led by William Mulligan and Judge Moynihan, were increasingly critical of the growth of the Order's home office and the high costs of administration. Included in the first draft of the insurgents' Reconstruction Program was a direct attack upon the commission: "[We] deplore the misdirected effort of the History Commission, which has failed to correct popular misconceptions of history, or to take any note of the propaganda in the guise of history syndicated through our metropolitan dailies in the last two years." The commission was also criticized for spending $80,000 on "such remote and impractical topics as Jay's Treaty, the Monroe Doctrine, Trade, and Foreign Policy." McSweeney reported to the committee that he had been "subjected to a campaign of personal vilification and slander based on utter falsehood, nationwide in scope, and even attempting to promote dissension within the commission itself, which was happily unsuccessful."[45] It is likely that the insurgents fully exploited McSweeney's close association with Pelletier, the *enfant terrible* of 1922–23. Though he delivered a report to the extremely hostile delegates at the 1923 Supreme Convention in Montreal, McSweeney had already tendered his resignation. Gaillard Hunt became chairman of the Historical Commission in January 1924 and almost immediately proposed a plan whereby the Order would publish a forty-seven-volume history of the Catholic Church in America. The project met firm disapproval. Hunt died in March 1924 and McSweeney returned to the chairmanship. But after all prior publishing commitments had been fulfilled, the commission was quietly terminated in 1925.[46]

McSweeney had never intended the Fourth Degree's Historical Commission to become a permanent office within the Order, but he appeared to have been stunned by the ways in which it became enmeshed in the political battles of 1922–23. The insurgents' criticism of the commission as being utterly remote from the immediate concerns of the membership was perhaps a consensus view. The works of Bemis and Nevins were certainly not intended for the edification of the membership, while the Racial Contribution Series appears to have had little appeal to the general reader. The Supreme Officers were generally supportive of the commission, but in reaction to the insurgents' attacks they felt called upon to display their fiscal responsibility. Though Flaherty paid tribute to the historical commission in his 1925 Report to the Supreme Council, he expressed equal concern for its replacement, a national essay contest for junior and senior high school students regardless of religious affiliation.[47]

In retrospect it can be recognized that the historical commission's publications were the Order's most significant contribution to the world of scholarship and to the principle of inter-ethnic understanding. However, with the revival of anti-Catholicism, the Order's anti-defamation character compelled the leaders to seek more practical ways—such as the essay contest—to combat anti-ethnic and anti-Catholic movements.[48] The commission's work was reflected even on the local level, particularly in Texas, where the State Council in 1923 established its own Historical Commission. After consulting with Peter Guilday, the dean of American Catholic Church historians, the Texas commission, chaired by Father Paul J. Frick, C.S.C., of St. Edward's University in Austin, began assembling historical source material. In 1934 the Texas Knights commissioned Dr. Carlos E. Casteñeda of the University of Texas to write a multivolume series under the title *Our Catholic Heritage in Texas.*[49] With four volumes published in the late 1930s, Casteñeda's seven-volume history spans four centuries and is still considered a major work in its field. Immediately prior to establishing the Texas Historical Commission, the delegates to the 1923 State Convention received a report on the growth of anti-Catholicism in the state, and this too helped engender strong support for presenting an accurate historical account of the Catholic heritage in Texas.[50] Indeed, by this time the entire Order had been alerted to the precipitous rise of anti-Catholic animus clearly underlined by the revival of the Ku Klux Klan and the bogus K. of C. Fourth Degree oath.

II

On Thanksgiving night, 1915, sixteen men assembled on the top of Stone Mountain near Atlanta, Georgia, to swear their allegiance as Brother Knights of the Invisible Empire of the Ku Klux Klan. *The Birth of a Nation,* the first full-length motion picture, which depicted the original Klan as responsible for heroically imposing law, order, and Christian righteousness upon the post–Civil War South, had electrified

Southern audiences and had been frequently viewed by William Joseph Simmons, the founder of the revived Klan.[51] Simmons was an ex-Methodist preacher who became an insurance salesman and a membership promoter for the Woodmen of the World as well as a member of the Masons and the Knights Templar. For several years he had envisioned establishing a fraternal society modeled on the old Klan, in which his father had been an officer in central Alabama.[52] During the first five years, Simmons's Klansmen were not night riders, nor were they overtly anti-Catholic and anti-Semitic; rather, they identified their "one hundred percent Americanism" in terms of anti-Negro Protestantism. When the United States entered World War I, Klansmen in Georgia and Alabama aimed to protect the nation against enemy aliens, draft dodgers, union leaders, and anyone who appeared to them to deviate from patriotic purity.[53] Limited to Georgia and Alabama and numbering no more than 2,000 members in early 1920, the Klan was a relatively insignificant order among the many "patriotic" fraternal societies of the day.

To bolster membership, Simmons joined forces with Edward Young Clarke and Elizabeth Tyler, who had formed the Southern Publicity Association, a successful fund-raising group cloaked in the guise of respectability and righteous determination. Clarke and Tyler, who were paid 80 percent commission on initiation fees and other benefits, soon effected quantitative and qualitative changes in the Klan's character. Shortly after they began their recruitment campaign, they were amazed at the popular appeal of the K.K.K. *The Birth of a Nation* contributed to this appeal, and Simmons, sensitive to the growing alienation among several groups in American society, exploited the widespread mood of social and economic disillusionment.[54]

By 1920, wartime idealism had given way to postwar cynicism. The anti-German sentiment which had been aroused by wartime propaganda became a general anti-foreign sentiment. The new immigrants from Eastern and Southern Europe were caricatured as greedy Jewish moneylenders, radical agitators, or Roman-Catholic conspirators plotting to harness America to the papal throne. The severe recession of 1920 engendered among poor whites a yearning for the mythical security of the past when Anglo-Saxon Protestantism dominated the life of the nation. Rural Americans viewed the increasingly dominant urban culture as the embodiment of everything contrary to the allegedly rural virtues of the clean-living, thrifty, hardworking, and patriotic yeoman farmer. City dwellers in once stable neighborhoods were frightened by the advance of foreign immigrants and migrant blacks from the South.

The "mongrelization" of America was viewed as symptomatic of a social malaise which required a total war between the Klan's "forces of righteousness" and the radical Jewish, Catholic, Negro, and alien "forces of evil." Though recruiters, called Kleagles, adjusted the Klan gospel to suit the salient hostilities of a particular locality, anti-Catholicism remained the strongest animus exploited by the Klan.[55] Little more than a year after Clarke and Tyler joined Simmons, the Invisible Empire numbered nearly one million Klansmen located in every region of the nation.

In early September 1921, while more than two hundred Kleagles were spreading the Klan creed, Rowland Thomas, a journalist on the staff of the *New York World*, wrote a series of articles in which he exposed the secret character of the order and its violent program.[56] The headlines of the *World's* September 14 edition featured the Kleagles' circulation of the K. of C. "Forged Oath." Besides including an original copy of the bogus oath, the *World* also reported that the Kleagles had circulated the oath in their membership campaigns throughout the country.[57] With eighteen other newspapers carrying the exposé, Congress was influenced to investigate the Klan in late 1921. Simmons testified to the patriotic, law-abiding character of the Invisible Empire and successfully prevented the House of Representatives from recommending punitive action. Atlanta Representative W. D. Upshaw supported Simmons when he introduced a bill seeking an investigation of the K. of C. and other "secret" fraternal orders.[58] John B. Kennedy, editor of *Columbia*, doubted the effectiveness of the *World's* "series of sensational articles" in exposing the depth of religious and racial prejudice in American society. Besides providing the Klan with valuable publicity, the *World*, according to Kennedy, stressed the economic motives of the Imperial Wizard and his Kleagles and the ways in which they exploited "modern improvisations"—i.e., new techniques of sales and showmanship. Unmasking the Klan's drive for profit, the *World* disregarded the Invisible Empire's exploitation of the strong veins of anti-Catholic, anti-Semitic, and anti-black prejudice, as if those who joined the Klan were merely gullible rather than hate-filled.[59] One of the first students of the Klan, John M. Mecklin, shared Kennedy's assessment of the *World's* series of articles.

If the Klan were utterly un-American it could never have succeeded as it has. The Klan was not alien to American society. If it were, the problem would be simpler. The Klan was but the recrudescence of forces that already existed in American society, some of them recent, others dating from the more distant past. It gives a totally false idea of the social significance of the Klan . . . to liken it, as does the *World,* to an alien and destructive force "tunneling, mole-like, under the whole structure of American institutions." The Klan drew its inspiration from ancient prejudice, classical hatreds, and ingrained social habits. The germs of the disease of the Klan, like germs in the human body, have long been present in the social organism and needed only the weakening of the social tissue to become malignant.[60]

Basic to the Klan's recruitment strategy was the staging of membership campaigns at Protestant churches. Though most national leaders of what would now be called "mainline" Protestant denominations condemned the Klan, it nevertheless received enthusiastic support from many fundamentalist ministers. For example, when 52 percent of the Methodist clergy, who were pro-Klan, were confronted by their anti-Klan bishop and board, they refused to submit.[61] As one writer who penetrated the Klan remarked, "I believe the keynote of the Klansmen [sic] spirituality is that they should hold rigidly to the fundamental idea of Protestantism. . . . They feel the Klan is the power by which they, Klansmen, can do their best work for America and Protestantism itself."[62]

The Hearst newspapers also exposed the Klan's principles, strategy, and tactics. In October 1921, a Knight of Columbus from Dixon, California, wrote to Supreme Advocate Pelletier, enclosing a clipping from a local newspaper in which the reporter attacked Hearst as well as the K. of C.[63] and noting that "a few of us believe that [the bogus] oath called upon [the Knights of Columbus] to flay, to bury alive, to boil, to kill and various other Christian? [sic] practices, when called upon by the proper authorities—Catholic of course—to do so. But surely no one would object to that form of treatment from a noble Christian Catholic Knight. God Forbid." The reporter continued to editorialize on Hearst's exposé of the Invisible Empire by lashing out at the K. of C. for their allegiance "to a foreign Hierarchy, whose very visible ruler is an Emperor, wearing a three storied crown and calling himself Pope of Rome, King of all Kings, Lord of all Lords, and ruler of the visible universe."[64]

Pelletier's strategy in combating the publication of the bogus oath was to circulate the K. of C. publication which included summaries of anti-Klan speeches by congressmen and others who defended the Order's loyalty and integrity. Since the bogus oath was so widely published in the United States, Canada, and Newfoundland, Pelletier concluded that the enormous expenses involved in litigation precluded his office from initiating prosecution for libel. Instead, he encouraged State Councils to assume responsibility for prosecution; but because such libel cases called for careful legal planning he urged caution.[65] Shortly after he became Supreme Advocate (July 1922), Luke E. Hart, with the approval of the Supreme Board of Directors, pursued a more aggressive campaign against the publishers and circulators of the bogus oath. Because he felt that the organizers behind the "violent wave of religious prejudice [were] actuated by mercenary motives," he was convinced that they would cease to publish the false oath if they were confronted by the threats of lawsuits, fines, and imprisonment. He appealed to members, all Catholics, and "every broad-minded fellow citizen to aid us in running down the circulators of this malign libel." During the prior wave of anti-Catholicism, the Order had successfully prosecuted several disseminators of the oath, but, in order to demonstrate that it was not motivated by a "vengeful spirit," the K. of C. lawyers urged the court to be merciful in its sentencing. Because the oath had been so widely circulated throughout North America during the early twenties, Hart announced that the Order would not seek clemency for those convicted of libel but would instead prosecute them to the limits of the law. Unlike the test cases of the earlier period, these suits were part of a larger campaign "to stamp out this pernicious propaganda which threatens the social peace of the Republic."[66]

One of the most vicious propaganda mills was the Rail Splitter Press, which published a long list of pornographic material by "expriests" and "ex-nuns." Among its publications was *The Ku Klux Klan or the Knights of Columbus Klan,* by Arthur H. Bell, which traced the origins of the K. of C. to the Molly Maguires, a group of Irish-American miners in Pennsylvania who had employed violent anti-management tactics. This publication was obviously intended to suggest that the Order was actually guilty of putatively violent Klan crimes while the K.K.K. itself was a law-abiding patriotic society. Bell quoted William Lloyd Clark, editor of the *Rail Splitter:* "[The] Knights of Columbus . . . represents the concentrated cussedness of all the treasonable organizations and all the infernalism of the papal system centralized on one body, whose slogans are: 'The Pope is King,' and 'To Hell with the government.' "[67] Besides attacking the Order's loyalty to the United States and quoting the bogus oath, Bell pursued the stereotypical anti-Catholic line as he elaborated on the Church's anti–public school position, its conspiracy to take over the nation, its opposition to separation of church and state, to religious freedom, to civil marriage, to all Protestant fraternal societies, and to freedom of speech and press.[68] Hart wrote to the Rail Splitter Press demanding that they "discontinue the publication and distribution" of the bogus oath or suffer the consequences of a legal suit. Editor Clark printed Hart's letter, which he said was in response to the pamphlet extolling the Klan and condemning the "K of C Klan." Referring to the pamphlet as the "greatest defense of Klancraft and the greatest unmasking of the K of C ever written," and to Hart's letter as "the most damnable piece of Papal insolence that has ever come into this office," Clark urged every Klansman, Mason, and patriot "to unite with the Rail Splitter and challenge the K of C to bring them to court."[69] James Malone, State Deputy of Kansas, informed Hart that the *Rail Splitter*'s publication of the bogus oath had been circulating throughout Topeka and urged him "to call this bird [i.e., Clark] and take him on for a round, and let the world know the difference between a real American eagle and a buzzard."[70] Hart agreed with Malone and told him that he doubted Clark would actually ever reprint the oath, but if he did then Hart promised to "give the liveliest law suit that 'The Rail Splitter' ever tackled.' "[71] Hart's thrust did not prevent Clark from continuing to attack the Order, but he never reprinted the bogus oath.

Hart's campaign against the publication of the bogus oath was not a complete reversal of Pelletier's rather cautious strategy. Hart initiated several libel suits against publishers and circulators during the period between 1923 and the Al Smith campaign of 1928, but, since state and local councils initiated their own suits in Oklahoma, Arkansas, Texas, California, and many other states, the Supreme Board decided not to finance every suit. The local, state, and national levels of the Order offered rewards to anyone who could prove the authenticity of the bogus oath.[72]

In 1923 the Supreme Board, prompted by the hierarchy and the State Council in Texas, authorized deposits of $5,000 in banks located in each of the five dioceses of Texas. State Deputy W. F. Hustmyre coordinated advertisements of the reward in newspapers throughout the state. After widespread coverage of the reward, Bishop Christopher E. Byrne of Galveston urged Hustmyre to advertise the fact that $25,000 "was clamoring to be claimed but no one came." Such an ad would prove that whoever circulated the oath was deliberately slandering the Order and the Church and "that ignorance, after such widespread denial and a generous offer for truth, can no longer be an excuse for any one who would use it again."[73] The Klan had been particularly active in publicizing the bogus oath in Texas. By the time the K. of C. offered its rewards in the spring of 1923, the Invisible

Empire had become quite visible as it shifted from clandestine vigilantism to open political warfare. With over 200,000 members in Texas, the Klan had become an extremely effective political force. In the 1922 elections a Klansman was elected governor, while his fellow members controlled a majority in the lower house of the state legislature and were elected judges and local officials.[74] The Klan's political strategies in Texas had been enunciated at the first annual "Klanvocation" held in Atlanta in November 1922. Throughout that year the Invisible Empire had experienced scandal, dissent, and open rebellion. The Klan's chief promoters, Edward Clarke and Elizabeth Tyler, had been arrested on several occasions on charges of intoxication and possession of liquor. During the Klanvocation, Imperial Wizard Simmons was forced to resign and was replaced by Hiram Wesley Evans, a dentist from Dallas. Though Simmons staged a temporary comeback in the spring of 1923, Evans maintained his control and remained in office seventeen years.[75] The new Imperial Wizard announced that the Klan was first and foremost a patriotic society which stood for "education, temperance, the flag, Protestantism, morality, and charity" and that he would not tolerate lawless night-riding. Under his direction, the Klan should pursue its "patriotic program" through established political processes. Because the reformed "respectable" Klan portrayed the Catholic Church as fostering disloyalty in its parochial schools, as advocating repeal of prohibition, as persecuting Protestants, as immoral, and as a self-serving, uncharitable institution, anti-Catholicism was the unifying theme of the political program.[76] Moreover, by attacking the Catholic parochial schools, the Klan could solidify its entire program and mine a rich vein of traditional nativism and anti-Catholicism among several non-Klan Protestant, and chauvinistic societies.

During the nineteenth century, the Catholic school was subjected to a barrage of ridicule; nativists circulated pornographic stories of immoral convent schools, and the American Protective Association in the 1890s juxtaposed the virtuous, patriotic "little red schoolhouse" with the disloyal papist parochial school. Though respectable Protestant spokesmen seldom uttered public criticism, they too generally viewed the Catholic school as divisive. In the mid-nineteenth century when public schools were infused with Protestantism, the American hierarchy had urged the development of parochial schools to protect Catholic youth from proselytization. With the rise of religious pluralism, public education lost some of its Protestant tincture and adopted secular humanitarian and patriotic goals. Though traditional Church belief held that religious education was vital to transmission of the faith, in response to secular public education the American-Catholic spokesmen saw Catholic education as necessary to maintaining belief in a culture rapidly relegating religion to a secondary place in its scale of values.[77]

In every section of the nation, various groups, including the leaders of the Scottish Rite Masons, the Klan, and self-styled patriotic nativistic and anti-Catholic societies, coalesced into political movements to pass state laws compelling students to attend public schools. During the same period other organizations, such as the National Education Association, were lobbying for the establishment of a federal department of education. Most Catholic leaders considered the latter to be, at worst, a covert effort ultimately aimed at the liquidation of their schools and, at best, an effort which would destroy local control of both public and private schools. The American Church, through the National Catholic Welfare Conference, lobbied against bills to establish a department of education, the most significant of which was the Smith-Towner bill.[78] The K. of C. mounted its own campaign against this bill and was directly involved in combating anti-Catholic compulsory public-education referenda, initiatives, and bills on the state level.

The first compulsory education measure was proposed in Nebraska in 1919, but Michigan was the center of the first major grass-roots effort. Detroit's automobile industry had lured immigrants, Negroes, and southern whites to its factories.[79] Large ghettos teeming with foreign-born Catholics posed a serious threat in the minds of those who feared the Church. Moreover, Detroit had a legacy of anti-Catholicism; during the 1890s it housed the national leadership of the American Protective Association.[80] In the spring of 1920, James A. Hamilton, head of the Public School Defense League, led the campaign for a state constitutional amendment which would require public-school education for all students between the ages of five and sixteen. Though the referendum failed by a two-to-one margin, Hamilton continued his efforts during the next three years.[81] By 1921, both the Klan and some Masons had joined the movement. The Diocese of Detroit under Bishop Michael Gallagher enlisted the Knights of Columbus in the fight for Catholic schools.

In July 1922, the Oklahoma Americanization Society proposed an amendment to the state constitution which would require all grade-school children to attend public schools. Armed with support from the Klan, the "Americanizers" sought to place the issue before the voters. The Church in Oklahoma, supported by many Protestant groups, most of which also sponsored their own parochial schools, waged an intense campaign against the proposed amendment. The school issue became involved in the gubernatorial election; the anti-Klan candidate won, and the supporters of the compulsory public-school petition never mustered the required number of signatures.[82] Though Catholics were victorious on this issue, they were unable to prevent anti-Catholic hiring practices in the public-school system. Since there are several documented instances of such discrimination, it is likely that the practice was widespread.

It was in Oregon that the advocates of compulsory public education mounted their most successful campaign. When Major Luther I. Powell, a Klan Kleagle from Louisiana, embarked on an Oregon recruitment effort in early 1921, he discovered a strong mix of anti-Catholicism, nativism, labor-capital hostility, and isolationism. One historian of the Klan entitled his chapter on Oregon, "Puritanism Repotted," because so many of Oregon's citizens were descendants of New Englanders who had moved to the Far West via the Mississippi Valley, as if fleeing from hoardes of invading immigrants.[83] The Federation of Patriotic Societies—composed of such fraternal orders as the Orange Lodge (of Protestant-Irish origins), Knights of Pythias, and the Masons, most of which were dedicated to compulsory public education —had paved the way for the "one hundred percent Americanism" of the Invisible Empire. Klan recruitment in Oregon followed a typical pattern. Major Powell would approach sympathetic Protestant ministers, one of whom would sponsor a lecture by an "escaped nun" and all of whom would help distribute Klan literature on the immigrant-papal threat to American democracy.[84] Soon the Klan was spreading throughout the state. In its first year it had prevented the establishment of a Newman Club at the University of Oregon and had developed a strong political base in Portland. Fred L. Gifford, who became the first Exalted Cyclops of Portland Klan No. 1 and later Grand Dragon of Oregon, also organized a very successful recruitment campaign. By the spring of 1922, there were fourteen thousand Klansmen in Oregon, half of them in Portland.[85] Though only 2 percent of Oregon's population were hooded Knights while 8 percent were Catholics, the Klan was more concentrated in its strategies. For example, when Portland Catholics protested the Klan's use of public facilities for its rallies, Mayor George Baker, who was suspected of harboring Klan sympathies, refused to take action. However, the Governor, Ben Alcott, was bitterly anti-Klan. He criticized the K.K.K. for "stirring up fanaticism, race hatred, religious prejudices, and all of those evil influences which tend toward factional strife and terror."[86] Though the Klan and other "one hundred percent American" societies failed to muster an anti-Alcott majority in the May 1922 Republican primary, they succeeded in unseating him in the November election; Walter Pierce became Oregon's first Democratic governor in the twentieth century. But the gubernatorial election was overshadowed by the compulsory-public-education initiative which was on the November ballot. Originating with the Scottish Rite Masons and supported by the Knights of Pythias, the Federation of Patriotic Societies, the Oregon Good Government League, the Loyal Orange Lodges, and the K.K.K., the proposal required all students from eight to sixteen to attend public schools.

Archbishop Alexander Christie of Portland organized a Catholic campaign against the initiative. Spokesmen for the Lutherans, Episcopalians, Seventh-Day Adventists, Presbyterians, and Jews, as well as several university presidents, condemned the measure, but nevertheless the initiative was incorporated into the laws of Oregon. Fortunately, because it was not to go into effect until 1926, the anti–compulsory-public-education forces had ample time to challenge the law's constitutionality in the courts.

The Supreme Board of Directors of the Order did not perceive the national significance of the compulsory-public-education measure until after it had been voted into law. For example, in the midst of the preelection campaign, the Board refused to donate to Christie's defense fund "on account of a similar situation existing in many other states."[87] Shortly after the November elections in Oregon, the State Deputy, P. J. Hanley of Portland, informed Luke Hart that "we are . . . preparing to bring this bill into the Courts . . . with a view of ultimately having it brought to the Supreme Court of the United States, in order that it be settled forever, and that it may strike a final blow at any effort to have this or similar measures enacted in any other state in the Union."[88] Alerted to the significance of the Oregon issue, Supreme Knight Flaherty wrote a letter to all the members, published in *Columbia,* in which he announced that the Oregon school law was a manifestation of a "national movement to abolish the parochial school." He urged all Catholics, "especially we Knights of Columbus . . . to unite to protect our rights" or suffer the return of the "old days of persecution."[89]

At the January 7, 1923, meeting of the Supreme Board in Chicago, Archbishop Christie addressed the Directors on the proposed legal suit to test the constitutionality of the law. The Board responded with the resolution that the Order would "provide the money that may be required" and authorized a payment of $10,000 to cover "the initial expense."[90] Roger Baldwin, associate director of the American Civil Liberties Union and a personal friend of Luke Hart, informed Hart that "we are entirely with you in this matter, because that law violates the principles of civil and religious liberty."[91] Four days after he appeared before the Supreme Board, Christie addressed the Administrative Board of the National Catholic Welfare Conference, which also met in Chicago. Chaired by Archbishop Edward J. Hanna of San Francisco and composed of six archbishops and bishops, the N.C.W.C. Board also resolved to subsidize the entire cost of the litigation and pledged to raise $100,000.[92] When the K. of C. and N.C.W.C. boards later discovered that each had passed essentially the identical resolution, the result was the kind of jealousy, and bitterness that had prevailed between the Order and the hierarchy's N.C.W.C. in World War I.

The officers were quite surprised, as we have noted, when the Catholic press reported the Oregon resolution of the N.C.W.C. in late January, as were members of the hierarchy when they heard that the K. of C. had pledged to finance the litigation. Utterly confused by the situation, the officers postponed sending a check to Christie until the matter was clarified. Archbishop Austin Dowling of St. Paul, a member of the Administrative Board of the N.C.W.C., was "quite wrought up" about the K. of C.'s role in the Oregon matter. He told Supreme Physician E. W. Buckley that he had heard that the Knights had pledged $50,000 to finance the case. Dowling and the N.C.W.C. did not want the Order to interfere, and insisted that whatever money it had given to Christie should be returned. Buckley told Luke Hart of his meeting with Dowling and advised that "we sit tight until we hear further from Portland."[93]

J. P. Kavanaugh, Archbishop Christie's lawyer, who was present at both the K. of C. and the N.C.W.C. meetings in Chicago, told Hart that Christie was expecting to receive an initial $10,000 from the Order and other payments in accord with the Supreme Board's resolution. He implied that there was some doubt as to the N.C.W.C.'s ability to raise $100,000.[94] Hart was willing to see the Order subsidize the entire cost "if the bishops will just let us do it and will give us credit for what we do."[95] Moreover, he was informed by Martin Carmody that several bishops were not in sympathy with the N.C.W.C. action in Chicago. Carmody also told Hart that he favored sending the $10,000, but not "as a contribution to the Welfare Council [sic] Fund."[96] Hart agreed with Carmody, doubted that the bishops would give the Order credit, but concluded that the Knights could gain some public esteem by making "a great deal of the fact that we had stepped into the trench and provided the moneys necessary to initiate this movement."[97]

On February 17, a special committee appointed by the Board and composed of Flaherty, Hart, and McGinley met in Chicago and decided to seek the advice of Archbishop Christie before allocating $10,000 for his legal fund. By this time Dowling had urged Portland's archbishop to rely entirely upon the N.C.W.C. and not to accept the money from the K. of C. After the committee had informed Christie by wire of its need for direction, the archbishop wired McGinley to "hold all promised contributions" until further notice. Then on the following day, February 18, he wired, WOULD GREATLY APPRECIATE CHECK TO QUICKEN ACTION. VERY SINCERE . . . APPRECIATION FOR THIS AND OTHER FAVORS.[98] Within a few days, Archbishop Christie received $10,000 from the Order. Since as late as July 26, Judge Kavanaugh reported Christie had not received any money from the N.C.W.C., and since the first complaint in the case of the Sisters of the Holy Names of Jesus and Mary vs. the State of Oregon was submitted on August 22, it is evident that the K. of C. subsidy was crucial in preparing the brief for the test case.[99] However, by September the N.C.W.C. had raised $60,000 for the struggle, $21,000 of which had been sent to Christie.[100]

Besides the Sisters of the Holy Names, who had operated a private school in Portland since the mid-nineteenth century, the Hill Military Academy also filed suit against the compulsory-public-school law. In March 1924, the Federal District Court declared the law unconstitutional on the basis of the Fourteenth Amendment's guarantees of equal protection. This decision was appealed to the Supreme Court, which on June 1, 1925, handed down its unanimous decision declaring the law unconstitutional. The Court's opinion, written by Justice James C. McReynolds, also elaborated on the Fourteenth Amendment guarantees: "We think it entirely plain that the Act of 1922 unreasonably interferes with the liberty of parents and guardians to direct the upbringing and education of children under their control." Because the defenders of the law based their argument on the legality of the democratic process by which the people of Oregon voted the measure into law, Justice McReynolds emphasized that "the child is not the mere creature of the State; those who nurture him and direct his destiny have the right, coupled with the high duty, to recognize and prepare him for additional obligation."[101]

The N.C.W.C. issued a press release in which it praised the American bishops for financing the successful battle against the Oregon law, without any mention of the Knights' contribution. Daniel A. Tobin, Supreme Director from New York, who had made several speeches lauding the Order's strong financial support of Christie's struggle, was one among many Knights angered by the N.C.W.C.'s failure to give credit to the Order. He wrote a long letter to *The Catholic News* (New York) in which he documented the K. of C. donations to challenge the Oregon law. In a July 25, 1925, editorial, *The Catholic News* explained the injustice done to the Knights by stating that the release of the N.C.W.C. News Service was "not based on fact."[102]

The Oregon Knights, under the leadership of State Deputy P. J. Hanley, also supported the Hill Military Academy's suit. Hanley appealed to Knights throughout the Order to help their Oregon brothers. He received nearly $9,000 from over 300 individual Knights and councils as well as over $6,000 from the Supreme Board.[103] In a letter to Cardinal Hayes, Hanley explained the Knights' subsidy for the Academy's suit: "It fell to my lot to finance the case of the Hill Military Academy, which we considered a very necessary auxiliary to the case of the Sisters, in order to show that the fight was not exclusively a Catholic one."[104] The Hill Academy case provided the Order with its own means for opposing the Oregon public school law free from embarrassing entanglements with the N.C.W.C.

By the time of the Supreme Court's decision on the Oregon school case, membership in the Ku Klux Klan in Oregon was declining. Internal and external factionalism had created distrust among those patriotic societies once allied with the Klan; public charges of corruption, and adverse publicity from the school case, also caused a severe loss of the Invisible Empire's patriotic credibility and social respectability. This was equally true nationally. After reaching its peak in 1924, with one and a half million members, the K.K.K. was a relatively insignificant political force by 1926. But in 1928, the nomination of Al Smith as the Democratic candidate for the Presidency ignited the smoldering coals of religious prejudice. Because he favored the repeal of prohibition, the three Rs of anti-Catholic animus—"Rum, Romanism, and Rebellion"—were revived. The K.K.K. experienced a brief revival, but several anti-Smith groups, particularly in the South, had more respectable spokesmen.[105] The Methodist Episcopal Church of the South, speaking through the *Wesleyan Christian Advocate*, stated, "Governor Smith has a constitutional right to run for President, even though a Catholic. This we confess. And we have a right to vote against him because he is a Catholic . . . we are strongly persuaded that Catholicism is a degenerate type of Christianity which ought everywhere to be displaced with a pure type of Christianity." One Lutheran official addressed a large gathering in New York: "Shall we have a man in the White House who acknowledges allegiance to the autocrat on the Tiber, who hates democracy, public schools, Protestant personages, individual rights, and everything that is essential to independence?"[106] On the other hand, many nationally prominent Protestant leaders, including two Methodist Episcopal Bishops of the South, denounced those who would inject religion into the campaign.[107] The Catholic Church reiterated its traditional position of neutrality. Though the K. of C. bogus oath circulated throughout the country (Smith was a member of the Order), the Supreme Officers limited their response to court action, and, in accord with its laws, the Order remained officially aloof from the political contests.

In their unofficial capacity, of course, the Supreme Officers were, like many Catholic leaders, deeply committed to Smith's campaign. Luke Hart, who had served on the St. Louis board of aldermen, was pro-Smith. "Much as I would love to see it, I cannot convince myself that he [Smith] has a chance." He referred to Herbert Hoover as the "World's Most Uninteresting Speaker."[108] As the Supreme Advocate responsible for the Order's litigation against the publishers and circulators of the bogus oath, Hart viewed the election of 1928 in terms of the Order's Catholic anti-defamation work. "However, win or lose, I think Smith's campaign has done much for Catholicity by dragging old man Intolerance out into the broad daylight where the public can have a good look at him."[109]

II

The Knights' Crusade
in Mexico

THOUGH CHAPTER 12 WILL BE CONCERNED with the Knights as they experienced the Great Depression, the New Deal, and the rise of dictatorships in Europe, these issues form a backdrop to the present chapter on their activities during the persecution of Catholics in Mexico. Because the Order pursued a consistent policy during this period, which spans James Flaherty's later years and nearly all of Martin Carmody's administration, I will postpone treatment of internal matters until the next chapter. However, it is important to recall that Supreme Knight Carmody had been Deputy Supreme Knight since 1909, and that most of the Supreme Officers during the Mexican involvement belonged to the pre–World War I generation whose goals for the Order were still to promote Catholic culture and to defend the Church against the attacks of bigoted Masons, Socialists, Protestants, and Anglo-Saxon racists.

Martin Carmody, a lawyer, joined Grand Rapids (Michigan) Council No. 389 in 1902 and was State Deputy when elected Deputy Supreme Knight in 1909. William McGinley, charter member of New Amsterdam Council No. 217 (instituted in April 1897) was a deputy postmaster in New York City when he was elected Supreme Secretary in 1909. John Martin, elected Deputy Supreme Knight in 1927, was a lawyer and First Grand Knight of Green Bay Council No. 617 (instituted in November 1901). Daniel J. Callahan, Supreme Treasurer since 1909, achieved prominence as an organizer of councils throughout the South and as an executive of a steamboat company. Callahan moved to Washington, D.C., where he became a well-known civic leader and was an officer in the Riggs Bank. Dr. Edward W. Fahey, who became Supreme Physician shortly after the death of Dr. Buckley in late 1923, was educated in Canada, settled in St. Paul, and joined the Knights in 1905. Father John McGivney became Supreme Chaplain in 1928 upon the death of his brother Patrick. We have seen in Chapter 9 that Luke Hart joined Kenrick Council No. 686 in 1908 and was a prominent St. Louis attorney when elected Supreme Advocate in 1922. Hence, most of these officers joined the Order when it was in its infancy within their own jurisdiction. They were pioneers who served on degree teams dedicated to promoting Columbian idealism through the medium of the ceremonials. Second- and third-generation Irish Americans and members of the professional middle class, they were imbued with a sense of pride in the progress of American Catholicism and were acutely conscious of the Order's Catholic anti-defamation character. When these Knights of the pre–World War I generation determined to defend the Church in Mexico, they drew upon decades of experience as crusaders against religious persecution.

When the first K. of C. council was instituted in Mexico in 1905, the Catholic Church was beginning to respond to the issues endemic in a rapidly changing society characterized by massive poverty and illiteracy. Her opponents claimed that the Church was motivated by a desire to compete with the Protestant agencies and with the secular policies of the regime of Porfirio Díaz rather than by an authentic spirit of social concern, a criticism which reveals the widespread distrust of an institution which had been so closely allied with the traditional oligarchy. Indeed, since the promulgation of the 1857 Constitution— which deprived the Church of her privileges and confiscated her property—anticlericalism was infused into nearly every political group in Mexico with the exception of the National Catholic Party. Though Díaz had unofficially allowed the hierarchy and religious orders to regain some property, the Church's situation as an institution was precarious during the first decade of the twentieth century.[1]

It is impossible to determine the extent to which the Church was persecuted during the revolution of 1910–17, but there were frequent outbursts of anti-Catholicism. Octavio Paz portrays the revolution in terms of a festival of violence, one which revealed the "brutal, resplendent face of death and fiestas, of gossip and gunfire, of celebration and love (which is rape and pistol shots)."[2] When radical factions controlled various regions during the civil war, there were incidents in which churches were seized and communion wafers desecrated, while priests and nuns were subjected to abuse and frequently forced into exile without warning. A large segment of the Mexican hierarchy formed an unofficial church-in-exile in the United States.

The anti-Catholic atrocities were publicized in the United States during 1914–15 by Father Francis C. Kelley, editor of *Extension* (later bishop of Oklahoma City), and Father Richard H. Tierney, editor of

America. Though Cardinal Gibbons assumed a moderate position, other members of the American hierarchy, such as Bishop James A. McFaul of Trenton, New Jersey, and Bishop Joseph Schrembs of Toledo, Ohio, publicly expressed their outrage over the religious persecution in Mexico. Ever sensitive to the cause of religious liberty, the Knights of Columbus, through its Supreme Council, officially condemned the Mexican revolutionaries. When the Wilson Administration supported the Constitutionalist forces of Venustiano Carranza and ordered the American fleet to Vera Cruz to obstruct arms shipments to Victoriano Huerta in April 1914, the latter was forced to resign and go into exile. When the United States recognized the Carranza government in 1915, American Catholic spokesmen, believing Huerta to be less antagonistic to the Church than Carranza, lashed out at the interventionist policies of President Wilson and Secretary of State William Jennings Bryan.[3] By the end of 1916, Carranza had begun to consolidate the resolution, and, with the restoration of law and order, those Mexican prelates who had taken refuge in the United States returned to their dioceses.

Because Catholicism was viewed as inimical to the revolution, the Carranza government inserted several severe anti-ecclesiastical provisions into the Constitution of 1917 aimed at curbing its economic, political, and social power. The Church was forbidden to own property, and all ecclesiastical institutions became the property of the state; primary education became a monopoly of the state; religious orders, which had been protected by previous constitutional amendments, were forbidden; priests could not vote, hold office, or participate in politics; non-Mexican priests were barred from exercising their ministry; broad authority was granted to the legislatures of state governments to determine the precise number of priests and ministers to suit local needs; religious ceremonies and devotions were restricted to churches and private homes; public processions and other devotional practices were forbidden.[4] In response to those peasants and workers who had rallied to the radical colors of Francisco (Pancho) Villa and Emiliano Zapata, Carranza's constitution also included land reforms and work laws. Though this constitution was never placed before the voters for ratification, most scholars agreed that it was representative of the deep aspirations of the majority of Mexican people.[5] However, because its immediate implementation would have engaged the State in an impossible restructuring of the entire society, the constitution did not reflect the social realities of the present, but rather the revolutionary hopes of the future. And so, confronted with the need to impose order, Carranza did not enforce the anti-ecclesiastical laws.

Álvaro Obregón, who led a successful military revolt against Carranza in 1920, moved the government further to the left, exacerbated tensions with the United States (which withheld recognition out of fear of the rise of Bolshevism on its borders), and intensified the anti-Catholic posture of the revolution.[6] Though scholars concentrate on the church-state conflict during the presidency of Plutarco Elías Calles (1924–28), there were several acts of anti-Catholic harassment and violence during Obregón's term in office. In 1921 a bomb was set off at the door of Archbishop José Mora y del Rio, who, as the ordinary of the Archdiocese of Mexico City, had bitterly opposed the Constitution of 1917. Late in 1921, a bomb destroyed much of the shrine of Our Lady of Guadalupe, without, however, damaging the famous picture of the Virgin. Other incidents of violence occurred in 1922, including an armed fight between the Catholic Association of Mexican Youths and a group of leftists. The church-state issue reached a dramatic crescendo in early 1923 when over 40,000 pilgrims journeyed to the hill of Cubilete to witness Monsignor Ernesto Filippi, the Apostolic Delegate, and eleven other prelates bless the cornerstone of a monument dedicated to Christ the King. The Obregón government expelled the Apostolic Delegate for violating the constitution's provision proscribing "public worship," and future work on the monument was prohibited.[7]

William F. Buckley wrote an article for *Columbia* in which he reported that Monsignor Filippi, upon his arrival in the United States, "declared that . . . the real reason for his expulsion was the growth in Mexico of the Knights of Columbus and Daughters of Isabella." Buckley, who had large oil interests in Mexico and who was then president of the American Association of Mexico, quoted in full a Mexican-Catholic "manifesto of protest" against Obregón's expulsion of the pope's representative in Mexico. Signed by Luis G. Bustos, K. of C. State Deputy of Mexico, and five other executives of Catholic lay organizations, the "manifesto" listed the anti-Catholic outrages of the past few years and defended the legality of the Christ the King ceremonies on the basis that this did not constitute public worship since the ceremonies had taken place on private property.[8] The "manifesto" concluded with an attack upon the arbitrary conduct of the Mexican government and with a plea for religious liberty and a warning that the Catholic people of Mexico "will not endure these wrongs forever."[9] Buckley lashed out at the "Bolshevist" character of the Mexican government and documented the many anti-Catholic atrocities committed by Obregón during the previous ten years. Just as American Protestants were urging the United States to recognize officially the Obregón government, so Buckley urged the American Catholics to approve the nonrecognition policy of the Harding Administration until the Mexican government would guarantee religious liberty and the rights of American citizens.[10]

The Mexican Masons were jubilant over the expulsion of Filippi. William L. Vail, an American living in Mexico City, wrote what appears to have been a circular letter to his Masonic associates in the United States (addressed "Dear Noble") about the "considerable . . . heluvabaloo" which was raised in American newspapers regarding the Filippi affair and which was perpetrated by "the Knights of Columbus organization, whose methods here are the same as in the United States and are probably too well known to you to require any explanation on my part." Vail defended the Mexican government's action, contending that the government had warned the Church "against pulling the stunt off," i.e., the Christ the King ceremonies. He explained his reason for keeping American Masons informed: "the Knights of Columbus are turning Heaven and Earth to put the Government in the wrong abroad, and knowing how they love our Masonic institutions, I feel that our own people in the United States should know the facts and not be caught unawares."[11] Signed "Yours in the Faith, W. L. Vail," this letter was circulated in the South during the period when the Order was struggling against a large faction of Masons supporting the Oregon public-school law. Not only does this letter illustrate the traditional K. of C.–Masonic conflict but also the growth of the Order in Mexico. In fact, religious persecution in Mexico resulted in a rapid rise in K. of C. membership. In early 1918 there was only one council with four hundred Mexican Knights. By April 1923 there were forty-three councils with nearly six thousand members. Concurrent with this rise in membership, a Spanish translation of the bogus oath was being circulated south of the Rio Grande.

There were several church-state conflicts during the first years of Calles's presidency. He supported the schismatic Mexican Catholic-Apostolic Church, which declared celibacy immoral and which refused to recognize the authority of the pope. In early 1926, amid a confusing situation characterized by church leaders and politicians each suspecting the other of plots and intrigue, a leading newspaper quoted Archbishop Mora y del Rio's condemnation of the anti-Catholic provisions of the 1917 Constitution. Calles soon retaliated by implementing these provisions more fully. The situation became polarized when the government expelled more than two hundred priests, closed the remaining Catholic primary schools, and required all priests to register with the civil authorities. The Mexican hierarchy refused to comply with these laws, which, though constitutional, had never been fully enforced, and announced that effective July 31, 1926, the Catholic Church in Mexico would cease performing all public religious ceremonies.[12]

The National League for the Defense of Religious Liberty, or Liga Nacional, which was founded in 1925 in retaliation for Calles's support of schismatic Catholics, was a lay organization which played a significant role in the struggle against Calles. With State Deputy Bustos as one of its presidents, the League organized a Catholic economic boycott during the latter half of March in order to pressure the government to rescind the anti-Catholic laws. Bustos and other leaders were arrested on charges of sedition. The boycott continued but with only short-lived success.[13]

A few days after the Catholic Church had ceased public services in Mexico, Supreme Knight Flaherty declared that "the religious crisis in Mexico will be the most important question discussed by this [1926 Supreme Council] Convention." He considered the U.S. government's silence on the issue as tantamount to approval of the Mexican government. Flaherty disagreed with the Coolidge Administration's view that the religious question was entirely a domestic issue. Since the Calles government had expelled Bishop George J. Caruana, papal observer in Mexico, who was an American citizen, Flaherty was hopeful that this incident "can be the opening wedge" in effecting a change in U.S. policy. Twenty-five thousand Knights were in Philadelphia for the August 3–5 convention. In his annual address, Flaherty reported that "the Knights of Columbus in Mexico have been persecuted, their schools and halls there have been closed, and their purposes have been maligned. And why? . . . because they are Catholics, members of a Church which the present government of Mexico harasses and despoils." On behalf of the Order he vigorously protested the anti-Catholic persecution, which he considered to be "Communistic in origin [and] anti-religious in principle."[14] On August 5, the delegates unanimously passed a resolution by which the Supreme Council protested Calles's "despotic anti-Catholic persecution," warned Americans of the Bolshevik presence "at their very doorsteps," called upon the American Federation of Labor to cooperate in the Order's Mexican campaign, condemned the U.S. government for its support of the Carranza and Obregón governments, and implied that the United

States should deny recognition to the Calles government until it guaranteed religious liberty.[15] The resolution concluded by authorizing the Supreme Board of Directors to assess the members "to the extent of $1,000,000 for a campaign of education, to the end that the policies of Soviet Russia shall be eliminated from the philosophy and ideals of liberty of conscience [sic], and democratic freedom may extend to our afflicted human beings beyond the Rio Grande."[16]

The following day, copies of the resolution were sent to President Coolidge and Secretary of State Frank B. Kellogg; Flaherty wired Coolidge requesting an interview. Supreme Treasurer Daniel Callahan, who lived in Washington and was very active in civic affairs there, had three meetings with Kellogg during August. Because the resolution had been widely interpreted as a demand for American intervention in Mexico, Flaherty issued a press release on August 23 in which he reiterated the Order's position on the "Communist Regime" and on the Knights' campaign to enlighten public opinion on the despotic character of the Calles government. He also criticized the American government's recognition of the Carranza, Obregón, and Calles regimes. Flaherty stated that the K. of C. resolution "did not demand that the American government intervene in Mexico, [nor did it] specify the manner or form which governmental action should take."[17]

In September, Flaherty, Hart, McGinley, Carmody, Assistant Supreme Secretary John Conway, and Supreme Director William Prout of Massachusetts met with President Coolidge. Flaherty recorded his impression of Coolidge's views in the minutes of a special September 5 Board meeting. He recalled that, after the President informed the Order's leadership of the necessity of maintaining diplomatic relations with Mexico, he declared that his Administration was "committed to bringing about a solution to the troubles which beset the people of Mexico."[18] Luke Hart told a reporter for the *St. Louis Post Dispatch* that the leaders were "quite satisfied" with Coolidge's interest "in the struggles of the people of Mexico for rights denied to almost no other people on earth." Hart said that they did not recommend a policy of interference but rather urged one of noninterference, because the Mexican political situation "was brought about largely by the meddling of [the Wilson and Harding] Administrations." Hart reported that the discussion with Coolidge included lifting the U.S. arms embargo on Mexico but that the Order did not specifically request such an action, though certainly favoring it.[19] If the arms embargo were lifted, then anti-Calles rebels could receive supplies from the United States.

The "campaign of education" on the Mexico issue entailed the publication of nearly five million copies of various pamphlets, all of which included selections from eyewitness reports on the extent to which the Church was persecuted by the Mexican government. In a pamphlet entitled "Mexico," David Goldstein, the K. of C. anti-Socialist lecturer, quoted pro-Calles, anti-Catholic statements made by the K.K.K.'s publication, *The Truth Seeker;* by Margaret Sanger, a leading spokesperson of the American birth-control movement; and by spokesmen for the International Workers of the World (I.W.W.), the American Socialist Party, and the Communist Party.[20] Though the A. F. of L. did not assume an anti-Catholic position, it too strongly sympathized with Calles's policies. The latter came as a blow to Goldstein, who had been a leading figure in the trade-union movement. The pamphlet also elaborated on the heroic efforts of the National League for the Defense of Religious Liberty. Drawing the analogy between the anti-Calles forces and the American revolutionaries, it referred to the defenders of Catholic rights as "Mexican Minute Men." It mistakenly evaluated the National League's economic boycott as "tremendously successful" and quoted in full the circular calling for the national Catholic boycott, which was prefaced by the following manifesto:

> Catholics! Nero has passed!
> Caligula has died!
> Diocletian has disappeared!
> And thus all enemies of the Church will end!
> Only God does not die; nor
> will the Church ever die.
> Christ lives! Christ Reigns! Christ rides![21]

The leaders of the National League, who had been working closely with the hierarchy, formed the leadership of the armed rebellion which had developed with the cessation of Catholic services. Dedicated to "Cristo Rey," the rebels, who included hundreds of Knights of Columbus, were called *Cristeros* (Christers) by their enemies. Though the hierarchy did not officially condone the rebellion, neither did it condemn it. Hence, the League proceeded to lead the rebellion with what it considered to be the implicit approval of the Church. With the hierarchy and the Calles regime at an impasse, the *Cristeros* movement represented the laity's refusal to surrender to the state's demands. Robert E. Quirk views the National League as the Catholic power base during this period: "The fate of Mexican Catholicism then passed into the hands of laymen and especially of the Liga Nacional. . . . There was no talk of . . . conciliation in the lay circles."[22]

Pope Pius XI portrayed the struggles in Mexico as a Christian crusade against the forces of "barbarism." In his encyclical *Iniquis Afflictisque* (November 18, 1926), he praised the courageous work of the Mexican laity but consistently advocated peaceful resistance to the religious persecution. Among those organizations which he singled out as deserving of specific praise, the Knights of Columbus headed the list. "First of all we mention the Knights of Columbus, an organization which is found in all states of the Republic and fortunately is made up of active and industrious members who, because of their practical lives and open profession of the Faith, as well as by their zeal in assisting the Church, have brought great honor upon themselves." He was particularly impressed with the Mexican Knights' catechetical program and its defense of religious education in general. Pope Pius credited the Order with the establishment and promotion of the Liga Nacional, aimed at presenting "a unified invincible front to the enemy."[23] The Supreme Board of Directors, extremely grateful for the Pope's recognition of the Order's work in Mexico, passed a resolution (January 9, 1927) by which 500,000 lire were sent to Pius XI "for such purposes and uses in relieving the distress of our afflicted fellow-Catholics in Mexico as His Holiness may determine."[24]

Throughout 1927, the Order continued to circulate anti-Calles pamphlets as well as the American hierarchy's Pastoral Letter on the religious persecution in Mexico. A portion of the $1 million Mexican Fund was sent to Patrick Cardinal Hayes of New York, who distributed money to dioceses which cared for refugees from Mexico. The Supreme Office sent thousands of dollars to those K. of C. councils that were engaged in relief work for Mexican associates and their families. For example, to the family of Manuel de la Peza, the State Secretary of the Mexican Knights who died in the United States after two years in exile, the Order paid the burial expenses, a remittance of $200 to his dependents, and $100 monthly allowance to his widow.[25] Though rumors have persisted to circulate that a part of the Order's Mexican Fund went for the purchase of arms for the *Cristeros,* there is no evidence of such direct support. Because the Mexican Knights were so identified with the *Cristero* rebellion, the Order was officially proscribed in Mexico and the Spanish edition of *Columbia* was banned from the Mexican mail.

During 1927–29, while the *Cristeros* pursued guerrilla warfare against the Calles government, the Coolidge Administration, through the diplomacy of its ambassador to Mexico, Dwight W. Morrow, vigorously pursued a *modus vivendi* satisfactory to the leaders of Church and state. Though Morrow was a Wall Street lawyer, he defied the stereotype by his genuine interest in Mexican culture and by his openness to the aspirations of the revolutionaries. Gradually he gained Calles's confidence and respect. Secretary of State Kellogg told him that he could not officially discuss the church-state struggle, but he did encourage him to broach the issue on a personal plane. On November 13, 1927, shortly after Morrow arrived in Mexico, the intensity of the religious issue was dramatically demonstrated when three members of the National League unsuccessfully attempted to assassinate General Álvaro Obregón. The police arrested Humberto Pro Juarez, a regional delegate of the League, and his brother, Miguel Pro, a Jesuit priest. Though Humberto had sold his automobile to the assassins a few days before the event, both he and his brother were innocent of complicity in the crime. In spite of a confession by the man responsible for the attack on Obregón, the chief of police ordered the immediate execution of the Pro brothers without trial (November 23, 1927). Determined to deter Catholics from further terroristic activities, the chief of police publicly circulated photographs of the executions, including one of Father Pro facing the firing squad with his arms outstretched in Christlike posture. Such photographs were cherished as holy pictures by devout Catholics and engendered further hostility toward the Calles regime among Father Pro's co-religionists throughout North America.[26] Prior to the Pro executions, Morrow and Calles had scheduled a tour through Mexican agricultural districts. Though Morrow knew that "some Catholics would consider my trip an endorsement" of the barbaric acts of the government, he nevertheless met with Calles in the wake of the executions.[27] Morrow's realism achieved results. He succeeded in winning Calles's confidence, and shortly after the tour he quietly initiated a line of diplomacy which ultimately led to a resolution of the Catholic issue.

In preparation for his first official visit to Mexico, Morrow had met with Father John J. Burke, C.P., general secretary of the National Catholic Welfare Conference, to discuss the volatile religious situation south of the Rio Grande. The diplomat and the scholar priest developed a sense of mutual trust which led ultimately to a Burke-Calles meeting. Though Burke had received authority from Monsignor Pietro Fumasoni-Biondi, the Apostolic Delegate in the United States, to meet with Calles in early April 1928, he had no authority to negotiate a settlement. During the next fourteen months Morrow continued to serve as liaison between the conflicting parties, but because the diplomatic lines ran through the Vatican, the Mexican hierarchy, Mexican political circles, the League, and the *Cristeros,* negotiations were frequently delayed and at times appeared hopelessly entangled in the irreconcilable and impassioned positions of the various factions.

The Mexican Knights of Columbus condemned any diplomatic approach, and with the League and the Catholic Youth Organization they wrote to Pope Pius XI (May 31, 1928) a long letter in which they identified any accord with the government as a capitulation to the forces of despotism.[28] When General Obregón, who was designated to succeed Calles in 1928 and who was committed to the Calles-Burke overtures, was assassinated by a Catholic extremist (July 9, 1928), a peaceful accord appeared hopeless. After a lengthy eight-month impasse, signs of moderation surfaced among the conflicting groups.[29] Finally on June 21, 1929, Archbishop Leopoldo Ruiz y Flores, the Apostolic Delegate in Mexico, and President Emilio Portes Gil issued a declaration which formed the basis for a *modus vivendi.* The bishops agreed to allow their clergy to register with the government and to reopen the churches for religious services. Portes Gil stipulated that the government would register only those clergymen approved by the hierarchy, that religious education within the churches would be allowed, and under constitutional guarantees all citizens, including churchmen, would possess the right to petition the government for changes in the laws. Hence, in return for the Church's recognition of the revolution, the government allowed the Church to maintain its identity. The Mexican government continued to enforce the exile of militant bishops and some of the leaders of the League, including Luis G. Bustos, and hundreds of those *Cristeros* who surrendered were summarily executed. Though the American press praised the eleventh-hour role of Edmund A. Walsh, S.J., vice-president of Georgetown University, John J. Burke was the indispensable figure in placating Calles (still the power behind the presidency) through the determined efforts of Dwight Morrow.[30]

The Order never changed its policy on Mexico during the Burke-Calles meetings, but it did alter its strategies. Supreme Knight Martin Carmody's first report to the Supreme Council included a lengthy list of grievances against the "Bolshevist" government of Mexico. After he reviewed the Order's noninterventionist policy in Mexico, he condemned the tendency of the American press to allow "its columns to be used constantly as an agency for the Mexican authorities to spread through the U.S. its opposition to Catholics, the Catholic Church, and the Knights of Columbus, by associating . . . these names with every happening in Mexico, whether it be a case of common banditry or military demonstration."[31] He believed that such public distortions of the role of the Order in Mexico served to intensify religious tensions in the United States. Obviously, he could not comment on the strong K. of C. representation within the ranks of the *Cristeros,* which in a sense would have justified the Mexican press attack upon the Knights; nor could he comment on the strong pro-*Cristero* support among the Supreme Officers, particularly Luke Hart, who, through various intermediaries, attempted to influence Bishop Díaz to reject a diplomatic solution to the conflict. Joseph N. Fining, head of Fining Press Syndicate, which the Order employed to handle its anti-Mexican campaign, wrote to Hart late in May 1928, stating that he had been in touch with Bishop Díaz and that "conditions are favorable for carrying out ideas which you and I have discussed. I think you will find a sentiment among the [Mexican] Bishops kindly toward these ideas. . . . It is absolutely foolish to flatter ourselves [the U.S.] with the hope that anything may be gained by parleying with Calles and Obregón. While negotiations proceed, persecutions continue."[32] There is no other corroborative evidence to place the leadership of the American Knights in the militants' camp. However, Supreme Secretary William McGinley recalled that the Order "waged a vigorous campaign [against Mexico] until negotiations were opened by Father Burke." Since there was a notable decline in anti-Calles articles in *Columbia* concurrent with the Burke negotiations, it would appear that Burke had a restraining influence upon the Order. On the other hand, the leadership was not sympathetic to the 1929 accord; McGinley further remarked that Burke's "settlement [i.e., the 1929 *modus vivendi*] tied the hands of . . . the Knights of Columbus."[33]

Several K. of C. leaders who were active in the League were forced into exile. Hundreds of Mexican Knights were killed fighting for the *Cristero* cause. Referred to as martyrs by militant Catholics, these K. of C. *Cristeros* have been portrayed as villainous counterrevolutionaries in a mural which dominates the Plaza de Populo in Mexico City. At the August 19, 1929, meeting of the Supreme Board and at the subsequent meeting of the Supreme Council, Edelmiro Traslosheros and George Nuñez, State Deputy and State Secretary of the Mexican Knights, reported on the condition of the Order in their jurisdiction. They noted that all but five councils had suspended work during the period of church-state conflict, and that "since the persecution ended" they had urged the reorganization of councils. Twenty-five percent of the fifty-one councils had been reconstituted during the previous two months, and they had hoped to have another 50 percent reconstituted by the end of the year. The remaining 25 percent "will be hard to get going, as they are located in places where the persecution was so strong that there are no members of the Order left there." Nuñez and Traslosheros conveyed Archbishop Díaz's gratitude to the Knights for all their efforts on behalf of the Church in Mexico. Díaz sought the Order's support for a peaceful resolution to the civil-religious conflicts in those states "where the situation has not been settled" and emphasized the need for the Knights to work with the Mexican hierarchy in their attempt to respond to the nation's many social problems.[34] The 1929 settlement was, at best, only a precarious truce between the Church and the central government, one which several state governments ignored either by banning religious services altogether or by severely restricting the numbers of priests permitted to pursue their pastoral duties.

II

Beginning in 1931 the central government revived its anticlerical policies. General Calles, who was the power behind the President, had shifted to the right on economic and social issues, but in order to appear loyal to the principles of the revolution, he lashed out at the Church for its disloyalty. In 1933, the government announced a six-year education plan which was aimed at removing the nation's youth from the Church's catechetical programs. Anticlericalism was injected into the election campaign of 1934 as the future President, General Lázaro Cárdenas, pledged that he would "not permit the clergy to intervene in any manner in the education of the people."[35] Former President Calles declared war on the Church's education program: "We must now enter into and take possession of the minds of the children, the minds of the young . . . because they do belong and should belong to the Revolution."[36] After Cárdenas had been elected, a government commission called for a constitutional amendment prohibiting Catholic schools and all religious instruction.

During this period of renewed anticlericalism, the American Catholic hierarchy condemned the persecution of the Church in Mexico (January 1933), and shortly after Franklin D. Roosevelt entered the White House he was beset by a barrage of Catholic protests against the behavior of the U.S. Ambassador to Mexico, Josephus Daniels. Because Daniels had campaigned for Al Smith and had opposed the K.K.K. in his home state of North Carolina, Catholics were shocked when, in an address in Mexico City (July 1934), Daniels praised and quoted Calles's remark, "we must enter and take possession of the mind of childhood, the mind of youth," as bespeaking the tradition of Thomas Jefferson on public education. Unaware of the anticlerical context in which Calles uttered this remark, Daniels was soon subjected to attack from a variety of American Catholic spokesmen, several of whom called for his immediate resignation.[37]

In the fall of 1934, Catholic criticism mounted as many Mexican priests and nuns again sought refuge from persecution in the United States. Roosevelt publicly defended his friend Daniels but was in frequent private consultation with Father John J. Burke as to the appropriate diplomatic approach to the Mexican government. Though he was determined to maintain his "Good Neighbor Policy" by avoiding any public statement which implied intervention in the domestic affairs of any Latin-American nation, Roosevelt told Burke that he would nevertheless underline his administration's commitment to religious liberty.[38]

During October, Luke E. Hart and Daniel J. Callahan were urging Supreme Knight Carmody to speak out on the Mexican situation.[39] On November 3, after a meeting of the Supreme Officers in Detroit, Carmody issued a press release in which he declared that the Mexican government was "a blotch and a stench to the family of nations."[40] He labeled the Mexican government "totalitarian," one which harbored hopes "to out-Russia Russia in making men chattels of the State"; to illustrate his point, he referred to an incident in Mexico City in which Catholics were forced out of their churches by armed soldiers.[41] On behalf of the Order, Carmody issued a "vigorous protest" against the religious persecution in Mexico and sought the support of "all fair-minded Americans" to join in denouncing the "Communist, atheistic regime at our very doors."[42]

At the January 13, 1935, meeting, the Supreme Board passed a resolution which denounced the behavior of the Mexican government as "opposed to religion, morality, justice, and liberty, and as a menace and a peril to this nation," and which called upon the U.S. government to "make representations to the government of Mexico." On the same day, Carmody wired Roosevelt requesting a meeting with the Resolutions Committee of the Supreme Board (i.e., the Supreme Officers) at the President's "earliest convenience."[43] Roosevelt replied that, because of the heavy demands upon his time, he was unable to meet with the representatives of the Order but referred them to Secretary of State Cordell Hull.[44] On January 21, the committee, except for Luke Hart, met with Hull. Callahan described the Secretary of State as "quite sympathetic, but there was nothing definite he could promise us so far as the relationship between the two countries was concerned. He rather intimated they had lots of data and were keen to take whatever steps they could in a diplomatic way to alleviate the situation."[45] Callahan also reported that Carmody told Hull of the Order's 1926 resolution on Mexico and of the favorable response of President Coolidge, the obvious inference being that Roosevelt himself could have met with the committee.

Prior to the meeting with Hull, the Supreme Officers had decided to appeal to friendly Senators in support of a resolution calling for a special congressional investigation of the situation in Mexico. After leaving Hull's office, they met with ten Senators, including Robert Wagner, David I. Walsh, and Key Pittman, chairman of the Senate Committee on Foreign Relations. Carmody told Luke Hart that these Senators gave "assurances that they will promote and support vigorously the plan of introducing a resolution in the Senate, asking for an investigation of the conditions in Mexico . . . with the object in mind that if persecutions in Mexico are not discontinued and assurances [given] that they will not be renewed then diplomatic relations will be terminated with that country." He also referred to a telephone conversation with Senator Walsh, who reported that he had just visited with the President and had informed him of the Order's intention to organize a national grass-roots effort on behalf of the Senate resolution and of the need for the President to meet with the leaders of the K. of C. and give them "definite assurances." While the President seemed amenable to such a meeting, Walsh had told Carmody that Roosevelt's secretary was not very encouraging, and Carmody had indicated his fear that a meeting with Roosevelt could end up with the President uttering "soft words" which would tend to obstruct the Order from pressuring for the resolution.[46]

On January 29, Callahan informed Hart that Senator William E. Borah of Idaho, the ranking minority member of the Foreign Relations Committee, would call for the investigation.[47] Scholars have been puzzled by Borah's willingness to offer this resolution, which was called the Borah Resolution, to the Senate, because he had so few Catholic constituents and because he was the Senate's leading isolationist. The Callahan-Hart correspondence sheds new light on the issue as it substantiates the fact that the resolution originated with the

Knights of Columbus and that Senator Walsh was the key figure in winning Borah's support. Though one may speculate about Borah's motives, the leaders of the Knights, who had many contacts with Borah, were convinced that the Senator was animated only by a sincere concern for human rights in Mexico. Carmody then wrote to all the American Grand Knights, urging them to wire their Representatives and Senators on the critical need for a Senate investigation of the situation in Mexico. Luke E. Hart wrote to T. J. Pendergast, Democratic political leader in Kansas City and a member of the Order, asking him to seek Senator Harry Truman's endorsement of the resolution. Truman informed Pendergast that he favored the resolution—he saw the Mexican government as analogous to the "Bolshevist" organization in Russia—and told Pendergast, with characteristic candor, "It has always been my opinion ever since I was a school kid that James K. Pope [sic] made a mistake when he didn't make the Panama Canal the southern boundary of the United States."[48]

To supplement the political campaign, *Columbia* waged an incessant propaganda battle to expose the religious persecution and the need for implementation of the Borah Resolution. Editorials frequently cited historical precedent for the U.S. government's defense of religious liberty in foreign nations. One such editorial referred to President Harrison's tacit condemnation of the revival of anti-Semitic laws in Czarist Russia.[49] The Order's support for the Borah Resolution also resulted in the establishment of an office in Washington. In response to the Roosevelt Administration's contention that the situation in Mexico was entirely a domestic affair and that the rights of American citizens were not violated, and to illustrate that the Order's motives were not limited to the protection of Catholic interests, the K. of C. lobbying office was entitled the National Committee for the Defense of American Rights in Mexico. Under the direction of an attorney, Matt Mahorner (son-in-law of Daniel Callahan), the committee was an ad hoc response to the Administration's anti-Borah pressure upon the Senate Foreign Relations Committee. Its major work to that effect was a lengthy memorandum intended "to establish a *prima facie* case in support of an investigation by a Senatorial Committee."[50] Prefaced by a historical account of religious persecution against persons of all denominations, the memorandum charged the American government with intervention in defense of the Mexican government. "The so-called 'Cristero' War of 1929 [sic] . . . would undoubtedly have succeeded, in the opinion of competent observers, but for the help given by the American Secretary of State to the radical government by put-

ting an embargo on arms." Implicitly condemning the Burke-Calles
modus vivendi of 1929, it documented cases of anti-Protestant, anti-
Semitic, anti-Catholic persecution between 1929 and 1935, and summarized numerous precedents for a strong American protest against
violations of religious liberty.[51]

The Friends of Catholic Mexico, with Robert R. Hull of *Our Sunday
Visitor* as chairman and Dorothy Day of *Catholic Worker* as first vice-
president, congratulated the Knights for their strong pro-Borah position. In a letter to Hart, Hull referred to the "diabolical policy that has
been pursued by our Government with regard to Mexico."[52] The
American Committee on Religious Rights and Minorities (an ecumenical group which included such religious leaders as Henry Sloane
Coffin, president of Union Theological Seminary; Bernard F. Rich-
ards, director of the Jewish Information Bureau; and Michael Williams,
editor of *Commonweal*) sent a deputation to Mexico to inquire into the
religious policies of the government. The Knights were aware of this
deputation but, according to Daniel Callahan, the committee would,
at best, only confirm what that Order had already brought to light.[53]
However, a *Columbia* editorial quoted extensively from the deputation's report, and this added a note of objectivity to the Knights'
cause.[54] Throughout its campaign to promote the Borah Resolution,
the Order was in communication with the exiled Apostolic Delegate to
Mexico, Archbishop Ruiz, with several members of the hierarchy, and
with the Vatican Secretary of State, Eugenio Cardinal Pacelli. In March
1935, at the suggestion of Hart, Ruiz wrote a pro-Borah letter to all
the American bishops and archbishops.[55] Though Ruiz reported that
the response was very encouraging, the American hierarchy was divided on the proper strategy. Archbishop Michael Curley of Baltimore
and Bishop Francis Kelley of Oklahoma City were the most vociferous
interventionists, advocating a congressional investigation as a way of
compelling Roosevelt to issue a public condemnation of the religious
persecution.[56]

In late April 1935, Hart and Bishop Kelley discussed the Order's
Mexican campaign. There was general agreement between them on
principles, particularly the Order's political support of the Borah Resolution, but Kelley advised "that the Knights of Columbus work
should be managed in such a way as to not identify our Order with it,
because of a feeling that our Order is tremendously powerful and
influential and that, therefore, it has aroused such antagonism in Mexico that it is more cordially disliked than is the Church itself."[57] Hart
disagreed, noting that the Order's public sponsorship provided it with

"color and standing which a covert campaign would lack."[58] Kelley's book, *Blood Drenched Altars, Mexican Study and Comment,* had just been published and had avoided any reference to either the Mexican Knights or the Supreme Officers. The book, in fact, is less polemical than its title suggests. Though Kelley developed an elaborate defense of the Catholic contribution to Mexican culture, he placed the revolution and the attack upon the Church in broad historical and philosophical perspective.[59]

Archbishop Curley was also in close contact with several leaders of the Order. He was of the opinion that the Catholic laymen of Mexico "will never accept anything like the so-called agreement of 1929" and that "no matter what the Church does, thinking laymen are determined to have liberty or nothing." Curley stated that his own personal "Mexican campaign contributions in the way of cash ran well into the four figures."[60] Curley was very disappointed when the N.C.W.C.'s Administrative Committee of Bishops refused to endorse the Borah Resolution.[61] He attacked Roosevelt for obstructing the Borah Resolution and for his refusal to see a delegation from the Knights of Columbus. In that context, on May 10, Curley told Supreme Treasurer Callahan that the "Knights of Columbus are being criticized very severely for their silence in connection with the refusal of the President to see them."[62] Upon the advice of Senator Walsh, the Knights had not sought an interview with the President during March and early April in the hope that the Order's campaign would be successful and that Roosevelt would invite the Supreme Officers to the White House.[63] When it became apparent that an invitation would not be forthcoming and that the Senate Foreign Relations Committee was succumbing to the Administration's anti-Borah pressure, the Order's leaders did attempt to see Roosevelt. Carmody wrote to the President on April 22, 1935, seeking an interview on April 29 "or as soon thereafter as convenient."[64] After Carmody had written several such letters to the White House, and after the bishops had publicly sought the Administration's condemnation of the persecution in Mexico, Roosevelt consented to meet with representatives of the Knights on July 8.

Though there is no transcript of this one-hour meeting between the Supreme Officers and Roosevelt, Hart summarized the discussion in letters to Archbishop Ruiz and Bishop Kelley. After Carmody reviewed the Order's reasons for requesting the interview, the President informed the Knights "that Mexico is dealing with an aggravated form of the trend away from religion that is world-wide in scope." He then told them of how his Good Neighbor Policy was a response to the strong feelings of anti-U.S. sentiment among the people of Latin America and that if his Administration "should take any decisive stand concerning the religious persecution in Mexico, it would be resented by all Latin America and it would probably have no other result than the killing of one hundred priests and nuns." Nevertheless, Carmody reiterated the Knights' position that the President should make a protest to the Mexican government and "that if it failed to grant the desired relief, diplomatic relations would be severed." Hart added that "we want the pressure that is keeping the Borah Resolution in the committee withdrawn so that the Resolution may be brought onto the floor and adopted." Hart also referred to the significant role of U.S. public opinion in effecting changes in the anticlerical provisions in the Mexican constitution, and told the President that American Catholics would be entirely dissatisfied with another *modus vivendi* like that of 1929. The President answered Hart by stating, "It is certain that we are not going to war with Mexico," as if to imply that if he adopted the Knights' position, war was inevitable. Hart retorted that the United States successfully pressured England to settle the Irish question without going to war, an inaccurate historical analogy which apparently did not elicit a response from the President. Roosevelt informed the Knights that he "was closely in touch with Rome, the Apostolic Delegate [Archbishop Amleto Cicognani, Apostolic Delegate in the United States], the hierarchy, the National Catholic Welfare Council [sic], and Father Burke, and that they approved entirely of the policy that had been pursued by him in connection with the Mexico situation." Because the Knights had also been in contact with Rome and had received encouragement from Archbishop Cicognani as recently as the day before this very meeting, Hart indicated to Kelley and Ruiz his disbelief in the accuracy of Roosevelt's remarks, saying that "certainly his statement concerning the Hierarchy is not consistent with what we know to be the attitude of Archbishop Curley and a great many other Archbishops and Bishops."[65]

The meeting ended as it had begun; both the President and the K. of C. leaders were confident of the correctness of their positions. The Order continued to pursue its political campaign on behalf of the Borah Resolution and to publicize the anti-Catholic atrocities in Mexico, while Roosevelt continued to fight the resolution on the grounds that an investigation of the Mexican situation would jeopardize his foreign policy. However, he implied his intention to follow the 1929 Morrow precedent of quiet diplomacy and agreed to make a public statement on the issue.

Father Burke, who was soon to become the Vatican's official representative on the Mexican situation, had been urging Roosevelt to make such a statement. On July 17, 1935, in response to a petition signed by many congressmen concerned with the religious situation in Mexico, Roosevelt publicly endorsed those who are making "it clear that the American people and the Government believe in freedom of religious worship, not only in the United States, but also in other nations."[66] Though the Catholic press generally praised Roosevelt's statement, the Supreme Officers did not even respond to it. They continued to hold Roosevelt responsible for disregarding the sentiments of millions of Catholics. Delegates to the Supreme Council (August 21, 1935) unanimously adopted a strong letter of protest addressed to President Roosevelt. The letter condemned "the Administration's sustained attack upon the Borah amendment and the failure of the United States to extend to the oppressed people of Mexico that solace and comfort which has been so often held out to the persecuted peoples of other races and religious beliefs."[67]

On October 2, Roosevelt issued another statement aimed at the Mexican government's religious policy: "Our national determination to keep us free . . . of foreign entanglements cannot prevent us from feeling deep concern when ideals and principles that we have cherished are challenged. We regard it as axiomatic that every person shall enjoy the free exercise of his religion according to the dictates of his conscience."[68] Since he uttered these remarks in San Diego, just twenty miles from the Mexican border, many Catholic newspapers praised the President for his attack upon the Cárdenas government. However, the Order's leaders considered Roosevelt's statement "a small sop to Catholics."[69] The Supreme Board of Directors, which met on October 5–6, authorized another letter of protest to the President. (Though it appeared over the signatures of Carmody and McGinley, Luke Hart had drafted it.) Dated October 25, the letter was a severely astringent expression of the Order's disappointment at the President's failure to fulfill his assurance made at the July 8 meeting that he would make a public statement "expressing the attitude of our Government concerning conditions in Mexico." According to the Knights, the San Diego speech did not fulfill that promise because "you made no reference to Mexico. You refrained from expressing sympathy for the weak and down-trodden people of that oppressed land." After listing fourteen Presidents who remonstrated against the oppressed minorities in foreign countries, the Knights asserted that Roosevelt's Good Neighbor Policy could not be used as "an excuse for non-action on this great crisis, involving the liberty of conscience, of person and property of sixteen million people. . . . Have you shut your eyes to the sufferings of those millions of oppressed peoples who are our immediate neighbors on the south? Do you not hear their cries for mercy and succor?" The letter quoted from the November 1934 statement of the American hierarchy on the Mexican situation, which, though it did not include a plea for a presidential statement, did imply that the Order's strategies were in accord with the bishops'. The letter concluded with a series of charges blaming Roosevelt for "throttling the Borah Resolution" and, in sum, for his policy of "non-action in behalf of bleeding and oppressed Mexico."[70]

Roosevelt's reply (undated but received on November 14) opened with the remark that he would not comment on the "language of your communication;" instead, he included the entire section of his San Diego speech dealing with the U.S. commitment to religious liberty, as well as a quote from Theodore Roosevelt substantiating his position of nonintervention in the domestic affairs of a foreign government. He noted that since not one incident of Mexican violation of American rights had been reported in the past year, there was no legitimate reason for him to make a protest to the Mexican government. He also defended his Good Neighbor Policy, which he said "can in no sense be construed as indifference on our part," but rather as the principle for maintaining "peaceful conditions" between the two nations, with the obvious implication that the policy advocated by the Knights could lead to war with Mexico.[71] On November 17, Carmody issued a press release acknowledging receipt of the President's letter, denying the charge that the Knights sought intervention, and reiterating the Order's commitment to the Borah Resolution. The two positions were irreconcilable, as Roosevelt considered a Senate investigation of the Mexican situation tantamount to meddling in that government's domestic affairs.

The national wire services reported fully on the K. of C.–Roosevelt correspondence. Carmody wrote another condemnatory letter to the President on December 16, but by then Roosevelt had decided that the Knights' case was closed and he did not reply. Indeed, James A. Farley, a Catholic and chairman of the Democratic National Committee, considered Carmody's letter undeserving of a reply: "This crowd in New Haven has been terribly discourteous and I wouldn't bother with them at all."[72] Many Catholic newspapers and periodicals, particularly *America,* sided with the Order during this period of confrontation. The editor of *America,* Wilfrid Parsons, S.J., who had been in close touch with the Order's leadership throughout its struggle on behalf of the Borah Amendment, considered Roosevelt's reply to the Knights "providing comfort to the enemies of religion."[73] However, Archbishop John T. McNicholas of Cincinnati reacted unfavorably to the October 25 letter to Roosevelt. In a public statement, read from the pulpit in the churches of his archdiocese on November 3, he said that the Knights "in no sense speak for the priesthood or for the Catholic laity of the Archdiocese of Cincinnati on the persecution of religion in Mexico, or on any other subject having religious implication, unless they have a commission from us."[74] Since McNicholas stated that he was not in agreement with Roosevelt's Mexican policy, he was particularly alienated by the Knights' tacit presumption that they could speak for the Church in America. The leadership of the Order was quite annoyed at McNicholas's behavior. Hart wrote to Wilfrid Parsons that the archbishop's statement was a "wholly unwarranted and volunteered affront to the Knights of Columbus." He said the McNicholas "challenge" to the Order concerning the right of the organization to speak for the Catholics of his diocese was "entirely gratuitous and tended to minimize the worth and the effect of our letter."[75]

Deputy Supreme Knight Francis Matthews had private meetings with Bishop Bernard Mahoney of Sioux Falls, South Dakota, and Archbishop Joseph F. Rummel of New Orleans regarding the hierarchy's attitude toward the Order's Mexican campaign. Mahoney told Matthews that "the attitude of Archbishop McNicholas of Cincinnati was not the general attitude of the Hierarchy."[76] Rummel did not mention McNicholas but informed Matthews that "there seems to be a feeling among the hierarchy that the Knights of Columbus are attempting to anticipate what the bishops themselves are trying to do, and that they take action in advance of the bishops, somewhat to their confusion."[77] He recommended greater communication and coordination between the Order and the Administrative Committee of the N.C.W.C. After receiving these communications, Hart wrote to Matthews, "I had at no time any fear of the attitude of the Bishops concerning our Mexican activities. They simply could not go back on us and the one who attempted it, Archbishop McNicholas, has received more criticism, direct and indirect, for what he did in this regard than for all the other things that he did since he became Archbishop."[78] The hierarchy was clearly divided on the role of the Knights in the Mexican situation. Archbishop Samuel Stritch of Milwaukee supported McNicholas. The University of Notre Dame presented an honorary degree to Roosevelt on December 9, which was an indirect blow to the Order. At the ceremonies, George Cardinal Mundelein of Chicago was enthusiastic in his praise for Roosevelt, and he implicitly endorsed the McNicholas letter when he stated that no one had the authority to speak for the Church in America. Arthur Krock, political editor of the *New York Times,* viewed the Mundelein statement as a direct rejection of the Order's anti-Roosevelt campaign.[79]

Hart seems to have been uttering the sentiments of all the Supreme Officers when he wrote that "we would be glad to assist in carrying out any plan that might be agreed upon by the Bishops. Up to this time no such plan has been agreed upon and on account of the divergence of views held in Baltimore, San Antonio, Chicago, and elsewhere, I think it very doubtful whether any plan to assist the Mexican cause can be agreed upon." Since Hart considered the Order's Mexican campaign to be in accord with the principles contained in the bishops' pastorals of November 1934 and May 1935, he failed to grasp why the bishops "complain about our doing what they asked everyone to do."[80] He was confident that the hierarchy would not interfere with the Order's program, and he counted on the support of Archbishop Curley and William Cardinal O'Connell of Boston. Judge John E. Swift, Supreme Director from Boston, sought the advice of Cardinal O'Connell, who suggested that a representative meet with the Apostolic Delegate to ascertain Rome's views on the Order's Mexican campaign.[81] O'Connell also wrote a very encouraging letter to the Supreme Board of Directors, which met in New Orleans January 12 and 13 of 1936. The Board published this letter, along with the declaration to "continue to fight" for religious liberty in Mexico.[82]

According to the January 13, 1936, minutes of the Administrative Board of the N.C.W.C., Father Burke reported that Archbishop Rummel of New Orleans met with representatives of the Supreme Board and had "spoken to the members of the necessity of cooperation with the bishops." The N.C.W.C. Board proposed a conference between the leadership of the Order and themselves which "might prevent further irregularity and misunderstanding on the part of the Knights of Columbus in the Mexican crisis."[83] In a February 2 editorial in *Our Sunday Visitor,* Bishop John Francis Noll, a member of the Administrative Board, called for "a unified policy of action in regard to Mexico on which all Catholics can agree." Noll indicated that such unity was "gradually taking shape. The lead has been taken by the Knights of Columbus. They should be careful to remain in accordance with the Bishops' plan." He reiterated that the Order's policy hinged upon the success of the Borah Resolution and was critical of the Roosevelt Administration's "giving comfort and support to the persecutors of religion and human rights" and obstructing the Borah Resolution in the Senate. Noll made a plea for a "unified Catholic front" and invited "every liberty loving American" to join in and fight for "fundamental American and human rights" in Mexico. "It is either Americanism in Mexico or Communism. It is either democracy or tyranny, Washington or Moscow, the State or God." He implicitly opposed relying on quiet diplomacy. "The fight from now on must be in the open. No more private agreements. No more settling out of court!"[84] Such a statement ran contrary to the Vatican's policy as conveyed through Archbishop Cicognani, who had designated Father Burke as the Holy See's representative in negotiating a peaceful settlement for Mexico.[85] Roosevelt had assigned Assistant Secretary of State Sumner Welles as his representative on the Mexican issue. At the suggestion of the President, Welles had several meetings with Burke.[86] Though Hart had urged Carmody to seek Cicognani's direction on the Mexico issue, Carmody refused to confer with him on the grounds that it would be "impolitic" to make a protest on the public utterances of members of the hierarchy.[87] However, in March of 1936, Callahan and Hart suspected that Cicognani would urge the Order to moderate its campaign while the Order, through *Columbia,* had been openly critical of the Burke-Morrow diplomacy of 1929 as a tacit capitulation to the Bolshevist persecutors.

Immediately after the Order's inauguration of its Mexican campaign, Supreme Knight Carmody informed the Vatican Secretary of State, Eugenio Cardinal Pacelli, of the Supreme Board's resolution and of the Order's new membership campaign. In his response, the Cardinal Secretary of State congratulated the Knights on the "magnificent example of fraternal assistance and support which . . . you are giving by your prayers and by your campaign of publicity to your persecuted fellow Catholics of Mexico."[88] Carmody also reported the progress of the Order's campaign to its agent in Rome, Enrico Galeazzi, who was very close to Cardinal Pacelli. Galeazzi wrote to Carmody on December 7, 1935, "I have also reported in detail about everything to the Secretary of State office."[89] Later that month Galeazzi informed Pacelli of the McNicholas letter and of Mundelein's Notre Dame statement praising President Roosevelt. He also reported that the Knights had been "accused of political partisanship in favor of the Republicans . . . of meddling with matters which were not their business; of claiming an introduction of the American Government into the internal affairs of another country and so forth."[90] Hence, while Burke was negotiating for a settlement behind the scenes and the Bishops' Administrative Board of the N.C.W.C. was attempting to harness the Order's Mexican campaign to the N.C.W.C., the Order was maintaining its own lines of communication with the Vatican. Furthermore, because the Order received encouragement from Cardinal O'Connell, Bishop Noll, and Archbishop Curley, and because the bishops did not unite behind a common strategy, the Knights continued to pursue their public campaign against the Cárdenas government.

In March 1936, Luke Hart admitted that he was "in a quandary as to just what is to be done with . . . reference to the conditions in Mexico." Though he was committed to the campaign and was encouraged by Noll's February 2 editorial, he was apprehensive about the "danger" of becoming embroiled in politics as "we get closer to the Presidential campaign." He was reluctant to continue explicitly to promote the Borah Resolution because Borah was then seeking the Republican nomination for the presidency. There is substantial evidence to indicate that the Supreme Officers' Mexican policy was not politically motivated, but because Carmody and Hart were active Republicans they were sensitive to charges of political partisanship. Hart was convinced that the Apostolic Delegate, "influenced . . . by Father Burke, was very sympathetic to the President." He indicated that another letter to Roosevelt would be a way of "arousing public opinion," but because of political and ecclesiastical issues he deferred to the Supreme Board for a decision.[91] Though *Columbia* continued to publish articles and editorials on the Mexican situation, the Board decided not to write the President until after the August meeting of the Supreme Council in Toronto. The delegates unanimously adopted a resolution deploring the continued religious persecution in Mexico, but instead of authorizing another letter to the President, the resolution called upon the U.S. government "to remonstrate against the persecution in Mexico." To assert that the Order's strategy was in accord with the principles enunciated by the American hierarchy, the resolution quoted from the bishops' pastoral letters, from the *Baltimore Review*'s endorsement of the Order's campaign, and from Cardinal O'Connell's praise of the Order's struggles for religious liberty.[92]

The Roosevelt Administration did not respond to this resolution, but the President was concerned about the political ramifications such Catholic anti-Administration statements might have upon the November elections. By autumn of 1936 the Cárdenas government began to shift. When Cárdenas broke away from Calles in early 1935, he

stressed social and economic reform and tended to veer away from
Calles's brand of extreme anticlericalism. Ambassador Daniels, contrary to his image among the Knights and other militant anti-Cárdenas
Catholic groups, had been urging the Mexican President to initiate a
policy of religious liberty. As he wrote to Roosevelt, "My thought has
been to quietly convince the authorities that the first thing to do is
permit churches to be opened and priests to officiate in those states
where the churches are now closed. That is the most important
step."[93] Colonel Patrick H. Callahan of Louisville, the irrepressible
critic of the Order and a close friend of Josephus Daniels, publicly
defended the latter's commitment to religious liberty and lashed out
at the Order's Mexican policy as politically naive.[94] Meanwhile, Father
Burke was working closely with the State Department to achieve another *modus vivendi* based upon the return of an Apostolic Delegate to
Mexico, which would signify some normalization of relations between
Mexico and the Vatican and between the Church in Mexico and the
Mexican government. However, Burke died on October 30 before he
could witness the results of his labors.[95] Never sympathetic with
Burke's strategies, the leadership of the Order continued its Mexican
program throughout the Landon-Roosevelt election campaign in the
hope of influencing the Catholic vote. But because Catholic leadership
was so obviously divided on Mexico, because the religious situation in
Mexico had improved, and because social and economic issues were
paramount, there was no distinctive Catholic vote registered on the
Mexican issue as Catholics joined the vast majority in reelecting
Roosevelt for a second term.[96]

Father Burke's legacy to the Catholic cause in Mexico became
evident when Archbishop Ruiz was restored to his position as Apostolic Delegate to Mexico in February 1937. The Administrative Committee of the N.C.W.C. was also attempting to achieve another of
Burke's major goals: to harness the Knights of Columbus to the
N.C.W.C. so that there would be but one national voice on the Catholic
position. At its November 19, 1936, meeting, the Administrative Board
adopted principles and procedures for the Catholic organization's affiliation with the N.C.W.C. Catholic societies of national scope were
required to submit their programs to the Administrative Board of the
N.C.W.C. in order to ascertain "the common mind of the Bishops."
Though this latter directive was particularly aimed at the K. of C., the
largest national lay organization, the following principles appear to
have originated in the McNicholas dispute with the Order. "A Catholic

organization is acting out of harmony with Catholic action if it, without this readily available guidance [from the bishops], takes a public position on a matter legislative or otherwise—which affects Catholic interests."[97]

Several weeks before this meeting of the bishops, Cardinal Pacelli had visited the K. of C. Supreme Office in New Haven. Since such a visit symbolized the Vatican's high regard for the Order and since the Cardinal Secretary of State did not visit Washington, D.C., where the N.C.W.C. was located, the leadership of the Knights felt confident in dealing with the N.C.W.C.'s attempt to bring the Order under closer control of the representatives of the hierarchy. According to Hart's correspondence, the bishops' action was aimed at aligning the Order's Mexican position with that of the N.C.W.C. Supreme Director Swift conferred with Cardinal O'Connell, who was of the opinion that the N.C.W.C. was more concerned with the activities of Father Charles E. Coughlin, the controversial radio priest, than with the Knights' Mexican program. However, he told Swift that the Adminsitrative Board of the N.C.W.C. may "feel that nothing more should be done" by the Order on the Mexican question.[98] In his report to the 1937 Supreme Council meeting in San Antonio, Carmody stated that "for reasons that need not be stated here, it may appear advisable that further action should not now be taken" on the situation in Mexico.[99]

Shortly after the convention, Carmody met with Archbishop Ruiz, who told him that churches had been opened and priests were functioning freely in Mexico City and other parts of the Federal District but that persecution continued in most of the states. Ruiz concluded that "present conditions in Mexico . . . are not improving but rather growing worse."[100] Graham Greene, who had witnessed the religious persecution in Tabasco, the most stridently anticlerical state in Mexico, recalled the experience. "It was in Mexico too that I discovered some emotional belief among the empty and ruined churches from which the priests had been excluded. At the secret Masses . . . I had also observed for myself how courage and a sense of responsibility had revived with the persecution. I had seen the devotion of peasants praying in priestless churches and I had attended Masses in the upper rooms where the Sanctus bell could not sound for fear of the police."[101] By 1937 the "sense of responsibility" among lay activists urged them to establish the National Sinarquista Union, which was aimed at restoring religious liberty through passive resistance and civil disobedience. In mid-1938 the *Sinarquismo* (meaning "without anarchy") movement dramatically resisted attempts to prevent a public Mass in Tabasco.[102] Though anticlerical laws remained substantially unchanged by 1940, the *modus vivendi* appeared stable. Symbolic of the peaceful coexistence between church and state, Cárdenas's chosen successor, General Manuel Ávila Comacho, was a "believing Roman Catholic."

12

The Impact of the Great Depression

THE POLITICAL AND DIPLOMATIC ENTANGLEMENTS of the Mexican campaign were the Order's paramount concern during the Great Depression and the first phases of the New Deal. While the Knights played a central role in the ecclesiastical and political dramas associated with the defense of the Church in Mexico, they failed to create an affirmative social policy during the most severe economic crisis in the history of the United States. Unlike the specific and clearly definable issues of the twenties, the economic and social issues of the thirties were of such magnitude that there was no single factor to which the Order could address itself with even the probability of modest success.

President Hoover's response to the Depression stressed local and philanthropic programs for relieving economic and social distress, while Roosevelt's New Deal initiated myriad federal programs and projects. As a major voluntary society which had for decades developed its own relief projects, the Order participated in Hoover's scheme to foster employment. Because the role of voluntarism was deemphasized within the New Deal and because the Order was in the throes of a severe membership crisis by 1933, the K. of C. remained almost entirely aloof from the Roosevelt Administration's domestic program. Private correspondence among the leaders contains only passing references to the New Deal while public addresses, Supreme Council resolutions, and the like reveal that the Order did not take a stand on Roosevelt's remedies for the nation's economic ills. A law forbidding party politics within the Order may explain the Knights' reluctance to officially endorse the Administration, but it does not explain their refusal to support particular New Deal programs publicly. Had these programs included the explicit incorporation of such Protestant voluntary organizations as the Y.M.C.A. or the Salvation Army, as in World War I, the Order would have sought recognition as the Catholic service organization. The Order's clash with F.D.R.'s application of his Good Neighbor Policy in Mexico was a sign of its strong anti-defamation character. However, the lack of any religious component in the New Deal programs precluded any expression of the Knights' Catholic interests in domestic policy. This chapter explores the ways in which the Order coped with the impact of the Depression, responded to Pope Pius XI's call to Catholic Action, and reacted to what the leadership considered the major threat to the Church in Europe and the United States, international communism.

The strong proliferation of social and education projects on the national level during the twenties, which was matched by state and local councils, was the result of the growth in prestige and membership during the immediate postwar period; between 1919 and 1924, 600,000 men became Knights of Columbus. This rapid growth in membership also allowed state councils to expand the K. of C. presence into a wide variety of local social and educational projects. Among the many programs sponsored by state councils during the twenties were: Home Finding Association and Newman Club work in Illinois; Catholic student centers at the state universities in Missouri, Michigan, Wisconsin, and Iowa; religious and social work among migrant Mexican workers in Colorado; the erection and maintenance of a high school for girls in St. John's, Newfoundland; a home for sailors at Halifax and $100,000 for annual college scholarships by the Nova Scotia State Council; college scholarship programs in Connecticut, New York, Massachusetts, and Maryland; a tuberculosis sanitarium in New York; endowment of hospital beds in Massachusetts; the Columbian Cadets program with summer camps and recreation centers in New Jersey; Catholic historical research in Texas; Catholic radio programs in Maryland, Michigan, Rhode Island, and Utah; a K. of C. immigrant aid society supported by all jurisdictions in Canada; the erection and maintenance of the Gibault Home for Boys in Indiana; and dissemination of Catholic literature in California, Georgia, and Florida. Local councils and chapters also expanded their social activities. For example, by the end of the 1920s there were over forty councils and chapters which provided overnight accommodations, some in large multistory K. of C. hotels such as those in New York City and Baltimore.

As seen in Chapter 8, membership more than doubled as a result of the Order's war work: 1917—389,000; 1922—782,400. However, of the nearly 400,000 new members, 75 percent joined as associate members. In 1923, associate membership began to decline, while insurance membership experienced a steady increase. Noting a decline of almost 42,000 members between 1922 and 1925, Supreme Knight Flaherty remarked in his 1925 report to the Supreme Council that this marked a "wholesome evaporative process" which represented the withdrawal of men "insufficiently inspired with the meaning of membership in the Order and the retention of more substantial recruits." Flaherty had designated 1924–25 as the "Insurance Year" and proudly reported substantial progress in recruiting insurance membership. He pointed to statistical evidence which verified the fact "that the insurance member sticks" and urged councils to stress the Order's insurance feature, "which is, in essence, its legally abiding justification for existence, and in practice, the hinge upon which all other activity depends."[1]

The following year the Supreme Board approved several changes in the rates, structure, and benefits of the insurance program which went into effect on January 1, 1927, raised the age requirement for associate membership to twenty-six, and required those members entering the Order between the ages of eighteen and twenty-five to carry a $1,000 insurance policy at a cost of 80 cents or less per month.[2] In his last report to a Supreme Council (1927), James Flaherty reviewed the causes for adopting these new membership rules. Because he considered the rapid surge in membership in the immediate postwar years to have occurred during "abnormal" times when thousands of ex-servicemen motivated by dutiful gratitude to the K. of C. secretaries "stormed our doors," he concluded that associate membership would continue to decline.[3] Hence, Flaherty was not alarmed at the prospect of new rules retarding the growth of associate membership; "we have learned, through the past five years, that a large gain in associate membership does not constitute healthy growth." The rationale for mandatory insurance was predicated on the basis that anyone under twenty-six entering as a noninsurance member "may reasonably be suspected of deficiency in his understanding of the nature and obligation of Knighthood" and would tend to drop his membership after a few years. As a corollary, the prospective associate member over twenty-six was presumed to be mature enough to realize the character of Knighthood and, therefore, was more loyal to the Order. Though he admitted that only one percent of young men seriously considered purchasing insurance, he viewed that one percent as the ideal group for membership in the Order: "the man who sees something more than a picnic in life, the man who, without being glum, indicates . . . serious interest in the security of his future . . . can be relied upon to take serious interest in the work of the Order." Flaherty concluded his vigorous defense of the reforms in characteristic rhetorical style:

We now stand at the threshold of a new era in the life of the Order. We have it within our power to determine that from this time forward, our membership shall be a solid, serious, loyal, dependable body of men. We have it within our power to protect ourselves against the inevitable loss of prestige that occurs when lukewarm members drop out of the Order and publish mythical reasons for their defection. One member who says "I used to be" hurts the Order more than a hundred who say "I never was." The present requirements for candidates constitute a definite step forward. It is possible that they make for slower growth, but it is certain that they make for healthy, permanent growth. I am old enough to value permanence more highly than speed.[4]

On the basis of the growth of insurance membership, Flaherty's projection proved accurate: Between 1923 and 1929, when associate membership dropped by nearly 140,000, insurance membership increased by more than 20,000. In August 1929, on the eve of the Great Depression, total membership was 637,122, with over 40 percent insurance members. In contrast to 1915, when total membership was 346,560, with less than 30 percent insurance members, the 1929 figures represented the "healthy permanent growth" Flaherty sought. The Order's insurance, which was placed on an actuarial basis in 1902, entailed no risk to the policyholders. In 1927 there was $275 million worth of insurance in force. There were no K. of C. insurance agencies; the financial secretary of each council was responsible for enrolling members and collecting assessments. The Supreme Physician's office was responsible for processing applications, while the Supreme Advocate passed on all death claims and then notified the Supreme Treasurer to issue a check for each valid claim. Though it was a cumbersome process entailing an abundance of correspondence among officers located in various regions of the country, the insurance program, the backbone of the Order, was believed to be very efficient. Indeed, the Order's solvency was so great that it waived assessments (premiums) twenty-four times between 1909 and 1927. With assets of over $25 million, the Order was in excellent financial condition during the twenties.

Since the Depression caused a severe drop in membership, Supreme Knight Carmody, along with the entire leadership, was burdened with the economic and social plight of the era while facing within the Order a steadily declining fiscal base. During his eighteen years as Deputy Supreme Knight, Martin Carmody participated in the formation of policies on a wide variety of fraternal, insurance, and ecclesiastical issues. Shortly after assuming office in September 1927, Carmody initiated a "Selective Membership Extension Program" by which the Supreme Office attempted to enlist local, district, and state officers in a national campaign to publicize the benefits of joining the Knights. Carmody attempted personally to motivate the local leaders through a speaking tour. Though he was confident of its ultimate success, the campaign did not stem the decline; more than 32,000 associate members withdrew from the Order during his first year in office. He reported such statistics at the 1928 Supreme Council Convention in Cleveland but also pointed to the rise in insurance members by nearly 3,500 as a hopeful sign and a vindication of the effectiveness of the insurance reforms. Characteristic of his view of the religious motif of Columbian fraternalism, Carmody urged the members to cherish the virtue of fraternal charity: "The Holy Grail may be sought over land and sea in many climes without avail, and may be found in the cup of cold water extended to the thirsty at our doorstep."[5]

At the 1929 convention, Carmody's only reference to the Selective Membership Extension Program was to urge local councils to guard against overextending themselves by purchasing "extravagant" new council homes which were beyond their needs and which placed an undue financial burden upon members, many of whom withdrew because of high dues.[6] To stimulate the campaign, the Supreme Board of Directors set a quota of 10 percent increase in membership for each council and offered awards on a competitive basis to councils which achieved the highest percentage of increase in each jurisdiction.[7]

At the 1930 Supreme Council Convention, Supreme Knight Carmody spoke at length on Pius XI's call for Catholic Action, first enunciated in the encyclical *Ubi Arcano Dei Consilio* (1922), and copies of that encyclical were distributed to the convention delegates. Though Carmody did not allude to the Depression within this context, he did focus on the Order's obligation to follow the leadership of the hierarchy in promoting the principles of Catholic Action, and he implied that the Order's work was in accord with the organized Lay Apostolate.[8] When he did comment on the Depression, he urged the delegates to consider the current crisis as a challenge: "It is from such adverse conditions that a people or a nation rises to its full powers. Then are produced those elements that toughen the fibre, strengthen the backbone, steel the courage, and gird that stamina that was possessed by the hardy pioneers who three hundred years ago founded here the Massachusetts Bay Colony."[9]

This peroration on the virtues of the Pilgrim fathers may have been in accord with President Hoover's philosophy of rugged individualism, but it was a marked departure from James Flaherty's speeches during the economic crises of the early twenties which lashed out at the social irresponsibility of the moneyed class. Though Carmody encouraged individual Knights to be charitable to those in distress, he made no reference to the cause of the Depression or to its social and economic consequences.

As the leader of a voluntary society which had responded to war and to natural disaster (the Order had donated $50,000 for flood relief in 1927), Carmody placed the Order at the service of the Administration in its attempt to initiate and coordinate the work of private organizations—vis-à-vis state agencies—in relieving the distressed. On October 27, 1931, after President Hoover had established a commission on employment, Carmody wired the President, offering the services of 2,600 K. of C. councils to the commission.[10] The following day Hoover replied with a letter of gratitude for the Order's "fine spirit of cooperation." Prior to this exchange, Carmody had urged all Grand Knights to appoint "strong and active employment committees" in their councils.[11] During early November the Order established a central Bureau of Employment in New Haven, and Peter Collins, who had been head of the Order's postwar employment bureau, was appointed director. By the end of July 1931, the 1,056 committees established by local councils had placed 43,128 unemployed into jobs.[12] This figure did not include the job placements made by K. of C. committees which were attached to other civic and voluntary societies. Some councils had been actively engaged in employment services throughout the twenties. In St. Louis, the twenty councils affiliated with the St. Louis Chapter had hired a full-time secretary for an employment bureau which had been in operation since the end of World War I. Collins was a well-known national spokesman on labor-capital issues. Though he was an impassioned anti-Socialist he was, nevertheless, a strong advocate of social reform. Under his leadership nearly 100,000 persons were placed in jobs during the bureau's first eighteen months. Collins died in April 1932, just as his national employment work had achieved some momentum. The Supreme Board's resolution on his death included an appropriate tribute: "He was a protagonist of Catholic doctrine, a militant Knight in the field of Catholic action, and a champion of the cause of every man who earns his bread by the sweat of his brow."[13]

In October 1931, President Hoover appointed Carmody to the Administration Organization on Unemployment Relief. The Supreme Officers passed a resolution to support the organization, while Carmody's role on two subcommittees was to help publicize the unemployment campaign. Two pages in *Columbia* were devoted to promoting the President's organization, and the Supreme Office addressed 3,000 envelopes to State and District Deputies and Grand Knights which the organization used for letters urging the local K. of C. leaders to cooperate with the President's measures against unemployment.[14] In his NBC radio broadcast on March 29, 1932, the Golden Anniversary of the Order, Carmody proudly informed his listeners of the Order's employment services and of its commitment to voluntary rather than to government-controlled remedies for the nation's economic ills. "Men do not want the dole. They wish to be independent and work out their livelihood with the least possible interference. They do not want to be patronized as subjects, or have their personal actions regulated by law." According to Carmody, Columbian fraternalism which engenders a "spirit of fellowship, neighborliness . . . and teamwork" was desperately needed during so difficult a period.[15] In his congratulatory note on the Order's Jubilee, President Hoover commended the Knights for the "many helpful contributions to education, fraternal benevolence, and the relief of human distress."[16]

The Depression, as noted earlier, seriously affected the Order's revenues. Though Carmody pointed out that the Order's insurance program was 120 percent solvent, the decline in membership resulted in a cash-flow problem which necessitated borrowing money from the principal of the Italian and other funds to meet expenses. However, since the budgets for *Columbia* and for the entire Supreme Office had already been considerably reduced to cut expenses, diminishing revenues were regarded as a serious though temporary problem. Nevertheless, the interest on its many bonds and mortgages, combined with the fact that its stock-market investments had always been minimal, meant that the Order was able to survive, particularly since insurance membership had not drastically fallen. Because its Golden Anniversary provided the Order with a broad public forum from which to publicize its unemployment works and to promote membership, the leaders decided to celebrate the occasion, even though in a definitely restrained manner. Indeed, Carmody in his nationwide Golden Anniversary broadcast dedicated the Order to the relief of all those hurt by the Depression.

During these trying days through which we are passing, let there be such affectionate and meritorious service on behalf of our neighbor, our fellow-member in the great common fraternity of mankind, who is out of employment, out of money, out of touch with his fellow-man, that he, like the dough-boy in the trench, may know that he is not forgotten and that fraternity still lives, not merely in the handclasp of friendship, but in the supporting, sustaining, helping hands and hearts of those that generously share with others, both themselves and their possessions.[17]

Besides this broadcast, the celebration of the Golden Anniversary included "Commemoration Week," June 24–30, which was dedicated to the Order's Founder, Michael J. McGivney; the unveiling of the Cardinal Gibbons Memorial on August 14 in Washington, D.C.; Columbus Day celebrations; and a membership drive to recruit 50,000 new Knights, combined with a "Welcome Home" program aimed at retrieving lapsed members.[18] Though the last was limited to the local councils, State Councils sponsored many programs in tandem with those of the Supreme Office. Council No. 1507 in Guelph, Ontario, commissioned an original one-act drama on the foundation of the Order which was first presented on April 19, 1932. Carmody, who was present for the occasion, was so impressed with the production that he had copies of the script printed and distributed to the subordinate councils and urged them to present the play during Commemoration Week. Despite this short notice, more than 400 councils managed to stage the drama during that week.[19] Other local programs included banquets, Pontifical High Masses, local radio broadcasts, Communion breakfasts, and council open-house celebrations. San Salvador Council No. 1 sponsored a banquet at the Taft Hotel in New Haven with several prominent speakers, including Bishop John J. Nilan of the diocese of Hartford and Governor Wilbur Cross of Connecticut. A similar banquet was sponsored by the Massachusetts State Council at the Copley Plaza Hotel in Boston which featured speeches by Cardinal O'Connell, Governor Joseph P. Ely, and Mayor James M. Curley. Commemoration Week was celebrated in Waterbury, the birthplace of Father McGivney, with a solemn Pontifical High Mass, several services at the Founder's grave, and a large banquet with senior representatives of the American hierarchy and of state and local governments in attendance.[20]

The Cardinal Gibbons Memorial originated with the Washington, D.C., Knights. In 1927, State Deputy Charles W. Darr initiated a movement to seek the donation of a plot of land from the city, which, after both the Supreme Knight and the State Deputy had petitioned Congress, was granted to the Order. Situated on Sixteenth and Pine

Streets and Park Road Northwest, the plot lay dormant until the Supreme Council in 1930 decided to underwrite the entire cost of the memorial through a per-capita tax on the membership. A special committee chaired by Archbishop Michael Curley of Baltimore commissioned Leo Lentell of New York to sculpt the statue, which was ready for unveiling in time for the Golden Anniversary Supreme Council Convention in mid-August. After a large parade, including Fourth Degree corps from eight provinces, had passed the reviewing stands, Archbishop Pietro Fumasoni-Biondi, the Apostolic Delegate, led the Invocation. With President and Mrs. Hoover and congressmen, cabinet members, ambassadors, and members of the hierarchy in attendance, the celebrations highlighted speeches by Carmody, Hoover, and Bishop John M. McNamara, auxiliary of the archdiocese of Baltimore, followed by the statue's unveiling by Margaret Gibbons Burke of New Orleans, a grandniece of Cardinal Gibbons.[21]

Supreme Knight Carmody recalled that Cardinal Gibbons was the Order's "loyal friend and affectionate Counselor, exercising towards the Knights of Columbus the fond and kindly relation of a father to his children." President Hoover, who had had frequent meetings with the Cardinal, mentioned how Gibbons had "won the personal affection of thousands of Americans of every race and every creed." He spoke of his work on behalf of "labor in moments of crisis," of his "interest in the welfare of the Negro race," and of the way he impressed "the power that gentleness, kindliness, and homely wisdom" can have "in influencing the affairs of the community and the nation." Bishop McNamara remarked on the appropriateness of the Knights' enshrining the memory of the Cardinal in bronze, since Gibbons embodied the principles upon which the Order stood.[22]

Carmody urged the local councils to celebrate Columbus Day by publicizing the Discoverer's "claim to respect of everyone who lives in this hemisphere" and by sponsoring "Welcome Home" programs to draw lapsed members back to the Order.[23] But the Golden Anniversary's 50,000 membership drive was a total disaster. Not only did the Order lose nearly 42,000 associates and over 4,000 insurance members, but 1932 marked the first year in its history that many local councils were discontinued; thirty-two went out of existence. Perhaps these figures would have been even more disastrous had there not been a concentrated membership drive. But within these extremely adverse economic and social conditions, it was apparent the Order could not afford to expand its activities. Indeed, it was hard-pressed to maintain existing programs. Though the Roman playgrounds were maintained on the interest received from the investment of the $1 million - fund, there was a period in 1931 when it appeared that the Order would even terminate the playground program.

II

Past Supreme Knight Edward Hearn, who had administered the construction and maintenance of the five K. of C. playgrounds in Rome since 1922, had experienced several communication problems both with the Supreme Officers and with Vatican officials, particularly on budgeting issues. According to Robert I. Gannon, S.J., the official biographer of Francis Cardinal Spellman, Hearn and Monsignor Francisco Borgongini-Duca, Secretary for Extraordinary Affairs and the Pope Pius XI's representative to the Knights of Columbus in Rome, held opposing views on the purpose of the playgrounds. "The Italian [i.e., Vatican] ideal of lay work was to build chapels on all playgrounds. The Americans [i.e., K. of C.], while equally devout, were by nature and experience more realistic."[24] Spellman, who had been Borgongini-Duca's student while at the North American College and who was visiting Rome during the Jubilee year of 1925, was approached by his former professor to help him in his negotiations with Hearn. Spellman noted in his diary for September 2 that he had lunch with Hearn, who indicated to him that "he had his troubles, but he appreciates the fact that I have approved the situation and have talked frankly."[25] The following day Borgongini-Duca asked the young priest to accept a permanent appointment as a liaison with Hearn. With the latter's approval and with the Pope's strong endorsement, Spellman was appointed playground director at St. Peter's Oratory, directly responsible to Borgongini-Duca, and was given the title of Addetto alla Segreteria di Stato—la Sezione, i.e., attaché in the first section of the Secretariat of State. Hearn offered him an annual salary of $2,400, "but for many reasons I was willing to work for . . . $900 a year and my board."[26]

Spellman's first impression of Hearn was that he was a "fine, intelligent, broad-minded, and square Catholic gentleman." He summarized his role as mediator between the K. of C. Commissioner and the Monsignor: "Monsignor Borgongini-Duca and Mr. Hearn are both big men and smart men. They are both forceful, but they have opposite views on many things and neither one is very anxious to yield and each expects me to convince the other that his viewpoint is correct. That is only one of many things. But in the meantime everything is advancing smoothly and a few more months ought to see a great development."[27]

Hearn's abundant correspondence with various Supreme Officers included frequent references to problems, but they were of a general nature with no mention of the role of Father Spellman. Since Hearn was elevated to the status of a papal count and Spellman was made Monsignor during the period between 1925 and 1930, we may infer that the American priest had successfully achieved his mission. However, relations between Hearn and Borgongini-Duca once again erupted in a dispute in 1930–31 which, within the context of the Italian state–Vatican conflict in June of 1931, precipitated a crisis. The dispute derived from the Order's purchase of two pieces of property adjacent to St. Peter's Oratory. Though Hearn and Borgongini-Duca agreed on the necessity of developing a girls' wing of the Oratory on the property, which was directly across from the sacristy of St. Peter's Cathedral, the Monsignor became impatient with the long delay in beginning the project. Hearn pleaded with the Supreme Officers to expedite the flow of extra funds but, reluctant to invade the principal of the Italian Welfare Fund, the Board of Directors decided to allot only a semiannual payment of $5,000 from the interest of the fund to the Oratory project.[28]

Hearn, who had urged the Officers to borrow funds from the General Expense Account to be paid back with accumulated interest from the Italian Fund, responded to news of this decision by writing to Supreme Secretary McGinley, "It cannot be that you are serious in this matter." He then reported how embarrassed he was when Monsignor Borgongini-Duca "walked in on me" with the news that the Order planned to erect a memorial to Cardinal Gibbons. "His Excellency then said to me, 'Is it not strange that the Knights of Columbus should disregard the urgent appeal of the Holy Father in the matter of this small building here in Rome and take up the matter of building a monument in Washington that will certainly cost the Order a great deal more money?' I said, 'Your Excellency, there is no answer I can give you. I am not in a position to know what influence has been brought to bear upon the Board of Directors of the Knights of Columbus.' "[29]

Hearn's letter arrived too late for the Board to consider his plea immediately. Since in April he stated that "the situation here is unbearable and I am about at the end of my patience,"[30] he must have been disturbed by the continuous delay, particularly as he was not notified until October that the Board had agreed to fund the project immediately rather than extend the payment over a three-year period. Though construction of the girls' section on the newly added area of the Oratory commenced in the fall of 1930, relations between Borgongini-Duca and Hearn remained strained. In March 1931 the Monsignor notified Hearn that the Oratory owed the Holy See more than 2,600 lire in back taxes.[31] After waiting nearly six weeks to respond to this surprising information, Hearn wrote a forceful letter in which he told the Monsignor that "it does not seem reasonable that we should be expected to pay taxes on St. Peter's Oratory, a property that we do not own and do not control. . . . We are under the necessity of saying to Your Excellency that if this matter is not adjusted and our funds are used for this purpose we will refrain in future from advancing funds and will only pay bills after we have had the opportunity of reviewing them."[32]

Before the tax issue could be resolved, a conflict erupted between the Italian government and the Vatican in which the government accused the Catholic Young Men's Association of illegal competition with the Fascist youth program, the Balilla, and retaliated by closing many of the association's clubhouses. Catholic athletic associations, many of which used the K. of C. playgrounds, were thus unsure of the legality of their status. During the discussions leading to the Lateran Treaty of February 1929, by which the sovereignty of the Vatican State was recognized by the Italian government, the issue of Catholic athletic activities was somewhat clarified. However, the Balilla asserted its authority in 1930 on the ground that Catholic athletic teams were engaging in illegal athletic training and team competition.[33] On May 31, 1931, the Vatican was notified "that the situation was so grave that the Police Commissioner thought it wise to close the Knights of Columbus Playgrounds." Spellman, who had met with the police commissioner, went directly to Hearn's office with the news, whereupon Hearn instructed Enrico Galeazzi, the Order's architect, to "go at once to all our playgrounds and close them in order to avoid an unpleasant situation, in fact to save the Government from taking aggressive action against American citizens."[34] Galeazzi was able to close the playground without incident, except that when he arrived at the San Lorenzo grounds he found the police had already locked the gates and had confiscated the K. of C. papers and files. The following day, June 1, Hearn informed the American ambassador, John W. Garrett, of the events of May 31 and of the fact that these playgrounds were the property of American citizens, were individually administered by loyal Italian citizens, were for the use of young children, and were closed to all meetings of Catholic action. "With these facts in mind, it would be difficult for anyone to believe that these grounds of ours were the nursery of propaganda of any kind inimical to the Government or Good Order." He requested the ambassador to bring this matter to the attention of the proper officials of the Italian government, "that we be favoured with some explanation why this unpleasant situation should have developed."[35]

In his June 8 letter to Carmody, Hearn told the Supreme Knight that he had been "inundated by newspaper correspondents" but that he had made "no statement of any kind" other than to confirm the fact that the playgrounds were closed.[36] However, the Paris edition of the *New York Herald* for June 1 included several statements by Hearn in which he declared that he viewed the Order's recreation centers as separate from the Vatican's Catholic Action program. "We have no connection whatever with the Azione Cattolica [Catholic Action Association]. Our activities in Italy are purely philanthropic through furnishing children's playgrounds, which are open to all sects and creeds. . . . We are in no way interested in domestic troubles between the Government and the Vatican. It is none of our business, and therefore I cannot understand this unprecedented action, which came without a single warning."[37] Though Hearn later denied he had made this statement, it is difficult to believe that he did not make a statement similar to this—perhaps off the record—because the language, tone, and content are in accord with the general character of his correspondence during this period.[38]

Vatican officials assumed the *Herald*'s article was accurate and concluded that Hearn had disassociated the K. of C. from the cause of Catholic Action. Because Hearn's position was that of an official of a Catholic organization, his comments to the press were regarded as the blunder of a naif. His naiveté evidenced itself later that month when he refused a request by Borgongini-Duca that the new wing of St. Peter's Oratory be opened on June 29 (the Feast of Saints Peter and Paul), because "the [Fascist] government might take offense at our action."[39] Since Borgongini-Duca had been raised to the rank of archbishop and was the Vatican's first nuncio to the Italian state, engaged in constant negotiations with the Fascist government, Hearn was hardly in a position to instruct the prelate on diplomatic behavior. On June 23, Hearn reported to McGinley that while the Supreme Officers might consider him too loyal to the interest of the Holy See, the Vatican considered him too loyal to the Knights of Columbus. Because he suspected the government of censoring his mail, he could not divulge "the exact difficulties confronting your enterprise over here." However, he told McGinley to conjure up the most "drastic things you can and be prepared to act quickly when the moment comes."[40]

The day before Hearn wrote this letter, Archbishop Fumasoni-Biondi, Apostolic Delegate in the United States, received a cable from Cardinal Pacelli, Vatican Secretary of State since 1930, requesting that Supreme Knight Carmody "immediately recall Count Hearn."[41] In his letter to Carmody, the Apostolic Delegate quoted from Pacelli's cable: "In view of certain statements which he made and which were published in the Paris edition of the *New York Herald* on Monday, June 1st, his presence in Rome is very embarrassing and dangerous both to the Holy See and to the works of the Knights of Columbus." He also conveyed the Holy See's advice that "the Order appoint as his [Hearn's] successor one who is acceptable to the Holy See and capable of justly appreciating the Azione Cattolica in all its aspects."[42] No doubt the Hearn–Borgongini-Duca conflict influenced the decision to have him recalled. According to Enrico Galeazzi, this conflict reached an impasse when Hearn refused Borgongini-Duca's request that the Order fund a new chapel for the girls' section at St. Peter's Oratory.[43]

Since Carmody was visiting Newfoundland when Pacelli's cable arrived in Washington, he did not receive the Apostolic Delegate's letter until June 27. On June 30, after meeting with the Supreme Officers and visiting Archbishop Fumasoni-Biondi, he cabled Hearn to place the Rome office under the care of Galeazzi. Both were to leave for Paris, where Hearn was to receive a letter of instruction in care of American Express.[44] Hearn waited for more than two weeks in the company of Galeazzi in Paris until Carmody's letter arrived.[45] According to Hearn it contained a full explanation of events and a clear expression of the "kindest sentiments of affection and consideration coupled with the deepest regret that the action which was made mandatory must be taken." Hearn soon returned to the United States, but there is no extant correspondence revealing his views. Minutes of the January 9–10, 1932, Board of Directors meeting indicate that after the playground issue had been resolved, Pacelli urged Hearn to return, but according to the Board minutes Hearn, who had publicly announced at the 1929 Supreme Council meeting that he wanted to retire as soon as construction at the Oratory was completed, tendered his resignation.[46]

The Vatican–Italian state conflict was resolved in late August, and on September 6 a coded cable from Monsignor Alfredo Ottaviani to the Apostolic Delegate in Washington, D.C., contained a message from Galeazzi to Carmody in which he notified the Supreme Knight that the government had turned over the keys to the San Lorenzo gates and that upon receiving authorization he would reopen all the playgrounds.[47] In a letter to the Apostolic Delegate, Pacelli explained the ways in which the settlement affected the Order's playgrounds: "The Holy See intends to accord this Institution [i.e., the Order's centers in Rome] its personal patronage in placing these playgrounds at the disposal of the parishes of Rome, of the Youth Associations of Catholic Action, and of Catholic Schools and Colleges."[48] Galeazzi later recalled that the issue was settled on the basis that the Catholic-sponsored groups could participate in recreational activities but not athletic training, which meant that no athletic contests could take place on the K. of C. playgrounds, and that they must be limited to Catholic groups. This directive was a drastic departure from Hearn's putative position cited in the *Herald,* which clearly separates the playgrounds from Catholic Action. Pacelli also noted that the new building of the Oratory had been completed and that the Holy See desired to have it opened without further delay. He closed with an invitation to Carmody to visit Rome in order to "partake in personal discussion of the works here."[49]

In November 1931, Carmody did visit Rome, where he was the guest of honor at dinners hosted by Archbishop Borgongini-Duca and by Monsignor Giuseppe Pizzardo, Vatican Undersecretary of State for Foreign Affairs. Monsignor Spellman was instructed to introduce the Supreme Knight and Mrs. Carmody officially at a private audience with Pope Pius XI on November 11. Galeazzi reported that Carmody informed the Pope of his concern that improvements (the chapel addition which Hearn had disapproved) begin at St. Peter's Oratory. "The Holy Father was greatly moved and repeatedly expressed his thanks." Both Carmody and his wife received papal honors during their visit, and Archbishop Borgongini-Duca later remarked to Galeazzi, "Mr. Carmody has heart and intellect, and he has certainly won us all to his heart."[50]

Shortly after he returned to the United States (January 9–10, 1932), Carmody reported to the Supreme Board of Directors on his visit to Rome. By that time, Hearn had officially resigned, but in light of his ten years of service in Rome the Board approved a temporary annual salary of $5,000 for him as a consultant. At this January meeting, Carmody informed the Board of his high regard for Galeazzi. However, the Supreme Knight reported that "it is understood by Mr. Galeazzi that he is in no position to speak for the Order, not having powers that Brother Hearn had, and not being in a position to make decisions as to matters of policy."[51]

The young Italian architect appears to have been quite satisfied with these terms; he had professional concerns of his own which were quite demanding. Since he had designed the playgrounds and had frequent dealings with the Italian and Vatican authorities, he was thoroughly familiar with the intricacies of both bureaucracies. Almost immediately after he had replaced Hearn, he negotiated the relocation of the Tiber River playground, which was on land owned by the Italian government and leased by the K. of C. Through such negotiations he gained the respect and friendship of several prominent persons, particularly in the Vatican. Monsignor Francis Spellman and Galeazzi became very close friends. In late September 1932, shortly after Spellman was consecrated bishop and was about to depart for Boston, Galeazzi wrote to McGinley of the bishop's valuable service to the Order during his seven years in the Vatican Secretary of State's office. He recalled that Spellman had been the Pope's representative to the Order in Rome and had been "of tremendous help all the time, as he is such an intimate and good friend of all high officials at the Vatican, so that everything was made very easy for me all the time for every necessity."[52] Spellman's closest friend among the Vatican authorities was Cardinal Pacelli, to whom he introduced Galeazzi. When the Cardinal Secretary of State needed to break away from the demands of his office, he and Spellman were vacation companions. Galeazzi and Pacelli became such good friends that the Cardinal asked Galeazzi to accompany him on his 1936 four-week tour of the United States and on several other official and unofficial visitations during the mid-1930s.

Pacelli dedicated the new Tiber River playground on May 27, 1934. The former Tiber River playground, which eventually became sandwiched between two state recreational facilities erected later on, was turned over to the government after the Order had negotiated for another site farther from the central section of the city. At the dedication of the new playground, the Cardinal Secretary of State referred to the Knights as "the standard bearers of Catholic action, collaborating in the hierarchical apostolate for the defense and triumph of the Faith."[53]

III

The Order incorporated this Catholic Action theme into an extensive membership drive inaugurated in January 1935. Entitled Mobilization for Catholic Action, the campaign was endorsed by many members of the hierarchy as well as by Cardinal Pacelli, who stated, "It is my earnest and fervent prayer that this laudable endeavor to enroll the Catholic manhood of North America in the ranks of the Knights of Columbus may be a brilliant success so that by a greatly enlarged and carefully selected membership you may be enabled, in devoted cooperation with the hierarchy, to address yourselves . . . to the social and civil life which puts to such severe tests the souls of men today."[54]

With the approval of the Supreme Board of Directors, Carmody contracted the service of the American City Bureau to manage the campaign. To lead the volunteer force an international committee was established, composed of prominent Knights throughout the Order and chaired by William P. Larkin, former Supreme Director from New York. The professional campaigners trained thirty-nine regional directors to be responsible for organizing local solicitation, with the goal of recruiting 50,000 new members. The campaign was officially opened on March 17, 1935, with a national radio broadcast featuring addresses by Carmody and Larkin and songs by the Irish tenor John McCormack, who was a Knight of Columbus. Carmody stated that the purpose of the campaign "was not for the mere augmentation of our manpower but solely that the Knights may continue to have the strength and the disposition to discharge [their] service of Church and country."[55] Larkin opened his address by noting the appropriateness of inaugurating the campaign on the feast of St. Patrick, "one of the world's outstanding exemplars of Catholic Action." Larkin declared that "never since the dawn of recorded history" had there been a greater need for Catholic Action than in the Depression era, when "false prophets and purveyors of anti-American propaganda . . . would set class against class, blot out the deity from the heavens, introduce the ethics of the barnyard into every relation in life, and trample under foot the Constitution of our country."[56]

At the August meeting of the Supreme Council, Carmody told the delegates that the result of the campaign "was most gratifying." Nearly 51,000 were enrolled, which, though it did not represent a net increase, did reduce the rate of decrease in membership from 9 percent to 8.3 percent.[57] The success of this campaign managed by professionals led to the establishment of the Order's Service Department, which was authorized to develop new programs for local councils. Under the direction of Charles Ducey, who had received a graduate degree in Boy Leadership from Notre Dame in 1928 and who had directed the Order's Boy Life Bureau, the Service Department inaugurated in January 1936 a "Five Point Program of Progress." This program was not intended to impose a specific course of action upon all the councils but was, rather, a set of aims and objectives for the councils to pursue, buttressed by the promotional and public-relations efforts of the Service Department. The Five Points—Catholic Activity, Council Activity, Fraternal Protection, Publicity, and Maintenance of Manpower—established the local council as something more than a mere social club. The Service Department circulated literature highlighting those successful Catholic and council activities sponsored by councils, such as a Catholic radio and public-lecture series. The new department devised ways of improving the council's public relations and promoting the Order's insurance programs. The success of point five, Maintenance of Manpower, was dependent on implementing the other points of the program, since the goal was to stimulate the members to participate actively in the Catholic, fraternal, and insurance life of the Order. As Carmody stated in his introduction of this program, the Five Points had been stressed from the foundation of the Order. By regularly publicizing council activities, *Columbia* had traditionally fulfilled the role of a clearinghouse for information on the Order's Catholic and Council activities as well as its insurance program.[58]

The Service Department helped the councils play a greater role in parish, diocesan, and civic activities. Among the suggestions to local councils were: the formation of study clubs in "Catholic doctrine and philosophy; . . . in social, economic, and political principles of Christian government; in catechetical training to impart knowledge of the Faith to others and prepare non-Catholics for reception into the Church." The councils were also to foster corporate communion and retreat programs, sponsor youth programs, support the Legion of Decency and other efforts aimed at ridding movies and literature of obscenity, and support the Catholic position on divorce and birth control, which "are tending to . . . destroy the strength of the nation."[59] The Order's Mexican campaign was at its height during the period of the mid-thirties, when it was attempting to stimulate fraternal and civic life by inspiring the local councils with the principles of Catholic Action. Though the leaders based this campaign for religious liberty on the principles of the Declaration of Independence and the American Constitution, it may also be viewed as the Order's most intensive Catholic Action effort. It was also militantly anti-Communist, because Carmody was convinced that radical Socialist movements were inherently anti-Catholic.

In the mid-thirties, Communist parties in Europe and in the United States responded to the threat of fascism by advocating a

United Front with all parties and groups dedicated to the struggle against the ideologies embodied by Hitler and Mussolini. The Spanish Civil War was viewed by many American Catholics as a religious war because Franco purported to be defending the Church against the anti-Catholicism of the left-wing parties dominating the republic. When Italy and Germany intervened on behalf of the rebels, the United Front strategy was vigorously promoted and many European and American non-Communists—along with Communists—volunteered in the Republican army. Though several Catholic liberals such as George Schuster, editor of the *Commonweal,* refused to support Franco and urged Catholic neutrality on the ground that the forces of the right were just as anti-Christian as those of the left, such views represented a minority.[60] The American Catholic Press (later buttressed by the 1938 pro-Franco pastoral of the American bishops) tended to identify the Franco rebellion with the American Revolution and the United Front Government of the Republic with the totalitarianism of the U.S.S.R. The Order also stressed the anti-Catholic, anti-Democratic, Bolshevist character of the Spanish Republic and portrayed Franco as defender of Christian civilization. The United Front strategy in the United States, which was clearly expressed in the American Communist Party's recruitment of volunteers for the Republican forces in Spain, served to convince the leadership of the Order that the threat of Communist dominance of American society was not imaginary. Thus, the Order blended its militant anti-communism with its Five Point Program to form the Knights' Crusade Program. Each council was instructed to conduct four major meetings during February and March: Knights' Crusade Meeting on "Communism the Destroyer," Catholic Activity Meeting on "Irreligion the Destroyer," Family Defender Meeting on "Family Destroyers" (sponsored by the Council's insurance committee), and a Crusade Rally with the theme "The Crusade Conquers Destroyers." Carmody inaugurated the crusade with a flamboyant declaration of religious war against communism.[61]

> Combat Communism—our common foe. Feel,
> think, speak and live against it.
> Fall not a prey to its bewitching promises
> nor succumb to its beguiling trickeries.
> Be alert to recognize its many-colored
> and multiform masks as it seeks entrance
> into the lives of your communities and of
> your children.
> Strip bare the fallacies of its ever-present

and over-active agents and expose them for what
they are—enemies of civilization and of men's
souls.
To the allies of Communism, grant no peace.
Atheism and irreligion are the bed-rocks of
this curse of man.
Family destroyers—Birth Control, Divorce,
Lax Parents and Lawlessness—are but stepping
stones to the Communistic citadel of the Kremlin.
Injustice to man is the seed of Communistic growth.
Against all these, put your forces. With
Truth and Charity as your weapons, go forth as
a Crusade.
Conquer Destroyers![62]

It is perhaps significant that Carmody did not call upon the U.S.
government to investigate communism in the United States as he did
in his letters to Roosevelt seeking an investigation into the violations
of religious liberty in Mexico. In preparation for the March 21 crusade
rally in Detroit, the Knights had considered asking Father Charles E.
Coughlin, the famous radio priest, to address the rally, but because
Coughlin had, by 1937, alienated many representatives of the Catholic
hierarchy and the Catholic press by his anti-Roosevelt, anti-union, and
anti-Semitic statements, Carmody rejected the suggestion. This action
was in keeping with the general position of the Order. During the
thirties, *Columbia* remained entirely aloof from Coughlin, never once
commenting on any of his positions.[63] On March 19, the feast of St.
Joseph, just two days before the date upon which Council Crusade
rallies were scheduled, Pius XI issued his encyclical *Divini Redemptoris*
on atheistic communism. After discussing how the theory and practice
of communism are in opposition to the doctrine of the Church, the
Pope called upon the faithful to detach themselves from worldly
goods, to practice Christian charity, and to be committed to social
justice and Catholic Action as the remedies for the advance of communism. The Supreme Office had nearly one million copies of the encyclical printed and distributed among the local councils.[64]

At the Supreme Council meeting in August 1937, held in San
Antonio, the crusade was unanimously endorsed by the delegates.
Carmody reported that the *Daily Worker,* the official voice of the Ameri-
can Communist Party, had frequently vented "its wrath against the
Knights of Columbus."[65] And, indeed, there were several reports of
local councils successfully exposing campaigns for "Spanish Democ-

racy" as Communist-dominated United Front projects.[66] Shortly after the convention, the Supreme Board of Directors approved Carmody's proposal to hire an anti-Communist lecturer, George Hermann Derry, who had been a member of the K. of C.'s Historical Commission and who had recently resigned as President of Marygrove College in Detroit. Derry's lecture program, which was subject to the prior approval of the hierarchy, included a general public address sponsored by local Knights and an address to the clergy of the diocese on anti-Communist leadership.[67] Though he was a fervent anti-Communist, he was also anti-Fascist.

Communism hides behind the smokescreen of name calling. Everyone who opposes Communism is labeled a "Fascist." If I don't like Russian caviar, that is no proof that I like Italian spaghetti. Everything objectionable in Fascism is found in Communism, exaggerated to an extravagant degree. Politically, both stand for the omnipotent, totalitarian, bureaucratic state. Both contend that man exists for the State, not that the State is a servant to man. Economically, Communism abolishes private property. Fascism maintains it, but nationalizes the most important industries and principal banks. Communism destroys all religion. Fascism, in the form of Nazism, has declared war on Christianity.[68]

Derry summarized the Catholic position on social justice:

The restriction of monopoly, the curbing of the money power, the establishment of cooperative work, and the wide distribution of private property are explained by the Popes in proposing the Christian solution. . . . The problem facing Americans is to know and understand what Communism is—what it stands for—and how the problems of the day can be met in the Christian manner.

The Knights of Columbus, through its Crusade against Communism, with its local study clubs, its public forums, its open meetings, its exposition of Communistic tricks, is making a definite contribution to democracy.[69]

Between November 4 and June 30, 1938, Derry addressed more than 100,000 persons in public meetings and nearly 10,000 priests and religious at the special clergy meetings. While Derry was lecturing on the evils of communism and fascism, Carmody responded to a request by the Jewish War Veterans of the United States that the Order urge the President to take diplomatic action in support of Jewish refugees seeking homes in Palestine. On October 17, 1938, Carmody wrote an impressive letter to Roosevelt.

The Order of the Knights of Columbus, embracing five hundred thousand members, moved by the same sentiments of fair play and justice that have prompted it to protest on different occasions persecution by governments and fanatical groups of peoples of various faiths who sought only the enjoyment of their God-given right to worship their Creator in accordance with the dictates of their conscience, expresses the deepest sympathy for the distressed Jews of Europe, and most respectfully urges our Government to use its influence to preserve in its full meaning, force, and intent the Palestine mandate that guarantees to the Jews, now sadly persecuted in Europe, the right unhampered to seek refuge and protection in the homeland of their forefathers. In order that the bonds that bind all peoples in human fellowship may not be destroyed, we urge in the name of humanity that prompt action be taken.[70]

Unfortunately, this, like other pleas, had little effect on Roosevelt's policy toward the first refugees.

A new crusade, the Knights' Crusade for Social Justice, was inaugurated in 1938, which emphasized a more positive program than mere anti-communism. Since Derry and, later, Paul McGuire, a noted Catholic Action lecturer from Australia, organized their lectures on social-justice themes, they continued to lecture during the period of the new crusade. The Social Justice crusade was viewed as the necessary outgrowth of the anti-Communist campaign. "It will not be sufficient that these destructive forces [of communism] be merely exposed. . . . The public must be aroused to realize that only by the application of Christian principles, in private and public affairs, will there be eliminated, so far as humanly possible, the distress and suffering upon which these forces thrive."[71] The Service Department listed a number of suggested topics for study clubs, debates, and other council-sponsored programs. These topics emphasized the opposition of socialism, communism, and fascism to the Church's teaching on social justice and stressed the programs advocated by Pius XI in his social encyclicals: a living wage, credit unions, the cooperative and social responsibilities of employers, bankers, and property owners. The Order also distributed 2,000 copies of a bibliography, *A Key to Sources on Christian Social Reconstruction,* edited by Fathers Joseph F. MacDonnell, S.J., and Joseph F. Duane, S.J., of Weston College, which was topically arranged and was intended for the use of the K. of C. study clubs.[72] Buttressed by the Service Department, the local councils were continuously supplied with material to stimulate the membership to study and implement social encyclicals.

In March 1939, Cardinal Pacelli was crowned Pope Pius XII. The Order was represented by Supreme Director John F. O'Neill of New Jersey. The Holy Father assigned Enrico Galeazzi as Papal Secret Chamberlain and Escort to Joseph P. Kennedy, the American representative to the Coronation. The elevation of his close friend to the

Pilgrimage to Europe

On August 21, 1920, French civic and ecclesiastical dignitaries assembled for the Knights of Columbus presentation of an equestrian statue of Lafayette to the City of Metz.

Pope Benedict XV visiting with the Knights of Columbus in the Vatican gardens, Sunday, August 29, 1920

Youth Activities

Brother Barnabas McDonald, F.S.C., founder of the Columbian Squires, junior order of the Knights of Columbus

The first class of Boy Guidance graduates in the Knights of Columbus postgraduate course at the University of Notre Dame, June 13, 1926

Golden Anniversary

James Cardinal Gibbons, Archbishop of Baltimore and a patron of the Order

President Herbert Hoover attends the dedication ceremony in 1932 of the Knights of Columbus' Cardinal Gibbons Memorial statue, Washington, D.C.

Five Supreme Knights gather at the Golden Anniversary Supreme Convention. LEFT TO RIGHT: John J. Cone, John J. Phelan, Martin H. Carmody, James A. Flaherty, Edward L. Hearn.

A Knights of Columbus military "hut" or recreation center Montreal, Quebec

Gibbons Council No. 2285, Newport, Vermont, opens its War Bond drive.

Dedication of the National Shrine of the Immaculate Conception. The campanile or "Knights' Tower" was subsidized by $1,000,000 in contributions from members of the Order.

Supreme Knight Luke E. Hart and Father Paul C. Reinert, S.J., president of St. Louis University, unveil a bronze plaque honoring the Order's Vatican Film Library housed at Pius XII Memorial Library.

A Knights of Columbus delegation meets with President Calvin Coolidge on the issue of religious persecution in Mexico. LEFT TO RIGHT: Supreme Advocate Luke E. Hart, Deputy Supreme Knight Martin Carmody, Supreme Knight Flaherty, President Coolidge, Supreme Secretary William J. McGinley, Supreme Director William C. Prout, Assistant Supreme Secretary John Conway. (The Presidential retreat in the Adirondacks, New York, September 1, 1926.)

Supreme Knight Luke E. Hart visits with President Dwight Eisenhower. Columbus Day, October 12, 1953.

Supreme Knight Hart and President Kennedy at the Columbus Day celebration in Washington, D.C., October 11, 1961

President Richard M. Nixon attends the banquet of the 89th Supreme Convention presided over by Supreme Knight John W. McDevitt at the Waldorf-Astoria in New York City, August 17, 1971.

papal throne was a deeply touching experience for Galeazzi. He wrote to Carmody shortly after the Coronation, "I have been through the most thrilling glorious days of my life."[73] The Order's agent in Rome was most grateful to the Knights, for it was through them that he had formed such strong attachments to Bishop Francis Spellman, who was soon to be consecrated Archbishop of New York, and Eugenio Pacelli, who reigned as Pope for twenty years. Enrico Galeazzi remained the Pope's loyal confidant and close friend. During the war, he made three visits to the White House as the Pope's personal envoy. He also maintained the Roman playgrounds out of his personal finances during the period when the United States and Italy were at war.

In his last address as Supreme Knight, Carmody quoted from Pius XII's 1939 Easter sermon, "Since external peace cannot but be a reflection of internal peace of conscience, procure it if one does not have it, guard it and cultivate it if one has it." Carmody also quoted from Washington's farewell address, in which the first President urged the young Republic to "observe good faith and justice toward all nations. Cultivate peace and harmony with all. Religion and morality enjoin this conduct." Carmody's last speech was in a sense a call for a crusade for peace based upon and infused with Columbian principles of loyalty to God and country. His strategy for peace was based upon Washington's warning against "permanent alliances with any portion of the foreign world." After referring to the deep disillusionment which Americans suffered after World War I, he urged the United States not to join "in the hates, the greeds and alliances that repeatedly breed turmoil in Europe. There is only one policy which we can safely or justly follow, and that is to keep out of it all."[74] Two weeks after Carmody's last speech, Hitler invaded Poland.

13

The Ordeal of War and the Politics of Leadership

IN 1939, LUKE HART, DANIEL CALLAHAN, and a majority of the Board of Directors decided that the Order needed a Supreme Knight who would be a strong fraternalist like Carmody but who would also play an active role in business and insurance affairs.[1] Because Supreme Secretary William McGinley had been incapacitated by illness since 1937, the New Haven Office was in need of an efficient administrator. Led by Hart, the Board supported Deputy Supreme Knight Francis Matthews of Omaha, Nebraska, an effective orator and a lawyer with insurance experience, as its candidate for Supreme Knight. The Directors leaned toward Supreme Director Daniel Tobin of New York for Supreme Secretary, but because he had suffered injuries in an accident at the convention, New York State Deputy Joseph Lamb became the Board's candidate. Lamb was an engineer with Texaco Oil Company, had an excellent reputation as a good administrator, and was extremely popular in New York, one of the Order's largest jurisdictions. Supreme Director John Swift of Massachusetts, a judge in the Superior Court and a close associate of Cardinal O'Connell, was the Board's candidate for Deputy Supreme Knight. Supreme Chaplain Monsignor John McGivney, brother of the Order's founder, had died in 1938, and his nephew, Father Leo M. Finn, was chosen as his replacement. (Though the office of Supreme Chaplain had traditionally been limited to moral leadership and spiritual guidance, since the early forties the Supreme Chaplain was also a member of the Executive and Finance Committee.) The election of Supreme Officers developed according to Hart's design except for the contest for Deputy Supreme Knight. John Swift was opposed by Patrick J. Moynihan, Past State Deputy of Massachusetts.

Moynihan, who made a dramatic entrance on the first day of the convention, had the support of many anti-administration delegates. At the conclusion of the Supreme Secretary's report, Moynihan moved that a special committee be formed to investigate the Supreme Officers' and Directors' management of the mortuary reserve, with particular scrutiny of the practice of drawing funds from the earnings of the mortuary reserve to pay for the fees for investment of that fund. He contended that all such fees should be paid from the general fund rather than decrease the solvency of the insurance members' mortuary reserve. Had Moynihan limited his dissent to such criticism, the issue would have been easily resolved. However, in support of his motion to establish the investigating committee, he lashed out at the general leadership of the Order, referring to the Officers and Directors' "mass negligence . . . incompetence . . . selfishness" and charging them with violating "the ethical and moral obligations of their trusteeship." He also summarily indicted the leaders for "cajoling convention after convention" to perpetuate themselves in office. Moynihan, with the cooperation of William Mulligan of Connecticut and delegates from several other states, also supported resolutions limiting the tenure of Directors and Officers, as well as the salaries of the latter. At a lengthy caucus that evening, Hart responded to Moynihan's charges. Though such caucuses were not recorded, Hart's later comments indicate that his defense rested on four major positions: The Order's principles and practices of managing its mortuary reserve were common among fraternal insurance societies; the insurance commissioners of Connecticut and of several other states had approved such practices; to pay for the administration of the mortuary reserve from the general fund, to which noninsurance members contributed, would be unfair to the associate members; the officers' salaries were commensurate with and, in some cases, lower than salaries paid to officers of other fraternals.[2] Hart convinced the membership. Realizing that his motion would not carry, Moynihan withdrew it. Nevertheless, he came within twenty votes (139 to 119) of defeating Swift for Deputy Supreme Knight.[3]

The 1939 convention was just the first phase of the Moynihan affair. Shortly afterward, Moynihan renewed his attacks upon the administration, and on behalf of the insurance members of Massachusetts he lodged a complaint with the State Insurance Commissioner's office on the grounds that the management of the Knights of Columbus mortuary reserve fund violated laws regulating fraternal and commercial insurance companies. Before he had received word of Moynihan's complaint, Supreme Knight Matthews suspended him for breaking the Order's rules on public slander.[4] After Moynihan was found guilty by a committee of the Board in early 1940, he brought suit against the Order in the Massachusetts Superior Court on the grounds that the Order followed illegal processes in expelling him. Hart won the case, as he argued by citing precedent cases in which fraternal organizations successfully defended their authority to initiate extraordinary committee hearings comparable to that established by the Knights of Columbus in the Moynihan affair.[5]

Moynihan was, in 1940, the State Commissioner of Administration and Finance and was close to his Brother Knight, the State Commissioner of Insurance, Charles F. J. Harrington. From January 1940 to May 1948, Commissioner Harrington and representatives of the Order held numerous meetings on the legality of the Order's administration of the mortuary fund. There were official hearings and an appeal to a judicial tribunal. Hart's correspondence on the Massachusetts insurance issue during these years included several hundred letters to and from state commissioners supporting the Order's management of the mortuary reserve fund, other fraternal leaders sympathetic to the Order's case, and numerous letters to his fellow Supreme Officers, particularly John Swift, with whom he worked closely in attempting to resolve the issue. From the outset Hart and others were convinced that political motives were at the basis of Harrington's persistency. In August 1941, Hart wrote to his close friend Timothy Galvin, "I am a little surprised to know that Harrington is still continuing his efforts to punish the Order for the disciplining of Pat Moynihan. There is nothing else behind his attitude."[6]

The Massachusetts debacle finally culminated in Harrington's directive of June 14, 1948, which revoked the Order's license to sell insurance in the Bay State. From Harrington's point of view, he was not persecuting the Order but rather protecting its policyholders from improper expenditures which he considered as threats to the security of their insurance. However, since three previous Massachusetts commissioners and many other insurance commissioners in the United States and Canada had approved the Knights' investment practices, and since Harrington did not question other fraternal benefit societies which employed the same practices, one has to conclude that there was discrimination against the Order. The *Insurance Index*, which published five articles prior to the revocation of the Order's license, supported this conclusion.[7] After Harrington revoked the Order's license, the *Index* published "an open letter to the members of the Knights of Columbus" by the publisher, James E. Dunne, also editor of *Dunne's Reports*. Dunne considered Harrington's action "shocking," assured the membership "that you can do no better than to carry your [insurance] certificate with the Knights of Columbus," and urged the Knights "to become militant in your protest against what we regard as unwarranted action on the part of the Commonwealth of Massachusetts."[8] Since Dunne was a 32nd Degree Mason, his brief on behalf of the Knights of Columbus insurance program carried strong weight. Dunne also supported the Order in its efforts to pass bills in the Massachusetts legislature which would explicitly allow fraternal benefit societies to allocate funds from their mortuary reserve to cover the costs of investment of the reserve.[9]

The Order's major lobbyist in the State Legislature was John W. McDevitt, Massachusetts State Deputy. A former teacher turned administrator, McDevitt was highly regarded as an effective speaker and a shrewd political strategist. Though Supreme Knight Swift directed the lobbying campaign, McDevitt was charged with polling the members of the legislature. Since his State Council was generally sympathetic to the Moynihan-Harrington faction, McDevitt was forced to pursue the cause with little or no assistance. Thus, during the winter and spring of 1949, Hart and Swift relied almost entirely upon him for the tedious and time-consuming detail work.[10] Armed with an abundance of data on every aspect of the Order's case, McDevitt successfully lobbied the passage of the legislation, and less than a year after Harrington had revoked the Order's license the Knights of Columbus insurance once again achieved legal status. In his report to the Supreme Convention of 1949, Supreme Knight Swift praised McDevitt for his "constant and untiring efforts" in the campaign.[11] Luke Hart was so impressed with McDevitt's service that he later encouraged him to stand for election as a Supreme Director, urged his candidacy for Deputy Supreme Knight, and appears to have favored McDevitt to succeed him as Supreme Knight.

The Massachusetts insurance issue initiated by Moynihan lasted for nearly ten years. Not only did it entail a vast amount of time and effort on complex legal questions, it also involved the Supreme Officers and Directors in an enormous public-relations task to repair the damage of Moynihan and Harrington's attack upon the legality of the Knights' insurance program. Indicative of the damage is the fact that between December 31, 1939, and December 31, 1946, there was a 13-percent net increase in the Order's insurance certificates, but in Massachusetts the K. of C. insurance in force declined by 13 percent. In other words, had Massachusetts kept pace with Orderwide trends during those years, by the end of 1946 the Order would have had $6.5 million more insurance in force.

II

While the Massachusetts insurance issue festered, Supreme Knight Francis Matthews led the Order as it passed out of the Great Depression and into the most destructive war in human history. That war is the harbinger of profound change is a truism. Those changes which have occurred in the Church and American society since 1939 were reflected in the history of the Knights of Columbus. Though its Catholic fraternalism was revived during and after the war, symbolized by a growth in membership and the development of ambitious programs, the Order's business, insurance, and governance structures were strained as a result of the need for modernization. Internal political conflicts about the role of the Supreme Knight within this modernization process, about the role of the Order in the war, and about its relationship to modernization in the Church created a crisis of leadership. As these conflicts intensified, Supreme Knight Matthews encountered strong opposition, which culminated in his refusal to seek reelection in 1945. Thus, while the Knights were attempting to play a significant role in the war, intensive battles occurred behind the scenes which severely distracted the leadership during this world conflagration.

The foreign-policy attitude of American Knights reflected the general anti-interventionist sentiments of American society. The German seizure of Austria in 1938 and of the Sudetenland in March 1939, the Japanese invasion of China in 1938 and expansion in the Pacific in 1939, and the German blitzkrieg in Poland in September 1939 moved the world to total war, but the American people were generally resolved to remain isolated from the conflagrations of Europe and Asia.[12] The American bishops manifested this spirit of cautious neutrality in their November 1939 pastoral message:

We beg our people neither to be carried away by intemperate emotion, nor to become victims of hate mongers who set loose the evils of anger, envy, and revenge. The first line of defense against the involvement of our own nation in the misery of war is aloofness from emotional entanglements. Our primary duty is that of preserving the strength, stability, and sincerity of our own nation, not indeed in a spirit of selfish isolation, but rather in a spirit of justice and charity to those people whose welfare is our first and chief responsibility.[13]

As late as October 1941, 91.5 percent of the 13,000 Catholic priests who responded to a poll conducted by the Catholic Laymen's Committee for Peace opposed American entrance into the European war.[14]

In response to Pope Pius XII's petition for prayers for peace, the Order sponsored an international prayer-for-peace program on Armistice Day 1939 and a radio prayer-for-peace broadcast on May 19, 1940. While the American Knights fastened their hopes on U.S. neutrality, many of their brothers in Canada and Newfoundland were combatants. On September 13, 1939, less than two weeks after war was declared in Europe, Supreme Director Dr. Claude Brown wired all State Deputies in Canada that he had formed an ad hoc committee to work with civic and church leaders in formulating a policy to guide the Canadian Knights in the establishment of a welfare program comparable to the K. of C. huts program in World War I. By the end of October, the Canadian government had approved the Order's welfare program and established a united organization composed of the K. of C., the Y.M.C.A., the Salvation Army, and the Canadian Legion. To direct the Order's welfare program, the Canadian Knights created a Board of Directors composed of Bishop C. L. Nelligan, head of the national Catholic Chaplains; two other Catholic chaplains; Archbishop A. A. Vachon of Ottawa; and K. of C. leaders from each of the nine provinces of Canada. The ad hoc committee, which initiated the Order's program, became the Executive Committee of the Board with Claude Brown of London, Ontario, President; Supreme Director Francis Fauteux of Montreal, Vice President; Ontario State Deputy Philip Phelan, Secretary; and Quebec State Deputy Ludger Faguy. Charged with administering the national program, the Executive Committee reflected the Knights' numerical strength in Ontario and Quebec; of the approximately 33,000 Canadian Knights, nearly 26,000 resided in these two provinces.[15]

Dr. Claude Brown, a dentist who achieved the rank of lieutenant colonel in World War I, had been Grand Knight of London Council, District Deputy, Master of the Fourth Degree, and State Deputy of Ontario before becoming Supreme Director in 1927. At his own expense he toured Canada to spur on the Order's activity, and in early 1940 he went to England to direct the overseas welfare work. With its headquarters established in Ottawa, the nation's capital, the Order's program was developed in close cooperation with government agencies. Between December 1939 and April 1940 the Knights raised almost $230,000, an extraordinary amount considering the fact that there were relatively few Knights in Canada. In March 1941, all service organizations participated in a joint campaign which raised $7 million, $750,000 of which were allocated to the K. of C. huts program. From

1942 to the end of the war, the Canadian government assumed full responsibility for fund-raising.[16]

The Knights' program was extremely diverse: Recreation centers were set up in the large cities; the Order provided for morale programs in a designated number of training camps, and K. of C. hostels were established in Halifax and Sydney, Nova Scotia; Campbellton, New Brunswick; and St. John's, Newfoundland. Canadian K. of C. hostels provided hospitality and entertainment for servicemen on furlough in England and, later, as the Allied armies drove eastward, on the Continent as well. The most hazardous volunteer work was assigned to those Knights who became recreation supervisors in theaters of war. One K. of C. supervisor, F. O'Neil, who was stationed in Hong Kong in December 1941, was, along with Canadian and British forces, imprisoned by the Japanese. In his journal he recorded the many ways in which he and other supervisors fulfilled their responsibility as morale officers. They organized softball, volleyball, and soccer games, directed musical and comedy shows, taught night courses, and established a library. Nearly two hundred Knights served as volunteers. As an indication of the Canadian government's strong support, these volunteers were paid a salary at a captain's rank and qualified for pensions and disability pay. Six K. of C. volunteers lost their lives during the war, including Claude Brown, who died apparently as a result of injuries during a bombing raid on London in 1941.[17]

The Canadian Knights, rather than the government, provided all the chapel supplies for Catholic chaplains, including stations of the cross, kneeling benches, statues, and religious articles such as rosaries and prayerbooks. After touring the camps in Europe in 1942, Bishop Nelligan, Principal Catholic Chaplain, wrote, "In Canada the Knights of Columbus Canadian Army Huts stretch like a golden chain from coast to coast, connecting up all our military camps and a large number of our newly established training centers. In each and every one of them is to be found a genial and capable staff, always ready and anxious to serve the troops."[18]

With experience gained during World War I, the Canadian huts program was an extremely successful endeavor, one which was dependent upon the close cooperation of the Knights, the hierarchy, and the government. Its success was also dependent upon the cooperation of French- and English-speaking Knights. The clearest manifestation of the success of the program was the Order's growth during and after the war. Between 1939 and 1947, membership more than doubled. At the 1940 convention, Supreme Knight Matthews, on behalf of the entire Order, expressed a "feeling of pride" in the way in which the Canadian Knights "responded to the emergency demands" of war. With the German forces victorious in Denmark, Belgium, Holland, and France between April 9 and June 22, 1940, Matthews voiced the changing mood of the nation: U.S. entrance into the war appeared inevitable. He observed that the common ideals of democracy of the Canadian and American Knights were so interwoven that "as free people [we] will survive or perish together."[19]

III

The fall of France had, in the words of one historian, "revolutionized American thinking about defense."[20] Indeed, for the first time in the nation's history Congress passed (in mid-September 1940) a selective service act authorizing a peacetime draft. Anticipating the passage of this act, Supreme Knight Matthews visited with the Chairman of the Board of the N.C.W.C., Archbishop Samuel Stritch of Chicago, on August 23 (the day after the close of the 1940 Supreme Convention) to discuss the possibility of the Order's representing the Church as the ίcial Catholic welfare organization to serve the armed forces. Stritch informed Matthews that he must wait for a definite reply until after the November meeting of the bishops. Matthews was hopeful that the American Knights, following the lead of their Canadian brothers, would once again be designated by Church and government to establish a K. of C. military program.[21]

Matthews and Hart had attended an October 11 conference in New York with leaders of the Y.M.C.A., Salvation Army, and Jewish welfare organizations. Matthews wrote to Archbishop Stritch that the group had agreed to a "unified campaign for funds on behalf of all agencies which might be engaged in the work"; he also informed Stritch that the discussion centered on "the authority of those present to speak for the interests with which they are identified." Matthews strongly emphasized the need for some official Catholic representation at the next meeting of the group on October 18. "It is very evident, I think, that someone should be authorized to represent the Catholic group at this meeting. Although you have been kind enough to indicate that the Catholic hierarchy may designate the Knights of Columbus to act in this capacity, I hesitate to proceed further without a letter advising me that it is your wish that the Knights of Columbus should do so." Stritch once again informed Matthews that he must wait for a definite commitment until the bishops met in November.[22] In the meantime, he was asked to be an unofficial observer at the meetings of the group of voluntary organizations, which later was entitled "The National United Welfare Committee for Defense."[23]

Between October 11 and November 15, Matthews and Hart attended twenty-three meetings of the United Welfare Committee, but their authority was undefined until the bishops decided on a general policy. Because the Knights had alienated the N.C.W.C. during the Mexican campaign, the Order did not expect a strong endorsement of its proposal. Moreover, Monsignor Michael J. Ready, General Secretary of the N.C.W.C., had informed the bishops of the many lay societies which had also discussed ways of responding to the spiritual, moral, and social needs of Catholic soldiers and sailors in the training camps. Hence, when the bishops met on November 15, 1940, they did not designate the Order as the official Catholic welfare agency but rather created the National Catholic Community Service (N.C.C.S.), an organization with broad authority "to formulate programs for the work of the Church in defense, industrial centers, and areas adjacent to military camps [and] to provide for the setting up of social centers by Catholic agencies with the permission of the Ordinary."[24]

The bishops also supported the United Welfare Organization, which was later incorporated into the United Service Organization (U.S.O.). Archbishop Edward Mooney of Detroit became Chairman of the Administrative Board of the N.C.W.C. and President of the Board of Trustees of the N.C.C.S. During the two months following the November 15 establishment of the N.C.C.S., Matthews and Hart were still confident that the Order would play a strong and visible role as the major sponsor of the social centers. However, the N.C.C.S. was reluctant to develop programs until the government had established its own policies for the voluntary organizations of the United Welfare Committee.

In a January 13, 1941, interview with Monsignor Ready, Matthews indicated his growing impatience with the N.C.C.S. position. In his notes on this meeting, Matthews recorded: "Mr. Matthews repeated to Monsignor Ready that the situation was becoming intolerable so far as the Knights of Columbus was concerned . . . owing to our inability to answer inquiries as to what the Catholic program is to be." In response to Ready's reiteration of the N.C.C.S. position to wait for government directives, Matthews reported that the other voluntary organizations, such as the Y.M.C.A., were preparing detailed programs. He expressed frustration at queries from "bishops, priests, Catholic laymen,

Army officers, public officials, and citizens generally who, in each instance, want to know what the Knights of Columbus are going to do."[25]

Shortly after Matthews visited with Ready, he and Luke Hart went to Detroit to confer with Archbishop Mooney. In a letter to Supreme Treasurer Daniel Callahan, Matthews reported, "I suggested to the Archbishop that the men at Washington [i.e., the N.C.W.C. staff] did not seem to appreciate the nature of the work which is needed or the extent of the program which we have set up. Luke and I explained to him that we felt that the Welfare Program should be turned over to the Knights of Columbus to handle and that it should be conducted in the name of the Knights of Columbus Society." According to Matthews, Mooney responded "that he was disappointed because we felt that way," but he advised the Knights "that the wisest course would be to accept the decision of the Bishops [i.e., the Administrative Board of the N.C.W.C.] that the welfare work should be conducted under the name of the National Catholic Community Service."[26] Mooney also assured the Knights that they had "full authority in direction of the work" and that it would certainly be to the Order's benefit to cooperate with the bishops. On January 24, Matthews wrote to Mooney a "written pledge of our unfailing loyalty and faithful compliance with your wishes and directions at all times."[27]

Though by this pledge the impasse between the K. of C. and N.C.C.S. seemed to have been resolved, Matthews's deferential posture toward the bishops was not representative of the attitude of his fellow Supreme Officers. Luke Hart was particularly opposed to the way in which Matthews had so deeply involved himself in the N.C.C.S. cause. "It has been made so plain to Frank [Matthews] and me in our conferences with Archbishop Mooney that the Knights of Columbus name and organization cannot be used in this work and that there is no use quibbling about it. Therefore, I think that the Bishops should be allowed to set up their organization and work that matter out in their own way. We cannot assume responsibility and do the work when we have no authority to make decisions and no freedom of action whatsoever." Mooney had indicated to Hart and Matthews that he desired to establish a "Laymen's Committee" with Matthews as chairman, but Hart was opposed to the idea because the committee would include representatives from other Catholic organizations, which would mean "such a variety of opinions and such a conflict of desires that I do not believe it can work." Hart contended that Matthews was "holding on to this work [with the N.C.C.S.] more tenaciously than he

should . . . it is not our job. It is the job of the Bishops and since they
will not turn it over to us, then I think we should go ahead with our
own program."[28]

Since its foundation as the National Catholic War Council during
World War I, there had been several conflicts between the N.C.W.C.
and the K. of C., particularly on policies relating to Mexico and Catholic Action. Because the N.C.W.C. had developed such authority by
1941, the Order could never have successfully pursued its own program. By right, the Knights of Columbus could have tried, but such an
action would have been viewed as a tacit act of defiance of Church
authority, and without the support of the hierarchy the morale of the
Order would have been seriously damaged. Hence, in practice, Hart's
idea to form an independent K. of C. welfare program appears entirely
unrealistic; once the leaders of the Order had sought the bishops'
approval for a Knights' huts program, they had no alternative than to
abide by the bishops' decision. In World War I days, Cardinal Gibbons
and other prelates had relied upon the Order as the only national body
of laity organized to meet the tasks of raising funds and initiating
programs to serve the Church. Now, the N.C.W.C. viewed the Knights
as only one of many lay organizations which, if they desired to maintain
the support of the bishops, had to acknowledge the authority of the
Administrative Board of the N.C.W.C. and defer to its wishes. Supreme Knight Matthews, though disappointed that the Order was not
recognized as the official welfare agency, seems to have sensed that the
administrative structure of the Church had so evolved as to preclude
independent lay initiatives, and that the future of the Order was dependent upon the ways in which it successfully related to an increasingly
unified hierarchy. As will be noted later in this chapter, the Hart-
Matthews conflict over the N.C.C.S. was only the first of a series. But
because Hart was loyal to the office of the Supreme Knight, his opposition to Matthews during this period was muted. Thus, when Matthews
was appointed chairman of the Executive Committee of the N.C.C.S.
and its representative in the U.S.O., Hart also accepted positions on
various committees in both organizations.

The role of the Order's general office in the N.C.C.S. included
staff support on budget and administrative problems and the release
of staff to be field supervisors. The N.C.C.S., along with all other
agencies incorporated into the U.S.O., established social centers
throughout the United States and in rest and recuperation areas behind the lines of battle. Many Knights served on local N.C.C.S. committees, while local K. of C. councils contributed to the support of the

centers, frequently opening their clubhouses for N.C.C.S.-sponsored events. Where there was no N.C.C.S. center, a local council tended to fill the vacuum. For example, the only Catholic social center for the armed forces in Atlanta, Georgia, was under the auspices of Atlanta Council. Francis Heazel reported to Luke Hart on his visit to Atlanta Council's Home in 1943:

The ladies of the various parishes are giving the members of the local council excellent support.... There were about 200 soldiers at the K. of C. Clubhouse Saturday evening for a dance. Sandwiches and coffee were served and everything was free. Atlanta Council had received an allotment of $5,000 from the local U.S.O. Committee in Atlanta. I, of course, got quite a thrill out of seeing this work for the soldiers operating under the auspices of the Order. I realized what a great job we could be doing everywhere in the country if we had been permitted to undertake this work.[29]

One of the Order's most significant wartime services was its blood bank. The Knights have been generally credited as the first national organization to sponsor a blood-donor program. The Supreme Council adopted the measure in 1938 after it had been successfully organized on the local level by St. Paul Council No. 397. Local councils also sponsored war-bond drives and other community projects to support the war effort.[30]

On January 17, 1942, shortly after the United States entered the war, the Supreme Board of Directors, at the suggestion of Deputy Supreme Knight John Swift, established a War Activities Committee which was authorized to keep a record of all the Order's wartime services. Though Matthews was appointed chairman of this committee, the authority devolved upon Swift to administer its programs. Pope Pius XII, in his Christmas message of 1939, had enuciated basic principles for a just peace which included respect for all nations' right to life, recognition of the aspirations of social and national minorities, commitments to disarmament and to international institutions to guarantee the peace, and pleas for charity and justice in personal and international life. The American bishops, through the Administrative Board of the N.C.W.C., had issued a pastoral letter in November 1942 which included the warning that "secularism cannot write a real and lasting peace."[31] In January 1943, the Supreme Board of Directors, influenced by these papal and episcopal statements and prompted by a proposal of John Swift, established a Peace Program Committee charged with the responsibility "to study the general subject matter of the Order undertaking a program for shaping and educating public opinion to the end that Catholic principles and Catholic philosophy will be properly represented at the peace table at the conclusion of the present war."[32]

As chairman of the committee, John Swift consulted with members of the hierarchy, including Cardinal O'Connell, on the need and propriety of a Catholic peace program promulgated by a lay organization. After the proposal was approved by these prelates, he sought out the views of leading Catholic scholars. From the lengthy essays submitted by theologians, philosophers, and sociologists, Swift's committee composed the Order's Peace Program, which was adopted by the Supreme Council Convention on August 19, 1943. The Order's program was structured on principles derived from the natural-law theory of St. Thomas Aquinas but expressed in traditional American political terms, with religious overtones but with not one reference to an explicitly Catholic principle. The program endorsed the establishment of international institutions for world peace but warned that their viability would be dependent upon the acceptance of the law of moral right vis-à-vis that of "material MIGHT" and upon an "ardent crusade of Christian forces to prevent the collapse of Christian civilization . . . and to bring God back into world government."[33]

The Knights' Peace Program was widely acclaimed by the Catholic press. Father John La Farge, S.J., wrote in *America* that the program "should be read by every statesman in the world." Father James M. Gillis, C.P., editor of the *Catholic World,* published the entire program in the October 1943 issue of the magazine. Both Gillis and La Farge referred to the publication of the "Inter-faith Declaration on World Order and Peace" composed by representatives of Protestant, Catholic, and Jewish communities but considered the Knights' program superior because it was more specific in its content than that of the "triple faiths." Indeed, in the January 1944 issue of the *Catholic World,* Gillis reported that he had read more than one hundred such peace proposals and concluded, "I can say in all good conscience that the Knights of Columbus program is superior to any other I have seen."[34]

Meanwhile, Matthews and Hart were extremely busy with committee assignments on the N.C.C.S. and the U.S.O. As chairman of the Executive Committee of the N.C.C.S., Matthews was far more active in the manifold responsibilities of his office than was Hart. The Supreme Knight was chosen to represent the N.C.C.S. abroad and was frequently unable to attend meetings of the Officers and Board. His absence at such meetings was understood as an unavoidable necessity. However, even before Matthews became so deeply immersed in

N.C.C.S. work, Hart and other leaders wre troubled by the Supreme Knight's frequent absences from the home office in New Haven. Because Hart had supported Matthews for Supreme Knight on the basis that he would make frequent visits to New Haven and because, given a new Supreme Secretary and the inauguration of a new insurance program, Matthews's presence in the home office was viewed as crucial to the affairs of the Order, Hart was particularly angered by Matthews's refusal to abide by the 1939 agreement.

IV

The Matthews-Hart conflict began in 1940, smoldered for more than a year, and reached its peak in 1943–45, when Hart unsuccessfully ran against Matthews in the election for Supreme Knight in 1943 and Matthews was compelled by an overwhelming opposition not to seek reelection in 1945. The conflict was exacerbated by disagreement on the role of the Order in World War II, but its tragic element lay in the fact that the two men had previously been the closest of friends. Indeed, Matthews bought a farm in southern Iowa close to the Hart farm where the Supreme Advocate had spent his boyhood. Upon his election as Supreme Knight in 1939, Matthews acknowledged his gratitude for Hart's friendship: "I must express my personal thanks to my beloved friend, Luke Hart, who, when I as a young man, a very young man, became a member of this Board, was kind enough to take an interest in me and give me the benefit of his counsel, his friendship, and his advice . . . ; it was his guiding hand on my shoulder that made it possible for me to render a better service to the Order than I could possibly have otherwise. . . . Therefore, to you, Luke Hart, I express my heartfelt and everlasting thanks."[35]

Hart's correspondence with Supreme Director Francis Heazel of Asheville, North Carolina, charts the deterioration of the Matthews-Hart friendship. In December 1940, Hart wrote Heazel, "There are some things for which I am responsible. One of these is the new insurance program. . . . The other is the election of the present Supreme Knight as head of our Order. That was done with the understanding that he would do the work and furnish the guidance that the Order's interests require. I know that he [Matthews] is not doing it. It can only be done at New Haven. He professes a great aversion to New Haven. I do not think that the fault is with New Haven. It is with his unwillingness to settle down to the task and apply himself to it."[36]

Hart considered the new insurance program, adopted in 1940, as vital to the Order's development as a fraternal benefit society. Intended to bring the Knights into step with commercial companies, the insurance reforms were in accord with Hart's general drive to modernize the business features of the Order. The new insurance program included five plans: whole life with level premiums payable to age 70, or with payments limited to a term of twenty years, or a term of thirty years; endowment insurance maturing at age sixty-five; and a modified step-rate plan for members who wished a plan somewhat similar to the one adopted in 1902. Premiums for all five plans were computed by actuaries using up-to-date methods; four plans offered insurance for the whole of life, while the endowment plan allowed the insured to receive the value of his insurance at age sixty-five. Prior to 1940, all premiums were computed on a step-rate basis and did not include the administrative costs of the Supreme Office staff responsible for bookkeeping and servicing claims. The new premiums included such costs. Because these reforms established an agency system, general and field agents replaced the Financial Secretaries of the local councils as the Order's insurance sales force (medical examiner's fees were then paid by the Supreme Office rather than by the local councils). Though Financial Secretaries continued to service members' insurance and collect premiums, the centralization of that program necessitated that they be appointed directly by the Supreme Knight. The pre-1940 custom of periodic waivers of premiums, which rewarded the older members paying higher premiums according to the step-rate plan, was replaced by the payment of dividends. The old system allowed members to receive a loan only to pay premiums, while the new provided for cash-loan features.[37]

According to Hugh MacDonald, who was chief accountant in New Haven in 1940, these reforms had a "drastic impact" upon the home office. The creation of the agency department required the establishment of a commissions department; the cash-dividend and cash-loan features necessitated the development of two more departments. These additional departments caused the expansion of the accounting department.[38]

The expansion of the insurance program and the subsequent growth of the home office engendered the need for enlarging the authority of the Supreme Knight and for rationalizing the executive structure of the Board of Directors. The Supreme Council of 1940 established the Executive and Finance Committee of the Board of Directors, composed of the Supreme Officers and one other member of the Board. This committee was authorized to act on behalf of the Board between meetings but was required to have all its decisions ratified by the Board.

As mentioned earlier, Hart had promoted Matthews's candidacy for Supreme Knight in 1939 after Matthews promised that he would make frequent visits to the home office to administer the implementation of the proposed insurance reform. When Matthews failed to live up to Hart's expectations, he lost Hart's support. On June 11, 1941, Hart wrote, "I am not able to deviate from the attitude which I have assumed for years and with which every member of the Board, including Frank [Matthews], was in complete agreement, to the effect that the duties of the Supreme Knight must be performed at the Supreme Office. Apparently, Frank has changed his mind about this, and I refuse to go along with him in that regard."[39]

On June 21, 1941, Hart expressed his views "frankly" to Matthews. Hart recorded this conversation: "I told him that the Order is in bad shape from lax leadership, management, and direction and that it cannot be operated from the Hotel Astor . . . a lot of things were discussed but nothing resulted from it."[40] Matthew Birmingham, business manager of *Columbia,* was extremely distressed by the rupture between the two Supreme Officers. He told Hart that "you must do everything humanly possible to have the officers, the Board, the Supreme Council appreciate that Frank is your best friend—a great Supreme Knight and the kind of fellow you always said he was. You must do this for the good of the Order and for all of us who appreciate that harmony among good . . . friends."[41]

In his reply to Birmingham, Hart revealed his commitment to the principle of loyalty to friends and that he had been "doing a lot of worrying." However, his attachment to the Order ran just as deep, if not deeper, than loyalty to friends. "You know that nearly the best friend that either you or I ever had was the Order.It is being imposed upon and its interests are being neglected. That is a matter which I cannot overlook and I will not pretend to anyone that he is doing a good job when I know the contrary. If my refusal to acquiesce in such a condition or to pretend something that is not true hurts anyone, it cannot be helped."[42]

Matthews was reported to have been very dejected by Hart's criticism, but the Supreme Knight appears to have been confident that the rupture would be healed in time and that the two would reconcile their differences. Indeed, at the 1941 Supreme Convention, Matthews paid tribute to Hart for his "outstanding contribution of invaluable worth to the establishment of both the United Service Organization and the National Catholic Community Service" and his "unfailing wisdom . . . which he renders so successfully as Supreme Advocate of our Order."[43] Each Supreme Officer and the five administration candidates for Supreme Director were unanimously elected to office, but such collegiality proved to be, at best, merely a temporary display, for in the next few years there occurred the most serious internal struggles in the Order's history.

Matthews felt that Hart was making a personal assault upon him during 1942 and 1943 when the Supreme Advocate challenged him at Board meetings.[44] The conflict became more acrimonious in April 1943, when Supreme Director Ray T. Miller of Cleveland introduced a resolution against Matthews for violating the trust of his office as Supreme Knight. The resolution listed the grievances stemming from Matthews's failure to fulfill his 1939 promise regularly to administer the affairs of the Order at New Haven. It also noted that officers and board members had several conferences with the Supreme Knight regarding his responsibility to abide by the 1939 agreement, conferences which "aroused the resentment of the Supreme Knight and on that account have developed an ever-widening breach between the Supreme Knight and . . . officers and eventually between the Supreme Knight and practically all of the Supreme Board of Directors." The resolution concluded that since Matthews had failed to provide "proper leadership," the Board should authorize the Supreme Secretary to compile a statement recording the dates on which Matthews had visited New Haven on business, together with a complete record of all his expenses as Supreme Knight from September 1, 1939, to April 1, 1943. Miller's resolution passed by a vote of 18 to 2 with two abstentions.[45] The resolution became the legal basis upon which Hart developed his case against Matthews. The expense-account statement was the central issue in a campaign aimed at forcing Matthews to refuse to stand for re-election at the 1943 Supreme Convention in Cleveland.

However, Matthews was not intimidated, and armed with Luke Hart's expense account for the same period, he reported to the convention delegates at the opening session that he had been subjected to a relentless attack by Hart, Miller, Heazel, and others. After listing the charges against him contained in the Miller resolution, he challenged his opposition to produce the secretly circulated expense-account statement. Matthews then revealed figures from a certified expense statement of Luke Hart which seems to have resulted in such confusion that the undecided delegates were compelled to side with one or the other on the basis of an act of faith.[46]

Matthews accused his opponents of conspiring to ruin his reputation, while he himself "found it impossible to return the bitterness and merciless attitude which they so persistently exhibited toward me." He did not explicitly answer the charge against him but rather pledged that he had been "conscious of [the] duty and high responsibilities" of his office and dedicated himself "to leading the Order in the direction which will win for it an ever-increasing measure of confidence on the part of the clergy and the members of the hierarchy."[47]

Prior to the 1943 convention, Matthews had sought the support of several members of the hierarchy in his struggle against "the machination of power" against him. Archbishop Mooney of Detroit, chairman of the Administrative Board of the N.C.W.C., gave him his unequivocal support and promised to attend the convention in the event that Matthews needed such a visible symbol of the hierarchy's endorsement of his candidacy.[48] Bishop Thomas K. Gorman of Reno, Nevada, and Rodrigue Cardinal Villeneuve, O.M.I., of Quebec promised him that each would instruct the delegates from their jurisdictions to vote for Matthews.[49] Perhaps Hart also sought the hierarchy's endorsement but, given his general resentment of any ecclesiastical interference in the affairs of the Order, such action would have been out of character. The crux of the 1943 conflict came when Hart announced himself as a candidate for Supreme Knight. The election results reveal that the convention was nearly equally divided: Matthews received 142 votes, Hart 121. After the latter had moved that the election be made unanimous, a customary symbol of fraternal unity, Matthews proceeded to address the delegates on the implications of this "historic convention," calling it "the climax of many grueling experiences which I have encountered in recent months." He referred to his election as a vindication of his views on the direction of the Order but he did promise to "improve upon the handling [the business side] of the Order's affairs." Though he referred to his "friend, Luke Hart," he asked the delegates to consider electing officers and directors who would support him.[50]

Joseph Lamb was unopposed as Supreme Secretary. After his defeat as Supreme Knight, Hart accepted the nomination for Supreme Advocate. In the event that Hart had won, Ray Miller would have been the anti-Matthews candidate for Advocate. William Mulligan of Connecticut, who had been the Reconstruction candidate against Hart in 1922, was Matthews's choice to replace the incumbent, but Hart managed to muster a majority vote and defeated Mulligan, 132 to 129.

John Swift also defeated Matthews's candidate for Deputy Supreme Knight, John W. Babcock, Past State Deputy of Michigan; but Dr. William McNamara of Fair Haven, Vermont, defeated Dr. Edward W. Fahey of St. Paul, Minnesota, who had been Supreme Physician since 1923. Another pro-Matthews candidate, Leo M. Flynn of Chicago, was victorious in the election for Supreme Treasurer. Because the incumbent, Francis Heazel, was Hart's closest associate among the officers, Flynn's election came as a severe blow.[51]

Hart may have felt isolated and perhaps disappointed, but his correspondence immediately following this dramatic convention reveals that he had assumed a remarkably dispassionate attitude and that he was developing his strategies for the next two conventions, where he planned to have elected Supreme Officers and Directors who would be sympathetic to his views on the direction of the Order. Throughout the next two years Matthews and Hart maneuvered for support. Dr. McNamara established the Supreme Physician's office in New Haven, which, because that office handled the underwriting for the Order's insurance, was an expression of Matthews's renewed concern for the administrative work of the Order. In 1944 Hart was removed from the Executive Committee of the N.C.C.S.; this he viewed as Matthews's way of isolating him from the hierarchy. In accord with the code of fraternalism, they never allowed their conflict to interrupt the duties of their offices, but Matthews's position as chairman of the N.C.C.S. provided him with a very prestigious platform. Moreover, he was a far better orator than his opponent, though Hart would prove to be a consummate political strategist behind the scenes. He seldom revealed his plans until the last moment and thereby prevented his opposition from developing an organized counter-strategy. As Supreme Advocate for over thirty years, Hart had a masterly command of every facet of the Order, and he had a broad network of friends and allies. Thus, at the 1944 Convention he successfully managed the election of five anti-Matthews Directors, which gave him nearly unanimous support on the Board. Throughout the next year, crucial votes on the Board of Directors revealed only a minority of two or three members supporting Matthews. One significant vote arose in April 1945 when the Board considered a proposal, submitted by Wilbert J. O'Neill, President of the National Council of Catholic Men (N.C.C.M.), which was a request that the Order become an affiliate of his organization. To have affiliated with the N.C.C.M. would have threatened the Order's independent identity and would have placed the Knights under the N.C.W.C.; thus the Board rejected the proposal but voted that subordinate councils be urged to affiliate on the local level. Matthews was the only Director in opposition to the vote, which indicated that his general views on the Order's role within the Church were in direct opposition to the governing consensus.[52]

Matthews also registered a negative vote on the issue of the convention of 1945. Originally scheduled for August 19–21 in Montreal, it was postponed because Canadian authorities had prohibited large conventions, reserving all hotel space for returning troops. Matthews and McNamara were opposed to a convention in 1945, ostensibly because it would be unpatriotic to attempt to deprive troops of much needed hotel space. The majority of the Board obviously felt that political motives prompted this opposition and, led by Luke Hart, voted to convene in Montreal on October 23–25. They defended this position on the ground that U.S. authorities had announced the ban would be lifted on October 1 and that the Canadian government was expected to follow suit. Even after Canada announced a November 1 date for the termination of its restrictive hotel policy, the Board decided to hold to the date, confident that something could be arranged. Such confidence proved misplaced, and after convening on October 23 in St. Patrick's parish, the delegates approved a motion to adjourn and meet the following day in Plattsburg, New York. Matthews's supporters had unsuccessfully attempted to pass a motion to adjourn the convention until August 1946.[53] Though the Supreme Knight's report, which contained his views on the entire convention issue, was not included in the printed proceedings, his correspondence immediately after the convention shows that he had told the delegates that he considered the meeting at Plattsburg to be illegal. On that basis he announced that he was not a candidate for office. As a result, Matthews's candidate for Supreme Knight was soundly defeated by Judge John Swift and all of Hart's slate of candidates were elected: Dr. Edward Fahey, Supreme Physician; Francis Heazel, Treasurer; and Hart's close friend, Timothy Galvin of Hammond, Indiana, Deputy Supreme Knight. Even William Mulligan, who felt that Matthews had misrepresented his case in 1943, ended up in Hart's camp. He succeeded Galvin in the Office of Supreme Master of the Fourth Degree.

Matthews had consulted with Archbishop Mooney before he attended the climactic 1945 convention.[54] Mooney was in full accord with his decision not to be a candidate for Supreme Knight, an opinion which Matthews considered to be a vote of no confidence in the Hart forces. The Archbishop also assured Matthews that the hierarchy wished him to remain as chairman of the Executive Committee of the

N.C.C.S. and to represent them on the U.S.O. and other government boards. Not long after the Plattsburg convention, Archbishop Stritch told Matthews that "you may be assured that we shall call upon you to assist us as we called upon you so often in the past. You have done an excellent work for us, and we appreciate it beyond expression."[55]

There is no doubt that both Hart and Matthews were dedicated to the good of the Order. Hart held so strongly to his views that the Supreme Knight should be virtually a resident administrator in New Haven that he was willing to break his long friendship with Matthews. Since Hart held himself responsible for Matthews election in 1939, he considered it a parallel duty to drive him out of office. As shown in his voluminous correspondence and in interviews with those who worked with him, Luke Hart was a powerful personality with an overwhelming sense of identity with the Knights. Because Hart jealously guarded the Order's autonomy, he considered Matthews's support of the N.C.C.S. as a betrayal of his office as Supreme Knight. Hart intimated that Matthews's fatal flaw was his drive to pursue personal ambitions, symbolized by his willing association with the hierarchy during World War II. On the other hand, Hart's major weakness was his self-righteous intolerance of any one who did not rise to his own rigidly high standards of loyalty, dedication, and zeal.

Francis Matthews was a gifted leader, but once he lost Hart's trust he lost the basis of his power in the Order. Matthews's achievements after his retirement illustrate his many qualities; in 1946 he was appointed to President Truman's Civil Rights Committee, and in 1948 he headed the Nebraska delegation at the 1948 Democratic Convention. In May 1949, Truman appointed him Secretary of the Navy. During his twenty-six months in that post he was engaged in such significant issues as the developing arms race and the Korean war. On June 27, 1951, Truman appointed him U.S. Ambassador Extraordinary and Plenipotentiary to Ireland, where he died October 18, 1952. Ten months later, Luke Hart became Supreme Knight and the first resident administrator of the Order, thereby embracing those high standards of leadership which he had enforced on others.

14

John E. Swift and the Cold-War Years

JOHN E. SWIFT WAS UNANIMOUSLY ELECTED SUPREME KNIGHT at the convention of 1945. The entire Hart slate emerged victorious in the election of Supreme Officers, which effected a return to unity after a three-year period of discord. The Supreme Physician, Dr. Fahey, in accord with the pattern established by his predecessor, Dr. McNamara, moved his residence to New Haven, but it was understood that Swift, a judge in the Massachusetts Superior Court, could not be a resident Supreme Knight. However, it appears that Luke Hart assumed that Swift would make frequent visits to the Supreme Office, since it was only two-hours by train from Swift's Boston home.

Swift was born of Irish parents in Milford, Massachusetts, on December 7, 1879. He was a graduate of Boston College and the Law School of Boston University. He joined Valencia Council No. 80 in 1912 and after serving as Grand Knight, District Deputy, State Secretary, and State Deputy, he was appointed to the Supreme Board of Directors in 1927 to fill a vacancy created by the death of William C. Prout, also of Massachusetts. Swift's encounter with Patrick J. Moynihan in the election of Deputy Supreme Knight in 1939 and the subsequent struggle with the Massachusetts Insurance Commissioner, which finally terminated in 1948, were significant internal issues during his period in office as Deputy Supreme Knight as well as Supreme Knight.

The major external concerns of the Order during Swift's terms as Supreme Knight, 1945–53, were related to what the American Church considered the major evils of the day, the expansion of Communist power in Europe and Asia and the advance of secularism in modern culture.

In his first major address as Supreme Knight (January 20, 1946), Swift lashed out at American capitulation to Soviet expansionism, saying that all the world knows that Godless Russia has torn the Atlantic Charter to tatters, and enslaved millions of our fellow Catholics all the way from Finland and Poland to Catholic Austria and Czechoslovakia and almost to the gates of Rome. By one shameless appeasement after another we have failed to uphold our American ideals. . . . Has not the time arrived for some group or some leader to arise in forums of the world and in challenging tones cry out to Russia —'thus far thou shalt go, and no farther.' "[1]

After reviewing the Order's Peace Program, with its commitment to a crusade for the establishment of the "social reign of the Prince of Peace," Swift elaborated on the Knights' $1 million scholarship fund for the children of members who died in the war. He urged the graduates of Catholic colleges and universities to join the Order, to become lay apostles, and to defend Christian civilization against the evils of communism.[2] This speech, which was delivered at a Boston testimonial dinner honoring Swift upon his election as Supreme Knight, was widely publicized. Coincidentally, the U.N. site-finding committee was visiting Boston during this period. Though the Soviet members of the committee had previously indicated that Moscow favored a New York site for the United Nations, a Soviet representative announced that Russia had rejected Boston because of Swift's speech. The *Boston Post* defended Swift and pointed out that he did not condemn the U.N. as the Russians charged; " 'On the contrary,' he said, 'we offer UNO our humble prayer for success.' "[3]

John Swift's first report to the Supreme Council Convention in 1946 was, in a very real sense, a uniquely American Catholic anti-Communist manifesto. After a lengthy disquisition on the evils of the "Satanic scourge" of Bolshevist imperialism and of the philosophy of Marxist Leninism, Swift focused on the Communist conspiracy within the United States.[4] He referred to reports of the F.B.I. and of congressional committees which, he said, proved the Communist penetration of the government, labor unions, and college faculties. He deeply lamented the proliferation of hundreds of Communist Front organizations: "in every industrial city CELLS of young communists are forming and furiously debating in every city block!" Swift associated the rise of Communist infiltration with the decline in the moral fiber in American life, particularly evidenced in the disintegration of family life. To illustrate the Order's dedication to the struggle against communism, Swift reported that the Knights had sponsored a full-page advertisement in twelve large metropolitan newspapers in the United States and five in Canada which highlighted the dangers of communism and offered free copies of Monsignor Fulton J. Sheen's pamphlet *Communism, the Opium of the People.* Though this advertising campaign had been very successful, Swift devised an even more extensive campaign to combat communism and to "counteract the un-American philosophies that seem to be advancing throughout the United States."5

Swift's plan originally called for the establishment of a "Commission for the Preservation and Promotion of our American Ideals," but when it was finally approved it was called "The Knights of Columbus Crusade for the Preservation and Promotion of American Ideals."6 The crusade was based upon such precedents as the Order's Commission on Religious Prejudices, the Knights of Columbus Historical Commission, and the Knights' defense of the Church in Mexico. That section of the plan which dealt with American ideals was similar to the Peace Program of 1943, except that it explicitly identified those ideals with Catholic philosophy and applied them to the rights of the workingman. It pointed out that the Declaration of Independence and the Bill of Rights, as well as the utterances of Adams, Jefferson, and Lincoln, resounded with the natural-law theories of "our Suarez and St. Thomas," particularly those theories based upon the moral law. The plan listed the rights of the workingman as including the right "to a job, to a family living wage, to collective bargaining, and to strike, to *Joint-Management,* enroute to Joint Ownership of Industry" and, until the latter condition is reached, the right to all forms of social security: unemployment compensation and disability and old-age insurance.7

Though these rights of labor were derived from social encyclicals, they distinguished the Knights' Crusade from other prevalent varieties of anticommunism. Indeed, in its treatment of the causes of Communist ferment and social unrest, the plan listed the "Abuses of Unrestricted Capitalism":

(a) Unfair distribution of wealth.
(b) "Rich are getting richer and the poor are getting poorer."
(c) Wretched condition, misery of industrial workers in many parts of the world.
(d) Oppression of the poor by the *Four Capitalistic Dictators:*
   1. Over wages.
   2. Over prices.
   3. Over other people's money.
   4. Over money, the medium of exchange itself.
(e) Insufficiency for today, insecurity for tomorrow.
(f) Unemployment.
(g) Industrial Crises: alternating booms and depressions.
(h) "Economic Royalists" and stubborn opponents of all reform.

(i) Economic Liberalism of the 19th Century—opposing all reform through legislation.

(j) The pseudo-*"Scientific"* Socialism of Karl Marx.[8]

Just as President Roosevelt had lashed out at "malefactors of great wealth" as selfish opponents of the New Deal reforms, so Swift's plan attacked the capitalist opponents of Catholic social-justice principles. However, there was other rhetoric more indebted to the conservative and reactionary anticommunism of the day: attacks on those "High Brow" fellow travelers who were "culturally veneered, powerfully influential, and reportedly above suspicion." The elite groups that included "Millionaire 'angels,' the do-gooders' . . . Crackpot idealists, dreamers, 'perfectionists . . . 'brain-trusters,' so-called 'bright young men,' 'social planners,' *self-styled* 'Intelligentsia' . . . 'Liberals' in every style . . . college students—strutting as 'advanced' thinkers in this 'scientific age' . . . [and] *Their agnostic professors."* Other enemies included official *"Communist Propagandists"* and "Tired Liberals," who were "pretentious, white-collared aristocratic Communists," well motivated but who, because they had no religious faith, advocated "brute force to bring about their starry millennium and what they call 'The Kingdom of God on Earth.' "[9] But the plan's anti-elitist rhetoric may also have been indebted to that Catholic populism derived from the Knights' traditional hostility to the Anglo-Saxon upper-class groups that were thought to be dedicated to remaking American society according to modern secular blueprints.

The practical operation of the plan was based upon the discussion-group principle, with the council chaplain as the most appropriate local leader. To illustrate the high regard which had traditionally been paid to the discussion group, the plan quoted from an eclectic range of "famous thinkers" such as Thomas Aquinas, William Gladstone, Hilaire Belloc, and Robert Hutchins, then president of the University of Chicago. Though Knights of Columbus councils were envisaged in the plan, the primary focus was upon college students and seminarians, who would thus become lay apostles adept at defending American ideals against attacks by Communists and who also would be drawn to join the Knights of Columbus and perpetuate the crusade for "faith and fatherland."[10] The crusade was officially launched in December 1946 under the directorship of George Hermann Derry, Ph.D., leader of the Knights' 1930s crusade against communism. At the 1947 Supreme Council Convention, Swift proudly reported that most councils were developing discussion groups and that more than three hundred were in operation. He was also quite pleased that President Truman had strongly endorsed the crusade and had expressed his hope that the entire membership "will join in support of that campaign with zeal and enthusiasm. Our goal must be to drive out of our American life every movement which aims to promote within our borders any form of totalitarianism or any subversive movement."[11]

Swift presented a lengthy summary of the principles and strategies of the crusade and introduced the *Manual for Discussion Groups* written by Dr. Derry, which Auxiliary Bishop John J. Wright of Boston said was "an amazing production, profoundly thought-provoking and admirably condensed."[12] The crusade gained momentum during 1947–48, and by August 1948 there were thirteen hundred K. of C. discussion groups. The Yugoslav government's persecution of Archbishop Alojzije Stepinac in 1946–47 no doubt stimulated Catholic interest in the Knights' crusade. The Order vigorously protested against such persecution and amplified its crusade in 1947 with the broadcast over a network of several hundred radio stations of the K. of C. programs "Safeguards of America" and "Foundations of Our American Ideals." The "Safeguards" series was divided into six fifteen-minute dramatizations, beginning with an exposition of the harshness of life in Communist Russia and concluding with a treatment of the struggle against the Communist effort in the United States.[13] The "Foundations" series was also divided into six programs and emphasized the natural-law roots of American idealism, the divine source of the state's authority, religious liberty, and the contrast between democratic freedom and Communist tyranny.[14] Swift announced to the 1948 Supreme Council a third series, "The Future of America," which was to focus on America's "place as the moral leader in the family of nations, the great benefactor of the human race."[15]

The "Safeguards" series elicited a rejoinder from *The Daily Worker.* In his column on the "Broadway Beat," Barnard Rubin announced that the "K of C Plans Big Radio Hoax on Communists" and warned that "this fantastic hoax will be the signal for the greatest crackdown and terror campaign on unions, free speech, liberals, and Communists that this country has witnessed in recent times."[16] The *Knights of Columbus News* proudly featured Rubin's articles and proclaimed that the program "is hitting the commies where it hurts." The *News* did not dignify the *Daily Worker* article by responding to the charge that the Knights were fostering a witch hunt, but it did question "which dream book Comrade Rubin used for some of the colorful details of the story."[17] Nevertheless, while the six scripts for the "Safeguards" series warned listeners of the dangers of Communist-front organizations, it also included a defense of First Amendment freedoms.[18] However, by persistently sounding the alarm about the Communist enemy within, the Order opened itself to charges that it was fostering terrorist tactics.[19] Indeed, in 1947 the Supreme Council passed a resolution condemning the "Soviet conspiracy" which had "established beachheads of corruption and disloyalty among employees of our government, among the members of our labor unions, among the ranks of American citizens engaged in the practice of the professions and in the education of our children."[20] The resolution called upon the administration and Congress "to take all measures necessary to defeat" this conspiracy.

In May 1950, shortly after Joseph McCarthy's anti-Communist campaign had achieved national notoriety, the editor of *Columbia,* John Donahue, responded to McCarthy's critics. Donahue did not defend McCarthy's tactics but did affirm that criticism of McCarthy was "premature." Donahue specifically defended the Senator against the charge that he was using guilt-by-association tactics. "That disaster has not occurred and is not likely to occur. What does happen . . . is that a man's association can make him the object of reasonable suspicion." Donahue concluded, therefore, that those people that have long been associated with "individuals or groups known to foster the communist 'line' are, we submit, reasonably subject to suspicion and inquiry before they are admitted to, or permitted to remain in, positions of public trust."[21]

The Supreme Council of 1950 passed a strongly worded anti-Communist resolution which included the "petition" that the President and Congress "take every necessary step to check the treasonable activities of the communists and their sympathizers." The resolution seems to have been not only supportive of McCarthy's aims but of his strategy as well, as it concluded with the assertion that the "rights provided in our constitution for the protection of loyal citizens [were] never intended for the solace of traitors and conspirators against our freedom."[22] However, in 1951 the Supreme Council did not even consider such an implicitly pro-McCarthy resolution; rather, the delegates adopted a resolution recommending that all citizens "seriously study the saving principles expounded in the social Encyclicals . . . to the end that the social order may be reconstructed," thereby removing the social evils exploited by the Communists. This resolution was prefaced by remarks honoring the sixtieth anniversary of *Rerum Novarum* and the twentieth anniversary of *Quadragesimo Anno.*[23]

The 1952 and 1953 Supreme Councils adopted anti-Communist

resolutions which were vague and without any reference to internal subversion or congressional investigations. During the entire McCarthy period, only two *Columbia* editorials defended the Senator. However, because McCarthyism had by 1953 engendered tensions among the pro and anti forces within the Church, as well as hostility between Catholics and Protestants, the editor of *Columbia* portrayed McCarthy under the fictional name "O'Clavichord." After elaborating on O'Clavichord's penetrating questions of those persons he suspected as engaged in a conspiracy "to overthrow . . . their country's government by violence," Donahue told of how O'Clavichord had been accused of spreading the disease of "O'Clavichordism," which inevitably leads to a "loss of freedom of the press, speech, and assembly." The editor doubted that the disease led to anything more than "severe headaches," perhaps induced by "bumps acquired while ducking under a protective barrier called the Fifth Amendment." Donahue had little sympathy for those who were subjected to McCarthy's style of questioning; he concluded his editorial with the remark that "the moral, if any, is that confession, which is good for the soul, may be rough on the ego."[24] The following September, Donahue once again asserted his doubt that O'Clavichordism was a dangerous disease: "we have not been aware of any heaped-up piles of murdered reputations or slaughtered innocents. We have not sniffed the smoke of distant bonfires, stoked—or so it is rumored—by O'Clavichord's horde of eager book-burners."[25]

Two months after this editorial appeared in *Columbia,* McCarthy initiated his investigation of subversion in the Army, a course of action which ultimately led to his condemnation by the Senate on December 2, 1954. The Supreme Council of that year adopted a resolution which did support the need for continuing the congressional investigation of the internal threats of a Communist conspiracy.[26] Because McCarthy was then under attack for his investigations of Communists in the U.S. Army, such a resolution, though more restrained than that of 1951, was definitely a defense of the Senator. Even John Swift, who was the Order's leading crusader for the Promotion and Preservation of American Ideals (which had lost its momentum by 1951), toned down his anticommunism during the McCarthy period. However, on one occasion, at the annual States Dinner in conjunction with the Supreme Council of 1953, Swift lashed out again at the "fellow travelers" and other groups which "find vices in all our virtues and seeds of death in our harvest of plenty."[27] Paradoxically, he severely criticized those who sought the protection of the First and Fifth amendments, yet urged all Americans to "learn to live in *charity* [his italics] with Russians and communists, everywhere," and affirmed that he was not recommending "witch hunts."[28] Instead, he called upon the Knights and all "God-serving individuals" to proclaim their pride in the American heritage and in American ideals. It is obvious then that Swift was pro-McCarthy, though it is possible that he was not always uncritical of his means.

II

It is not possible to assess the grass-roots sentiment of the Order, but one may assume that a majority was pro-McCarthy. The Order's forty-year history of anti-socialism, its various anti-Communist crusades, and the Church's strongly anti-Communist position in the Cold War years must have had a deep impact upon the members. The anti-McCarthy minority within the Order was as anti-Communist as the majority but was disillusioned with his red-baiting style or was composed of loyal party Democrats. One representative of this minority was Leonard F. Schmitt, who ran against McCarthy in the 1952 primary. Like McCarthy, Schmitt was a Knight of Columbus, but he was attached to the liberal La Follette wing of the Republican Party. Schmitt's liberal-Catholic anti-McCarthyism was similar to that of *Commonweal* and to such liberal Catholic spokesmen as Auxiliary Bishop Bernard J. Sheil of Chicago; George Schuster, President of Hunter College; and Jerome Kirwin of the University of Chicago. The majority of the Order may have been pro-McCarthy but, as Donald F. Crosby, S.J., points out, those who were Democrats would have tended to vote along party rather than religious lines.[29] Crosby's conclusion, however, represents a curious subordination of historical fact to stereotyped banalities. He writes, "The Knights' pro-McCarthy policy was completely congruent with their long history of political conservatism, their failure to support civil rights and social legislation, their flag-waving patriotism, and their abiding distaste for Protestants, liberals, and intellectuals of every religion."[30] The foregoing chapters are a point-blank refutation of Crosby's careless clichés, which display total unawareness of the significance of the Knights, of the ecumenism of the Commission on Religious Prejudices, of the Order's general support for trade unionism, of the broad array of intellectuals, including George Schuster, who wrote for *Columbia* magazine, of the Knights of Columbus Historical Commission, which published books by Samuel

Flagg Bemis, Allan Nevins, and W.E.B. DuBois, of the liberal social thought of George Hermann Derry, and of the Order's vigorous promotion of the social encyclicals. Though Martin Carmody and Luke Hart were political conservatives, John Swift's 1946 attack on capitalist manipulators of prices and on all those who advocated a free market and his strong support for economic democracy and social-welfare legislation marks him as a fairly representative New Deal anti-Communist. Crosby asserts that the pro-McCarthy Catholics, which could have included the majority of the Knights, tended to be of the "hands-off school of thought," those who believe that the Church should limit its concerns to churchly matters rather than speak out on the social issues of the day. Crosby identifies the liberals with the activist, interventionist school in the fifties, *Commonweal* Catholics who urged the bishops to assume moral leadership on major social questions.[31] But the conflict between the two schools is historically grounded in the rift between Archbishop John Ireland and Archbishop Michael Corrigan in the 1890s. The Americanism of Ireland, one will recall, was interventionist in its drive to embrace American democracy and culture as congruent with Catholic ideals. The anti-Americanist held fast to a hands-off view of American culture because of its essentially Protestant and materialistic character. Now, as this history of the Knights makes clear, every major phase in the evolution of Columbianism embraced the Americanist or interventionist vision. In the 1890s, Thomas H. Cummings described the Knights as heralding "a new type of Catholic manhood . . . a new spirit within the Church" and as acting as a leaven in American life.[32] The Commission on Religious Prejudices (1914–17) was interventionist in its assertion of the un-American nature of religious bigotry. The Historical Commission (1920–25) was Americanist in its promotion of the ethnic contributions to American history. The Mexican campaign (1926–37), the Peace Program, and the Crusade for the Promotion and Preservation of American Ideals were all rooted in the ideals of American civil liberty and of the alleged Catholic origins of the natural-law theories enshrined in the Declaration of Independence and in the general political thought of the founding fathers. If Columbianism displayed a conservative tenor, it was not political conservatism but rather cultural conservatism.

The Knights' defense of eighteenth-century ideals was lodged in the foundation of the Republic and their attachment to the Catholic contribution to American culture derived from their Catholic minority consciousness which in its public expression was distinctly interventionist. The rapid social changes of the post–World War I period, characterized by the increasing divorce rate, the promotion of birth control, and the breakdown of traditional sexual mores, held the Order back from a thorough Americanist embrace of American culture and impelled the Knights to assume a conservative (but still moderately interventionist) position on these cultural issues. However, the Knights rationalized their criticism of these social changes on both Catholic and Americanist grounds as symbolizing not only a departure from traditional moral teaching but also representing the advance of secularism, which was viewed as a deviation from the idealism of the founding fathers.

The Knights' antisecularism was expressed in their anticommunism. One of the major reasons for the advancement of communism, according to Swift, was "the de-Christianized conscience and paganized heart of modern man."[33] Because Catholics more visibly demonstrated their faith by their high church-attendance rates and by their loyalty to the institutional fabric than members of other religions, it was incumbent upon Catholic spokesmen, particularly of such interventionist character as the Knights, to demonstrate Catholicism's strongly antisecularist character. In the process, they expressed themselves in the rhetoric of what scholars have called "civil religion," which portrays the United States as the refuge of the homeless and oppressed, the promised land, America the land of liberty destined by God to play a redemptive or salvific role in the world. Civil religion, which by definition embraces Protestants, Catholics, and Jews alike, does not replace institutional religion but rather permeates the consciousness of all Americans.[34] However, according to the Columbian belief in the Catholic baptism of the nation, the Knights placed special emphasis upon Catholicism's role in "this *almost* chosen people" (italics added). John Swift called upon "all God created and God-redeemed individuals [of all faiths] to be proud of our American heritage, our American ideals, our American contributions. Together we can save America and save the World."[35]

Swift's strong assertion of Catholic self-confidence, though apologetic and defensive in tone, was indicative of the general sense of institutional maturity of the Church in America. The *Christian Century* pointed out in late 1944 that, with almost twenty-three million members, the Catholic Church in America was nearly three times larger than the largest Protestant denomination. The author of the article, Harold Fey, sounded the alarm at the numerical growth and organizational strength of Catholics. "They have cast off the inferiority complex which naturally characterizes an alien minority and have begun boldly and aggressively to assert their power. It is only within this generation that the Roman Catholic Church has come to feel at home in the United States. Now that it speaks the 'American' language and has raised up native leaders who are loyally followed by millions, it is for the first time in a position to make history—American history." There is no evidence of a K. of C. response to Fey's remarks. But the Knights would have sensed Fey's rather patronizing attitude, particularly since Columbianism was born of pride in the Catholic makers of American history. However, Fey's views appear to have been characteristic of the Protestant concern over the growth of Catholic influence, and reflected the traditional Protestant fear that these millions of Catholics represented a singular threat because they were "subject to the spiritual direction of an Italian pontiff who represents a culture historically alien to American institutions."[36]

Such Protestant-Catholic tensions in the postwar period, which Fey's article reflects, were most visible on the issue of federal aid to education. The N.C.W.C. had been traditionally opposed to all forms of federal aid to education on the grounds that such funding represented a threat to the autonomy of private schools and that the proponents of such aid were usually anti-parochial-school spokesmen. Prompted by a sense of Catholic self-confidence, by a lessening fear of federal power after the New Deal, and by budgetary problems caused by postwar inflation, the Education Department of the N.C.W.C. reversed its position. In 1947 Catholics were encouraged by the Supreme Court case *Everson v. Board of Education,* which permitted children of parochial schools to ride public-school buses. As a result of this decision and the growing fear among many Protestant groups that the Catholic Church, allied with the alien power in the Vatican, was threatening Protestant hegemony over American institutions, sixty Protestant leaders issued a manifesto on the "Separation of Church and State" in November 1947. This group, which referred to itself as Protestants and Other Americans United for the Separation of Church and State (P.O.A.U.), declared in its manifesto that it was "anti-Catholic only in the sense that every Catholic is anti-Protestant." However, the *raison d'être* of the P.O.A.U. was explicitly to struggle against the growth of what it considered to be the Vatican-based power of the Catholic Church in America, a Church which was by its nature driven to dominate America's democratic institutions and, at the expense of the principle of the separation of church and state, to seek privileges for its sectarian educational system.[37]

The Knights of Columbus vigorously supported federal aid to

parochial schools. In response to those who decried the *Everson* case as a blow at the "wall of separation" between church and state, the editor of *Columbia* cited John Courtney Murray, S.J. The latter considered the proponents of the "wall" as advocates of a "barrier deflecting American democracy toward a disastrous development alien to its primitive spirit and . . . [deflecting] all government aid singly and solely towards the subsidization of secularism as the one national 'religion' and culture, whose agent of propaganda is the secularized public school."[38]

On January 3, 1948, John Swift replied to the P.O.A.U. manifesto in the form of a very widely circulated press release. Swift viewed the manifesto as an insult to the patriotism of Catholics, Protestants, and Jews "who do not subscribe to its biased and inaccurate interpretation of the First Amendment." The Supreme Knight expressed his confidence that the American people would not be swayed by P.O.A.U.'s drive to stir up "religious bigotry."[39] John Donahue, editor of *Columbia,* who referred to the P.O.A.U. as the P.U. and Co., lashed out at the organization and defended the Order's position on federal aid in several editorials in the late 1940s and early '50s on the ground that the religious character of the parochial school was a major weapon in the battle with materialism and secularism.[40] The 1949 Supreme Council unanimously adopted two resolutions implicitly opposed to the P.O.A.U.'s manifesto. The resolution "on Church and State" condemned the "wall of separation" concept as "far-fetched, unwarranted, and prejudicial." Stating that the First Amendment merely prohibits laws "respecting the establishment of religion," the resolution stated that the opponents of public aid for services such as transporting parochial children on public-school buses had "misled people . . . into accepting a figure of speech as a principle of law." The resolution on federal aid to education asserted that "Catholics support unequivocally the principle of the separation of Church and State."[41]

The Resolution concluded: "Catholics do not desire Federal aid for Parochial schools. . . . Catholics insist upon the right of all children to participate on an equal basis in benefits provided by the Federal government; if such benefits are provided for school children they should be provided for all school children without discrimination."[42]

Protestant hostility to the growth of Catholic influence in America was singularly expressed in Paul Blanshard's *American Freedom and Catholic Power.* Blanshard, a former official in the State Department, launched his polemic in 1947 with a series of articles for the *Nation* which gained such widespread support that he was prompted to write a book exposing the alleged Catholic conspiracy.[43] Though he claimed to be objective and scholarly, Blanshard invoked nearly every anti-Catholic slur, excepting only the pornographic luridities of the ex-priest ex-nun genre. The Pope was portrayed as a "world monarch who rules a synthetic moral empire that overlaps and penetrates the sovereignty of all earthly governments."[44] The Catholic bishops were foreign agents, and the U.S. government should force them to register as such. The laity were considered subjects of the pope, while Catholic Action groups, such as the Knights of Columbus, were, like Communist cells, infiltrating secular organizations and representing the advance of creeping Vaticanism. Blanshard severely criticized the Knights of Columbus Catholic Advertising Program. (The Order sponsored advertisements in secular newspapers aimed in part at dispelling public ignorance of the Church.) He considered the K. of C. advertisements an attempt "to disguise the worst feature of their own faith by adroit double-talk."[45] He viewed Catholic education as fostering undemocratic separatism, and he identified the public school as the unifying element in America's pluralistic society.

Blanshard's first book was so popular that it went into fourteen printings in less than two years. His second book, *Communism, Democracy, and Catholic Power,* was nearly as popular.[46] Both books were hailed by the majority of leading Protestants and favorably reviewed in *Newsweek,* the *Nation,* and the *Saturday Review.* Regardless of their place on the liberal-conservative spectrum, Catholics condemned Blanshard for his deeply biased appraisal of the Catholic threat to democracy. The scholarly trappings of his book and his proud claim that he was not anti-Catholic were singularly offensive to Catholics, particularly because so many Protestants were deceived, or wanted to be deceived, by his claim to objectivity. In 1951 John Cogley, editor of *Commonweal,* commented on Blanshard's vast popularity. "The name Blanshard means something in American life today, and to different kinds of people who have one thing in common, that they don't like the Catholic Church. The man has become the spokesman for a motley crew, and he seems to work on the something-for-everybody principle." Cogley was deeply disturbed that reviewers of *Communism, Democracy, and Catholic Power* "treated it as serious and unbiased. But I know of no Catholic who would agree, from Jacques Maritain to the latest high school graduate. Even the most critical Catholics, the most liberal of the 'liberal' Catholics . . . are on record as believing that Mr. Blanshard has presented a distorted, biased caricature of their religious beliefs and has done so with sneers and snipings."[47] James M.

O'Neill's book *Catholicism and American Freedom* was a Catholic response to Blanshard's *American Freedom and Catholic Power.* O'Neill devoted three chapters to the historical contribution of Catholicism in America, which he said substantiated "the consistent record of American Catholic endorsement of our total constitutional situation. This approval, both lay and clerical, has been substantially unbroken for 160 years."[48] *Columbia* strongly endorsed O'Neill's "long awaited reply" and pointed out that O'Neill had taught for forty years in public schools, and had served for twelve years on the Committee on Academic Freedom of the American Civil Liberties Union, experiences which illustrated O'Neill's "commitment to the First Amendment freedoms."[49]

Blanshard's books exacerbated Protestant-Catholic tensions in the late 1940s and early '50s by an appeal to the secularist mentality of certain academic and intellectual elites who tended to lump together Catholic "authoritarianism," the antics of Senator McCarthy, and the Church's position on divorce and birth control into a single anti-Catholic caricature. The revival of anti-Catholicism in the postwar period was unaccompanied by any new wave of nativism. Hence, it was not motivated by strong grass-roots fears of the immigrant-Catholic conspiracy. However, because the Church had, in the words of the *Christian Century,* "come to feel at home in the United States" and had "cast off the inferiority complex which naturally characterizes an alien minority,"[50] postwar anti-Catholicism represented hostility to the Church's ascendancy as a major religious force in American society. Conservative Protestant groups tended to resent the fact that America was losing its roots, while liberal Protestants and secularists resented the Church's strong assertion that a culture without religion was analogous to a body without a soul. From its birth, the Knights of Columbus had been struggling against the various forms of anti-Catholicism and nativism. The enemy had appeared in the form of hooded Klansmen, of frustrated populists (*The Menace* and the Rail Splitter Press), of self-designated one-hundred-percent American patriots, and of the traditional Masonic cant. The most dangerous form appeared in the sophisticated cloth of the secularistic elites who were beginning to find a new voice in the universities and the media. These were the days when Catholic youth were warned to fortify themselves for the battle against the atheism in non-Catholic colleges and universities, when Newman Centers were cherished as refuges of belief in an agnostic environment.

The Order's anti-elitism or Catholic populism was in the tradition of the Church's nearly two-century struggle against that aspect of the modern intellectual world view which excluded the role of Providence and stressed the inevitability of progress. Another aspect of the Knights' Catholic populism was in the tradition of the Order's struggle against the dominant white Anglo-Saxon Protestant elite—the New England Yankees, the reformers of the Progressive movement, the immigration restrictionists—who portrayed themselves as the pure-blooded guardians of the American way of life which, in the process, was perceived as strongly inimical to Blacks, Jews, Catholics, and southern and eastern European immigrants; in short, those potential pollutants of the pure stream of Protestant-American culture. Thus the K. of C. crusade against American secularism and communism represented to John Swift and others another phase in the struggle for the preservation of genuine American ideals based upon the Catholic roots of the founding fathers' political vision.

John Swift's leadership of the Order's anticommunism and antisecularism was not a knee-jerk conservative defense of capitalism, nor was it mindless flag-waving. When Swift lashed out at all those fellow-traveler groups in his anti-Communist speeches and at the P.O.A.U. in his antisecularist attitudes, he was asserting the Columbian commitment to the Catholic component in American culture, derived, as he considered it to have been, from the Catholic soul of western civilization.

15

Luke E. Hart and the Confrontation with Modernity

THE STORY OF THE KNIGHTS OF COLUMBUS from 1953 to the present can only be told from the vantage point of New Haven. From the time Luke Hart became the first full-time Supreme Knight, the history of the Order has been determined almost exclusively by the administrative policies and programs of each of the Supreme Knights residing in New Haven. Though Luke Hart, John W. McDevitt, and Virgil C. Dechant worked closely with other Supreme Officers and Directors, each placed his own distinctive imprint upon the Order in accord with the ways in which each perceived the needs of the membership and responded to the prevailing trends in Church and society. Hence the recent history of the Knights is best understood by examining the point of view, the administrative character, and the style of leadership of each of the Supreme Knights.

Luke E. Hart was the most thoroughly prepared man ever to hold the highest office in the Order. He became a Knight in 1908, during Hearn's administration, Supreme Director in 1918 and Supreme Advocate in 1922. No other officer had ever matched his length of service or his breadth of experience. Though he was closely identified with the insurance program, he was actively engaged in the formation of policies governing the Order's major fraternal programs ranging from the huts in World War I to the anti-Communist crusades in the Cold-War years. By the time he became Supreme Knight he had attended thirty-one Supreme Council conventions, many of which expressed the heights of idealism, symbolized by the establishment of the Squires and the Mexican campaign, and a few of which were riven by the political conflicts illustrated by the emergence of the dissident movements of William Mulligan in the twenties and Patrick Moynihan in the thirties, and by his conflict with Matthews in the forties. When he became Supreme Knight in 1953, Hart was confident that he could maintain the Order's traditional anti-defamation character, with its patriotism and with its general promotion of Catholic interests, but he also sensed the need for modernizing the governance structure as an antidote to the virus of internal conflict.

Just as Swift's administration reflected the postwar tensions in American society and the sense of maturity in the American Church, so Hart's administration reflected contemporaneous trends in social, political, and ecclesiastical history. The Eisenhower years have been perceived as a period of rapid modernization of economic structures within a society reluctant to depart from traditional values. It was also a time when the American Catholic Church modernized its educational, health-care, and other charitable institutions in response to rapidly changing conditions in America's complex society. Hart became Supreme Knight seven months after the inauguration of Dwight D. Eisenhower and died three months after the assassination of John F. Kennedy. His administration also spanned the time between the end of the Korean conflict and the period immediately preceding the escalation of the Vietnam war. Though he confronted the civil rights movement, he never witnessed its triumph, nor did he experience the impact of the Second Vatican Council. Hart was a conservative Republican who mounted periodic, short-lived, anti-Communist campaigns, but he was not a romantic crusader. Just as he was driven to blend the Order's traditions with modern forms, so he also attempted to integrate his religious and Irish-American sensibilities with his business and legal acumen.

When Hart was elected Supreme Knight, he informed the delegates at the 1953 convention that he would be moving to New Haven to assume his duties. "For many years I have had the notion that the best interests of the Order require that the business of the various Supreme Officers should be conducted from the Supreme Headquarters in New Haven. I intend to establish a precedent by conducting the business of my office from New Haven."[1] The other officers followed suit, and this marked a new phase in the corporate development of the Order's home office. However, Hart was determined to modernize the governance structure further by removing the election of Supreme Officers from the general convention and placing it in the hands of the Board of Directors. Thus, the Supreme Council delegates were to become analogous to stockholders by electing board members who would elect officers from their membership.

The convention which elected him Supreme Knight passed such

an amendment, in the form of three resolutions, which authorized the Board to appoint six Supreme Officers (Supreme Chaplain and Warden were appointees) from its membership and which expanded the number of Board members from fifteen to twenty-one, thereby providing seats for the six Supreme Officers, formerly ex-officio Board members.[2] Because constitutional amendments had to be passed by two consecutive Supreme Council conventions, the measure was resubmitted in 1954. Amid some debate and an unsuccessful attempt to pass a substitute amendment providing for the direct election of Supreme Knight, Secretary, and Warden, the original amendment passed by more than a three-to-one margin.

Supreme Advocate Harold J. Lamboley, a Past State Deputy from Wisconsin and a former judge, introduced the 1954 amendment by tracing the history of the then present law back to 1895 and the history of similar amendments proposed since 1939. After elaborating on the Order's nearly $500 million dollars of insurance in force, its large home-office staff of over four hundred employees, its large investment portfolio, and its myriad Catholic Action programs, Lamboley concluded that the traditional elective principle would not guarantee that the best administrative talent would rise to positions of leadership of so complex an organization. He reminded the delegates that under the proposed amendment the Supreme Council would still possess the authority to elect officers indirectly through its direct election of all board members. On behalf of the Board of Directors, Lamboley offered several changes to the original 1953 amendments which stipulated annual election of the six Supreme Officers, new election procedures for board members in 1955, and other constitutional changes in accord with the character of the amendment. One such change further illustrated the stockholder-delegate analogy: Only delegates designated as representing insurance members were allowed to vote on questions affecting insurance matters. However, because the Supreme Officers were not merely officers of a corporation but also the leaders of the entire fraternal membership, delegates representing associate members were entitled to vote for all board members. According to the constitutional amendment, eleven Supreme Board members were to be elected at the 1955 convention. Terms of office were to be based upon the number of votes for the candidates. The top seven were elected for a three-year term, the next two for a two-year term, and the remaining two for a one-year term. With the expansion of the Board to twenty-one, this procedure would mean that every year delegates would elect seven members, or one third of the Board. The results of the 1955 elections must have been a blow to Hart, as he received a two-year term while the other Supreme Officers and two board members were elected to three-year terms.[3]

Because he had been closely identified with the Order's insurance program for thirty-one years as Supreme Advocate and because he had been extremely active in the National Fraternal Congress (he served as president in 1952), Hart saw the need for continuous modernization of this program. Besides the reforms of 1940, he introduced innovations eventually leading to insurance plans for the families of members, and he also initiated national meetings of general agents. Hart strongly identified insurance with fraternalism and emphasized the importance of the insurance members in his first report as Supreme Knight in 1954. Associate members had traditionally far outnumbered insurance members, except during the period between 1934 and 1943, when the Depression caused large numbers of associates to drop out of the Order. The return of prosperity and the revival of the Order's idealism in the postwar period engendered a rapid rise in new associate membership, which nearly doubled in size between 1945 and 1954 from 312,000 to 594,000. However, in 1954 there were nearly 325,000 insurance members, which represented a growth of 100,000 since 1945.[4] The subsequent growth of the mortuary reserve fund had a strong impact upon the Order's investment portfolio, while the growth in associate membership allowed the leaders to launch, on a per-capita tax basis, ambitious programs to promote Catholic interests.

Hart's experience with the Order's insurance program was matched by his involvement in its investments. In his 1954 report he explained that the viability of the mortuary reserve fund was dependent upon annual earnings of 3 percent. Because interest rates had declined to 2 1/2 percent in the immediate postwar period, the average earnings of the Order's investment portfolio dipped slightly below 3 percent in 1950. Consequently, Hart urged John Swift and the other officers who composed the Board's Executive and Finance Committee to shift from the policy of investing in low-yield bonds to the more aggressive policy of investing in real estate.[5]

Shortly before he became Supreme Knight, Hart developed a new investment plan "as a result of my close contacts with heads of other large insurance societies."[6] According to this new policy, called the lease-back investment plan, the Order purchased several pieces of property which it leased back to the seller "upon terms generally that would bring to our Order a net rental equal to the normal mortgage interest rate."[7] Leases were arranged on a time basis so that the

Order's investment would be entirely amortized by rent within a given period, at which time the Order could sell the property or renew the lease.

The most dramatic of the Order's lease-back investments was its purchase of the property on which Yankee Stadium stood. In late 1953 Supreme Treasurer Francis Heazel had been informed that the property was for sale. On December 9, 1953, eight days before the purchase was consummated, the story broke in the news media and "was in every paper from Hong Kong to Cairo, Egypt. The favorable reaction to the publicity was almost unanimous and some members and councils sent us telegrams of congratulations and appreciation."[8] Hart recorded the details on the transaction in his diary for December 17, 1953. "We all met in the Board Room of the Bankers Trust Company in Rockefeller Center. . . . The various documents incident to the Yankee deal were executed and I delivered a check for $2,500,000. . . . It was, of course, the largest check I ever signed. The Knights then acquired title to the ground on which Yankee Stadium is built. We then leased it back . . . for an initial term of twenty-eight years at $182,000 per year and with the privilege . . . of three renewable terms of fifteen years each at $125,000 per year."[9] The Yankee Stadium land was just one of eighteen pieces of property purchased between 1952 and 1962. In 1963, Hart reported that the total invested in lease-back property had reached nearly $29 million.[10]

Under Luke Hart, the Order continued to respond to requests for mortgage loans by parish priests, members of the hierarchy, and heads of Catholic institutions. In 1954 the assets of the Order's mortuary reserve fund included $17.5 million in notes secured by such mortgages. Indeed, from the late 1890s, when it made the first such loan to St. Rose's Church in Meriden, Connecticut, to 1954, the Knights had loaned over $300 million to Catholic churches and institutions and "never lost one cent of principal or interest."[11] Though only a small percentage of the Order's investments was in preferred and common stock, Hart increased the amount during his tenure as Supreme Knight.

II

Luke Hart did not limit his concerns to the modernization of the insurance, governance, and investment structures. He was particularly proud of two major Catholic activities which came under his direction and which evidenced the infusion of the Order's traditional Catholic spirit into modern programs: the Catholic Advertising Program, and the Knights of Columbus Foundation established to support the Vatican microfilm library at St. Louis University. Both programs originated in St. Louis before Luke Hart moved from that city to New Haven. Though John Swift was Supreme Knight during the origins of these projects, the Order adopted them because of Hart's close association with the Church in St. Louis.

The Catholic Advertising Program was conceived by Charles F. Kelley, a member of Marquette Council No. 606 and an executive in the advertising firm of Kelley, Zahrndt & Kelley. In 1943, Kelley proposed that the Missouri Knights erect a radio station in St. Louis "for the purpose of broadcasting the truths concerning the Catholic religion."[12] After a committee was formed, composed of Kelley, Hart, Missouri State Chaplain Father Edward Rogers, State Deputy Amos A. Govero, chapter chairman Robert M. Guion, and other prominent Missouri Knights, the proposal was submitted to Archbishop John Glennon. Though Glennon supported the proposal, he was not enthusiastic. Eventually, the committee decided to abandon the radio station idea in favor of newspaper advertising in the secular press, a plan which met with the "hearty approval" of Archbishop Glennon. Originally the committee had envisioned that Father Rogers and a group of priests would answer the replies to the ads, but Glennon suggested Father Lester L. Fallon, C.M., a theology professor at Kenrick Seminary of the Archdiocese of St. Louis and founder of the Confraternity Home Study Series in 1938.[13] Fallon had perceived the need for the latter program after several summers in the Missouri Ozark Mountain area, where he had received many favorable responses to his street preaching on Catholicism. The confraternity was quite popular during the war years, when more than 25,000 servicemen were enrolled.[14]

The Missouri K. of C. advertising campaign was launched on June 18, 1944, with an ad in the Sunday issue of the *St. Louis Post Dispatch;* this was the first of fifty-two ads scheduled to appear in that paper. The advertisements were highlighted by a bold-print headline in the form of a thematic question, below which was a small illustration and a two-hundred- to three-hundred-word editorial aimed at encouraging the reader to learn more about the Catholic view on the chosen theme by contacting the Religious Information Bureau (R.I.B.) sponsored by the Knights of Columbus.[15] The tone of the ads was generally apologetical but seldom polemical. Many were aimed at clarifying ignorance of Catholic teaching regarding the sacraments, purgatory, the role of Mary, prayers to the saints, indulgences, and the Mass. Some ads, such as "Is Religion a Racket?," were intended to expose the dangers of secularism, while others presented Catholic views on the need for social justice and on the inroads of modern materialism. Many ads were designed to dispel traditionally American anti-Catholic myths about Catholic loyalty to the pope, and about Catholic attitudes to public education and to the separation of church and state.[16]

One ad on the Bible, entitled "The World's Best Seller—The Book of Disunity," engendered some controversy as it implicitly criticized the Protestant view of the Bible as the "sole guide in matters of religious faith." The ad concluded with the assertion that the "Catholic Church alone is the authorized interpreter of the Bible."[17] Several Protestant spokesmen were offended by what they considered to be a clear expression of Catholic triumphalism. In a letter to a Georgia Knight, Charles Kelley noted that several Protestant magazines had been extremely critical of the Bible ad, and he concluded that such attacks revealed that the ad had effectively expressed the fallacies of the "Bible only" theory.[18] Kelley stated that he expected criticism from Protestant ministers who "objected to the idea of Catholics daring to advertise in newspapers of wide circulation. We have some opposition from similar sources here. . . . The significant thing to us is that while these ministers object to the publication of Catholic advertisements, the rank and file of Protestants of good will are showing a very healthy interest in our campaign." He substantiated this interest by noting that during the first nine months of the campaign the Catholic Information Bureau (C.I.B.) received 12,248 requests for free pamphlets and that over three hundred non-Catholics were enrolled in the C.I.B.'s religious-instruction program.[19] Not all Protestant groups were critical of the Knights' ads. For example, *The Lutheran Witness,* the official organ of the Evangelical Lutheran Synod of Missouri, noted that "these advertisements [which] were very carefully worded so as to avoid conflict with official Roman teaching, cannot fail to impress public sentiment."[20]

Archbishop Glennon was so pleased with the Missouri Knights' campaign that he contributed $1,000 to the program in May 1945. Though the Missouri State Council had endorsed the project from its origin, the first phase was limited to the archdiocese of St. Louis. However, Knights throughout Missouri responded with strong financial support, and in 1945 ads appeared eventually in many newspapers in the state. The Indiana Knights adopted the Missouri ad program in 1945, but they initiated their own counterpart to the R.I.B. The Washington State Council also placed the ads in newspapers, but referred their readers to the St. Louis R.I.B. for pamphlets and correspondence courses.[21] Father Rogers, the treasurer of the Missouri program, vigorously promoted the ad campaign among the clergy by sending them copies of each ad before it appeared in the press.

Hart appears to have been eager to elevate the Missouri campaign to the level of an Orderwide project. At his request, Father Rogers addressed the delegates to the Supreme Council in 1946 on the role and scope of the program.[22] Then, at the 1947 convention, the Missouri delegates submitted a resolution that "the Supreme Council adopt a program of Catholic advertising similar to the program that has been conducted by the State Council of Missouri the past three years with great success."[23] The resolution was recommended to the Board of Directors and, with Hart as its major advocate, was approved. In October 1947, Hart elaborated on the need for a "continent-wide ad campaign," which led to a $125,000 allocation for the placing of six ads in 1948. A Board committee, chaired by Hart, selected two magazines for the Supreme Council ads, the *American Weekly,* a Sunday supplement to large metropolitan newspapers with estimated circulation of 23 million, and the *Pathfinder,* which had circulation of over 2 million, chiefly among the rural population where Catholic teaching was most misunderstood.[24] In 1948 the Board passed an 80-cent annual per-capita tax for the funding of this program, which provided over $500,000 for annual operating costs of the ads and the R.I.B. office in St. Louis. Over the next five years, ads were placed in many U.S. magazines such as *Collier's, Newsweek,* and *Atlantic Monthly* and in such Canadian weeklies as *Liberty, Maclean's, Star Weekly,* and *Weekend.* By 1954 Father Fallon's office staff had grown to thirty employees, including three Vincentian priests, and by that year the office had received over 1.5 million requests for information on the Catholic Church. Several hundred local councils placed the ads in their hometown newspapers, while prison and hospital chaplains and missionaries supplemented their catechetical work with the R.I.B.'s series of pamphlets which were written by Catholic scholars in a popular style.

The hierarchy and clergy enthusiastically embraced the Order's project. There is no way to measure accurately the number of people who became Catholics as a result of the ads and the program, but according to the thousands of letters received by the R.I.B., the number of converts had been substantial. Though Hart frequently quoted from such letters to illustrate the deep impact of the program, its major goal was to expand the general public's understanding of Catholicism.

Luke Hart's summary of the program placed it squarely within the historical character of the Order:

In sponsoring this advertising program the Knights of Columbus is performing direct and highly essential service to the Church . . . a service which is performed by no other agency . . . our advertisements go into the homes of those who will not visit a Catholic Church. They reach people who do not read our Catholic literature, magazines, and newspapers. . . . They correct false notions about our faith. They discredit long-standing anti-Catholic propaganda and refute current falsehoods which are calculated to turn decent people against us. They compel even those who will not join us to respect us. They bring Catholic teaching right out into the open, where people may accept or reject as they wish . . . but where no person of common sense and fairness can misunderstand or misinterpret it."[25]

Before an ad was approved for publication, both Hart and Monsignor Leo Finn, the Supreme Chaplain, discussed its suitability. They were particularly concerned that the ads not reveal any expression which might needlessly offend Protestants. The Catholic Advertising Program also provided the Order with a permanent link with the media by which it could elaborate the Catholic as well as the Order's position on social and moral issues. Throughout the fifties, when there were many requests for the Order to pursue a vigorous anti-Communist crusade, Hart refused to comply on the grounds that the Order's Catholic Advertising Program included ads on the Church's teaching on communism and that many other organizations were committed to anticommunism. The size of the Order's financial outlay for advertisements and pamphlets, which reached over $10 million by the time of Luke Hart's death in early 1964, represents the Order's largest commitment among its many Catholic Action programs and clearly symbolizes Hart's drive to express the Knights' traditional character in contemporary forms.

In its early years the Order had been a supporter of Catholic University and had always been a champion of Catholic education in general. Its $1 million trust fund for the education of children of members who had died in World War II—one of John Swift's most ambitious programs—evolved into a scholarship fund for attendance at Catholic colleges and universities. The education project closely associated with Luke Hart was the Vatican microfilm library housed at St. Louis University. Hart was very close to the Jesuit university and had headed its $500,000 fund-raising campaign among Missouri Knights. The idea of microfilming portions of the Vatican Library originated with Lowrie Daly, S.J., who had been influenced by the University of Michigan's British Museum microfilm project. Father Daly received strong encouragement from Paul C. Reinert, S.J., president of the university, and from Joseph P. Donnelly, S.J., head librarian. After the Vatican had given its approval, the St. Louis Jesuits turned to several foundations for funds but received little encouragement. In April 1951, at a meeting of the Supreme Board of Directors, Father Bernard W. Dempsey, S.J., regent of the School of Commerce and Finance, represented St. Louis University in its appeal for funds from the Order. Dempsey informed the Directors that the microfilming project was aimed at preserving selected manuscripts of the Vatican Library in the event that war, revolution, or natural disaster might lead to their destruction. He also explained that many of the manuscripts dated back to the pre-Christian era and were irreplaceable and that the proposed microfilm library at St. Louis University would be of immense interest to scholars in various fields. Dempsey estimated that the cost would be about $140,000. The Board voted favorably but referred the project to its Executive and Finance Committee.[26] Though Hart was very supportive of the project, he and the other officers were concerned that the Knights' contribution be viewed as a donation for the Vatican Library microfilm project rather than as a donation to the university itself. To guarantee this, the Board established the K. of C. "Foundation for the Preservation of Historic Documents at the Vatican Library" which was to be funded by a 15-cent per-capita tax to be collected over a two-year period.[27]

John Swift reported to the delegates on the establishment of the foundation and elaborated on the many ways in which this project was in accord with the Order's historical character as the lay organization dedicated to promoting the Catholic contribution to western civilization.[28] James C. Dunn, U.S. Ambassador to Italy, wrote to Luke Hart congratulating the Order on this "dramatic gift" by which scholars will be "inspired with a sense of world community and common devotion to ageless ideals."[29] Archbishop Giovanni B. Montini (later Pope Paul VI), Vatican Undersecretary of State, wrote that His Holiness Pope Pius XII was very grateful that the Order had made such a valuable contribution to "Christian learning," symbolic of the Knights' "genuine Catholic spirit" and their service to "true Christian humanism."[30]

Father Daly, assisted by the staff of the Vatican Library, completed the microfilm project in June 1956. For more than four years 6,900 rolls of microfilm were processed; 9,500,000 manuscript pages were made available for research at St. Louis University. The project cost

$350,000, a figure which far exceeded the original estimate of $140,-000.[31] With the completion of the project, the foundation was dissolved. The repository of the microfilm was entitled "The Knights of Columbus Vatican Film Library, at St. Louis University." On May 18, 1959, St. Louis University's Pius XII Memorial Library opened its door to students. The Order contributed $250,000 for those rooms which were to be used for the Vatican Film Library and for conferences. The latter was named "the Knights' Room" and is still one of the major conference rooms on the campus.[32] Later, Luke Hart drew the analogy between the Knights' Room at St. Louis University and the Knights' Tower at the National Shrine of the Immaculate Conception in Washington, D.C., as appropriate designations for the contribution of hundreds of thousands of Columbians.

The Knights' Tower at the National Shrine was also a project which originated in 1957, when the Board of Directors agreed to finance the construction of the campanile. The National Shrine was initiated by Cardinal Gibbons, who had laid the cornerstone for the crypt church at Catholic University on September 23, 1920. Depression and war delayed construction, and it was not until the 1950s that work proceeded on an uninterrupted schedule. Though the church was nearly completed and the foundation for the campanile had been constructed by 1957, funds were exhausted. On March 22, 1957, the Most Reverend Patrick A. O'Boyle, Archbishop of Washington and Chancellor of Catholic University, and Monsignor Thomas J. Grady, Supervisor of the National Shrine, approached Luke Hart with the message that "it was the unanimous wish of the Cardinals, Archbishops, and Bishops that the opportunity to erect the Campanile should be presented to the Order."[33] Convinced that the Order "should avail itself of this privilege," Hart and the Supreme Board agreed to propose to the 1957 Supreme Council convention that the Knights contribute $1 million, through a $1.25 per-capita tax spread out over a five-year period, for the construction of this 329-foot belltower attached to the largest Catholic church in America.[34] On November 20, 1959, two days before the dedication of the Pius XII Memorial Library, the shrine was dedicated with more than one thousand Fourth Degree Knights forming an honor guard for the guests. Inside the entrance to the campanile, a bronze tablet was erected upon which was inscribed, "The Knights' Tower/Gift of The Knights of Columbus to The National Shrine of the Immaculate Conception as a Pledge of the Devotion of Its Members To Our Blessed Lady Patroness of The United States."[35]

The Knights' Tower remained a silent witness to the Order's deep loyalty to the Church until a carillon of fifty-six bells was solemnly blessed by Archbishop O'Boyle on July 7, 1963. The Order financed the installation of the carillon at a cost of $150,000. The largest bell was named after Mary, while the second largest was named the Christopher bell in tribute to the Saint, to the Order's patron, and to the Knights. Luke Hart proudly remarked that "throughout all the ages, the Knights' Tower will be a monument to the Order, giving evidence of the undying loyalty of our members to Mary, Mother of God . . . and these bells will forever ring out the glory of man's redemption."[36]

III

Like his predecessor, John Swift, Hart vigorously promoted anti-secularist and anti-Communist programs. He was particularly proud of the Order's role in amending the Pledge of Allegiance to include "under God" after the phrase "one nation." The movement for the amendment originated in April 1951, when the Supreme Board of Directors adopted a resolution providing that the amended pledge be recited at meetings of the 750 Fourth Degree Assemblies in the United States. Urged by five State Councils—Delaware, Florida, Michigan, New York, and South Dakota—the Supreme Council of 1952 passed a resolution urging Congress to amend the pledge. Copies of the resolution were sent to the President, the Vice-President, and the Speaker of the House. As president of the National Fraternal Congress, Hart successfully urged the 110 fraternal societies to adopt the resolution.[37]

Congressman Louis C. Rabaut of Michigan introduced in the House of Representatives a resolution to amend the pledge in the Public Law on April 20, 1953. After sixteen other such resolutions were submitted to Congress, the amended pledge was finally passed and on Flag Day, June 14, 1954, President Eisenhower signed it into law.[38] Later the President wrote to Luke Hart, extending his gratitude to the Knights for their "part in the movement to have the words 'under God' added to our Pledge of Allegiance." Patriotism, one of the Order's four cardinal principles, was the predominant motive behind the movement for the amended pledge. Though such patriotism has been construed to symbolize "worship of the state," the Knights' patriotism was in accord with the traditional symbolism of "In God We Trust." In his letter to Hart, Eisenhower emphasized the Knights' patriotic loyalty vis-à-vis state idolatry. "These words, 'under God,' will remind Americans that despite our great physical strength we must remain humble."[39]

The Order's promotion of religious values in the nation's public life frequently touched foreign policy. In response to the Hungarian revolution of 1956, Hart telephoned Presidential Assistant Sherman Adams on October 27, 1956, to urge the Eisenhower Administration to bring the issue of the Hungarian revolution to a special session of the U.N. with the hope that it would "take action with reference to the massacre of the people of Hungary by the Communist government of the Soviet Union." That same day the Supreme Board adopted a resolution "expressing the sympathy of our Order for the Hungarian people" and urging the U.N. "to take immediate steps to restrain the murderous assault of the armed troops of the Soviet Union." Hart was certain that the Order had "contributed much to the sentiment that was aroused and to what will, I confidently believe, be an end of the Communist misrule of weak and defenseless nations."[40]

During 1956 and 1957, when rumors circulated that President Eisenhower was planning to invite Marshal Josip Broz Tito of Yugoslavia to visit the United States, Hart responded with a vigorous protest. On December 19, 1956, Hart wired Eisenhower expressing his "amazement that he should consider inviting to this country the jailer of Cardinal Stepinac, the tyrant of Yugoslavia, the persecutor of religion, and the accomplice of the murderers of Budapest."[41] Hart's blistering wire was widely reported in the press and was followed by an appeal from Hart to the members to join in the Order's anti-Tito campaign.

On January 14, 1957, Hart telephoned the White House for an appointment to visit the President, who was then on a trip to the Southwest. Three days later the State Department informed Hart of the President's tour and imminent inauguration and asked if he would be willing to discuss the Tito matter with Undersecretary of State Robert T. Murphy. The following day Hart and Dan Daniel, the National Commander of the American Legion, met with Murphy at the State Department. Hart recalled, "Mr. Murphy told me that up to this time no invitation has been extended to Mr. Tito and although he gave us no assurance that an invitation may not be extended to him I am convinced of the sincerity of his statement that up to the present no such invitation has been extended. Mr. Murphy is a Catholic and I am confident that he is in sympathy with our viewpoint and that the decision, when it is made, will not be his but that of the President."[42] He was also confident that through public and congressional protest the Order's viewpoint would prevail.

Congressman John W. McCormack of Massachusetts, majority leader of the House and a Knight of Columbus, "cooperated in a wonderful way by himself issuing a public protest" and by sponsoring a congressional anti-Tito petition.[43] Though several other organizations also sponsored protests, when the Eisenhower Administration announced on January 31, 1957, that Tito would not be visiting the United States, Hart claimed a victory for the Order. "The entire undertaking was led by the Knights of Columbus. Without the leadership that our Order provided, the protest would have amounted to little and except for what was done by our Order and in its name, Tito . . . would have partaken of our hospitality and would have returned to Belgrade with added prestige."[44] *Time* magazine credited the Knights with a leading role but implied that even without the Order's participation the anti-Tito movement would have been successful.[45] In mid-December 1956, Hart wrote to Secretary of State John Foster Dulles, informing him of his opposition to the Secretary's statement to the effect that no situation would warrant the United States "going to war to protect an oppressed people from a tyrant."[46] Hart told Dulles that there were several historical precedents for defending oppressed people from a tyrant. "I told him we did it in Cuba and there is no question that it was pressure of sentiment in this country that brought about the relief of Ireland in 1921 and helped the Mexicans in the middle twenties and again in the middle thirties."[47]

Hart incorporated his victory over Tito into the general celebration of the Order's Diamond Jubilee. The Order's anniversary was highlighted by the dedication of a statue of Father Michael McGivney in his hometown of Waterbury, by a *Life* magazine cover story on the Knights, and by the Supreme Council meeting in Chicago. On March 29, 1957, the 75th anniversary of the incorporation of the Order in Connecticut, nearly ten thousand people gathered to witness the dedication of the bronze statue of the Order's founder. Sculpted by Joseph A. Coletti of Boston, the statue portrayed Father McGivney, in the words of Coletti, "as a spiritual leader of his people. He is garbed in a simple cassock and cloak and with his left hand holds the book of the gospel. . . . His right hand is raised heavenward to represent the Kingdom of God. . . . His gaze, too, is upward and his face expresses spiritual bliss and vision. The bronze reliefs of the four principles of the Knights of Columbus—Charity, Unity, Fraternity, and Patriotism, which adorn the pedestal—are conceived to be allegorical representatives of the Christian fabric of our society and life."[48]

The *Life* cover story of the Order's Diamond Jubilee originated at the suggestion of Luke Hart. Since *Life* had featured the Masons in its October 8, 1956, issue, the editors were vulnerable to the suggestion that the magazine feature the 75th anniversary of the Knights.[49] After several months of preparation, the article appeared in the May 27, 1957, edition. Like the piece on the Masons, that on the Knights was a pictorial essay which highlighted the ceremonial character of the Order. Other photos included ceremonies of the Fourth Degree, the Squires, the Columbiettes (an unofficial women's auxiliary), and the Zouave Drill Team of the St. Louis, Missouri, Knights. Because the latter organizations were on the remote fringes of the Order, Hart and others were somewhat disturbed by *Life*'s presentation. However, photos and texts on Hart in his office and at Yankee Stadium, and coverage of the Catholic Advertising and Vatican Film Library programs, struck the Supreme Knight as representative of the Order's broad interests and influence.[50] Though Hart publicly admitted that his views and those of *Life*'s editors "did not in every way coincide," he was extremely gratified that a magazine with an estimated readership of 28 million "brought our Order favorably to the attention of millions of people who previously had known little or nothing at all about it."[51]

At the Diamond Jubilee meeting of the Supreme Council in Chicago, Hart reviewed the year's celebrations on both the Supreme and local levels. The Order had reached a membership of one million during the previous year, but over forty thousand men became Knights during the Diamond Jubilee. The insurance program under Hart grew enormously; between 1953 and 1957 the amount of insurance in force grew from $420 million to nearly $690 million, while total assets exceeded $124 million. In his report Hart answered the rhetorical question, "What are you trying to do, make an insurance organization out of the Knights of Columbus?" by stating, "Of course. . . . Father McGivney made an insurance organization out of it. That was its primal purpose and it has never been otherwise."[52] Once again he recalled the days of the Great Depression, when associate membership declined by 67 percent while insurance members remained committed to the Order. He was particularly proud of the Order's growth in the noninsurance jurisdictions.

Two years before the Order celebrated its Diamond Jubilee, the Philippines and Mexico jurisdictions celebrated their Golden Jubilee. As mentioned in Chapter Five, Manila Council No. 1000 was founded in 1905 by American Knights attached to the U.S. Civil Service administering affairs in the Philippines. By 1920, membership in the council was predominantly Filipino. World War II wrought such havoc that the council ceased all activity. With the liberation of Manila, Council No. 1000 became an official welfare agency, but its offices and supplies had been destroyed by fire. On March 21, 1945, Grand Knight Gabriel Lao wrote to the Supreme Office seeking financial aid, whereupon Supreme Knight Matthews turned to the N.C.C.S. for welfare funds. Though the American Catholic agency responded by wiring money, wartime complications prevented its reaching Manila Council. Assisted by Council Chaplain George J. Willmann, S.J., Lao once again wrote to New Haven for financial assistance. The Supreme Board immediately responded with an appropriation of $10,000 to assist the council's welfare work.[53]

In the immediate postwar years, Manila Council gradually revived. Father Willmann, who envisioned the Order as the paramount lay society in the Philippines, set out to recruit members and establish new councils. During a visit to the United States in 1947, he convinced Hart of the need for the Order's expansion and proposed the establishment of three new councils in the Islands. Hart recalled the visit with Willmann. "I was somewhat dubious about agreeing to the proposal, but when it was stated that unless we afforded the Filipino men an opportunity to join the Knights of Columbus, they would join the Masons, I agreed to make the recommendation to the Supreme Board of Directors on condition that Willmann would himself act as District Deputy and have supervision of the councils."[54] In October 1947 the Board approved Willmann's proposal, which turned out to be so successfully implemented that by the time Hart visited Manila Council (April 1955) there were more than fifty councils in the Philippines. In the pages of *Columbia* and at the 1955 Supreme Council meeting, Hart reported that the Filipino membership "embraces men from every walk of life, including many of influence and high standing in the affairs of the nation." As if to testify that Father Willmann's dream had been realized, Hart noted that the "Hierarchy and the clergy . . . regard it [the Order] as a most important factor in the lives of the people and in the welfare of the Church."[55] Indeed, unlike Knights in other jurisdictions (except Mexico), the Filipino K. of C. was placed on a canonical basis as the Church's official Catholic Action society. Though the Order in the Philippines achieved unique status and developed as a parish society, its growth there was in accord with its origins as a Catholic response to the general drift toward proscribed secret societies such as the Masons. Father Willmann's successor, Oscar Ledesmá, was a former ambassador to the United States. He and Monsignor Francisco Tantoco, Jr., National Secretary, have presided over the continued growth of the Order in the Islands. In 1980, when Supreme Knight Virgil Dechant visited the jurisdiction on its Diamond Jubilee, there were 40,000 Filipino Knights.

During the Order's Mexican Campaign (1926–37), Hart had been the chief strategist in the Knights' lobbying efforts. In his report on his September 1955 visit to Mexico, he included many references to the previous period of religious persecution and to the suppression of the Knights of Columbus. He recalled his own role in the Order's Mexican Campaign and expressed his gratitude that the Mexican Knights were flourishing with over five thousand members in forty-three councils.[56] Hart's tour of several Mexican councils was highlighted with several religious ceremonies, but unlike the Philippines, where he met with President Ramon Magsaysay, the political climate in Mexico precluded visits with civil dignitaries. However, the historic alliance between the Knights and the Mexican hierarchy was closely evidenced in Hart's several meetings with Church officials, including the Apostolic Delegate, Archbishop Guillermo Piani, who twenty-five years earlier had become a Knight while in the Philippines.[57]

Cuba was another jurisdiction which celebrated its Golden Anniversary during Luke Hart's tenure of office. Havana Council was founded in 1909 by American Knights stationed in Cuba during the second U.S. intervention. By the 1920s the composition of its membership was predominantly Cuban. Because the Spanish colonial government and the Church had been united, anticlericalism and Cuban patriotism were nearly synonymous. Hence the Order's anti-defamation character became the unifying force among practicing Catholics eager to assert the compatibility of Catholicism with loyalty to the anticolonialist basis of the Cuban political ethos.

By the time of its Golden Jubilee in 1959, Cuba numbered twenty-nine councils with nearly three thousand members. Though the revolutionary government of Fidel Castro had come to power in late 1958, it had yet to turn to the extreme left. Since many Knights had joined in the struggle against President Fulgencio Batista, the Order confidently invited Castro to attend a Fourth Degree banquet in honor of the Golden Jubilee. At the banquet Castro was represented by an aide who listened to several patriotic speeches by leading Knights. One speaker, a Past State Deputy, spoke of the Knights' participation in the revolutionary army and attempted to dispel rumors that the revolutionary government was Marxist-dominated.[58] Hart did not attend the ceremonies, but at the 1959 Supreme Council meeting the State Deputy of Cuba, Julio Jover Vidal, presented him with a plaque in gratitude for his role in "making the people of the United States acquainted with the truth about what went on in Cuba after the recent revolution in that country."[59] The Cuban Knights honored Hart because *Columbia* had published an article (March 1959) by Richard Pattee, who had documented the Catholic participation in the revolution and expressed hope in Castro's government.[60]

Hart was also impressed with Castro during this period. In April 1959 he attended a luncheon in Castro's honor sponsored by the Overseas Press Club. The following August, Hart wrote Castro that he was disappointed that he did not have "the privilege" of meeting with the Prime Minister. However, the purpose of the letter was to inquire about the imprisonment of a Knight of Columbus and to assure Castro that he "did not believe he would be guilty of any offense against your government."[61] The Chief Director of the Prime Minister's office responded that "serious charges" had been posted against the Cuban Knight, but he assured Hart "that no injustice will be done to him by the Revolutionary Government."[62] Within a year after Hart wrote his cordial letter to Castro, the Cuban revolution entered its radical Communist phase and refugees began streaming into Florida. Many Cuban Knights sought refuge in Miami, among whom were fourteen Grand Knights of Councils in Cuba. Hart and Florida State Deputy John W. Adamson agreed that the situation required the institution of a new council in Miami. Our Lady of Charity Council No. 5110, led by Grand Knight Luis Felipe Lay, a son of a Past State Deputy of Cuba, became a virtual Cuban council in exile.[63] Though there were thirty councils in Cuba in 1980, they are isolated from the Supreme Office.

From its origins the Order had struggled against myriad forms of anti-Catholicism. With the elections of Pope John XXIII and President John F. Kennedy, two anti-Catholic caricatures were exposed as shams. The warm jovial earthiness of Pope John XXIII dispelled the anti-Catholic myth which portrayed papal power in terms of a design for world conquest, while the generally esteemed leadership qualities of John Kennedy put to rest the bias that Catholicism and American democracy were inherently contradictory. The Knights had mourned the death of Pope Pius XII, who had been so intimately associated with the Order's welfare work in Rome. But the strong K. of C.–Vatican association continued during the reign of John XXIII. Luke Hart and Joseph Lamb were in the first row at his coronation, and six months later John XXIII became the first pope to visit a K. of C. playground.[64] On May 10, 1959, he toured St. Peter's Oratory with Count Galeazzi and Alfredo Cardinal Ottaviani. *L'Osservatore Romano* reported that the Pope had been familiar with the work of the Order in Rome through his close friendship with Cardinal Borgongini-Duca, a former director of the Oratory.[65] The Pope's gentle, unassuming, pastoral manner led Hart to "dream of what a wonderful thing it would be" if Pope John would visit the United States for the dedication of the National Shrine.[66] The Supreme Knight, on behalf of the Supreme Council, did invite the Pope to make such a visit, but Hart's dream never materialized. However, in the spring of 1961 the entire Supreme Board visited Rome to inspect the playgrounds and was privileged to be received in a papal audience, during which time Hart informed the Pope of the Order's history and programs. Pope John responded with praise for the Knights' "manifold works," which he compared to "the harmonious notes of a musical melody filling the air all around him."[67]

Though Pope John's informality endeared him to the American public, the P.O.A.U. persisted in publicizing its opinion that the Church was un-American and anti-democratic, and, during 1960, it and several other groups injected the issue of Catholic loyalty into the election campaign. The Order's constitution precluded its official endorsement of political candidates, but it was particularly vigilant in countering the role of religious prejudice in the campaign. Thus the Order did not hesitate to respond when anti-Catholics circulated the Fourth Degree bogus oath—John F. Kennedy was a Fourth Degree Knight.

Luke Hart and Supreme Advocate Harold Lamboley were inundated with letters from members on the widespread circulation of the bogus oath. Though early in the campaign Hart was of the opinion that "everybody is pretty much alive now to the fact that this document is a bogus," during the last few months before the election he and Lamboley had to dedicate "a tremendous amount of time" responding to its circulation.[68] Hart's policy did not include legal prosecution unless the printer or publisher of the "oath" refused to retract, to apologize, and to give assurances that its publication would be discontinued. W. L. King, an ordained minister who published *The Voice of the Nazarene* in Elizabeth, Pennsylvania, was one publisher whom the Order was compelled to prosecute. He distributed many thousands of copies of the bogus oath throughout the country. On September 16, 1960, a Pennsylvania court issued a preliminary injunction against King.[69] In its August 22 issue, *Time* magazine reported on the history of the bogus oath, "an old and notorious piece of anti-Catholic propaganda," and noted its circulation in many states. At the 1960 Supreme Council meeting in Atlanta, the delegates adopted a resolution that an official letter be sent to the editor of *Time* commending the magazine for publishing the "excellent and timely article, 'The Fake Oath.' "[70]

In his campaign against the bogus oath, Hart consulted with the leaders of the Anti-Defamation League of B'nai Brith. "They were quite pleased with the way in which we have undertaken to suppress the bogus oath. They have a very kindly feeling for Catholics, because they feel that both groups are discriminated against and it is their opinion that the vast majority of the Jewish people will vote for Kennedy."[71] Hart was convinced that the election of Kennedy "would do more to eliminate bigotry in this country than anything else that ever happened."[72] Though he was a conservative Republican, Hart was enthusiastic in his support for Kennedy. He was not concerned with Kennedy's close ties "with the so-called liberal element" because he was "confident that he [Kennedy] would take advice from his father and this is pretty much of a guarantee that he would keep his feet on the ground."[73]

Kennedy's now famous address to the Greater Houston Minister-ial Association on September 12 included several comments reflecting the Order's traditional notions of Columbianism. He referred to the battle of the Alamo: "side by side with Bowie and Crockett died McCaffey and Bailey and Carey, but no one knows whether they were Catholics or not. For there was no religious test at the Alamo." Kennedy also pledged his belief in an America "that is officially neither Catholic, Protestant, nor Jewish . . . and where religious liberty is so indivisible that an act against one church is treated as an act against all."[74] Historians generally agree that the Houston speech greatly reduced the significance of the religious issue. Though the editor of *Columbia* insisted that there was no large "Catholic vote" in the election, it is very likely that many Republican Knights, like Luke Hart, were drawn to Kennedy as an excellent representative of a man of their faith and Order, one whose election would mark a new era in Catholic life in America.[75]

On October 11, 1961, Luke Hart visited the President at the White House. Kennedy greeted Hart with the remark, "Hello, Chief, you know I am a Fourth Degree member of the Knights of Columbus." Kennedy was a member of Bunker Hill Council No. 62 and Bishop Cheverus General Assembly Fourth Degree. The President informed the Supreme Knight that his younger brother Edward had received "his Third Degree in our Order three weeks before." Hart presented Kennedy with a Fourth Degree emblem, which "he immediately put . . . in his lapel," and with a special picture of the American Flag with the Pledge of Allegiance, which also included the story of how the Order achieved the "under God" amendment.[76] Hart invited Kennedy to speak at the Supreme Council meeting in Boston the following August and reminded him that his grandfather, John F. Fitzgerald, had addressed the 1913 meeting in that city.[77]

The Supreme Chaplain, Monsignor Leo M. Finn, never witnessed the Kennedy years, as he died suddenly on October 30, 1960. Hart lost not only a valuable adviser on ecclesiastical affairs but a close confidant as well. "I consulted with him freely and he knew my innermost thoughts."[78] To replace Finn, Hart turned to Bishop Charles P. Greco, ordinary of the diocese of Alexandria, Louisiana. On November 22, Hart visited with Bishop Greco in Shreveport. When Hart broached the topic of Supreme Chaplaincy, the bishop stated that he was greatly honored, and the Supreme Board officially appointed Bishop Greco the following January 14. Greco had joined the Order in 1918 at the invitation of the Knights of Houma Council No. 1317. He became Council Chaplain, and after his appointment as Bishop of Alexandria in 1946 he was appointed State Chaplain. The Louisiana Knights worked closely with the bishop on several projects in his diocese, particularly the K. of C. Morey Hill Youth Camp. He came to the attention of the Supreme Officers at the Supreme Council meeting of 1954 in Louisville, Kentucky, where he addressed the delegates on the honorable principles and programs of the Order.[79] Upon assuming the office of Supreme Chaplain, Bishop Greco initiated a Religion Outline Program for chaplains. A warm, jovial person like John XXIII, Bishop Greco was the first member of the hierarchy to serve as Supreme Chaplain. His amiable, peaceful personality was well suited for the position, particularly since his appointment occurred during a period when Hart was severely criticized by other prelates for his poor handling of a strike by the home office employees in New Haven.

The employees, predominantly women, organized their union in May 1955. Perhaps the organizers would have been unable to muster a majority had Hart imposed a standardized wage scale and had he not arbitrarily removed two paid holidays. Unaccustomed to managing a large office staff of over four hundred employees, Hart tended toward paternalism, and when confronted with what he considered to be disloyalty or insubordination he would become all the more intransigent. Because contract negotiations had broken down, the union went on strike on August 15, 1955, a day before the 1955 Supreme Council meeting. Though the strike was settled within four days, Archbishop Henry J. O'Brien of Hartford, as well as Monsignor Joseph Donnelly, his spokesman on labor issues, and other clergymen issued statements to the effect that the strike was an embarrassment to the archdiocese of Hartford and explicitly sided with the union. Hart considered such action unjust ecclesiastical interference, and after the strike had been settled he placed his case before the Apostolic Delegate, Archbishop Amleto Cicognani, who strongly supported Hart's position: "The Knights of Columbus is not an organization of the Church. It is a body of Catholic men having an independent status and its own program and its own objectives. It has a right to conduct its business as it sees fit without interference from the hierarchy or the clergy."[80] The second office strike lasted from November 1, 1959, to February 1, 1960. The primary issue was working conditions—sick leave, etc.—rather than money. Apparently deterred by Cicognani's 1955 statement, Archbishop O'Brien and Monsignor Donnelly remained aloof from the strike, but *America* and *Ave Maria* were severely critical of the Order.[81]

A 1962 strike of the Pressmen's Union at the Order's printing plant, one which lasted over ten months, received national attention. The major issue was wages, but there were several factors which contributed to the strike's complexity. There were only twelve pressmen, and the two other unions at the printing plant did not respect their picket line. Moreover, Hart was determined to see the Order's publications—*Columbia* and the *K. of C. News*—published on time, so he contracted for the printing to firms outside of New Haven, which invited charges of hiring strikebreakers. The *Catholic Transcript,* official newspaper of the archdiocese of Hartford, lashed out at Hart, as did the association of Catholic Trade Unionists. In response, Hart had *Columbia* publish a chart illustrating the fact that the K. of C. pressmen were offered higher wages and better fringe benefits than pressmen at other New Haven shops.[82] On October 26, 1962, the Supreme Board adopted a resolution which confirmed the right of the Order to handle its business affairs "without interference of others regardless of their position or rank."[83] The editors of *Ave Maria* (a publication of the Holy Cross Fathers of the University of Notre Dame) concluded that the resolution "sounds as though it was composed in a moment of unthinking anger at the K. of C. critics."[84] Indeed, Hart's anger was frequently vented when the Order was under attack by ecclesiastics and Catholic journalists, who criticized the Knights for not abiding by the moral precepts of the Church. Hart's standard defense, that the

Order is an organization of Catholics, not a Catholic organization, was unconvincing. For example, the *St. Louis Review,* the newspaper of that archdiocese, pointed out that the K. of C. sought good press coverage and praise for its Catholic Action projects but considered adverse criticism as interference. "Presumably it was permissible for . . . diocesan papers to publish accounts of . . . Mr. Hart's speech on the lay apostolate. This would be coverage of 'an organization of Catholics.' But when the same organization is accused of strikebreaking and kindred evils the diocesan press must remember that it is not a Catholic organization, and hence is exempt from this type of publicity." The editors concluded with the remark that, regardless of how the Knights choose to define themselves, "Christian principles are involved and the simple question is: Are the Knights observing them or not?"[85] To Hart the question was a simple business issue involving adversary relations between management and labor. Since he offered the pressmen higher wages than other union shops, he felt that he had been fair. As for the charges of strikebreaking, he felt a higher duty to publish the Order's magazine for its members than he did toward the union. However, the far larger issue for Hart was that his critics among the Catholic press never consulted with him privately.

Throughout Hart's term as Supreme Knight, the Order was frequently accused of racism. Traditionally the Knights responded to such charges by noting that the Order's constitution did not prohibit black members, that its application for membership did not inquire as to the candidate's race or color, and that the members of the local council voted on the candidate according to their consciences, with five no votes constituting a rejection of the candidate. By the late 1950s, Hart was encouraging councils to accept black candidates, but he refused to advocate mandatory reforms. Father John La Farge, S.J., founder of the Catholic interracial movement, stated in 1959 that "we badly need a new and enlightened policy on the part of . . . the Knights of Columbus, even though fragments of its honor are saved by the interracial membership of some of its councils." By 1961 Hart was boasting that the Order included thousands of black members; however, when asked to publish photos of black members, he refused on the grounds that it would be patronizing. "I think Negroes should come in just as the other people come in and that from the Supreme Council's standpoint it should not be regarded as something that is extraordinary."[86]

Obviously, Hart was far from an enthusiastic integrationist. His conservative gradualist approach prevented him from advocating a change in the blackball system, which allowed a tiny minority to discriminate against black candidates. He withstood the severe criticism of hundreds of ecclesiastics and journalists until late 1963. In the spring of that year he attended a special meeting of religious leaders at the White House to discuss the civil rights issue. Though his attitudes may have been affected by the discussion led by the President he greatly admired, the immediate occasion for his change in attitude was an incident which occurred in Chicago in mid-November. When a black candidate for membership, a graduate of the University of Notre Dame, was rejected, six council officers resigned in protest. The incident achieved national notoriety; Bishop Cletus F. O'Donnell, auxiliary of the Chicago archdiocese, and the Chicago Catholic Interracial Council spoke out against the blackball system. Apparently moved to consider the good of the Order within such a dramatically controversial situation, Hart announced that he favored a "full airing of the membership proceedings" at the August 1964 meeting of the Supreme Council.[87]

Hart never participated in that discussion, for on February 19, 1964, he died at the age of eighty-four. As will be detailed in the next chapter, the racial issue was resolved under the direction of Supreme Knight John W. McDevitt. Hart bequeathed several items of unfinished business to his successor, but he also left a legacy of over one million members and over one billion dollars of insurance in force. Though he was an extremely complex person, his manifold character was integrated by his deep sense of loyalty to the Order. The fact that he was a Supreme Officer for nearly forty-two years is not as significant as the way in which he interpreted his role as Supreme Advocate and as Supreme Knight. Because he was such a powerful and outspoken leader, he engendered opposition within the Order and the Church. However, he had such a profound impact upon the Order that by 1964 the Knights of Columbus and Luke Hart were synonymous.

16

John W. McDevitt and
the Preservation
of Catholic Fraternalism

JOHN W. McDEVITT, who had been the first home-office-resident
Deputy Supreme Knight since 1961, was elected Supreme Knight
shortly after Hart's funeral in St. Louis. Though he was greatly influenced by Hart, nearly two generations separated McDevitt from his
octogenarian predecessor. While Hart was a State Deputy during
World War I, McDevitt did not hold that position until after World
War II. Indeed, McDevitt was the first Supreme Knight born in the
twentieth century. A native of Malden, Massachusetts, a town in the
greater Boston area, McDevitt was born in December 1906. After he
received an undergraduate degree in 1928 and an M.A. in 1929 from
Boston College, he became a teacher and later principal at Malden
High School. From 1942 to 1961 he was Superintendent of Schools in
Waltham, Massachusetts, served on various school boards, and was
chairman of the Massachusetts State Board of Education. A member
of Santa Maria Council No. 105, McDevitt served in various local and
state offices but, as mentioned in Chapter 13, gained national attention
during the Massachusetts insurance debacle in 1948 when he was State
Deputy. His experience in this extremely volatile situation seems to
have influenced his style of leadership, which was that of a broker of
consensus who nevertheless was not reluctant to take a firm position
on issues. These qualities became extremely valuable as the leadership
of the Order passed into the hands of a new generation.

Supreme Advocate Harold Lamboley, who followed Hart into the
office in 1953, had also been a State Deputy during the post–World
War II period and was well known for his ability as a facilitator of
compromise. Supreme Secretary D. Francis Sullivan had succeeded
Joseph Lamb, who died just three weeks before Hart. Sullivan was the
first Supreme Officer to have risen within the home office rather than

within the state council offices. Because he had been Lamb's Assistant Supreme Secretary since 1948 and was of Luke Hart's generation, he represented continuity during a period of rapid change. Upon Sullivan's retirement in 1967, his young assistant, Virgil C. Dechant, Past State Deputy of Kansas, became Supreme Secretary. By this time Francis Heazel had retired and Daniel L. McCormick was Supreme Treasurer. Born in Newark, New Jersey, in 1913, McCormick was Grand Knight of South Orange Council No. 1831 in 1945–46 and State Deputy in 1956–57. In February 1964, he was appointed to fill the unexpired term of Luke Hart on the Board of Directors, and in October of the next year he became Supreme Treasurer after a brief period as Heazel's assistant. John H. Griffin, M.D., a Supreme Director since 1960, succeeded John McDevitt as Deputy Supreme Knight. Though a native of Peabody, Massachusetts (born in 1914), and a graduate of Boston College and Tufts Medical School, Dr. Griffin entered the Order in Maryland in 1947 after he left the U.S. Navy Medical Corps. After serving as Grand Knight of Bryantown Council No. 2293, he rose to State Deputy in 1960. Upon the retirement of Dr. Gerald Lunz, he was elected Supreme Physician in October 1966.

Thus, within a short time after he became Supreme Knight, John McDevitt was assisted by officers far removed from the generation of Luke Hart. However, each of them was influenced by and deeply indebted to Hart, for he had bequeathed to them a membership of over one million, assets in the hundreds of millions, a thriving insurance program, and a modern corporate structure through which they could govern the Order effectively. Though McDevitt and the other officers were, like Hart, traditionalists in their Columbianism, they had not experienced that period in the Church when Cardinal Gibbons strengthened the Knights' autonomy by relying so strongly upon the organization, nor had they witnessed the Knights of Columbus–N.C.W.C. struggles during the twenties and thirties. Unlike Hart, McDevitt did not view the N.C.W.C. or the bishops as a threat to the Order's independent status. Nevertheless, he was soon to be put to the test in resolving difficult issues with the hierarchy. He was also called upon to lead the Order during the crises of the sixties, when every Catholic organization was compelled to justify its existence in light of the Second Vatican Council, when every patriotic organization was confronted with a barrage of radical protests, and when every defender of traditional morality was criticized in the light of the general permissiveness of the era. McDevitt vigorously responded to these crises by anchoring the Order in the relatively conservative consensus of the

American hierarchy, by reiterating the Order's traditional antipathy to elitist reformers (i.e., John Swift's Catholic populism), and by reasserting the Knights' cultural conservatism on the role of women and on divorce, birth control, abortion, and pornography.

II

Next to establishing a smooth transition of leadership, McDevitt's first priority was to heal the ruptures with the hierarchy. The Order's black-ball admissions policy, which had alienated many bishops, was a pressing concern. Ten days before the opening of the 1964 Supreme Council meeting, both *America* and *Ave Maria* published editorials urging the Order to change that policy. Though Hart had planned for a revision of the laws, McDevitt's fresh style of leadership engendered a sense of hope that finally something would actually be done to remedy the situation. In a preface to his statement on the issue at the 1964 convention in New Orleans, McDevitt said that "the hierarchy of the United States and Canada, yes, and the hierarchy in Rome await our thoughts on this matter."[1] His statement included a commitment to local democratic procedures on admissions as well as several references to the fact that justice and charity demanded that the Order amend its rules on the process of admissions and "thereby remove forever the opportunities of prejudice that tend to dilute our judgment."[2] McDevitt referred to Bishop Greco's *Pastoral on Race Relations,* which had been placed in each delegate's packet of convention material. The Supreme Chaplain's pastoral letter was a moderate piece of social commentary appended to a firm theological statement on racial justice. Though he was characteristically compassionate to those who may have opposed integration, he concluded, "If some choose to criticize my efforts . . . that is their concern; bringing you to Christ is mine, and all else is of little consequence."[3]

Twelve state delegations submitted resolutions to amend the admissions rule, but the Resolution Committee composed a substitute which was passed by the convention. The rules were changed to the effect that to reject an applicant a negative vote of one third of those present, rather than five blackballs, was required.[4] Because racial discrimination persisted as a factor in the selection process, the Supreme Council of 1972, at the strong urging of McDevitt, changed the rules so that it took a majority of those present to negate a candidate for membership.[5]

Supreme Knights Visit the Holy See

Eugenio Cardinal Pacelli, Vatican Secretary of State (later Pope Pius XII), visits the Supreme Office in New Haven, Connecticut, October 13, 1936. LEFT TO RIGHT, SEATED: Bishop Francis J. Spellman, Cardinal Pacelli, Supreme Knight Martin Carmody; STANDING: Assistant Supreme Secretary John Conway, Supreme Secretary William McGinley, Enrico Galeazzi, Knights of Columbus representative in Rome.

A private audience with Pope Pius XII, June 2, 1950. LEFT TO RIGHT: Monsignor Leo Finn, Supreme Knight John Swift, Supreme Advocate Luke Hart and Count Enrico Galeazzi.

A private audience with Pope John XXIII, April 14, 1961. LEFT TO RIGHT: Supreme Chaplain Bishop Charles P. Greco, Supreme Knight Hart and Deputy Supreme Knight McDevitt.

Supreme Knight McDevitt and Bishop Greco meet with Pope Paul VI, June, 1966.

Supreme Board of Directors meet with Pope Paul VI, April 10, 1978.

A private audience with Pope John Paul II. LEFT TO RIGHT: *Mrs. Ann Dechant, Supreme Knight Dechant, Pope John Paul II, Bishop Greco, Mrs. Mary Louise Griffin, Supreme Physician John Griffin, Count Enrico Galeazzi.*

Three of the Seven Knights' Playgrounds in Rome

San Lorenzo playground

Oratory of San Pietro

*Valle Giulia playground—in the backgro
the Basilica of St. Eugenio, patron se
Pope Pius XII.*

For devotion to Mary

For vocations

For the retarded. Bishop Greco's dedication to provide for the retarded has become the Knights' special charity.

For family life. Mother Teresa of Calcutta and Supreme Physician Griffin chat at Family of the Americas Conference. (Guatemala City, August, 1980.)

For the deaf. In Texas, a choir sings with hand signs.

For the senior citizens

For the North American hierarchy. One of several meetings of Bishops sponsored by the John XXIII Medical-Moral Research and Education Center and funded by the Knights of Columbus. (Dallas, Texas, January, 1980.)

For devotion to the Holy Family. This chapel in the Supreme Office, New Haven, Connecticut, was erected in 1980 and dedicated to the Holy Family.

Though Hart had frequently observed that there were 10,000 black Knights in the early sixties, he never presented any evidence to support that figure. The racial issue at the 1964 convention was not limited to this significant reform of the admissions policy. A few days before the convention was to meet in New Orleans, McDevitt received word that the Roosevelt Hotel, the scheduled site of the convention, had a color-bar restriction for guests; McDevitt immediately threatened to move the convention to another hotel. Archbishop John P. Cody of New Orleans also applied pressure upon the management. Ultimately the hotel changed its policy; to symbolize the victory over racial discrimination, a black priest, Father Harold R. Perry, who later became an auxiliary bishop of New Orleans, sat at the head table at the annual States Dinner held at the Roosevelt during the convention.[6]

Relations between the Supreme Office and the Archdiocese of Hartford had been deteriorating ever since Archbishop Henry O'Brien had criticized Hart's handling of the strike of 1955. After John McDevitt became Supreme Knight, he sought a rapprochement with the archbishop which culminated in the restoration of harmony and good will between the Order and the archdiocese. In April 1965 the Knights and O'Brien co-sponsored the Archbishop's Conference on Human Rights held at Yale University. More than two thousand people attended the conference, which, under the theme "From Words to Action," was dedicated to discerning ways of achieving interracial justice. The Supreme Board of Directors was so impressed with the conference that it successfully introduced a motion at the 1965 Supreme Council urging state and local councils to sponsor similar conventions.[7]

At the 1964 convention, McDevitt announced to the delegates that he had settled another dispute with the hierarchy, one he had inherited from Luke Hart. During the latter years of the Hart administration, the Supreme Knight placed rigid controls upon the modest insurance program which the Mexican State Council had established in the 1920s to conform to laws prohibiting the sale of American insurance policies. By the early 1960s, Hart was so convinced that the Mexican program, which had developed a rather large mortuary fund, was not based upon sound business principles that he imposed strict rules for its management to protect both the Mexican Knights and the Order's business reputation. However, in the process he appointed a Knight to a responsible position who was not a state official and who was *persona non grata* to the Mexican hierarchy, particularly to Archbishop Miguel Dario Miranda of the archdiocese of Mexico City. Hence, the conflict over the insurance program, which was itself very complex, was compounded by political conflict between Hart and the State Council and by the role of the hierarchy in this issue. Hart bitterly resented Miranda's interference and insisted that the State Council conform to his demands. Miranda responded by advising the State Officers to disregard Hart's orders when they met at the State Convention of May 1962. When Hart heard this he successfully urged the Supreme Board to suspend the entire Mexican State Council.[8]

Over the next ten months the situation was polarized as both Hart and the Mexican State Council, supported by Archbishop Miranda, held firm to their positions. At its April 1963 meeting, the Supreme Board suspended all the Mexican Knights who had been engaged in the management of the insurance program. In retaliation the State Council, with prior approval from a special meeting of the Mexican Knights, announced (on April 23) that the jurisdiction was no longer affiliated with the Supreme Council.[9] By this time the apostolic delegates to Mexico and to the United States had entered the conflict, as well as the leaders of the Mexican hierarchy. Hart's insistence that his appointees manage the insurance program and his assertion of the Order's independence from the hierarchy were the central points of conflict. Hart himself appeared to have been unaware of the fact that, since the Order in Mexico was an authorized Catholic Action society, it came under the direction of the hierarchy. Though Hart had attempted to persuade his opponents both in correspondence and during a visit to Mexico, he died with the crisis still unresolved. Indeed, a month before his death he vigorously defended the Order's autonomy in a letter to the Archbishop of Guadelajara, José Cardinal A. Garibi.[10]

Five weeks after he became Supreme Knight, John McDevitt, accompanied by Bishop Greco, met with Cardinal Garibi, Archbishop Miranda, and the Apostolic Delegate in Mexico, Archbishop Luigi Raimondi, at the latter's home in Mexico City. Greco, who had attempted to persuade Hart to alter his position, had informed McDevitt that months earlier the Pope had indicated his concern with the Order's Mexican problems. The new Supreme Knight expressed his eagerness to achieve a peaceful solution to the conflict and his regrets over the recalcitrant behavior of his predecessor. Since McDevitt deferred to the wishes of the hierarchy and indicated that he would be bound neither by Hart's unpopular appointments nor by the suspension of leading Knights, those points of conflict were quickly resolved, allowing the group to discuss the rules governing proper management of the insurance program. John McDevitt reported to the delegates to the 1964 convention on the results of this and subsequent meetings with the leaders of the Mexican jurisdiction. "Discussions were guided by charity and discipline," and mutual respect and harmony had been achieved.[11] To symbolize that peace had been restored and to assure the Mexican Knights that the needs of their jurisdiction would be represented on the highest level, McDevitt successfully supported the candidacy of José Cardenas Stille, a Mexican Knight, for a position on the Supreme Board.

After McDevitt responded to those members of the hierarchy alienated by Hart's policies on racial integration, industrial relations, and the Mexican issue, he developed his own agenda for the Knights in the 1960s. However, to assure that the Order would never again be led by a Supreme Knight whose age might obstruct his vision of the future, McDevitt successfully urged the 1964 Supreme Council convention to pass a mandatory retirement age of seventy for all Supreme Officers, and to make anyone who had reached the age of seventy ineligible for election to the Board.

At the 1965 and 1966 meetings of the Supreme Council, he set forth the principles upon which the Order's programs would be developed. Opposed to what he perceived as the new individualism and "rebellious spirit" in Church and society, McDevitt interpreted *aggiornamento* in accord with Pope Paul VI's admonitions to proceed with reform and renewal gradually, cautiously, and with fidelity to the changeless core of faith.[12] Therefore, McDevitt stated that the Knights, within the context of the Second Vatican Council, "shall be characterized by respect, reverence, and relevance."[13] In contrast to various secular and ecclesiastical dissidents, the Order would respect all legitimately constituted authority, with particular reverence for the bishops and the pope. In response to these "unenlightened critics" of the Order's conservatism, McDevitt committed the Knights to "a dynamism which is willing to adapt, to explore, and to act."[14] Subsequently, he advocated improving the role of women and the family in the programs of the Order and reforming the ceremonials in the light of "present spiritual and liturgical concepts."[15]

When the Supreme Knight referred to "unenlightened critics," he must have had in mind William J. Whalen, a former Knight, who wrote an article for *U.S. Catholic* entitled "The Knights of Columbus: Are They Obsolete?" Though Whalen applauded the Knights for finally eliminating the blackball system and for their various Catholic Action endeavors, he concluded that the Order was facing obsolescence. In light of the general decline of fraternalism and the challenges of Vatican II, Whalen urged the Knights to shed their ceremonial character, establish rigid attendance requirements for council meetings, and shift their emphasis from insurance programs to ecumenical, liturgical, and social justice projects.[16]

Whalen was a relatively mild critic in contrast to Edward Wakin and Joseph Scheuer, authors of *The De-Romanization of the American Catholic Church,* which was published in 1966 before the Supreme Council meeting. Wakin and Scheuer criticized the Order's racial and labor policies and concluded that it was an outmoded "secret society [which] long outlived the usefulness of its original service as a lodge." They indicted *Columbia* for its "corny Catholicism" and interpreted the Order's character as more dependent upon the secular environment than Catholicism. Accordingly, they viewed the Knights as "well-meaning, middle-class, mediocre, and conformist."[17]

At the 1966 Supreme Council convention, McDevitt responded to Wakin and Scheuer by noting that "as you know there are self-professed prophets on the American scene who equate criticism with progress and who see our Society in a state of helpless obsolescence and doomed to drawing its last gasps in the imminent future. They charge that death is overtaking us because we have succumbed to the disease of do-nothingness, social irresponsibility, and racial prejudice."[18] To illustrate the vitality of the Order, the Supreme Knight referred to the elimination of blackballing and the Order's co-sponsorship of the Human Rights Conference at Yale and announced to the delegates that the Order would help sponsor the John La Farge Institute, an ecumenical research and dialogue center dedicated to the solution of economic and social problems on the basis of Judeo-Christian moral principles. The Supreme Knight indicated that the Order would directly benefit from the Institute, as it would provide state and local councils with discussion material.[19] Since Father La Farge had admonished the Knights to abolish the blackball system a few years prior to this announcement, the Order had clearly made significant progress in a short time.

At the 1966 convention, McDevitt also noted that the evolution of American Catholicism had had an enormous impact upon the Order. Whereas in its infancy the Order "served principally as a fortress where members could gather and find mutual encouragement and strength against the slings of a society still hostile to both their religion and their nationality," by the 1960s the Catholic Church "has taken firm root and has become the leading Christian body in the land."

Therefore, McDevitt announced that "it is high time we abandon the concept of our Order as mainly a fortress to protect us from a hostile world. We are not a besieged minority."[20] He concluded by urging the Knights to embrace Vatican II's Pastoral Constitution on the Church in the Modern World *(Gaudium et Spes)*, which he likened to "a veritable banquet table from which our councils can choose additional programs to fit their interests and capabilities."[21] At the 1967 Supreme Council meeting, McDevitt reported that the La Farge Institute, "encouraged by the Knights of Columbus," had sponsored several ecumenical and social-action dialogues. "The entire purpose of this cooperation between the Knights of Columbus and the John La Farge Institute is to insure that our Order does ever more to bring the forces of our religious heritage to bear upon the many thorny problems of the modern world."[22] However, by 1967, developments within the American Church were reaching a condition of polarization. Thus in 1966, Father Gommar De Pauw, an embittered conservative, was severely critical of Church authority and was suspended by Lawrence Cardinal Shehan of Baltimore; while Father William A. Dubay was suspended by James Francis Cardinal McIntyre of Los Angeles because of his excessively liberal criticisms and behavior.[23]

Within the context of this polarized situation, McDevitt posed the question, "Is the Knights of Columbus a conservative or a progressive society?" He answered by stating that the Knights were "both progressive and conservative and we are neither." He explained that the Knights were progressive in their "efforts to shake the country free from any prejudice . . . to create conditions which will give every American a chance to obtain decent money . . . to eliminate poverty . . . [and to foster] interreligious and interracial understanding." The Knights' conservatism was exemplified by their deep attachment to Judeo-Christian morality, their anti-secularism, their patriotism, their loyalty to the bishops and the pope, and their disregard of "the haughty harangue or deceiving sophism of Father So and So's latest recital on 'Why I Left the Church.'" McDevitt rejected that type of progressivism which is based upon an "enchantment with the popular idea of change as such" as well as that form of conservatism which is dedicated "to the static philosophy of traditionalism." The Knights thus remained progressive on social issues but conservative on cultural issues, particularly on those related to the authority of the Church. In that time of "confusion and turbulence," McDevitt placed the Order squarely behind the hierarchy's responsibility "for teaching, sanctifying, and guiding the Church." In light of this commitment, the Order made a financial contribution of $60,000 to the Center for Applied Research in the Apostolate (C.A.R.A.), which was chaired by John Cardinal Krol and dedicated to a scientific study of the most effective ways of designing the Church's ministries to meet the new religious needs of the various groups within the Church.[24]

One expression of the Order's own *aggiornamento* was the sort of fraternal ecumenism which developed between the Knights and the Masons. Cooperation between the two fraternal societies had been occurring at the grass-roots level during the mid-1960s. The movement reached the national level in 1967 when, on Washington's Birthday, Supreme Knight McDevitt, accompanied by Deputy Supreme Knight Charles Ducey and Supreme Advocate Harold Lamboley, met with George M. Newbury, Sovereign Grand Commander of the Northern Jurisdiction of the Scottish Rite of Freemasonry; Frank C. Staples, Grand Master of Masons, State of New York; Irving Partridge, Deputy for Connecticut; and several other officials. At this "fraternal summit" the leaders discussed ways in which both societies could unite as "loyal dedicated citizens" in a common struggle "to combat and overcome the forces whose degenerative influence is becoming a crippling menace to our way of life."[25] Therefore, the Knights and the Masons agreed to join together in promoting patriotism, engendering "positive programs" of good citizenship and respect for constitutional authority, law, and order, and encouraging programs for youth to train citizens for responsible leadership in the democratic way of life.[26] This movement toward fraternal détente symbolized that the Order had truly shed its fortress mentality, but, more significantly, it also represented the Knights' recognition of the need for uniting with other fraternal organizations in the struggle against the disintegration of traditional notions of patriotism and morality.

Another development aimed at making the Order more relevant was the movement to revise the ceremonials. In 1965, McDevitt appointed a ceremonials commission chaired by the then Assistant Supreme Secretary, Charles J. Ducey. At the 1966 Supreme Council Convention, the Supreme Knight reported that the commission had prepared new ceremonies for the installation of various state and subordinate council officers and was studying ways to revise the initiation ceremonies which would be "consistent with modern day philosophy of social justice and religious practice."[27] The commission was spurred on by an incident which occurred during an initiation held at Pavia Council No. 48 in Bethel, Connecticut, in February 1966 when a candidate was injured. The candidate, who was hospitalized for minor injuries and who allegedly was psychologically traumatized by the event, received no compensation from the local council. The Supreme Office denied any responsibility for the behavior of the degree team, because the latter had violated the authorized code for conducting the Third Degree. (Eventually the candidate brought suit against the Order and the person who injured him. The incident received national publicity, and in 1970 the Court ruled that the Knights pay $60,000 in damages.)[28] Though some degree teams had violated the rules by engaging in excessive roughhousing, the traditional Third Degree was extremely popular among the membership. Indeed, at the first Supreme Council meeting (1969) following the Supreme Board's adoption of the revised ceremonials, a group of traditionalists hired a plane to fly over New Haven trailing a sign, "Preserve the Old." However, the revisions were officially approved and gained widespread acceptance over the years. The new ceremonials contained the traditional spirit of Columbianism, such as pride in one's Catholic roots, but modern social-justice principles were also incorporated into the initiation.

At the 1969 Supreme Council meeting in New Haven, Supreme Knight McDevitt defended the revised ceremonials within the historical evolution of the Order. He pointed out that they were originally designed to provide Catholic men with severe challenges to help sustain them in a hostile anti-Catholic environment. Because by the 1960s Catholics were no longer confronted with overt prejudice and discrimination and because the Second Vatican Council urged the laity to become a "vital force" in society, the older ceremonials were, according to McDevitt, unsuitable to contemporary Catholics. "Today's Catholic man, whatever his background or social class, is more sophisticated than ever before. He is more literate and more conscious of the psychological factors that motivate him and his society. He tends to be more moved by ideas than by rituals and to resent being forced into contrived situations of crisis. . . . We feel that the new ceremonials, properly performed, can talk to this modern man on his own terms and can give him sufficient motivation to persuade him to develop into an apostle ready for today."[29]

The development of structures to suit contemporary Catholics was visibly expressed in the Order's new home office building, which was completed in 1969. Located adjacent to the city's new civic and sports center, the twenty-three-story building, designed by Kevin Roche–John Dinkeloo and Associates, an internationally known architectural firm, was a part of Mayor Richard Lee's ambitious urban-renewal complex for downtown New Haven. Unlike Luke Hart, who remained aloof from New Haven's civic life, McDevitt involved the leadership of the Order in the local Chamber of Commerce and the United Way, while he himself became a director of several banking and philanthropic institutions. The former home office, which was in the old New Haven Railroad Building, was too small for the Order's staff. The large new glass-faced building which now dominates the city's skyline is set off by four 320-foot towers which symbolize the four principal ideas of the Order: Charity, Unity, Fraternity, and Patriotism.

In his address at the 1969 annual States' Dinner of the Supreme Council, John McDevitt stressed the notion of knightly devotion and loyalty to Church and country. However, he remarked that the defense of the faith was no longer limited to warding off the antireligious influences of secularism and atheism, nor was the defense of the fatherland limited to protecting the nation from enemy invasion; rather the enemy was located "within the border of our country [and] within the walls of our church." The Supreme Knight identified the enemy forces within the nation as "lawlessness . . . injustice, poverty, discrimination . . . neglect, lack of concern, and lack of dialogue." He portrayed the enemies within the Church as those who act as if every believer is "his own theologian and enjoys the infallible guidance of the Spirit" and as those whose behavior reveals a "false freedom of conscience which licenses the individual to do not as God says but as the person pleases."[30] He believed that the reason why monasteries and convents were being emptied and closed was because America's "affluent, permissive, and indulgent society—even among our Catholic people—has failed to cultivate the spirit of discipline, self-denial and dedication required to prepare youth for full consecration to the service of God."[31] Hence, McDevitt lashed out at those Catholics who in the name of relevance had capitulated to modern forms of materialism and individualism. The Supreme Knight's agenda for a new defense of faith and fatherland included fostering such programs as the La Farge Institute and the fulfillment of the goals of the Second Vatican Council under the guidance of the papacy and the hierarchy.[32]

Supreme Knight McDevitt not only restored harmony with the hierarchy but, within a condition of social and ecclesiastical polarization, he explicitly committed the Order to the Church's magisterium for direction on all moral and theological issues. Archbishop Luigi Raimondi, Apostolic Delegate in the United States, acknowledged this commitment at the 1969 dedication ceremonies for the new home office building. "The Knights of Columbus have clearly and unmistakably closed ranks around the hierarchy and particularly around the Vicar of Christ. We feel that this has been their merit and their strength."[33] At the 1969 Supreme Council meeting, this commitment was concretely expressed in John McDevitt's announcement that the Order was contributing $75,000 to the United States Catholic Conference's Task Force on Urban Problems to help heal the lingering sores of poverty and discrimination.[34] More significantly, on the explosive issue of Pope Paul VI's encyclical *Humanae Vitae,* the Supreme Knight illustrated the Order's "loyalty for those whom God has set in position of decision-making and responsibility sharing in the Church" by reprinting a booklet based on the encyclical entitled *Sex in Marriage.*[35]

Another symbol of the Knights' loyalty to the Holy See was the Order's 1965 gift of the property of St. Peter's Oratory to the Holy See for the site of a new audience hall for the pope. In 1968 the buildings of the new St. Peter's Oratory were blessed, at which time Pope Paul VI acknowledged his gratitude for the Order's gift of land and for the expansion of its traditional playgrounds program. "To the Supreme Knight John McDevitt and to his collaborators and to the entire flourishing and meritorious association we express our gratitude, our applause, and our best wishes."[36] The Order's most valued contributions to the Holy See were in the area of communications. In 1966, John McDevitt attended the dedication ceremonies of two new shortwave transmitters for the Vatican radio station, one of which was donated by the Order and the other by Francis Cardinal Spellman.[37] Then in 1975 the Order agreed to pay the cost of every "uplink" signal for major worldwide satellite telecasts from the Vatican. McDevitt explained to the delegates at the 1975 Supreme Council meeting that Bishop Andrew-Maria Deskur, president of the Pontifical Commission for Social Communications, had invited the Knights to fund this undertaking "not only because our Order has a long history of coming to the aid of the Holy See but also because it has carried on for more than a quarter-century a program of disseminating Catholic teachings and values."[38] The Supreme Knight stated that "a world floundering on the sands of shifting morality" desperately needed the messages of the Holy Father.[39]

For years Supreme Knights had communicated with the Vatican through their trusted friend, Count Enrico Galeazzi, who attended the 1969 Supreme Council meeting. Count Galeazzi had been the chief architect at the Vatican since 1934, had been closely associated with the Vatican's investments, and since 1939 had served as the delegate to the Cardinals' committee for the governance of Vatican City. From his office on the Via Veneto, he administered the six K. of C. play-grounds with the assistance of his nephew, Sergio Galeazzi, and his secretary, Cecilia Gospodinoff. He also served as the Order's "ambas-sador" to the Holy See. In his address to the 1969 delegates, Galeazzi referred to his role as "pleasant and easy because the Order of the Knights of Columbus has always been and is particularly now the pure model of Catholic Action." As one of the most distinguished laymen in the service of the Vatican, Galeazzi had conveyed to the Order the great prestige associated with his dedication to the Holy See and had been an invaluable source of communication between New Haven and the Vatican. In 1969, John McDevitt announced that the Board of Directors had elected him to honorary membership in the Order, and in 1978 Supreme Knight Virgil C. Dechant awarded him his Third Degree. In July 1981, Count Galeazzi celebrated his golden anniver-sary as director of the Knights' Roman operations, and in 1982 he marked nearly sixty years as the Knights' engineer architect for their historic recreation projects in Rome.

One of the bishops closest to the Order was John J. Wright, whom John McDevitt knew from Wright's early days as a priest in the archdi-ocese of Boston. By the time he appeared at the 1969 Supreme Council meeting he had been elevated to the College of Cardinals and was prefect of the Vatican's Congregation for the Clergy. Cardinal Wright proudly remarked that he and McDevitt "were lifelong friends."[40] Both began their careers as educators and shared many characteristics in common. They were highly acclaimed speakers, well versed in secu-lar and ecclesiastical history, and both embraced *aggiornamento* only to be disillusioned with what they considered extremism in the wake of Vatican II.

Wright's address to the 1969 convention, which was printed in the *Supreme Council Proceedings* and later published by the Order under the title *A Church of Promise,* included a lengthy tribute to the Order's many contributions to the Church, but it was primarily an explication of Pope Paul's vision of the mission of the Church in the modern world. To allay fears of the "morbid solicitude which grips your hearts at the moment," Cardinal Wright sought to place the crisis in the post–Vatican II Church in the perspective of history in order to illustrate the Church's survival in previous critical periods. He then stressed the need for a strong religious commitment to the defense of life to coun-teract the anti-life forces of abortion, sterilization, and war.[41] John McDevitt reflected Cardinal Wright's call to leadership as he drew the Order into the forefront of what was widely known as the "pro-life movement." At the 1970 Supreme Council convention he spoke on the sanctity of life in opposition to abortion, euthanasia, and other anti-life movements. McDevitt recalled how Father McGivney decided to "call our society an organization of Knights" because Knighthood had "long been equated with the role of protector." He then concluded that the Knights of today must become protectors of life: "we must protect right; we must protect innocence; we must protect truth."[42]

Catholic education had been a persistent concern of the Order for years. McDevitt manifested this concern by successfully urging the Board of Directors and the leadership of the Fourth Degree to sponsor a scholarship program at Catholic University to be called the Pro Deo and Pro Patria Scholarship Fund.[43] The Order awarded scholarships to those sons and daughters of members who had achieved the highest scores in a competitive examination. He also expanded the Order's Educational Trust Fund—originally established to provide free college education to the children of members who lost their lives in World War II—to include the children of police and full-time firemen members who had died in the line of duty. Since 1970 the scholarship program has been under the direction of Father T. Everett McPeake, S.J., former dean at Fairfield University. The major educational concern during the 1970s was the shrinking financial base of the Catholic parochial school system. McDevitt explained to the delegates to the 1971 Supreme Council that "it is no reproach to our public school systems, in which I played a directive role for many years, to state that they simply are not equipped to develop strong religious commitment or moral discipline. . . . This can be done most effectively if parents, Church, and [Catholic] school cooperate in the task."[44] He was also concerned that without Catholic schools there would be a serious decline in vocations to the priesthood, to the religious life, and to the lay apostolate. To bolster the financial condition of parochial schools, he favored some form of tax subsidies for parents of parochial school children or a federal educational voucher system.

President Richard M. Nixon, who gave the major address at the States' Dinner at the 1971 Supreme Council convention in New York, surprised his listeners by indicating his support for Catholic education. Secretary of Transportation John Volpe, a member of the Order and a friend of John McDevitt, was responsible for this first appearance of a President at a Supreme Council gathering. Nixon's speech touched a wide variety of topics in a very general way. He did specifically mention that the Knights "can count upon my support" to reverse the trend of Catholic school closings.[45] The major theme of his address, however, was a plea for the revival of the moral character of the nation, which he said was best exemplified in Vince Lombardi, a recently deceased football coach and a Roman Catholic.[46] In one sense the President's appearance was more significant than his address, as it represented his perception of the strong role of the Order in American Catholic life. Though McDevitt was grateful for the honor the President bestowed upon the Order, he had hoped that Nixon would have affirmed the pro-life position, would have been more specific in his support of Catholic education, and would have vigorously endorsed the Order's campaign against pornography.

In 1969, the Supreme Council adopted a resolution affirming the justice of U.S. aims and objectives in the Vietnam war.[47] Editorials in *Columbia* written by Elmer Von Feldt, who replaced John Donahue as editor in 1966, were also generally supportive of Presidents Johnson and Nixon's goals in Southeast Asia, but as the U.S. commitment escalated and the South Vietnamese government appeared to lack strong resolve, the editorials questioned the effectiveness of the American military effort. John McDevitt never spoke out on the propriety of the war. However, he was very emphatic on the impropriety of massive antiwar protests, based upon what he perceived as the undemocratic principle of civil disobedience. In several of his Columbus Day addresses, McDevitt enunciated a strongly conservative theory of American government. Shortly before the 1972 election he stated that the representative character of our government "means that all the people participate in government in the sense that they elect candidates of their choice to positions of responsibility. It does not mean that the changing opinions and preferences of the voters always must find reflection in the votes and actions of the elected. In representative government the elected official's prime obligation is to his conscientious judgment of what is best for the common good, not what might please the common crowd." To substantiate his political vision, the Supreme Knight cited Aristotle's four "political virtues, i.e., justice, temperance, courage, and prudence," and explained their meaning. "Justice is truth in action. Temperance keeps a rein on passions. Courage implements the conviction of conscience. Prudence dictates the choice of the better course of action."[48]

McDevitt described the Bill of Rights as a preventive against both the "tyranny of the majority, and the tyranny of the minority." To those who lauded civil disobedience, McDevitt responded by stating that "no orderly society can exist if everyone acts as if he had the privilege of observing only those laws which he thinks are good and violating those that he considers bad. This does not assure a regime of exclusively good laws but a jungle of bad laws."[49] The Supreme Knight's political theory was congruent with his notion of Church governance; just as elected representatives in a republic hold a trust to follow their conscience rather than the whims of the most vocal group of constituents in the streets, so too the magisterium is obliged to uphold Church doctrine rather than to satisfy the most vocal group of believers in the pews.

III

John McDevitt's positions on the issues of pro-life, Catholic education, and respect for political and ecclesiastical authority gained him great popularity among the members. Though there was a slight decline in membership during the late 1960s and early 1970s when every Church institution was subjected to internal introspection and external disenchantment, membership since 1974 has set record highs each year. By 1969 Supreme Secretary Virgil C. Dechant had been entrusted with the "job of monitoring and guiding" the insurance program. Dechant, who had achieved a fine business reputation in the management of his own automobile agency in Hays, Kansas, was assisted by John O'Brien, a former general agent in Dallas, Texas. The previous year, 1968, the Order had abolished the rule which required members under twenty-six years of age to purchase a minimum $1,000 life insurance policy.[50] As mentioned in Chapter 12, this law was intended to challenge the sincerity of young members by requiring them to make an economic pledge. Though there were several attempts to abolish the rule, by 1968 there was an abundance of statistical evidence to prove that most young members purchased only the minimum and that many field agents tended to be satisfied with commissions on this more or less captive group of members.

Under Virgil Dechant, John O'Brien, and the latter's assistant, Joseph Mauro, the insurance program was expanded and improved, particularly in the computer operations at the home office, and the Order's insurance experienced a period of extraordinary growth. In 1960 the Knights reached one billion dollars of insurance in force, in 1971 two billion, and in 1975 three billion. By 1975 there were 85 general agents and 550 field agents serving the members.[51] Not every Catholic fraternal society had developed such a strong insurance program. Indeed, in 1967 the Order absorbed the insurance membership of the Catholic Benevolent Legion (C.B.L.), because that group had dwindled to less than a thousand members and because its insurance program was sorely in need of the Order's expertise. (As mentioned in Chapter 1, Father McGivney had visited with the leaders of the C.B.L. in Brooklyn in late 1881, to learn from their experience and to discuss the possibility of establishing a C.B.L. Council in New Haven.)

McDevitt also authorized the centralization and modernization of the Catholic Advertising Program. Because he believed that in the post–Vatican II era the program needed to be monitored at the home office, where the Supreme Officers could better influence its character and where it could be coordinated with the Service Department and with *Columbia* magazine, in 1969 he successfully negotiated with the Vincentians of St. Louis for its relocation to New Haven. Since the Missouri Knights continued to fund their own Religious Information Bureau, the Supreme Council's program was called the Catholic Information Service. Father John V. McGuire, C.SS.R., who had served as a pastor, a missionary, and a writer, was appointed program director. Under Father McGuire's leadership the advertising program emphasized "larger and more attractive pictures and shorter and simpler copy."[52] The catechetical pamphlet series was also updated in light of the perceived need for a basic doctrinal approach within the context of the post–Vatican II Church. For example, in 1975 the following pamphlets were published: "Faith and Common Sense (How Much We Need Them Both)," "Purgatory (Reasonable and Consoling)," "The Early Years of the Church (Christianity Is More than the Bible)," and "Christ and His Church (A Simplified Version of the Second Vatican Council's Document on the Church)."[53] In 1975, the Catholic Information Service received over 87,000 requests for such pamphlets, and nearly 6,000 persons were enrolled in its ten-lesson correspondence course on the Catholic faith.

Statistics revealing the strength of the Order's membership, insurance, and fraternal programs clearly showed the vitality of the Knights during a period when many had predicted that they would die of obsolescence. John McDevitt was the first Supreme Knight to lead the Order after the demise of the Catholic "ghetto" and during a time when Catholics were almost fully assimilated into American society. However, it was also a time of deep tensions in Church and civil society. McDevitt attempted to reconcile the Order's traditional spirit with the changing character of Catholicism after Vatican II and of the American social scene, but when the ecclesiastical and social pace of change reached rapid acceleration and when polarization disturbed the equilibrium, he guided the Order with a set of rigid principles. He was progressive on several social-justice issues such as the admission of blacks to the Order, the La Farge Institute, and the early programs of C.A.R.A., on changes in the ceremonials, and on incorporating the entire family into the life of the Knights, but on the cultural issues of birth control, abortion, and the sexual revolution and on the nature of political and ecclesiastical authority, John McDevitt assumed a strongly conservative position.

In a very real sense his principles and priorities were a reflection of those expressed by the papacy and the majority of the American hierarchy. Catholics were assimilated into the mainstream of American society, but the Knights of Columbus under John McDevitt were not fully absorbed into American culture. The Knights, like the American Church, included liberals and conservatives, transformationists and preservationists. However, the leadership of the Knights and the Church throughout the 1960s and '70s still tended to be socially progressive, and culturally and ecclesiastically conservative.

17

Virgil C. Dechant and the Prologue to the Second Century

JOHN W. McDEVITT RETIRED IN JANUARY 1977. The Board of Directors convened for its quarterly meeting in San Juan, Puerto Rico, on January 22 of that year to select his successor. Virgil C. Dechant was elected unanimously. Forty-six years old when he assumed the office, Dechant's rise to national prominence had been rapid. Now a member of LaCrosse (Kansas) Council No. 2970, he entered the Order in Liebenthal, Kansas, in 1949 at the age of eighteen, and served as Grand Knight of St. Augustine Council No. 2340 there from 1951 to 1952. He was appointed District Deputy, 1952–57, elected State Treasurer for 1957–59, and appointed State Membership Director, 1959–60. Delegates to the Kansas State Convention chose him as State Deputy in 1960, and he was reelected in 1961. At age twenty-nine, Dechant was one of the youngest men to hold this office in the Order's history.

Luke Hart noted Dechant's leadership abilities, as evidenced by large increases in insurance and associate membership during his terms as Kansas State Membership Director and as State Deputy. His "Every Council Active" program saw each Kansas council bring in at least one new member during his term. Accordingly, at the 1961 Supreme Council meeting, Hart assigned him to chair the Good of the Order Committee and to deliver its report to the delegates. In 1963 Hart successfully recommended Dechant's election to membership on the Supreme Board; in fact, he was the last director named before Hart's death. In October 1966 he was elected Assistant Supreme Secretary and Supreme Master of the Fourth Degree. A year later he was chosen Supreme Secretary to succeed D. Francis Sullivan, who had retired for reasons of health.

Virgil Dechant's background as a seminarian (he attended the Pontifical College Josephinum in Worthington, Ohio), as a businessman (owner of an automobile and farm-equipment agency and in real estate), as a farmer, and as a second-generation Volga German American with deep roots in the Kansas plains—all these permeated his perspectives on the Order as it approached its second century. His business background made certain a keen interest in the insurance and investment programs. As Supreme Secretary, he advocated the installation of a sophisticated computer system which streamlined many transactions associated with the growing insurance operation. In these and in other ways, he brought to the office characteristics of his own generation, particularly a more personal style of leadership. Nevertheless, he maintained strong ties to the Order's traditions, evincing a personal devotion to Father McGivney and recognizing the need to reinvigorate the Order's ceremonials. He also initiated the present history project and laid plans for a museum at the home office. Thus, though his business background contributed to a pragmatic approach to innovative projects, his pragmatism was tempered by an abiding loyalty to tradition. From the outset of his administration, he projected a deep respect for the priesthood and a conviction about the family character of the Order. Indeed, his first initiative as Supreme Knight was to draw back into the extended family circle of the Order the widows and children of deceased members. Upon learning of a brother Knight's death, the Supreme Knight forwarded a letter of condolence to the widow and family, inviting her to continue her husband's council's activities. She was offered a free lifetime subscription to *Columbia* magazine, was informed of the Order's scholarship and student-loan programs, and was told that her husband would be remembered daily at a Mass offered at the Knights' Altar at St. Mary's Church in New Haven.

Dechant's administration was composed of some officers who served during the McDevitt years. John H. Griffin, M.D., and Daniel L. McCormick continued to hold the offices of Supreme Physician and Supreme Treasurer, respectively. However, Deputy Supreme Knight Charles J. Ducey had retired in April 1976 and Supreme Advocate Harold J. Lamboley the previous October. Supreme Director Ernest J. Wolff of Peterborough, Ontario, was elected as Ducey's replacement, but he retired after two terms. He was succeeded by Frederick H. Pelletier of San Bernardino, California. Neither Deputy Supreme Knight took up residence in New Haven. John M. Murphy, Lamboley's assistant since 1965, was elected Supreme Advocate in 1975 upon Lamboley's retirement. John K. McDevitt was designated Assistant Supreme Advocate. When Dechant was elected Supreme Knight, he was succeeded as Supreme Secretary by Supreme Director Richard B. Scheiber of Huntington, Indiana, a Catholic journalist who had been editor of *Our Sunday Visitor* and a Past State Deputy of Indiana. Hence, the Officers brought to their tasks a depth of fraternal experience and a wide variety of geographical and professional backgrounds.

Dechant's first term began by stressing the Knights' religious character. Shortly after his election, he visited the National Shrine of the Immaculate Conception in Washington, D.C., where he placed his administration under the Virgin Mary's protection. At the Supreme Council meeting in August 1977, the Supreme Knight reiterated this dedication and also placed the Order under her care. He announced the implementation of a program by which all new members, upon joining the Order, would receive a special Knights of Columbus rosary blessed by Bishop Greco, the Supreme Chaplain. Further, he told the delegates of his intention to establish a chapel in the home office building.[1] In June 1980, the chapel was solemnly blessed by Auxiliary Bishop John F. Hackett of Hartford in the presence of Officers, Directors, and State Deputies and their families. In accordance with the Order's objective of strengthening Catholic family life, the chapel was dedicated to the Holy Family.[2]

The new Supreme Knight frequently expressed the Order's loyalty to the Holy See. He was especially proud of the Knights' support of the evangelization efforts of the Holy Father, particularly in relation to what has come to be known as the "satellite uplink" program. Essentially, this project was initiated to provide the transmission (uplink) of television signals of papal ceremonies at least three times annually to the four INTELSAT satellites circling the globe. In mission lands, too, the Order agreed to pay for recapturing this signal (the down link) so the telecasts could be seen in those countries. During a 1975 Holy Year pilgrimage to Rome for the Knights of Columbus insurance agents, Dechant, accompanied by Bishop Greco and Elmer Von Feldt, editor of *Columbia,* met with Bishop Andrew-Maria Deskur, president of the Pontifical Commission for Social Communications. At this session, he negotiated an agreement with Bishop Deskur for the uplink program. The Christmas Midnight Mass from St. Peter's Basilica, a Holy Week ceremony, and one other papal event would be telecast worldwide each year. This papal project was expanded considerably when, upon the death of Pope Paul VI on August 6, 1978, Dechant received a telegram from Bishop Deskur asking if the Order would underwrite the cost of televising the pontiff's funeral, the conclave, and the investiture of his successor. A hastily called meeting of the Executive and Finance Committee acceded to this request. Thirty-three days after Pope John Paul I's pontificate began, the "Smiling Pope" died and again Bishop Deskur requested the Order's support for televising the funeral of Pope John Paul I and the first words and installation Mass of his successor, who was to be Karol Cardinal Wojtyla. Again, the Order responded affirmatively. It has been estimated that each of these special telecasts was seen by more than 800 million people.[3]

In 1977, Bishop Deskur visited New Haven to report on the progress of the uplink program to the Supreme Officers. He brought with him two additional proposals which subsequently received the Board's approval. The first was the establishment of a Knights of Columbus Vatican Film Library, which would seek to collect all extant movie-film footage of the popes. The films collected would be made available to scholars, journalists, and other interested parties. The second project, called Radio Veritas, was initiated to beam religious broadcasts to the quarter of the world's population which lives behind the Bamboo Curtain.[4]

As the undertaking of such projects by the Order came to the attention of the pontiffs, they showed an eagerness to express their appreciation personally to the Knights. In 1978, the Supreme Board was invited to hold its April meeting in the Vatican. Pope Paul VI met the Directors and their wives in audience and congratulated them on the Order's works for the Church.[5] Later that year, Supreme Knight and Mrs. Dechant and Bishop Greco represented the Order at the installation of Albino Cardinal Luciani as John Paul I. Three days before the formal installation of the new pope, the party was summoned to the Vatican, accompanied by Count Galeazzi, for a private audience. It was the first audience granted by Pope John Paul I to any layman.[6] Similarly, the Dechants, Bishop Greco, and Dr. and Mrs. Griffin attended the installation of Cardinal Wojtyla as Pope John Paul II. Three days after the installation Mass, the Holy Father received the Supreme Knight and party in a private audience.

One mark of Pope John Paul II's pontificate has been his historic pastoral journeys to various lands, and the Knights have played an important role in several. When the Pope traveled to the Dominican Republic and Mexico in 1979, the Archbishop of Santo Domingo, Octavio Antonio Cardinal Beras Rojas, invited Supreme Knight Dechant to be present to welcome John Paul II to the Americas. During the stay, Dechant and Supreme Treasurer McCormick were requested by the Cardinal to establish the Order in the Dominican Republic.

Following the Mexican journey, the Order produced an English-language film covering this event. After the Pope's return to his homeland, again in 1979, Bishop Paul C. Marcinkus, President of the Institute for the Works of Religion at the Vatican, approached Supreme Knight Dechant at the funeral of Cardinal Wright with the information that raw film footage of the Poland trip was available but that money was lacking to edit it into usable form. With funds supplied by the Order, several films were produced which, it was later learned, were shown on Polish television and even in movie theaters.

Pope John Paul II's trip to the United States in October 1979 generated great enthusiasm among the Knights. While preparations for the journey were under way, the Supreme Knight was asked by the National Conference of Catholic Bishops (N.C.C.B.) to underwrite the cost of filming the papal journey. The Board readily agreed, and so the film of the Holy Father in the United States was soon made available to posterity. At every city on the papal itinerary Knights were in evidence—in Boston, New York, Philadelphia, Des Moines, Chicago, and Washington, D.C.—whether as honor guards composed of Fourth Degree members in regalia, or as members serving as ushers and guides or monitoring crowds.

The Washington phase of the papal journey was of special significance to the Order. Word came to the Supreme Office that His Holiness would receive the Supreme Officers and representatives of the Board in a special audience at the Apostolic Delegation on October 7. It was the only such audience granted to a lay organization during the Holy Father's visit. At the audience, Pope John Paul II received a sizable gift from the Order for his personal charities, along with a porcelain bas-relief of the Infant of Prague created by Cybis Studios. Accepting the gifts from Supreme Knight Dechant, the Pope said, "Whatever is in this envelope will be used"—turning then to the Infant —"for this Child." In his formal message, especially prepared for the audience, the Holy Father stated, "Many times in the past, and again today, you have given expression to your solidarity with the mission of the Pope. I see in your support a further proof—if further proof were ever necessary—of your awareness that the Knights of Columbus highly value their vocation to be part of the evangelization effort of the Church."[7]

However, it was not only in evangelization that the Order was acting in support of, and in concert with, the Church. Shortly after he became Supreme Knight, Dechant met with Archbishop Joseph L. Bernardin, president of the N.C.C.B., to assure him that the Knights would be privileged to consider aiding the bishops insofar as possible in projects that would come before them. Under Dechant's leadership, the Order continued to fund annually the N.C.C.B.'s pro-life effort, and in 1979 this project was assumed by the Fourth Degree. Since 1977, the Order has been providing similar support for the Canadian Conference of Catholic Bishops (C.C.C.B.). At the Supreme Council meeting in 1979, the delegates reasserted the Order's ties to the National Shrine of the Immaculate Conception by establishing the Luke E. Hart Memorial Fund. Dedicated to the "purposes of promoting increased devotion to Our Blessed Mother and for the preservation of the shrine in perpetuity," the $500,000 trust was raised by a 50-cent per-capita tax on members of U.S. councils.[8]

In the aftermath of Pope John Paul II's visit to Mexico, Supreme Knight Dechant launched the "Pilgrim Virgin—Marian Hour of Prayer" program at the 1979 Supreme Convention. Images of Our Lady of Guadalupe, blessed by the Pope, were delivered to the State Deputy of each of the Order's jurisdictions at the convention during a Marian hour of prayer. The images were carried by the State Deputies to their home states, where a schedule was arranged for the pictures to be displayed at each local council, at which time the Marian service would be held. At the conclusion of the program, some five thousand councils had sponsored prayer programs attracting more than two million participants.[9]

Following up on resolutions advocating the Order's support for tuition tax credits for parents of children attending private schools, the Board voted in 1979 to fund the office of the N.C.C.B.'s Advisory Committee on Public Policy and Catholic Schools. This office was established in the N.C.C.B.'s Division of Education to help promote passage of legislation to alleviate the tax burdens faced by parents with children in parochial and other private schools. On behalf of the National Catholic Education Association (N.C.E.A.), the Supreme Knight was instrumental in arranging a special filmed message, the first of its kind, from Pope John Paul II to the delegates to the 1979 N.C.E.A. convention in Philadelphia. The Holy Father stressed the importance of Catholic education and the need for it to flourish.[10]

In 1980, the Supreme Knight reported to the delegates at the Supreme Council meeting in Atlanta, Georgia, that the Order had been approached by Monsignor John F. Meyers, N.C.E.A. president, and Archbishop Joseph L. Bernardin, chairman of N.C.E.A.'s Board of Directors, to support research on ways to meet the challenges confronting Catholic education. Monsignor Meyers was particularly concerned with the need to strengthen the religious spirit of the lay faculty, the Catholic component of the curriculum, and the managerial skills of the administrators. Dechant remarked that, after many hours of discussion with Monsignor Meyers, the Board had prepared a proposal to the Supreme Council for its consideration. The plan suggested establishment of a fund within Knights of Columbus Charities, Inc., of $1 million, the earnings of which would subsidize in perpetuity the N.C.E.A.'s research efforts.[11] The fund would be raised by a $1.00 per-capita levy on members of the U.S. and Canadian councils. The delegates approved the proposal unanimously, and the following October the Board officially established the Father Michael J. McGivney Memorial fund for New Initiatives in Catholic Education. By this fund the Knights demonstrated their commitment to continued involvement in the future of Catholic education.[12] On April 21, 1981, the N.C.E.A. responded to the Knights' long-time concern for Catholic education by honoring the Order with the prestigious C. Albert Koob Merit Award. Presented by Archbishop Bernardin and accepted by Supreme Knight Dechant, the award commended the Knights for their endowment of the chair of American History at Catholic University, the financing of the 1925 Oregon school case, and the McGivney Fund —all cited, among other initiatives, as part of their "long record . . . of endorsement of Catholic education."[13]

Supreme Knight Dechant's emphasis upon the need to bring the Knights closer to the clergy was manifested in his vocations program, in his successful efforts to change the rule on membership which provided all priest members with honorary life membership (non-dues-paying status) and to restructure the council meeting agenda to give greater prominence to the chaplain's message, and in his promotion of the Knights of Columbus parish-round-table program. This last project, conceived in 1977 and implemented the following year in dioceses where it was approved by the ordinary, was an attempt to place the local resources of the Order at the disposal of parish clergy. In small towns and rural areas, subordinate councils were virtually parish-oriented councils closely allied with the pastor. However, in the cities one council might draw from several parishes, which often meant isolation from the needs of particular local communities. Hence, this program encouraged the leaders of these councils to establish a round table of Knights to strengthen the Order's ties to the basic ecclesiastical unit of the Church. It gave the Order an effective means of placing the local resources of councils at the disposal of pastors in accordance with the intention of the founder, Father McGivney.[14]

The vocations program was aimed at deepening the sense and awareness of vocations and at motivating the laity to create a proper climate for nurturing the Christian life in all its dimensions. The Supreme Council Vocations Committee, chaired by Father John V. McGuire, C.SS.R., provided guidance and direction to state and local council vocation committees by suggesting ways to implement the program's goals.[15] Father McGuire's committee developed a "Vocations Handbook," forwarded to state and local committees, and, in conjunction with the Catholic Information Service, sponsored an advertising campaign in college and high-school publications and in the college editions of *Time* and *Newsweek* offering free information on the priesthood and religious life.[16] The entire April 1978 issue of *Columbia* was devoted to vocations and included several reports on vocation programs on the local level, such as the New Jersey "Adopt a Seminarian" project intended to provide moral and financial support for candidates to the priesthood.[17] To help seminarians, priests, and religious with financial assistance toward completing their educations, the Supreme Council opened its student-loan program to them, regardless of membership.[18]

In 1978, Dechant added new dimensions in the area of vocations by commissioning the National Opinion Research Center (N.O.R.C.) of Chicago, Illinois, to study the attitudes of young Catholics in the United States and Canada. This research charted the youths' thinking on subjects such as the Church, vocations, Catholic education, and Church-related service organizations and fraternal societies. The idea for the survey was generated by the Supreme Council Vocations Committee, which felt the need for current empirical data as it sought to establish programs to promote vocational awareness among the laity.[19] The N.O.R.C. survey, published by the Sadlier Company in 1981, was widely acclaimed as an invaluable tool in work with the young.[20] As a result of the Order's vocations initiatives, in April 1981, Supreme Knight Dechant and Father J. V. McGuire were invited by William Cardinal Baum, Prefect of the Sacred Congregation for Catholic Education at the Vatican, to attend the International Congress of Bishops Delegated by the Episcopal Conferences and of Others Responsible for Ecclesiastical Vocations, which was held at the Vatican on May 10–16, 1981. The Supreme Knight was one of three laymen invited to participate in the congress.

During this visit to Rome, the Supreme Knight concluded arrangements with Archbishop Lino Zanini, delegate for the Office of Administration of St. Peter's Basilica, for the construction in the grottoes of the Basilica of a new chapel dedicated to Saints Benedict, Cyril and Methodius, co-patrons of Europe. An additional project included the enlargement of the adjoining chapel of Our Lady of Czestochowa, to one and a half times its present size.

Located in the new chapel will be a bronze celebrant's chair, a bronze bas-relief of the three saints, and a Carolingian cross, all sculptured by Tommaso Gismondi. Archbishop Zanini presented the Supreme Knight with replicas of the latter two artworks for placement in the Order's museum in New Haven. An exact replica of the cross will be placed behind the main altar at St. Mary's Church, the birthplace of the Order, and a smaller replica of the cross will be given to the delegates to the centennial convention in August, 1982. Archbishop Zanini also proposed that a plaque be erected in the new chapel stating that it is "the generous gift of the Order of the Knights of Columbus."[21]

In prior consultation with Agostino Cardinal Casaroli, papal secretary of state, Archbishop Zanini was informed that the project was approved by His Holiness Pope John Paul II "because it realizes His very desire." Supreme Knight Dechant thanked Archbishop Zanini for the privilege of participating in this project in these words:

"In participating in this tribute to the glorious patron saints of Europe, we have a sense of repaying, in a small way, a long-standing debt of gratitude. It was from Europe, starting with Columbus, that the countries now under the patronage of these three great saints sent missionaries to the new world. The roots of the present Christian faith of the Knights of Columbus are deep in the soil once walked upon and evangelized by Saints Benedict, Cyril and Methodius, and all who shared in their preaching of the Gospel."[22]

After visiting with Archbishop Zanini, the Supreme Knight Dechant, Father McGuire, and Count Galeazzi proceeded to St. Peter's Square for the general audience which would take place that afternoon. The Holy Father's vehicle entered the square, the pontiff waving to and blessing the crowd, and began a second turn. Suddenly shots rang out. His Holiness fell, wounded. Dechant was close enough to hear the shots, and recalled that the pigeons in the square flew off in fright. He heard several bishops in the crowd begin prayers for the Pope and, after praying for a while, left with Father McGuire and Count Galeazzi for the apartment of Archbishop Deskur, a close personal friend of the Holy Father. The group comforted the distraught prelate and prayed with him for about an hour in his private chapel.

Referring to the Holy Father's motto, "Totus Tuus, Maria," the Archbishop said: "Mary will watch over him."[23]

The 98th Supreme Council had passed a resolution inviting Pope John Paul II to honor the Order with his presence at the centennial convention in Hartford in 1982. Then the 99th Supreme Council passed a motion empowering the Board of Directors to establish an irrevocable $10 million endowment, "the Knights of Columbus Vicarius Christi foundation," the earnings of which will be presented each year to the Pope for whatever charitable purpose he views as most appropriate. The foundation's funds will be invested in Church loans with the intention of providing financial assistance to local bishops in tandem with the annual gift to the Holy Father. At current earnings, this gift should amount to $1 million. Never has the Order so dramatically and so substantially manifested its fealty to the Holy See than through the establishment of the Vicarius Christi foundation.

II

Dechant also felt the need to expand the Order's programs in the area of Christian family life. In his first report to the Supreme Council in Indianapolis, Indiana, he disclosed that the newly created position of Family Life Director had been added to the "Surge with Service" Program, thereby helping state and local councils to create more programs for the family. He was convinced the time had arrived to mold the Knights of Columbus into an organization for the benefit of the family. Dechant already had formulated a policy that enabled wives to wear the emblem of the Order in jewelry fashion for the first time. It also permitted children of members to wear the emblem in badge form. The program of recognizing a local council's "Family of the Month" was initiated, and, at the 1980 Supreme Convention in Atlanta, Dechant personally presented the first "International Family of the Year" at the States' Dinner.[24] The Order's commitment to youth, which originated with the work of Brother Barnabas, has been expressed in several forms. Its traditional Squires program for boys twelve to eighteen years of age (in 1976 the minimum age was lowered from thirteen to twelve) has been growing steadily during the seventies and early eighties. Since its origin, nearly 200,000 young men have entered the Squires, while its membership in April 1981 was nearly 20,000. Brother Barnabas had also encouraged the Knights to sponsor

Boy Scout troops; in 1981, 875 councils in the United States were sponsoring troops with an enrollment of nearly 21,000 scouts. Since 1974, the Order has subsidized the entire cost of the National Catholic Workshop on Scouting held at Philmont, New Mexico. Established to train clerical and lay leaders in the ways in which scouting relates to the Church's general apostolate to the young, the workshop has deepened the Order's commitment to youth.

The Order also began to subsidize projects sponsored by the Pope John XXIII Medical-Moral Research and Education Center in St. Louis, Missouri, aimed at exploring the impact of science and technology upon questions of life and death in light of the Church's moral teaching on birth control, abortion, euthanasia, and related issues. As a result, the Order supplied a grant to the center in January 1980 which subsidized a workshop in Dallas, Texas, entitled "The New Technologies of Birth and Death: Medical, Legal, and Moral Dimensions" held for bishops of the United States and Canada. The Supreme Knight attended the opening day of the workshop and told the gathering that the Order considered it a privilege "to assist the Bishops in carrying out their apostolate." He stated that any program that benefited the bishops would, in turn, benefit the Knights of Columbus. The Order provided another grant for the center's 1981 meeting, which was also held in Dallas and which focused on the topic "Human Sexuality and Personhood." Bishops from the United States and Canada, numbering more than two hundred, attended the meeting and praised it as an unqualified success.[25]

Dechant took particular interest in and endorsed natural family planning. He told the delegates to the 1980 Supreme Council that he believed "the Knights of Columbus have the manpower, facilities, and resources to invest in natural family planning, not only for Catholics, but for all people of good will. The time has come to put our manpower—our family power—our facilities and our resources on the line."[26] Dechant felt that, in cooperation with the hierarchy, the Knights could and would be successful in disseminating natural family planning information. With this in mind, the Board of Directors voted to cooperate with the World Organization of the Ovulation Method—Billings (W.O.O.M.B.), by helping to finance W.O.O.M.B.'s "Congress for the Family of the Americas" held in Guatemala City, Guatemala, in July 1980. The congress was attended by a personal representative of the Holy Father, Archbishop Simon Lourdusamy, President of the Sacred Congregation for the Propagation of the Faith. Those present, including a Knights of Columbus delegation headed by

Dr. Griffin, heard Mother Teresa of Calcutta give the keynote address.[27] The Order's support of natural family planning extended beyond its support of W.O.O.M.B. At a meeting in February 1981 in Edmonton, Alberta, Supreme Knight Dechant met with Archbishops Joseph N. MacNeil and Henri Legaré, president and vice-president respectively of the Canadian Catholic Conference of Bishops (C.C.C.B.), in the company of the Canadian Supreme Directors and State Deputies. The topic was an "All-Canadian Project" for the Knights that would be most acceptable to the Canadian hierarchy. The choice was natural family planning, and the Knights agreed to fund a natural family planning office in the C.C.C.B. which would be charged with coordinating efforts in this area.

Dechant also drew on extensive personal experience as a ceremonials officer in Kansas by raising a question as to whether the time for a change in the Order's ceremonials had arrived. He was concerned that the ceremonials, as revised in 1968, were not achieving the desired goal of imparting effectively the lessons of charity, unity, and fraternity in a positive way. In accord with his general respect for Knights at the grass-roots level, he sponsored a series of regional seminars conducted by the Committee on Ceremonials of the Board.[28] The results of the meetings supported his observations, and soon after, Dechant appointed Samuel L. Dambrocia, Past State Deputy of Pennsylvania, as director of ceremonials at the Supreme Council office.[29] With the widespread support for revisions, Dechant and his personal staff set about the tasks of restructuring the degree rites. Working personally with ceremonial teams at the home office, he immersed himself in developing ceremonials which would be an effective learning experience for new members. The new ceremonials were released in 1981 and met with widespread acclaim. Dechant once stated that ceremonials are so important that he regarded them as one of the four pillars of the Order, all resting on the foundation of Catholicity. He described the other three pillars as membership, insurance and, investments, uniquely tied together. All four pillars were strengthened during Dechant's years in office.[30]

Between 1977 and June 30, 1981, with recruitment campaigns designed to attract new members, the Order's membership grew annually, adding 120,000 men to its rolls during this period to achieve an all-time high level of more than 1.35 million members. Adding to this total the wives and children of members, the Order's family was near the 5 million mark. As Pope John Paul II himself declared to the Officers at the audience in Washington, D.C., "That is a nation!"[31]

Meanwhile, in this same period, the Fourth Degree, the patriotic arm of the Knights, registered a gain of 20,000 members. Dechant also revived the new-council development program, which had previously been merged with the service department. Under the direct supervision of the Supreme Knight, Donald J. Dreiling, Kansas State Membership Chairman when Dechant was State Deputy and himself a Past State Deputy of Kansas, was named to administer this program. With this renewed interest in expanding the Order's base, more than one thousand new councils were instituted between 1977 and the end of 1981, the greatest period of growth for any similar period in the Order's history. The fraternal year ending June 30, 1980, saw 266 new councils instituted, for a net gain of 253, the highest single year on record. In January 1981, Thomas P. Smith, Jr., became administrator of the new council development program.

The insurance program of the Order continued to experience record-breaking growth under the direction of Dechant. Insurance in force climbed from $3.6 billion at year end 1976 to more than $6.4 billion by the end of 1981, placing it in the top 7 percent of the entire insurance industry of more than eighteen hundred companies. The agency department, under Joseph R. Mauro, expanded its staff to include 4 regional directors, 111 general agents, 3 special agents, 747 field agents, and 5 field training instructors. In 1979, L. Timothy Giles was appointed resident actuary.

As the Order's insurance grew, so did its assets and investment portfolio. In 1974, Charles C. Walden was appointed director of the investment department, and subsequently experts in bonds, mortgages, and real estate were added to the staff. Because post–Vatican II Catholicism experienced institutional decline and a reordering of its ministerial priorities, there were fewer Church investments during McDevitt's years in office. By the late 1970s, however, several dioceses and Catholic institutions were suffering from severe fiscal problems. In response to this condition, which was exacerbated by rising interest rates, Dechant revived Luke E. Hart's emphasis on Church-related investments by greatly expanding the Order's loans to dioceses and religious institutions. At the 1980 convention, Dechant reported that the statement once made by Supreme Knight Hart—that not a single penny of principal or interest has been lost in Church loans—held just as true, even though the total of such loans since 1904 added up to more than $1 billion.[32] By 1981, approximately 10 percent of the Order's assets were committed to Church-related loans. Between year-end 1976 and the summer of 1981, the Order's assets grew from $656 million to more than $1 billion. With this tremendous growth in assets, the investment department's responsibility grew accordingly, while the authority remained vested in the Executive and Finance Committee of the Board.

The Order's expanding structure was firmly rooted in state and local councils, Fourth Degree assemblies, and Columbian Squires circles. The service department—headed by William L. Piedmont until 1977, when Harvey G. Bacqué became director upon Piedmont's promotion to Assistant Supreme Secretary—provided a continuous flow of program materials, stimulating local units of the Order to reach out to the hierarchy, clergy, parishes, and secular community. In 1980, Supreme, state, and local councils contributed nearly $32 million and over nine million man-hours to a wide variety of charitable causes benefiting the underprivileged, the deaf, the blind, the aged, and the retarded.[33] One of the most popular and visible of these projects is the State Council–sponsored drives for the mentally retarded. Bishop Greco, who had founded two institutions for mentally retarded children in the diocese of Alexandria, Louisiana, was largely responsible for this charitable undertaking.

With the growth and development of every facet of the Order's fraternal and insurance programs, Dechant expanded his administrative staff to include one administrative assistant to the Supreme Knight, first Howard E. Murphy and then William J. Van Tassell, a Supreme Director from New York, and two personal assistants, Paul M. McGlinchey, a former associate editor of *Columbia,* and Donald J. Dreiling, former administrator of new council development. The Board also designated a new Assistant Supreme Treasurer, John F. Barrett, a Supreme Director from Virginia. In September 1980, Supreme Secretary Richard B. Scheiber resigned, and in his place the Board elected Supreme Director Howard E. Murphy. Upon the retirement of William L. Piedmont in June 1980, Edward J. Maloney was promoted from Chief Accountant to Assistant Supreme Secretary. At the April 1981 meeting of the Board, W. Patrick Donlin was designated Assistant Supreme Advocate.

The expansion of membership, new councils, insurance in force, investments, and home office administration strengthened the Order's structure, but the Order was also experiencing some of the strains affecting American fraternalism in general. The flight to suburbia, the distractions of the mass media, the social apathy and cynicism characteristic of the post-Vietnam and post-Watergate era, and the decline in volunteerism brought on by overdependence upon governmental solutions to social problems all contributed to an atmosphere that did little to foster fraternal societies. But there always was a tremendous amount of diversity among Knights of Columbus councils. Indeed, this diversity was a source of strength in the Order's traditional commitment to aid Church and society. There had long been a tendency by some to view the council only as a social club with little consideration of its role as a cell in the apostolate of the Church. In response to these conditions, Dechant attempted to stimulate the membership to a greater awareness of the religious and moral issues confronting the Church. The Order's Catholic anti-defamation character, on the wane since the 1960s, no longer united the membership.[34] However, the Order's struggle against what the Church viewed as the secularistic, materialistic, and anti-life drift of American culture did appear to mobilize a majority of the Knights. The positive side of this contemporary crusade was evidenced in the variety of new programs reflecting the proliferation of the new social ministries of the Church.

III

On assuming the office of Supreme Knight, Dechant expressed optimism for the Order's idealistic and practical character. His strong devotion to Mary resulted in the free distribution of more than half a million rosaries in the first five years of his administration, while his dedication to the family led to a variety of innovations, including, as already noted, the extension of specific privileges to widows of deceased members. As the leader of the largest Catholic fraternal society, Dechant fostered a spirit of close communication with Catholic organizations modeled on the Order in other lands: the Knights of St. Columbanus in Ireland, the Knights of St. Columba in England and Scotland, the Knights of the Southern Cross in Australia and New Zealand, and the Knights of Da Gama in the Union of South Africa. Dechant's collegial style of leadership led to the expansion of Board committees from nine to sixteen, a development which also symbolized the growth of K. of C. programs. This horizontal extension was complemented by a vertical relationship with membership at the grassroots level. While tightening the procedures of local-council accountability to the Supreme Office, he also was attentive to the views of the membership, as evidenced by his several tours to local councils, even to the remote regions of the Philippines, Guam, Hawaii, as well as to sparsely settled areas of Canada and the United States. Dechant frequently declared that the basis for his hope in the future was his faith in the vision of Father McGivney. Indeed, he was so dedicated to the priest founder that he initiated preliminary procedures for his beatification in consultation with the pastor of St. Mary's Church and with Archbishop John Francis Whealon of Hartford. Dechant also took steps to provide for the renovation of St. Mary's Church, the shrine and birthplace of the Order, during the Centennial year in the hope of having Father McGivney's remains reinterred there. The Columbian Squires will participate in the renovation of St. Mary's by underwriting the cost of an access facility for the elderly and handicapped in accord with the spirit of the international year of the handicapped.

As the Supreme Knight attempted to engender lay, religious, and moral leadership on the local level through the Service Department, membership campaigns, and the ceremonials, and as he continued to develop programs responsive to the needs of the Holy See, the bishops, and the clergy, he likewise was committed to instilling the spirit of the founding Knights, particularly of Father McGivney, into the life of the Order. Indeed, McGivney fashioned a unique Catholic fraternal benefit society with a singular blend of idealism and practicality which allowed the Order to develop in harmony with the evolution of the American Church. The Columbian motif, which had symbolized the Order's celebration of the American Catholic heritage in a society given to outbursts of anti-Catholic hysteria, also evolved. Still grounded in a strong pride in the Catholic roots of North America, Columbianism developed into a conscious cultivation of traditional Catholic loyalties to authority and of Catholic social and moral values in a society characterized by the decline of tradition and decreasing Church attendance.

Since the period of international expansion at the turn of the century, each administration has confronted the tensions between the Order's Columbian idealism and the practical business side of the Order. The very fact that the Order's associate and insurance membership has continued to experience quantitative growth and qualitative change strongly suggests that this has been a creative tension. Had idealism dominated to the neglect of the insurance program, the Order would have evolved into a social club without the economic strength to provide leadership and direction in the service of the Church and the community. Conversely, had the insurance program dominated, the Order would have developed into a business corporation without the idealism to attract a large membership and to provide the strong basis upon which the Knights' many fraternal programs were developed. The history of the Knights of Columbus mirrors the history of the American Catholic Church. In the post–Vatican II period, when fraternalism has been viewed as a relic of a previous era, the Order has continued to flourish not only because of its ability to thrive on creative tension but also because it has vigorously attached itself to the cause of the Church. Proud of their orthodoxy, their defense of Church authority, and their record of service, the Knights of Columbus still reflect the spirit of their priest founder with a unique blend of Catholic idealism and American practicality.

Pope Paul VI greets Supreme Chaplain
Bishop Charles P. Greco in 1975.

Supreme Knight Virgil Dechant, Mrs. Ann Dechant and Bishop Greco are honored by Pope John Paul I in his first private audience after his election as Pope (September 1, 1978).

Supreme Knight and Mrs. Dechant, together with Bishop Greco, are received by Pope John Paul II (1978).

During his 1979 visit to the United States, Pope John Paul II meets with Supreme Officers at the apostolic delegation office in Washington, D.C. Shown are Supreme Knight Dechant, Count Enrico Galeazzi, Archbishop Jean Jadot and Bishop Greco.

Supreme Council Headquarters Building
in New Haven, Connecticut, dedicated in 1969

Notes

KEY TO ABBREVIATIONS

ARCHIVES

AAB	Archdiocese of Baltimore
AABo	Archdiocese of Boston
AACh	Archdiocese of Chicago
AAD	Archdiocese of Detroit
AAH	Archdiocese of Hartford
AANY	Archdiocese of New York
AAP	Archdiocese of Philadelphia
AASF	Archdiocese of San Francisco
AASL	Archdiocese of St. Louis
ACUA	Catholic University of America
ADBel	Diocese of Belleville
ADPr	Diocese of Providence
AKC	Knights of Columbus, New Haven
AKCR	Knights of Columbus, Rome
AUND	University of Notre Dame
AUSCC	United States Catholic Conference

COLLECTIONS CONTAINED IN THE KNIGHTS OF COLUMBUS ARCHIVES, NEW HAVEN

BO	Bogus Oath File
CA	Catholic Advertising File
HC	Historical Commission
JWM	John W. McDevitt Papers
LEH	Luke E. Hart Papers
MF	Mexico File
OSC	Oregon School Case
RBD	Record of Supreme Board of Directors
RP	Roman Playgrounds File
SCMB	Supreme Council Minute Book
SCP	Supreme Council Proceedings
SSM	San Salvador Council Minutes
WAF	War Activities File
WWII	World War II Files

OTHER SHORT FORMS

CC	*Connecticut Catholic*
Col	*Columbia(d)*

Chapter 1: Origins in New Haven

1. Archives, Knights of Columbus, New Haven (hereafter cited as AKC), Geary Papers, "The Founder."
2. Austin Francis Munich, *The Beginnings of Roman Catholicism in Connecticut* (New Haven, 1935), 8. For the history of the Catholic Church in Connecticut see Thomas S. Duggan, *The Catholic Church in Connecticut* (New York, 1930); James H. O'Donnell, *History of the Diocese of Hartford* (Boston, 1899); Dolores Ann Liptak, "European Immigration and the Catholic Church in Connecticut, 1870–1920" (unpublished doctoral dissertation, University of Connecticut, 1979).
3. Duggan, op. cit., 134.
4. Munich, op. cit., 22.
5. Frank Andrews Stone, ed., *The Irish in Their Homeland, in America* (Storrs, Connecticut, 1975), 60.
6. Ibid., 78.
7. Thomas N. Brown, "The Origins and Character of Irish-American Nationalism," *Review of Politics* 18 (July 1956), 328–29.
8. Laurence J. McCaffrey, *The Irish Diaspora in America* (Bloomington, Indiana, 1977), 37. Also see John B. Duff, *The Irish in America* (Belmont, California, 1971); Andrew M. Greeley, *That Most Distressful Nation* (Chicago, 1973); Edward M. Levine, *The Irish and Irish Politicians* (South Bend, Indiana, 1966); Daniel P. Moynihan, "The Irish," in *Beyond the Melting Pot*, eds., Nathan Glazer and Daniel P. Moynihan (Cambridge, Massachusetts, 1963); Joseph P. O'Grady, *How the Irish Became American* (New York, 1973); William V. Shannon, *The American Irish* (New York, 1974); Carl Wittke, *The Irish in America* (New York, 1970).
9. Quoted by Patrick T. Conley and Matthew J. Smith, *Catholicism in Rhode Island: The Formation Era* (Providence, 1976), 126.
10. Ibid.
11. McCaffrey, op. cit., 85.
12. Ibid.
13. Ibid. Also see Ray Allen Billington, *The Protestant Crusade, 1800–1860* (Chicago, 1964); J. Humphrey Desmond, *The Know-Nothing Party: A Sketch* (Washington, 1904); Oscar Handlin, *Immigration as a Factor in American History* (Englewood Cliffs, New Jersey, 1959); John Higham, *Strangers in the Land: Patterns of American Nativism, 1860–1925* (New York, 1965);

Richard Hofstader, *Anti-Intellectualism in American Life* (New York, 1963); John Carrol Noonan, *Nativism in Connecticut* (Washington, 1938).

14. McCaffrey, op. cit., 93.
15. Ibid., 94.
16. Ibid., 32.
17. Quoted by Noonan, op. cit., 190.
18. Ibid., 189–90.
19. Ibid., 202.
20. Emmett Larkin, "The Devotional Revolution in Ireland, 1850–1875," *American Historical Review* 77 (June 1972), 625–52.
21. Jay P. Dolan, *The Immigrant Church: New York's Irish and German Catholics 1815–1865* (Baltimore, 1975), 46.
22. Ibid., 45–61.
23. William J. Whalen, *Handbook of Secret Organizations* (Milwaukee, 1960), 69.
24. Ibid., 70–79.
25. Colman J. Barry, O.S.B., *The Catholic Church and German Americans* (Milwaukee, 1953), 27n.; also see Mary L. Brophy, B.V.M., *The Social Thought of the German Roman Catholic Central Verein* (Washington, 1941).
26. Dorothy Ann Lipson, *Masonry in Federalist Connecticut* (Princeton, New Jersey, 1977); Allec Mellor, *Our Separated Brethren, the Freemasons* (London, 1967). Also see Henry Wise Beville, *History and Triumph of Fraternalism* (Norfolk, Virginia, 1920); William J. Whalen, *Christianity and Freemasonry* (Milwaukee, 1958); E. J. Dunn, *Builders of Fraternalism in America* (Chicago, 1924); Noel Pitts Gest, *Secret Societies: A Cultural Study of Fraternalism in the United States* (Columbia, Missouri, 1946); Arthur Schlessinger, *The Rise of the City, 1878–1898* (New York, 1933).
27. Daniel Colwell, "The Knights of Columbus," *Columbiad* (hereafter cited as *Col*) XVII (January 1910), 4.
28. The Sarsfield Guards were named after the Irish-Catholic soldiers, led by Patrick Sarsfield, who made the last stand against the British at the battle of the Boyne. See McCaffrey, op. cit. Note 8, p. 21.
29. Colwell, "The Knights of Columbus," loc. cit.
30. AKC, Geary Papers, "Red Knights."
31. AKC, "Constitution of the Sarsfield Council No. 1, Order of Red Knights."
32. AKC, Geary Papers, "Red Knights."
33. AKC, newspaper cuttings, *New Haven Morning Journal and Courier*, March 18, 1875.
34. Geary papers, "Red Knights."
35. AKC, *St. Vincent's Mutual Burial Association* (copy).
36. AKC, unidentified newspaper cutting. Quoted in an interview with William H. Sellwood, a charter member of the K. of C.
37. Sister Joan Bland, S.N.D., *The Story of the Catholic Total Abstinence Union of America* (Washington, 1951).
38. Daniel Colwell, "Knights of Columbus," *Col* XX (January 1913), 12.
39. AKC, unidentified newspaper cutting. Sellwood, op. cit.
40. Colwell, op. cit.
41. AKC, William Geary, Cornelius T. Driscoll, and other unnamed incor-

porators' recollections on the origins of the Order. Unpublished manuscript (hereafter cited as Geary and Driscoll).

42. AKC, Michael Tracy's Minutes, October 2, 1881. (Because this group evolved into San Salvador Council, these minutes will be hereafter cited as SSM.)

43. Ibid., November 6, 1881.

44. Ibid., November 20, 1881.

45. Ibid., December 4, 1881.

46. Ibid., December 18, 1881.

47. Colwell, op. cit. Note 38.

48. AKC, Geary and Driscoll.

49. Hence the five major primary sources relate conflicting stories on the events leading up to the foundation of the Knights of Columbus. There are the minutes of the St. Mary's group, recorded by Michael Tracy but copied sometime later in another hand; the minute book of the Church Street group, which was copied in its present form in 1909 and 1913; the recollections of William Geary, C. T. Driscoll, and other charter members, compiled in 1914; and William Geary's notes on the history written in the late 1920s. Though chronological and other problems abound, each of these sources is in agreement on the following points. The Foundation of the Knights of Columbus came after a period of trial which included Father McGivney's visits to Brooklyn and Boston; without Father McGivney's persistence neither the St. Mary's group nor the Church Street group could have sustained themselves. The Church Street group emerged as the Supreme Council of the Knights of Columbus; a smattering of the St. Mary's group, which continued to meet throughout the winter and spring of 1882, emerged as San Salvador Council No. 1, Knights of Columbus. Indeed, except for Daniel Colwell, and perhaps James Mullen, the other men in attendance at the first Church Street meeting were members of the previously convened St. Mary's group: Father McGivney, C. T. Driscoll, William Geary, John T. Kerrigan, and Dr. M. C. O'Connor. Since Mullen and Colwell were former officers of the Red Knights, perhaps this meeting does symbolize not only the evolution of the leadership of the Order but that point in its development when the fraternal and social aspects were strongly injected into the life of the young organization.

50. AKC, Supreme Council Minute Book (hereafter cited as SCMB), January 9, 1882.

51. AKC, SSM.

52. AKC, copy of this application.

53. AKC, Geary and Driscoll.

54. AKC, SCMB, February 2, 1882.

55. AKC, newspaper cuttings, *New Haven Journal Courier,* February 8, 1882.

56. "New Haven," *Connecticut Catholic* (hereafter cited as *CC*) VI (February 11, 1882), 1.

57. Daniel Colwell, "The Knights of Columbus," *Col* XVII (March 1910), 4.

58. AKC, Geary and Driscoll.

59. AKC, Dr. O'Connor's recollections, handwritten manuscript.

60. AKC, Geary Papers.
61. "Christopher Columbus—Discoverer of the New World," *CC* III (May 25, 1878), 4.
62. AKC, McGivney Papers, M. J. McGivney to Michael Edmonds, June 7, 1882.
63. AKC, SCMB, February 2, 1882. However, William Geary, who was present at the February 2 meeting, noted that the election was not held until May. AKC, Geary Papers.
64. Daniel Colwell, "Knights of Columbus," *Col* XVII (April 1910), 4.
65. AKC, Charter File, Articles of Incorporation.
66. AKC, McGivney Papers, M. J. McGivney to Reverend Pastor, April 1882.
67. Ibid.
68. AAH, McMahon Papers, Bishop Lawrence T. McMahon to Francis J. Reynolds, September 7, 1885.
69. Ibid.
70. AKC, McGivney Papers, M. J. McGivney to Michael Edmonds, June 7, 1882.
71. AKC. The entire constitution is included in the SCMB.
72. AKC, *Connecticut Knights of Columbus . . . Objects, Benefits, and Instructions for Forming New Councils.*
73. Once again sources conflict regarding the chronology and the content of the events related to the formation of the first council. William Geary recalled that the minutes of the St. Mary's group, which ultimately became the first council, records a December 4 (1881) election in which C. T. Driscoll was elected President for six months. Geary noted that Driscoll was elected Grand Knight on June 11, 1882. The Supreme Council's book on subordinate councils instituted records John T. Kerrigan as the Grand Knight with May 15 as the council's date of institution. According to the minutes of the St. Mary's group, Kerrigan was not elected Grand Knight until November 1882. The roll book of Council No. 1, which does not list the officers, refers to June 15 as the date of the initiation of the twenty-five charter members. Out of all of this confusion the following represents the most probable reconstruction of events:

   1. C. T. Driscoll was the first temporary chairman (president) of the council.

   2. May 15 is the consensus date of the council's institution.

   3. James T. Mullen was the first Grand Knight. June 15 is the likely date of the first initiation, as on that day the Constitution and By-laws of the Order were accepted by the Supreme Council.
74. AKC, Arthur J. Riley papers, Father Arthur J. Riley, historian of K. of C., 1950–54, unpublished notes on an interview with Miss Jane Curran, daughter of Michael Curran, Incorporator of K. of C., June 1950.
75. AKC, Geary Papers.
76. The oldest charter member of San Salvador was Father Patrick T. Lawlor, the first Supreme Council Chaplain as well as the first Chaplain for Council No. 1. Though his age was not listed, he was ordained a priest in 1863, which leads one to conclude that he was in his mid-forties in 1882. Patrick Madden, "wood worker," was the oldest among those

whose age was listed, while the youngest was the founder of the Order, Father McGivney, age twenty-nine.

James T. Mullen, first Supreme Knight, a native of New Haven, was born in 1847. He served for one year in the Union Army (Company C, Ninth Regiment, Connecticut Volunteers). Mullen served as fire marshal, constable, and other posts in the civic life of New Haven. One of the founders of the Red Knights, Mullen was an enthusiastic fraternalist and one of the three men responsible for designing the first set of ceremonials for the Order.

Deputy Supreme Knight John T. Kerrigan, also a native of New Haven, was chief mailing clerk in the city post office when the Order was founded.

Supreme Physician Matthew C. O'Connor was born in Staten Island, New York, in 1849. After training in New York City, Dr. O'Connor settled in New Haven, where he established his practice. Besides his volunteer efforts for the Knights of Columbus, he freely gave his services to the St. Francis Orphan Home for thirty-two years.

Cornelius T. Driscoll, first Supreme Advocate, was born in County Kerry, Ireland, in 1845 and spent his boyhood on a Connecticut farm. He graduated from Yale College in 1869 and received his law degree from Yale in 1871. A leading figure in the Democratic Party, his political career began in 1877 when he was president of the Board of Aldermen. He was elected to the State Legislature in 1881 and served as Corporation Counsel throughout the 1880s. In 1900 he became the first Catholic mayor of New Haven.

Supreme Lecturer (1882–84) and Supreme Secretary (1884–1909) Daniel Colwell was a native of North Adams, Massachusetts. In 1865, at the age of eighteen, Colwell moved to New Haven, where he began his apprenticeship in the bootmaker trade. Later he opened his own shoestore on Congress Street, but his work for the Democratic Party led him to run successfully for Town Constable in 1877, an office he held when the Order was founded.

William M. Geary, an incorporator, was born in New Haven in 1852. After working in his father's grocery and liquor store for a few years, Geary, an ardent Democrat, was appointed clerk to the Board of Selectmen and Town Agent in 1874, a position he held for twelve years.

Little has been written on Michael Curran, first Supreme Treasurer. His age and place of birth were not recorded in any of the official books. He was an undertaker who, according to Geary, was "highly esteemed by clergy and laity."

The strong parish loyalties of the first-generation Knights were clearly expressed in the choice of their pastor, Father Patrick T. Lawlor, as Supreme Chaplain. Before he became pastor of St. Mary's in 1879 he had served at St. John's Parish, New Haven, and at parishes in Mystic, Rockville, and New London. Father Lawlor, assisted by his curate, Father McGivney, was an energetic administrator, a determined fundraiser, and a concerned pastor. According to William Geary, Father Lawlor "did not enthuse over the plan adopted for the new association of degree work, ceremonials, passwords, etc." Though he originally preferred the character of the Catholic Foresters, "he became hopeful of the success of the new Order and gave his counsel and advice unreservedly and was an active member of San Salvador."

77. AKC, Geary Papers.
78. Archives of St. Mary's Seminary, Register Book I, 220, Registrant No. 648.
79. Archives of Niagara University. Catalogue of Seminary of Our Lady of the Angels. Also see Jean-Claude Drolet, *L'Ordre des Chevaliers de Columb* (Ottawa, 1962), 32.
80. AAH, Galberry Papers, Joseph P. Dubruel, S.S., to Thomas Galberry, December 19, 1877.
81. AKC, Geary Papers.
82. Quoted by Cornelius Maloney, *History of Sheridan Council No. 24.*
83. "New Haven," *CC* VII (July 29, 1882), 1.
84. Quoted by Maloney.
85. "New Haven," *CC* VII (September 2, 1882), 2.
86. Rev. Joseph Gordian Daley, "The Personality of Father McGivney," *Col* VII (June 1900), 1.
87. Ibid.
88. Quoted by Maloney.
89. "The Knights of Columbus," *CC* VII (February 3, 1883), 4.

Chapter 2: Conflict and Expansion in Connecticut

1. AKC, SSM, July 2, 1882.
2. Ibid., August 6, 1882.
3. Ibid., August 20, 1882.
4. Ibid., September 21, 1882.
5. Ibid., October 5, 1882.
6. Ibid., October 19, 1882.
7. Ibid., November 2, 1882.
8. AKC, Matthew C. O'Connor's notes on origins of the Order.
9. AKC, SSM, November 2, 1882.
10. Ibid., November 16, 1882.
11. AKC, McGivney Papers, M. J. McGivney to P. J. Ford, March 9, 1893, photocopy.
12. AKC, McGivney Papers, M. J. McGivney to P. J. Ford, April 17, 1883, photocopy.
13. Ibid.
14. "Meriden," *CC* VII (April 28, 1883), 2.
15. "Meriden," *CC* VIII (May 26, 1883), 2.
16. Daniel Colwell, "The Knights of Columbus," *Col* XVII (July 1910), 8.
17. AKC, Geary and Driscoll.
18. The Supreme Board of Directors was, and still is, solely responsible for the development of the ceremonials. Though the minutes of the Board of Directors do not include an official adoption of the three-stage initia-

tion rite, there is a reference to the Third Degree, "brotherly love," in an 1885 manual for the ceremonials of the First and Second Degrees.

19. "New Haven," *CC* VIII (February 23, 1884), 3.
20. AKC, SCMB, "Supreme Knight's Report, June 15, 1883."
21. Ibid.
22. Ibid.
23. AKC, Geary Papers, "Red Knights."
24. Michael J. McGivney to the editor, *CC* ViII (August 25, 1883), 3.
25. Ibid.
26. A reprint of this *Catholic Forester* article appears in *CC* VII (February 3, 1883), 4.
27. "Editorial," *CC* VIII (August 25, 1883), 3.
28. "Meriden," *CC* VIII (November 24, 1883), 2.
29. "Meriden," *CC* VIII (December 1, 1883), 2.
30. "Meriden," *CC* VIII (December 29, 1883), 2.
31. "Wallingford," *CC* VIII (January 19, 1884), 2.
32. "Meriden," *CC* VIII (March 8, 1884), 2.
33. Sister M. Claudia Carlen, I.H.M., *A Guide to the Encyclicals of the Roman Pontiffs from Leo XIII to the Present Day* (New York, 1939), 44–46.
34. Quoted in *CC* IX (May 31, 1884), 1.
35. Fergus MacDonald, *The Catholic Church and Secret Societies in the United States* (New York, 1946), 105–6. Also see John Tracy Ellis, *James Cardinal Gibbons, Archbishop of Baltimore 1834–1921* (Milwaukee, 1952), I, 441–42.
36. Quoted by MacDonald, 105.
37. D. J. Donohue to the editor, *CC* IX (May 10, 1884), 3.
38. Ibid.
39. *Constitution and By-Laws of the Knights of Columbus* (New Haven, 1884).
40. Ibid., 9–10.
41. AKC, SCMB, Supreme Knight's Report, June 15, 1884.
42. Ibid.
43. Ibid.
44. AKC, SCMB, Supreme Treasurer's Report, June 15, 1884.
45. Quoted by D. J. Donohue and William M. Geary to the editor, *CC* IX (June 7, 1884), 7.
46. Ibid.
47. William M. Geary to the editor, *CC* IX (June 14, 1884), 5.
48. D. J. Donohue to the editor, *CC* IX (June 28, 1884), 2.
49. "Green Cross Council," *CC* IX (September 20, 1884), 7.
50. "Bishop Galberry's Memorial Mass," *CC* IX (September 20, 1884), 1.
51. "Green Cross Council," loc. cit.
52. "New Haven," *CC* IX (November 15, 1884), 2.
53. Ibid.
54. "New Haven," *CC* IX (December 6, 1884), 6.
55. AKC. The original of this testimonial is in the museum collection.
56. "Minutes of Sheridan Council No. 24, April 27, 1885," Sheridan Council Minutebook, Waterbury, Connecticut.
57. Ibid., May 1, 1885.
58. Ibid., May 3, 1885.

59. Ibid.
60. AKC. The statistics are abstracted from *K. of C. Roll, Supreme Council, 1884.*
61. AKC, SCMB, "Supreme Secretary's Report, May 5, 1885."
62. "Meriden," *CC* X (May 9, 1885), 5.
63. "Clericus" to the editor, *CC* X (May 16, 1885), 4.
64. "Editorials," *CC* X (May 16, 1885), 4.
65. Father Michael J. McGivney to the editor, *CC* X (May 30, 1885), 4.
66. Ibid.
67. Ibid.
68. "Clericus" to the editor, *CC* X (June 6, 1885), 4.

Chapter 3: **The Vitality of the Order and the Death of the Founder**

1. Quoted in "The Knights of Columbus," *CC* IX (November 1, 1884), 5.
2. AKC, SCMB, October 29, 1885.
3. "Knights of Columbus," *CC* X (May 9, 1885), 5.
4. AKC, SCMB, May 12, 1885.
5. Ibid., June 9, 1885.
6. Ibid., October 29, 1884.
7. "Editorial," *CC* X (February 6, 1886), 4.
8. Ibid.
9. Quoted in "K. of C. Parade," *CC* X (July 11, 1885), 4.
10. Quoted in "K. of C. Parade," *CC* X (August 15, 1885), 4.
11. Ibid.
12. Ibid.
13. Ibid.
14. AKC, SCMB, May 17, 1886.
15. AKC, Geary Papers, William M. Geary and William M. Sellwood to the editor of *CC,* May 5, 1886 (copy).
16. Ibid.
17. AKC, SCMB, May 3, 1886.
18. Ibid., May 17, 1886.
19. Ibid.
20. "Knights of Columbus," *CC* XI (May 22, 1886), 8.
21. AKC, Geary Papers, "James Mullen."
22. *Park City Council No. 16, Golden Jubilee 1885–1935* (Bridgeport, Connecticut, 1935), n.p.
23. AKC, SCMB, Supreme Knight's Report, June 14, 1887.
24. Ibid.
25. Ibid.
26. T.F.C. to the editor, *CC* XIII (June 23, 1888), 4.
27. AKC, SCMB, June 26, 1888.
28. Ibid.
29. Ibid.
30. "Tempus" (pseudonym for a Knight from Providence, Rhode Island), *CC* XIII (April 6, 1889), 5.

31. Ibid.
32. "Knights of Columbus address by Father McGivney and Honorable John J. Phelan," *Providence Visitor* XIII (January 28, 1889), 4.
33. "Tempus," loc. cit. Note 28.
34. AKC, SCMB, June 27, 1889.
35. Ibid.
36. "The Reverend M. J. McGivney," *Waterbury Republican* (August 15, 1890), 4.
37. Ibid.
38. "Funeral Services of Father McGivney—at Thomaston," *Waterbury American* (August 18, 1890), 1.
39. "Funeral of Founder of K. of C.," *New Haven Union* 35 (August 18, 1890), 1.
40. "Funeral Services. . . ," loc. cit.
41. Ibid.
42. "An Impressive Funeral," *Waterbury Republican* (August 19, 1890), 1.
43. Quoted in "Knights of Columbus: A Parade and Services in Honor of Deceased Members," *CC* XVI (June 20, 1891), 1.

Chapter *4*: Columbianism, Anti-Catholicism, and Americanism

1. "Philip J. Markley," *New Haven Union Souvenir of the 400th Anniversary of the Discovery of America* (October 11, 1892), 1.
2. AKC, Charter File, Charter of the Knights of Columbus, 1889.
3. AKC, SCMB, Supreme Knight's Report, June 24, 1890.
4. M. F. Sullivan, "Reminiscences," *The Observer,* a publication of Rodrigo Council No. 44, 1 (March 1926), 6.
5. AKC, SCMB, Supreme Knight's Report, June 24, 1890.
6. AKC, SCMB, June 25, 1890.
7. AKC, SCMB, Supreme Knight's Report, June 25, 1891.
8. AKC, SCMB, June 26, 1891.
9. "Bridgeport," *CC* XVI (July 4, 1891), 8.
10. "Knights of Columbus Notes," *CC* XVI (July 4, 1891), 8.
11. S. D. Cronin to the editor, *CC* XVI (January 30, 1892), 8.
12. AKC, *The Record of the Catholic Benevolent Legion* X (January 1892).
13. D. M. Morey, *Fiftieth Anniversary Souvenir Edition,* Hornell Council No. 243 (Massachusetts, 1947), 46.
14. "Knights of Columbus," *CG* XVI (March 19, 1892), 1.
15. M. F. Sullivan, loc. cit. Notes 4, 6.
16. Charles S. O'Neill, *History of the Knights of Columbus* (New York, 1897), 106.
17. Ibid., 107.
18. AKC, SCMB, May 31, 1892.
19. "A Suggestion to the Knights," *CC* IX (March 28, 1885), 2.
20. AKC, SCMB, Supreme Knight's Report, May 3, 1892.
21. AKC, SCMB II, Supreme Knight's Report, October 24, 1893.
22. AKC, SCMB, June 24, 1891.

23. AKC, SCMB, Supreme Knight's Report, May 3, 1892.

24. "Columbian Celebration," *CC* XVII (October 1, 1892), 1.

25. "New Haven Celebration, Elm City in the Hands' of the Knights of Columbus," *CC* XVII (October 15, 1892), 1.

26. Ibid.

27. O'Neill, op. cit. Notes 16, 106.

28. AKC, SCMB II, Supreme Knight's Report, October 24, 1893.

29. Another scholar of melodrama, Michael Booth, stated, "As long as people enjoy uncomplicated characters, thrilling situations, throbbing emotions, and happy endings, as long as they are willing to lose themselves in a dream world of the imagination corresponding to their own reality, melodrama in one form or another will never cease to appeal." Quoted by Michael Kilgarriff, *The Golden Age of Melodrama: Twelve 19th Century Melodramas* (London, 1974), 24.

30. AKC, Ceremonial File, *Ritual and Manual of the Second Degree in Three Forms,* 1891.

31. "Archbishop Williams," *CC* XVIII (May 20, 1893), 4.

32. Robert H. Lord, John E. Sexton, Edward T. Harrington, *History of the Archdiocese of Boston, 1604–1943* (Boston, 1944), III, 101.

33. Ibid.

34. Ibid.

35. Donald L. Kinzer, *An Episode in Anti-Catholicism: The American Protective Association* (Seattle, 1964), 35. During an 1886 strike for the eight-hour day, anarchists held a meeting in Chicago's Haymarket Square during which time a bomb exploded.

36. Ibid.

37. "Armed Know-Nothings," *CC* XVII (April 3, 1893), 4.

38. Thomas H. Cummings, "The Knights of Columbus," *Donahoe's Magazine* XXIX (May 1893), 557.

39. *Col* I (November 1893), 1. Also see "The Secret Oath of the American Protective Association, October 31, 1893," in John Tracy Ellis, ed., *Documents of American Catholic History* (Milwaukee, 1955), 499–501.

40. "William J. Coughlin addresses Lowell Council No. 72," *Col* I (January 1894), 1.

41. Ibid.

42. Ibid.

43. Ibid.

44. Thomas H. Cummings, "Gentlemen in Fraternity," *Donahoe's Magazine* XXXIII (November 1895), 1240.

45. Ibid., 1239–40.

46. Ibid., 1240.

47. Ibid., 1241–42.

48. Ibid., 1242.

49. Ibid., 1243.

50. Ibid.

51. Timothy Smith, "Religion and Ethnicity in America," *The American Historical Review* 83 (December 1978), 1161.

52. Quoted by Walter Elliott, *The Life of Father Hecker* (New York, 1894), 292–93.

53. Ibid., 293. Also see Vincent F. Holden, C.S.P., *The Yankee Paul, Isaac Thomas Hecker* (Milwaukee, 1958).

54. John Ireland, in the Introduction to Elliott, *The Life of Father Hecker*, xxi.

55. Ibid., xii. Also see John Ireland, *The Church and Modern Society* (St. Paul, 1905), II, 221–50.

56. Ibid., II, 226.

57. See Patrick A. Ahern, *The Life of John J. Keane, Educator and Archbishop* (Milwaukee, 1955); Robert Cross, *The Emergence of Liberal Catholicism in America* (New York, 1971); Robert Emmett Curran, *Michael Augustine Corrigan and the Shaping of Conservative Catholicism in America, 1878–1902* (New York, 1978); John Tracy Ellis, *Perspectives in American Catholicism* (Baltimore, 1963), 107–26; Gerald P. Fogarty, S.J., *The Vatican and the Americanist Crisis: Denis J. O'Connell, American Agent in Rome, 1885–1903* (Rome, 1973); Andrew M. Greeley, *The Catholic Experience* (New York, 1969); Thomas T. McAvoy, C.S.C., *The Great Crisis in American Catholic History* (Chicago, 1957).

58. Quoted by John Tracy Ellis, *James Cardinal Gibbons, Archbishop of Baltimore 1834–1921* (Milwaukee, 1952), II, 6.

59. McAvoy, 45–93.

60. Quoted by McAvoy, 282.

61. See Chapter 5, "International Expansion."

62. "Prosperous K. of C.," *CC* XXI (August 21, 1896), 1.

63. Ellis, *Gibbons*, I., 478.

Chapter 5: **International Expansion**

1. Charles S. O'Neill, "The Story of Columbian Knighthood," *Donahoe's Magazine* LIX (February 1908), 147.

2. Quoted by Donna Merwick, *Boston Priests 1848–1910: A Study of Social and Intellectual Change* (Cambridge, 1973), 146.

3. John Tracy Ellis, *James Cardinal Gibbons, Archbishop of Baltimore 1834–1921* (Milwaukee, 1952), II, 601.

4. Charles S. O'Neill, *History of the Knights of Columbus* (New York, 1897), 325.

5. Fergus MacDonald, *The Catholic Church and Secret Societies in the United States* (New York, 1946), 162–63.

6. O'Neill, *History of the Knights of Columbus*, 331.

7. John K. Sharp, *History of the Diocese of Brooklyn, 1853–1953* (New York, 1954), I, 237.

8. Quoted by Charles S. O'Neill, "The Story of Columbian Knighthood," *Donahoe's Magazine* LIX (February 1908), 149–50.

9. AANY, Corrigan Papers G8, John J. Derry to Corrigan, June 5, 1895.

10. AANY, Corrigan Papers G8, Richard L. Walsh to Corrigan, June 15, 1895.

11. AKC, SCMB II, "Supreme Knight's Report, October 15, 1895."
12. Ibid.
13. "The Prosperous K. of C.," *CC* XXI (August 21, 1896), 1.
14. James E. Foley and Nicholas Virgadamo, eds., *The Knights of Columbus in the State of New York 1891–1968* (New York, 1968), 164.
15. Frederick J. Zwierlein, *The Life and Letters of Bishop McQuaid* (Rochester, New York, 1926), II, 474.
16. AKC, Record of Supreme Board of Directors (hereafter cited as RBD), I, March 8, 1898.
17. ADPr, Diary of Bishop Matthew Harkins, May 6–7, 1896.
18. O'Neill, *History,* 363.
19. Ibid., 364–67.
20. Dennis J. Clark, "The Irish Catholics," in *Immigrants and Religion in Urban America,* eds., Randall M. Miller and Thomas D. Marjek (Philadelphia, 1977), 59.
21. Maurice Francis Egan and John B. Kennedy, *Knights of Columbus in Peace and War* (New Haven, 1920), I, II.
22. John B. Bauernschub, *Columbianism in Maryland, 1897–1964* (Baltimore, 1949), 34.
23. Joseph J. Thompson, *A History of the Knights of Columbus in Illinois* (Chicago, 1921), 110–11.
24. Ibid., 111.
25. Ibid., 112.
26. Ibid.
27. *Remembrance of the Knights of Columbus, Commemorating the Twenty-fifth Year of Its Organization* (Sandusky, Ohio, 1906), 80.
28. "Editorials," *Col* VI (December 1899), 10–11.
29. "Proceedings of the National Convention," *Col* VII (March 1900), 16–17.
30. Paul A. Joyce, ed., *Sixty Years of Columbianism in Tennessee* (Nashville, 1962), 18.
31. Ibid.
32. Roger Baudier and Millard F. Everett, *Knights of Columbus in Louisiana* (New Orleans, 1962), 24.
33. "Alabama," *Col* IX (January 1902), 15.
34. AKC, Arthur J. Riley File, James Reardon to Arthur J. Riley, October 31, 1951.
35. "The Progress in Minnesota," *Col* VIII (May 1901), 9.
36. Ibid.
37. Horton J. Roe, ed., *Fifty Golden Years—The History of the Knights of Columbus in Wisconsin, 1902–1952* (Milwaukee, 1953), 43–44.
38. "Indiana," *Col* VI (August 1899), 12.
39. "Indiana," *Col* VI (November 1899), 12.
40. "Missouri," ibid., 16.
41. AKC, *Minute Book, Mt. Pleasant Council, No. 98,* 46–47.
42. Ibid.
43. Quoted in "Editorials," *Col* VI (November 1899), 8.
44. "Editorials," ibid.

45. "The K. of C.," *The Sunday Watchman* (St. Louis, Missouri) III (February 25, 1900), 5.
46. AKC, *Minute Book of Kansas City Council No. 527,* 3 (copy).
47. Ibid.
48. Herbert J. Tholen, ed., *The Knights of Columbus: Their First Fifty Years in Kansas* (1950), 11.
49. AKC, *Minute Book of Kansas City Council No. 527,* 10.
50. Ibid.
51. Tholen, op. cit., 11.
52. Ibid., 13.
53. AKC, *Minute Book of Kansas City Council No. 527,* 13.
54. Ibid., 16.
55. "Colorado," *Col* VII (December 1900), 12.
56. "Utah," *Col* VIII (September 1901), 13.
57. Ibid.
58. AKC, Arthur J. Riley File, Right Reverend Duane G. Hunt to Arthur Riley, April 23, 1950.
59. "Editorials," *Col* VI (November 1899), 9.
60. Joseph Scott, "Pioneer Days of the Knights of Columbus in California," *Knights of Columbus Historical Review* (Los Angeles, 1934), 15.
61. Peter T. Conmy, *Seventy Years of Service, 1902–1972: History of the Knights of Columbus in California* (Visalia, California, 1972), 13–20.
62. Joseph Scott, "The Mission of the Order in the Land of the Missions," *Col* XI (February 1904), 5.
63. "Editorials," *Col* VII (August 1900), 10.
64. "Colorado," *Col* IX (April 1902), 10.
65. James J. Gorman, "Out West," *Col* XI (March 1904), 5.
66. Ibid.
67. AKC, New Mexico File, unidentified newspaper cutting, "How Columbianism Came to New Mexico."
68. William H. Oberste, *Knights of Columbus in Texas, 1902–1952* (Austin, 1952), 22–23. Also see Brother William S. Dunn, C.S.C., *Knights of Columbus in Texas* (Austin, 1978), 1.
69. Ibid., 24–25.
70. Ibid., 25.
71. "The Indian Territory," *Col* XI (January 1904), 10.
72. Quoted in *Catholic Fortnightly Review* (St. Louis, Missouri) XV (June 1, 1908), 335.
73. "The Indian Territory," loc. cit., 10.
74. Quoted by Jack Muldoon, "Historical Supplement, No. 1," *Nevada Knight Letter,* I, 6.
75. "The Knights of Columbus in Canada," *Montreal Council Review* (Montreal, 1934), 55.
76. Ibid.
77. Quoted in "Proceedings of the General Council 1899," *Col* VI (March 1899), 11.
78. "Canada," *Col* VII (February 1900), 12.
79. "Prince Edward Island," *Col* XI (January 1904), 11.

80. For the American administration of the Philippines, see Pedro S.De Achútegui, S.J., and Miguel A. Bernad, S.J., *Religious Revolution in the Philippines: The Life and Church of Gregorio Aglipay 1860–1960* (Manila, 1961), I, 313–48. Also see Gregorio F. Zaide, *Catholicism in the Philippines* (Manila, 1937), 196–200.

81. Mario Gotbonton, "God's Foot Soldiers," *The Cross* (Manila) 6 (May 1951), 7–9.

82. "Editorials," *Col* VII (October 1900), 9.

83. "Grand Ceremony in Mexico," *Col* XIII (March 1906), 5.

84. Ibid.

85. "Knights of Columbus in Mexico," *Col* XII (November 1905), 4.

86. Ibid.

87. "Grand Ceremony . . . ," loc. cit.

88. Ibid.

89. Paul V. Murray, *The Catholic Church in Mexico* (Mexico City, 1965), I, 290–313.

90. AKC, Oral History File, interview with Eugene Donahoe, Detroit, June 27, 1979.

91. AKC, *Ceremonials of the Knights of Columbus* (handwritten copy).

Chapter 6: Insurance Reforms, Patriotism, and Catholic Culture

1. AKC, Supreme Knight's Report, *Proceedings of the National Council,* March 5, 1895 (New Haven, 1895), 7. (Hereafter all National and Supreme Council Proceedings are cited as SCP.)

2. AKC, SCMB, II, "Supreme Knight's Report, October 24, 1893."

3. AKC, SCP, 1895.

4. AKC, SCP, 1902.

5. AKC, SCP, 1895.

6. "Fifty Years of Forestry," *Golden Jubilee Year, M.C.O.F., 1879–1929* (Boston, 1929), 35.

7. AKC, SCP, 1905, 7.

8. Ibid.

9. "Fifty Years of Forestry," loc. cit.

10. AKC, Daughters of Isabella File. "United States Court of Appeals for the Second Circuit, National Circle, Daughters of Isabella, Complainant, against the National Order of the Daughters of Isabella, Defendant." Reprint of the decision, 4.

11. Ibid., 2.

12. Ibid., 4–5.

13. Ibid., 6.

14. P. K. Kerwin, "Catholic Daughters of America," *Catholic Encyclopedia* (New York, 1967), III, 267.

15. AKC, SCP, 1897, 12.

16. Ibid.

17. Ibid., 11–12.

18. Ibid., 12.

19. Ibid., 4.
20. Ibid., 14.
21. Ibid., 7–8.
22. Ibid., 9–11.
23. "James E. Hayes," *Col* V (March 1898), 3.
24. AKC, SCP, 1898, 8.
25. Charles S. O'Neill, *History of the Knights of Columbus* (New York, 1897), 197.
26. AKC, RBD, June 10, 1898.
27. AKC, SCP, 1899, 7–8.
28. AKC, Edward Hearn Files, *Memories of Edward Hearn.*
29. "Proceedings of the National Council," *Col* VI (April 1899), 9.
30. Ibid., 10.
31. Ibid., 8–12.
32. O'Neill, 197.
33. Edward Hearn, "True Knighthood," *Col* V (October 1898), 6.
34. Ibid.
35. "Proceedings of the National Council," *Col* VI (April 1899), 9–10.
36. Ibid., 10.
37. AKC, SCP, 1901, 41.
38. Fackler was one of the five co-founders of the Actuarial Society of America. See Terence O'Donnell, *History of Life Insurance in Its Formative Years* (Chicago, 1936), 524.
39. AKC, SCP, 1901, 44.
40. Joseph L. Thompson, *A History of the Knights of Columbus in Illinois* (Chicago, 1921), 50.
41. AKC, *Proceedings of the Connecticut State Council,* 1907.
42. Timothy Crowley to the editor, *Catholic Transcript* (Hartford, Connecticut) IX (May 23, 1907), 4.
43. Quoted by Thompson, 54. Also see Maurice Francis Egan and John B. Kennedy, *The Knights of Columbus in Peace and War,* I, 104–10.
44. O'Donnell, op. cit. Note 38, 677.
45. Ibid., 660.
46. "Knights of Columbus in Uniform," *CC* XI (July 26, 1886), 4.
47. Ibid.
48. AKC, SCP, 1900, 6.
49. James E. Foley and Nicholas Virgadamo, eds., *The Knights of Columbus in the State of New York 1891–1968* (New York, 1968), 19.
50. Ibid., 14–16.
51. AKC, Fourth Degree File, historical notes.
52. AKC, Fourth Degree Ceremonial (handwritten copy).
53. Ibid.
54. Thomas H. Cummings, "Catholic Gentlemen in Fraternity," *Donahoe's Magazine* XXXIII (November 1895), 1249.
55. John Tracy Ellis, *James Cardinal Gibbons, Archbishop of Baltimore 1834–1921* (Milwaukee, 1952), II, 90.
56. AKC, "State Deputy's Report, Fourth Annual Convention, Maine State Council," Reprint in SCP 1899, 74.

57. Ibid.
58. Dorothy Dohen, *Nationalism and American Catholicism* (New York, 1967), 147.
59. "Editorial Notes," *Col* VII (April 1900). 5
60. Ibid., 11–12.
61. Ibid., 10.
62. Ibid.
63. Ibid., 11.
64. Personal interview with John W. McDevitt, May 20, 1979.
65. "The National Council," *Col* VI (March 1899), 11.
66. Ibid., 15.
67. Ibid.
68. Edward Gerard, "A Celtic Chair at Washington," *Donahoe's Magazine* XXXIII (January 1895), 51–55.
69. Peter E. Hogan, *The Catholic University of America, 1896–1903: The Rectorship of Thomas J. Conaty* (Washington, D.C., 1949), 22, 46.
70. "The National Council," loc. cit. Note 65, 15.
71. John Tracy Ellis, *The Formative Years of the Catholic University of America* (Washington, D.C., 1946), 307, 369.
72. AKC, SCP 1901, 9.
73. "Presentation Ceremonies at Washington," *Col* XI (May 1904), 4.
74. Ibid.
75. Ibid.
76. Ibid., 5.
77. Ibid. Also see M. B. O'Sullivan, "The Knights at Washington," *Donahoe's Magazine* LI (May 1904), 487–91.
78. ACUA, Records of the Rector, Conaty File, K-M, 1899. Thomas J. Conaty to Thomas B. Lawler, April 27, 1899.
79. AUND, John J. Ewing Papers, D. P. Toomey to John J. Ewing, Boston, March 5, 1904; T. J. Duane to John J. Ewing, Peoria, May 2, 1904.
80. Quoted by Arthur Preuss, *The Review* II (July 7, 1904), 428.
81. ACUA, Papers of the Faculty, Charles H. McCarthy File, "Notes from the Knights of Columbus Chair in Church History."
82. Ellis, *Gibbons,* II, 149–57. Also see Colman J. Barry, O.S.B., *The Catholic University of America, 1903–1909: The Rectorship of Denis J. O'Connell* (Washington, D.C., 1950), 71–108.
83. Quoted by Thompson, op. cit. Note 40, 393.
84. Ibid., 394.
85. "The First Graduate," *Col* XV (April 1908), 8.
86. Ibid.
87. Quoted in "Supreme Knight's Report," *Col* XIV (September 1907), 2.
88. Ibid.
89. AKC, Luke E. Hart Papers (hereafter cited as LEH), John S. Leahy to Dr. R. E. Kane, October 6, 1924 (copy).
90. AKC, RBD, August 15, 1907.
91. AKC, Leahy to Kane, loc. cit.
92. "Proceedings of the National Council, 1907," *Col* XIV (September 1907), 8.

93. Ibid.
94. AAB, 105425401, Edward L. Hearn to James Cardinal Gibbons, December 7, 1907.
95. AASL., Glennon Papers, John J. Glennon to James Cardinal Gibbons, December 11, 1907.
96. AAB, Edward L. Hearn to James Cardinal Gibbons, November 9, 1908.
97. Ibid.
98. *The Fellows of the Knights of Columbus Catholic University Endowment Record of Students 1914–1922* (Washington, D.C., 1922), 2.
99. Ibid., 2–3. Also see "Presentation of Catholic University Fund," *Col* XXI (February 1914), 4. According to the *Fellows* booklet, the date of presentation was January 1. *Columbiad*'s date of January 6 is the more likely, as January 1 was a holy day of obligation.
100. "Presentation . . .", 5.
101. Ibid.
102. Ibid.
103. Ibid.
104. *Fellows . . .* , 4–5.

Chapter 7: The Catholic Anti-Defamation Projects

1. Quoted by Edward E. Grusd, *B'nai B'rith: The Story of a Covenant* (New York, 1966), 15.
2. Ibid., 20.
3. Ibid., 150.
4. Colman J. Barry, O.S.B., *The Catholic Church and German Americans* (Milwaukee, 1953), 188.
5. Arthur Preuss, "An Extract from the Ritual of the Catholic Elks," *The Review* VIII (December 5, 1901), 562.
6. In the Americanist controversy Janssen sided with the conservatives. Barry, 213.
7. Arthur Preuss, "The Bishop of Belleville on The Knights of Columbus," *The Review* VIII (September 5, 1901), 367.
8. Quoted in "Editorial Notes," *Col* VIII (August 1901), 9.
9. Ibid.
10. Quoted in Ibid.
11. Arthur Preuss, "The Rights of the Ordinary Concerning Catholic Societies," *The Review* VIII (October 3, 1901), 418.
12. John Walsh, *Some Words Explanatory and Defensive of the Knights of Columbus Against a Recent Episcopal Censure* (Troy, New York, 1901).
13. Ibid., 7.
14. "Editorial Notes," *Col* VIII (October 1901), 9.
15. ADBel, August Barthel, "Brief Sketch of Belleville Council No. 1028 and the Entry of the Knights of Columbus into the Diocese," unpublished manuscript. Also see Joseph L. Thompson, *A History of the Knights of Columbus in Illinois* (Chicago, 1921), 162, 224.
16. Barthel, "Brief Sketch. . . ."

17. Ibid.
18. Quoted in "Catholic, Not Masonic," *Catholic Transcript* I (May 12, 1899), 4.
19. Ibid.
20. Ibid.
21. Arthur Preuss, "Growing Opposition to the Knights of Columbus," *The Review* XI (April 21, 1904), 241.
22. Quoted in Ibid.
23. Ibid.
24. "Meeting of the Board of Directors," *Col* XI (May 1904), 16.
25. "Coughlin vs. the K. of C.," *Col* XIII (April 1906), 5.
26. "Cardinal Satolli on the Order," *Col* XI (August 1904), 3.
27. "Archbishop Bruchési's Tribute," *Col* XIII (June 1906), 1, 14.
28. "Order's Greatest Triumph," *Col* XIII (July 1906), 4.
29. Ibid., 5.
30. Lyman Faxon, "Knights of Columbus Headquarters," *Col* XI (October 1904), 2.
31. James E. Foley and Nicholas Virgadamo, eds., *The Knights of Columbus in the State of New York 1891–1968,* 35–38. Also see Thomas J. Comerford, "A Magnificent Permanent Home," *Col* XI (October 1904), 5.
32. Comerford, 8.
33. Foley and Virgadamo, 135–38; also AKC, New York File, "Minutes of the Long Island Chapter" (copy).
34. Foley and Virgadamo, 14–15.
35. "The Kansas Relief Fund," *Col* X (October 1903), 10.
36. "San Francisco Relief Fund," *Col* XV (September 1908), 9.
37. Quoted by Adele Francis Gorman, O.S.F., "Federation of Catholic Societies in the United States" (unpublished doctoral dissertation, Notre Dame, 1962), 113.
38. Thomas T. McAvoy, *A History of the Catholic Church in the United States* (Notre Dame, Indiana, 1969), 345.
39. Ibid., 345–46.
40. "The National Convention," *Col* XV (September 1908), 6.
41. Dennis A. McCarthy, "Unveiling a Magnificent Success," *Col* XIX (July 1912), 3.
42. Ibid., "Addresses Delivered at the Unveiling," 6.
43. Ibid., 8.
44. Ibid., McCarthy, 4.
45. Ibid., "The Grand Banquet," 5.
46. Ibid., Edward Hearn, "Proud of Knights," 11.
47. "News from Councils, Iowa," *Col* XV (December 1908), 9.
48. "An Extraordinary Triumph," *Col* XVI (March 1909), 3.
49. "Supreme Knight's Report," *Col* XVI (August 1909), 19.
50. "Professor Monaghan's Lectures," *Col* XVII (February 1910), 15.
51. "The Good of the Order," *Col* XVII (September 1910), 32.
52. Edward L. Hearn, "The Knights of Columbus," *The Catholic Encyclopedia* (New York, 1913) VIII, 6713.
53. "The New York Celebration," *Col* XIII (November 1906), 7–8.

54. Ibid., 8.
55. James C. Monaghan, "Conservation," *Col* XVIII (December 1911), 8.
56. John Higham, *Strangers in the Land: Patterns of American Nativism, 1860–1925* (New York, 1965), 117.
57. Quoted by Higham, 124.
58. Ibid.
59. Thomas H. Cummings, "The Knights of Columbus," *Donahoe's Magazine* XXIX (May 1893), 557. For a discussion of the triple melting-pot theory, see Milton M. Gordon, *Assimilation in American Life: The Role of Race, Religion, and National Origins* (New York, 1964), 115–32.
60. Cummings, "The Knights of Columbus," 557.
61. Higham, 17.
62. Ibid., 179.
63. Ibid., 179–80.
64. Quoted by Higham, 182.
65. "The Guardians of Liberty," *Col* XIX (April 1912), 10.
66. Leo Christopher Donohue, "The Alleged Fourth Degree Knights of Columbus Oath" (unpublished dissertation, Boston College, 1938), 43–44.
67. AKC, Bogus Oath File (hereafter cited as BO), reprint of the Bogus Fourth Degree Oath.
68. *Knights of Columbus vs. Libel and Malicious Bigotry* (New Haven, 1914), 19.
69. AKC, Fourth Degree Files, Fourth Degree Pledge.
70. *Knights of Columbus vs. Libel and Malicious Bigotry*, 19.
71. Ibid., 2. Also see "Philadelphia Knights Take Action on Bogus Oath," a reprint from the *Philadelphia Ledger*, February 21, 1913, in *Col* XX (March 1913), 4.
72. *Criminal Libels Against the Knights of Columbus Exposed* (hereafter cited as *Criminal Libels*), (New Haven, n.d.), 9.
73. Ibid.
74. Quoted in Ibid.
75. *Criminal Libels*, 10.
76. Ibid., 11.
77. Quoted in Ibid., 12.
78. *Criminal Libels*, 21.
79. Quoted in Ibid.
80. *Criminal Libels*, 13–14.
81. Ibid., 14. Also see Peter T. Conmy, *Seventy Years of Service, 1902–1972: A History of the Knights of Columbus in California* (Visalia, California, 1972) 34.
82. Conmy, op. cit., 34; *Criminal Libels*, 48–49.
83. Conmy, 33; *Criminal Libels*, 49.
84. Conmy, 34; *Criminal Libels*, 49.
85. Conmy, 34.
86. *Criminal Libels*, 18.
87. Ibid., 17.
88. "The Knights of Columbus Oath," *The Menace* (September 12, 1914), 1.
89. "Proceedings," *Col* XV (October 1908), 34.
90. Ibid.

91. "Proceedings," *Col* XVI (September 1909), 9.

92. *The National League for the Protection of American Institutions,* Document No. 28 (New York, 1896).

93. AKC, Flaherty File, "James A. Flaherty," unpublished manuscript.

94. The full text of these resolutions is included in "Politics and Religion," Education Briefs, No. 25 (January, 1909); *Ecclesiastical Review* (Philadelphia, 1909), 72.

95. James A. Flaherty, "Future of the Knights of Columbus," *Col* XX (January 1913), 3.

96. "A Fearless Knight's Triumph," *Col* XX (January 1913), 10.

97. "Tool of Socialism," a reprint from the *Catholic Columbian* (Columbus, Ohio), in *Col* XX (April 1913), 10.

98. Edwin A. Daly, "How to Successfully Combat Socialism," *Col* XX (October 1913), 4.

99. David Goldstein, *Autobiography of a Campaigner for Christ* (Boston, 1935), 112.

100. Ibid., 120–21.

101. "Great Lecture Tours Planned," *Col* XXI (February 1914), 10.

102. John Reddin, "Columbianism Today and Tomorrow," *Col* XXI (March 1914), 3.

103. Ibid.

104. Goldstein, 145.

105. "Educational Campaign Thoroughly Appreciated," *Col* XXI (May 1914), 10.

106. Ibid., 4.

107. "Supreme Knight's Report," *Col* XXI (September 1914), 11.

108. Ibid., 27.

109. Ibid., 32.

110. P. H. Callahan's "Introduction" to an address by Washington Gladden, "Patriotism" reprint in *Col* XXIV (February 1917), 4.

111. Washington Gladden, "Anti-Papal Panic," *Col* XXI (August 1914), 4, 13. Condé B. Pallen, Ph.D., L.L.D., a prominent Knight and an editor of the *Catholic Encyclopedia,* responded to Gladden's article with qualified praise; ibid., 5.

112. Sydney Ahlstrom, *A Religious History of the American People* (Garden City, New York, 1975), II, 257, 260–62.

113. Joseph E. Green, "Patrick Henry Callahan (1866–1940)," unpublished dissertation, Catholic University of America, Studies in Sociology, 54. (Washington, D.C., 1964), 57–58.

114. *Report of Commission on Religious Prejudices* (New Haven, 1915), 4.

115. Ibid., 1.

116. Ibid., 14.

117. Ibid., 4.

118. Ibid., 21.

119. Ibid., 5.

120. Ibid., 16.

121. Ibid., 17.

122. Ibid., 18.

123. Ibid., 10.
124. Ibid., 27.
125. Ibid., 28–30.
126. Ibid., 30.
127. Ibid., 30–31.
128. Ibid., 31.
129. Ibid., 32.
130. "Supreme Knight's Report," *Col* XXII (October 1915), 13.
131. *Report of Commission on Religious Prejudices* (Davenport, Iowa, 1916), 14.
132. Ibid., 6.
133. *A Message to All Patriotic Citizens* (Louisville, 1916).
134. *Report . . .*, 1916, 8–9.
135. Quoted by Green, op. cit. Note 112, 18.
136. Ibid., 88.
137. Ibid., 69.
138. Ibid., 89.
139. *Report . . .*, 1916, 21.
140. Ibid., 22.
141. Ibid., 25.
142. Ibid.
143. Quoted in *Report . . .*, 1916, 43.
144. Ibid., 45.
145. "Supreme Knight's Report," *Col* XXIII (September 1916), 11.
146. *Report of the Commission on Religious Prejudices* (New Haven, 1917), 3.
147. Ibid.
148. Ibid., 4.
149. Ibid., 5.
150. Ibid.

Chapter 8: Serving the Servicemen in World War I

1. AKC, War Activities File (hereafter cited as WAF), James A. Flaherty to Woodrow Wilson, April 17, 1917.
2. AKC, WAF, James A. Flaherty to Woodrow Wilson, May 23, 1917.
3. Frederick Katz, "Pancho Villa and the Attack on Columbus, New Mexico," *American Historical Review* 83 (February, 1978), 101–30.
4. William H. Oberste, *Knights of Columbus in Texas, 1902–1952* (Austin, Texas, 1952), 207–12; Maurice Francis Egan and John B. Kennedy, *Knights of Columbus in Peace and War* (New Haven, 1920), I, 201–10; "Knights on Border Service," *Col* XXIII (August 1916), 11.
5. "Knights on Border Service," 11.
6. C. Howard Hopkins, *History of the YMCA in North America* (New York, 1951), 486.
7. Quoted by Hopkins, 486.
8. W. J. Moriarty, "Solving Soldier Problems," *Col* XXIII (September 1916), 7.
9. Ibid., 9. Such reports accurately reflected the problems; in 1916 there

were only nine Catholic chaplains attached to the National Guard and only three or four attached to the regular Army units assigned to Mexican border duty; see *United States Catholic Chaplains in the World War* (Army and Navy Chaplains Ordinate, New York, 1924), XIV. For further information on the chaplains problem see AACh, Mundelein Papers, "Minutes of the Meeting of the Archbishops 1916." There were severe shortages of local priests as well; in the diocese of Corpus Christi, forty-four priests administered to over 75,000 Catholics within an area of 22,391 square miles; see Egan and Kennedy, I, 202.

10. "Guardsmen on the Border," *Col* XXIII (October 1916), 15.
11. "Along the Mexican Border," *Col* XXIII (November 1916), 16.
12. "Guardsmen on the Border," 16.
13. "Along the Mexican Border," 16.
14. AKC, WAF, Flaherty to Wilson, May 23, 1917.
15. Quoted by Hopkins, 487.
16. AKC, WAF, Bagley to McGinley, April 14, 1917.
17. AKC, WAF, Bagley to McGinley, April 14, 1917.
18. Ibid.
19. AKC, WAF, McGinley to Bagley, April 20, 1917.
20. P. H. Callahan, "The K. of C. War Activities," *Good of the Order* XIV (March 1, 1919), 6. This was originally a publication of Louisville Council No. 390 but in 1919 was published and edited by Callahan. For a general study of American society during the war, see David M. Kennedy, *Over Here: The First World War and American Society* (New York, 1980).
21. AKC, WAF, E. W. Buckley to McGinley, April 28, 1917.
22. AKC, WAF, P. H. Callahan to McGinley, May 9, 1917.
23. AKC, WAF, William P. Larkin to McGinley, May 9, 1917.
24. AKC, WAF, John J. Wynne to Larkin, May 7, 1917.
25. AKC, WAF, William J. Mulligan to McGinley, May 7, 1917.
26. "News from the Councils, Missouri," *Col* XXIV (June 1917), 18.
27. "The Work in Missouri," *Col* XXIV (June 1917), 21.
28. "News from the Councils, Vermont," *Col* XXIV (June 1917), 21.
29. "The 1917 State Conventions," *Col* XXIV (June 1917), 12.
30. P. H. Callahan, "The K. of C. War Activities," *Good of the Order* XIV (March 1, 1919), 5.
31. P. H. Callahan, "The K. of C. War Activities," *Good of the Order* XIV (July 15, 1919), 14.
32. AKC, WAF, Raymond B. Fosdick to Flaherty, June 1, 1917.
33. AKC, WAF, Flaherty to Fosdick, June 12, 1917, a rough draft.
34. AKC, WAF, Flaherty to Grand Knight, June 12, 1917; also see *Col* XXIV (July 1917), 3.
35. AKC, WAF, McGinley to Thomas A. Lawler, June 15, 1917.
36. P. H. Callahan, "The K. of C. War Activities," *Good of the Order* XIV (April 15, 1919), 5.
37. Reprinted in "Approval from the War Department," *Col* XXIV (July 1917), 4.

38. AKC, WAF, James Cardinal Gibbons to Reverend Lewis J. O'Hern, May 19, 1917 (copy).
39. P. H. Callahan, "The K. of C. War Activities," *Good of the Order* XIV (May 1, 1919), 5.
40. Ibid., 7.
41. Ibid., 5.
42. "Proceedings of the Supreme Council," *Col* XXIV (September 1917), 16.
43. P. H. Callahan, "K. of C. War Activities," *Good of the Order* XIV (May 1, 1919), 7.
44. AKC, SCP 1917, 16.
45. AKC, WAF, Gibbons to Frederick Ullrick, District Deputy, July 4, 1917.
46. P. H. Callahan, "The K. of C. War Activities," *Good of the Order* XIV (May 1, 1919), 7.
47. Ibid., June 1.
48. Ibid., June 15, 6.
49. Ibid., 15.
50. Ibid., July 1, 1919, 6.
51. Ibid.
52. Ibid., 14.
53. Ibid. Also see Elizabeth McKeown, "War and Welfare, A Study of American Catholic Leadership" (unpublished dissertation, Divinity School, University of Chicago, 1972), 107–17; Elizabeth McKeown, "The National Bishops' Conference, an Analysis of its Origins," *Catholic Historical Review* LXVI (October 1980), 565–83.
54. AKC, WAF, Callahan to John J. Burke, September 10, 1917 (copy).
55. AKC, WAF, Callahan to Joseph Pelletier, September 10, 1917 (copy).
56. Ibid., September 18, 1917 (copy).
57. AKC, WAF, Callahan to John Agar, September 18, 1917 (copy).
58. AKC, WAF, Agar to Callahan, September 20, 1917 (copy).
59. AKC, WAF, W. P. Larkin to John Wynne, S.J., September 24, 1917 (copy).
60. AKC, WAF, Extracts from minutes of the Supreme Board of Directors, September 30–October 1, 1917 (copy).
61. P. H. Callahan to the *Post Standard* of Syracuse, New York, reprinted in *Good of the Order* XIV (July 15, 1919), 1.
62. Ibid.
63. Ibid.
64. AKC, WAF, Copy of Baker's statement quoted in Press Release #3, September 22, 1917, Knights of Columbus Committee of War Activities.
65. P. H. Callahan, "K. of C. War Activities," *Good of the Order* XIV (August 1, 1919), 5.
66. Ibid., 14.
67. Ibid., 15.
68. Ibid.
69. AKC, WAF, Callahan to William Jennings Bryan, September 17, 1917 (copy).

70. AKC, WAF, Callahan to William Fox, September 11, 1917 (copy).
71. P. H. Callahan, "K. of C. War Activities," *Good of the Order* XIV (July 15, 1919), 6.
72. Ibid., 7.
73. AKC, WAF, Callahan to the editor of the *Catholic Transcript,* October 13, 1917 (copy).
74. AKC, WAF, H. P. Wilkinson to A. G. Bagley, August 21, 1917 (copy).
75. AKC, WAF, War Activities Memorandum, December 1, 1917.
76. Joseph L. Thompson, *A History of the Knights of Columbus in Illinois* (Chicago, 1921), 725.
77. Ibid., 726–77.
78. P. H. Callahan, "K. of C. War Activities," *Good of the Order* XIV (June 11, 1919), 5.
79. AKC, WAF, H. DeShivers, John J. Burke, and Francis C. Beckley to McGinley, September 17, 1917 (copy).
80. AKC, WAF, Callahan to Walter N. Kernan, September 20, 1917 (copy).
81. AKC, WAF, Pontur to O'Hern, October 5, 1917 (copy).
82. AKC, WAF, Callahan to War Activities Committee, October 9, 1917.
83. AKC, WAF, Callahan to Pontur, October 11, 1917, copy of a letter which includes the complete cable.
84. AKC, WAF, "Report of Walter Kernan, Overseas Commissioner, to the Board of Directors," New York, January 6, 1918, 1.
85. Dumas Malone and Basil Rauch, *War and Troubled Peace, 1917–1939* (New York, 1960), 39.
86. John J. Pershing to Walter N. Kernan, copy in *Col* XXV (February 1918), 6.
87. AKC, WAF, "Report of Walter Kernan . . .," loc. cit. Note 113, 2.
88. AKC, WAF, Callahan to Kernan, November 9, 1916 (copy).
89. "Our Work Abroad," *Col* XXV (February 1918), 5–6.
90. AKC, WAF, cable, Callahan to Kernan, December 7 (copy).
91. AKC, WAF, cable, Kernan to Callahan, December 11.
92. AKC, WAF, Kernan Report to "The Officers and Supreme Board of Directors and Committee on War Activities of the Knights of Columbus, February 19, 1918" (copy).
93. Ibid.
94. AKC, WAF, Callahan to Pelletier, February 2, 1918 (copy).
95. AKC, WAF, Callahan to Sir Charles Fitzpatrick, February 15, 1918 (copy).
96. AKC, WAF, Pelletier to Callahan, February 16, 1918 (copy).
97. AKC, WAF, Callahan to Pelletier, February 28, 1918 (copy).
98. AKC, WAF, Callahan to Kernan, February 25, 1918 (copy).
99. AKC, WAF, Callahan to War Activities Committee, February 26, 1918 (copy).
100. AKC, WAF, Callahan to Pelletier, February 28, 1918 (copy).
101. P. H. Callahan, "K. of C. War Activities," *Good of the Order* XIV (September 15, 1919), 7.
102. AKC, WAF, Pelletier to Callahan, April 10, 1918 (copy).
103. AABo, K. of C. File, 1918, extracts from Minutes of Meeting of Supreme

Board of Directors, Knights of Columbus, held at Hotel LaSalle, Chicago, Illinois, May 29, 1918.

104. AKC, WAF, Callahan to Flaherty, April 20, 1918 (copy).

105. AABo, K. of C. File, 1918, Flaherty to Callahan, May 29, 1918 (copy).

106. AABo, K. of C. File, 1918, Callahan to Father Thomas Oakley, June 3, 1918.

107. AKC, WAF, Father Thomas F. Oakley, "Dear Editor," May 6, 1918, copy of letter which was never published.

108. AABo, K. of C. File, 1918, Callahan to Oakley, June 3, 1918.

109. AKC, WAF, Pelletier to John Kernan, June 21, 1918 (copy).

110. AKC, WAF, Kernan to Flaherty, December 31, 1918 (copy); cable quoted in this sixteen-page letter, 3.

111. Ibid., 3–16.

112. Ibid., 16.

113. Ibid.,

114. AKC, WAF, "Larkin, Victim of Gas, Returns," *Sunday American,* May 18, 1919, copy of newspaper cutting donated by Mr. Frank A. Larkin, Queens Valley, New York.

115. AKC, WAF, Diary of Frank A. Larkin, copy of original owned by Frank A. Larkin.

116. Ibid., 22.

117. Ibid., 23–24.

118. Ibid., 39.

119. Ibid., 40.

120. "Larkin, Victim of Gas, Returns," loc. cit. Note 114.

121. AKC, WAF, Joseph Tumulty to Flaherty, September 18, 1917 (copy).

122. AKC, WAF, Flaherty to Wilson, October 10, 1917 (copy).

123. AKC, WAF, Wilson to Flaherty, October 23, 1917.

124. "Some Great War Fund Drives," *Col* XXV (March 1918), 11.

125. "Our Great New York War Fund Drive," *Col* XXV (May 1918), 9, 16.

126. AKC, WAF, "Remarks of Bishop Muldoon at Meeting, Supreme Board of Directors, May 26–27, 1918" (copy).

127. AKC, WAF, Muldoon to Flaherty, August 3, 1918.

128. "The Victory Convention," *Col* XXV (September 1918), 8.

129. "Proposed Combined Drive?" *Col* XXV (September 1918), 4.

130. Ibid.

131. "One Drive for War Funds," *Col* XXV (October 1918), 3.

132. Egan and Kennedy, op. cit. Note 4, I, 304.

133. AKC, WAF, Knights of Columbus Theater, Antwerp, Program, July 3, 4, 5, 1919.

134. "A K. of C. Club in Rome," *Col* XXVI (March 1919), 17.

135. Leo Hillman, "Under High Pressure," *Col* XXVI (July 1919), 7.

136. "K. of C. Huts for Gobs in Turkey," *Col* XXVII (July 1920), 12.

137. Egan and Kennedy, I, 367.

138. "Everything Free," *Col* XXVI (March 1919), 10.

139. AKC, WAF, a cutting. D. J. McCarthy, "A Query Concerning the K. of C.," *America.*

140. William Almon Wolff, "Keep Coming, Casey!" *Col* XXVI (May 1919), 9.

141. AKC, WAF; this story is included in Mulligan, "Reports," March, April, 1919.
142. Ibid.
143. AKC, WAF, Report of Commissioner Fox to the Supreme Secretary, July 12, 1920.
144. AKC, WAF, William Fox, unpublished diary, January 29, 1920, 102.
145. AKC, WAF, "Minutes of Special Meeting, Supreme Board of Directors, November 22, 1918."
146. AKC, WAF; this letter was quoted in full in McGinley to Directors and Examiners in Charge, U.S. Employment Service.
147. AKC, WAF, McGinley to K. of C. Secretaries Aboard Transports, January 28, 1919.
148. "Heads Employment Work," *Col* XXVI (May 1919), 21.
149. Collins and Mulligan met with Burke and O'Grady in May 1919; see Collins's eleven-page report, AKC, WAF, Report, May 1919. Also see ACUA, John J. Burke File 06B, McGinley–Burke correspondence, May 1919.
150. Peter W. Collins, "From Battlefield to Workshop," *Col* XXVII (January 1920), 7.
151. Quoted by Egan and Kennedy, op. cit. Note 4, I, 388.
152. Collins, 7–10.
153. AKC, WAF, McGinley to State Deputies, April 19, 1921.
154. AKC, WAF, *Report of the Supreme Board of Directors, Educational and Welfare Work* (New Haven, 1920), 10.
155. James A. Flaherty, "A Red Letter Year," *Col* I (September 1921), 22.

Chapter 9: Mission Abroad and Divisions at Home

1. Supreme Knight's Report," *Col* XXVI (September 1919), 13.
2. Ibid.
3. "The Bishops' Program of Social Reconstruction," in *American Catholic Thought on Social Questions,* ed. Aaron I. Abell (New York, 1968), 325–48.
4. "Report of Committee on the Good of the Order," *Col* XXVI (September 1919), 29.
5. Ibid., 30.
6. "The Proposed Statue at Metz," *Col* XXVI (September 1919), 8.
7. AKC, Metz File, newspaper cutting. "Ein Freimaureheiliger und Die Knights of Columbus," *Familien Blatt.*
8. AKC, Metz File, J. M. Weinzapfel to McGinley, May 27, 1920.
9. AKC, Metz File, McGinley to Weinzapfel, June 3, 1920.
10. "Supreme Knight's Report," *Col* XXVII (October 1920), 12.
11. AKC, Metz File, John Reddin, unpublished diary, 11.
12. Ibid., 59–60.
13. Ibid., 3.
14. Ibid., 4.
15. Quoted in "The Pilgrimage to Europe," *Col* XXVII (October 1920), 3.
16. "The Audience with the Pope," *Col* XXVII (October 1920), 16.

17. Ibid., 17.
18. Ibid.
19. AKC, Metz File, John Reddin's diary, 73.
20. Ibid.
21. Ibid., 77. For newspaper accounts of the Order's audience with Benedict XV, see "Pope's Allocution in Praise of Work of Knights of Columbus," *The Monitor* (San Francisco) XXII (October 2, 1920), 21.
22. "Board of Directors," *Col* XXVII (November 1920), 5.
23. John W. Maynard and Carlo M. Ferrari, *The Methodist Episcopal Church in Italy* (Rome, 1930), 8.
24. AKC, Roman Playgrounds File (hereafter cited as RP), "Extracts from Letter of European Commissioner, Edward L. Hearn." Received in Supreme Office August 26, 1921.
25. Arthur Benington, "Rome's Call to the K. of C.," *Col* I (November 1921), 9, 23. Tom Watson, a former U.S. senator from Georgia, published *Watson's Magazine,* which contained frequent anti-Catholic articles similar to those of *The Menace.* See Comer Vann Woodward, *Tom Watson, Agrarian Rebel* (New York, 1938).
26. Maynard and Ferrari, op. cit. Note 35, 16–22.
27. James A. Flaherty, "A Red Letter Year," *Col* I (September 1921), 23.
28. Quoted by John B. Kennedy, "War and Those Who Make It," *Col* I (February 1922), 17.
29. AKC, RP, a cutting. "The Battle of Rome," *Literary Digest* (September 15, 1923), 35–36.
30. AKC, RBD, January 15, 1922.
31. Ibid., IV, January 14, 1922.
32. Ibid., 155.
33. AABo, K. of C. File, 1922, Hearn to Flaherty, April 5, 1922 (copy).
34. AABo, K. of C. File, 1922, Hearn to McGinley, May 14, 1922 (copy of cable).
35. "Edward F. Hearn, Pope Pius and the K. of C.," *Col* I (July 1922), 23.
36. AKC, RP, McGinley to Hearn, June 29, 1922.
37. "K. of C. Italian Fund Will be Prorated," *The Pilot* (Boston) XXXVIII (February 2, 1922), 1.
38. AKC, RP, *Knights of Columbus Welfare Work in Rome 1923–1927* (brochure, 1928), 8.
39. Ibid., 10–11.
40. "The Voice from the Vatican," *Col* III (June 1924), 15.
41. Ibid., 3.
42. Ibid., 15.
43. J. Joseph Huthmacher, *Massachusetts People and Politics 1919–1933* (Cambridge, Massachusetts, 1959), 14.
44. "Watch and Ward Society Move to Oust Prosecutor," *Boston Evening Record* XXXI (November 13, 1919), 1.
45. Ibid., 2.
46. AKC, J. Pelletier File, memo to McGinley anonymously written by "a prominent lawyer and friend of Mr. Pelletier."
47. AKC, J. Pelletier File, "Argument for District Attorney Joseph C. Pelle-

tier" by James A. Reed (U.S. Senator) and Louis C. Boyle (Ex-Attorney General of Kansas), 1–5.

48. Ibid.

49. Ibid., 58.

50. AKC, J. Pelletier File, untitled newspaper cutting, *Boston American,* February 22, 1922.

51. Ibid. The secondary literature does not include one reference to the possible innocence of Pelletier. In his biography of Godfrey Lowell Cabot, Leon Harris devotes an entire chapter on the Cabot-Pelletier conflict in which Pelletier's guilt is considered a truism not requiring one footnote; see Leon Harris, *Only to God; The Extraordinary Life of Godfrey Lowell Cabot* (New York, 1967), 230–51. Also see John Henry Cutler, *Honey Fitz: The Life and Times of John F. Fitzgerald* (Indianapolis, 1962), 236.

52. Ibid.

53. "An American Dreyfus Case?" *Col* I (March 1922), 17.

54. "The Knights of Columbus and the Pelletier Case," *The Nation* 114 (April 12, 1922), 423.

55. ACUA, Bishop Muldoon's Rockford File, William J. Mulligan to P. J. Muldoon, July 18, 1923.

56. AKC, LEH, Minutes of the Supreme Board of Directors, April 8–10, 1922 (copy).

57. AKC, J. Pelletier File, *Resolutions Presented for Consideration of the Supreme Council Knights of Columbus, Atlantic City, N.J., August 1–3, 1922* (copy).

58. AABo, K. of C. File, 1922, William C. Prout to Bernard J. Rothwell, March 16, 1922 (copy).

59. AABo, K. of C. File, 1922, Edward A. Hickey, Secretary of the Catholic Laymen's Committee, Boston, to the Delegates Supreme Convention, The Knights of Columbus, July 29, 1922 (copy).

60. AKC, J. Pelletier File, Pelletier to Flaherty, June 29, 1922 (copy).

61. Quoted in "Calls Protest Impertinent," *Catholic Transcript* XXV (August 3, 1922), 5.

62. AKC, LEH, Hart to Dr. T. E. Purcell, March 20, 1922.

63. AKC, LEH, Hart to Purcell, March 30, 1922.

64. AKC, LEH, biographical notes on Luke E. Hart.

65. "Pelletier Sends Resignation," *The Columbian News* (New York) XI (July 5, 1922), 1.

66. AASF, K. of C. File, 1922, William J. Mulligan to Most Reverend Edward J. Hanna, July 15, 1922.

67. AKC, LEH, Hart to Carmody, July 15, 1922.

68. Most Reverend John J. Glennon, "University of Knighthood," *Col* II (September 1922), 24.

69. Quoted in "Deus ex Machina," *Catholic Transcript* V (August 3, 1922), 4.

70. Ibid.

71. James A. Flaherty, "Still Hewing to the Line," *Col* II (September 1922), 26.

72. AKC, LEH, "J. G. Hargrove to the Members of the Supreme Council of the Knights of Columbus" (printed pamphlet).

73. ACUA, P. H. Callahan Papers, 1922. See Coyle–Callahan correspondence, November 1922.

74. AKC, LEH, Callahan to LaVega Clements (State Deputy, Kentucky), March 7, 1923 (copy).

75. AKC, LEH, "Knights of Columbus Reconstruction Program" (copy).

76. AKC, LEH, Callahan to LaVega Clements, March 7, 1923 (copy).

77. AKC, LEH, "Knights of Columbus Reconstruction Program."

78. Ibid.

79. AKC, LEH, "Memorandum . . . Concerning Knights of Columbus Reconstruction Program."

80. AKC, LEH, "Notes on the Reconstruction Program."

81. AASL, K. of C. File, 1923, "A Bishop's Warning to The Knights of Columbus" (extracts from a sermon delivered by the Right Reverend M. J. Gallagher, Bishop of Detroit at Detroit Assembly's Communion Mass in his cathedral May 13, 1923), reprinted from the *Fortnightly Review*, July 1, 1923.

82. AAD, Gallagher Papers, "Hearing, April 8, 1923, Resolution Adopted by Board of Directors Knights of Columbus" (printed copy).

83. Ibid., 15.

84. Ibid., 17–19.

85. Ibid., 20.

86. Ibid., 21.

87. Ibid.

88. "A Bishop's Warning . . . ," loc. cit. Note 81.

89. ACUA, Muldoon Papers, Box 10, Folder 15, Joseph Schrembs to Muldoon, May 26, 1923.

90. AKC, LEH, D. J. Callahan to Luke E. Hart, May 17, 1923.

91. AKC, LEH, Hart–Callahan correspondence, March–May 1923.

92. AKC, LEH, J. F. Martin to William J. McGinley, June 8, 1923 (copy).

93. AKC, LEH, Hart to Hearn, June 13, 1923.

94. ACUA, Muldoon's Rockford File, Mulligan to Muldoon, July 18, 1923.

95. ACUA, Flaherty to Muldoon, September 17, 1923, Muldoon's Rockford File; also, AABo, K. of C. File, 1923, Flaherty to Cardinal O'Connell, September 11, 1923.

96. Ibid.

97. James A. Flaherty, "Progress and Prosperity" (Supreme Knight's Report), *Col* III (September 1923), 6.

98. Ibid., 7.

99. Ibid., 11.

100. Ibid., 12–16.

101. AKC, LEH, Hart to P. J. McCarthy, September 1, 1923.

102. "Resolution No. 75, Texas" (Proceedings of the 1922 Supreme Convention), *Col* II (September 1922), 19.

103. Quoted in "K. of C., Planning Boy's Clubs," *Michigan Catholic* (August 10, 1922), 1.

104. AKC, LEH, Minutes of the meeting of Supreme Board of Directors, June 23–25, 1923 (copy).

105. "Proceedings of the Supreme Convention," *Col* III (September 1923),

11–12; also, W. J. Battersby, *Brother Barnabas, Pioneer in Modern Social Service* (Winona, Minnesota, 1920), 113–15.

106. Quoted by Battersby, op. cit., 115.
107. Ibid., 117.
108. AABo, K. of C. File, 1923, Flaherty to O'Connell, February 11, 1924.
109. Battersby, op. cit., 117.
110. Ibid., 145.
111. Quoted by Battersby, 156.
112. AKC, LEH, Brother Barnabas to Hart, July 25, 1929.
113. Battersby, op. cit., 156.
114. Ibid., 159.
115. Ibid., 160.
116. Ibid.
117. Ibid., 164.
118. Ibid., 187.
119. Ibid., 187–96.
120. AKC, LEH, Brother Barnabas to Hart, July 25, 1929.
121. Quoted by Battersby, op. cit., 209.

Chapter 10: Historical Revisionism and the Ku Klux Klan

1. Bessie Louise Pierce, *Public Opinion and the Teaching of History in the United States* (New York, 1970), 208.
2. Ibid., 77.
3. AKC, Historical Commission (hereafter cited as HC), McSweeney biography.
4. Edward F. McSweeney, *De-Americanizing Young America: Poisoning the Sources of our National History and Traditions* (Boston, 1920).
5. Ibid., 2.
6. Ibid., 6.
7. Ibid. Parenthetical remarks were McSweeney's.
8. Pierce, op. cit., 206. Also see John Higham, *History* (Englewood Cliffs, N.J., 1965).
9. AKC, HC, copy of resolution passed by Supreme Assembly, May 28, 1921.
10. James A. Flaherty, "A Red-Letter Year" (Supreme Knight's Report), *Col* I (September 1921), 23.
11. John H. Reddin, "The American History Contest," *Col* I (September 1921), 12.
12. "Knights Correct False Impression," *The Pilot* (Boston) 92 (September 24, 1921), 1.
13. Ibid.
14. Edward F. McSweeney, "American History for Americans," *Col* I (August 1921), 10.
15. David M. Chalmers, *Hooded Americanism: The First Century of the Ku Klux Klan, 1865–1965* (New York, 1965), 33.
16. AKC, HC, rough draft of Chairman's Report, 1923.

17. AKC, RBD, Minutes of Meeting of Board of Directors, New Orleans, January 3, 1922.
18. Edward F. McSweeney, "The Anger of the Anglophiles," *Col* I (April 1922), 10.
19. AKC, HC, copy of McSweeney address to the Supreme Convention of 1922.
20. Quoted by Pierce, 223.
21. Ibid., 226.
22. Charles Edward Russell, "Behind the Propaganda Scenes," *Col* II (September 1922), 5–6, 26.
23. Frances FitzGerald, *America Revised* (Boston, 1979), 59–70.
24. John H. Reddin, "The American History Contest," loc. cit. Note 11, 23.
25. "Proceedings of the Supreme Convention 1922," *Col* II (September 1922), 10. Also see S. A. Keenan, "Making History in Walla Walla," *Col* II (December 1922), 11.
26. Samuel Flagg Bemis, *Jay's Treaty: A Study in Commerce and Diplomacy* (New York, 1923), ix–x.
27. Ibid., 270–71.
28. Charles Edward Russell, *The Origins of the Propaganda Movement* (New Haven, 1922).
29. Thomas A. Mahony, "What Is the Monroe Doctrine?" *Col* I (January 1922), 20.
30. Rear Admiral William S. Benson, *The Merchant Marine* (New York, 1923).
31. Mengchien Joseph Bau, *The Open Door Doctrine in Relation to China* (New York, 1925).
32. AKC, HC, Edward F. McSweeney, Report to the Supreme Board of Directors, October 1923.
33. George Abel Schreiner, *Cables and Wireless* (New York, 1924).
34. AKC, HC, McSweeney, Report . . . 1923, "Introduction," 1.
35. "Proceedings of the Convention," *Col* III (September 1923), 22.
36. Allan Nevins, *The American States During and After the Revolution, 1775–1789* (New York, 1924).
37. Edward F. McSweeney, "Racial Contribution to America," *Col* III (June 1924), 8.
38. Edward F. McSweeney, "Introduction," in W.E.B. DuBois, *The Gift of Black Folk: Negroes in the Making of America* (Boston, 1924), 28.
39. Ibid., 1.
40. Ibid., 2.
41. Herbert Aptheker, ed. *The Correspondence of W.E.B. DuBois* (Boston, 1973), I, 311.
42. George Cohen, *The Jews in the Making of America* (Boston, 1924), 237–61.
43. Frederick Franklin Schrader, *The Germans in the Making of America* (Boston, 1924).
44. AKC, HC, Minutes of Meeting of Special Committee on Historical Commission Matters, June 2, 1923.
45. AKC, HC, quoted by McSweeney in his "Memorandum for Special Committee, May 5, 1923."
46. However, as late as August 1924 Supreme Knight Flaherty circulated a

form letter elaborating on the rationale underlying the Racial Contribution Series and announcing that three books in the series had been published and others were to follow. See AANY, 012, James Flaherty to your Excellency, August 15, 1924.

47. James A. Flaherty, "A Goal of Progress" (Supreme Knight's Report), *Col* V (September 1925), 42.

48. John H. Reddin, "Annual Prize Essay Contest," *Col* IV (April 1925), 42.

49. Brother William H. Dunn, C.S.C., *Knights of Columbus in Texas 1902–1977* (Austin, Texas, 1978), 7–9; and William H. Oberste, *Knights of Columbus in Texas 1902–1952* (Austin, Texas, 1952), 165–206.

50. Oberste, op. cit., 171.

51. Kenneth T. Jackson, *The Ku Klux Klan in the City 1915–1930* (New York, 1967), 4.

52. Chalmers, op. cit. Note 20, 28–29.

53. Chalmers, 31; Jackson, 18–23.

54. Chalmers, 32.

55. Chalmers, 110–11, Jackson, 18–23.

56. Jackson, 11.

57. "Ku Klux Salesman Circulated a Forged Oath of Treasonable and Murderous Obligations. They say Knights of Columbus take . . ." *The World* (New York) LXII (September 14, 1921), 1.

58. Jackson, 11–12.

59. John B. Kennedy, "The Profits of Prejudice," *Col* I (October 1921), 13.

60. John M. Mecklin, *The Ku Klux Klan* (New York, 1924), 124–25.

61. Michael Williams, *The Shadow of the Pope* (New York, 1932), 134.

62. Quoted by Williams, 134–35.

63. AKC, Anti-Catholicism File, W. J. Weyland to Joseph Pelletier, October 21, 1921.

64. Ibid., unidentified newspaper cutting attached to letter.

65. AKC, Anti-Catholicism File, Joseph Pelletier File, 1921.

66. "K. of C. Bogus Oath Circulators Will Be Prosecuted," *NCWC News Sheet* III (February 5, 1923), 1.

67. Arthur H. Bell, *The Ku Klux Klan or the Knights of Columbus Klan* (Milan, Illinois, n.d.), 4–5.

68. Ibid., 10–18.

69. AKC, Bogus Oath File (hereafter cited as BO), William Lloyd Clark Case, copy of Hart's letter (March 20, 1923) and Clark's response printed by Rail Splitter Press in form of a handbill entitled "The Knights of Columbus Exposed."

70. AKC, BO, Clark Case, James Malone to Luke E. Hart, June 26, 1923.

71. AKC, BO, Clark Case, Hart to Malone, June 28, 1923.

72. Dr. Peter T. Conmy, *Seventy Years of Service, 1902–1972: History of Knights of Columbus in California* (Visalia, California, 1972), 32–25; Roger Baudier and Millard F. Everett, *Anchor and Fleur-de-lis: Knights of Columbus in Louisiana, 1902–1962* (New Orleans, 1965), 146–47; Thomas Elton Brown, *Bible Belt Catholicism: A History of the Roman Catholic Church in Oklahoma 1905–1945* (New York, 1977), 45–55; *Twentieth Annual Convention of the Connecticut State Council, Knights of Columbus, Danbury, Connecticut, May 13,*

1913 (Hartford, 1913), 20–21; *Twenty-First Annual Convention of the Connecticut State Council, Knights of Columbus, Greenwich, Connecticut, May 13, 1914* (New London, 1914), 24–25; Joseph J. Thompson, *A History of the Knights of Columbus in Illinois* (Chicago, 1921), 45 and 401; Herman J. Tholen, *The Knights of Columbus: Their First Fifty Years in Kansas* (Kansas State Council, May, 1950), 97–99; Brother William H. Dunn, *Knights of Columbus in Texas, 1902–1977* (Austin, Texas, 1978), 5; *Report of the Eleventh Annual Convention of the Colorado State Council, Knights of Columbus, Pueblo* (May 26, 1913), 4; William H. Oberste, *Knights of Columbus in Texas, 1902–1952* (Austin, Texas, 1952), 121–40; Horton L. Roe, *The History of the Knights of Columbus in Wisconsin from Their Beginnings in the Year 1900* (Oshkosh, Wisconsin, 1952), 69–71.

73. AKC, LEH, C. E. Byrne to W. F. Hustmyre, June 30, 1923.
74. Chalmers, op. cit. Note 15, 39–44.
75. Jackson, op. cit. Note 51, 13–16.
76. Ibid., 17.
77. Douglas Slawson, "The Attitudes and Activities of American Catholics Regarding the Proposals to Establish a Federal Department of Education Between World War I and the Great Depression" (unpublished doctoral dissertation, Catholic University of America, 1980).
78. Ibid.
79. Ibid., 124.
80. Jackson, 127–28.
81. Slawson, 128.
82. Thomas Elton Brown, op. cit. Note 72, 99–116.
83. Chalmers, 85.
84. Chalmers, 85–86.
85. Chalmers, 88.
86. Quoted by Jackson, 202.
87. AKC, LEH, Minutes of the Meeting Supreme Board of Directors, July 30, 31, 1922 (copy).
88. AKC, Oregon School Case (hereafter cited as OSC), P. J. Hanley to Luke E. Hart, November 29, 1922.
89. James A. Flaherty, "The New Year Call to Duty," *Col* II (January 1923), 3.
90. AKC, LEH, Minutes of Meeting, Supreme Board of Directors, January 6–7, 1923 (copy).
91. AKC, OSC, Roger Baldwin to Hart, January 22, 1923.
92. AUSCC, Files of the General Secretary, Minutes of the Administrative Board, N.C.W.C., January 11, 1923, in *Minutes of the Administrative Board, N.C.W.C., April 25, 1919, to November 7, 1929*.
93. AKC, OSC, E. W. Buckley to Hart, January 30, 1923.
94. AKC, OSC, Hart to McGinley, January 29, 1923.
95. AKC, OSC, Hart to McGinley, January 30, 1923.
96. AKC, OSC, Carmody to Hart, February 7, 1923.
97. AKC, OSC, Hart to Carmody, February 9, 1923.
98. AKC, OSC, Archbishop Christie to McGinley, February 17, 1923. William Mulligan sent copies of the February 18 telegram from Christie to

McGinley to Cardinal O'Connell of Boston. See AABo, K. of C. File, 1923.

99. AKC, OSC, Kavanaugh to Hart, July 26, 1923.

100. AKC, OSC, Carmody to Hart, September 22, 1923.

101. Quoted by Frank J. Lonergan, "The Oregon School Decision," *Col* IV (July 1925), 25.

102. AKC, OSC, Daniel A. Tobin to William J. McGinley, July 14, 1925. Also see "Knights of Columbus Gave Financial Aid to Fight Oregon School Case," *The Catholic News* XXXIX (July 25, 1925), 2, and "The K. of C. and the Oregon Law," in the same edition.

103. AKC, OSC, P. J. Hanley, Financial Account of the Hill Military Academy Case.

104. AANY, 2–15 (39), P. J. Hanley to Cardinal Hayes, June 27, 1925.

105. Jackson, op. cit. Note 51, 251–55.

106. Quoted by Williams, op. cit. Note 61, 193.

107. Ibid., 195.

108. Ibid.

109. AKC, LEH, Hart to John F. Martin, November 3, 1928. Hart may not have voted for Smith, as at the time of the 1960 election he was supposed to have said, "This is the first election in which I have voted Democrat."

Chapter *11*: The Knights' Crusade in Mexico

1. Paul V. Murray, *The Catholic Church in Mexico: Historical Essays for the General Reader* (Mexico City, 1965), I, 334–68.

2. Octavio Paz, *The Labyrinth of Solitude: Life and Thought in Mexico,* translated by Lysander Kemp (New York, 1961), 148–49.

3. Daniel James, *Mexico and the American* (New York, 1963), 154–74.

4. Robert E. Quirk, *The Mexican Revolution and the Catholic Church, 1910–1929* (Bloomington, Indiana, 1973), 40–79.

5. Ibid., 60–61.

6. Ibid.

7. John W. F. Dulles, *Yesterday in Mexico: A Chronicle of the Revolution, 1919–36* (Austin, Texas, 1961), 298–99.

8. William F. Buckley, "What's Wrong in Mexico?" *Col* III (March 1923), 7.

9. Ibid., 9.

10. Ibid.

11. AKC, Mexico File (hereafter cited as MF), W. L. Vail to "Dear Noble." This undated letter, signed "Yours in the Faith, W. L. Vail," was given to Supreme Treasurer Daniel J. Callahan by a friend of his in Alexandria, Virginia.

12. Dulles, 304.

13. Ibid., 303–4.

14. AKC, SCP, 1926, 16.

15. Ibid., 69–70.

16. Ibid., 70.
17. AKC, LEH, Minutes of Special Meeting of the Supreme Board of Directors, September 5, 1926 (copy).
18. Ibid.
19. AKC, MF, newspaper cuttings, *St. Louis Post Dispatch,* September 10, 1926.
20. David Goldstein, *Mexico* (New Haven, 1926), 3–10.
21. Ibid., 11.
22. Quirk, op. cit. Note 4, 18.
23. Quoted in "Pope Pius in Tribute to the Work of the Knights in Mexico," *Col* VI (January 1927), 30.
24. AKC, LEH, Minutes of the Supreme Board of Directors, January 8–9, 1927 (copy).
25. AKC, LEH, Minutes of the Supreme Board of Directors, June 30, 1928 (copy).
26. Quirk, 212–18.
27. Quoted by Harold Nicholson, *Dwight Morrow* (New York, 1931), 319.
28. Ibid., 320; also see Quirk, 219.
29. Quirk, 230.
30. For a detailed account of Burke's role in the negotiations, see John B. Sheerin, C.S.P., *Never Look Back: The Career and Concerns of John J. Burke* (Paramus, New Jersey, 1975), 108–44.
31. AKC, SCP, 1928, 22–23.
32. AKC, MF, J. N. Fining to Hart, May 29, 1928.
33. AKC, MF, McGinley to Michael Kenney, September 15, 1935.
34. AKC, LEH, Minutes of the Supreme Board of Directors, August 19–21, 1929 (copy).
35. Quoted by E. David Cronon in "American Catholics and Mexican Anti-Clericalism, 1933–1936," *The Mississippi Valley Historical Review* XLV (September 1958), 206.
36. Ibid.
37. Ibid., 207–19.
38. Sheerin, op. cit. Note 30, 161–64.
39. AKC, MF, Hart–Callahan correspondence, October 1934.
40. "Supreme Knight's Condemnation of the Acts of the American Government," *The Record. Religious Liberty: The Mexican Government* (New Haven, 1935), 5.
41. Ibid., 6.
42. Ibid., 9.
43. Ibid.
44. George O. Flynn, *American Catholics and the Roosevelt Presidency 1932–1936* (Lexington, Kentucky, 1968), 162. Also see George O. Flynn, *Roosevelt and Romanism* (Westport, Connecticut, 1976).
45. AKC, MF, Callahan to Hart, January 22, 1935.
46. AKC, MF, Carmody to Hart, January 23, 1935. For biographical information on Senator Walsh see Dorothy G. Wayman, *David I. Walsh, Citizen Patriot* (Milwaukee, 1952).

47. AKC, MF, Callahan to Hart, January 29, 1935.
48. AKC, MF, Harry S. Truman to T. J. Pendergast, February 16, 1935. Pendergast sent this original Truman letter to Hart.
49. "Editorials," *Col* XIV (March 1935), 12.
50. "Supreme Knight's Condemnation . . .," *The Record. Religious Liberty: The Mexican Government,* 5.
51. Ibid., 15.
52. AKC, MF, Robert R. Hull to Hart, August 16, 1935.
53. AKC, MF, D. J. Callahan to Michael J. Curley, June 3, 1935 (copy). Also see *Religious Liberty in Mexico: Report of a Deputation to Mexico appointed by the American Committee on Religious Rights and Minorities* (New York, 1935), 4.
54. "Editorials," *Col* XV (October 1935), 13.
55. AKC, MF, Hart–Ruiz correspondence, March 1935.
56. AKC, MF, Hart to Francis Matthews, April 10, 1935.
57. AKC, MF, Hart to Joseph J. Driscoll, May 1, 1935.
58. Ibid.
59. Francis Clement Kelley, *Blood Drenched Altars, Mexican Study and Comment* (Milwaukee, 1935), 390. For a thorough study of Kelley's deep involvement in the Mexican Church, see James P. Gaffey, *Francis Clement Kelley and the American Catholic Dream* (Bensonville, Illinois, 1980), II, 3–103.
60. AKC, MF, Curley to Callahan, May 31, 1935 (copy).
61. Sheerin, op. cit. Note 30, 165. Also see U.S.C.C., General Secretary's Files, Minutes of the Administrative Board, N.C.W.C., November 17, 1935.
62. AKC, MF, Curley to Callahan, May 10, 1935.
63. AKC, MF, Walsh to Hart, March 27, 1935.
64. "Supreme Knight's Condemnation . . .," *The Record. Religious Liberty: The Mexican Government,* 6.
65. AKC, MF, Hart to Ruiz, July 10, 1935, and Hart to Kelley, July 13, 1935.
66. Quoted by Flynn, op. cit. Note 44, 160.
67. "Protest Mexican Persecution," *Col* XV (October 1935), 17.
68. Quoted by Flynn, 166.
69. This phrase was lifted from a newspaper article and included in an October 25 letter of protest reprinted in "Non-Action in Mexican Persecution Protested by Supreme Board" *Col* XV (December 1935), 11.
70. Ibid.
71. AKC, MF, Roosevelt to Carmody, received November 15, 1935.
72. Quoted by Cronon, op. cit. Note 35, 221.
73. Ibid.
74. AKC, MF, Hart to M. T. Birmingham, November 6, 1935.
75. AKC, MF, Hart to Parsons, November 8, 1935.
76. AKC, MF, Matthews to Hart, November 23, 1935.
77. Ibid.
78. AKC, MF, Hart to Matthews, November 30, 1935.
79. Flynn, op. cit. Note 44, 185.
80. AKC, MF, Hart to Parsons, December 19, 1935.
81. AKC, MF, Swift to Hart, January 4, 1936.
82. "The Fight in the Open," *Knights of Columbus News* (March 9, 1936), 2.

83. AUSCC, General Secretary's Files, *Minutes of the Administrative Board, NCWC,* January 13, 1936.
84. Quoted in "The Fight in the Open."
85. Sheerin, op. cit. Note 30, 16. Though Sheerin gives the impression that Burke was not appointed to the position until February 1936, Burke told the Administrative Board of the N.C.W.C. that Cicognani had requested him to enter negotiations in 1934. *Minutes of the Administrative Board, NCWC,* January 13, 1936.
86. Sheerin, 167.
87. AKC, MF, Hart to Carmody January 2, 1936; Carmody to Hart, January 4, 1936.
88. AKC, MF, Cardinal Pacelli to Martin H. Carmody, January 31, 1935.
89. AKC, MF, Galeazzi to Carmody, December 7, 1935.
90. AKCR, Galeazzi to Pacelli, January 15, 1936, English translation.
91. AKC, MF, Hart to Michael J. Kenny, S.J., March 16, 1936.
92. "Mexican Stand of Order Given Vigorous Support" (reprint of the resolution), *Col* XVI (October 1936), 8–9.
93. Quoted by Cronon, op. cit. Note 35, 225.
94. ACUA, Callahan Papers, 1936. Several editions of the *Callahan Correspondence* during 1936 include pro-Daniels letters.
95. Sheerin, op. cit. Note 40, 160–71.
96. Cronon, 228–30, and Flynn, 191–94.
97. AUSCC, General Secretary's Files, *Minutes of the Administrative Board of the NCWC,* November 19, 1936.
98. AKC, MF, Swift to Hart, January 2, 1937.
99. "The Crusade Goes Forward," *Col* XVII (October 1937), 5.
100. AKCR, Carmody to Galeazzi, August 27, 1937.
101. Graham Greene, "The Birth of a Catholic Writer," *Commonweal* CVIII (January 16, 1981), 12–13.
102. Joseph Lidet, S.J., "Sinarquismo Victory in Tabasco" in *Revolution in Mexico,* edited by James W. Wilkie and Robert L. Michaels (New York, 1969), 222–26.

Chapter 12: **The Impact of the Great Depression**

1. James A. Flaherty, "A Year of Progress," *Col* V (September 1925), 3.
2. AKC, SCP, 1927, 118.
3. Ibid., 17.
4. Ibid., 18.
5. Martin H. Carmody, "The Order Advances" (Supreme Knight's Report), *Col* VIII (October 1928), 25.
6. Martin H. Carmody, "We Face the Future" (Supreme Knight's Report), *Col* IX (October 1929), 6.
7. Ibid.
8. AKC, SCP, 1930, 23.
9. Ibid., 25–26.
10. AKC, SCP, 1931, 21.

11. Ibid.
12. AKC, LEH, Carmody to Woods, November 24, 1930 (copy).
13. "Peter W. Collins," *Col* XI (July 1932), 31.
14. AKC, LEH, Minutes of the Supreme Board of Directors, October 10, 1931 (copy).
15. "Supreme Knight's Radio Message," *Col* XI (May 1932), 28.
16. AKC, LEH, Herbert Hoover to Martin Carmody, March 18, 1932 (copy).
17. *The Golden Anniversary of the Knights of Columbus, 1882–1932,* souvenir booklet (New Haven, 1932), 34.
18. Ibid., 35.
19. Ibid., 35–36.
20. Ibid., 25.
21. Ibid.
22. Ibid.
23. Ibid.
24. Robert I. Gannon, S.J., *The Cardinal Spellman Story* (Garden City, New York, 1962), 43–44.
25. Quoted by Gannon, 44.
26. Ibid., 49.
27. Ibid., 50.
28. AKC, RP, McGinley to Hearn, January 16, 1930 (copy).
29. AKC, RP, Hearn to McGinley, April 28, 1930 (copy).
30. Ibid.
31. AKC, RP, Borgongini-Duca to Hearn, March 31, 1931 (copy).
32. AKC, RP, Hearn to Borgongini-Duca, May, 1931 (copy).
33. In a letter to Assistant Supreme Secretary Conway, Galeazzi related at length the fifteen-year history of the K. of C. playgrounds. AKC, RP, Enrico Galeazzi to John S. Conway, August 20, 1937.
34. AKC, RP, Hearn to Carmody, June 8, 1931 (copy).
35. AKC, RP, Hearn to His Excellency, the American Ambassador—i.e., John W. Garrett (copy).
36. AKC, RP, Hearn to Carmody, June 8, 1931.
37. AKC, RP, newspaper cutting, "American K. of C. Seeks Protest on Fascist Ban," *New York Herald* (Paris, June 1, 1931), 1.
38. AKC, LEH. Hearn denied he had made this statement at the August 16, 1931, meeting of the Supreme Board of Directors; Minutes of the Supreme Board of Directors, August 16, 1931 (copy).
39. AKC, RP, Hearn to McGinley, June 22, 1931 (copy).
40. AKC, RP, Hearn to McGinley, June 23, 1931 (copy).
41. AKC, RP, P. Fumasoni-Biondi to Carmody, June 21, 1931 (copy).
42. Ibid.
43. In an interview on October 13, 1979, Count Galeazzi told this author that the Borgongini-Duca conflict was intensified by Hearn's refusal to fund renovations in the chapel at St. Peter's Oratory. Hearn never commented on this aspect of his feud with the Monsignor, but because when Carmody visited the Oratory the following November he agreed to an expenditure of $4,000 for such renovation, Galeazzi's recollection of the conflict is substantiated.

44. AKC, RP, Carmody to Hearn, June 30, 1931 (copy of cable).

45. AKC, RP, Carmody to Hearn, July 1, 1931.

46. The only extant letters of Hearn's after his dismissal were written in 1939. By this time he had developed a bizarre conspiracy theory which included a severe indictment of Borgongini-Duca and the American ambassador aimed at forcing the K. of C. to turn over the playgrounds to the Italian government, St. Peter's Oratory to the Vatican. Since the Oratory was virtually a Vatican institution in all but name, Hearn's retrospective conspiracy theory appears to have been deeply jaundiced by his bitter experience during 1931. AKC, RP (copy).

47. AKC, RP, cablegram quoted by Monsignor Paul Marella in: Marella to Carmody, September 10, 1931.

48. AKC, RP, letter and cable quoted in: Marella to Carmody, September 10, 1931 (copy). Marella was the auditor at the apostolic delegate's Office.

49. Ibid.

50. AKC, RP, Galeazzi to McGinley, November 13, 1931 (copy).

51. AKC, LEH, Minutes of Meeting of the Supreme Board of Directors, January 9–10, 1932 (copy).

52. Galeazzi to McGinley, September 26, 1932 (copy).

53. Quoted by Carmody in Supreme Knight's report, "Forward with New Spirit," *Col* XIV (October 1934), 6.

54. AKC, RP, Pacelli to Carmody, January 1935.

55. AKC, LEH, Minutes of the Meetings of Supreme Board of Directors, January 12–13, 1933 (copy).

56. "Our March 17 Mobilization Broadcast," *Col* XIV (April 1935), 19.

57. "Victory on all Fronts" (Supreme Knight's report), *Col* XV (October 1935), 6.

58. "K. of C. Forward Movement—Five Point Program of Progress," *Col* XV (February 1936), 14–16.

59. Ibid.

60. David J. O'Brien, *American Catholics and Social Reform: The New Deal Years* (New York, 1968), 86–89.

61. "Knights' Crusade—Your Part," *Col* XVI (February 1937), 14–15.

62. Ibid., 14.

63. For a thorough discussion of Father Coughlin's role in the New Deal Years, see O'Brien, 150–81.

64. *Encyclical Letter of His Holiness, Pope Pius XI (Divini Redemptoris) Atheistic Communism* (New Haven, 1937).

65. "The Crusade Goes Forward" (Supreme Knight's Report), *Col* XVII (October 1937), 16.

66. "The Knights of Columbus Crusade Marches On," *Col* XVI (March 1937), 14–15.

67. Martin Carmody, "Knight Crusaders," *Col* XVI (February 1937), 1.

68. George Hermann Derry, *The Peril of Communism* (New Haven, 1938), n.p.

69. Ibid.

70. AKC, LEH, Minutes of the Supreme Board of Directors, October 17, 1938 (copy).

71. *Knights' Crusade for Social Justice,* Council Schedule and Organization, (New Haven, 1939).
72. Joseph F. MacDonnell and Joseph F. Duane, *A Key to Sources on Christian Social Reconstruction* (New Haven, 1939).
73. AKCR, Galeazzi to Carmody, March 17, 1939.
74. "Make Peace our Watchword" (Supreme Knight's Address at the States Dinner, August 17), *Col* XIX (October 1939), 14.

Chapter 13: **The Ordeal of War and the Politics of Leadership**

1. AKC, LEH, Hart–Callahan correspondence, March–June 1939.
2. AKC, LEH. Moynihan's charges were included in Francis A. Matthews to Edwin Boehler, Los Angeles, California Chapter, May 3, 1940, printed in pamphlet form entitled *Personal and Confidential and Not for Publication.* After the Order had expelled Moynihan, he sued the Order to reinstate him. Moynihan's charges and Hart's responses are quoted at length in the following brief submitted to the Massachusetts Superior Court, Suffolk County (Equity): *Patrick J. Moynihan vs. Knights of Columbus, N 051680—Copy of Defendants' Reply Memorandum on Demurrer and Plea to the Jurisdiction,* 12–18.
3. AKC, SCP, 1939.
4. Patrick J. Moynihan *vs.* Knights of Columbus.
5. AKC, RBD, 1940–48.
6. AKC, LEH, Hart to Galvin, August 7, 1941.
7. *Reprint of Articles Published in the Insurance Index* (published by the Supreme Council, Knights of Columbus), New Haven, Connecticut, 1948.
8. James E. Dunne, "An Open Letter to the Members of the Knights of Columbus," reprinted from the Insurance Index, July 1948 (published by Supreme Council, Knights of Columbus), New Haven, Connecticut, 1948).
9. AKC, LEH, James E. Dunne to Luke E. Hart, January 14, 1949.
10. AKC, LEH, Hart–Swift correspondence, January–May 1948.
11. AKC, SCP, 1949.
12. William F. Leuchtenburg, *Franklin D. Roosevelt and the New Deal 1932–1940* (New York, 1963), 295.
13. Quoted by Thomas T. McAvoy, *A History of the Catholic Church in the United States* (Notre Dame, Indiana, 1969), 429.
14. Roger Van Allen, *The Commonweal and American Catholicism: The Magazine, the Movement, the Meaning* (Philadelphia, 1974), 89–90.
15. *War Services of the Canadian Knights of Columbus* (Montreal, 1948), 5.
16. Ibid., 16–22.
17. Ibid., 205.
18. Ibid., 198–99.
19. AKC, SCP, 1940, 30.
20. Leuchtenburg, op. cit., 299.
21. AKC, World War II Files (hereafter cited as WWII), Matthews to Stritch, October 13, 1940.

22. Ibid.

23. Rita L. Lynn, *The National Catholic Community Service in World War II* (Washington, D.C., 1952), 8.

24. Quoted by Lynn, 10.

25. AKC, WWII, Memorandum, Interview of Supreme Knight with Monsignor Ready at his office in Washington, January 13, 1941.

26. AKC, WWII, Matthews to Callahan, January 18, 1941.

27. AKC, WWII, Matthews to Mooney, January 24, 1941.

28. AKC, WWII, Hart to Francis J. Heazel, January 27, 1940. (Heazel, a Supreme Director, was Hart's close confidant.)

29. AKC, WWII, Heazel to Hart, May 18, 1943.

30. AKC, WWII, excerpts from Board of Directors Meetings Related to War Activities Committee.

31. McAvoy, op. cit. Note 17, 433–39.

32. AKC, RBD, January 10, 1943.

33. AKC, WWII, *Peace Program Proposal by the Knights of Columbus* (New Haven, 1943), 3.

34. Quoted by George Hermann Derry, "Our Columbian Peace Crusade," *Col* XXIII (April 1944), 1.

35. AKC, SCP, 1939, 68.

36. AKC, LEH, Hart to Heazel, December 18, 1940.

37. Interview with Hugh MacDonald, former chief accountant; since 1980, research assistant and consultant.

38. Ibid.

39. Hart to Heazel, June 11, 1941.

40. AKC, LEH, Hart to Heazel, June 21, 1941.

41. AKC, LEH, Birmingham to Hart, June 7, 1941.

42. AKC, LEH, Hart to Birmingham, June 11, 1944.

43. AKC, SCP, 1941, 27.

44. AKC, LEH, Hart–Heazel and Hart–Raymond Miller correspondence, 1942.

45. AKC, RBD, April 11, 1943.

46. This portion of Matthews's report was not printed in the Proceedings but was quoted in *The Case of James J. McMahon and Theodore W. Osbahr, Past State Deputies New Jersey Knights of Columbus* (Montclair, New Jersey, 1950), 34–41.

47. Ibid.

48. AAD, Mooney Papers, Matthews to Mooney, August 12, 1943. In this letter, Matthews indicated that it might be necessary for Mooney to attend the Supreme Council meeting.

49. AAD, Mooney Papers, Matthews to Mooney, July 14, 1943, and July 27, 1943.

50. AKC, SCP, 1943.

51. Ibid.

52. AKC, RBD, April 15, 1945.

53. AKC, RBD, October 21–22, 1945.

54. AKC, SCP, 1945, 18.

55. Truman Library, Francis Matthews Papers, "Mission to Rome," Folder 2, Matthews to Enrico Galeazzi, January 7, 1946.

Chapter 14: John E. Swift and the Cold-War Years

1. "Testimonial to Supreme Knight," *Col* XXV (March 1946), 15.
2. Ibid., 23.
3. "UNO Bars Free Speech," *Boston Post* (February 5, 1946), 10; also Editorial, *Col* XXV (March 1946), 1.
4. "Report of the Supreme Knight," *Col* XXVI (October 1946), 5–6.
5. Ibid., 15.
6. Ibid.
7. Ibid., 16.
8. Ibid.
9. Ibid.
10. Ibid., 17.
11. "Report of the Supreme Knight," *Col* XXVII (October 1947), 14.
12. Ibid., 18.
13. "Report of the Supreme Knight," *Col* XXVIII (October 1948), 5.
14. Ibid., 5–6.
15. Ibid., 6.
16. This article was quoted in its entirety, along with a rejoinder article, "Truth Makes Commie Squad," in *Knights of Columbus News* XXI (March 10, 1947), 1.
17. "Truth Makes Commie Squad."
18. AKC, Anti-Communism File, "Safeguards for America." John Swift sent a copy of the Knights of Columbus Memo to Cardinal Dougherty as "evidence of the effect of the radio series"; John E. Swift to Dennis Cardinal Dougherty, March 6, 1947.
19. AAP, Dougherty Papers, 86.6617.
20. AKC, SCP, 1947, 135–36.
21. "Editorial," *Col* XXIX (May 1950), 1.
22. AKC, SCP, 1950, 131.
23. AKC, SCP, 1951, 146.
24. "Strange Case of O'Clavichord," *Col* XXXII (June 1953), 1.
25. "Footnote on O'Clavichord," *Col* XXXIII (September 1953), 1.
26. AKC, SCP, 1954, 159.
27. AKC, SCP, 1953, 192–94.
28. Ibid.
29. Donald F. Crosby, *God, Church, and Flag: Senator Joseph R. McCarthy and the Catholic Church, 1950–1957* (Chapel Hill, North Carolina, 1978), 92–94.
30. Ibid., 235.
31. Ibid., 248–51.
32. Thomas Harrison Cummings, "Catholic Gentlemen in Fraternity," *Donahoe's Magazine* XVL (November 1895), 1249.
33. AKC, SCP, 1953, 194.

34. Robert N. Bellah, *The Broken Covenant: American Civil Religion in Time of Trial* (New York, 1975). John Murray Cuddihy, a social theorist of religion and culture, developed a theory on the religion of civility best exemplified by the comment, "I happen to be a Catholic," rather than "I am a Catholic." According to Cuddihy, the American condition of religious pluralism engendered a strong sense of restraint among religious believers of all faiths. To avoid conflict and to get along, American Protestants, Catholics, and Jews, almost unconsciously, cultivated a distaste for religious triumphalism as lacking civility as if, regardless of one's religion, we must all be, above all, civil and mannerly to one another. John Murray Cuddihy, *No Offense: Civil Religion and Protestant Taste* (New York, 1978), 12–30. When, in 1957, upon the death of Joseph McCarthy, John Donahue, the editor of *Columbia*, expressed his admiration for the Senator, he said that the reason for McCarthy's fall was because he offended the elites by his garish, uncivil behavior. "What he did was this: at a time when his country was being ever so politely, graciously, and ignorantly betrayed, he blew the police whistle—loudly and rudely and effectively—and right in the middle of a fatally soothing program of chamber music, with a Moscow motif, being rendered by some of the nicest people. And for this the Senator was killed. . . . The conviction here is that this country, and the world, is much better off thanks to the fact that Senator Joe had the courage to stand in the minority until the majority came to understand the essence of the matter." "Editorial Comment," *Col* XXXVII (June 1957), 22.

35. AKC, SCP, 1953, 194.

36. Quoted by Lerond Curry, *Protestant-Catholic Relations in America: World War I Through Vatican II* (Lexington, Kentucky, 1972), 43.

37. Ibid., 56.

38. Quoted in "Editorials," *Col* XXVI (March 1947), 43.

39. "To Protestants and Other Americans," *Col* XXVII (February 1948), 1.

40. When, in 1949, Representative Graham Barden introduced an education bill which explicitly denied federal aid to parochial schools, the Protestant-Catholic conflict intensified. Cardinal Spellman referred to Barden as a "new disciple of bigotry" and displayed posters in St. Patrick's Cathedral which portrayed the bill as "unjust, unAmerican, and divisive," quoted by Curry, op. cit. Note 48, 54.

41. "On Church and State," reprinted in *Col* XXIX (October 1949), 11.

42. Ibid.

43. Paul Blanshard, *American Freedom and Catholic Power* (Boston, 1951).

44. Ibid., 48.

45. Ibid., 297.

46. Paul Blanshard, *Communism, Democracy, and Catholic Power* (Boston, 1951).

47. John Cogley, "Something for Everyone," *Commonweal* 54 (July 13, 1951), 326.

48. Quoted by John S. Kennedy, "Blanshard Brought to Book," *Col* XXXI (June 1952), 10.

49. "Editorials," *Col* XXXI (May 1952), 1.

50. Curry, op. cit., Note 36.

Chapter *15*: Luke E. Hart and the Confrontation with Modernity

1. AKC, SCP, 1953, 117–18.
2. Ibid., 57–58.
3. AKC, SCP, 1954, 136–42.
4. Ibid., 23–29.
5. Ibid., 35–36.
6. Ibid., 32.
7. Ibid., 37. Hart reported that the *New Haven Journal-Courier* sent a reporter to interview Hart on December 8, and the next morning its headlines read "K. of C. Buys Yankee Stadium."
8. Ibid.
9. AKC, LEH, Luke E. Hart Diary, December 17, 1954.
10. AKC, SCP, 1963, 41.
11. AKC, SCP, 1954, 37.
12. AKC, Catholic Advertising File (hereafter cited as CA), Luke E. Hart to Thomas E. Comber, CSP, November 3, 1954. Extracts from this letter are included in Thomas E. Comber, *Some Considerations of the Merits of the Knights of Columbus Advertising this Faith Campaign in the Light of Certain Predetermined Criteria*, M.A. thesis, St. Paul's College, Washington, D.C., 1954 Appendix III.
13. Ibid.
14. AKC, CA, Virgil Kelley to Stephen A. Cain, February 7, 1945.
15. Ibid.
16. AKC, CA, galleys of early ads.
17. AKC, CA, "The World's Best Seller: The Book of Divinity," galley.
18. AKC, CA, Kelley to Cain, February 7, 1945.
19. Ibid.
20. Quoted by Virgil Kelley, *The Truth About Catholics* (New York, 1954), 17.
21. AKC, CA, Kelley to Cain, February 17, 1945.
22. AKC, SCP, 1946, 176–78.
23. AKC, SCP, 1947, 153.
24. "Advertising the Truth," *Col* XXVII (January 1948), 3.
25. AKC, SCP, 1952, 123.
26. AKC, RBD, April 21, 1951.
27. AKC, RBD, August 20, 1951.
28. AKC, SCP, 1951.
29. Ibid., 37.
30. Ibid., 17–18.
31. For detailed information on the Vatican film library, see Lowry S. Daly, S.J., "The Vatican Film Library, Mirror of History," *Col* XXXII (July 1953), 5, 19–20.
32. AKC, LEH; see Hart–Paul C. Reinert, S.J., correspondence, 1952–54.
33. AKC, SCP, 1957, 47.
34. AKC, SCP, 1957, 48.
35. AKC, SCP, 1960, 39.
36. AKC, SCP, 1963, 43.
37. Hart recalled the story of the pledge in his report. AKC, SCP, 1962, 44.

38. Dwight D. Eisenhower to Luke E. Hart, August 6, 1954, quoted in AKC, SCP, 1954, 318.

39. Ibid. Because George M. Docherty had delivered a sermon on the "under God" amendment in Washington, D.C., shortly before the pledge was amended, several reporters mistakenly attributed the origin of the amendment to him. Luke Hart wrote several letters tracing the origins of the amendment to the Knights of Columbus. As late as 1979 an article appeared in *America* which was based on the mistaken reports of Docherty's role in the movement. See Robert M. Senkewicz, S.J., "Twenty-five Years Under God," *America* (June 9, 1979), 469–70. Senkewicz's interpretation was based upon the mistaken notion that the "under God" insertion meant *one state* rather than *"one nation* under God." My italics.

40. AKC, RBD, July 1, 1962.

41. AKC, SCP, 1957, 44.

42. AKC, LEH, Hart to Members of the Supreme Board of Directors, January 21, 1957.

43. AKC, SCP, 1957, 43; also, Hart–John McCormack correspondence, January 1957. Senator Keating of New York and Mayor Wagner of New York City joined in the protest.

44. AKC, SCP, 1957, 43.

45. "Tito, Stay Home," *Time* LXIX (February 11, 1957), 6.

46. AKC, LEH, Hart to John J. Gillis, January 8, 1957.

47. Ibid., 4.

48. "Our Great Day," *Col* XXXVII (May 1957), 4–5.

49. "Busy Brotherly World of Freemasonry," *Life*, 41 (October 8, 1956), 104–22.

50. "Knights of Columbus in 75th Year," *Life* 42 (May 27, 1957), 54–66.

51. AKC, SCP, 1957, 49.

52. Ibid., 34.

53. AKC, RBD, June 30, 1945.

54. AKC, LEH, Hart to Galeazzi, March 10, 1955. Hart relayed this information to the Order's agent in Rome.

55. AKC, SCP, 1955, 37. Luke E. Hart, "Knighthood in the Philippines," *Col* XXXV (July 1955), 44–45.

56. AKC, SCP, 1956, 41.

57. AKC, SCP, 1956, 42.

58. This anecdote was told to me by George Hyatt, a Past Grand Knight of Havana Council who was present at this banquet. After Castro turned to the left, Hyatt emigrated to Miami. In 1960, Hart persuaded him to take a position at the home office.

59. AKC, SCP, 1959, 127.

60. Richard Pattee, "Report on Cuba," *Col* XXXIX (March 1959), 6, 10–12, 34, 44.

61. AKC, LEH, Hart to Fidel Castro, August 13, 1959 (copy).

62. AKC, LEH, Juan D. Orto to Hart, August 26, 1959.

63. AKC, SCP, 1960.

64. AKC, SCP, 1959, 39.

65. "A Visit from His Holiness," *Col* XXXIX (July 1959), 57.
66. AKC, SCP, 1959, 182.
67. AKC, SCP, 1961, 47–48.
68. AKC, LEH, Hart to John J. Gillis, May 31, 1960.
69. AKC, SCP, 1960, 46–48. "Injunction Issued Against Circulator of Bogus Knights of Columbus Oath," *Col* XL (October 1960), 16, 38.
70. AKC, SCP, 1960, 173.
71. AKC, LEH, Hart to John J. Gillis, October 4, 1960.
72. AKC, LEH, Hart to John J. Gillis, May 31, 1960.
73. AKC, LEH, Hart to Gillis, July 25, 1960.
74. Quoted by Van Allen, *The Commonweal and American Catholics*, 136–37.
75. "Editorial Comment," *Col* XL (December 1960), 16. Also see John Cogley, *Catholic America* (New York, 1973), 116–42; Edward Duff, S.J., "The Church and Public Life," in *Contemporary Catholicism in the United States,* Philip Gleason, ed. (Notre Dame, Indiana, 1967), 97–126; H. Fuchs, *John F. Kennedy and American Catholicism* (Des Moines, Iowa, 1967); Andrew M. Greeley, *The Catholic Experience* (New York, 1969), 280–98; Thomas F. O'Dea, *American Catholic Dilemma* (New York, 1961).
76. AKC, LEH, quoted in Hart to Galeazzi, October 19, 1961.
77. "The Supreme Knight at the White House," *Col* XL (November 1960), 4, 44.
78. AKC, LEH, Hart to Gillis, October 31, 1960.
79. AKC, SCP, 1954, 133–35.
80. AKC, LEH, quoted in an unmailed letter, Hart to Reverend Theodore Hessburgh, C.S.C., March 10, 1960.
81. AKC, LEH, reprints of editorials in *America* and *Ave Maria,* n.d.
82. "The Pressmen's Strike at Our Printing Plant," *Col* XLII (October 1962), 5.
83. "Board of Directors Re-elects Supreme Officers, Approves Management of Order's Affairs," *Col* XLII (December 1962), 5.
84. Quoted in "Editorial Comment," *Col* XLIII (January 1963), 16.
85. AKC, LEH, newspaper cutting, "Bad Days for the Knights," *St. Louis Review* (September 21, 1962).
86. AKC, LEH, newspaper cutting, quoted in "End Discrimination, Catholics Are Urged," *Chicago Daily News,* October 26, 1959.
87. AKC, LEH, newspaper cutting, "K. of C. Chief Would Air Membership," *Catholic Chronicle* (Toledo, Ohio), November 22, 1913, 1.

Chapter *16*: John W. McDevitt and the Preservation of Catholic Fraternalism

1. AKC, SCP, 1964, 44.
2. Ibid., 45.
3. Ibid., 196.
4. Ibid., 138–40.
5. AKC, SCP, 1972, 54–56.
6. Interviews with John W. McDevitt, 1977–80.

7. AKC, SCP, 1965, 145; also see "Order Co-Sponsor—Archbishop's Conference on Human Rights," *Col* XLV (May 1965), 4–5. Interview with John W. McDevitt, November 14, 1980.

8. AKC, John W. McDevitt Papers (hereafter cited as JWM), Memorandum, "Insurance Question in Mexico."

9. Ibid.

10. AKC, JWM, Hart to Jose Cardinal Garibi, January 13, 1963.

11. AKC, SCP, 1964.

12. AKC, SCP, 1965, 177–78.

13. Ibid., 178.

14. Ibid., 178–79.

15. Ibid., 179.

16. William J. Whalen, "The Knights of Columbus: Are They Obsolete?" *U.S. Catholic* XXX (December, 1964), 6. For replies to Whalen's article see *U.S. Catholic* XXX (April 6, 1965), 55.

17. Edward Wakin and Father Joseph Scheuer, *The De-Romanization of the American Catholic Church* (New York, 1966), 215.

18. AKC, SCP, 1966, 45.

19. Ibid., 46–47.

20. Ibid., 173.

21. Ibid., 174.

22. AKC, SCP, 1967, 45.

23. For analyses of the problems of the changing Church in America see Daniel Callahan, *The Mind of the Catholic Layman* (New York, 1963); John Tracy Ellis, *American Catholicism* (Chicago, 1970), 304–7; Philip Gleason, ed., *Catholicism in America* (New York, 1970) and *Contemporary Catholicism in the United States* (Notre Dame, 1969); Andrew M. Greeley, *The Catholic Experience* (New York, 1969); James Hitchcock, *The Decline and Fall of Radical Catholicism* (New York, 1971); Francis J. Lally, *The Catholic Church in a Changing America* (Boston, 1962); Michael Novak, *The Open Church* (New York, 1964).

24. AKC, SCP, 1968, 189.

25. Ibid., 37.

26. Press release quoted in AKC, SCP, 1967, 51.

27. AKC, SCP, 1966, 41.

28. Paul Good, "McManus vs. the Knights of Columbus," *Harper's Magazine* 243 (September 1971), 66–80.

29. AKC, SCP, 1969, 51.

30. Ibid., 215.

31. Ibid., 216.

32. Ibid., 216–18.

33. Quoted in "The 87th Supreme Council Meeting," *Col* XLIX (October 1969), 9.

34. AKC, SCP, 1969, 49.

35. Ibid., 43–44.

36. AKC, SCP, 1965, 38–40.

37. AKC, SCP, 1966, 43–44.

38. AKC, SCP, 1975, 52.

39. Ibid., 53.
40. AKC, SCP, 1969, 125.
41. Ibid., 126–29.
42. AKC, SCP, 1970, 204.
43. AKC, SCP, 1965, 44–46.
44. AKC, SCP, 1971, 45.
45. Ibid., 212. Daniel Schorr, reporting on the address for CBS, quoted a Catholic source who criticized Nixon's pro-Catholic education remarks as intended only for "political or rhetorical effect." Schorr traced several White House abuses of his civil liberty to his report of Nixon's address to the K. of C. See Daniel Schorr, *Clearing the Air* (Boston, 1977), 71–82.
46. Ibid., 212–13.
47. AKC, SCP, 1969, 182.
48. John McDevitt, "Conscience and Public Trust," *Col* LII (November 1972), 29.
49. John W. McDevitt, "Democracy: Liberty or License?" *Col* LI (November 1971), 23.
50. AKC, SCP, 1969, 42–44.
51. AKC, SCP, 1975, 40.
52. AKC, SCP, 1971, 51.
53. AKC, SCP, 1975, 49.

Chapter *17*: Virgil C. Dechant and the Prologue to the Second Century

1. AKC, SCP, 1977, 48–49.
2. "Report," *Col* LX (August 1980), 33.
3. "Report," *Col* LVIII (December 1978), 42–43.
4. AKC, SCP, 1978, 66.
5. "Report," *Col* LVIII (June 1978), 39–45.
6. "Report," *Col* LVIII (November 1978), 40–41.
7. "Report," *Col* LIX (November 1979), 40–41.
8. AKC, SCP, 1979, 314.
9. "Report," *Col* LIX (August 1979), 41.
10. AKC, SCP, 1979, 58.
11. Virgil C. Dechant, "Family: The Domestic Church" (Supreme Knight's report), *Col* LX (October 1980), 53–54.
12. "Report," *Col* LX (December 1980), 40.
13. *Knights of Columbus News* LVI (May 8, 1981), 1.
14. AKC, SCP, 1977, 49–53; AKC, SCP, 1978, 56–57; AKC, SCP, 1979, 54.
15. John V. McGuire, C.SS.R., "The Knights and Vocations," *Col* LVIII (April 1978), 38–40.
16. AKC, SCP, 1978, 6.
17. "Report," *Col* LVIII (April 1978), 41.
18. AKC, SCP, 1977, 53.
19. AKC, SCP, 1978, 65. For an analysis of a portion of this survey, see Andrew M. Greeley, *The Young Catholic Family* (Chicago, 1980).

20. Joan L. Fee, Andrew M. Greeley, William C. McCready, and Teresa A. Sullivan, *The Young Catholics* (New York, 1981).

21. AKC, quoted in news release, Public Relations of the Knights of Columbus, May 27, 1981.

22. Ibid.

23. Interview with Virgil C. Dechant, June 12, 1981.

24. AKC, SCP, 1980, 312.

25. Quoted in *The New Technologies of Birth and Death: Medical, Legal, and Moral Dimensions* (St. Louis, 1980), xi–xii. Also see Elmer Von Feldt, "Where Is Life? When Is Death," *Col* LX (July 1980), 6–15.

26. Dechant, "Family: The Domestic Church," loc. cit. Note 11, 32.

27. *Knights of Columbus News* LV (September 19, 1980), 1.

28. AKC, SCP, 1977, 57.

29. AKC, SCP, 1979, 78.

30. AKC, SCP, 1978, 54.

31. "Report," *Col* LIX (November 1979), 41.

32. AKC, SCP, 1980, 44.

33. Dechant, "Family: The Domestic Church," loc. cit. Note 11, 26.

34. For a stimulating study of contemporary anti-Catholicism, see Andrew M. Greeley, *An Ugly Little Secret* (Kansas City, 1977).

Index